S0-ACR-686

Pennsylvania Land Applications

Volume 2:

New Purchase Applications, 1769-1773

Pennsylvania Land Applications

Volume 2:
New Purchase Applications, 1769-1773

by

Kenneth D. McCrea, Ph. D.

Published by

Genealogical Society of Pennsylvania
215 South Broad Street, 7th Floor
Philadelphia, PA 19107-5325

Library of Congress Control Number: 2003106838

International Standard Book Number: 0-9718357-1-3

Available from:

Genealogical Society of Pennsylvania
215 South Broad Street, 7th Floor
Philadelphia, PA 19107-5325

Cover Illustration: The cover illustration showing two women washing laundry on the banks of the Susquehanna River is a wood cut engraving by Granville Perkins entitled "North Branch of the Susquehanna, at Hunlocks," which is located south of Wilkes-Barre, in Luzerne County, within the area included in the New Purchase Applications. It was published in 1873 in the book *Picturesque America*, by D. Appleton & Co., New York.

Manufactured in the United States of America
using acid-free paper
by Sheridan Books, Inc.

An Internet Interactive Book

AncestorsLand.com

Have you ever been tempted to add a notation in a library book next to a reference to that elusive ancestor of yours in order to seek additional information from other researchers? This web site will be a way to do that without getting arrested for defacing a library book (and without visiting all libraries owning this book).

This book is interactive through the web site AncestorsLand.com. The web site will allow readers of this book to add information on their ancestors mentioned in the book, to submit and view corrections of any errors they may find in the book, and to contact other researchers working on the same relatives. The web site also has a freeware program that can be downloaded that will allow readers to find the D-M code for a surname not listed in the phonetic cross-reference section of the book.

The information submitted to the web site will be placed into an online database that can be used to exchange genealogical information via email and/or personal genealogical web site links. This site will be maintained for at least five years from the date of publication.

Acknowledgments

This book would not have been possible without the help of the following people:

Jonathan Stayer, who provided corrections and other improvements to the manuscript, and helped obtain the microfilm and other materials used in the preparation of this book.

Michael Reichwein, and Jared Parvin assisted with the typing and data entry for the book.

Gladys Sowers and James Beidler assisted with the proofreading of the manuscript.

And finally, I wish to thank the Genealogical Society of Pennsylvania, without whose support it would not have been possible for me to prepare and publish this book.

Kenneth D. McCrea, Ph. D.
Stevens, Pennsylvania
July 2003

CONTENTS

Introduction

Pennsylvania Land Settlement and the Treaty of Fort Stanwix

William Penn, and subsequently his children and grandchildren, followed a policy of preventing settlers from acquiring land in areas not yet purchased from the Indians. This policy was only partially effective since many "squatters" did settle in those areas prior to treaties being signed. However, no legal title could be obtained for this land until it was purchased from the Indians.

The Purchase of 1768, or the "New Purchase" as it was called at that time,[1] consisted of land obtained from the Indians by the Treaty of Fort Stanwix. Signed at Fort Stanwix near Rome, New York, on 5 November 1768, this treaty deeded lands in New York, Pennsylvania and south of the Ohio River, in what was at that time Virginia, to the Proprietary Government of Pennsylvania. The report of the signing of the Treaty of Fort Stanwix was read to the Pennsylvania Assembly in January 1769 as follows:[2]

GENTLEMEN,

I HAVE the Pleasure to acquaint you that, at a General Congress held last Fall at Fort Stanwix by Sir William Johnson, his Majesty's Superintendant for Indian Affairs in the Northern District, with the Indians of the Six Nations, and their Nephews, the Delawares and Shawanese, a general Boundary Line was happily settled between the Indians and his Majesty's middle Colonies; and that a Purchase was made, by the Proprietaries of this Province, of a large Tract of Country, lying within the general Boundary, and contained within the following Limits, viz. Beginning in the said Boundary Line, on the East Side of the East Branch of the River Susquehanna, at a Place called Owegy; and running with the said Boundary Line down the said Branch on the East Side thereof, till it comes opposite to the Mouth of a Creek called by the Indians Awandae; and across the River, and up the said Creek, on the South Side thereof, and along the Range of Hills called Burnet's Hills by the English, and by the Indians on the North Side of them, to the Head of a Creek which runs into the West Branch of Susquehanna, which Creek is called by the Indians Tiadaghton; and down the said Creek, on the South Side thereof, to the said West Branch of Susquehanna; then crossing the said River, and running up the same, on the South Side thereof, the several Courses thereof, to the Fork of the same River, which lies nearest to a Place on the River Ohio, called Kittanning; and from the said Fork by a strait Line to Kittanning aforesaid; and then down the said River Ohio, by the several Courses thereof, to where the Western Bounds of the said Province of Pennsylvania cross the same River; and then with the said Western Bounds to the South Boundary thereof; and with the South Boundary aforesaid to the East Side of the Alleganey Hills; and with the same Hills, on the East Side of them, to the West Line of a Tract of Land purchased of the said Proprietaries from the Six Nation Indians, and confirmed by their Deed bearing Date the Twenty-third Day of October One Thousand Seven Hundred and Fifty-eight; and then with the Northern Bounds of that Tract to the River Susquehanna, and crossing the River Susquehanna to the Northern Boundary Line of another Tract of Land purchased from the Indians, by Deed bearing Date the Twenty second Day of August, One Thousand Seven Hundred and Forty-nine; and then with that Northern Boundary Line to the River Delaware; at the North Side of the Mouth of a Creek called Lechawacsein; then, up the said River Delaware, on the West Side thereof, to the Intersection of it by an East Line to be drawn from Owegy aforesaid to the said River Delaware; and then with that East Line to the Beginning, at Owegy aforesaid.

I am also to Inform you, that the Right Honourable the Earl of Hillsborough, his Majesty's Secretary of State for the American Department, hath signified to me, that his Majesty In his Wisdom has been pleased to alter Part of the Plan heretofore adopted for the Management of Indian Affairs; and to order, that the Regulation of the Indian Trade shall be left to the respective Colonies, whose Legislatures must be the best Judges of what their several Situations and Circumstances may require.

And as the unjust Settlements made on the Lands unpurchased of the Indians, and the Abuses committed by the Traders, were the principal Causes of the Disaffection of the Savages, it is his Majesty's Royal Expectation, that a due Attention will be given by the Colonies to these important Objects; and that they will frame proper and adequate Laws not only for preventing any Settlements being made on the Indian Lands beyond the general Boundary Line, but also for the Controul and Punishment of those atrocious Frauds which have been practised by the

[1] The term "New Purchase" was used at that time to describe the area covered by these applications. However, the Purchase of 1784, to the west of this purchase, was also sometimes referred to as the "New Purchase" in later land records.

[2] Votes of Assembly. Pennsylvania Archives, Eighth Series, Volume VII, pp. 6311-6313.

Advertiſement.

THE LAND-OFFICE will be opened on the Third Day of April next, at Ten o'Clock in the Morning, to receive Applications from all Perſons inclinable to take up Lands in the New Purchaſe, upon the Terms of Five Pounds Sterling per Hundred Acres, and One Penny per Acre per Annum Quit-Rent. No Perſon will be allowed to take up more than Three Hundred Acres, without the ſpecial Licence of the Proprietaries or the Governor. The Surveys upon all Applications are to be made and returned within Six Months, and the whole Purchaſe-Money paid at One Payment, and Patent taken out within Twelve Months from the Date of the Application, with Intereſt and Quit-Rent from Six Months after the Application. If there be a Failure on the Side of the Party applying, in either procuring his Survey and Return to be made, or in paying the Purchaſe-Money and obtaining the Patent, the Application and Survey will be utterly void, and the Proprietaries will be at Liberty to diſpoſe of the Land to any other Perſon whatever. And as theſe Terms will be ſtrictly adhered to by the Proprietaries, all Perſons are hereby warned and cautioned not to apply for more Land than they will be able to pay for in the Time hereby given for that Purpoſe.

By Order of the Governor,

PHILADELPHIA, LAND-OFFICE, *Febr.* 23, 1769.

JAMES TILGHMAN,
Secretary of the Land-Office.

N. B. *So long a Day is fixed to give the Back Inhabitants Time to repair to the Office.*

Figure 1. Original Advertisement for New Purchase Application Program.

Indian Traders. As the Grounds and Reasons of his Majesty's Resolutions, upon these Subjects, are In general set forth in a Report of the Board of Trade, transmitted me by the Right Honourable the Earl of Hillsborough, which points out what his Majesty expects of the Colonies in these Matters, and explains what will be hereafter the Nature of the Office of Superintendant, which is not wholly to be laid aside; I have ordered the Secretary. for your better Information, to lay that Report before you.— I am persuaded, Gentlemen, I need not labour to convince you of the Reasonableness of his Majesty's Expectations, nor to shew how greatly both the Interest and Safety of the Colonies depend upon a close Attention to the Objects recommended; nor can I doubt of your earnestly setting about, and prosecuting, with all possible Dispatch, a Work of so much Consequence to the Colonies in general, and this Province in particular.
JOHN PENN
January 16, 1769.

In Pennsylvania, the East Side and West Side Application programs were still active. The first legal titles to land within the New Purchase were granted through a similar application process. The Assembly acted quickly to establish a means for settlers to begin the process of obtaining title to land within the New Purchase:

At a special Meeting at the Governors on Wednesday the 25th Day of January Ao. di. 1769.[3]
Present: The Governor, Mr. Hamilton, The Sec'ry Mr. Tilghman, The Rec'r Gen'l Mr. Hockley, The Rec'r Gen'l Mr. Physick, The Surveyor Gen'l Mr. Lukens.

The Board assisted by Mr. Hamilton took into Consideration the Terms on which the Office should open for the late new purchase and are of Opinion that the Application plan in general be continued but are of Opinion that there shou'd be some Alteration as to the time of returning the Surveys & paying for the Land and taking out Patents which is referred to further Consideration.

At a Meeting at the Governors the 24th Feb'y, 1769:[4]
Present: The Governor, The Sec'ry Mr. Tilghman, The Auditor Gen'l Mr. Hockley, The Rec'r Gen'l Mr. Physick, The Surveyor Gen'l Mr. Lukens.

The Governor with the Advise of the Board orders that the Land Office be not opened for receiving Applications to take up Land in the new Purchase till the 3d of April next in order that the back Inhabitants may have sufficient time to bring in their Applications And the Secretary immediately give Notice of the opening the Office on that day by separate Advertizem'ts to be distributed as soon as may be & by inserting them in the next weeks papers.

A copy of the original advertisement for the New Purchase Applications (Figure 1) is attached to the inside cover of the original New Purchase Application Register. Some controversy developed over the delay of the acceptance of applications until April 3rd, since the Officers' and Gentlemen's tract applications were accepted before the general public had a chance to submit applications. See below for more details on the Officers' and Gentlemen's tracts.

Geographic Area Included in the New Purchase Applications

The area of Pennsylvania covered by the New Purchase is described in John Penn's report of 16 January 1769, presented above. The land formed a strip across the State from the southwest corner to the northeast corner (Figure 2). It included all or part of 26 of the 67 present-day counties in Pennsylvania. At the time of the purchase, the new land was annexed to the existing counties of Cumberland, Berks and Northampton (Figure 3).

In 1770, soon after the purchase, a map of the newly expanded Province of Pennsylvania was prepared by William Scull (who was one of the surveyors of land within the purchase). This map shows many of the features that were used to describe the locations of the land in the applications. Many of the place names have changed since 1770, making the locations of the applications more difficult to determine. A copy of this map (Figure 4), prepared in 1775 for the British Government, is shown here in six sections.[5] This was the best map of Pennsylvania that the British Army would have had during the Revolutionary War.

An interesting announcement for William Scull's map was published in the Philadelphia newspapers. It was a for a "pre-publication" sale, similar to that done for this book:[6]

[3] Minutes of the Board of Property. Pennsylvania Archives, Third Series, Volume 1, p. 251.
[4] Minutes of the Board of Property. Pennsylvania Archives, Third Series, Volume 1, p. 255.

[5] The original map, in the collection of the Pennsylvania State Archives, has split into six separate sections as shown here.
[6] Pennsylvania Journal and The Weekly Advertiser, 26 JAN 1769.

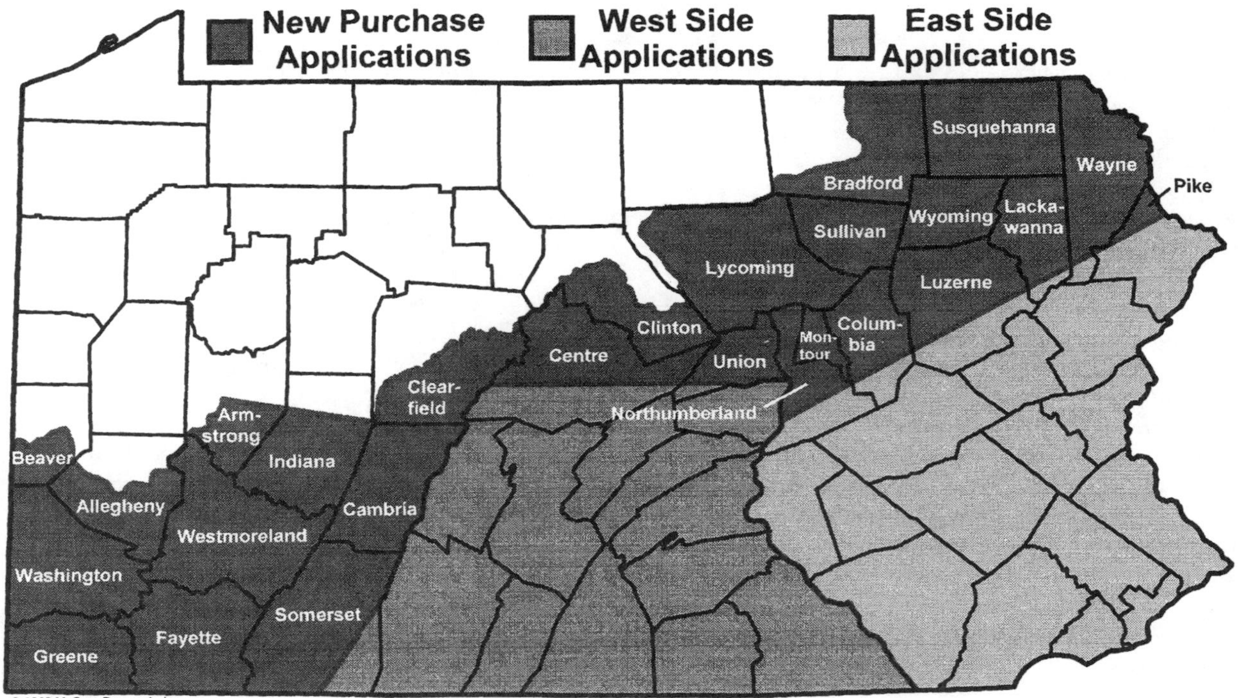

Figure 2. Map showing the locations of the three Application programs.

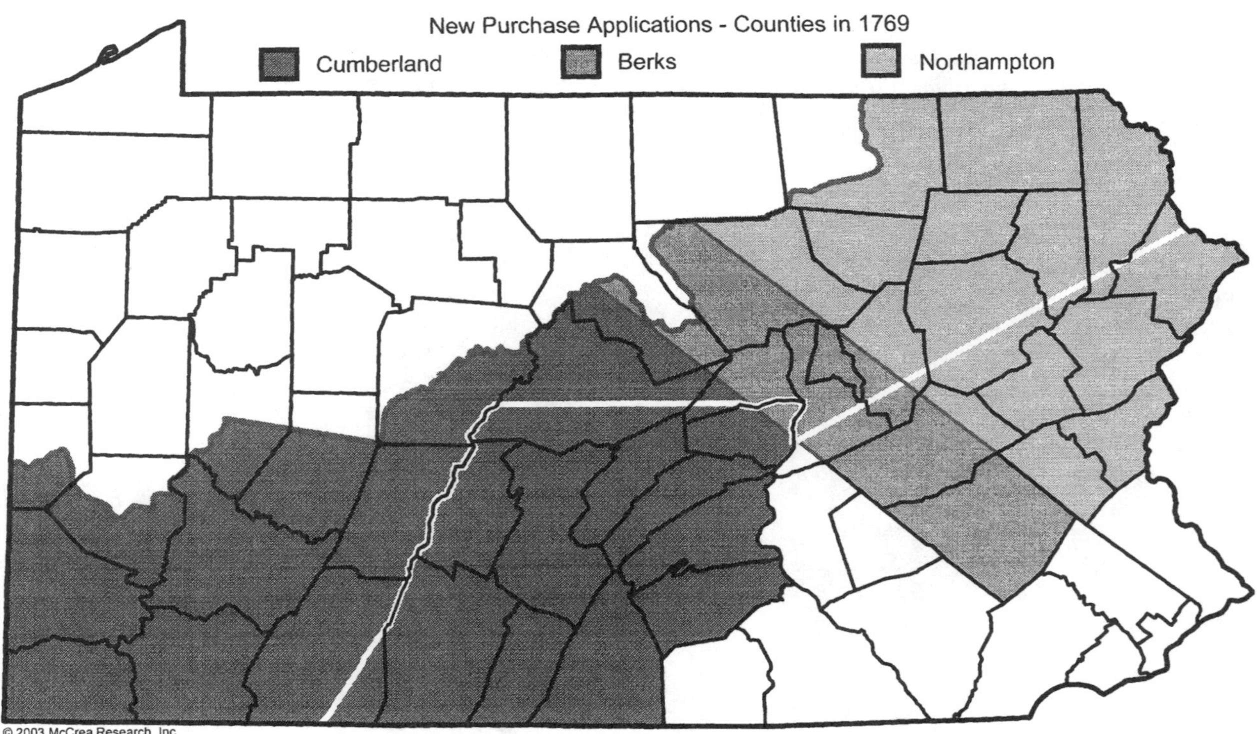

Figure 3. Counties within the New Purchase in 1769.

A MAP OF

PENNSYLVANIA

EXHIBITING

not only THE IMPROVED PARTS of that PROVINCE, but alſo

ITS EXTENSIVE FRONTIERS:

Laid down FROM ACTUAL SURVEYS,

and Chiefly FROM THE LATE MAP of W. Scull *Published in 1770;*

And Humbly Inscribed

TO THE HONOURABLE

THOMAS PENN AND RICHARD PENN ESQUIRES

TRUE AND ABSOLUTE PROPRIETARIES & GOVERNORS *OF THE*

PROVINCE OF PENNSYLVANIA

and the *TERRITORIES* thereunto belonging.

English Miles 69½ to a Degree.

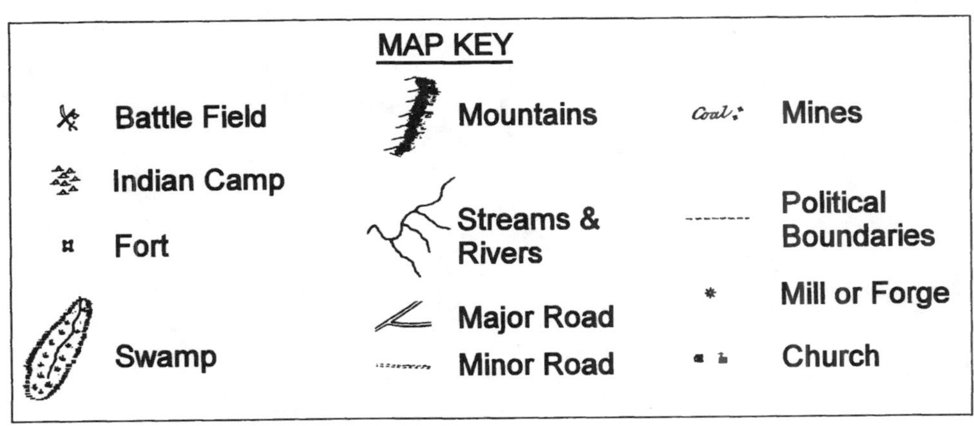

Figure 4. Map of Pennsylvania in 1770.

Map printed in London, England in 1775 based on William Scull's 1770 map of Pennsylvania. This version of Scull's map would have been used by the British during the Revolutionary War. The map is reproduced in six parts on the next six pages. Pennsylvania State Archives, MG-11, Map 88.

Figure 4. Pennsylvania in 1770, Western section.

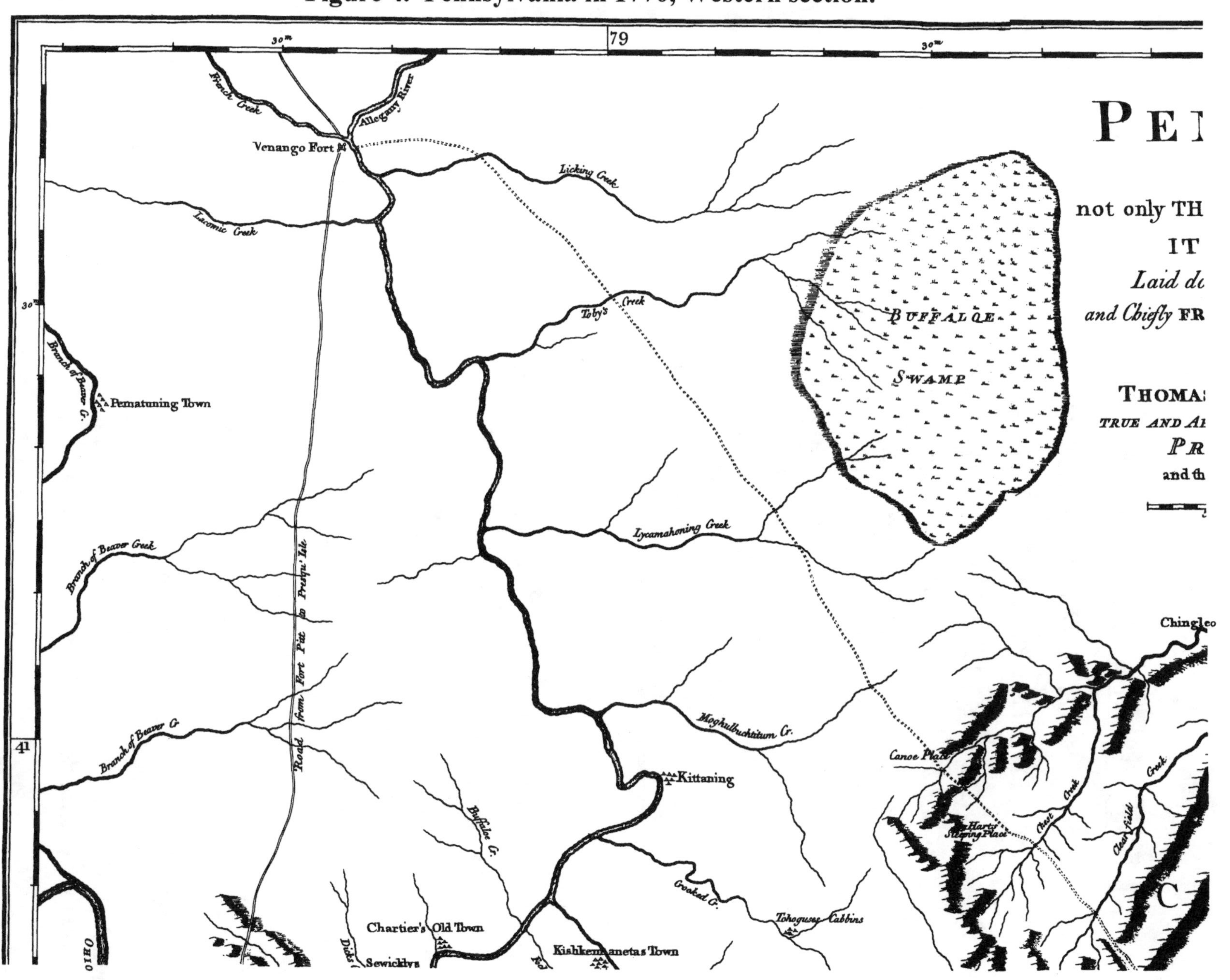

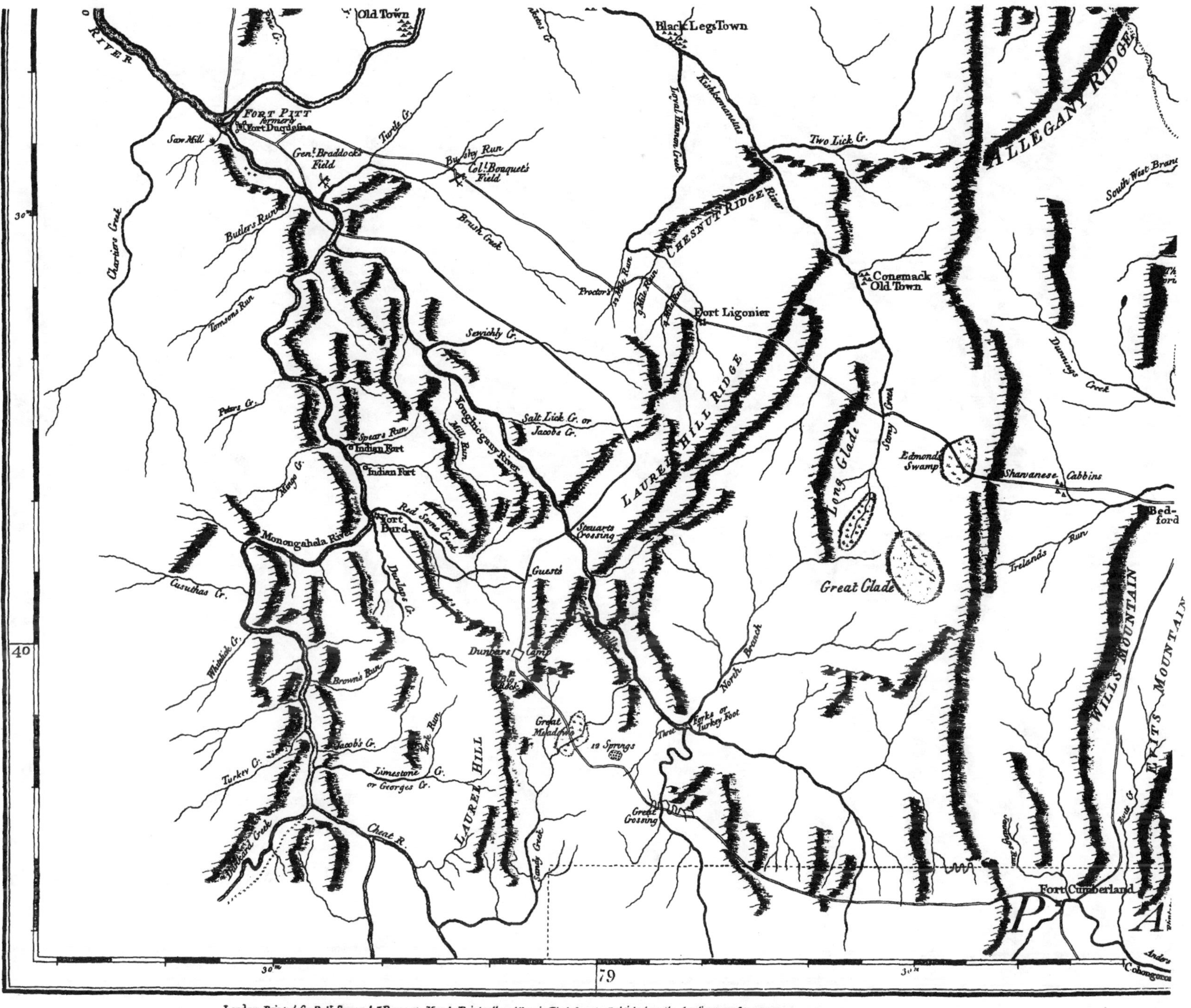
RIVER
Old Town
Black Legs Town
ALLEGANY RIDGE
FORT PITT formerly Fort Duquesne
Saw Mill
Turtle Cr.
Genl. Braddocks Field
Bushy Run
Col. Bouquets Field
Loyal Hannon Creek
Kishkemanetas River
Two Lick Cr.
South West Branch
Chartiers Creek
Butlers Run
Brush Creek
CHESNUT RIDGE
Proctors
Conemack Old Town
Fort Ligonier
Tomsons Run
Sewickly Cr.
Dunnings Creek
LAUREL HILL RIDGE
Peters Cr.
Salt Lick Cr. or Jacobs Cr.
Yoghiogany River
Mill Run
Spears Run
Indian Fort
Long Glade
Sandy Creek
Edmonds Swamp
Shawanese Cabbins
Mingo Cr.
Red Stone Creek
Fort Burd
Monongahela River
Stewarts Crossing
Bed-ford
Guests
Great Glade
Trelands Run
Cusuthas Cr.
Dunlaps Cr.
WILLS MOUNTAIN
40
Dunbars Camp
North Branch
Browns Run
Great Meadows
12 Springs
Forks or Turkey Foot
Jacobs Cr.
Turkey Cr.
Limestone Cr. or Georges Cr.
LAUREL HILL
Great Crossing
Cheat R.
Fort Cumberland
30m
79
London Printed for Robt. Sayer & J.Bennett, Map & Printsellers No. 53 in Fleet Street, Published as the Act directs 10 June 1775

Figure 4. Pennsylvania in 1770, Central section.

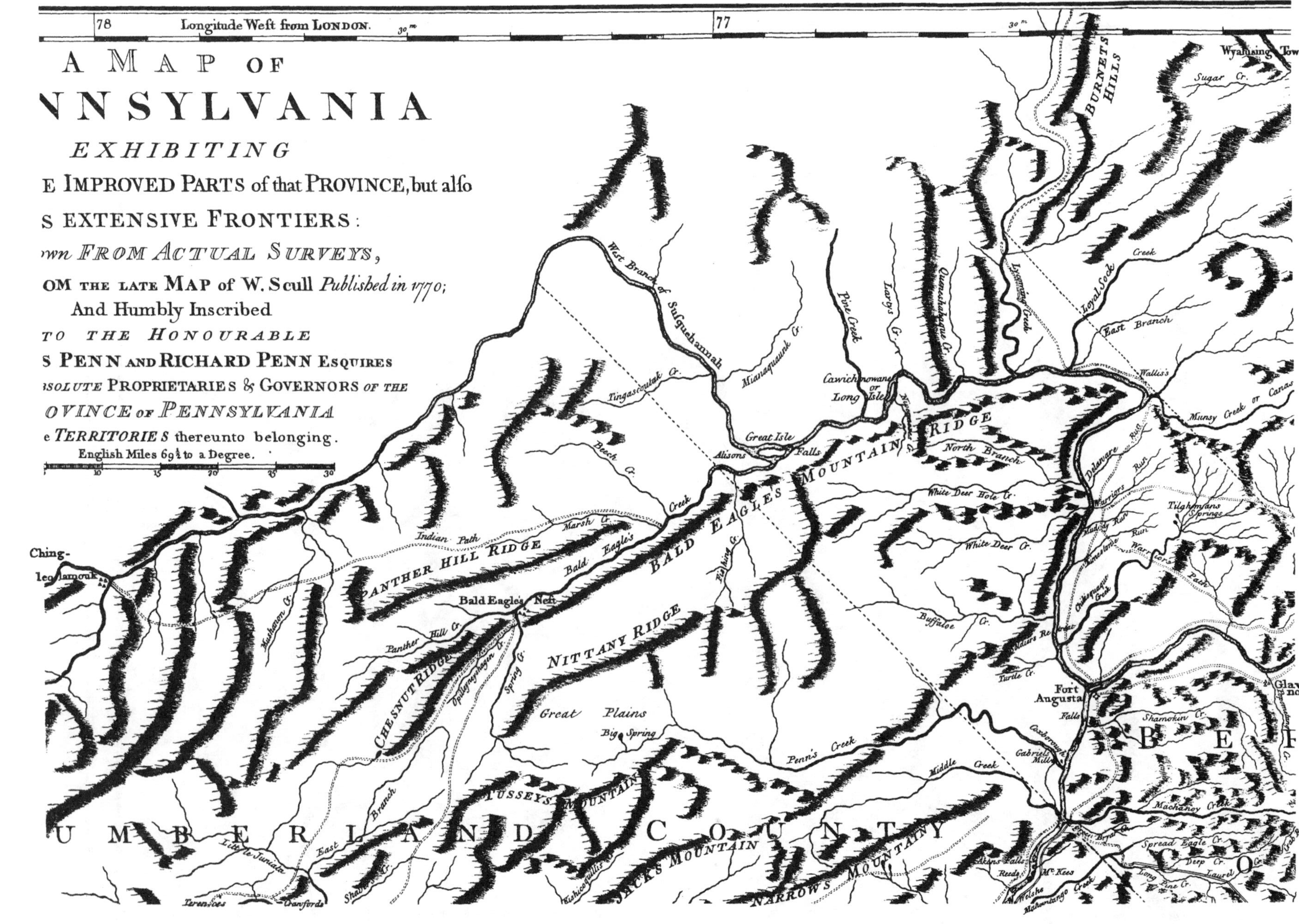

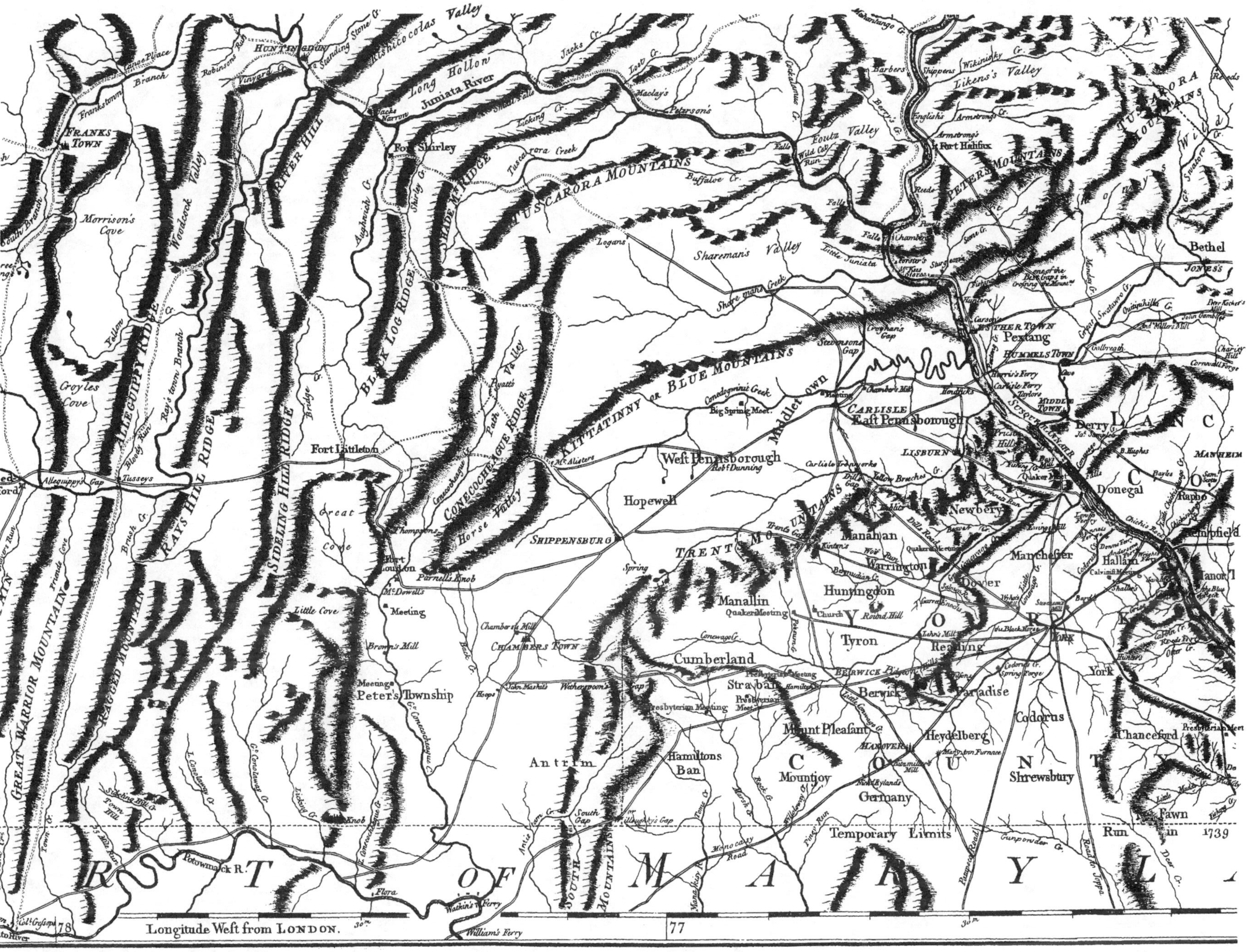
GREAT WARRIOR MOUNTAIN
RAGGED MOUNTAIN
ALLEGUIPPY RIDGE
RAYS HILL RIDGE
SIDELING HILL RIDGE
BLACK LOG RIDGE
SHADE MTN RIDGE
TUSCARORA MOUNTAINS
CONECOCHEAGUE RIDGE
KITTATINNY or BLUE MOUNTAINS
PETERS MOUNTAINS
SOUTH MOUNTAIN
Franks Town
Morrison's Cove
Groyles Cove
Bedford
Fort Littleton
Great Cove
Little Cove
Long Hollow
Juniata River
Fort Shirley
Huntingdon
Kishicocolas Valley
Shippensburg
Chambers Town
Carlisle
Peter's Township
Antrim
Hopewell
West Pensborough
Middleton
East Pensborough
Cumberland
Manallin
Tyron
Huntingdon
Mount Pleasant
Mountjoy
Germany
Heydelberg
Paradise
Codorus
Shrewsbury
Manchester
Hallam
Chanceford
Newbery
Warrington
Dover
Donegal
Derry
Pextang
Fort Halifax
Sharemans Valley
Tuscarora Creek
Williams's Ferry
Hamiltons Ban
Strabane
Berwick
York
Temporary Limits
Longitude West from LONDON.
77
78
London Printed for Robt. Sayer & J.Bennett Map & Printseller No. 53 in Fleet Street Published as the Act directs 11 June 1775

Figure 4. Pennsylvania in 1770, Eastern section.

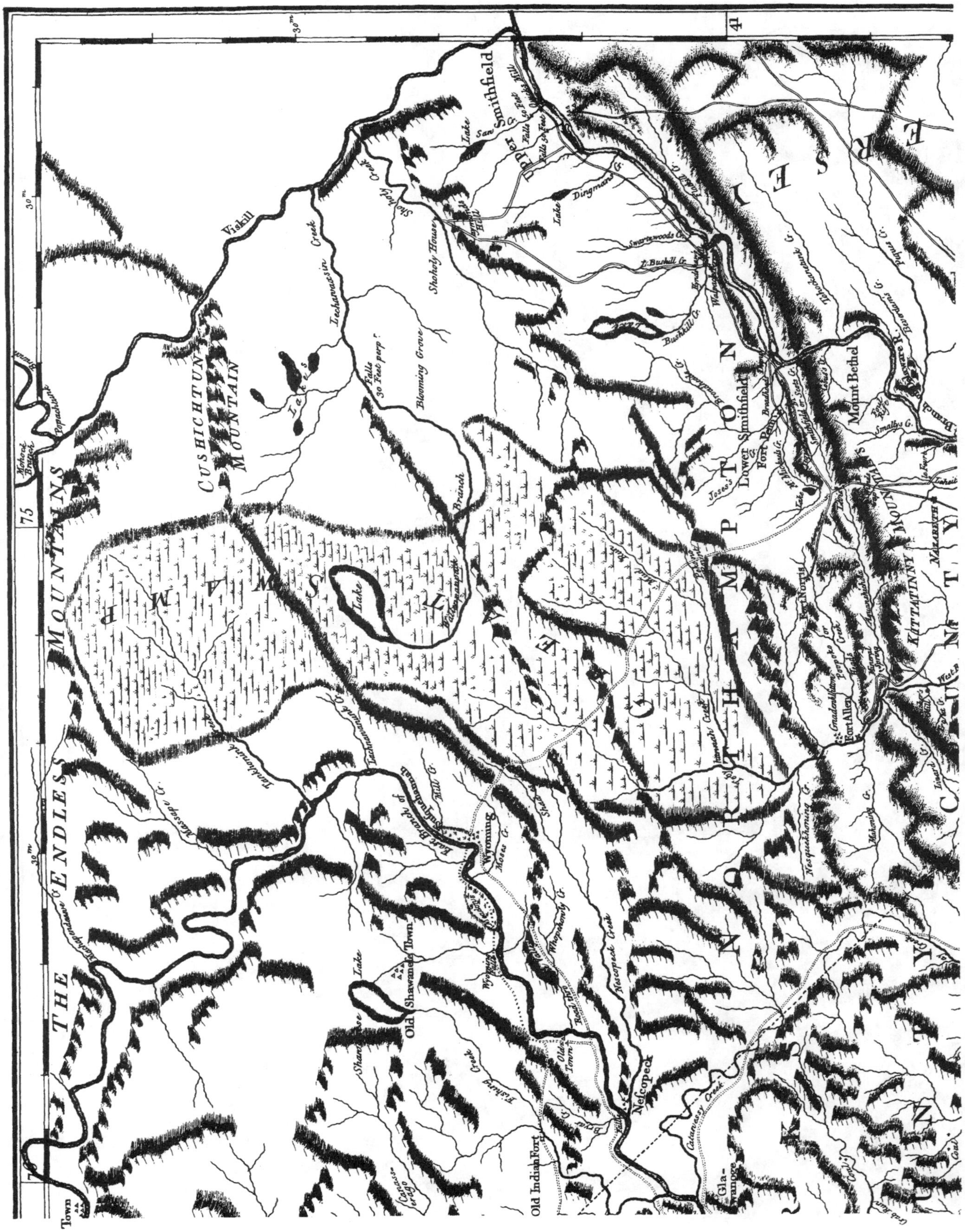

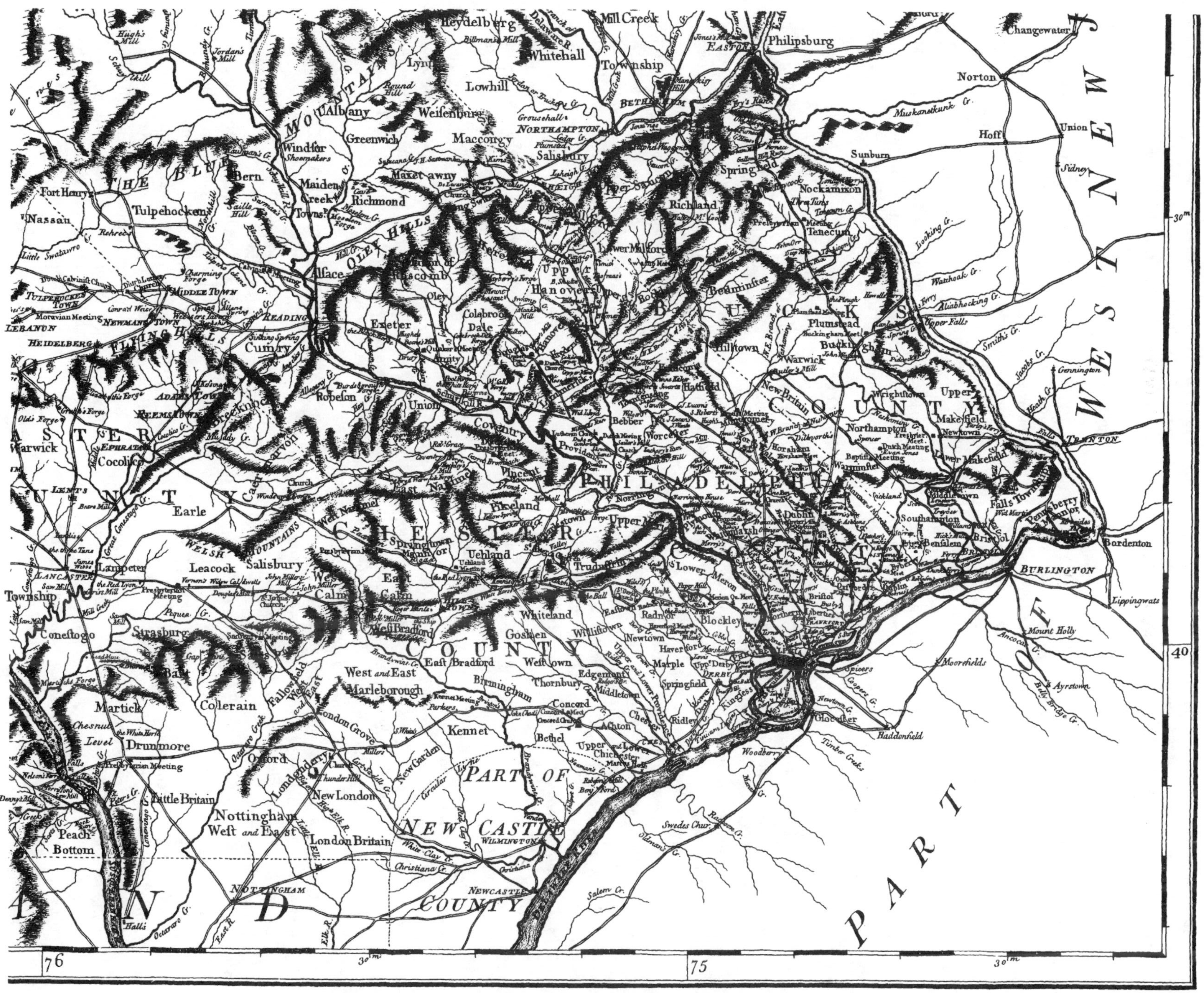
London Printed for Robt. Sayer & J.Bennett Map & Printsellers. No 53 in Fleet Street. Published as the Act directs 10 June 1775.

Advertisement

The Map of the Province of Pennsylvania, published by the late Mr. Nicholas Scull, notwithstanding great care and pains were taken to render it compleat, yet being an extensive work, hath been found not only imperfect but erroneous in many parts which were laid down from the best information he could then obtain. The Subscriber, who was employed in that useful work, has had great opportunities of correcting its errors, and supplying its defects, and spent a great deal of time for that purpose. Having communicated his intentions to several ingenious gentlemen, who kindly assisted him with materials, he is induced by their advice and encouragement of many others, who have seen his improved Map, (now nearly finished) to publish the same by subscription according to the following proposals,

First. It being objected that the large scale on which the former Map was laid down, made it expensive at the same time that it only extended a little beyond the improved parts of the province, this map is laid down on a scale of ten miles to an inch, and will comprehend the whole extent of the province; describing the situation of all the towns, villages, and remarkable places, and courses of the roads, rivers, creeks, and mountains, with great precision, on one sheet of paper, of about thirty inches in length, and about twenty inches in breadth.

Second. The map to be printed on good paper, and delivered to the subscribers at the price of Seven Shilling and Six-pence, on or before the first day of October next. The expectation he has of being soon enabled from the actual surveys and accurate observations to lay down the back country, now lately purchased of the Indians with great exactness, (for which he is determined to exert his utmost industry,) occasions the postponing his intended publication to so late a day. And in the meantime he takes this opportunity of earnestly requesting those gentlemen, who can furnish him with any draughts or observations of any part of the province that may be serviceable to his design, to communicate the same as early as possible, and their favours shall be gratefully acknowledged.

William Scull

Those who are inclined to encourage this undertaking, are requested to subscribe their names with John Lukens, Esq. Surveyor General, Messrs. Hall and Sellers, William and Thomas Bradford, William Goddard, Henry Miller, James Biddle, and Peter Miller, in the city of Philadelphia; Mr. John Hart, in Southwark; Mr. William Masters, in the Northern Liberties; Mr. Christopher Sower, in Germantown; George Ross, and James Ralfe, Esquires in Lancaster; Samuel Johnston, Esq. in York Town; Mr. Richard Tea, and Mr. James Polke, in Carlisle; Lewis Gordon, Esq. in Easton; Henry Hale Graham, Esq. in Chester; and Dr. John DeNormandie, Esq. in Bristol.

As can be seen in the description of the area covered by the Treaty of Fort Stanwix, the boundaries of the purchase are subject to some interpretation, especially in areas where the boundary was an artificial line, rather than a distinct feature such as a river. Judging from my mapping of the locations of some of the surveys, there were New Purchase Applications surveyed which were outside the Treaty area. The Minutes of the Board of Property demonstrated this confusion:[7]

Land Office Feb'ry 27th 1775

There being many Applications for Warrants on the heads of Crooked Creek, Two Lick Creek, Cowan Shannock, Laurell Run, Stump Creek, Sugar Creek, and other Waters thereabouts which it is not certain are within the late Indian purchase of Fort Stanwix The Governor orders that Thomas Smith and Joshua Elder the two Deputy Surveyors in that part of the Country do immediately before they enter upon the surveying of any more Warrants this Season run a traverse from the Canoe place on Sasquehanna to Kittaning & then carefully calculate & run a direct Line to the Canoe place & mark it so that they may know when Warrants are to be surveyed whether the Land be within or without the purchase. If it be more convenient to begin the Traverse from the Kittaning they may do it and run the line from Sasquehanna to Kittaning. That they do not execute any Warrants or run any Surveys which are out of the purchase That they report to the Secretary when they have completed the Line And that in the mean time the Secretary do not issue any Warrants upon the Lands of the Waters aforesaid.

New Purchase Application Lottery

Applications for land in the New Purchase began to arrive at the Land Office in Philadelphia well before the April 3rd date that had been set for the acceptance of applications. This created a problem of two or more applications being submitted for the same tract of land. The normal solution was to accept the application with the earliest date. A total of 2,802 applications had reached the Land Office by April 3rd, so a lottery system was devised to alleviate the problem. All of the applications received by

[7] Minutes of the Board of Property. Pennsylvania Archives, Third Series, Volume 1, pp. 396-397.

April 3rd were placed in a box and drawn out one at a time. They were numbered in the order in which they were drawn, starting with number 1. In any disputes over the land, lower application numbers took precedence.

The New Purchase was divided into eleven surveying districts. A deputy surveyor was assigned to each district. Applicants were required to have their land surveyed within six months by the deputy surveyor for the district where the land was located. Only a small number of applications were surveyed within the six month time limit. Surveys turned in to the Land Office more than six months after the application date were still accepted. The applicants also were required to pay the remaining fees and obtain a patent within twelve months from the date of the application. This deadline also was not enforced. In many cases returns were filed much later than twelve months after the application date. The latest date found in the New Purchase register was 12 March 1941, when application NP-3392 for Thomas Gibson was patented.

A good example of the consequences of the lottery system can be seen in an action of the Board of Property on 28 June 1774:[8] "*The Board took into Consideration the Pretensions of Seth McCormick [NP-450], Mary Rees [NP-601], and Richard Irwin [NP-1787] to a Tract of Land on Chillisquaque Creek And it appearing to them that their several Applications were for the same place. That Seth McCormicks is the earliest it is ordered by the Governor that he hath an exceptance of survey and a Patent.*" A return was filed on Seth McCormick's application on 8 July 1774 by Col. Francis; the other two applications were not returned.

Judging from notes in the New Purchase register, there were many cases in which more than one person submitted an application for the same piece of ground. Because of the large number of applications dated 3 April 1769, the lottery system provided a solution to this problem by allowing the application with the lowest assigned number to be accepted when more than one application had the same date.

Documents Created by the Application Process

1) Application

The first step in the Application process was to bring an "application" to the Land Office in Philadelphia. The application usually consisted of a small slip of paper (as paper was very expensive in that era). The New Purchase Applications were handled differently than the East Side Applications (Volume 1 of this series).[9] The "Lottery System" developed for the New Purchase required that only one application be written on each slip of paper. As in the East Side Applications, many of the applications originally were submitted on sheets of paper with more than one on a sheet of paper. These sheets were cut into individual slips with only one application on each section. Some of these applications had individual entries on both sides. In those cases, the one on the back was copied onto a new slip of paper and the original one crossed out. An example of this procedure can be seen in Figure 5.

The original New Purchase Applications are filed together in numerical order, and have been microfilmed. All but 41 of the original applications (or their copied replacements) were found.

2) Order to Survey

An additional document was prepared when the application was accepted. This was an Order to Survey which was sent out to the deputy surveyor in the district where the land was presumed to be located. These documents were not kept by the Land Office, but became the property of the individual surveyors. Some of these documents survive in county courthouses. Others apparently fell into private hands. An example of a New Purchase Order to Survey, purchased by the author on eBay (Internet auction site), is shown in Figure 6. These orders are not found in the collections of the Pennsylvania State Archives, where the other referenced documents can be found.

3) Survey

The survey is a map of the property prepared from the field notes of the surveyor. Each side of the property is described using its starting point (often a tree, but sometimes a post or pile of stones), its direction (described by a deviation in degrees from either North or South), and its distance measured in "perches." A perch is equal to 16.5 feet and is the same as a "rod." Thus a side of a property may be described as "South 25 degrees East, 100 perches," meaning a line 100 perches long running in a direction 25 degrees east of south. It also includes the names of the owners of the adjacent properties, and usually shows small streams and rivers. Beginning in the first half of the nineteenth century, the original surveys, which are on loose sheets of

[8] Minutes of the Board of Property. Pennsylvania Archives, Third Series, Volume 1, p. 382.

[9] McCrea, Kenneth D., 2002, Pennsylvania Land Applications, Volume 1: New Purchase Applications, 1765-1769, Pennsylvania Chapter, Palatines to America, Strasburg, PA.

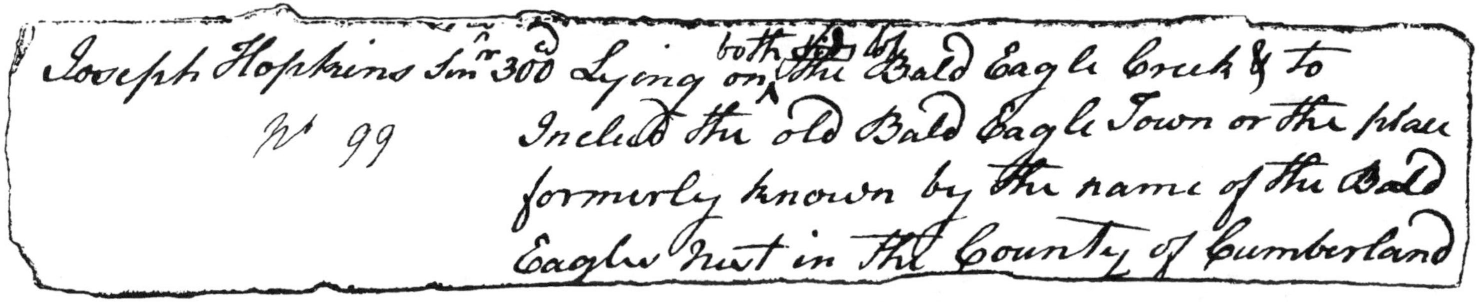

Joseph Hopkins Junr 300 Lying on both sides of the Bald Eagle Creek & to Include the old Bald Eagle Town or the place formerly known by the name of the Bald Eagles Nest in the County of Cumberland

No 99

A. New Purchase Application Number 99.

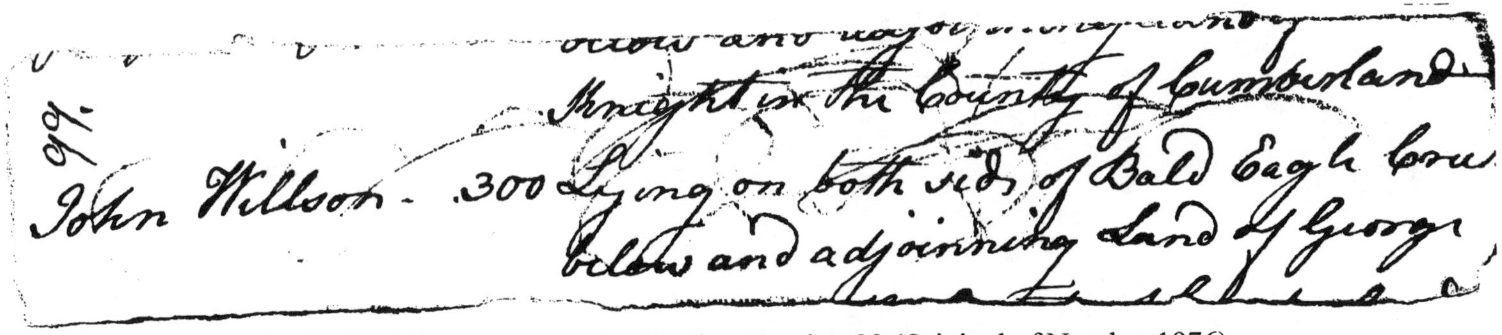

John Willson - 300 Lying on both sides of Bald Eagle Creek below and adjoining Land of George Knight in the County of Cumberland

99.

B. Back of New Purchase Application Number 99 (Original of Number 1976).

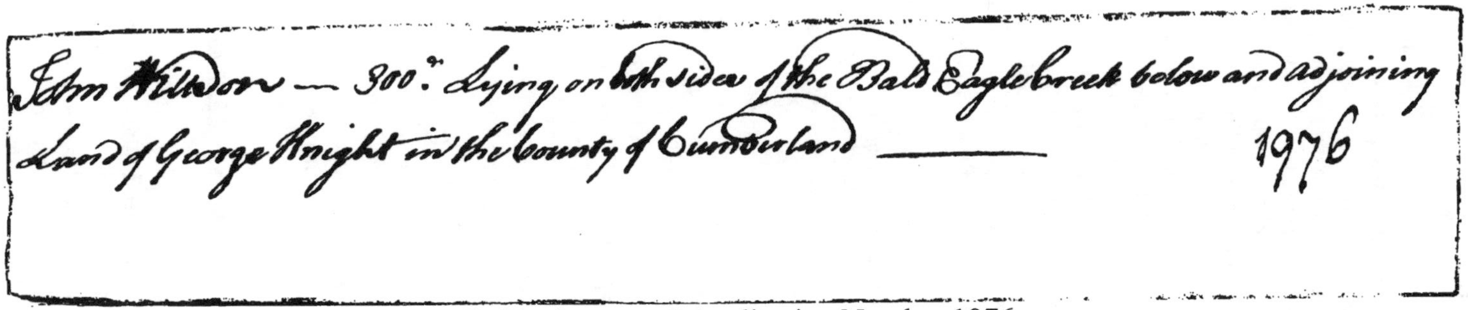

John Willson — 300a Lying on both sides of the Bald Eagle creek below and adjoining Land of George Knight in the County of Cumberland ———

1976

C. "Replacement" Application Number 1976.

Figure 5. Original New Purchase Applications and a "Replacement" Application used for the Lottery Drawing.

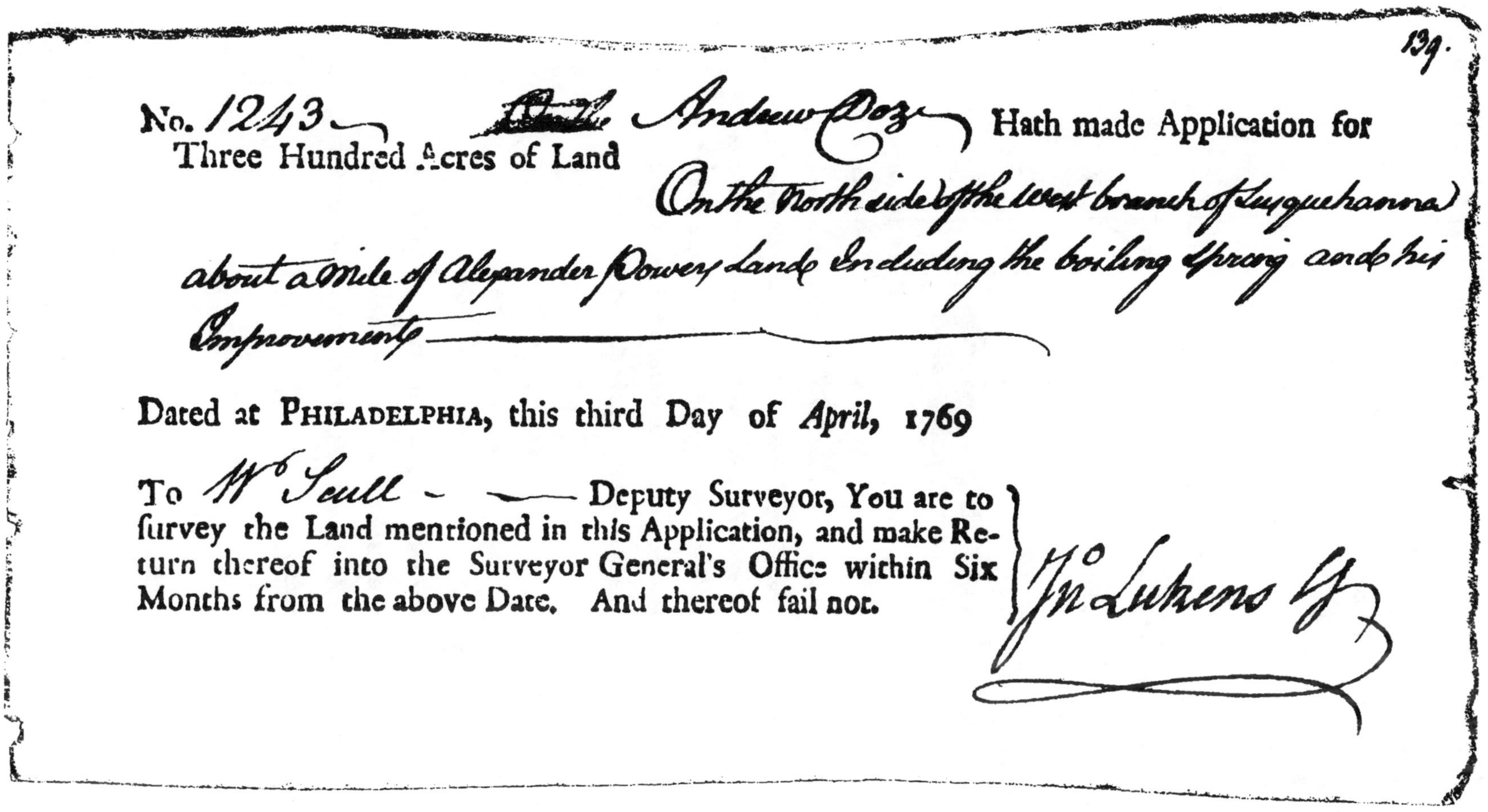

139.

No. 1243 Andrew Doz Hath made Application for
Three Hundred Acres of Land On the North side of the West branch of Susquehanna about a Mile of Alexander Powers Land Including the boiling Spring and his Improvements

Dated at PHILADELPHIA, this third Day of *April*, 1769

To Wm Scull — Deputy Surveyor, You are to survey the Land mentioned in this Application, and make Return thereof into the Surveyor General's Office within Six Months from the above Date. And thereof fail not.

Jno Lukens SG

Figure 6. Order to Survey for Andrew Doz, NP-1243.

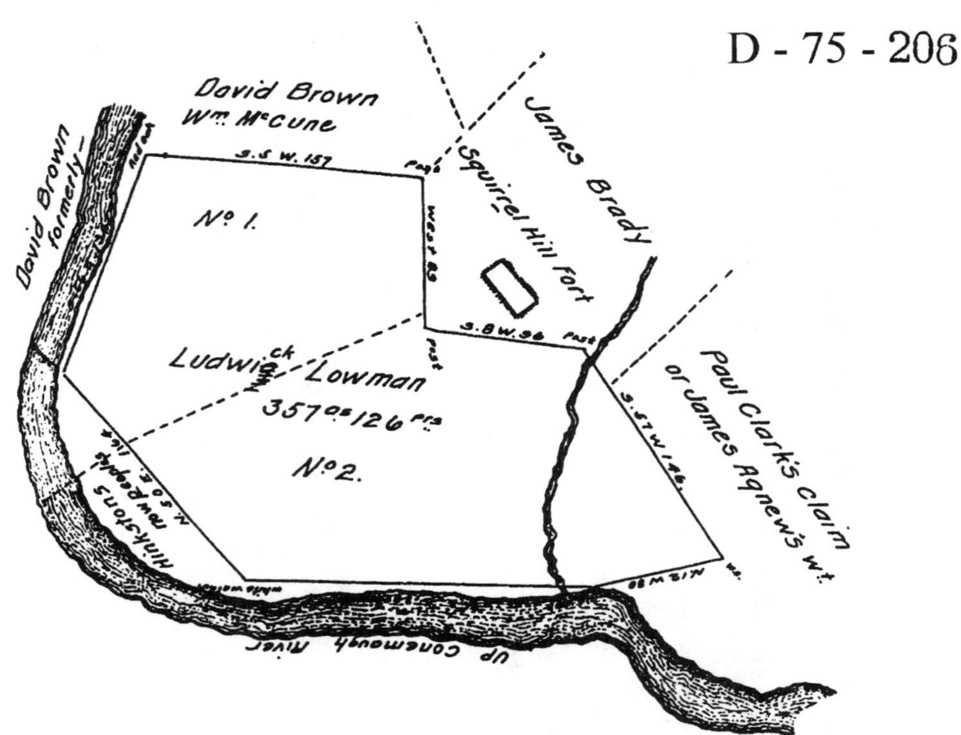

Inpursuance of an Application granted to Ludwick Lowman. No. 467 dated 3d April 1769. Surveyed on the 3d of February 1829 the above described tract of land containing three hundred fifty Seven Acres. one hundred and twenty Six perches and the allowance proportioned at Six per Cent for Roads &c. Situate on the South Side of Conemaugh River at the old Fort of Squirrel Hill. in Fairfield Township in the County of Westmoreland Pa.

Gabriel Hiester Esqr. — S.L. Carpenter D.S.

Surveyor General of Pa. — D. Brown. Patd.

[struck out] — No. 277 not Patd.

N.B. No. 1. Was Surveyed on Warrant to David Brown. dated 19th of March 1789 and also an appn. in the name of Wm. McCune. No. 527. Patented. No. 2. was Surveyed on order No. 277 granted to John Hinkson. not Patented yet James Peoples claims under Hinkson.

S.L.C.

For Report see Appln. No. 1594.

Figure 7. Example of a Copied Survey. New Purchase Application NP-467, Ludwick Lowman. This survey conflicted with other surveys and was not returned.

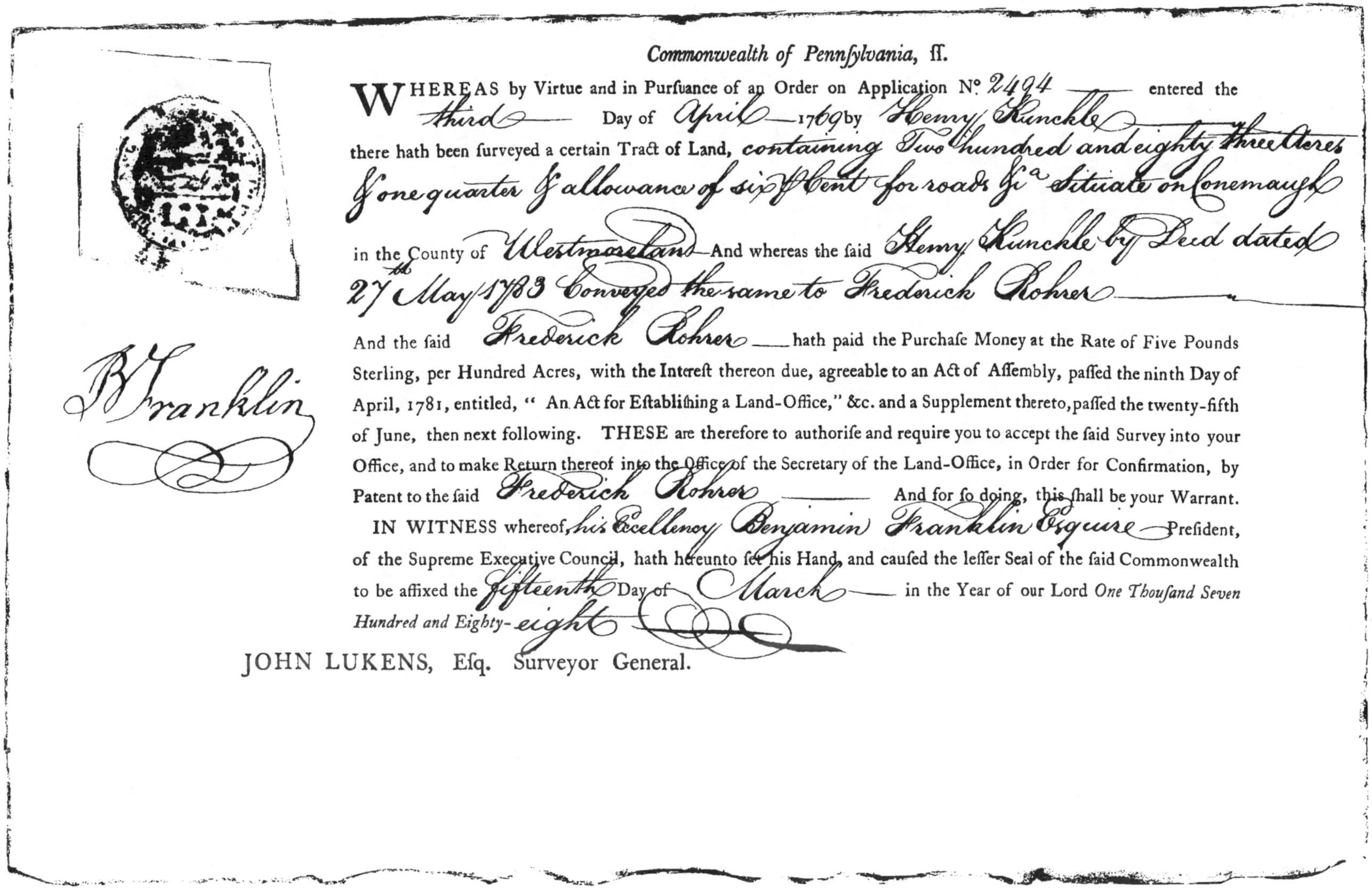

Commonwealth of Pennſylvania, ſſ.

WHEREAS by Virtue and in Purſuance of an Order on Application N° 2494 —— entered the third —— Day of April — 1769 by Henry Kunckle —— there hath been ſurveyed a certain Tract of Land, containing Two hundred and eighty three Acres & one quarter & allowance of six P Cent for roads &c.a Situate on Conemaugh in the County of Westmoreland And whereas the ſaid Henry Kunckle by Deed dated 27th May 1783 Conveyed the same to Frederick Rohrer ——

And the ſaid Frederick Rohrer —— hath paid the Purchaſe Money at the Rate of Five Pounds Sterling, per Hundred Acres, with the Intereſt thereon due, agreeable to an Act of Aſſembly, paſſed the ninth Day of April, 1781, entitled, " An Act for Eſtabliſhing a Land-Office," &c. and a Supplement thereto, paſſed the twenty-fifth of June, then next following. THESE are therefore to authoriſe and require you to accept the ſaid Survey into your Office, and to make Return thereof into the Office of the Secretary of the Land-Office, in Order for Confirmation, by Patent to the ſaid Frederick Rohrer —— And for ſo doing, this ſhall be your Warrant.

IN WITNESS whereof, his Excellency Benjamin Franklin Esquire President, of the Supreme Executive Council, hath hereunto ſet his Hand, and cauſed the leſſer Seal of the ſaid Commonwealth to be affixed the fifteenth Day of March —— in the Year of our Lord *One Thouſand Seven Hundred and Eighty-* eight

B Franklin

JOHN LUKENS, Eſq. Surveyor General.

Figure 8. Frederick Rohrer's Warrant to Accept on Application NP-2494 of Henry Kunckle.

paper, were copied into ledger books by the Land Office. A typical survey is shown in Figure 7 (the copied survey).

4) Warrant to Accept

Prior to this application program, when an individual wanted to start the process of obtaining title to a parcel of land, he would submit an application to the Land Office along with payment of a fee based on the acreage of the land for which a warrant was being requested. The Land Office would then issue a warrant allowing the individual to have the land surveyed by the Deputy Surveyor. In this application program the Land Office issued a "warrant to accept" after the survey was filed at the Land Office and the appropriate fees were paid. These warrants were filed with the regular warrants for the county where the land was located at the time of the warrant, which may be different than the county when the application was issued due to boundary changes and new county formations. The name on the warrant was not necessarily the same as the one on the application. If the land had been sold prior to obtaining the warrant, the warrant would be issued to the current owner and indexed under that person's name. An example of a warrant to accept where the ownership had changed is given in Figure 8.

5) Return

A return was prepared by the Surveyor General from information provided by the applicant and from the survey of the property. The purpose of the return is to certify the accuracy of the survey. It included a reference to the original application, a description of the "metes and bounds" of the property, the names of the neighbors to the property, and the history of the ownership of the property if the person for whom the return was being filed was not the original applicant. The text of a typical return (for NP-737) is transcribed here:[10]

State of Penns. SS.

Whereas by virtue and in pursuance of an order on application No. 737 dated the 3rd day of April 1769 there hath been surveyed the 24th day of October 1769 to James Stringer a certain tract of land called "Dundee" situate about ten miles from Fort Pitt now Allegheny County And whereas the said James Stringer by deed dated the 21st December 1769 conveyed the above mentioned tract to Elias Davidson who by deed dated the 22nd September 1797 conveyed the same to William McCrea. Now in pursuance of a warrant dated the eighth day of December 1807 requiring me to accept the said survey into my office and to make return thereof into the Secretary's Office in order for confirmation by Patent to the said William McCrea I do hereby certify that the said tract is bounded as follows, viz, Beginning at a black oak thence by poor hilly land North three hundred perches to a post, thence by the same and land of one Smith West one hundred and sixty one perches to a post, thence by a hill south one hundred and fifty five perches to an ash west eighty two perches to a white oak thence by vacant land south one hundred and forty five perches to an ash, and thence by hilly land east, two hundred and forty three perches to the beginning containing three hundred fifty four acres one hundred and fifty one perches and the allowance of six percent for roads &c. Returned into the Secretary's office this 8th day of December 1807.

Saml Cochran, S[urveyor] G[eneral]

6) Patent

The patent was the final step in obtaining full title to the land. After the warrant to accept was returned and the fees paid (at the rate of five pounds Sterling per hundred acres, and one penny per acre per year quit rent), the Land Office issued a patent for the land. This document is similar to a deed except that the transaction occurred between the Commonwealth and an individual rather than between two individuals. A transcript of a typical patent follows:[11]

THE SUPREME EXECUTIVE COUNCIL OF THE COMMONWEALTH OF PENNSYLVANIA. To all to whom these presents shall come greeting. Know ye that in consideration of the sum of Forty three pounds eighteen shillings lawful money paid by Eleazer alias Eli Myers into the Receiver General's Office of the Commonwealth there is granted by the said Commonwealth unto the said Eleazer alias Eli Myers a certain tract of land called "The Widow's Dower" situate on Turtle Creek waters in the County of Westmoreland Beginning at a birch thence by vacant land South thirty eight degrees West one hundred & forty two perches to a post thence by land of Mr. Boyd North twenty five degrees West forty three perches to a white oak South fifteen degrees West one hundred & forty one perches to a black oak North thirty nine degrees & an half West by vacant land one hundred & eighteen perches & an half to a white oak North seventy seven degrees West sixty six

[10] Return, 8 DEC 1807, NP-737

[11] Patent P-11-449. New Purchase Application Number 3368 to Martha Myers.

perches to a white oak thence by vacant hills North nineteen degrees West one hundred & four perches to a thorn tree North fifty two degrees East ninety five perches to a post North seventy eight degrees East sixty eight perches to a white oak North fifty degrees East one hundred & twenty four perches to a post thence by land of George Brotherton South forty degrees East one hundred & fifty six perches to the place of Beginning containing three hundred & thirty five acres and one hundred & forty perches and allowance of six percent for roads & with the appurtenances (which said tract was surveyed in pursuance of an Application No. 3368 entered the 13 June 1769 by Martha Myers who by deed dated 3d February 1776 conveyed the same to the said Eleazer alias Eli Myers in fee for whom a Warrant of Acceptance issued the 5 December Instant) To have and to hold the said tract or parcel of land with the appurtenances unto the said Eleazer alias Eli Myers and his heirs to the use of him the said Eleazer alias Eli Myers his heirs & assigns forever free and clear of all restrictions and reservations as to mines royalties quitrents or otherwise excepting & reserving only the fifth part of all gold & silver ore for the use of this commonwealth to be delivered at the pits mouth clear of all charges In Witness whereof the honorable Peter Muhlenberg, Esq., Vice President of the Supreme Executive Council hath hereto set his hand & caused the State Seal to be hereto Affixed in Council the tenth day of December in the year of our Lord One Thousand Seven Hundred & Eighty Seven and of the Commonwealth the twelfth. P. Muhlenberg. Attest Chas. Biddle, S. G. Inrolled 13th Decr. 1787.

Surveyors of the New Purchase

The New Purchase was divided into eleven surveying districts (Figure 9). Each district was assigned to a deputy surveyor, or in the case of one of the western districts, to three members of the McClean family. There does not appear to be any existing contemporary maps showing the surveyors' districts. Figure 9 was created partly from the descriptions of the districts recorded with the instructions given to each surveyor[12] and from a map in a book on the life of Thomas Smith who was one of the deputy surveyors.[13]

A document[14] found with the correspondence of the Surveyor General dated May 1769 listed the number of survey that had been sent to each deputy surveyor. In April 1769, the first month of the New Purchase Application program, 3,183 survey orders had been issued, representing nearly 83 percent of the total number of applications. There was considerable variation in the number of survey orders sent to each surveyor. This reflects the rates at which settlers were moving into each of the respective districts. Table 1 shows the number of survey orders that had been sent to each Deputy Surveyor by the end of April 1769.

A letter from William Maclay, one of the Deputy Surveyors, talks about his being called on to survey land for the "Officers" (see the section on the Officers' and Gentlemen's Tracts below) in the New Purchase.[15] The Treaty of Fort Stanwix, which opened the New Purchase for settlement, was signed on 5 NOV 1768. In theory, settlers should have been able to start "taking up" land at that time. However, the Provincial Government did not start accepting applications until 3 APR 1769. This letter discusses the problems this delay caused for the government and the Deputy Surveyors.

Content on Juniata, Feby 13th, 1769
Sir,

As some difference in sentiments happened between the Surveyor General and myself with regard to the number of orders now in my hands unexecuted; I have this day carefully examed all of my orders, and find that in all there have come to my hands about 1190 about 44 of these (as near as I can recollect) were in Mr. Tea's and Col. Armstrong's Districts. But as I did not keep an exact acc^{t}. of those that I sent, I cannot to a single one, tell how many I have in all rec^{d}. But there are now in my hands in all 1146 of which 584 are executed; 364 no land can be got for in this number are those which were out of the former purchase remain 198 unexecuted, and of uncertain fate. But as it is likely they will share the same chance as the others. I cannot expect to execute or find land for more than about 123 of them. And as I have executed 584 in about 2 years these 123 would not last me more than 5 months; new ones will be issued no doubt but will fail greatly in point of numbers. The above is very nearly the state of my district, as to the assertion that I had 600 to execute it was a very wide mistake. I expect in a few days to be called to survey for the Officers on Buffalo Creek,

[12] Pennsylvania State Archives, RG-17 (Records of the Land Office), Records of the Surveyor General, List of Deputy Surveyors, 1713-1850, microfilm LO 25.29.

[13] Konkle, Burton A., 1904, The Life and Times of Thomas Smith 1745-1809, Campion & Company, Philadelphia.

[14] Pennsylvania State Archives, RG-17 (Records of the Land Office), Records of the Surveyor General, General Correspondence, 1687-1853, Reel 3982.

[15] Ibid.

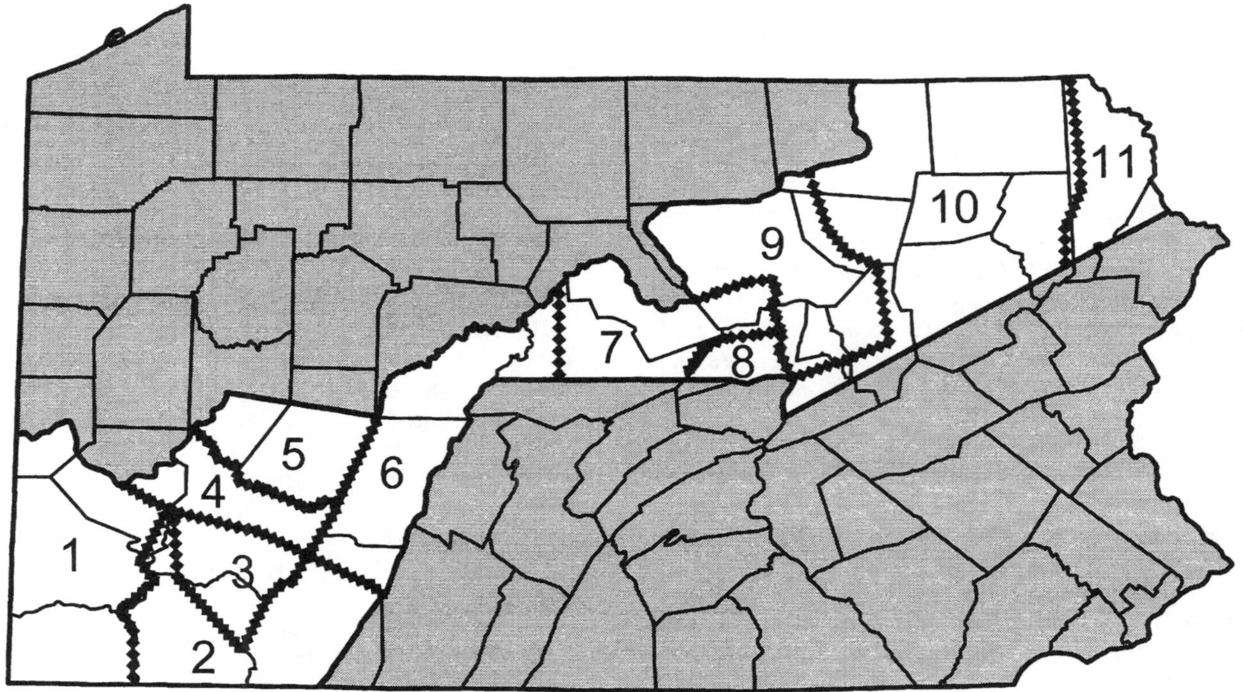

Figure 9. Deputy Surveyors' districts within the New Purchase in 1769. This map, showing the approximate boundaries of the Deputy Surveyors' districts, was created from the descriptions of the districts given when they were assigned and from mapping the locations of surveys done by the individual surveyors.

Table 1. District Surveyors.

District	Deputy Surveyor	Applications sent by May 1769
1	James Hendricks	143
2	Archiblad McClean, Jr., Moses McClean, and Alexander McClean	216
3	William Thompson	382
4	Robert McCrea [5th great uncle of the author of this book]	283
5	Joshua Elder	107
6	Thomas Smith	85
7	Charles Lukens	580
8	William Maclay	308
9	William Scull	706
10	Charles Stewart	361
11	John Biddle	12

and doubt little of our having some broils as we hear it is almost all settled or rather taken up or marked by people who hover about in order to protect it. I am in haste and hope you will excuse my troubling you with this unimportant letter and am

Sir, your most Obed^t. & Hble. Servt.
Wm Maclay
[To:] Ja^s Tilghman, Esqr.

Officers' and Gentlemen's Tracts

A group of officers from the French and Indian War had requested that the Provincial Government grant them land for their service. This group was headed by Col. Turbutt Francis. A total of 24,000 acres of land in the New Purchase was granted to them prior to the acceptance of applications from ordinary citizens. As can be seen in the letter from William Maclay, there was some difficulty in finding enough continuous unsettled land in which to survey the Officers' Tracts.

The locations of the three groups of "Officers' Tracts" are shown in Figures 10 through 13. Since a single location for 24,000 could not be found, three tracts of about 8,000 acres each were chosen.[16] Figure 10 shows the location of these three tracts. The connected draft located along Bald Eagle Creek shown in Figure 11 is recorded as survey BB-1-2 .[17] Figures 12 (along the Susquehanna River) and 13 (in Buffalo Valley in Union County) were created by the author of this work. These tracts were some of the best land available in the New Purchase.

A second set of applications were accepted prior to the official start of the New Purchase application program on 3 April 1769. These were called the "Gentlemen's Tracts." They were granted to prominent individuals, most of whom were officers in the government or friends of the Proprietors. These tracts are not all in one location and only one, GT-3,[18] is mapped here at the southern end of the Susquehanna River Tract in Figure 12.

Details of the granting of the Officers' Tracts can be seen in the following item from the Pennsylvania Archives: [19]

At a Meeting at the Governors the 3d Feb'y 1769.

Present: The Governor, The Sec'ry Mr. Tilghman, The Auditor Gen'l Mr. Hockley, The Rec'r Gen'l Mr. Physick, The Surveyor Gen'l Mr. Lukens

Ordered that Col'o Francis and the Officers of the 1st & 2d Battalion of the Pennsylvania Regiment be allowed to take up 2400 A's [this is an error – it should read 24,000 acres] *to be divided amongst them in the district Surveys on the Waters of the West Branch of Sasquehanna to be seated with a Family for each 300 A's within two Years from the time of Survey paying 5£ Sterling per hundred & 3d. Stg. per Acre. The Land to be taken as near as may be together and in bodys of Eight Thousand Acres at least. If more that eight Thousand Acres can be had in one place they may have the Liberty of taking it & laying out the Residue into other places, if it can't be got in one. The whole paid for before patents issue for any Parts Surveys to be made & returned in nine Months and Settlements made and Money paid in 15 Months after returns made. Int. & Quit Rent to commence in nine Months after Application, If all cannot pay for their parts in time patents to issue for the whole to such as will pay the whole Money still seated as above.*

The terms for the Gentlemen's Tracts are also found in the Pennsylvania Archives: [20]

At a Meeting at the Governors the 22nd Feb'y 1769 Present: The Governor, The Sec'ry Mr. Tilghman, The Auditor Gen'l Mr. Physick, The Surveyor Gen'l Mr. Lukens

The Board taking into Consideration the Application of Dr. Morgan and Major Smallman in behalf of themselves and other Officers of the Pennsylvania Regiments of the Years 1756, 1757, 1758, 1759, & 1760 (a List of whose Names they delivered in) to be allowed to take up Eighty Thousand Acres of Land beyond the Mountains upon the Terms on which the Application of Col'o Francis and his Corps have been allowed to take up Lands on the Sasquehanna are of Opinion that they shall be allowed to take up by way of Application when the Land Office opens fifty Thousand Acres (being nearly the proportion allowed Col'o Francis & Company) upon the same terms vizt. 5£ Sterling p. 100 A's & 1d Stg. p. Acre p. Annum Quit Rent to be taken up as near together as may be and in body of eight Thousand Acres each and Two thousand or in larger Bodys if it can be had the whole to be paid for at one payment before Patents issue for any parts. The Tracts to be divided amongst the Officers into district Tracts and a Family to be settled on each 300 A's in two Years from the time of Application. The Surveys

[16] Munger, Donna B. 1991. Pennsylvania Land Records, Scholarly Resources, Inc., Wilmington, DE, p. 80.
[17] Survey BB-1-2.
[18] Surveys D-57-242 and B-7-116 for Col. Turbutt Francis. This tract adjoins one of his two Officers' Tracts (OT-1).
[19] Minutes of the Board of Property, Pennsylvania Archives, 3rd Series, Volume 1, p. 253
[20] Minutes of the Board of Property, Pennsylvania Archives, 3rd Series, Volume 1, p. 254

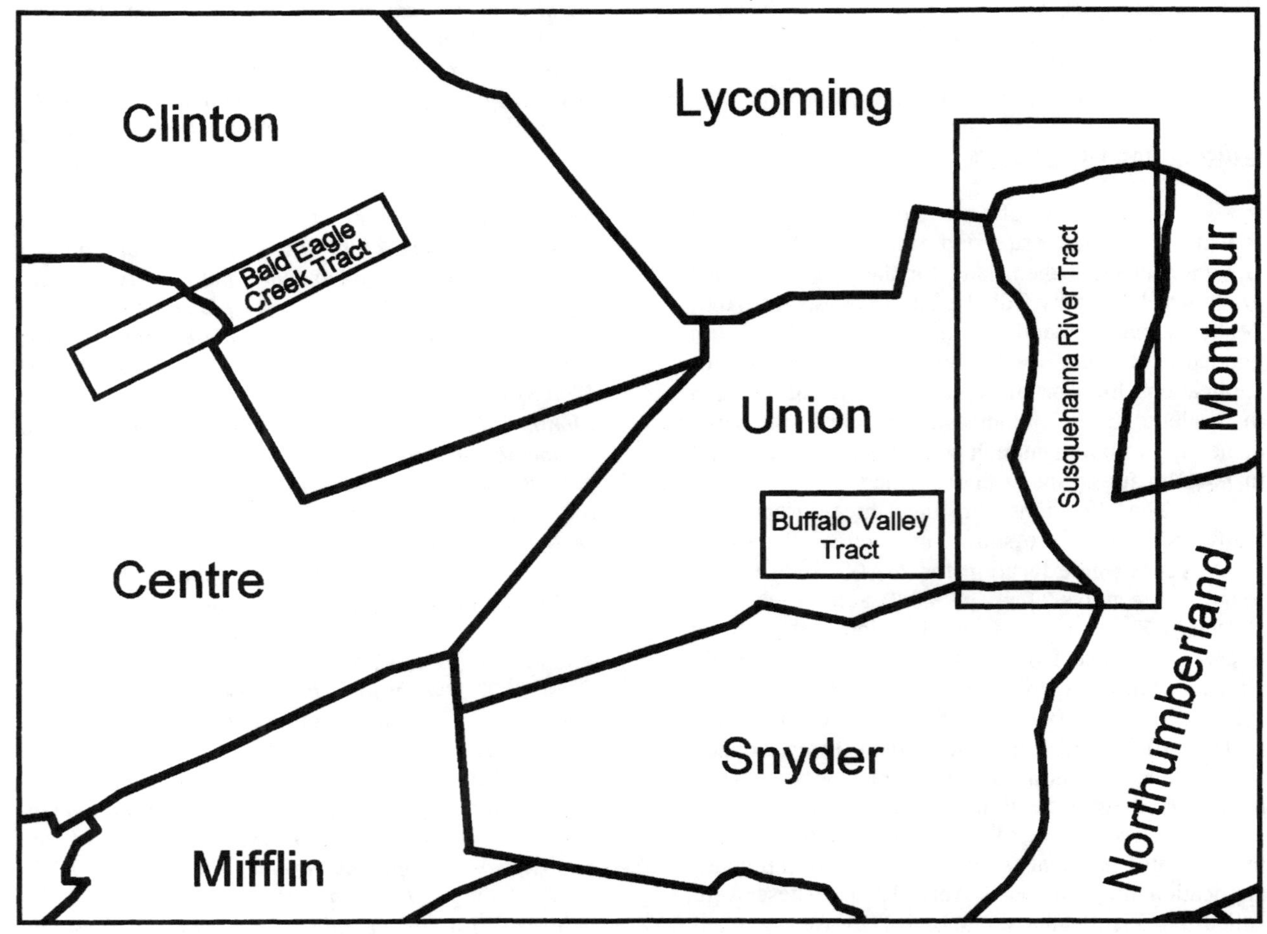

Figure 10. Map showing the location of the three sections of the Officers' Tracts.

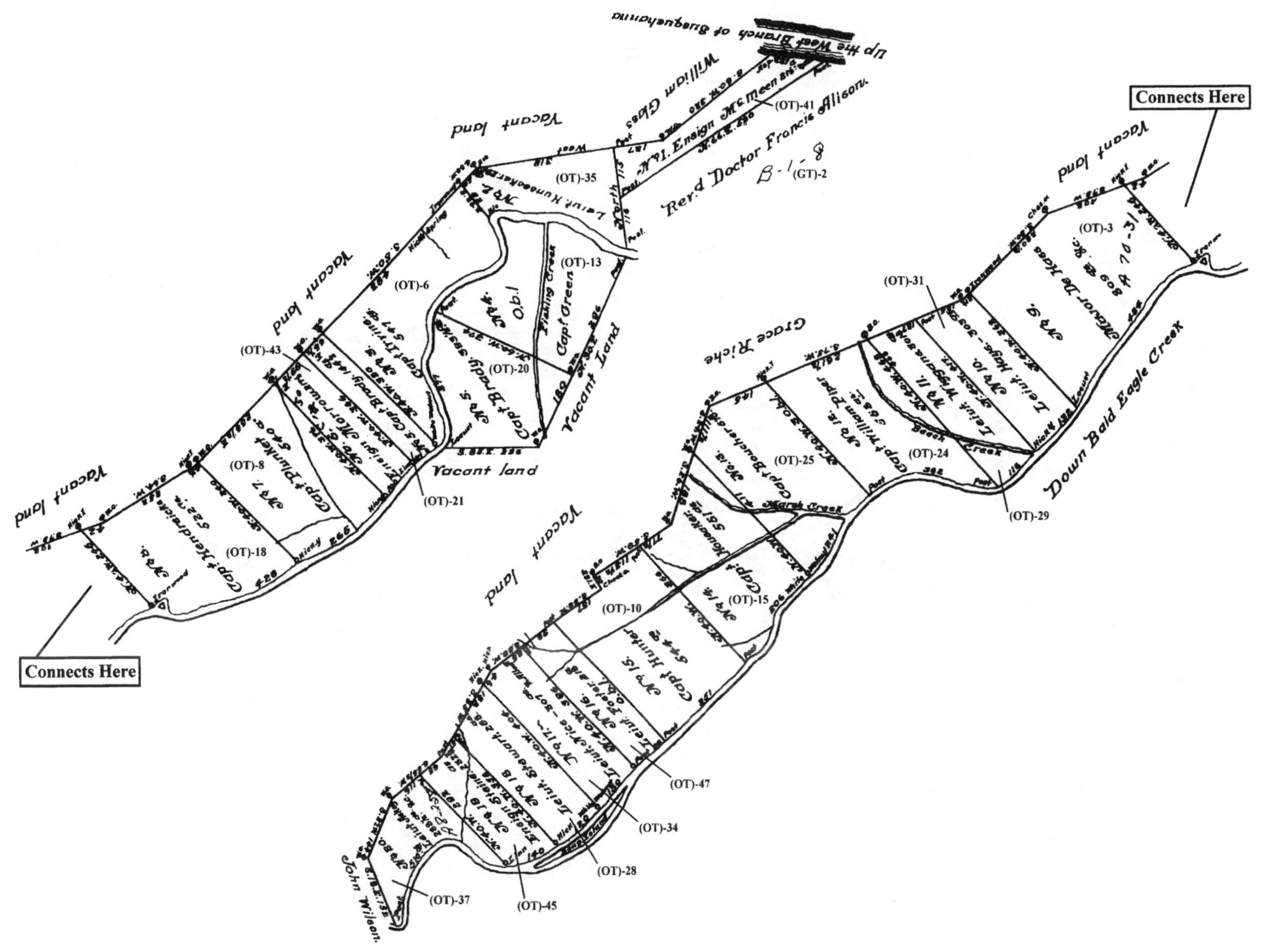

Figure 11. Bald Eagle Creek section of the Officers' Tracts. From Copied Survey BB-1-2.

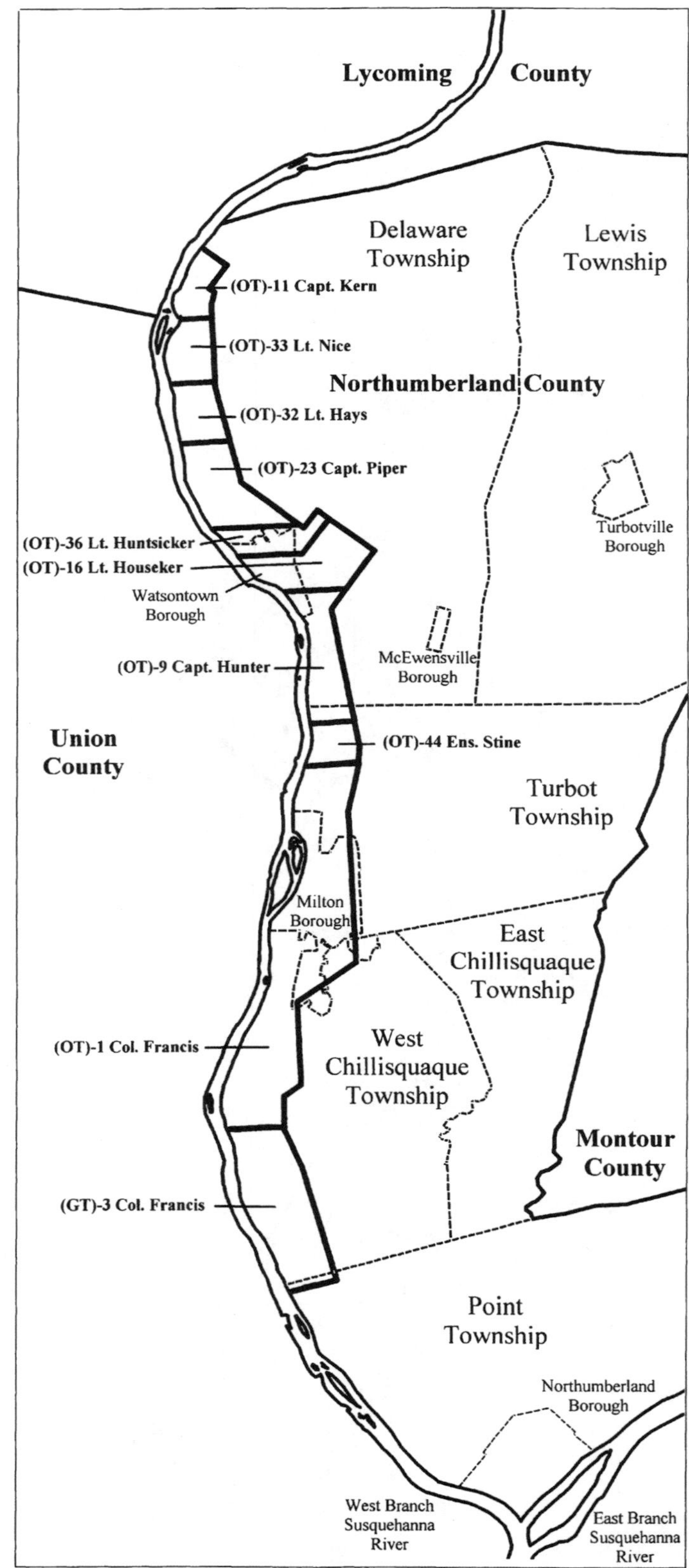

Figure 12. Susquehanna River Section of the Officers' Tracts.

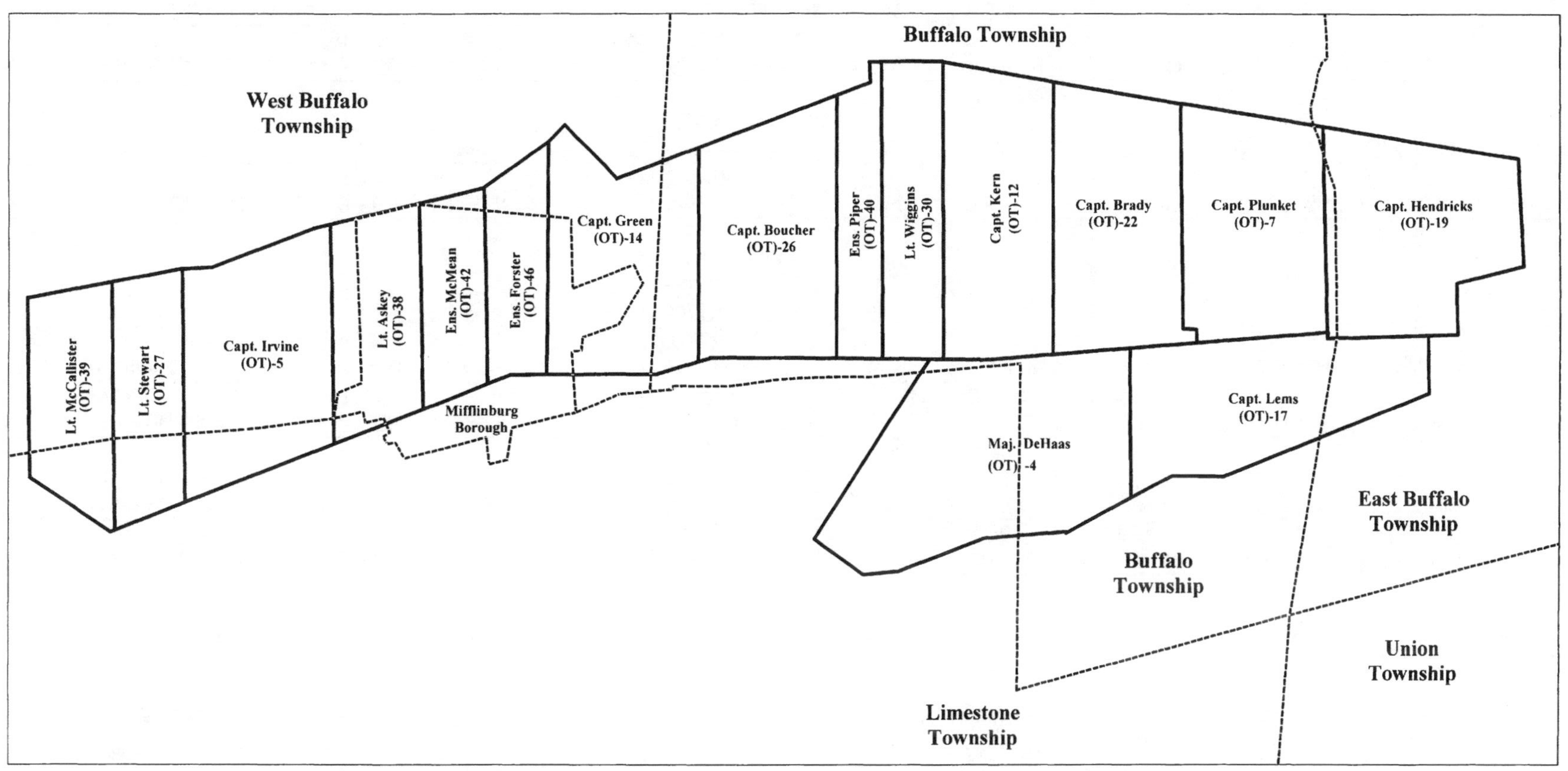

Figure 13. Buffalo Valley section of the Officers' Tracts.

Table 2. Officers' (OT) and Gentlemen's (GT) Tracts.

Tract	Applicant	Date	Orig. Place	Later Place	Acres	Survey	Neighbors, Notes, etc.
(OT)-1	Francis, Col. Turbutt	3 FEB 1769	Berks	Turbot & West Chillisquaque Twps. & Milton Borough, Northumberland	2775	B-6-64	(r8 MAR 1774)/(p10 MAR 1774)/[patent AA-14-479]
(OT)-2	Clayton, Col. Asher	3 FEB 1769			---		
(OT)-3	Dehaas, Maj. John Philip	3 FEB 1769	Berks	Beech Creek Twp., Clinton	809	BB-1-2 A-70-31	(r31 MAY 1774)/(p14 JUN 1774)/[patent AA-14-487]
(OT)-4	Dehaas, Maj. John Philip	3 FEB 1769	Berks	Buffalo & Limestone Twps., Union	922.62	A-70-36	(2 JUN 1774)/(p15 JUN 1774)/[patent AA-14-488]
(OT)-5	Irwin, Capt. James	3 FEB 1769	Berks	West Buffalo & Limestone Twps., Union	622	A-70-38	(r17 MAR 1774)/(p21 MAR 1774)/[patent AA-14-269]
(OT)-6	Irwin, Capt. James	3 FEB 1769	Berks	Bald Eagle Twp., Clinton	547	BB-1-2 A-26-125	(r17 MAR 1774)/(p21 MAR 1774)/[patent AA-14-265]
(OT)-7	Plunket, Capt. William	3 FEB 1769	Berks	Buffalo & East Buffalo Twps., Union	619	D-57-263 D-57-276 A-70-27	(r8 MAR 1774)/(p9 MAR 1774)/[patent AA-14-202]
(OT)-8	Plunket, Capt. William	3 FEB 1769	Berks	Bald Eagle Twp., Clinton	540	BB-1-2 C-146-297	(r8 MAR 1774)/(p10 MAR 1774)/[patent AA-14-201]
(OT)-9	Hunter, Capt. Samuel	3 FEB 1769	Berks	Delaware & Turbot Twps. & Watsontown Borough, Northumberland Co.	609	C-78-36	(r7 MAR 1774)/(p7 MAR 1774)/[patent AA-14-152]
(OT)-10	Hunter, Capt. Samuel	3 FEB 1769	Berks	Liberty Twp., Centre	544	BB-1-2 C-78-56	(r7 MAR 1774)/(p7 MAR 1774)/[patent AA-14-153]
(OT)-11	Kern, Capt. Jacob	3 FEB 1769	Berks	Delaware Twp., Northumberland	246	D-60-236 D-60-237 C-102-226	(r3 JUN 1774)/(p15 JUN 1774)/[patent AA-14-496]
(OT)-12	Kern, Capt. Jacob	3 FEB 1769	Berks	Buffalo Twp., Union	616.5	A-70-39	(r3 JUN 1774)/(p15 JUN 1774)/[patent AA-14-494]
(OT)-13	Green, Capt. Timothy	3 FEB 1769	Berks	Bald Eagle Twp. & Mill Hall Borough, Clinton	542	BB-1-2 Q-112	(r18 MAR 1774)/(p22 MAR 1774)/[patent AA-14-268]

Table 2. Officers' (OT) and Gentlemen's (GT) Tracts.

Tract	Applicant	Date	Orig. Place	Later Place	Acres	Survey	Neighbors, Notes, etc.
(OT)-14	Green, Capt. Timothy	3 FEB 1769	Berks	Buffalo & West Buffalo Twps. & Mifflinburg Borough, Union	616.6	A-70-37	(r17 MAR 1774)/(p22 MAR 1774)/[patent AA-14-264]
(OT)-15	Houseker, Capt. Nicholas	3 FEB 1769	Berks	Liberty Twp., Centre	551	BB-1-2 C-220-183	(r17 MAR 1774)Thomas Willing, Esq./(p22 MAR 1774)/[patent AA-14-287]
(OT)-16	Houseker, Capt. Nicholas	3 FEB 1769	Berks	Delaware Twp. & Watsontown Borough, Northumberland	609	C-220-182	(r17 MAR 1774)Thomas Willing, Esq./(p22 MAR 1774)/[patent AA-14-286]
(OT)-17	Lems, Capt. Christopher	3 FEB 1769	Berks	Buffalo & East Buffalo Twps., Union	623.7	D-57-42 D-57-43 D-57-45 D-56-281 D-56-82 A-70-33	(r8 MAR 1774 & p11 MAR 1774)Turbutt Francis [patent AA-14-172]
(OT)-18	Hendricks, Capt. James	3 FEB 1769	Berks	Beech Creek Twp., Clinton	522	BB-1-2 D-57-44 A-70-24	(r31 MAY 1774)John Philip Dehaas/(p14 JUN 1774)/[patent AA-14-486]
(OT)-19	Hendricks, Capt. James	3 FEB 1769	Berks	Buffalo & East Buffalo Twps., Union	639	A-70-32 D-57-45	(r8 MAR 1774)Turbutt Francis/(p9 MAR 1774)/[patent AA-14-159]
(OT)-20	Brady, Capt. John	3 FEB 1769	Berks	Bald Eagle Twp. & Mill Hall Borough, Clinton	393.5	BB-1-2 Q-38	(r30 MAY 1782)Samuel Atlee, Esq./(p20 JUN 1782)/[patent P-1-254]
(OT)-21	Brady, Capt. John	3 FEB 1769	Berks	Bald Eagle Twp., Clinton	144.5	BB-1-2 Q-38	(r30 MAY 1782)Samuel Atlee, Esq./(p20 JUN 1782)/[patent P-1-254]
(OT)22	Brady, Capt. John	3 FEB 1769	Berks	Buffalo Twp., Union	629.5	D-57-291 D-57-292 A-70-26	(r18 FEB 1789)Samuel McClay, Esq./(p18 FEB 1789)/[patent P-14-429]
(OT)23	Piper, Capt. William	3 FEB 1769	Berks	Delaware Twp., Northumberland	609	B-324	(r31 MAY 1794)James Irwin/(p7 JUN 1794)/[patent P-22-220]]
(OT)24	Piper, Capt. William	3 FEB 1769	Berks	Beech Creek Twp., Clinton & Liberty Twp., Centre	553	BB-1-2 A-70-25	(r26 MAY 1774)John Philip Dehaas/(p14 JUN 1774)/[patent AA-14-493]
(OT)25	Boucher, Capt. Conrad	3 FEB 1769	Berks	Liberty Twp., Centre	570	BB-1-2 A-70-23	(r31 MAY 1774)John Philip Dehaas/(p14 JUN 1774)/[patent AA-14-489]
(OT)26	Boucher, Capt. Conrad	3 FEB 1769	Berks	Buffalo Twp., Union	619.7	A-70-35	(r5 MAR 1774)John Philip Dehaas/(p7 MAR 1774)/[patent AA-14-151]

Table 2. Officers' (OT) and Gentlemen's (GT) Tracts.

Tract	Applicant	Date	Orig. Place	Later Place	Acres	Survey	Neighbors, Notes, etc.
(OT)27	Stewart, Lieut. Charles	3 FEB 1769	Berks	West Buffalo & Limestone Twps., Union	340.6	A-70-29	(r19 MAR 1774)/(p22 MAR 1774)/[patent AA-14-270]
(OT)28	Stewart, Lieut. Charles	3 FEB 1769	Berks	Howard & Liberty Twps., Centre	288	BB-1-2 A-10-72 D-56-76	(r18 MAR 1774)/(p22 MAR 1774)/[patent AA-14-266]
(OT)29	Wiggins, Lieut. Thomas	3 FEB 1769	Berks	Beech Creek Twp., Clinton & Liberty Twp., Centre	301.4	BB-1-2 C-220-184	(r18 MAR 1774)/(p22 MAR 1774)/[patent AA-14-262]
(OT)30	Wiggins, Lieut. Thomas	3 FEB 1769	Berks	Buffalo Twp., Union	339.1	A-62-298	(r19 MAR 1774)/(p22 MAR 1774)/[patent AA-14-263]
(OT)-31	Hays, Lieut. James	3 FEB 1769	Berks	Beech Creek Twp., Clinton	303	BB-1-2 C-78-60	(r7 MAR 1774)/(p7 MAR 1774)/[patent AA-14-157]
(OT)-32	Hays, Lieut. James	3 FEB 1769	Berks	Delaware Twp., Northumberland	334	C-78-59	(r7 MAR 1774)/(p7 MAR 1774)/[patent AA-14-156]
(OT)-33	Nice, Lieut. John	3 FEB 1769	Berks	Delaware Twp., Northumberland	334	B-354	(r3 JUN 1774)Jacob Kern/(p15 JUN 1774)/[patent AA-14-495]/[incorrectly assigned to Lt. James Hays in register]
(OT)-34	Nice, Lieut. John	3 FEB 1769	Berks	Liberty Twp., Centre	307	BB-1-2 C-102-224	(r2 JUN 1774)Jacob Kern/(p15 JUN 1774)/[patent AA-14-497]
(OT)-35	Huntzicker, Lieut. Daniel	3 FEB 1769	Berks	Allison & Bald Eagle Twps. & Lock Haven Borough, Clinton	292	BB-1-2 C-78-62	(r8 MAR 1774)Rev. John Hoge/(p8 MAR 1774)/[patent AA-14-160]
(OT)-36	Huntzicker, Lieut. Daniel	3 FEB 1769	Berks	Delaware Twp. & Watsontown Borough, Northumberland	334	C-78-63	(r11 MAR 1774)Rev. John Hoge/(p11 MAR 1774)/[patent AA-14-160]
(OT)-37	Askey, Lieut. Thomas	3 FEB 1769	Berks	Howard Twp., Centre	288.5	D-56-218 A-8-258 BB-1-2	(r18 MAR 1774)John Clark/(p29 MAR 1774)/[patent AA-14-221]
(OT)-38	Askey, Lieut. Thomas	3 Feb 1769	Berks	West Buffalo & Limestone Twps. & Mifflinburg Borough, Union	348	A-70-21	(r18 MAR 1774)John Clark/(p29 MAR 1774)/[patent AA-14-291]
(OT)-39	McCallister, Lieut. James	3 FEB 1769	Berks	West Buffalo & Limestone Twps., Union	340.62	A-70-40	(r15 MAR 1774)Samuel McClay/(p19 APR 1774)/[patent AA-14-319]/(r5 APR 1796)William Chamberlain
(OT)-40	Piper, Ensign William	3 FEB 1769	Cumberland	Buffalo Twp., Union	247.5	D-60-208 A-70-28	(r7 MAR 1774)/(p7 MAR 1774)/[patent AA-14-155]

Table 2. Officers' (OT) and Gentlemen's (GT) Tracts.

Tract	Applicant	Date	Orig. Place	Later Place	Acres	Survey	Neighbors, Notes, etc.
(OT)-41	McMean, Ensign William	3 FEB 1769	Cumberland	Lock Haven Borough, Clinton	216	BB-1-2 C-78-76	(r3 MAY 1774)Alexander Hamilton/(p4 MAY 1774)/[patent AA-14-309]
(OT)-42	McMean, Ensign William	3 FEB 1769	Cumberland	West Buffalo Twp. & Mifflinburg Borough, Union	248	A-70-30	(r10 MAY 1774) George Nagle, Esq./(p10 MAY 1774)/[patent AA-14-550]
(OT)-43	Morrow, Ensign James	3 FEB 1769	Cumberland	Bald Eagle Twp., Clinton	217.5	C-179-50 BB-1-2 C-199-252	(r19 MAR 1774)John Misser[this return was not found]/(p22 MAR 1774)/[patent AA-14-208]/(r11 JAN 1813)Adam Spangler & Henry Spangler/(p12 JAN 1813)/[patent H-8-420/[Note: this tract was patented twice]
(OT)-44	Stine, Ensign Augustine	3 FEB 1769	Cumberland	Turbot Twp., Northumberland	246	C-78-61	(r8 MAR 1774)Rueben Haines/(p19 APR 1774)/[patent AA-14-468]
(OT)-45	Stine, Ensign Augustine	3 FEB 1769	Cumberland	Howard Twp., Centre	232.75	A-89-127 BB-1-2	(r17 MAR 1774)Jesse Lukens/(p19 APR 1774)/[patent AA-14-556])
(OT)-46	Forster, Ensign James	3 FEB 1769	Cumberland	West Buffalo Twp. & Mifflinburg Borough, Union	246.5	D-56-232 A-70-22	(r31 MAY 1774)John Philip Dehaas /(p14 JUN 1774)/[patent AA-14-490]
(OT)-47	Forster, Ensign James	3 FEB 1769	Cumberland	Liberty Twp., Centre	218	A-70-34 BB-1-2	(r31 MAY 1774)John Philip Dehaas/(p14 JUN 1774)/[patent AA-14-491]
(GT)2	Allison, Francis Dr.	4 FEB 1769	Cumberland	Lock Haven Borough, Clinton	1500	B-1-8	(r7 APR 1772)/[original application with regular applications for 1769.]
(GT)3	Francis, Turbutt	4 FEB 1769		West Chillisquaque & Point Twps., Northumberland	1000	B-6-63 D-57-54 D-57-55	(r12 DEC 1774)/Henry Montour/[original application with regular applications for 1769.]
(GT)4	Tilghman, James	4 FEB 1769		Northumberland, Lycoming, Montour	5000	D-57-242 B-7-116	(r15 JAN 1770)/[original application with regular applications for 1769.]
(GT)5	Tilghman, James	4 FEB 1769		Loyalsock, Lycoming	500	D-62-265 D-62-281 A-40-98	(r27 SEP 1803)William Tilghman/Andrew Montour
(GT)6	Allen, Andrew	4 FEB 1769	Northampton	Wayne	2000	D-46-72 D-46-74 D-46-75 D-46-76 D-46-77	(p24 MAY 1949)Charles N. Whitson [patent H-80-87]/[original application with regular applications for 1769. Filed under name "A. Allen"]

Table 2. Officers' (OT) and Gentlemen's (GT) Tracts.

Tract	Applicant	Date	Orig. Place	Later Place	Acres	Survey	Neighbors, Notes, etc.
(GT)7	Allen, Andrew	4 FEB 1769		Northumberland & Luzerne	3000	B-6-65 B-6-66 B-6-67 B-6-68 B-23-127 BB-3-16 BB-4-15	(r24 FEB 1774)Francis Turbutt, Esq./(r13 June 1774)Francis Turbutt, Esq./[original application with regular applications for 1769. Filed under name "A. Allen"]
(GT)8	Purviance, Samuel Jr.	4 FEB 1769		Luzerne	2000	B-1-62 B-15-126	(p18 OCT 1873)John T. Everhart/[original application with regular applications for 1769. Filed under name "A. Allen"]
(GT)9	Allen, John	4 FEB 1769		Northumberland, Montour, & Columbia	5000	D-57-235 D-56-54 W-69 B-1-47 B-3-184 C-31-251 C-157-91	(r20 JUL 1815)J. Rees/(r3 SEP 1822)Thomas Copper, M.D./(r3 AUG 1848)J.J. Mulligan & J.W. Duncan/--- Tilghman
(GT)10	Purviance, Samuel Jr.	4 FEB 1769		Muncy, Lycoming	4000	D-56-205 D-56-217 D-56-235 D-56-245 D-56-275 D-57-256 D-62-248	[original application with regular applications for 1769. Filed under name "A. Allen"]
(GT)11	Ewing, John Rev.	7 FEB 1769	Berks	Kellt, Union	1000	D-62-242 A-49-82	(r2 AUG 1770)/[original application with regular applications for 1769.]
(GT)12	Ewing, John Rev.	7 FEB 1769	Berks	Buffalo, Union	500	D-57-260 A-49-66	(r6 JAN 1773)/[original application with regular applications for 1769.]
(GT)13	Allen, John	9 FEB 1769	Chillisquaque Creek		5000		--- Tilghman/[original application with regular applications for 1769.]
(GT)14	Montgomery, John, Esq. & Stewart, Alexander	9 FEB 1769	Washington, Westmoreland		1000 (925)	A-86-259 A-30-196 G-157 A-86-259 B-13-129 C-105-151	(r4 MAR 1773)John Montgomery/(r2 APR 1795)John Briney[patent P-23-385]/(r29 APR 1800)Martin Birch[patent P-43-38]/(r23 DEC 1830)John Dougherty[patent H-30-15]/(r5 APR 1849)James R. Johnston/[original application with regular applications for 1769. Also (GT)15.]
(GT)15	Montgomery, John & Stewart, Alexander	9 FEB 1769	Westmoreland	Indiana	1000	C-166-82 A-2-2	(r4 MAR 1773)John Montgomery/(r29 APR 1800)John Hindman/[see (GT)14 for original application]

Table 2. Officers' (OT) and Gentlemen's (GT) Tracts.

Tract	Applicant	Date	Orig. Place	Later Place	Acres	Survey	Neighbors, Notes, etc.
(GT)16	Purviance, Samuel Jr.	9 FEB 1769		Fairfield, Lycoming	4000	D-62-263 B-21-117 C-16-280 C-16-295 C-138-198 B-21-116	(r4 MAR 1796)Sarah Connally/(r4 AUG 1800)Samuel Mifflin/(r13 APR 1805)Henry Drinker/[original application with regular applications for 1769.]
(GT)17	McKee, Alexander	14 FEB 1769		St. Clair, Allegheny	500	D-62-83 B-7-39 B-7-40	(r12 APR 1827)James McKee
(GT)18	Stewart, Alexander	17 FEB 1769	Cumberland		1000	F-152	(r30 DEC 1773)/[original application with regular applications for 1769.]
(GT)19	St. Clair, Arthur	9 FEB 1769		Donegal, Westmoreland	300	D-56-103 C-207-29	(r17 OCT 1788)
(GT)20	Croghan, George	1 APR 1769		Pitt, Allegheny	1500 (1352.59)	B-1-52 D-62-93 A-37-82 A-88-350 A-87-106 B-1-52 D-50-90 B-9-93 C-51-171 A-21-158	(r29 DEC 1787)Conrad Winebiddle/(r6 FEB 1812)J. Brandon/(r6 FEB 1812)John Fritchman & wife/(r13 JUL 1815)James Ross/(r10 DEC 1844)George A. Bayard/(r19 MAY 1818)John Ewalt/(11 APR 1845)James Young/[original application with regular applications for 1769, undated, near the start of the letter "C". Also (GT)21-27 on same original application.]
(GT)21	Croghan, George	1 APR 1769	Westmoreland	Plum Creek, Allegheny	400	D-57-66 D-62-98 D-56-173 A-35-53 A-35-54 C-60-200	(r22 SEP 1815)Robert Elliot/(p23 JUN 1869)James Vorner[patent H-64-69]
(GT)22	Croghan, George	1 APR 1769		Pitt, Allegheny	400	D-56-177 C-75-204	(r22 APR 1789)William Heath[patent P-15-6]/Richard McMahon
(GT)23	Croghan, George	1 APR 1769		Pitt, Allegheny	400	A-217 A-86-21	(r23 MAR 1799)C. & C. Winebiddle
(GT)24	Croghan, George	1 APR 1769	Cumberland		600	H-179	
(GT)25	Croghan, George	1 APR 1769	Cumberland	Donegal, Westmoreland	400	D-57-68 D-57-69	
(GT)26	Croghan, George	1 APR 1769		Wilkins, Allegheny	500	B-23-13 A-77-162 A-77-163	John Frazier

Table 2. Officers' (OT) and Gentlemen's (GT) Tracts.

Tract	Applicant	Date	Orig. Place	Later Place	Acres	Survey	Neighbors, Notes, etc.
(GT)27	Croghan, George	1 APR 1769		Versailles, Allegheny	500	B-23-14	William Powell/widow Myers
(GT)28	Franks, David	1 APR 1769		South Huntingdon, Westmoreland	500	D-56-102 D-56-237 E-562 G-373	(r20 JUL 1781)Bernard Gratz/(r20 FEB 1787)Mary Plumtsead
(GT)29	Franks, David	1 APR 1769		South Huntingdon, Westmoreland	500	E-560 C-237	(r20 FEB 1787)Mary Plumstead/(r30 AUG 1796)Bernard Gratz
(GT)30	Franks, David	1 APR 1769		South Huntingdon, Westmoreland	500	E-559 C-233	(r20 FEB 1787)Mary Plumsted/(r6 JAN 1796)Bernard Gratz
(GT)31	Franks, David	1 APR 1769		South Huntingdon or Sewickley, Westmoreland	500	G-374 G-375	(r20 JUL 1781)Bernard Gratz
(GT)32	Franks, David	1 APR 1769	Sewickley Creek	Westmoreland	500	G-373 G-376	(r20 JUL 1781)Bernard Gratz
(GT)33	Franks, David	1 APR 1769	Youghiogheny River, Westmoreland	Allegheny	500	Z-72 C-206-167	(r19 FEB 1801)Robert Smith
(GT)34	MacKey, Aneas	1 APR 1769		Plum, Allegheny	300	D-62-82 G-10-112	Lt. Col. Reid
(GT)35	Meyers, Mrs. (widow)	1 APR 1769		Plum, Allegheny	300	A-54-283	(r19 JAN 1844)Henry & Ananias Chalfant, Administrators Of Thomas Chalfant
(GT)36	Beyerly, Andrew	1 APR 1769		Hempfield, Westmoreland	300	D-56-219 D-64-187 D-64-189 D-64-213 X-195	
(GT)37	Laughlin, Robert	1 APR 1769		Salem, Westmoreland	300	D-57-279	
(GT)38	Procter, Capt. John	1 APR 1769		Unity, Westmoreland	300	D-57-214 D-57-215 D-58-276 D-58-277 C-71-220 D-12-76 C-6-250 D-12-76	(r25 MAR 1802)James Guthrie/(r4 MAR 1819)George Smith

Table 2. Officers' (OT) and Gentlemen's (GT) Tracts.

Tract	Applicant	Date	Orig. Place	Later Place	Acres	Survey	Neighbors, Notes, etc.
(GT)39	Campbell, John	1 APR 1769		Derry, Westmoreland	300	F-231	Samuel Duncan/--- McGee
(GT)40	Frazier, John	1 APR 1769		North Versailles, Allegheny	300	A-89-167 C-225-241	(r5 JUL 1797)George Wallace, Esq.
(GT)41	Ormsby, John	1 APR 1769		St. Clair, Allegheny	300	O-157	(r15 APR 1813)Oliver Ormsby & other heirs of John Ormsby[patent H-9-385]/[original application with regular applications for 1769 - undated, at start of letter "O".]
(GT)42	Ormsby, John Jr.	1 APR 1769		St. Clair, Allegheny	300	A-88-349	(r23 FEB 1815)Thomas Baird & Joseph McClurgh/John Ormsby, Sr./[original application with regular applications for 1769 - undated, at start of letter "O".]
(GT)43	Ormsby, Oliver	1 APR 1769	Monongahela River	Allegheny	300	C-160-16	(r3 MAR 1800)/John Ormsby, Jr./[original application with regular applications for 1769 - undated, at start of letter "O".]
(GT)44	Thompson, William	1 APR 1769		Pitt, Allegheny	300	D-494	William Elliot/Alexander McGreegar/(r11 OCT 1802)Ephraim Blaine, Esq.
(GT)45	Thompson, Robert	1 APR 1769		Pitt, Allegheny	300	D-10-20	John Frazer/Peter Rolletes/Capt. Edmunson/(r4 MAR 1791)George Wallace, Esq.
(GT) 46	Auchmuty, Arthur	1 APR 1769	Berks	Augusta, Northumberland	250	A-22-21 D-56-206 B-1-181	(r1 APR 1810)Samuel Auchmuty/William Smith/[original application (dated 13 MAR 1769) with regular applications for 1769.]

to be made in nine Months from the time of Application & purchase Money paid with Interest from the Expiration of the nine Months in two Years from the time of Application. If all Officers cannot pay for their parts Patents to issue for the distinct Tracts to such as will pay the whole, still seating as above. And the Governor accordingly allows of their Applications on the above Terms.

A newspaper advertisement[21] dated shortly after the opening of the Land Office for the acceptance of New Purchase application calls for the Officers to meet in what is now Harrisburg to arrange details and to pay for the surveying of the tracts:

April 13, The following Officers, who served in the Pennsylvania Regiment in the year 1764, viz. Captains Hunter, Kern, Green, Housseggor, Lems, Hendricks, Brady, W. Piper, and Bucher; Lieutenants Stewart, Wiggins, Hays, Nice, Hunsicker, Askey, and McAllester; Ensigns W. Piper, McMeen, Morrow, Stiene, and Foster, are desired to meet at Mr. John Harris's in Paxton Township, Lancaster County, on the 15th day of May next in order that a division may be made of the land granted to them by the Honorable Proprietors, and are requested to be punctual in their attendance, that the expences attending the survey and other charges in prosecuting the applications, may be discharged.
TURBUT FRANCIS, Lt. Col.
J. P. De HAAS, Major,
WILLIAM PLUNKETT,
JAMES IRVINE, Captains

Table 2 lists the Officers' and Gentlemen's Tracts. The majority of these tracts were surveyed and patented.

Problems with the System – Caveats

A common problem found in many of the early Pennsylvania land records is that the description of the land on the application and the warrant is not precise enough to determine the exact location of the land. Often the description can be as simple as "adjoining John Smith." It was also a relatively frequent event for two surveys to overlap or for more than one person to attempt to claim the same tract of land. To deal with these problems any person who had a dispute over a tract of land could file a Caveat with the Board of Property. This entitled them to a hearing on the matter where the dispute could be resolved peaceably. These records often give an interesting insight into the land application process.

One noteworthy caveat was identified in which land applied for under a New Purchase application conflicted with a West Side Application. This land was located along Penns Creek in western Union County (see connected draft prepared by the author, Figure 14). In this area, Penns Creek was supposed to form the boundary between the areas of the New Purchase and the West Side Application. The text of the caveat is given here: [22]

On Caveat:
Administrators of Jacob Godshalk, deceased
vs. William Plunket

In this case it appears that Dr. Plunket claims under an Application No. 2783 [New Purchase Application] of John Harris entered Ano 1769 for 300 Acres of Land on Penns Creek Northward of Edward Lees & joining land of the said Harris purchaser of John Turner, Wm. Doran and Andrew Smith. And the Administrators of Jacob Godshalk claims under Stephen Wooleys Application No.1146 [West Side Application] entered 6th August, 1766 for 300 Acres of land at the Crab tree bottom and running down the Creek to Charles Stewarts Claim. It is ordered that the Surveyor General direct the Deputy Surveyor to execute the order of Wooley agreeable to its location in order to assist the Deputy in determining the location the depositions of Edward Lees is to be sent to him And to direct him to do the same as soon as possible.

Another caveat shows an example of a different kind of problem that can happen because of fraudulent activities. In this case another person with the same name tried to claim land applied for by a different person. Three entries in the Pennsylvania Archives give the details of this problem and how it was resolved:

Land Office, 28 JUL 1773[23]
George Albrecht enters a Caveat against the Acceptance of a survey made for John Foster and John Simpson on a piece of land on Penns Creek, in Northumberland County, Alledging that he hath an Application for the said Land and that he has been informed that a certain Geo. Albrecht, a name sake of the Caveator undertook to convey his the said Caveator's land to the said Forster and Simpson. The last Monday in November next is appointed for a hearing of the parties on this Caveat they having at least thirty Days Notice.

---

[21] Pennsylvania Journal, 20 APR 1769

[22] Minutes of the Board of Property, Pennsylvania Archives, 3rd Series, Volume 1, p. 431

[23] Caveat Book No. 5, Pennsylvania Archives, 3rd Series, Volume 2, p. 542

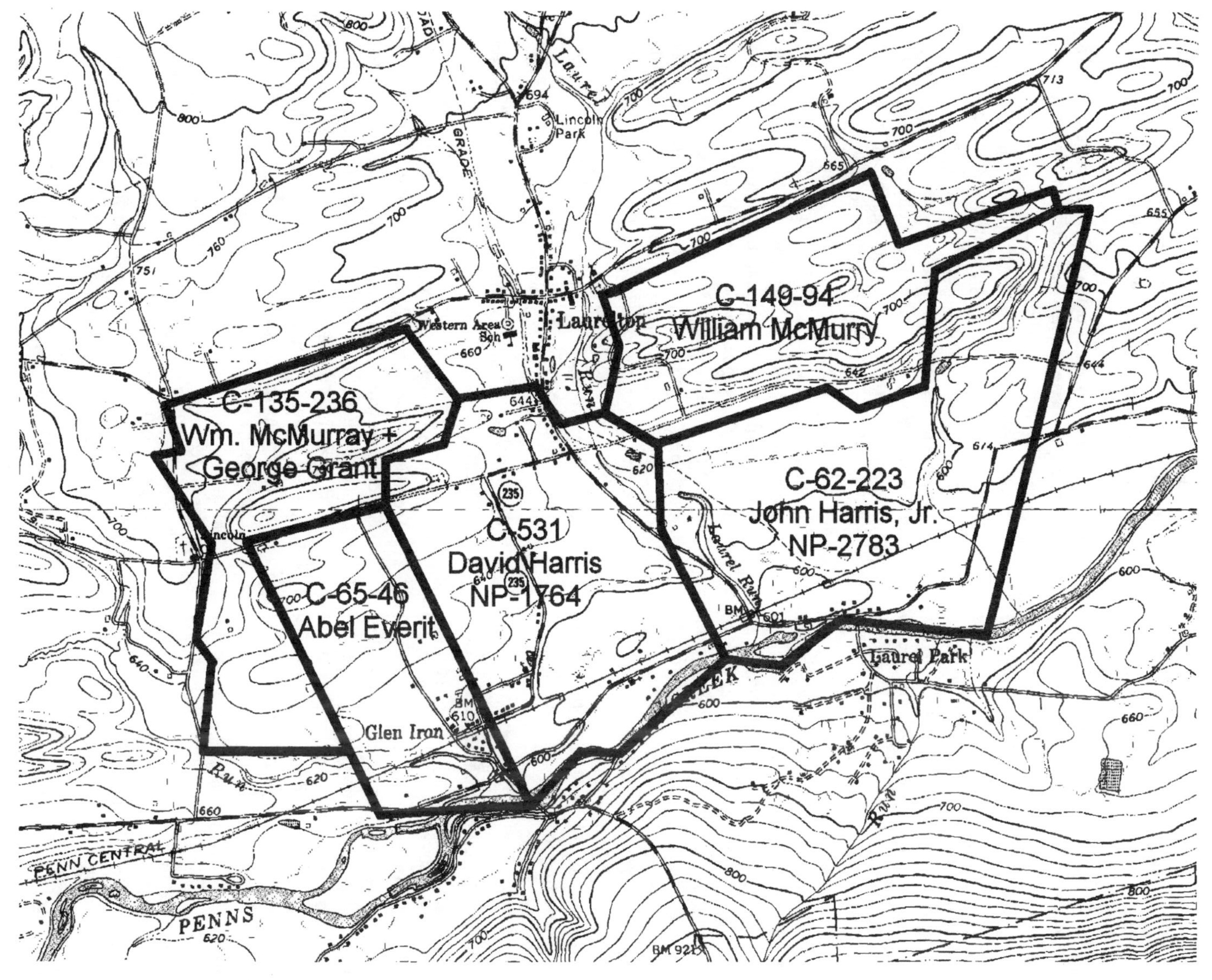

Figure 14. Connected Draft showing area of Caveat between a New Purchase Application and a West Side Application. Located on the north side of Penns Creek near Laurelton, Hartley Township, Union County.

30 NOV 1773[24]
George Albrecht agt. John Forster
John Forster having Notice of hearing & sending an Excuse by John Simpson the matter is postponed till the last Monday in April next.

28 JUN 1774[25]
Simpson and Foster
agt.
George Albrecht of Heidelberg Township
Simpson and Foster claim under an Appl'n of one George Albrecht, a different person from George Albrecht of Heidelberg Township, brother of Frederick. And there being heretofore some doubt which of the two persons the Application belonged to the matter is now cleared up by the Oath of Frederick Albrecht Brother of George of Heidelberg And a Patent is Ordered to him the same George & the Caveat of Simpson and Foster dismissed.

Table 3 shows those caveats printed in the Pennsylvania Archives that I was able to identify as relating to land applied for under New Purchase applications. As can be seen from the number of caveats listed here, disputes were fairly common. This table only lists those caveats that were filed in the years covered by the printed Pennsylvania Archives. There are most likely other caveats that were filed later and I undoubtedly missed some caveats from this time period because of the text of the caveats not mentioning that the land was obtained via a New Purchase application.

Potential for Fraud – Example of Samuel Wallis

An example of some of the potential problems with the application system as it was conducted is illustrated by the case of Samuel Wallis' attempt to combine 18 New Purchase applications into a single tract of land. Wallis purchased the rights to these applications from 18 different individuals. It is likely that he arranged with these people in advance of 3 April 1769 for his purchasing their applications. One of the original deeds was purchased on eBay (Internet auction site) by the author of this work. Table 4 lists the 18 applications and gives the full descriptions on each application. The deed is the sale of application NP-1558 (belonging to Peter Young) to Samuel Wallis. The deed is on a pre-printed form that had the purchase price of 5 shillings incorporated as part of the standard text. This deed is show in Figure 15. Several of the other 18 original deeds were also recently sold on eBay.

The main thing that the descriptions of these lands found on the applications have in common is their vagueness. Most of them only reference one neighbor's name. By virtue of the neighbors names, they all do appear to adjoin each other. However, in the Lien Docket (see below in the description of the column "Later Place") the lands were later thought to be in several different counties. Only three of the 18 tracts have surveys that were returned, and only one of the tracts was patented.

A county history of Lycoming County[26] gives a list of the 18 applications and details of Wallis' attempt to patent the land. While no survey of the tracts has been located, it is referenced as being in existence at the time the county history was written. The county history also gives the metes and bounds of the survey, and Figure 16 shows the location of the survey on a modern USGS topographic quadrangle.[27]

From the available information, there are two possible sources of the fraud involved in this example. It is possible that Samuel Wallis simply selected 18 applications that were so vague in their description of their location to allow him to claim that they were all adjacent and at this specific location. The other possibility is that the applications that had been surveyed were surveyed by others attempting to use an application that had failed. Which is the truth is not yet known.

The Controversy over the Delay in Opening the Land Office

Although the report of the conclusion of the Treaty of Fort Stanwix reached the Pennsylvania General Assembly on 16 January 1769, the Land Office was not opened for the receipt of applications until 3 April 1769. Prior to this date, a considerable number of acres within the New Purchase were taken up for proprietary manors, and the Officers' and Gentlemen's Tracts. Even though settlers were not allowed to take up land within areas not yet purchased from the Indians, many had already staked out claims within the New Purchase. When these settlers finally were able to file their applications on 3 April 1769, many of them found that the land they wanted had already been taken. An extremely informative exchange of letters on this issue was published in the Pennsylvania Gazette:[28]

---

[24] Minutes of the Board of Property, Pennsylvania Archives, 3rd Series, Volume 1, p. 371
[25] Ibid., p. 382

[26] Meginness, John F., 1892, History of Lycoming County, Pennsylvania, Brown, Runk & Co., Chicago, p. 199.
[27] USGS 7.5 minute maps, Beavertown, PA and Hartleton, PA quadrangles.
[28] Pennsylvania Gazette, 31 January 1771

Table 3. Caveats involving New Purchase Applications

App #	Ser (Vol) Page	Date of Caveat	Applicant	Others Named
(OT) all	PA (3) 2:518	8 DEC 1772	Lt. George Thompson	Caveats against any patents on the Officers Tracts since he should have had one.
(OT)18	PA (3) 2:462	20 JUN 1769	Capt. Christopher Lems	Rev. John Ewing
(GT)12	PA (3) 2:511	27 OCT 1772	Rev. John Ewing	John Hoge, Sr.
(GT)12	PA (3) 1:353	6 JAN 1773	John Ewing	John Hoge/William McClay/William Bale/James Shaddon
(GT)14	PA (3) 1:287	7 FEB 1770	John Montgomery & Alexander Stewart	Joseph Ellicott/Thomas Austin/Benjamin Austin
(GT)14	PA (3) 2:14	5 MAR 1792	John Montgomery & Alexander Stewart	Stephen Rybolt/Robert McCrea
(GT)14	PA (3) 2:126	1 SEP 1794	John Montgomery & Alexander Stewart	John Briney
(GT)15	PA (3) 2:459	31 MAY 1769	John Montgomery & Alexander Stewart	Benjamin Austin/Thomas Austin/Joseph Ellicott
(GT)15	PA (3) 1:287	7 FEB 1770	John Montgomery & Alexander Stewart	Joseph Ellicott/Thomas Austin/Benjamin Austin
(GT)23	PA (3) 2:465	20 JUL 1769	George Crogham	Casper Taub/Col. Bouquet
(GT)24	PA (3) 2:464	6 JUL 1769	George Crogham	William Elliot/Col. Reed
(GT)24	PA (3) 1:485	3 MAY 1786	George Croghan	William Elliott/Bernard Gratz (executor of George Croghan)
(GT)24	PA (3) 1:499	2 OCT 1786	George Croghan	William Elliott/Bernard Gratz (executor of George Croghan)
(GT)42	PA (3) 1:748	14 JUN 1791	John Ormsby, Jr	Oliver Ormsby
(GT)44	PA (3) 2:651	7 JUL 1784	William Thompson	John McKee
NP-1	PA (3) 2:540	13 JUL 1773	Abraham Smith	Dr. Francis Allison/Samuel Craig
NP-1	PA (3) 2:563	30 MAR 1774	Abraham Smith	Benjamin Allison/William Miller/Samuel Craig
NP-1	PA (3) 1:496	4 SEP 1786	Abraham Smith	Dr. Allison/William Miller
NP-6	PA (3) 2:585	18 NOV 1774	Jacob Weyland	William Patterson/Joseph Galloway/Peter Swartz/Dr. Smith/Michael Weyland/Joseph Hutchins/Thomas McFaden
NP-12	PA (3) 1:609	1 SEP 1788	Walter Beaty	William Beaty/Rebecca Carothers/James Carothers/James Hamilton, Esq./George Baird, Esq./Christopher Hays
NP-15	PA (3) 2:463	27 JUN 1769	Hugh Crawford	Jacob Bousman
NP-15	PA (3) 1:284	11 JAN 1770	Hugh Crawford	Jacob Bausman/Col. Croghan
NP-22	PA (3) 1:669	5 OCT 1789	Samuel Sloan	Robert Orr/George Clark/David Sloan (died by 5 OCT 1789)
NP-31	PA (3) 1:733	7 MAR 1791	Peter Boor	William Bonham/John Lowdon/Lawrence Boor
NP-32	PA (3) 1:295	1 MAY 1770	Michael Weyland	Joseph Hutchings/Mr. McClay/Mr. Lukens
NP-32	PA (3) 1:384	4 AUG 1774	Michael Weyland	Joseph Hutchins/Dr. William Smith/Peter Swartz (who intermarried the widow of Michael Weyland)/Robert Moodie, Esq./Robert Fruit/Mr. Lukens/Mr. McClay
NP-32	PA (3) 2:585	18 NOV 1774	Michael Weyland	William Patterson/Joseph Galloway/Peter Swartz/Dr. Smith/Jacob Weyland/Joseph Hutchins/Thomas McFaden

Table 3. Caveats involving New Purchase Applications

App #	Ser (Vol) Page	Date of Caveat	Applicant	Others Named
NP-44	PA (3) 1:293	26 MAR 1770	Elizabeth Brown	Rev. Thomas Barton/Samuel Wallis/Charles Lukens/Richard Peter Barton
NP-52	PA (3) 2:510	22 OCT 1772	James Dougherty	Nicholas Sheaffer
NP-52	PA (3) 1:352	28 DEC 1772	James Dougherty	Nicholas Sheaffer
NP-58	PA (3) 2:599	13 MAR 1775	Thomas Taylor	Robert Aiken/Richard Wallace
NP-60	PA (3) 1:586	3 MAR 1788	Simon Eaker	William Todd, Esq./Arthur St. Clair, Esq./William Findley, Esq./John Grant
NP-68	PA (3) 1:531	4 JUN 1787	Francis Foster, Jr.	Jacob Grojean/Thomas Rees/Philip Pfeffer/Jacob Gemberling/Martin Heffelfinger/John Sherrack
NP-76	PA (3) 1:442	26 NOV 1783	Henry Musser	John Alwood
NP-83	PA (3) 1:547	29 AUG 1787	Eneas Mackay	Samuel Mackay (son of Col. Eneas Mackay, deceased)/Andrew Hoy/Benjamin Lodge/Samuel Thompson
NP-83	PA (3) 1:640	3 MAR 1789	Eneas Mackey	Andrew Hoy/Col. Stephen Bayard/Elizabeth Bayard (wife of Stephen)/Samuel Mackey (son of Eneas)/B. Lodge/Jacob Bousman
NP-123	PA (3) 2:490	1 APR 1772	Thomas Doyle	David Robb/Cornelius Coxe
NP-123	PA (3) 1:459	4 APR 1785	Thomas Doyle	Daniel Robb/Cornelius Coxe
NP-124	PA (3) 2:487	-- FEB 1772	Daniel Elliott	Isaiah Althouse
NP-124	PA (3) 1:348	26 OCT 1772	Daniel Elliot	William Forster/Isaiah Althouse/--- Melone
NP-125	PA (3) 1:637	3 MAR 1789	John Cumpton	Alexander White (guardian of 3 daughters of John Hite, deceased)/Isaac White/John White/Alexander McClean/William White, deceased (father of Isaac and John)/Benjamin Whaley
NP-125	PA (3) 2:92	22 JAN 1794	John Cumpton	John Hite heirs
NP-128	PA (3) 1:295	1 MAY 1770	Joseph Hutchings	Michael Weyland/Mr. McClay/Mr. Lukens
NP-128	PA (3) 1:384	4 AUG 1774	Joseph Hutchins	Dr. William Smith/Peter Swartz (who intermarried the widow of Michael Weyland)/Robert Moodie, Esq./Robert Fruit/Mr. Lukens/Mr. McClay/Michael Weyland
NP-128	PA (3) 2:585	18 NOV 1774	Joseph Hutchins	William Patterson/Joseph Galloway/Peter Swartz/Dr. Smith/Michael Weyland/Jacob Weyland/Thomas McFaden
NP-149	PA (3) 2:520	29 DEC 1772	David Loning	James McGlaughlin/Samuel Nearson
NP-151	PA (3) 1:498	2 OCT 1786	Robert Newell, Jr	Joseph Chambers/Jacob Feagley/James Colvin
NP-152	PA (3) 2:615	23 FEB 1776	William Coxe	Thomas Cuthbert/James Hays/["I withdraw the above caveat as one of the Executors of my father, Thomas Cuthbert, deceased"]
NP-158	PA (3) 1:623	3 NOV 1788	Benjamin Brown	George Fry/Levi Hicks/Richard Gonsalus
NP-158	PA (3) 1:647	14 APR 1789	Benjamin Brown	Richard Gonzales/James Packer/Samuel Wallis, Esq.
NP-167	PA (3) 2:518	4 DEC 1772	William Montgomery	Stephen Porter
NP-172	PA (3) 2:486	13 FEB 1772	David Barr	Alexander Barr/Capt. James Potter/Hugh McKee
NP-180	PA (3) 1:697	7 JUN 1790	Richard Gist	John Little/Thomas Gist/John Woods, Esq./Isaac Meason/Cornelius Harity/Joseph Hunter/Enoch David/John Roberts/Daniel Edwards
NP-180	PA (3) 1:757	9 SEP 1791	Richard Gist	Joseph Hunter/John Little/Thomas Gist heirs/Christopher Gist (father of Thomas)/Nathaniel Gist/Cornelius Harety/Enoch David/John Roberts/Daniel Edwards
NP-180	PA (3) 2:51	5 NOV 1792	Richard Gist	--- Poe/--- Perry/Col. Isaac Meason/Thomas Gist

Table 3. Caveats involving New Purchase Applications

App #	Ser (Vol) Page	Date of Caveat	Applicant	Others Named
NP-201	PA (3) 1:531	4 JUN 1787	Martin Heffelfinger	Jacob Grojean/Thomas Rees/Philip Pfeffer/Jacob Gemberling/Francis Foster, Jr./John Sherrack
NP-211	PA (3) 1:302	26 JUN 1770	William Perry	John Coxe/Thomas Smith/Samuel Wallis
NP-212	PA (3) 1:283	26 DEC 1769	John Wright	Samuel Hughes/Benjamin Dean/John Ewing/Thomas Ewing (father of John)
NP-218	PA (3) 2:478	8 NOV 1771	Elias Reger or Reigar	John Lowdon
NP-227	PA (3) 2:544	13 AUG 1773	Miles Hillborn	Dr. Hugh Williamson/James Clark/Samuel Wallis
NP-243	PA (3) 2:508	23 SEP 1772	James Shadden	John Ewing/Neal McCoy
NP-243	PA (3) 1:353	6 JAN 1773	James Shaddon	John Ewing/John Hoge/William McClay/William Bale
NP-248	PA (3) 2:651	19 JUL 1784	Griffith Gibbons	Samuel Wallis/James Sharon/Samuel Coale
NP-252	PA (3) 2:508	23 SEP 1772	Neal McCoy	John Ewing/James Shadden
NP-254	PA (3) 2:511	27 OCT 1772	John Hoge, Sr. (son of Jonathan Hoge)	Rev. John Ewing
NP-254	PA (3) 1:353	6 JAN 1773	John Hoge	John Ewing/William McClay/William Bale/James Shaddon
NP-256	PA (3) 1:705	24 AUG 1790	Martin Laughman	John Gibson/James Hendricks/Thomas Smallman
NP-261	PA (3) 2:483	9 JAN 1772	John McClellan	Richard Baird/Elias Davison
NP-263	PA (3) 1:757	9 SEP 1791	Cornelius Harety	Joseph Hunter/John Little/Thomas Gist heirs/Christopher Gist (father of Thomas)/Nathaniel Gist/Enoch David/John Roberts/Daniel Edwards/Richard Gist
NP-289	PA (3) 2:473	12 AUG 1771	Henry Irisen	John Simpson
NP-292	PA (3) 1:733	7 MAR 1791	Lawrence Boor	William Bonham/John Lowdon/Peter Boor
NP-294	PA (3) 2:590	27 JAN 1775	Martin Schneider	Frederick Rohrer/John Elder
NP-297	PA (3) 2:469	2 OCT 1769	Hamilton Bell	Richard Smith/Dr. Francis Allison/Samuel Wallis
NP-297	PA (3) 1:281	29 NOV 1769	Hamilton Bell	Francis Allison/Samuel Wallis
NP-302	PA (3) 2:464	17 JUL 1769	Cornelius Swiper	Edward Shippen/Joseph Shippen, Jr.
NP-303	PA (3) 2:469	2 OCT 1769	Richard Smith	Hamilton Bell/Dr. Francis Allison/Samuel Wallis
NP-303	PA (3) 1:281	29 NOV 1769	Richard Smith	Hamilton Bell/Francis Allison/Samuel Wallis
NP-308	PA (3) 2:476	11 OCT 1771	Elizabeth Baldwin	John William Province/Rebecca Jenkins
NP-308	PA (3) 1:362	5 JUN 1773	Elizabeth Baldwin	Elias Stone (intermarried with Elizabeth Baldwin)/Aaron Jenkins/Rebecca Jenkins (wife of Aaron)/John William Province
NP-320	PA (3) 1:289	5 MAR 1770	John Sherer	William Sherer/Peter Resner
NP-325	PA (3) 2:540	21 JUL 1773	Margaret Stuart	James Goudy (of West Caln Twp., Chester Co.)
NP-326	PA (3) 2:574	8 JUL 1774	Joshua Mitchel	Robert Robb/Samuel Wallis/Susanna Robb (wife of Robert)/John Farmer
NP-326	PA (3) 1:566	28 SEP 1787	Joshua Michael [should be Mitchel]	Susanna Robb/Robert Robb (husband of Susanna)/Samuel Wallis/John Farmer
NP-326	PA (3) 1:586	3 MAR 1788	Joshua Mitchel	Robert Robb/Samuel Wallis
NP-336	PA (3) 2:508	21 SEP 1772	John Worthington	Thomas Johnston/Samuel Wallis/Samuel McWilliams
NP-336	PA (3) 1:374	29 MAR 1774	John Worthington	Samuel Wallis/Thomas Johnston
NP-338	PA (3) 2:631	15 MAR 1782	James Campbell, Jr.	Joseph Budd
NP-338	PA (3) 1:480	7 FEB 1786	James Campbell, Jr.	Joseph Budd/George Bryan

Table 3. Caveats involving New Purchase Applications

App #	Ser (Vol) Page	Date of Caveat	Applicant	Others Named
NP-348	PA (3) 1:350	26 OCT 1772	Hugh McClellan	Elias Davison/--- Beard/--- Guthry/--- Moore/Robert McCrea/John Allison/John Davison
NP-375	PA (3) 2:550	20 OCT 1773	Hannah Mason	William Clark/Dr. John Morgan
NP-375	PA (3) 1:401	29 AUG 1774	Hannah Mason	William Clark/Dr. John Morgan/Sarah Mason
NP-375	PA (3) 1:742	2 MAY 1791	Hannah Mason	William Clark/Dr. Morgan's heirs/William Scull/Charles Lukens
NP-377	PA (3) 2:648	26 APR 1784	James Stewart	Andrew Stewart (of Paxton Twp., Lancaster Co.)
NP-385	PA (3) 2:550	20 OCT 1773	William Clark	Dr. John Morgan/Hannah Mason
NP-385	PA (3) 1:742	2 MAY 1791	William Clark	Hannah Mason/Dr. Morgan's heirs/William Scull/Charles Lukens
NP-389	PA (3) 1:664	7 SEP 1789	Alexander Blaine	Ephtaim Blaine, Esq./--- Proctor/--- Todd/---Lochry/John Moore/--- Henry
NP-389	PA (3) 1:711	6 SEP 1790	Alexander Blaine	Ephraim Blaine/William Proctor/William Lochry/John Moore/William Finley/Archibald Lochry
NP-408	PA (3) 1:293	26 MAR 1770	Richard Peter Barton	Rev. Thomas Barton/Samuel Wallis/Charles Lukens/Elizabeth Brown
NP-450	PA (3) 1:382	28 JUN 1774	Seth McCormick	Mary Rees/Richard Irwin
NP-451	PA (3) 1:289	6 MAR 1770	James Cooper	George Irwin/Francis Irwin/William Johnson/Richard Irwin/Marcus Hulings/James McMahon/Adam Cooper/Robert Fowler
NP-455	PA (3) 2:528	2 MAR 1773	Lodowick Sprogell	James Claypoole/Jesse Lukens/William Patterson/Daniel Ryan
NP-458	PA (3) 2:476	11 OCT 1771	Rebecca Jenkins	John William Province/Elizabeth Baldwin
NP-458	PA (3) 1:362	5 JUN 1773	Rebecca Jenkins	Elizabeth Baldwin/Elias Stone (intermarried with Elizabeth Baldwin)/Aaron Jenkins (husband of Rebecca)/John William Province
NP-487	PA (3) 1:472	4 OCT 1785	William Barr	
NP-500	PA (3) 1:288	26 FEB 1770	Lawrence Shinney	John Clark/Joseph Shippen
NP-509	PA (3) 1:562	5 NOV 1787	John Reynolds	Charles Gibson/Thomas Campbell/William Finley, Esq./John Moore, Esq.
NP-545	PA (3) 2:488	11 MAR 1772	Alexander McCay	Alexander Blaine/Aeneas McCay
NP-549	PA (3) 1:623	3 NOV 1788	George Fry	Benjamin Brown/Levi Hicks/Richard Gonsalus
NP-551	PA (3) 2:574	8 JUL 1774	John Farmer	Robert Robb/Samuel Wallis/Susanna Robb (wife of Robert)/Joshua Mitchel
NP-551	PA (3) 1:566	28 SEP 1787	John Farmer	Susanna Robb/Robert Robb (husband of Susanna)/Samuel Wallis/Joshua Michael [should be Mitchel]
NP-551	PA (3) 1:586	3 MAR 1788	John Farmer	Robert Robb/Samuel Wallis
NP-560	PA (3) 2:534	11 MAY 1773	Galbraith Patterson	Thomas Rees/John Forster/William Patterson
NP-561	PA (3) 2:526	24 FEB 1773	Mary Field	Grace Little/Michael Troy/Ralph Forster
NP-562	PA (3) 1:311	29 OCT 1770	Andrew Forbes	John Caruthers (son of John)/John Nicholas/Capt. Thompson
NP-562	PA (3) 1:523	3 MAY 1787	Andrew Forbes	John Caruthers (son of John)/John Nicholas/Benjamin Lodge/William Shrater
NP-564	PA (3) 1:557	1 OCT 1787	Thomas Jordan	George Fry/Michael Troy
NP-564	PA (3) 1:570	3 DEC 1787	Thomas Jordan	Peter Miller/George Fry/Michael Troy
NP-575	PA (3) 1:610	1 SEP 1788	Joseph Yeates	Amos Ales/David England/James Bryson/Henry Dixon/--- Hooder
NP-594	PA (3) 1:376	29 MAR 1774	Charles Iredell	Jesse Lukens/Dr. Coxe/William McClay/Robert Iredell, Jr./William Norcross
NP-600	PA (3) 2:656	26 OCT 1784	John Boggs	Samuel Bell/William Smith
NP-601	PA (3) 1:382	28 JUN 1774	Mary Rees	Seth McCormick/Richard Irwin

Table 3. Caveats involving New Purchase Applications

App #	Ser (Vol) Page	Date of Caveat	Applicant	Others Named
NP-612	PA (3) 1:493	7 AUG 1786	Nicholas Mauer	Isaac Seely/Lewis Lewis/Gen'l Hiester/Mr. Dehaas/Thomas McKean/Mr. Bradford/Mr. Burd/George Landislyer/George Bryan/William Lewis/Charles Risk
NP-612	PA (3) 1:654	17 JUL 1789	Nicholas Mauer	Isaac Seely/Lewis Lewis/Gen'l Hiester/Mr. Dehaas/Joseph Wallis, Esq./Mr. Bradford/Mr. Burd/George Lautensliger/George Bryan/Charles Risk
NP-613	PA (3) 1:672	5 NOV 1789	William Sherer & Henry Shryock	Angus McDonald/William Schooly/Robert Adams/Col. Henry Bouquet/Stephen Field/Rees Cadwallader
NP-613	PA (3) 1:712	29 SEP 1790	William Sherer & Henry Shryock	William Schooly/Robert Adams/Joseph Thomas, Esq.
NP-613	PA (3) 1:729	7 FEB 1791	William Sherer & Henry Shryock	William Schooly/Robert Adams/Mr. Scott/Mr. Thomas/Col. Bouquet/Moses McClean/Thomas Banfield/Joseph Graybill/Josiah Crawford/--- Neeland/Angus McDonald
NP-618	PA (3) 1:705	24 AUG 1790	Thomas Smallman	John Gibson/James Hendricks/Martin Laughman
NP-637	PA (3) 1:757	9 SEP 1791	Enoch David	Joseph Hunter/John Little/Thomas Gist heirs/Christopher Gist (father of Thomas)/Nathaniel Gist/Cornelius Harety/John Roberts/Daniel Edwards/Richard Gist
NP-647	PA (3) 2:520	29 DEC 1772	James Robinson	Alexander Grant
NP-650	PA (3) 1:650	2 JUN 1789	William Allen	Jane Bee (intermarried with John Fitzgerald)/James Brison/Michael Huffnagle/William Beaty/Henry Beaty, Jr./David Merchant/Gen'l Thompson/Benjamin Lodge/William Finley, Esq.
NP-653	PA (3) 1:531	4 JUN 1787	Philip Pfeffer	Jacob Grojean/Thomas Rees/Martin Heffelfinger/Jacob Gemberling/Francis Foster, Jr./John Sherrack
NP-655	PA (3) 1:614	1 SEP 1788	John Frankson	John Bell/William Brown/Alexander Drummond
NP-681	PA (3) 2:639	8 MAR 1783	James Claypoole	Benjamin Freeman
NP-681	PA (3) 1:436	7 JUL 1783	James Claypoole	James Sherwood/Benjamin Freeman/Matthew Clarkson/Charles Lukens
NP-682	PA (3) 1:508	4 DEC 1786	James Ralse	John Woods, Esq./John P. Dehaas/Peter McKachney
NP-687	PA (3) 2:544	13 AUG 1773	James Clark	Miles Hillborn/Dr. Hugh Williamson/Samuel Wallis
NP-697	PA (3) 2:474	27 AUG 1771	James Wallace	Richard Wallace/Thomas Wilkins
NP-704	PA (3) 1:531	4 JUN 1787	John Sherrack	Jacob Grojean/Thomas Rees/Philip Pfeffer/Jacob Gemberling/Francis Foster, Jr./Martin Heffelfinger
NP-714	PA (3) 1:291	26 MAR 1770	Richard Edwards	Dr. Smith/John Casper
NP-723	PA (3) 1:723	16 DEC 1790	John Greg	Col. William Wilson/Samuel Hunter, deceased/Edward Milner/James Bell
NP-726	PA (3) 1:428	4 FEB 1783	James Breden	Dr. Ewing/Francis Irwin/Thomas Strawbridge/Nathaniel Gillespie/Frederick Antis, Esq./Col. Samuel Hunter
NP-775	PA (3) 2:520	29 DEC 1772	Samuel Nearson	David Loning/James McGlaughlin
NP-788	PA (3) 2:528	2 MAR 1773	Daniel Ryan	James Claypoole/Jesse Lukens/William Patterson/Lodowick Sprogell
NP-790	PA (3) 1:609	1 SEP 1788	Rebecca Carothers	William Beaty/James Carothers/Walter Beaty/James Hamilton, Esq./George Baird, Esq./Christopher Hays
NP-804	PA (3) 1:289	6 MAR 1770	James McMahon	George Irwin/Francis Irwin/William Johnson/Richard Irwin/Marcus Hulings/Robert Fowler/Adam Cooper/James Cooper

Table 3. Caveats involving New Purchase Applications

App #	Ser (Vol) Page	Date of Caveat	Applicant	Others Named
NP-818	PA (3) 1:283	26 DEC 1769	Samuel Hughes	Benjamin Dean/John Ewing/Thomas Ewing (father of John)/John Wright
NP-829	PA (3) 2:520	29 DEC 1772	Alexander Grant	James Robinson
NP-837	PA (3) 1:697	7 JUN 1790	Enoch David	John Little/Thomas Gist/Richard Gist/John Woods, Esq./Isaac Meason/Cornelius Harity/Joseph Hunter/John Roberts/Daniel Edwards
NP-873	PA (3) 2:585	18 NOV 1774	Thomas McFaden	William Patterson/Joseph Galloway/Peter Swartz/Dr. Smith/Michael Weyland/Jacob Weyland/Joseph Hutchins
NP-873	PA (3) 1:751	6 AUG 1791	Thomas McFaddion	George Weyland/William Cook, Esq./Andrew Stroup/Galbreath Patterson/William Maclay, Esq./John Lukens/Mr. Wells/--- Fisher
NP-873	PA (3) 2:9	6 FEB 1792	Thomas McFadian	Col. William Cook/Galbreath Patterson, Esq./James Miller
NP-877	PA (3) 2:599	14 MAR 1775	Peter Kechline	Jacob Shallus/John Weitzell/William Foster
NP-880	PA (3) 2:542	28 JUL 1773	George Albrecht	John Forster/John Simpson
NP-880	PA (3) 1:371	30 NOV 1773	George Albrecht	John Forster/John Simpson
NP-880	PA (3) 1:382	28 JUN 1774	George Albrecht (of Heidelberg Twp.)	--- Simpson/--- Forster/Frederick Albrecht (brother of George)
NP-885	PA (3) 2:506	9 SEP 1772	John Gillespie	Charles Pollock
NP-897	PA (3) 2:554	25 NOV 1773	Thomas Cavit	Jacob Miller/Matthias Miller (sons of Matthias Miller, killed by Indians in 1755)
NP-897	PA (3) 2:607	3 MAY 1775	Thomas Cavet	Peter Keester/Jacob Rerich/Sebastian Leyninger
NP-926	PA (3) 1:650	2 JUN 1789	Henry Beaty, Jr.	Jane Bee (intermarried with John Fitzgerald)/James Brison/Michael Huffnagle/William Beaty/William Allen/David Merchant/Gen'l. Thompson/Benjamin Lodge/William Finley, Esq.
NP-926	PA (3) 1:703	17 AUG 1790	Henry Beaty, Jr.	William Findley/David Marchant/Benjamin Lodge/Jane Bee (intermarried with John Fitzgerald)/James Brison
NP-946	PA (3) 2:541	22 JUL 1773	Thomas Kilcrist	Robert Armstrong
NP-954	PA (3) 1:531	4 JUN 1787	Jacob Gemberling	Jacob Grojean/Thomas Rees/Philip Pfeffer/Martin Heffelfinger/Francis Foster, Jr./John Sherrack
NP-962	PA (3) 1:303	26 JUN 1770	John Litton	William Smith/Samuel Wallis/John Montgomery, Jr.
NP-973	PA (3) 1:685	1 MAR 1790	Michael Byerly	Hanover Davis
NP-982	PA (3) 1:631	5 JAN 1789	James McMath	Oliver Duff/William Elliot/Eli Coulter/William Thompson/Thomas Caldwell/Jane Elliot/William Kearney
NP-1015	PA (3) 2:574	22 JUN 1774	Joseph Galloway	James Baskins/Capt. William Paterson
NP-1020	PA (3) 2:627	18 OCT 1781	John Augusta Washington	John Pearsall/Cornelius Hogeland
NP-1082	PA (3) 1:697	7 JUN 1790	Joseph Hunter	John Little/Thomas Gist/Richard Gist/John Woods, Esq./Isaac Meason/Cornelius Harity/Enoch David/John Roberts/Daniel Edwards
NP-1082	PA (3) 1:757	9 SEP 1791	Joseph Hunter	John Little/Thomas Gist heirs/Christopher Gist (father of Thomas)/Nathaniel Gist/Cornelius Harety/Enoch David/John Roberts/Daniel Edwards/Richard Gist
NP-1110	PA (3) 1:668	5 OCT 1789	John Boggs	David Fleming/John Campbell/Adam Gilfillen/John McKee/John Street

Table 3. Caveats involving New Purchase Applications

App #	Ser (Vol) Page	Date of Caveat	Applicant	Others Named
NP-1111	PA (3) 1:689	6 APR 1790	Frederick Miller	Michael Kessler/William Leetch/Thomas Hamilton/Samuel Hunter/John Beaty/--- Albright/--- Brillinger (taken captive by the Indians)
NP-1135	PA (3) 2:523	10 FEB 1773	John Singer	Michael Troy/Dr. Smith
NP-1189	PA (3) 1:662	7 SEP 1789	Andrew Lowers	William Waddle/William Brown/William Todd, Esq./Miers Fisher, Esq./Joshua Elder/Shadrack Muchmore (father of Jonathan Muchmore)
NP-1192	PA (3) 1:697	7 JUN 1790	John Roberts	John Little/Thomas Gist/Richard Gist/John Woods, Esq./Isaac Meason/Cornelius Harity/Joseph Hunter/Enoch David/Daniel Edwards
NP-1192	PA (3) 1:757	9 SEP 1791	John Roberts	Joseph Hunter/John Little/Thomas Gist heirs/Christopher Gist (father of Thomas)/Nathaniel Gist/Cornelius Harety/Enoch David/Daniel Edwards/Richard Gist
NP-1210	PA (3) 2:471	23 OCT 1769	John Robinson	Benjamin Dean/Levi Stephens/William Hanna/Mary Stephens/David Robinson
NP-1210	PA (3) 1:283	26 DEC 1769	John Robinson	Benjamin Dean/David Robinson/Samuel Hughes/Levi Stephens/William Hana/Mary Stephens
NP-1210	PA (3) 2:47	26 OCT 1792	John Robinson	Reuben Haines/James McLaughlin/Benjamin Dean
NP-1238	PA (3) 2:512	11 NOV 1772	Joseph Shute	Joseph Galloway/William Patterson/Samuel Wallis/Samuel Richards/John Gallagher
NP-1255	PA (3) 2:56	3 JAN 1793	John Umstead	James Forster (son of John Forster, deceased)/John Forsyth/William McClay, Esq.
NP-1259	PA (3) 1:697	7 JUN 1790	Daniel Edwards	John Little/Thomas Gist/Richard Gist/John Woods, Esq./Isaac Meason/Cornelius Harity/Joseph Hunter/Enoch David/John Roberts
NP-1259	PA (3) 1:757	9 SEP 1791	Daniel Edwards	Joseph Hunter/John Little/Thomas Gist heirs/Christopher Gist (father of Thomas)/Nathaniel Gist/Cornelius Harety/Enoch David/John Roberts/Richard Gist
NP-1263	PA (3) 1:493	7 AUG 1786	George Landislyer [Lautenslager]	Isaac Seely/Lewis Lewis/Gen'l Hiester/Mr. Dehaas/Thomas McKean/Mr. Bradford/Mr. Burd/Nicholas Mauer/George Bryan/William Lewis/Charles Risk
NP-1263	PA (3) 1:654	17 JUL 1789	George Lautensliger	Isaac Seely/Lewis Lewis/Gen'l Hiester/Mr. Dehaas/Joseph Wallis, Esq./Mr. Bradford/Mr. Burd/Nicholas Mauer/George Bryan/Charles Risk
NP-1266	PA (3) 2:534	11 MAY 1773	John Forster	Thomas Rees/Galbraith Patterson/William Patterson
NP-1282	PA (3) 1:289	6 MAR 1770	Marcus Hulings	George Irwin/Francis Irwin/William Johnson/Richard Irwin/Robert Fowler/James McMahon/Adam Cooper/James Cooper
NP-1282	PA (3) 2:580	16 SEP 1774	Marcus Hulings	Henry Hoffman/William McWilliams/Cornelius Atkinson/Samuel Boon
NP-1282	PA (3) 1:743	2 MAY 1791	Marcus Hewlings	John Coughran/Jacob Fulmer/--- Hoffman
NP-1293	PA (3) 1:547	29 AUG 1787	Samuel Thompson	Samuel Mackay (son of Col. Eneas Mackay, deceased)/Andrew Hoy/Benjamin Lodge
NP-1300	PA (3) 1:291	26 MAR 1770	John Casper	Richard Edwards/Dr. Smith
NP-1322	PA (3) 1:526	9 MAY 1787	John Patterson	Alexander McClean, Esq./--- Varner/Hugh Gilmore
NP-1337	PA (3) 1:665	7 SEP 1789	James Beard	John Irwin, Esq./John Henderson (surveyor, died before 30 OCT 1787)/Benjamin Lodge/James Guffie/Samuel Sturges
NP-1341	PA (3) 2:579	6 SEP 1774	George Ewing	James McLees/Rev. John Ewing/James Anderson/Andrew Kelly
NP-1341	PA (3) 1:682	1 FEB 1790	George Ewing	Dr. Ewing/John Kelly/Andrew Kelly/Alexander McCurdy/Edward Shippen/Joseph Shippen/James Anderson
NP-1383	PA (3) 2:602	6 APR 1775	George Espy	Evan Owen/James Hunter/Rev. Dr. Francis Allison
NP-1383	PA (3) 2:613	18 NOV 1775	George Espey	Evan Owen/Philip Johnston/John Hoofnagle

Table 3. Caveats involving New Purchase Applications

App #	Ser (Vol) Page	Date of Caveat	Applicant	Others Named
NP-1386	PA (3) 2:525	16 FEB 1773	Martin Trester, Jr.	Jacob Albright
NP-1390	PA (3) 1:401	29 AUG 1774	Sarah Mason	William Clark/Dr. John Morgan/Hannah Mason
NP-1431	PA (3) 2:93	29 JAN 1794	John Andrews	Rev. William Smith/Aaron Levy/Walter Stewart/Ann Stewart/John Palmer/William Moore
NP-1437	PA (3) 1:376	29 MAR 1774	William Norcross	Jesse Lukens/Dr. Coxe/William McClay/Charles Iredell/Robert Iredell, Jr.
NP-1439	PA (3) 2:651	19 JUL 1784	Samuel Coale	Samuel Wallis/James Sharon/Griffith Gibbons
NP-1451	PA (3) 2:506	9 SEP 1772	Charles Pollock	John Gillespie
NP-1463	PA (3) 1:748	22 JUN 1791	James Carnahan	Peter Light/Andrew Finley/Benjamin Lodge
NP-1486	PA (3) 2:90	6 JAN 1794	George Thompson	John Perry
NP-1534	PA (3) 1:765	7 NOV 1791	Thomas Sutherland	Hugh Beaty
NP-1560	PA (3) 2:506	9 SEP 1772	--- Foster	John Pollock/John Kilcriest/Mary Street/Joseph Allison
NP-1585	PA (3) 1:619	6 OCT 1788	Robert Pollox	Benjamin Ross/--- Huston
NP-1614	PA (3) 1:289	6 MAR 1770	Adam Cooper	George Irwin/Francis Irwin/William Johnson/Richard Irwin/Marcus Hulings/James McMahon/Robert Fowler/James Cooper
NP-1647	PA (3) 2:584	11 NOV 1774	Evan Hughes	Enoch Thomas
NP-1666	PA (3) 2:533	28 APR 1773	George Gabriel	John Cox, Jr./Abraham Heer
NP-1666	PA (3) 1:472	4 OCT 1785	George Gabriel	Elizabeth Reed/Abraham Heer/Christian Long (son-in-law of Abraham Heer)/Joseph Boude/George Conrad/Samuel Neave/David Heer/Frederick Weiser/Michael Sheafer
NP-1688	PA (3) 2:503	16 AUG 1772	Thomas Grant	Cornelius Cox
NP-1688	PA (3) 1:586	3 MAR 1788	Thomas Grant	Alexander Grant/Cornelius Cox
NP-1698	PA (3) 2:537	9 JUN 1773	James Kerr	John Kerr (of Carlisle, blacksmith)/William Scull/Jonathan Lodge/Robert Peoples, Jr.
NP-1724	PA (3) 2:526	24 FEB 1773	Ralph Forster	Grace Little/Michael Troy/Mary Field
NP-1733	PA (3) 1:376	29 MAR 1774	Robert Iredell, Jr.	Jesse Lukens/Dr. Coxe/William McClay/Charles Iredell/William Norcross
NP-1744	PA (3) 1:314	26 NOV 1770	Robert Conn	Michael Troy/George Leadley
NP-1758	PA (3) 1:631	5 JAN 1789	William Kearney	Oliver Duff/William Elliot/Eli Coulter/William Thompson/Thomas Caldwell/Jane Elliot/James McMath
NP-1766	PA (3) 1:575	7 JAN 1788	Thomas Christie	George Thompson, Esq./David Duncan
NP-1767	PA (3) 2:517	3 DEC 1772	Thomas Robb	Rebecca Mitcheltree/John Kerr
NP-1776	PA (3) 2:24	4 JUN 1792	James Robinson	James Snodgrass/Henry Small (now deceased)/John Small (son of Henry)
NP-1787	PA (3) 1:289	6 MAR 1770	Richard Irwin	George Irwin/Francis Irwin/William Johnson/Robert Fowler/Marcus Hulings/James McMahon/Adam Cooper/James Cooper
NP-1787	PA (3) 1:382	28 JUN 1774	Richard Irwin	Mary Rees/Seth McCormick
NP-1792	PA (3) 2:601	23 MAR 1775	Elijah Weed	William West, Jr./John Field/Joseph Merrill
NP-1792	PA (3) 1:453	7 JUL 1784	Elijah Weed	William West/Dr. Morgan/Joseph Merrill
NP-1807	PA (3) 2:503	14 AUG 1772	David Stephens, Sr.	Thomas Sutherland
NP-1820	PA (3) 2:24	4 JUN 1792	John Thompson	James Snodgrass/Henry Small (now deceased)/John Small (son of Henry)
NP-1864	PA (3) 1:584	3 MAR 1788	Ephraim Blaine, Esq.	William Lockry/John Proctor/William Proctor/William Todd/George Henry/Alexander Blaine/William Finley, Esq.
NP-1900	PA (3) 2:512	30 OCT 1772	Robert Wilkins	John Allison/John Ormsby/John Whitner/Simon Black

Table 3. Caveats involving New Purchase Applications

App #	Ser (Vol) Page	Date of Caveat	Applicant	Others Named
NP-1900	PA (3) 1:367	25 OCT 1773	Robert Wilkins	Simon Black/John Whitner/John Allison, Esq./John Ormsby/Robert Dill/Capt. Thompson/John Sampson
NP-1915	PA (3) 2:93	29 JAN 1794	John Palmer	Rev. William Smith/Aaron Levy/Walter Stewart/Ann Stewart/John Andrews/William Moore
NP-1923	PA (3) 2:651	19 JUL 1784	James Sharon	Samuel Wallis/Samuel Coale/Griffith Gibbons
NP-1933	PA (3) 2:521	8 JAN 1773	James Johnston, Sr.	John Lowdon/Samuel Davis
NP-1933	PA (3) 2:99	13 FEB 1794	James Johnston	John Lowdon/Thomas Rees/Samuel Davis
NP-1935	PA (3) 2:506	12 SEP 1772	Thomas Dobbins	Thomas Jordan/Michael Troy/Joseph Shippen, Esq.
NP-1981	PA (3) 2:508	21 SEP 1772	Samuel McWilliams	Thomas Johnston/Samuel Wallis/John Worthington
NP-1991	PA (3) 1:289	6 MAR 1770	Francis Irwin	George Irwin/Robert Fowler/William Johnson/Richard Irwin/Marcus Hulings/James McMahon/Adam Cooper/James Cooper
NP-1991	PA (3) 1:316	9 JAN 1771	Francis Irwin	George Irwin/Robert Fowler/William Johnson
NP-1991	PA (3) 1:428	4 FEB 1783	Francis Irwin	Dr. Ewing/James Breden/Thomas Strawbridge/Nathaniel Gillespie/Frederick Antis, Esq./Col. Samuel Hunter
NP-1995	PA (3) 2:539	6 JUL 1773	John Irwin	Peter Burns
NP-1999	PA (3) 2:471	23 OCT 1769	David Robinson	Benjamin Dean/Levi Stephens/William Hanna/Mary Stephens/John Robinson
NP-1999	PA (3) 1:283	26 DEC 1769	David Robinson	John Robinson/Benjamin Dean/Samuel Hughes/Levi Stephens/William Hana/Mary Stephens
NP-2003	PA (3) 1:669	5 OCT 1789	David Sloan (died by 5 OCT 1789)	Robert Orr/George Clark/Samuel Sloan
NP-2012	PA (3) 2:614	21 DEC 1775	Samuel Fisher, Jr.	David Hogg/Samuel Wallis/--- Biddle/Nathan Jones/Isaac Jones
NP-2024	PA (3) 2:474	27 AUG 1771	Thomas Wilkins	Richard Wallace/James Wallace
NP-2027	PA (3) 1:351	30 NOV 1772	Cornelius Atkinson	John Pollock/Robert Gilcreast
NP-2027	PA (3) 1:359	27 APR 1773	Cornelius Atkinson	John Pollock/Robert Gilcreast
NP-2039	PA (3) 1:584	3 MAR 1788	Benjamin Trapnall	Samuel Wallis/Samuel Hunter
NP-2076	PA (3) 2:518	10 DEC 1772	Josiah Galbreath (son of Bartram Galbreath)	John Philip Dehaas
NP-2093	PA (3) 2:542	6 AUG 1773	John Beaty	Andrew Glen/Thomas Sutherland/Jonas Vocht/Robert King
NP-2104	PA (3) 1:562	5 NOV 1787	Thomas Campbell	Charles Gibson/John Reynolds/William Finley, Esq./John Moore, Esq.
NP-2107	PA (3) 2:644	29 SEP 1783	Henry Boyles	James Finley/Samuel Lyon, Jr.
NP-2126	PA (3) 2:50	5 NOV 1792	Thomas Holliday	Moses Latta/Christopher Hays/Thomas Shields
NP-2159	PA (3) 2:517	3 DEC 1772	Rebecca Mitcheltree	Thomas Robb/John Kerr
NP-2164	PA (3) 2:486	13 FEB 1772	Hugh McKee	Alexander Barr/Capt. James Potter/David Barr
NP-2209	PA (3) 2:651	30 JUN 1784	James Jones	Alexander Hunter/John Philip Dehaas/Lewis Lewis/William Austin/John Scott
NP-2209	PA (3) 1:492	5 JUL 1786	James Jones	John Scott/Thomas Grant, Esq./Alexander Hunter/John Witmer/Lewis Lewis/Gen'l Dehaas/Zachariah Allen/Samuel Hopkins, Jr./William Austin
NP-2209	PA (3) 1:527	10 MAY 1787	James Jones	Alexander Hunter/Lewis Lewis/Gen'l Dehaas/Joseph Wallis

Table 3. Caveats involving New Purchase Applications

App #	Ser (Vol) Page	Date of Caveat	Applicant	Others Named
NP-2220	PA (3) 1:662	7 SEP 1789	Jonathan Muchmore	William Waddle/William Brown/Andrew Lowers/William Todd, Esq./Miers Fisher, Esq./Joshua Elder/Shadrack Muchmore (father of Jonathan)
NP-2228	PA (3) 2:520	29 DEC 1772	James McGlaughlin	David Loning/Samuel Nearson
NP-2230	PA (3) 1:697	7 JUN 1790	Thomas Gist	John Little/Richard Gist/John Woods, Esq./Isaac Meason/Cornelius Harity/Joseph Hunter/Enoch David/John Roberts/Daniel Edwards
NP-2230	PA (3) 1:757	9 SEP 1791	Thomas Gist	Joseph Hunter/John Little/Thomas Gist heirs/Christopher Gist (father of Thomas)/Nathaniel Gist/Cornelius Harety/Enoch David/John Roberts/Daniel Edwards/Richard Gist
NP-2230	PA (3) 2:51	5 NOV 1792	Thomas Gist	--- Poe/--- Perry/Col. Isaac Meason/Richard Gist
NP-2244	PA (3) 1:289	6 MAR 1770	Robert Fowler	George Irwin/Francis Irwin/William Johnson/Richard Irwin/Marcus Hulings/James McMahon/Adam Cooper/James Cooper
NP-2244	PA (3) 1:316	9 JAN 1771	Robert Fowler	George Irwin/Francis Irwin/William Johnson
NP-2280	PA (3) 2:564	9 APR 1774	Elizabeth Reed	Abraham Heer
NP-2280	PA (3) 1:472	4 OCT 1785	Elizabeth Reed	George Gabriel/Abraham Heer/Christian Long (son-in-law of Abraham Heer)/Joseph Boude/George Conrad/Samuel Neave/David Heer/Frederick Weiser/Michael Sheafer
NP-2296	PA (3) 2:615	27 FEB 1776	Ann Flahaven	James Johnston/Martha Johnston/Abraham Dewit
NP-2303	PA (3) 1:533	4 JUN 1787	Hugh Hunter	John McKee/Archibald McFadden/Thomas Shields/William Thompson/Benjamin Lodge
NP-2305	PA (3) 2:485	24 JAN 1772	Francis Allison, Jr.	James Miller
NP-2369	PA (3) 1:296	1 MAY 1770	John Duffield	Nicholas Sheaffer
NP-2385	PA (3) 2:463	27 JUN 1769	Jacob Bousman	Hugh Crawford
NP-2385	PA (3) 1:284	11 JAN 1770	Jacob Bausman	Hugh Crawford/Col. Croghan
NP-2389	PA (3) 1:477	29 NOV 1785	William Ewing	James McLees/John Musser/Adam Zantzinger
NP-2391	PA (3) 1:289	6 MAR 1770	George Irwin	Robert Fowler/Francis Irwin/William Johnson/Richard Irwin/Marcus Hulings/James McMahon/Adam Cooper/James Cooper
NP-2391	PA (3) 1:316	9 JAN 1771	George Irwin	Robert Fowler/Francis Irwin/William Johnson
NP-2408	PA (3) 2:539	6 JUL 1773	Peter Burns	John Irwin
NP-2408	PA (3) 1:493	14 JUL 1786	Peter Burns	Philip Davis/John Irwin
NP-2413	PA (3) 1:303	26 JUN 1770	John Montgomery, Jr.	John Litton/William Smith/Samuel Wallis
NP-2438	PA (3) 1:379	23 JUN 1774	Elizabeth Gardner	John Stevens/Theophilus Gardner (father of Elizabeth)
NP-2489	PA (3) 2:490	1 APR 1772	Jacob Snevely ("now deceased")	John Joseph Snevely/William Colvin/Adam Rove
NP-2502	PA (3) 2:506	9 SEP 1772	John Kilcriest	--- Foster/John Pollock/Mary Street/Joseph Allison
NP-2510	PA (3) 2:478	8 NOV 1771	John Lowdon	Elias Reger or Reigar
NP-2537	PA (3) 1:289	6 MAR 1770	William Johnson	George Irwin/Francis Irwin/Robert Fowler/Richard Irwin/Marcus Hulings/James McMahon/Adam Cooper/James Cooper
NP-2537	PA (3) 1:316	9 JAN 1771	William Johnson	George Irwin/Francis Irwin/Robert Fowler
NP-2546	PA (3) 2:505	28 AUG 1772	Joseph Bull	Cornelius Coxe/Mary Scull/Thomas Bull/Samuel Hunter
NP-2596	PA (3) 1:296	1 MAY 1770	Nicholas Sheaffer	John Duffield

Table 3. Caveats involving New Purchase Applications

App #	Ser (Vol) Page	Date of Caveat	Applicant	Others Named
NP-2596	PA (3) 2:510	22 OCT 1772	Nicholas Sheaffer	James Dougherty
NP-2596	PA (3) 1:352	28 DEC 1772	Nicholas Sheaffer	James Dougherty
NP-2598	PA (3) 1:311	29 OCT 1770	Abraham Lesher	John Caruthers (son of William)/Capt. Thompson/William Ferguson
NP-2598	PA (3) 1:322	29 APR 1771	Abraham Lesher	John Caruthers (son of William)/Capt. Thompson/William Ferguson/--- Duncan
NP-2636	PA (3) 1:374	29 MAR 1774	Thomas Johnston	Samuel Wallis/John Worthington
NP-2657	PA (3) 2:574	22 JUN 1774	James Baskins	Joseph Galloway/Capt. William Paterson
NP-2663	PA (3) 1:593	29 MAR 1788	Shadrach Muchmore	Gen'l St. Clair/William Moore
NP-2702	PA (3) 2:474	23 AUG 1771	James Erwin	Nathaniel Nelson/Joseph Erwin
NP-2710	PA (3) 1:668	5 OCT 1789	Samuel Beard	John Beard/Samuel Beard (father of Samuel & John)
NP-2731	PA (3) 1:609	1 SEP 1788	Henry Beaty, Jr.	Patrick Campbell/William Beaty
NP-2767	PA (3) 1:631	5 JAN 1789	Thomas Caldwell	Oliver Duff/William Elliot/Eli Coulter/William Thompson/Thomas Caldwell/Jane Elliot/William Kearney/James McMath
NP-2767	PA (3) 1:694	4 JUN 1790	Thomas Caldwell	William Elliot/Col. Abraham Smith/Oliver Duff
NP-2777	PA (3) 1:314	26 NOV 1770	George Leadley	Michael Troy/Robert Conn
NP-2782	PA (3) 1:751	6 AUG 1791	George Weyland	William Cook, Esq./Andrew Stroup/Galbreath Patterson/Thomas McFaddion/William Maclay, Esq./John Lukens/Mr. Wells/--- Fisher
NP-2783	PA (3) 2:578	19 AUG 1774	John Harris	Jacob Godshalk/Dr. Plunket/Stephen Wooley
NP-2783	PA (3) 1:416	30 OCT 1776	John Harris	John Harris/William Plunket/William McClay,Esq./Edward Lee
NP-2783	PA (3) 1:431	7 APR 1783	John Harris	Jacob Godshalk, deceased, administrators/Dr. William Plunket/Edward Lee/John Turner/William Doran/Andrew Smith/Stephen Wooleys [WS-1146]/Charles Stewart
NP-2788	PA (3) 2:535	24 MAY 1773	William Glass	Clary Campble/William McCrosky/William Brown
NP-2798	PA (3) 2:563	30 MAR 1774	William Miller	Benjamin Allison/Abraham Smith/Samuel Craig
NP-2798	PA (3) 1:496	4 SEP 1786	William Miller	Dr. Allison/Abraham Smith
NP-2811	PA (3) 1:585	3 MAR 1788	Henry Leef	Robert Tate/John Weitzel (administrator of Casper Weitzel)/William Gray/William Wilson/William Maclay, Esq.
NP-2849	PA (3) 1:569	3 DEC 1787	Phineas Killum	John Varvell/Edward Fox, Esq./David Bradford, Esq.
NP-2849	PA (3) 1:586	3 MAR 1788	Phineas Killum	John Varvell
NP-2849	PA (3) 1:607	4 AUG 1788	Phineas Killum	Hugh Brackenridge. Esq./John Varvell
NP-2849	PA (3) 1:663	7 SEP 1789	Phineas Killum	John Varvell/Hugh Brackenridge, Esq./David Bradford, Esq.
NP-2859	PA (3) 1:510	4 DEC 1786	Thomas Heiser	John Blackburn/Ephrain Blaine/Josiah Crawford
NP-2860	PA (3) 1:438	1 SEP 1783	James Byers	Alexander Ross ("having gone to the British")/E. Blaine
NP-2867	PA (3) 2:584	11 NOV 1774	Enoch Thomas	Evan Hughes
NP-2878	PA (3) 2:459	31 MAY 1769	Thomas Austin	Benjamin Austin/Joseph Ellicott/John Montgomery, Esq.
NP-2878	PA (3) 1:287	7 FEB 1770	Thomas Austin	Joseph Ellicott/Benjamin Austin/John Montgomery/Alexander Stewart
NP-2879	PA (3) 2:459	31 MAY 1769	Benjamin Austin	Thomas Austin/Joseph Ellicott
NP-2879	PA (3) 1:287	7 FEB 1770	Benjamin Austin	Joseph Ellicott/Thomas Austin/John Montgomery/Alexander Stewart
NP-2924	PA (3) 2:512	30 OCT 1772	John Whitner	John Allison/John Ormsby/Simon Black/Robert Wilkins

Table 3. Caveats involving New Purchase Applications

App #	Ser (Vol) Page	Date of Caveat	Applicant	Others Named
NP-2924	PA (3) 1:367	25 OCT 1773	John Whitner	Simon Black/John Allison, Esq./John Ormsby/Robert Dill/Robert Wilkins/Capt. Thompson/John Sampson
NP-2925	PA (3) 2:512	30 OCT 1772	Simon Black	John Allison/John Ormsby/John Whitner/Robert Wilkins
NP-2925	PA (3) 1:367	25 OCT 1773	Simon Black	John Whitner/John Allison, Esq./John Ormsby/Robert Dill/Robert Wilkins/Capt. Thompson/John Sampson
NP-2954	PA (3) 2:629	26 DEC 1781	George Reyer	[name on application is Sutfel Reyer, who is also named a neighbor on NP-2955]/Christ Knoble/Heiman Knoble/William Maclay/Robert McNair/Jacob Haverliny/Peter Harington/Thomas Barns/John Lugar/Capt. Weitzell
NP-2955	PA (3) 2:629	26 DEC 1781	Christ Knoble	Heiman Knoble/William Maclay/Robert McNair/Jacob Haverliny/Peter Harington/Thomas Barns/John Lugar/Capt. Weitzell/George Reyer
NP-2956	PA (3) 2:629	26 DEC 1781	Heiman Knoble	Christ Knoble/William Maclay/Robert McNair/Jacob Haverliny/Peter Harington/Thomas Barns/John Lugar/Capt. Weitzell/George Reyer
NP-2964	PA (3) 1:593	29 MAR 1788	William Moore	Gen'l. St. Clair/Shadrach Muchmore
NP-2969	PA (3) 1:586	3 MAR 1788	John Grant	William Todd, Esq./Arthur St. Clair, Esq./William Findley, Esq./Simon Eaker
NP-2981	PA (3) 1:571	3 DEC 1787	Robert Worthington, Jr., deceased heirs	Isaac Meason, Esq./Joseph Worthington/Elizabeth Worthington/Ralph Cherry
NP-2983	PA (3) 1:672	5 NOV 1789	Angus McDonald	William Schooly/Robert Adams/Col. Henry Bouquet/William Sherer/Henry Shryock/Stephen Field/Rees Cadwallader
NP-2983	PA (3) 1:696	7 JUN 1790	Angus McDonald	William Schooly/Robert Adams/Joseph Thomas, Esq.
NP-2983	PA (3) 1:712	29 SEP 1790	Angus McDonald	William Schooly/Robert Adams/Joseph Thomas, Esq.
NP-2983	PA (3) 1:729	7 FEB 1791	Angus McDonald	William Sherer/Henry Shryock/William Schooly/Robert Adams/Mr. Scott/Mr. Thomas/Col. Bouquet/Moses McClean/Thomas Banfield/Joseph Graybill/Josiah Crawford/--- Neeland
NP-3019	PA (3) 2:466	29 JUL 1769	William Elliott	Garret Pendergrass
NP-3019	PA (3) 1:485	3 MAY 1786	William Elliott	George Croghan/Bernard Gratz (executor of George Croghan)
NP-3027	PA (3) 1:631	5 JAN 1789	Jane Elliot	Oliver Duff/William Elliot/Eli Coulter/William Thompson/Thomas Caldwell/William Kearney/James McMath
NP-3046	PA (3) 1:336	25 FEB 1772	John Brownfield	John McKee/George England/Capt. Batt/Capt. Thompson
NP-3053	PA (3) 2:488	28 FEB 1772	Hugh Laughlin	Samuel McKee/Robert McCrea/Alexander Cook/James Dunrumple
NP-3084	PA (3) 1:713	4 OCT 1790	Mark Hardin	William Augustus Smith/John Masterson, deceased/James McDowell
NP-3086	PA (3) 2:499	4 JUN 1772	Susannah Harding	James McDowell
NP-3094	PA (3) 1:289	5 MAR 1770	Peter Resner	William Sherer/John Sherer
NP-3098	PA (3) 1:311	29 OCT 1770	Henry Speers	Thomas Crafts/Col. Monckton
NP-3116	PA (3) 1:438	1 SEP 1783	Alexander Ross	["A. Ross having gone to the British"]/James Byers/E. Blaine
NP-3130	PA (3) 1:336	25 FEB 1772	George England	John McKee/John Brownfield/Capt. Batt/Capt. Thompson
NP-3138	PA (3) 1:668	5 OCT 1789	John Street	David Fleming/John Campbell/Adam Gilfillen/John McKee/John Boggs
NP-3162	PA (3) 1:731	7 FEB 1791	James Renick	James Carnahan/Rev. John Elder/Joshua Elder (son of John)/John Beard, Esq.
NP-3167	PA (3) 1:547	3 SEP 1787	Robert Perry	John Kerr/Empson Brownfield

Table 3. Caveats involving New Purchase Applications

App #	Ser (Vol) Page	Date of Caveat	Applicant	Others Named
NP-3206	PA (3) 1:640	3 MAR 1789	Andrew Hoy	Col. Stephen Bayard/Elizabeth Bayard (wife of Stephen)/Samuel Mackey/Eneas Mackey (father of Samuel)/B. Lodge/Jacob Bousman
NP-3209	PA (3) 1:668	5 OCT 1789	David Fleming	John Campbell/Adam Gilfillen/John McKee/John Street/John Boggs
NP-3218	PA (3) 1:492	5 JUL 1786	John Scott	James Jones/Thomas Grant, Esq./Alexander Hunter/John Witmer/Lewis Lewis/Gen'l. Dehaas/Zachariah Allen/Samuel Hopkins, Jr./William Austin
NP-3218	PA (3) 1:574	7 JAN 1788	John Scott	Joseph Wallis/--- Dehaas/--- Whitmore/--- Grant/James Hendricks
NP-3227	PA (3) 2:590	27 JAN 1775	John Elder	Frederick Rohrer/Martin Schneider
NP-3230	PA (3) 2:502	3 JUL 1772	William Brown	Robert Miller/Joseph Brownlee/John Campbell
NP-3233	PA (3) 2:601	23 MAR 1775	Joseph Merrill	William West, Jr./John Field/Elijah Weed
NP-3233	PA (3) 1:453	7 JUL 1784	Joseph Merrill	Elijah Weed/Dr. Morgan/William West
NP-3239	PA (3) 1:639	3 MAR 1789	Samuel Martin	Robert Bleakley/John Nevill/Thomas Moorehead/Alexander Bolen/Rich Hill
NP-3245	PA (3) 2:528	19 MAR 1773	William McCleery	Henry Beason/Jacob Beason/Aaron Robertson/James Kendall/Isabella McCleery
NP-3246	PA (3) 2:528	19 MAR 1773	Isabella McCleery	Henry Beason/Jacob Beason/Aaron Robertson/James Kendall/William McCleery
NP-3263	PA (3) 2:655	24 SEP 1784	William Young	John White/Joseph Whary
NP-3263	PA (3) 1:520	2 APR 1787	William Young	Joseph Wharry/John White/Matthew Wilson/Thomas McDowell/James Alison, Esq./James Douglass, Esq./Matthew Richie, Esq.
NP-3263	PA (3) 1:564	5 NOV 1787	William Young	Joseph Wharry/John White/James Allison, Esq./John Douglas, Esq./Matthew Richie, Esq./Matthew Wilson/John Canon/Nathan Brown
NP-3264	PA (3) 1:606	4 AUG 1788	Alexander Young	George Thompson/William Young/John Anderson
NP-3280	PA (3) 2:91	22 JAN 1794	Thomas Braithwaite	Rev. William Smith/Thomas Gilpin/Asaph Wilson
NP-3286	PA (3) 2:104	24 MAR 1794	William Wilson	John Hoge/Christopher Sticker
NP-3291	PA (3) 2:112	5 MAY 1794	David Hall	John Montgomery, Esq./David McKee
NP-3296	PA (3) 2:476	11 OCT 1771	James Flenegan	John William Province/John Backus
NP-3301	PA (3) 2:53	3 DEC 1792	Samuel Wilson	John Giffen/John Hunter/Benjamin Lodge/Mr. Lovengier/Capt. Thompson/Nathaniel Hunt/Joshua Reynolds/Abraham Hendricks
NP-3303	PA (3) 2:502	3 JUL 1772	John Campbell	Robert Miller/Joseph Brownlee/William Brown
NP-3303	PA (3) 1:517	5 MAR 1787	John Campbell	Robert McKee/Adam Turner heirs/William Jack, Esq./Gen'l. Thompson/William Finley, Esq./Nehemiah Stokely
NP-3328	PA (3) 2:528 & 544	15 MAR 1773	John King	Edward Shippen/Joseph Shippen, Jr./Lazarus Young/Lydia King/Robert Young/Cornelius King/William Young
NP-3329	PA (3) 2:528 & 544	15 MAR 1773	Lazarus Young	John King/Edward Shippen/Joseph Shippen, Jr./Lydia King/Robert Young/Cornelius King/William Young
NP-3330	PA (3) 2:528 & 544	15 MAR 1773	Lydia King	John King/Edward Shippen/Joseph Shippen, Jr./Lazarus Young/Robert Young/Cornelius King/William Young
NP-3331	PA (3) 2:528 & 544	15 MAR 1773	Robert Young	John King/Edward Shippen/Joseph Shippen, Jr./Lazarus Young/Lydia King/Cornelius King/William Young
NP-3332	PA (3) 2:528 & 544	15 MAR 1773	Cornelius King	John King/Edward Shippen/Joseph Shippen, Jr./Lazarus Young/Lydia King/Robert Young/William Young

Table 3. Caveats involving New Purchase Applications

App #	Ser (Vol) Page	Date of Caveat	Applicant	Others Named
NP-3333	PA (3) 2:528 & 544	15 MAR 1773	William Young	John King/Edward Shippen/Joseph Shippen, Jr./Lazarus Young/Lydia King/Robert Young/Cornelius King
NP-3346	PA (3) 1:676	7 DEC 1789	Gen'l Edward Hand	David Scott/James Hendricks
NP-3352	PA (3) 2:644	29 SEP 1783	Samuel Lyon, Jr.	James Finley/Henry Boyles
NP-3357	PA (3) 1:716	4 OCT 1790	Dorsey Penticost	John Mullen/Jonathan Smith/Cumberland Dugan
NP-3371	PA (3) 2:50	5 NOV 1792	James Holliday	Moses Latta/Christopher Hays/Thomas Shields
NP-3381	PA (3) 1:311	29 OCT 1770	John Nicholas	Andrew Forbes/John Caruthers (son of John)/Capt. Thompson
NP-3381	PA (3) 1:322	29 APR 1771	John Nicholas	Andrew Forbes/John Caruthers (son of John)/Capt. Thompson
NP-3382	PA (3) 1:592	29 MAR 1788	Battle Harrison (died under age)	William Miller/Lawrence Harrison (father of Battle)
NP-3387	PA (3) 1:606	4 AUG 1788	John Anderson	George Thompson/William Young/Alexander Young
NP-3419	PA (3) 1:533	4 JUN 1787	Archibald McFadden	John McKee/Hugh Hunter/Thomas Shields/William Thompson/Benjamin Lodge
NP-3466	PA (3) 1:603	26 JUN 1788	George Grundy	John Patrick/Charles Burkham/Alexander McClean, Esq.
NP-3475	PA (3) 1:601	2 JUN 1788	William Grundy	Philip Rogers/Alexander McClean, Esq.
NP-3477	PA (3) 2:474	23 AUG 1771	Michael Harbet	Nathaniel Nelson/Peter Cassner
NP-3489	PA (3) 2:579	6 SEP 1774	James Anderson	Andrew Kelly/James McLees/Rev. John Ewing/George Ewing
NP-3489	PA (3) 1:682	1 FEB 1790	James Anderson	George Ewing/Dr. Ewing/Andrew Kelly/John Kelly/Alexander McCurdy/Edward Shippen/Joseph Shippen
NP-3504	PA (3) 2:579	6 SEP 1774	Andrew Kelly	James McLees/Rev. John Ewing/James Anderson/George Ewing
NP-3504	PA (3) 1:682	1 FEB 1790	Andrew Kelly	George Ewing/Dr. Ewing/John Kelly/Alexander McCurdy/Edward Shippen/Joseph Shippen/James Anderson
NP-3508	PA (3) 1:668	5 OCT 1789	Benjamin Kuykendale	James McDowell/John McKee/William Finley/John McDowell/Mr. Lodge
NP-3508	PA (3) 1:699	6 JUL 1790	Benjamin Kuykendale	James McDowell/John McDowell/John McKee/Benjamin Lodge/Abraham Smith, Esq./widow Kuykendale/Jonathan Smith
NP-3508	PA (3) 1:713	4 OCT 1790	Benjamin Kuykendale	James McDowell/Benjamin Lodge/John McKee
NP-3514	PA (3) 2:521	8 JAN 1773	Samuel Davis	James Johnston, Sr./John Lowdon
NP-3514	PA (3) 2:99	13 FEB 1794	Samuel Davis	John Lowdon/Thomas Rees/James Johnston
NP-3520	PA (3) 2:574	8 JUL 1774	Susanna Robb (wife of Robert)	Robert Robb/Samuel Wallis/Joshua Mitchel/John Farmer
NP-3520	PA (3) 1:566	28 SEP 1787	Susanna Robb	Robert Robb (husband of Susanna)/Samuel Wallis/Joshua Michael [should be Mitchel]/John Farmer
NP-3520	PA (3) 1:586	3 MAR 1788	Susanna Robb	Robert Robb/Samuel Wallis
NP-3528	PA (3) 2:502	3 JUL 1772	Joseph Brownlee	Robert Miller/John Campbell/William Brown
NP-3596	PA (3) 1:702	3 AUG 1790	John Vanderen	Thomas Smith, Esq.
NP-3599	PA (3) 2:4	3 JAN 1792	Mary McDowell	Henry Taylor/Levi Hollingsworth/Richard Yeates/Nathan McDowell
NP-3603	PA (3) 2:506	9 SEP 1772	Mary Street	--- Foster/John Pollock/John Kilcriest/Joseph Allison
NP-3605	PA (3) 2:506	9 SEP 1772	Joseph Allison	--- Foster/John Pollock/John Kilcriest/Mary Street
NP-3615	PA (3) 2:580	16 SEP 1774	Samuel Boon	Marcus Hulings/Henry Hoffman/William McWilliams/Cornelius Atkinson

Table 3. Caveats involving New Purchase Applications

App #	Ser (Vol) Page	Date of Caveat	Applicant	Others Named
NP-3615	PA (3) 2:581	28 SEP 1774	Samuel Boon	Henry Hoffman/Jacob Fulmer/Marcus Hullings
NP-3616	PA (3) 1:517	5 MAR 1787	Robert McKee	John Campbell/Adam Turner heirs/William Jack, Esq./Gen'l. Thompson/William Finley, Esq./Nehemiah Stokely
NP-3617	PA (3) 2:488	28 FEB 1772	James Dunrumple	Samuel McKee/Robert McCrea/Alexander Cook/Hugh Laughlin
NP-3643	PA (3) 1:553	20 SEP 1787	Samuel Elliot	Michael Gratz/John Elliot/Jacob Bousman
NP-3644	PA (3) 1:553	20 SEP 1787	John Elliot	Michael Gratz/Samuel Elliot/Jacob Bousman
NP-3663	PA (3) 1:640	3 MAR 1789	John Irwin	Mr. Brinigh/Mr. Painter/Conrad Shitler/D. Roberdeau
NP-3663	PA (3) 1:734	7 MAR 1791	John Irwin (Indian trader)	John Irwin, Esq./Benjamin Lodge/widow of William Lyon
NP-3668	PA (3) 1:640	3 MAR 1789	John Irwin	Mr. Brinigh/Mr. Painter/Conrad Shitler/D. Roberdeau
NP-3671	PA (3) 1:679	5 JAN 1790	William A. Lungan	Gen'l William Irvine (executor of Robert Calendar)/David Redick, Esq./John Hoge/Ephraim Blaine, Esq.
NP-3673	PA (3) 1:679	5 JAN 1790	Robert Calendar	Gen'l William Irvine (executor of Robert Calendar)/David Redick, Esq./John Hoge/Ephraim Blaine, Esq./William A. Lungan
NP-3694	PA (3) 1:614	1 SEP 1788	Alexander Drummond	John Bell/William Brown/John Frankson
NP-3695	PA (3) 2:649	27 MAY 1784	James Cunningham	John Bell (son of John Bell)/John Campbell
NP-3695	PA (3) 1:613	1 SEP 1788	James Cunningham	John Campbell/John Bell
NP-3697	PA (3) 2:537	9 JUN 1773	Robert Peoples, Jr.	John Kerr (of Carlisle, blacksmith)/William Scull/Jonathan Lodge/James Kerr
NP-3721	PA (3) 2:502	24 JUL 1772	Joseph Morton	John Brady
NP-3751	PA (3) 2:471	23 OCT 1769	William Hanna	Benjamin Dean/Levi Stephens/Mary Stephens/David Robinson/John Robinson
NP-3751	PA (3) 1:283	26 DEC 1769	William Hanna	Benjamin Dean/John Robinson/David Robinson/Samuel Hughes/Levi Stephens/Mary Stephens
NP-3753	PA (3) 2:471	23 OCT 1769	Mary Stephens	Benjamin Dean/Levi Stephens/William Hanna/David Robinson/John Robinson
NP-3753	PA (3) 1:283	26 DEC 1769	Mary Stephens	Benjamin Dean/John Robinson/David Robinson/Samuel Hughes/Levi Stephens/William Hana
NP-3764	PA (3) 1:586	3 MAR 1788	Vincent Colvin	John McDowell, Esq.
NP-3776	PA (3) 1:498	2 OCT 1786	James Colvin	Joseph Chambers/Jacob Feagley/Robert Newell, Jr.
NP-3776	PA (3) 1:626	25 NOV 1788	James Colvin	Elisha Teeters/John Hoge Redick
NP-3785	PA (3) 2:487	-- FEB 1772	Isaiah Althouse	Daniel Elliott
NP-3785	PA (3) 1:348	26 OCT 1772	Isaiah Althouse	Daniel Elliot/William Forster/--- Melone
NP-3834	PA (3) 1:436	7 JUL 1783	James Sherwood	James Claypoole/Benjamin Freeman/Matthew Clarkson/Charles Lukens
NP-3834	PA (3) 1:440	2 SEP 1783	James Sherwood	Benjamin Freeman/John Freeman (brother of Benjamin)/Matthew Clarkson/Lewis Stephens/Charles Lukens/James Claypoole
NP-3839	PA (3) 2:541	22 JUL 1773	Robert Armstrong	Thomas Kilcrist
NP-3847	PA (3) 2:656	21 OCT 1784	George Calhoon	William Cook, Esq./Mr. Montgomery

Table 4. Eighteen Applications Purchased by Samuel Wallis.

App. #	Applicant	Date	Description	Location	Acres	Survey
NP-107	Porter, William	3 APR 1769	"Adjoining land of Joseph Knight"	LD: Somerset	300	
NP-807	Paul, Joseph	3 APR 1769	"Adjoining land of William Porter"		300	
NP-2127	Paul, Henry Jr.	3 APR 1769	"Adjoining land of Joseph Paul"	LD: Somerset	300	
NP-1373	Taylor, Samuel	3 APR 1769	"Adjoining land of John Cumming"	South side Conemaugh Creek, Fairfield, Westmoreland	300	D-56-225
NP-2231	Knight, Joseph	3 APR 1769	"Adjoining land of Samuel Taylor"	LD: Fairfield, Westmoreland	300	
NP-608	Cathrall, Isaac	3 APR 1769	"Adjoining land of Joseph Hill"	Rostraver, Westmoreland	300	D-57-200
NP-1546	Cathrall, Benjamin	3 APR 1769	"Adjoining land of James Cathrall"	Rostraver, Westmoreland	300	D-56-136
NP-1558	Young, Peter	3 APR 1769	"Adjoining Benjamin Cathrall"	LD: Westmoreland	300	
NP-118	Settaford, Richard	3 APR 1769	"Adjoining Thomas Morgan"	Columbia/ LD: Columbia	300	
NP-318	Morgan, Thomas	3 APR 1769	"Adjoining land of John Sprogle"	Columbia/ LD: Columbia	300	
NP-592	Sprogle, John	3 APR 1769	"Adjoining land of William Wilson"/Northumberland	Fishing Creek, Columbia	300	C-207-7 (r12 JUN 1789)Henry Singer & Jacob Growell
NP-724	Hill, Joseph	3 APR 1769	"Adjoining land of Henry Paul Junior"	LD: Columbia	300	
NP-1147	Commings, John	3 APR 1769	"Adjoining land of Richard Sattaford"	Columbia/ LD: Columbia	300	
NP-327	Cowperthwait, Joseph	3 APR 1769	"Adjoining land of Thomas Bonnell on the east side of West Branch of Susquehanna below Pine Creek"	West Branch Susquehanna River, Lycoming/ LD: Lycoming	300	
NP-464	Willson, William	3 APR 1769	"Adjoining land of Joseph Cowperthwait east side West Branch Susquehanna below Pine Creek"	West Branch Susquehanna River, Lycoming/ LD: Lycoming	300	
NP-701	Bonnell, Thomas	3 APR 1769	"Adjoining land of Samuel Nicholas east side West Branch Susquehanna below Pine Creek"	West Branch Susquehanna River, Lycoming/LD: Lycoming	300	
NP-1573	Nicholas, Samuel	3 APR 1769	"On the easterly side of the West Branch of Susquehanna below and Adjoining the mouth of Tiadaughton or Pine Creek"	West Branch Susquehanna River & Pine Creek, Lycoming/ LD: Lycoming	300	
NP-1588	Nicholas, Samuel	3 APR 1769	"On the easterly side of the West Branch of Susquehanna below and Adjoining the mouth of Tiadaughton or Pine Creek"	West Branch Susquehanna River & Pine Creek, Lycoming	300	

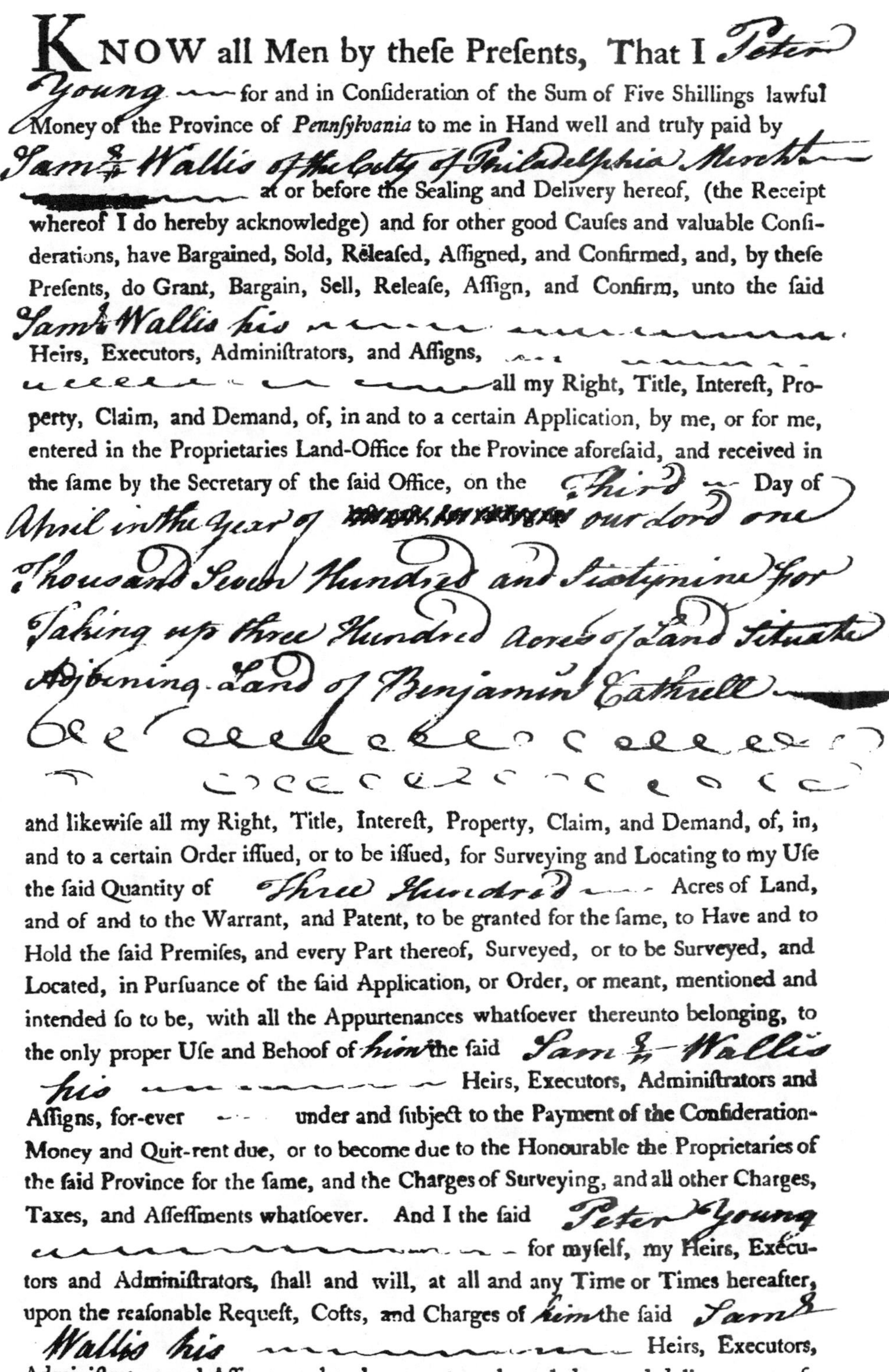

KNOW all Men by these Presents, That I Peter Young for and in Consideration of the Sum of Five Shillings lawful Money of the Province of *Pennsylvania* to me in Hand well and truly paid by Saml Wallis of the City of Philadelphia Merchant at or before the Sealing and Delivery hereof, (the Receipt whereof I do hereby acknowledge) and for other good Causes and valuable Considerations, have Bargained, Sold, Released, Assigned, and Confirmed, and, by these Presents, do Grant, Bargain, Sell, Release, Assign, and Confirm, unto the said Saml Wallis his Heirs, Executors, Administrators, and Assigns, all my Right, Title, Interest, Property, Claim, and Demand, of, in and to a certain Application, by me, or for me, entered in the Proprietaries Land-Office for the Province aforesaid, and received in the same by the Secretary of the said Office, on the Third Day of April in the year of our Lord one Thousand Seven Hundred and Sixtynine for Taking up three Hundred acres of Land Situate Adjoining Land of Benjamin Cathrell and likewise all my Right, Title, Interest, Property, Claim, and Demand, of, in, and to a certain Order issued, or to be issued, for Surveying and Locating to my Use the said Quantity of Three Hundred Acres of Land, and of and to the Warrant, and Patent, to be granted for the same, to Have and to Hold the said Premises, and every Part thereof, Surveyed, or to be Surveyed, and Located, in Pursuance of the said Application, or Order, or meant, mentioned and intended so to be, with all the Appurtenances whatsoever thereunto belonging, to the only proper Use and Behoof of him the said Saml Wallis his Heirs, Executors, Administrators and Assigns, for-ever under and subject to the Payment of the Consideration-Money and Quit-rent due, or to become due to the Honourable the Proprietaries of the said Province for the same, and the Charges of Surveying, and all other Charges, Taxes, and Assessments whatsoever. And I the said Peter Young for myself, my Heirs, Executors and Administrators, shall and will, at all and any Time or Times hereafter, upon the reasonable Request, Costs, and Charges of him the said Saml Wallis his Heirs, Executors, Administrators and Assigns, make, do, execute, acknowledge, and deliver, or cause

Figure 15. Page 1 of Original Deed from Peter Young to Samuel Wallis for NP-1558. This was one of the 18 tracts in the 9000+ acre tract that Wallis had surveyed in the area of Jersey Shore.

to be done, all and every ſuch further and other Conveyances, and Aſſurances in the Law, for granting and conveying the ſaid deſcribed Tract of Land and Premiſes, with all the Appurtenances, unto the ſaid Saml. Wallis his Heirs, Executors, Adminiſtrators, and Aſſigns, for-ever, as by him or them, them or their Counſel learned in the Law, ſhall be adviſed, deviſed, or required.

In WITNESS whereof, I the ſaid Peter Young have hereunto ſet my Hand and Seal this fourth Day of May in the Year of our LORD One Thouſand Seven Hundred and Seventy two

Peter Young

Sealed and Delivered in the Preſence of

Georg Senfft

Pennsylvania ss.

On the 29 day of July 1779 before me John Hambright Esqr. One of the Members of the Supreme Execut:ive Council of the State of Pennsylvania personally Came George Senff and being duly Sworn according to Law did depose & Say that he did see Peter Young Seal and as his Act and Deed Deliver the Above and within Deed of Conveyance or Instrument of Wrighting, & that the Name of this deponant thereunto Subscribed as a Witness is of his Own respective hand Wrighting and further Saith Not

Sworn the day & year Above Written Before me - Witness my hand & Seal

John Hambright

Figure 15, continued. Page 2 of Deed from Peter Young to Samuel Wallis.

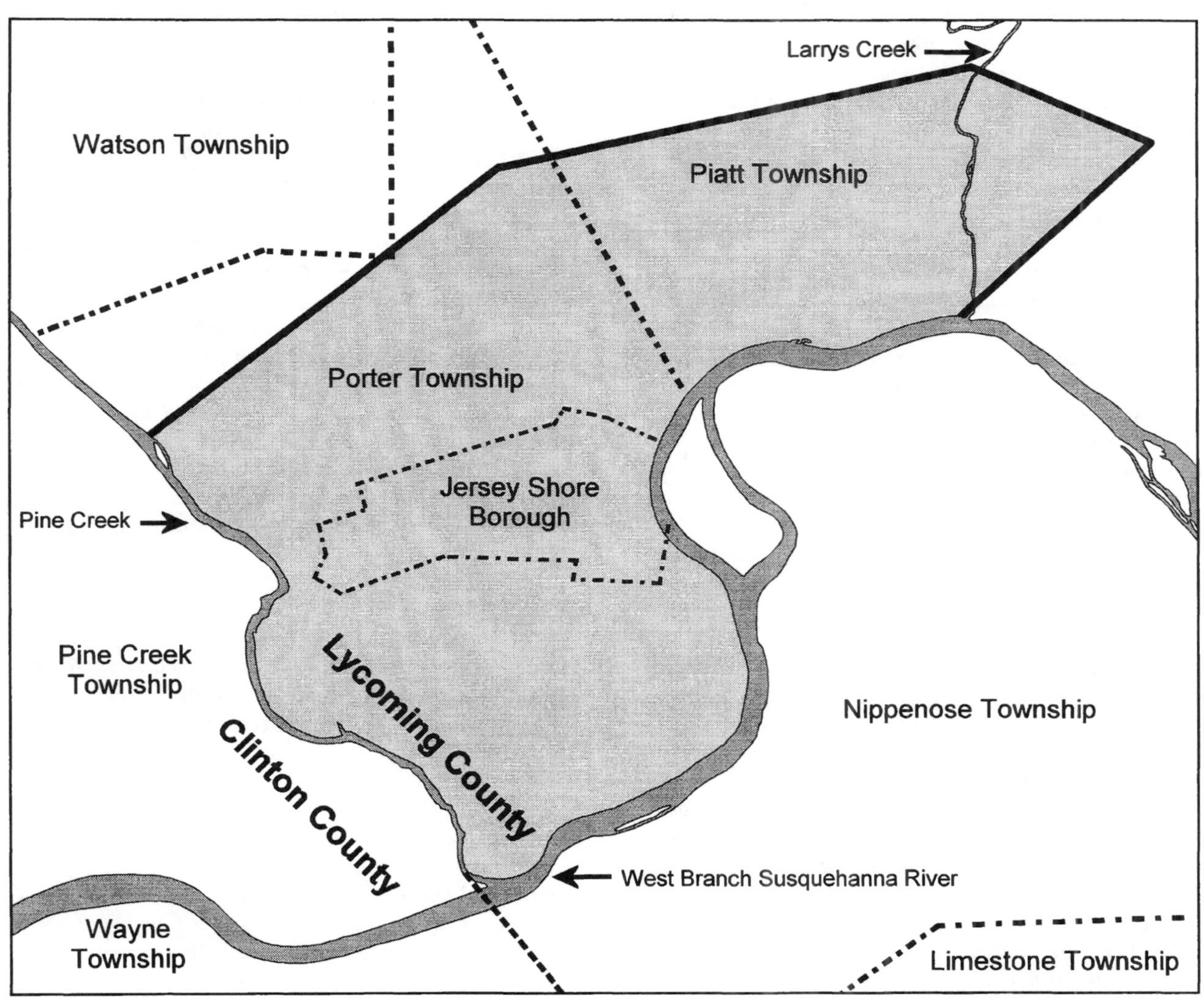

Figure 16. Lycoming County tract of Samuel Wallis. This tract was formed by combining 18 New Purchase Applications. The original survey was not located. This map was created using the description of the property given in the 1892 History of Lycoming County, Pennsylvania by John F. Meginness, page 199.

Part of a letter from Samuel Wallis:

"To the Public.

...The last grand Indian purchase was concluded in November, 1768. The Land-office was immediately opened for the exclusive benefit of the proprietary officers and friends, and before the end of February following, grants were made, of the best lands they had discovered, to the Secretary and his people, to the amount of near 150,000 acres, including a few surveys for the Proprietaries use. This quantity one would imagine a very plentiful repast; but it did not satisfy the hungry. The scheme however being disapproved by some of the officers, of greater virtue and fidelity, who refused to share in the plunder, and being loudly exclaimed against by the whole country, the Secretary was obliged to issue orders for surveying other large tracts, in the names of the Proprietaries, which might be shared amongst those who still remained ungratified, at leisure. This some of them have been honest enough to confess. Thus the names of the Proprietaries were prostituted to serve the avaricious purposes of their servants. The best of the land being thus secured, public notice was given, that the third day of April, 1769, the Land-office would be opened to receive applications for lands in the newly made purchase; and to multiply the fees, no person was allowed to enter an application in his own name for more than 300 acres. When the day, so long wished for by the country, arrived, great numbers attended to enter their applications. They were met at the State-House by the Secretary, who artfully persuaded them to enter their applications altogether, and let the fate of them be decided by way of lottery; promising, at the same time, that those who were unfortunate, should have liberty to take up any other vacant land, without the expence and trouble of a fresh application. Trusting to this fallacious promise, the people consented. Two thousand seven hundred and eighty-two applications were entered, for each one of which the Secretary received seven shillings --- not more than seven hundred of those applications proved fortunate. I have reason to believe, from the accounts of the several surveyors, the fortunate number was much less. The owners of the unfortunate applications, thinking nevertheless their money would not be lost, and depending on the Secretary's promise, immediately set themselves to search out other lands, and endeavoured to prevail on the several surveyors in whose districts they might be situated, to survey and make returns upon those applications. They were told no such orders had been given by their superiors --- such a promise had indeed been talked of, but it was not sufficient authority for them. Thus disappointed, those unfortunate people had recourse to the Secretary, reminded him of his promise, and pointed out the bad consequences of delay, by which they might a second time lose the land they had been at the expence and trouble of searching for. They were however put off with evasive answers, and kept in suspence for more than a twelve-month, by which means many of them suffered a second disappointment --- and they were at length told, that the removal of orders would be attended with bad consequences, and therefore could not be admitted. By the following short sketch it will appear, out of how much money he gulled the poor people, by this artifice and breach of faith.

2782 applications were entered, which had for their object only 700 tracts of lands, at 7 s. each --- £ 973 - 14 - 0.

700 orders of survey, which is more than just, by accounts received from the different deputy surveyors --- however we will allow that number were fortunate, it is all from the Secretary's promise, that he could have had a just right to detain his fees on --- at 7 s. each --- £ 245 - 0 - 0.

So that by the lottery scheme, and the breach of his promise, he detains unjustly £ 728 - 14 - 0."

Philadel. Jan. 17, 1771. SAMUEL WALLIS.

A very lengthy reply to Samuel Wallis' letter, written by James Tilghman, secretary of the Land Office, was published in the Pennsylvania Gazette.[29] James Tilghman's response reads, in part:

"To the PUBLIC.

...The charges against me are, my first opening the Land-office for the exclusive benefit of myself and my friends, my practices to multiply my fees, by my invention of the lottery, as it is called, and my breach of promise to the people, who put their locations or applications into it. To each of these I will answer distinctly.

The opening the office was not the sole act of the Secretary. It was a matter directed by the Board of Property, of which he is but one, and I have never singly taken any step of that kind. Samuel Wallis alledges at random, that "near 150,000 acres of land was, before the general opening of the Land-office, surveyed to the Secretary and his people, including a few surveys to the Proprietaries use;" by which he would intimate, that the principal part of this great quantity of land was surveyed for the Secretary and his people. There were warrants issued for about 80,000 acres for manors, in the different parts of the extensive New Purchase, of which about 60,000 acres have been surveyed, and

[29] Pennsylvania Gazette, 21 March 1771

these are what Samuel Wallis calls "a few surveys, for the use of the Proprietaries;" 24,000 acres, or thereabouts, were surveyed for the officers of the Pennsylvania regiment, in consequence of a petition to the honourable Proprietaries, and their concession, long before the New Purchase was made. About 25,000 acres were taken up on the common terms by gentlemen whom the Governor was pleased to gratify, and whom Samuel Wallis has the modesty to term "the Secretary's people." I myself had a tract of about 5000 acres, laid out by permission obtained of the Proprietaries, before the purchase was made of the Indians, and another tract of 500 acres, which the Governor was pleased to allow me to take up; and these are all the lands I have taken up, or been concerned in taking up, in Pennsylvania, either directly or indirectly. I had nothing to do with grants made to other people, nor did I solicit any of them, except one of 1500 acres for Doctor Allison. Thus have I given a fair account of what Samuel Wallis calls the Secretary's opening the Land-office, "for the exclusive benefit of himself and his friends."

I am next to consider the charge against me, for management to increase my fees, at the general opening the Land-office for the New Purchase. This management is made to consist in allowing each person to take up but 300 acres in his own name, and the contrivance of the lottery scheme, which Samuel Wallis would represent as the sole act of the Secretary. There is nothing more true than what has been before asserted, that the regulations of the Land-office are made by the Board of Property, and not by the Secretary himself, and no man knows better than Samuel Wallis, that the restriction of taking up 300 acres only by one person, was established before the present Secretary came into his office. And as to the lottery, the other gentlemen of the Board of Property will do me the justice to declare, that this was a scheme to which I was advised, to avoid disorder and confusion, and every appearance of partiality, and to give the numerous appliers an equal chance. For among the multitude who then attended with applications in their hands, whose application could the Secretary receive first, without giving offence to others? In a word, it was not only the opinion of the Agents, but of other gentlemen of judgment, intirely disinterested, that this was the fairest method, and it was executed to the general approbation of all concerned.

I will now state the matter of my promise to the people, respecting such applications as might prove unfortunate, and my conduct afterwards, both which Samuel Wallis very maliciously misrepresents. The office was opened on the 3d day of April, 1769, and as a great number of people attended to enter their locations, the receiving them in and rolling them up for drawing, took up the greatest part of that day and the night following. The drawing began on the fourth. In the morning of that day, as well as I can recollect at this distance of time, I was met in the street by one or two country people, who told me they intended to settle in the New Purchase, and that possibly their applications might prove unfortunate in the lottery by the prior drawing of others for the places they had in view, and that it would be hard upon them to lose the benefit of their applications; and asked me if they might not, in case their applications should prove unfortunate, have land surveyed in some other place, without new applications. I really thought their request but reasonable, and told them, I should have no objection to their having land surveyed any where in the same neighbourhood, upon such unfortunate applications; and that I, for my part, did not desire they should be put to the expence of new ones. This was probably told by them to others, and I believe my sentiments were known to most of those who put in applications. As to any absolute promise or engagement, I am positive I made none such, nor was any thing like it mentioned as terms, at the opening the office; for whatever was said by me, upon that occasion, was reduced to writing, and immediately afterwards entered in the application book, the tenor of which was to let the appliers know, "that such improvements or settlements as were made before the New Purchase, and at that time had families on them, or such as were made by licence from the commanding officer at Fort-Pitt, were not to be affected by applications. I did not make use of any persuasion to induce any man to put in his locations; there needed none; the eagerness of the people upon such occasions to get their locations entered was well known, and was what suggested the necessity of the lottery. And it appeared after the drawing was over, and the applications were entered up, that many had put in numbers of locations which they knew must prove unfortunate, in order to better their chances of obtaining the places they had in view.

A good while after the orders of survey had issued, and many, though not all the fortunate applications were surveyed, some of the deputy surveyors either spoke or wrote to me about orders for surveying for the people their unfortunate applications, and remembering the conversation which had passed between myself and several of the people, and being desirous that proper orders should be given, I applied to the other Agents upon the subject; but some of them were of opinion that there was already too much confusion, occasioned by the multitude of applications, and therefore did not incline to have any discretionary orders given to the deputy surveyors, especially as we had been informed that some of them, or their assistants, had been buying in the unfortunate applications, and might make an ill use of surveying them where they pleased. Before all the fortunate applications were surveyed, the Board of Property thought proper to put an end to the mode of taking up lands by applications or entries, and after this no orders could be given for surveying lands but by warrant. Before this alteration, there were very few, if any, instances of particular persons applying to the office about their unfortunate numbers. Since that time I think only one person applied for a warrant or two in August last (which was long before Samuel Wallis had any difference with me) in lieu of so many unfortunate locations, and upon that occasion I ordered the clerk of the Land-office to deduct the fees of those locations, and to do the same in all similar cases.

As to Samuel Wallis's ridiculous account stated between me and the people, I would just observe, that he has charged at least double the sum I received. It has been customary for the clerk of the Land-office, both before and since my time, to receive the Surveyor-general's as well as the Secretary's fees on applications. Three shillings and sixpence only was the Secretary's fee on applications; the other three and sixpence belonged to the Surveyor-general. This practice of the clerk's receiving the Surveyor-general's fee, was introduced not only to save the people the trouble of two payments at different offices, but because they did not themselves carry the locations to the Surveyor-general's office, as they do their warrants, but the locations being recorded in the Secretary's office, copies of them were by him sent to the Surveyor-general, and if the Surveyor-general's fees were not paid at the Secretary's office, he would lose the most, if not all of them. The fact, with regard to the fees, is as above stated, and it is hardly conceivable that a man who has had so much to do in the offices as Samuel Wallis, should not know it; but his aim seems to have been to escape in as much dust as he could possibly raise about the Secretary.

What might be the number of tracts which were the objects of all the locations which were put into the lottery, I am not able to determine, nor have I any thing to do with it. I had the same trouble in filing, recording and copying an unfortunate as a fortunate location; and I was obliged to file, record and copy them all, and was therefore entitled to the usual fees. But I have great reason to believe Samuel Wallis is much mistaken in the number of those tracts, as Captain Thompson, who has one of the six districts beyond the Allegheny Mountain, assures me he has surveyed at least half the number of tracts which Samuel Wallis mentions, on locations of the 3d of April, 1769, and there are five districts in the New Purchase on this side the mountain, and I am well assured a good number of tracts must have been surveyed in each of the eleven districts. I never enquired how many, as I had nothing to do with the affair, nor should I have known what I mention of the number of surveys in Captain Thompson's district, had he not told me of it, to show how much Samuel Wallis must have misrepresented that matter.

I have done with the reply, and I persuade myself I have satisfied every unprejudiced man of integrity and understanding, that I have been greatly misrepresented.

[This letter continues at a considerable length.]

March 12, 1771. JAMES TILGHMAN.

The Application program was ended in August 1769. No specific documents have been located to explain why the program was ended. It is not mentioned in the Minutes of the Board of Property. Fraud and other problems were the most likely cause for the end of the program. The mention of the end of the Application program in James Tilghman's letter (fifth paragraph) is the only explanation for the end of the program that I have been able to find.

Mapping and Land Settlement Patterns

Unlike the East Side Application program in which much of the area had been previously settled before the application program started, the New Purchase applications represented the first time that ordinary people could acquire title to land in that area. Because of this, much of the land in the New Purchase applications was prime land rather than previously unsettled (and presumably less desirable) land. To demonstrate this, I prepared a connected draft of an area along the Conemaugh River on the border of Westmoreland and Indiana Counties (Figure 17). As can be seen in the connected draft, the majority of the tracts are located along the river. An aerial photograph of part of this area (Figure 18) shows that some of the original boundary lines can still be seen as field edges or hedgerows.

Most of the New Purchase application tracts in this area are prime farm land. Figure 19 shows a "shaded relief" map of the same area shown in the aerial photograph.[30] Four of the five successful

---

[30] Created using the computer program Global Mapper. A limited feature version is available for free download at **http://mcmcweb.er.usgs.gov/drc/dlgv32pro/** by special agreement with the United States Geological Survey (USGS). The scanned USGS maps were downloaded from **http://www.pasda.psu.edu** and the digital elevation model data sets used with the program to create the

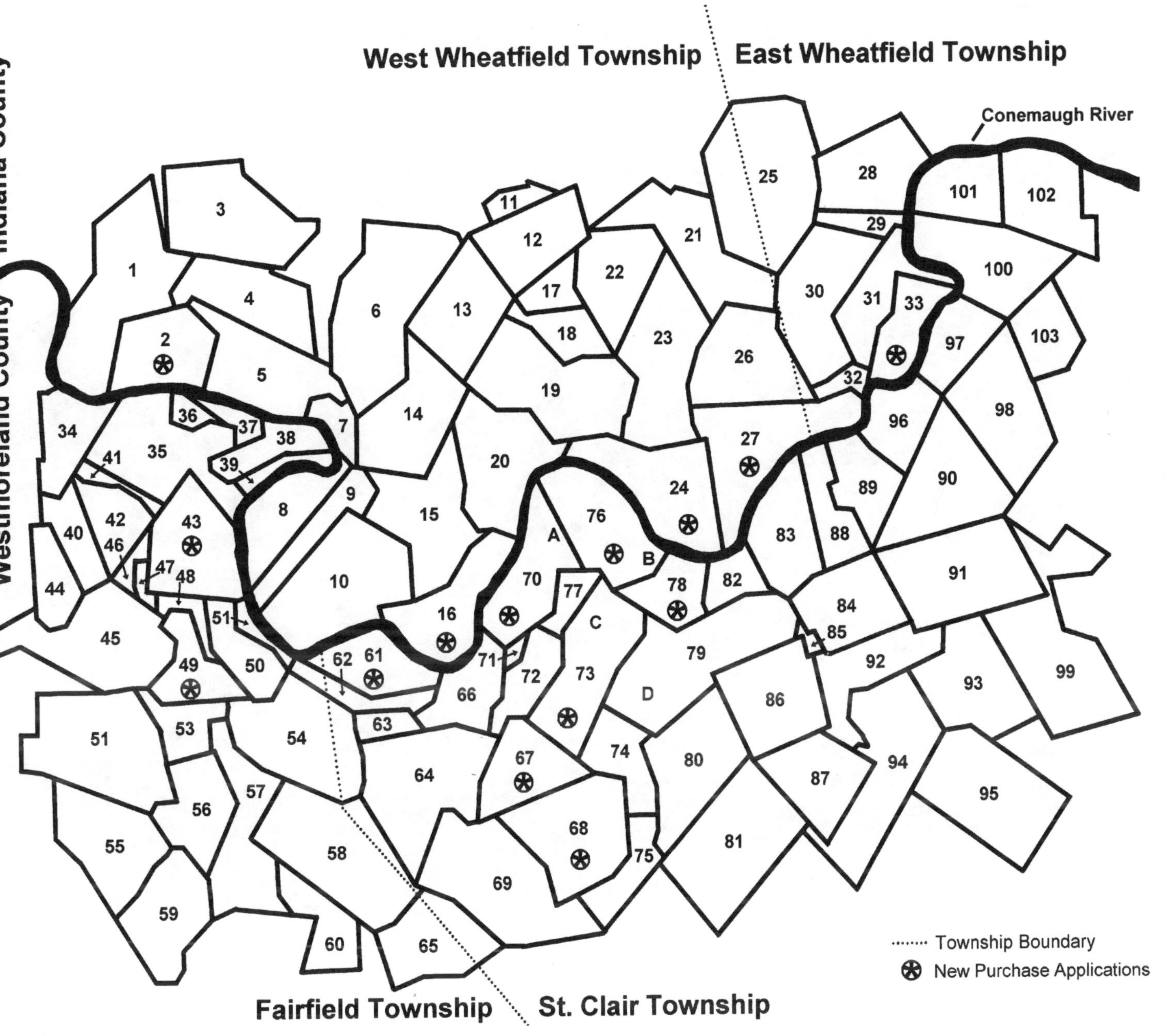

Figure 17. Connected draft along Conemaugh River on Indiana – Westmoreland County border.

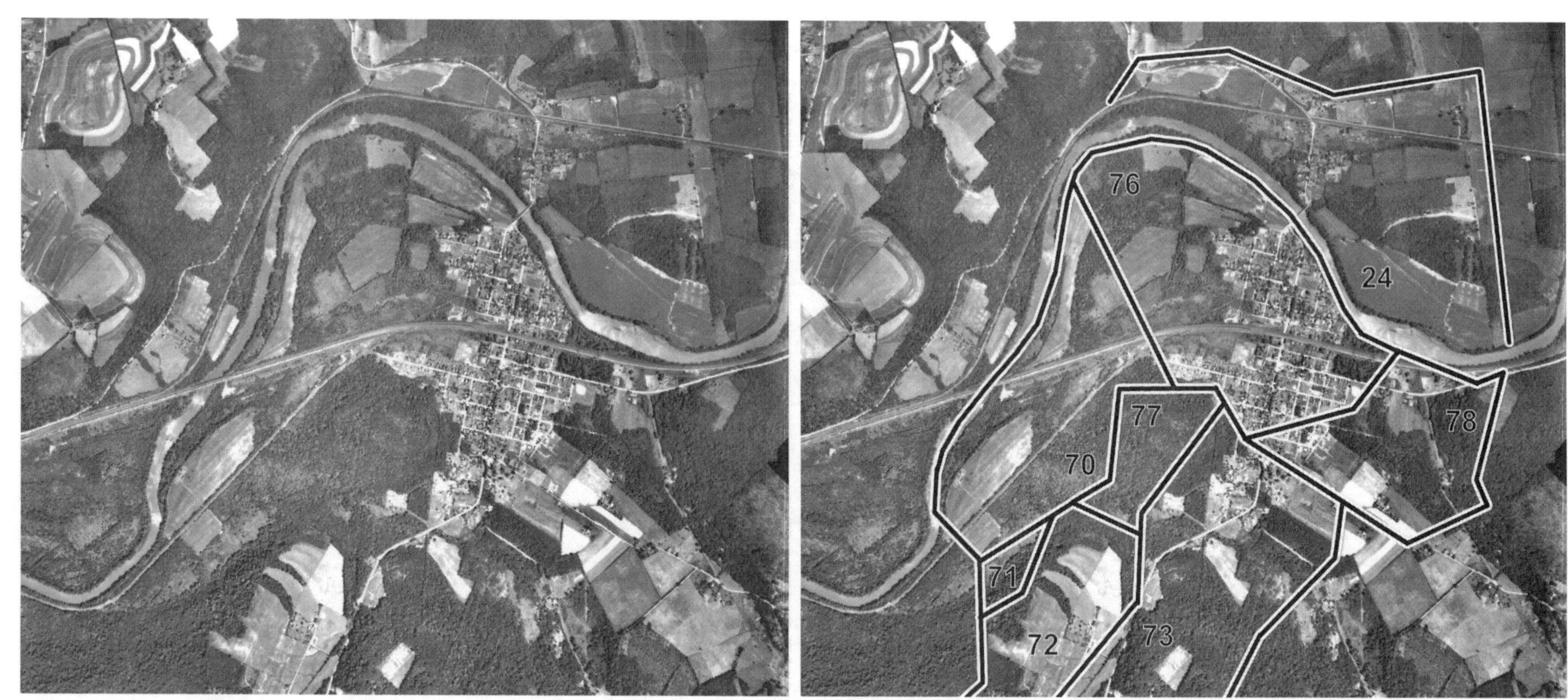

Figure 18. Aerial Photograph of the area around New Florence, PA. Photo on right shows tract boundaries from the Connected Draft shown in Figure 17. Aerial Photograph courtesy of Pennsylvania Geologic Survey Library in Middletown, PA. Their Web Site is located at: http://www.dcnr.state.pa.us/topogeo/library/lib.htm

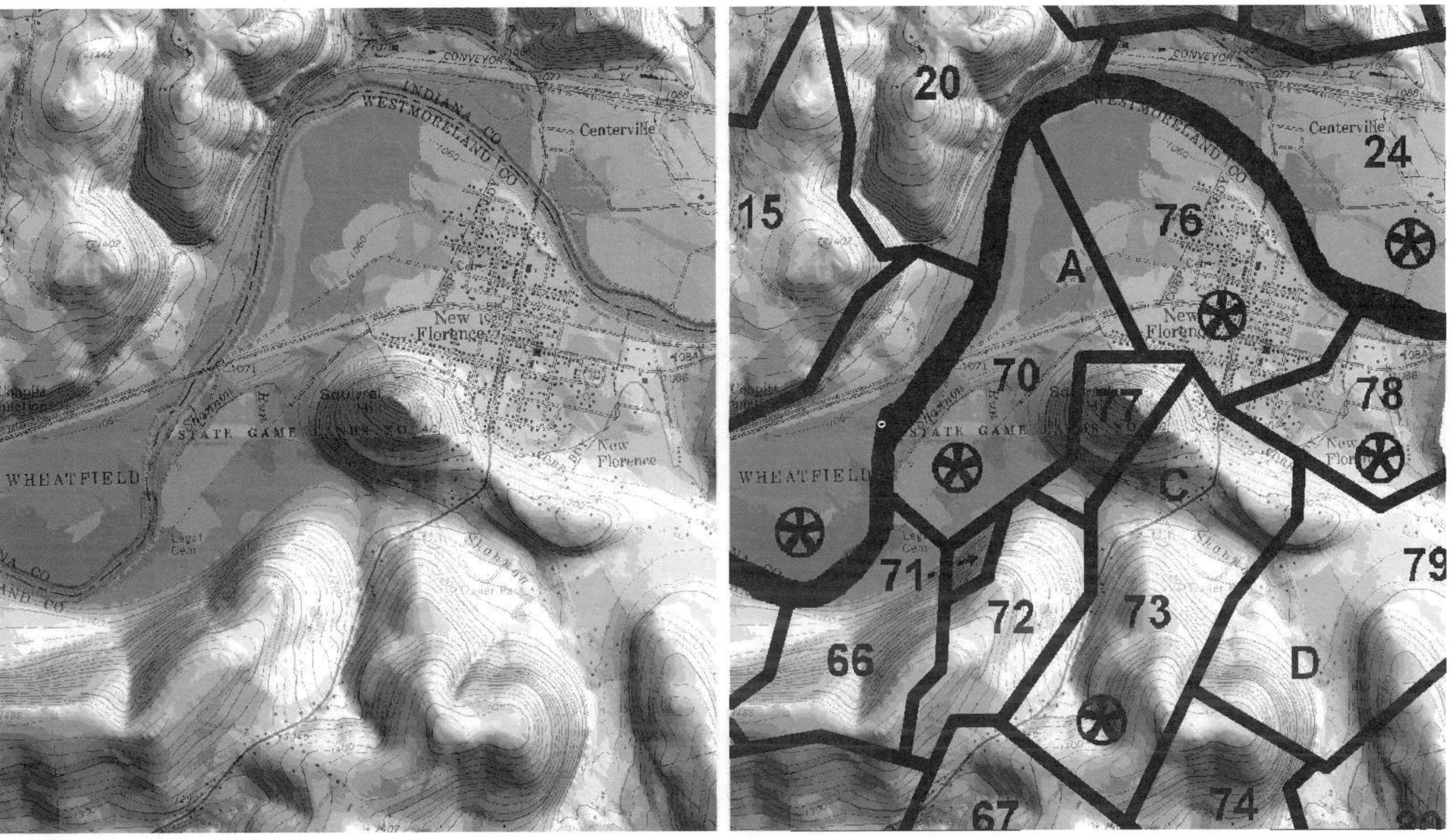

Figure 19. Shaded Relief Map of the area shown in Figure 18.

Table 5 - Key to Connected Draft along Conemaugh River, Indiana and Westmoreland Counties.

Tract #	Application # or Warrant	Applicant or Warrantee	Application or Warrant Date	Survey Reference	Later Owners
A	NP-467 (conflicting, not mapped)	Ludwick Lowman	3 APR 1769	D-57-206	[interferes with tracts 70 and 76]
B	NP-1594 (conflicting, not mapped)	John Reed	3 APR 1769	D-56-109	[interferes with tracts 76 and 78]
C	NP-1581 (conflicting, not mapped)	Robert Elliott	3 APR 1769	D-46-98	[interferes with tracts 72, 73 and 77
D	NP-1373 (conflicting, not mapped)	Samuel Taylor	3 APR 1769	D-56-225	[interferes with tracts 73, 74 and 79]
1	(Ind. Co.) R-18	Elliot Robinson in trust for Irwin Robinson heirs	10 DEC 1839	B-18-66	
2	NP-3634	Hugh Wiley	10 JUL 1769	A-42-211	(1793)William Todd, Esq.
3	(Ind. Co.) F-2	George Findley	19 NOV 1808	C-85-25	(1793)David Wilson
4	(Westm. Co.) H-275	James Hart	10 MAY 1792	C-68-175	
5	(Westm. Co.) J-81	Benjamin Jones	12 APR 1787	C-86-267	(1828)William B. Foster (1870)Andrew Robinson
6	(Westm. Co.) F-119	George Findley	15 NOV 1787	C-70-15	(1774)vacant (1848)Jacob & George Gamble[part] (1870)Archibald McCurdy, Samuel McClain, T. B. McGahan, W. A. McGahan, C. Hutcheson, Andrew Robinson, John B. Burkholder, George F. Gamble, Mary E. Lightcap, James M. McCurdy[part]
7	(Ind. Co.) R-3	David Reed, Esq.	22 SEP 1814	C-186-290	[interferes with tract 9] (1865)Ruth & Elizabeth Reed
8	(Westm. Co.) B-206	Adam Brittain	19 DEC 1785	B-16-5	(1853)George & Samuel Brittain
9	(Ind. Co.) B-4	Horace Bratain	9 SEP 1814	C-207-204	[interferes with tract 7] (1789)Adam Brattin (1853)William Ligat[part] (1854)George & Samuel Brittain[part] (1870)Ann McCoy[part]
10	(Westm. Co.) R-72	Andrew Reed	23 AUG 1784	C-170-234	(1815)David Reed (1853)J. Brown
11	(Ind. Co.) D-3	John Dick	8 DEC 1818	C-47-145	(1870)Robert Dick
12	(Westm. Co.) S-289	John Sheaver [Shaffer]	25 FEB 1788	(no survey found)	[mapping based on description in return dated 1 FEB 1813] (1817)John Dick

Table 5 - Key to Connected Draft along Conemaugh River, Indiana and Westmoreland Counties.

Tract #	Application # or Warrant	Applicant or Warrantee	Application or Warrant Date	Survey Reference	Later Owners
13	(Westm. Co.) F-28	Humphrey Fullerton	6 APR 1774	A-59-13	(1791, 1799)Archiblad Jamison
14	(Westm. Co.) K-17	William Kelly	6 APR 1774	C-111-121	(1832)William Rankin[part] (1838)Isabella Jameson[part] (1870)William Alexander
15	(Westm. Co.) F-134	Samuel Findley	5 MAR 1789	A-60-63	
16	NP-928	John Woods	3 APR 1769	C-117-92	
17	(Ind. Co.) D-1	Christopher Dumars	8 MAR 1815	C-29-194	(1791)vacant (1828)John Clarnen
18	(Westm. Co.) C-325	Samuel & Moses Crawford	14 NOV 1791	C-29-193	(1828)John Clarnen
19	(Westm. Co.) C-157	George Clymer	5 AUG 1785	C-28-267	[signer of the Declaration of Independence; major overlap with tract 13 and another warrant to James Dill dated 14 MAR 1788(survey D-50-118)] (1774)vacant (1832)Mary Clymer
20	(Westm. Co.) D-104	Neal Dougherty	20 MAR 1786	A-11-187	(1774)James McClintock (1789)Daniel McClintock (1794)William Graham
21	(Westm. Co.) B-196	Robert Barr	25 AUG 1785	B-7-38	(1811)John McCreary (1853)Isaac Rodgers & William Clark, heirs of Paul Clark, deceased
22	(Westm. Co.) M-249	William Moorhead	2 JAN 1786	A-72-52	(1790)Robert Dick (1815)Robert Smith
23	(Westm. Co.) F-78	Thomas Fitzsimons	5 AUG 1785	A-67-232	(1790)Edward Rily (1812)Charles Beard
24	NP-1640	Robert Hinkson	3 APR 1769	C-118-96	(1811)William McCune (1827)John B. Alexander & Abraham Horbach[part]
25	(Westm. Co.) C-292	William Crawford & Andrew Douglass	5 JUL 1788	A-89-186	(1787)vacant (1790)Robert Lawson (1797)Robert McCurdy
26	(Westm. Co.) H-155	Henry Hyse	28 NOV 1785	C-84-263	(1811)William Hise
27	NP-2648	James McCurdy	3 APR 1769	C-84-202	(1772)John Hinkson (1773)David Wilson (1784)Henry Hise (1827)William Hise
28	(Westm. Co.) H-273	John Hart	10 MAY 1792	A-72-32	(1787)vacant

Table 5 - Key to Connected Draft along Conemaugh River, Indiana and Westmoreland Counties.

Tract #	Application # or Warrant	Applicant or Warrantee	Application or Warrant Date	Survey Reference	Later Owners
29	(Ind. Co.) L-9	John Logan	31 MAR 1819	C-118-65	(1787)vacant (1828)Henry Taylor
30	(Westm. Co.) C-243	John Crawford, Sr. (of Bucks County)	15 FEB 1787	A-75-5	[interferes with tract 31] (1790)Samuel Mitchell (1820)William Steel
31	(Westm. Co.) K-23	John Kelly	28 FEB 1775	A-14-112	[interferes with tract 30] (1892)Charles Semple, William Kissinger
32	(Ind. Co.) P-5	Frederick Persian	8 NOV 1819	C-191-1	(1830)Thomas Clark, William Bracken, Mary Ann Galbreath, Daniel Persian, guardians of the minor children of Frederick Persian, deceased
33	NP-1224	Robert Gibb	3 APR 1769	A-75-13	(1787)Robert Roseberry
34	(Westm. Co.) M-390	Archibald McGuire	3 OCT 1787	A-59-49	(1795, 1799)Peter Justice (1808)David Williams (1838)William Hammond & James Murry
35	(Westm. Co.) S-422 & S-436	Jacob Stewart	11 FEB 1796 & 7 JAN 1799	C-202-76	(1799)Jacob Stewart, administrator of Andrew Harrison, deceased[part] (1815, 1829)Mathias States (1838)Joseph McBeth heirs[part] (pre-1838)Matthias States[part] (1838)Francis Marrion[part]
36	(Westm. Co.) C-517	Jacob Cavode	30 MAR 1829	C-30-180	(1815)Richard Hall (1871)John Covde heirs
37	(Westm. Co.) C-481	Jacob Cavode	31 MAY 1815	C-37-198	(1813)Ebenezer Brady
38	(Westm. Co.) B-218	Joseph Brady, Jr.	8 MAR 1786	C-35-7	(1799, 1815)James McCurdy
39	(Westm. Co.) M-668	James McCurdy	4 SEP 1815	C-152-192	
40	(Westm. Co.) M-471	Michael Myer	22 SEP 1790	C-141-115	(1788)Peter Snider (1793)Christian Eby
41	(Westm. Co.) K-142	William King	20 SEP 1838	C-110-274	(1875)David Coulter
42	(Westm. Co.) S-497	Robert Story	4 DEC 1822	C-210-193	(1874)--- Coulter & --- Dushane
43	NP-202	John Barr	3 APR 1769	O-267	[interferes with tract 51] (1823, 1826, 1829)James Parks (1838)Jacob Souders (1874)John Love
44	(Westm. Co.) M-347	Elias Miller & James Brady, Jr.	1 FEB 1787	C-128-275	(1802)Jacob Stewart

Table 5 - Key to Connected Draft along Conemaugh River, Indiana and Westmoreland Counties.

Tract #	Application # or Warrant	Applicant or Warrantee	Application or Warrant Date	Survey Reference	Later Owners
45	(Westm. Co.) A-73	John Alexander & James Lawson	7 FEB 1788	C-5-8	(1786)Abraham Reemer (1806)James & Thomas Lawson (1825)widow Tolbert (1829)Henry Tolbert heirs (1874)J. E. Baker
46	(Westm. Co.) G-251	Daniel Garland	12 MAR 1874	C-81-97	
47	(Westm. Co.) P-283	Alexander Park	7 JAN 1828	C-178-27	(1881, 1887)Joseph H. Love
48	(Westm. Co.) S-498	John Stewart	14 MAR 1825	C-230-99	(1773)John Burk (1874)Margaret Covode administrators
49	NP-1313	William Barr, Jr.	3 APR 1769	A-35-121	(1810)James Updegraff (1825)John Stewart
50	(Westm. Co.) H-207	Archibald Hanna	14 AUG 1786	A-62-62	(1826)James Huston
51	(Westm. Co.) B-369	James Buchanan	4 JUN 1794	C-27-270	[interferes with tract 43] (1870)William Huston
52	(Westm. Co.) L-77	Nicholas Lute	12 DEC 1785	C-116-16	
53	(Westm. Co.) E-81	Christian Eby	22 SEP 1790	A-27-130	(1786)vacant
54	(Westm. Co.) M-261	Archibald McGuire	1 MAR 1786	A-59-50	(1830)Archibald Huston
55	(Westm. Co.) C-237	Daniel Carmichael	19 DEC 1786	C-16-262	
56	(Westm. Co.) W-164	Thomas Woods	30 MAY 1786	D-6-201	
57	(Westm. Co.) P-150	Samuel Phipps	3 APR 1788	C-160-167	(1786)vacant (1830)William Galbreath heirs
58	(Westm. Co.) G-88	John Galbraith	2 JUN 1786	C-83-32	(1787)James & John Galbraith (1788, 1793)Thomas Galbraith heirs (1813)William & John Bennett (1822)William Myler[part] (1830)John Galbraith[part] (1830)Robert Boyd, Esq.[part] (1840)William Kennedy[part]
59	(Westm. Co.) T-95	Mary Todd	6 MAR 1786	A-84-253	(1787, 1794))Daniel Hendricks
60	(Westm. Co.) M-492	Robert Martin	27 FEB 1793	C-153-45	(1787, 1788)Charles Smock (1803)William Bennett (pre-1830)John Smock (1830)John Robison
61	NP-550	John Cummins	3 APR 1769	M-176	(1788, 1817)Archibald Maguire
62	(Westm. Co.) M-714	William Mathews	1 DEC 1829	C-140-220	

Table 5 - Key to Connected Draft along Conemaugh River, Indiana and Westmoreland Counties.

Tract #	Application # or Warrant	Applicant or Warrantee	Application or Warrant Date	Survey Reference	Later Owners
63	(Westm. Co.) D-143	Ellis Davis	17 APR 1789	C-45-235	(1815)Archibald Huston & Daniel Hendrix (1829, 1830)Archibald Huston (1834)John Hill & Paul Clark
64	(Westm. Co.) G-87	James Galbraith	2 JUN 1786	C-83-38	(1786)Thomas Galbraith heirs (1813)William & John Bennett (1817)John Matthews (1830)William Matthews (1830, 1840)William Kennedy (1829, 1832)John Bennett heirs[part]
65	(Westm. Co.) R-144	John Ramsey	20 NOV 1786	C-184-257	(1830)John Gilmer
66	(Westm. Co.) P-158	Robert Perry	14 JAN 1788	C-165-223	(1815)Archibald Huston & Daniel Hendrix (pre-1832)John Brown (1830)Col. Jacob D. Mathiot (1873)William M. Martin
67	NP-2674	John Rannels, Jr.	3 APR 1769	P-151	(1785)John Hinkson (1773, 1815)Samuel Gibb (1829)Thomas Trimble (1831)Thomas Trimble, James Trimble
68	NP-396	Samuel Gibbs	3 APR 1769	C-160-185	(1796)John Phipps (1822)William Matthews heirs
69	(Westm. Co.) H-117	John Huffnagle	22 JAN 1785	C-74-190	(1771)George Bratton (1787, 1815)Michael Huffnagle (1791)John Benninger (1822)Robert Brown (1829)Joseph Peoples (1830)Joseph Peoples heirs
70	NP-277	John Hinkson	3 APR 1769	C-191-20	(1829, 1831)James Peoples (1873)William Peoples
71	(Westm. Co.) M-784	William M. Martin	18 DEC 1873	D-43-45	
72	(Westm. Co.) C-324	Paul Clark	5 OCT 1790	C-42-22	(1773)John Hinkson (1873)John Campbell
73	NP-1212	Charles Cumings	3 APR 1769	D-490	(1787, 1811, 1822)James Brady (1828)George Hill (1830)William Brown
74	(Westm. Co.) B-309	Ebenezer & James Brady	27 SEP 1790	C-24-29	(1773)Robert Huthy (1827)Samuel Shannon (1837)Samuel Shannon heirs (1787, 1828)John Wallace

Table 5 - Key to Connected Draft along Conemaugh River, Indiana and Westmoreland Counties.

Tract #	Application # or Warrant	Applicant or Warrantee	Application or Warrant Date	Survey Reference	Later Owners
75	(Westm. Co.) H-221	William Hanna	14 AUG 1786	C-24-31	(1827)Robert Brown[part] (1837)Robert Brown, Jr. (1827)Samuel Shannon[part]
76	NP-527	William McCune	3 APR 1769	C-10-92	(1787, 1789, 1828)David Brown
77	(Westm. Co.) B-253	James Brady, Sr.	1 FEB 1787	C-25-5	(1773)John Hinkson (1830)James Hill
78	NP-789	Robert Barr	3 APR 1769	C-145	(1787, 1819)James Clark (1838)Paul & William Clark
79	(Westm. Co.) B-252	James Brady, Jr.	1 FEB 1787	B-7-86	(1773)Robert Huthy (1786)Robert Fulthy[probably the same person as above] (1819)George Srum heirs (1837)Catharine Shrum (1864)George Myers
80	(Westm. Co.) H-416	Robert Hice	4 AUG 1837	C-101-12	(1786)vacant (1787)John Wallace (1822)James Brady (1828)J. Matthews
81	(Westm. Co.) C-200	William Condy	20 MAR 1786	C-37-194	(1801)Peter Holtz (1815)Nicholas Requate (1822)Jeremiah Condy (1837)Jacob D. Mathiot & Co.
82	(Westm. Co.) B-326	James Brady	9 JAN 1794	C-13-270	(1786, 1787)James Clark (1838)Paul Clark
83	(Westm. Co.) W-156	William Woods	8 MAR 1786	A-13-1	(1786)James Clark (1819)Philip Milliron
84	(Westm. Co.) S-218	Charles Stewart	2 MAR 1786	A-3-198	(pre-1828)George Shrum (1828)Abraham Myers (1864, 1870)George Myers
85	(Westm. Co.) M-766	George Myers	18 JUN 1864	C-165-66	(1828)Samuel Elder
86	(Westm. Co.) B-217	John Brady	8 MAR 1786	A-66-46	(1837)John Brown[part] (1837)Ebenezer Decker[part] (1864)Patrick Daniels heirs
87	(Westm. Co.) S-452	Alexander Stewart	12 MAR 1808	C-204-25	(1786)vacant (1828)Baldwin Furnace land (1846)John White or Baldwin Furnace land
88	(Westm. Co.) W-250	James Wakefield	16 JUN 1794	A-13-2	(1813)Philip Millison

Table 5 - Key to Connected Draft along Conemaugh River, Indiana and Westmoreland Counties.

Tract #	Application # or Warrant	Applicant or Warrantee	Application or Warrant Date	Survey Reference	Later Owners
89	(Westm. Co.) W-231	John Williams	4 SEP 1793	A-69-146	(1790)William Steel (1794)Samuel Johnston (1806)George Steel (1832)James Steel
90	(Westm. Co.) D-145	Andrew Douglass & William Todd, Esq.	20 AUG 1789	C-44-250	(1786)vacant (1795)John Hart
91	(Westm. Co.) R-126	James Mitchell Raquet	20 MAR 1786	E-174	(1803)Lydia Raquet (1847)Jacob & George Myers
92	(Westm. Co.) H-209	Gasper Hill	9 JAN 1794	C-117-22	(1792)James Brady (1846)Thomas Kade & Samuel Hill, Daniel Decker (1864)Samuel Hill heirs (1907)Tillie C. Werder
93	(Westm. Co.) W-328	Thomas Wade	10 MAR 1847	A-3-206	(????)Jacob Hill (1846)James T. Hale & Co. (1901)Mathilda C. Werder
94	(Westm. Co.) H-430	Benjamin Hickock	4 AUG 1846	C-100-129	(1815)James Lemmon (1846)C. B. Callahan (1865)James T. Hale
95	(Westm. Co.) R-275	George Reed	4 AUG 1846	C-186-296	(1847)George M. Reed (1865)James T. Hale
96	(Westm. Co.) M-735	William McPherson	6 DEC 1836	A-3-193	(1790, 1794)William Steel
97	(Westm. Co.) D-146	Andrew Douglass & William Todd	20 AUG 1789	C-44-251	(1795)John Hart (1832)William Hart heirs
98	(Westm. Co.) M-196	James McCartney	2 FEB 1785	A-4-96	1795)John Hart (1837)--- Hart heirs
99	(Westm. Co.) R-274	Daniel H. Royer	29 AUG 1845	C-147-33	(1845, 1870)George Myers
100	(Westm. Co.) K-26	Samuel Kirkbride	30 JUL 1776	A-71-18	(1787)John Buchanan (1789)Samuel Pleasants (1837)Samuel McDonald
101	(Westm. Co.) D-157	Mary & Jane Douglass	10 MAY 1792	A-16-40	(1787)James Barr (1796)William Mabben
102	(Westm. Co.) F-85	John Findley	1 NOV 1785	C-55-174	(1837)Isaac Hill heirs
103	(Westm. Co.) H-418	Jane Hill	5 DEC 1837	A-3-207	

applications are relatively level bottom land ideally suited for farming. The other tract (number 73 in the connected draft) was located along one of the few roads in the area. That the land was in a prime location is probably true of most of the applications in the New Purchase. There are also four locations where unsuccessful applications had been surveyed. Table 5 shows the owners and warrant information for the tracts of land in the connected draft shown in Figure 17. Information on later ownership of these tracts (obtained from adjoining surveys done on different dates) is also presented in Table 5.

Format of the Data and Abbreviations

The information extracted from the New Purchase Applications is presented in Table 6. The eight columns in the table are:

1) Application Number – the applications were numbered as they were entered into the original register. The numbering was not perfect in the original. A few numbers were skipped and there were some that were used twice. If there were duplicate application numbers, they have been presented here with a letter following the number, for example the second application numbered NP-1123 is given the number NP-1123a.

2) Applicant's Name – the name of the applicant is recorded as it was written in the register, or if the original application was found, as it was written on the original. In some cases, a place or residence was given, and in a few, an occupation was stated. Most of these additional details were only found on the original application and not entered into the register.

3) Application Date – this is the date that appears in the register.

4) Original Place – this is the property location as mentioned in the description on the application. In most cases the county was specified. For properties that did not have later documents (survey, return, or patent), the township or other descriptive location (when no township was mentioned) is given.

5) Later Place – this is the county and township that were entered into the register as the location of the land when later documents were filed. County and township boundaries changed when new municipalities were formed. The place listed here is the one that had jurisdiction when the later documents were filed, and may not be the current municipality. The letters "LD:" indicate that there was an entry in the Lien Dockets for this application. The Lien Dockets were created to try to get the owners of unpatented land to obtain a patent for the land. The Lien Dockets were organized by county. The New Purchase Applications that had not yet been patented were entered into these dockets based on the preparer's best guess as to which of the current counties the land was located in. These may provide a clue as to the intended location of the application, but not all of these "guesses" are right, and some conflict with the location found on later documents.

6) Acres – this is the number of acres called for on the application. This is generally not the actual number of acres, but was the applicant's estimate of the area of the parcel. This was usually an underestimate. The actual number of acres was determined when the land was surveyed.

7) Survey – this is the reference to where the survey was copied. It consists of series-volume-page, as in C-193-239, or volume-page, as in M-226. The same reference was added to the original surveys, which were filmed in the same order. These numbers are random – there was no order to the way in which they were copied into the registers.

8) Neighbors, Notes, etc. – fields in this column are separated by a slash "/." This column includes the names of neighbors mentioned in the description of the land, and also some other names, such as relatives of the applicant. If a first name is not mentioned in the application, "---" was substituted. Dates within parentheses preceded with an "r" - (r6 MAR 1788) indicate that a return was filed on that date. If there is a name directly after the ")" instead of a slash, it indicates that the event was done by that person rather than the applicant. The letter "p" indicates a patent date. Other notes, including patent references, are included in square brackets "[ ]." "Original:" indicates the status of the original application. "(signed)" indicates that the original application appears to have been signed by the applicant. In some cases, it is possible that someone else wrote in the name of the applicant in such a way that it appears to be their signature. If there was a signature with the same surname as the applicant, this is noted, as it is likely that this person is a relative. If the signature is in German script, that is also indicated, as that can be a clue to the origin of the applicant (of course, German was used in countries other than "Germany," which did not yet exist as a political entity at that time). If a caveat was found that related

---

shaded relief map were downloaded from the site **http://data.geocomm.com/catalog/US/61062/sublist.html**, also for free.

to a New Purchase Application, there is a note to see the table of caveat data.

Phonetic Cross Reference

Because of the errors made in recording the names of the applicants and neighbors in the original documents, it is necessary to use a lot of leeway in searching the index. To assist with this, a phonetic cross reference section has been added to the book. Part one of this section lists all of the surnames found in the book alphabetically along with their Daitch-Mokotoff (D-M) codes. The D-M coding methodology was originally developed by Randy Daitch and Gary Mokotoff for use on German-Jewish surnames. They also work well on non-German surnames since they go beyond phonetic coding systems like soundex in that they encode the first letter of a surname, leading to a more robust search. Part two of the D-M phonetic cross reference sorts all the surnames by their D-M codes, thus grouping similar sounding surnames in the same area of the list. The instructions for the use of the D-M phonetic cross reference section are found at the beginning of that section.

Table 6 - New Purchase Applications (1769-1773)

Number	Applicant	Date	Orig. Place	Later Place	Acres	Survey	Neighbors, Notes, etc.
NP-1	Smith, Abraham	3 APR 1769		Derry, Westmoreland	300	C-193-239	(r6 MAR 1788)/[see caveat] Original: Missing
NP-2	Poultney, Thomas	3 APR 1769	Bald Eagle Creek, Berks	Northumberland	300	C-146-290	(r5 MAY 1774) Original: Missing
NP-3	Jenkins, Mary	3 APR 1769	Northumberland	Madison, Columbia	300	X-207 D-12-154	(r22 DEC 1818)T. Stewardson/Sharp Dunlaney Original: found
NP-4	Glen, Robert	3 APR 1769		Fishing Creek Twp., Northumberland	300		(r13 JAN 1775)William West, Jr./(r14 APR 1792 & p16 APR 1792)William West, Jr. Original: found
NP-5	Carpenter, Jacob	3 APR 1769	Hopewell, Berks	LD: Union	300	B-1-68	George Weaver Original: found
NP-6	Wayland, Jacob	3 APR 1769	Berks	Kelly, Union	300	D-57-29 F-86	(r6 OCT 1800)Richard Sherer/Michael Weyland/[see caveat] Original: found
NP-7	McCanahey, Robert	3 APR 1769		Mingo Run, Berks	300	M-226	(r4 SEP 1787)Ruth McCaskey Original: found
NP-8	Rees, Dieterick	3 APR 1769	Berks	White Deer, Union	300	D-56-134 D-56-246 D-60-237 C-140-102	(r16 JUL 1813)James McKessen/Ludwig Derr Original: found
NP-9	Quigley, John	3 APR 1769		West Buffalo, Union	200	D-57-273	Andrew Robinson Original: found
NP-10	Rohrer, Jacob	3 APR 1769	East Branch Susquehanna River	LD: Luzerne	300		John Rohrer Original: found
NP-11	Carrothers, John	3 APR 1769		Unity, Westmoreland	300	D-57-267	Original: found
NP-12	Beattey, Walter	3 APR 1769		South Huntingdon, Westmoreland	300	D-57-266	[see caveat] Original: Signed with initials "W B"
NP-13	Work, Robert	3 APR 1769		West Buffalo, Union	300	D-57-272	Original: found
NP-14	Zimmerman, John	3 APR 1769		White Deer, Union	300	D-56-75 D-56-134 D-56-163 D-60-237 C-166-61	(r18 DEC 1772)Robert McCorely Original: found

Table 6 - New Purchase Applications (1769-1773)

Number	Applicant	Date	Orig. Place	Later Place	Acres	Survey	Neighbors, Notes, etc.
NP-15	Crawford, Hugh	3 APR 1769		North Huntingdon, Westmoreland	300	C-172-78	(r22 OCT 1788)James Pollock/[see caveat] Original: Signed
NP-16	Tusler, David	3 APR 1769	Red Creek	Luzerne	200	C-222-274	(r9 AUG 1781)Joseph Wharton Original: Trissler on application, Trisler on survey.
NP-17	Kendrick, Henry	3 APR 1769	Berks	Ft. Augusta, Northumberland	300	C-197-190	(r10 SEP 1770)Matthias Slough/Abraham Keagy Original: found
NP-18	Ramsay, John Sr.	3 APR 1769	Stony Creek		150		Original: found
NP-19	Mitchell, Randell	3 APR 1769		Unity, Westmoreland	300	D-58-276 D-58-277 D-12-74 D-12-76	(r25 MAR 1802)James Guthrie/(r4 MAR 1819)George Smith Original: found
NP-20	Anderson, James	3 APR 1769	Chillisquaque Creek, Berks	Northumberland	300	A-39-218	(r24 JAN 1770)Isaac Duncan/Mr. Allen/Mr. Tilghman Original: found
NP-21	Smith, Robert	3 APR 1769	Cumberland	South Huntingdon, Westmoreland	300	A-44-47	(r17 NOV 1783) Original: found
NP-22	Sloan, Samuel	3 APR 1769		Unity, Westmoreland	300	C-109 C-192-48	(r15 MAR 1786)/[see caveat] Original: found
NP-23	Denny, Walter	3 APR 1769		Wilkins, Allegheny	300	D-62-81	Original: found
NP-24	Clayton, Edward	3 APR 1769	Berks	Chillisquaque, Northumberland	300	C-210-98	(r16 OCT 1787)Rev. Dr. William Smith & Thomas Calyton Original: found
NP-25	Whitmore, Jacob	3 APR 1769	East Branch Susquehanna River	Luzerne	300	C-162-133 C-162-134	(r 1840)S. Ovenshire Original: found
NP-26	Longe, John	3 APR 1769	Berks	Chillisquaque, Northumberland	300	C-222-251	(r6 JUL 1776)Robert & Joseph Wilson Original: found
NP-27	Wheeler, Joseph (of Lower Smithfield Township, farmer)	3 APR 1769	Mill Creek	LD: Wyoming	300		Original: found
NP-28	Erwin, William	3 APR 1769		White Deer, Union	300	D-57-271	[patented on NP-1025] Original: found

Table 6 - New Purchase Applications (1769-1773)

Number	Applicant	Date	Orig. Place	Later Place	Acres	Survey	Neighbors, Notes, etc.
NP-29	Poultney, Joseph	3 APR 1769	Bald Eagle Creek, Cumberland	Centre	300	A-3-43	(r19 JAN 1773)Matthias Slough Original: found
NP-30	Greer, John	3 APR 1769	Sewickley Creek, Bedford	Westmoreland/ LD: Westmoreland	300	D-57-214 D-57-215 X-174	--- Nicholson/James Greer Original: found
NP-31	Boor, Peter	3 APR 1769	Berks	Chillisquaque, Northumberland	300	L-409	(r2 MAR 1796)John Lowden/Lawrence Boor/[see caveat] Original: found
NP-32	Weyland, Michael	3 APR 1769	Berks	Kelly, Union	300	D-56-26 D-56-27 D-56-28 D-56-29 D-56-30 D-56-39 D-56-40 D-56-41 D-56-42 D-56-43 A-40-38	(r15 JUL 1785)Peter Schwartz/[see caveat] Original: found
NP-33	Richardson, Isaac Jr.	3 APR 1769	Nippenose Creek	LD: Lycoming	300		Original: Signed by James Richardson
NP-34	Stewart, Francis	3 APR 1769	Fishing Creek, Berks - Northampton	Northumberland	300	C-166-64	(r5 NOV 1772)James McClure/William Barton Original: found
NP-35	Gay, Robert	3 APR 1769	Northumberland - Berks	Muncy Creek Twp., Lycoming	300	D-56-188 D-56-236 C-53-287	(r12 DEC 1788) Original: found
NP-36	Hopkins, Elizabeth	3 APR 1769	Fishing Creek	LD: Columbia	300		A. Webster Original: found
NP-37	Jones, William	3 APR 1769	Cumberland	Findlay, Allegheny/ LD: Findlay, Allegheny	300	D-57-67	Sarah Irwin Original: found
NP-38	Field, John	3 APR 1769	Beaver Creek	Northumberland	300	D-13-276	(r13 JAN 1773)William West, Jr. Original: found
NP-39	Slough, George	3 APR 1769	Beaver Creek, Berks	Northumberland	300	C-197-188	(r10 SEP 1770) Original: Signed by Mathias Slough

Table 6 - New Purchase Applications (1769-1773)

Number	Applicant	Date	Orig. Place	Later Place	Acres	Survey	Neighbors, Notes, etc.
NP-40	Hunter, Joseph	3 APR 1769		Unity, Westmoreland	300	D-56-22 D-57-3 D-57-64 D-57-214 D-57-215 C-75-291 D-75-292	(r11 MAR 1790)/James Hunter/Captain Procter Original: Signed
NP-41	Hoofnagle, John	3 APR 1769	Susquehanna River, Northampton	Columbia	300	A-6-234	(r12 FEB 1770)Edward & Joseph Shippen Original: found
NP-42	Gough, Charles	3 APR 1769	Cumberland	Chest Creek, Bedford	300	A-75-236	(r11 MAY 1774)Robert Barckley/Alexander Barckley Original: found
NP-43	Graff, Casper	3 APR 1769	Berks	Turbot, Northumberland	300	C-166-100	(r21 APR 1774)Peter Miller, Esq. Original: found
NP-44	Brown, Elizabeth	3 APR 1769	Berks	Nippenose, Lycoming	300	D-57-34 D-57-251 D-57-252 D-57-298 D-56-199 D-56-200 D-62-226 D-62-299 D-55-63 D-60-239	(r6 JUL 1784)William Antes & Frederick Antes/[see caveat] Original: Signed by William Brown
NP-45	Dallam, Francis Sr.	3 APR 1769	Cumberland	Centre/ LD: Centre	300		Edward Ward, Sr. Original: found
NP-46	Graybill, Peter	3 APR 1769	Cumberland	Northumberland - Bald Eagle Creek, Centre	300	A-3-42	(r19 JAN 1773)Matthias Slough Original: Signed by Mathias Slough
NP-47	Hendricks, William	3 APR 1769		LD: Clinton	300		John Sugar Original: found
NP-48	Silver, Garsham	3 APR 1769	Berks	West Buffalo, Union	300	D-57-209 D-57-210 C-112-69	(r6 APR 1770)John Lowden Original: found
NP-49	Briniman, Adam	3 APR 1769	Bedford	Susquehanna, Cambria	300	A-22 C-169-40	(r23 FEB 1842)John G. Miller Original: found
NP-50	McConnell, George	3 APR 1769		Blacklick, Indiana	300	D-57-261 D-57-262	Original: found

Table 6 - New Purchase Applications (1769-1773)

Number	Applicant	Date	Orig. Place	Later Place	Acres	Survey	Neighbors, Notes, etc.
NP-51	Sheredine, Jeremiah	3 APR 1769	Cumberland	Bald Eagle Creek, Northumberland	300	C-48-22	(r15 OCT 1784)Jacob & Michael Dowdle Original: found
NP-52	Dougherty, James	3 APR 1769		Augusta, Northumberland/ LD: Northumberland	300	H-155	[see caveat] Original: found
NP-53	Spayd, Christian	3 APR 1769	Cumberland	Bald Eagle Creek, Northumberland	300	C-197-133	(r 8 AUG 1772)/Joseph Pauling Original: Signed "Christian Spadd"
NP-54	Hall, Catherine	3 APR 1769	Cumberland	LD: Somerset	300		Elihu Hall Original: found
NP-55	Chamberlain, Philip	3 APR 1769	Cumberland	Brushy Run, Westmoreland/ LD: Westmoreland	300		John Chamberain Original: found
NP-56	McNitt, Robert	3 APR 1769	West Branch Susquehanna River	LD: Clinton	300		John McCoron Original: signed
NP-57	Mauhan, Judah	3 APR 1769	Cumberland	Salem, Westmoreland	300	D-57-274	Mary Elder Original: found
NP-58	Taylor, Thomas	3 APR 1769		Plum Creek, Westmoreland	300	A-82-174	(r13 JUN 1787)Robert Aitkin/William Ramsey/[see caveat] Original: found
NP-59	Crider, John	3 APR 1769	Berks	Augusta, Northumberland	300	L-207 X-203	(r17 APR 1812)Isaac Kline Original: found
NP-60	Baker, Simon	3 APR 1769		Derry, Westmoreland/ LD: Westmoreland	300	H-488 C-2-209	(r3 MAR 1819)Andrew Allison/[see caveat] Original: name is Eaker on application, Acre on survey.
NP-61	Willson, Samuel	3 APR 1769	Cumberland	Bald Eagle Creek, Centre/ LD: Centre	300		Joseph Wilson, Jr. Original: found
NP-62	Moore, George	3 APR 1769		Raccoon, Beaver/ LD: Washington/ Allegheny	300	X-208	Original: found
NP-63	McClure, Richard	3 APR 1769	Fishing Creek	LD: Columbia	300		George Woods Original: found

Table 6 - New Purchase Applications (1769-1773)

Number	Applicant	Date	Orig. Place	Later Place	Acres	Survey	Neighbors, Notes, etc.
NP-64	Armstrong, Thomas	3 APR 1769		Derry, Westmoreland/ LD: Fairfield, Westmoreland	300	A-6-14	(p18 FEB 1870)William Gray Original: Signed by Joseph Armstrong
NP-65	Hoofnagle, George	3 APR 1769	Laurel Hill	LD: Somerset	300		Original: found
NP-66	Schneider, Abraham Jr.	3 APR 1769		White Deer, Union	300	D-57-265	Jacob Schneider Original: found
NP-67	Frick, Peter (of the Borough of Lancaster)	3 APR 1769	Penn, Northumberland		300	C-39-199	(r11 DEC 1772)Philip Deihl Original: found
NP-68	Foster, Francis	3 APR 1769	Berks	Buffalo Creek, Northumberland	300	D-62-105 E-358	(r23 DEC 1794)Jeremiah Parker/[see caveat] Original: found
NP-69	Ramsey, William	3 APR 1769		Kittanning, Armstrong/ LD: Armstrong	300	B-23-15	Benjamin Sutton Original: found
NP-70	Foster, Andrew	3 APR 1769		Bloom, Columbia	300	C-226-187	(r13 MAY 1816)Joseph Tremly/["I desire John Foster to take out a locaton in my name," signed Andrew Foster] Original: Signed
NP-71	Bruce, William	3 APR 1769	Peters Creek & Monongahela River		200		Original: found
NP-72	Duncan, David	3 APR 1769	Berks	Washington, Lycoming	300	D-62-193 D-57-21 D-56-36 D-56-131 D-56-269 D-60-226 C-39-225	Original: found
NP-73	Irwin, John	3 APR 1769		Turbot, Northumberland	300	A-42-9	(r31 MAR 1807)James Irwin Original: found
NP-74	Harris, John	3 APR 1769	Berks - Northumberland	Nippenose, Lycoming	300	C-234-29	(vacated by warrant of 8 SEP 1774 to Michael Troy in right of Jonathan Supplee on NP-264) Original: found
NP-75	Carpenter, John	3 APR 1769		Lawrence, Clearfield/ LD: Union	300	B-1-69	Jacob Carpenter Original: found

Table 6 - New Purchase Applications (1769-1773)

Number	Applicant	Date	Orig. Place	Later Place	Acres	Survey	Neighbors, Notes, etc.
NP-76	Musser, Henry	3 APR 1769	Berks - Northampton	Muncy, Lycoming	300	D-56-277 C-135-153	(r26 NOV 1783)John Alward/[see caveat] Original: found
NP-77	Snively, Andrew	3 APR 1769	Bedford	Youghiogheny River, Fayette	300	C-193-256	(r 26 MAR 1788)/Joseph Snively/--- Virgin/--- Pearsall Original: found
NP-78	Marchant, David	3 APR 1769		Franklin, Westmoreland	300	C-143-77	(r21 JAN 1817)Jeremiah Murray Original: found
NP-79	Gray, Elizabeth	3 APR 1769	Northampton	Fishing Creek, Northumberland	300	C-135-113	Levi Hollingworth/(r7 OCT 1782)John McKim & wife Original: found
NP-80	Erisman, Jacob	3 APR 1769		East Branch Susquehanna River, Luzerne	300	C-222-273	(r9 AUG 1781)Joseph Wharton/Vight Miller Original: found
NP-81	Webb, William	3 APR 1769		East Branch Susquehanna River, Luzerne/ LD: Salem, Luzerne	300	W-270	Original: found
NP-82	Cook, Charles	3 APR 1769	Northumberland	Muncy, Lycoming	300	E-352	(r24 MAR 1813)George Fague Original: Signed "Robert Cooke"
NP-83	MacKay, Aneas	3 APR 1769		17 miles east of Ft. Pitt, Allegheny	300	C-10-112	(r16 MAR 1789)Stephan Bayard, Esq. & wife/[see caveat] Original: found
NP-84	Wilson, John	3 APR 1769		between Youghiogheny & Monongahela Rivers, Fayette	300	A-14-90	(r16 JUN 1814)Joshua Hyle Original: found
NP-85	Hannah, James	3 APR 1769		Plum, Allegheny	300	D-57-66	John Hubley Original: found
NP-86	Dean, James	3 APR 1769	Westmoreland	Elizabeth, Allegheny	300	Y-231	Benjamin Appleby/James Sullivan/J. Devoir/(r20 JUN 1794)William Applegate Original: signed
NP-87	Summers, Henry	3 APR 1769	Cumberland	Hartley, Union	300	D-57-264	Original: found
NP-88	Davison, Robert	3 APR 1769		Unity, Westmoreland	200	Y-145	(r16 MAR 1791)Elias Davison Original: Signed
NP-89	Armstrong, William	3 APR 1769	Washington	Moon, Beaver	300	A-7-179	(r25 AUG 1852)Stephen Vankirk Original: Signed Joseph Armstrong

Table 6 - New Purchase Applications (1769-1773)

Number	Applicant	Date	Orig. Place	Later Place	Acres	Survey	Neighbors, Notes, etc.
NP-90	Prickit, Isaih	3 APR 1769	Whiteley Creek	LD: Greene	300		Original: found
NP-91	Snively, Michael	3 APR 1769	Monongahela River	LD: Cumberland, Greene	300		Benjamin Hokes Original: found
NP-92	Knight, Martha	3 APR 1769	Cumberland	LD: Somerset	300		Hannah Knight Original: found
NP-93	Hunter, James Sr.	3 APR 1769		Upper Burrell, Westmoreland	300	C-157-164	(r28 FEB 1782)A. Porter Original: found
NP-94	Baird, Archibald	3 APR 1769		Mt. Pleasant, Westmoreland/ LD: Mt. Pleasant, Westmoreland	300	D-57-278	Original: found
NP-95	McMachan, Richard	3 APR 1769	Washington	Monongahela River, Allegheny	300	T-96	John Coxs/(r10 JAN 1792)Sheshbarrar Bentley Original: found
NP-96	Worthington, Charles Jr.	3 APR 1769	Cumberland	Bald Eagle Creek, Northumberland	300	D-6-40	Joseph Hopkins, Sr./(r12 OCT 1783)Samuel Wallis Original: found
NP-97	Fisher, Elizabeth	3 APR 1769	Cumberland	LD: Westmoreland	300		Jemine Jones Original: found
NP-98	Downs, Thomas	3 APR 1769	Cumberland	Menallen, Fayette/ LD: Fayette	300	F-234 C-116-88	(r20 JUL 1790)William Linn Original: found
NP-99	Hopkins, Joseph Sr.	3 APR 1769	Cumberland	Bald Eagle Creek, Northumberland	300	K-177	Original: found
NP-100	Jones, Jehu	3 APR 1769		Muncy, Lycoming	300	E-437	William Jenkins/(r10 MAR 1841)Pearson Lloyd Original: found
NP-101	Perryman, John	3 APR 1769	Berks	West Buffalo, Union	300	D-55-76 C-112-70	Thomas Gilbert/(r6 APR 1770)John Lowdon Original: found
NP-102	Hunt, Ruth	3 APR 1769	Cumberland	LD: Somerset	300		James Hunt Original: found
NP-103	Carter, Spencer	3 APR 1769	Falls Brook	LD: Luzerne/ Columbia/ Bradford	300		Original: found

Table 6 - New Purchase Applications (1769-1773)

Number	Applicant	Date	Orig. Place	Later Place	Acres	Survey	Neighbors, Notes, etc.
NP-129	Warren, James	3 APR 1769		Limestone Run & Buffalo Creek, Union	300		[same as application NP-2005 to George Henton] Original: found
NP-130	Barton, Hester	3 APR 1769	Northumberland	Fishing Creek, Columbia	300	B-399	(r6 NOV 1801)Abraham Kline/William Anderson Original: found
NP-131	Havelitch, Jacob	3 APR 1769	Buffalo Run, Cumberland	LD: Union	150		George Miller/Simon Mirca/Christopher Man/George Essweiler Original: found
NP-132	Thauly, Abraham (of Newberry Township, York County)	3 APR 1769	Washington	Sawmill Run, Allegheny	300	D-62-83	Original: Signed
NP-133	Richards, William	3 APR 1769		Muncy, Lycoming	300	C-463	(r21 MAR 1805)Jacob Hill Original: found
NP-134	Bradford, William	3 APR 1769	Fishing Creek	LD: Columbia	300		Original: found
NP-135	Morgan, Morgan (near Mill Creek, Frederick County in Virginia)	3 APR 1769		Wharton, Fayette	300	C-139-111	(r16 MAR 1807)William McCall Original: signed
NP-136	Faree, Christopher	3 APR 1769	West Branch Susquehanna River	LD: Centre	300		Henry Good Original: found
NP-137	Elder, Mary	3 APR 1769	Cumberland	Salem, Westmoreland	300	C-28-270	Hannah Smith/(r6 SEP 1787)Alexaner Craig Original: found
NP-138	McDowell, Nathan (son of William)	3 APR 1769		Loyalhanna Creek, Westmoreland	300	C-129-215	(r25 APR 1787) Original: found
NP-139	Bayers, James	3 APR 1769		Washington, Westmoreland	300	D-68 C-152-170	(r13 DEC 1828)Daniel McKown & wife/(r4 MAR 1837)J. B. & S. Alexander Original: Signed
NP-140	Young, James	3 APR 1769		Allegheny River, Westmoreland	300	D-6-136	John King/(r9 AUG 1783)Samuel Watherill, Jr. Original: found
NP-141	Shaw, James	3 APR 1769		Northeast Branch Susquehanna River, Luzerne	300	P-156	(r5 MAR 1774)Archibald Stewart Original: found
NP-142	Irvin, Lawrence (of Cumberland County, farmer)	3 APR 1769	Bedford	Hempfield, Westmoreland	100	A-39-93	(r20 JUN 1810)Thomas Moore/--- Myer Original: found

Table 6 - New Purchase Applications (1769-1773)

Number	Applicant	Date	Orig. Place	Later Place	Acres	Survey	Neighbors, Notes, etc.
NP-143	Hepburn, Samuel	3 APR 1769	Berks	Chillisquaque Creek, Northumberland	300	C-388	(30 MAY 1795)/Joseph & Jonathan Haines, Exrs. of Bartholomew Haines/Dorrity Goz Original: found
NP-144	Church, Joseph	3 APR 1769		Turbot, Northumberland	300	K-428 C-82-250 C-135-227C-91-40	(r22 MAR 1808)Joseph Hutchinson/(r26 MAY 1814)Jacob Maxwell/(r23 MAR 1840)R. W. Hutchinson Original: found
NP-145	Montour, Henry	3 APR 1769		Moon, Allegheny	300	D-457	(r24 AUG 1826)Alexander Breckenridge Original: found
NP-146	Breckbill, John	3 APR 1769		West Branch Susquehanna River/ LD: Nippenose, Lycoming	300		Original: found
NP-147	Galbraith, Elizabeth	3 APR 1769	Berks	Derry, Columbia	300	C-144-202	(r26 APR 1827)Elizabeth Murray/James Tilghman Original: found
NP-148	Flipson, John	3 APR 1769	East Branch Susquehanna River	LD: Wyoming	300		Nicholas Flipson Original: found
NP-149	Laning, David	3 APR 1769	Northumberland	White Deer, Union	300	A-19-43 A-19-44	(r5 MAY 1789)John Cox, Esq./[see caveat] Original: found
NP-150	Miller, George	3 APR 1769		Loyalsock, Lycoming	300	D-57-242	Original: found
NP-151	Howell, Robert Jr.	3 APR 1769		Elizabeth, Allegheny	300	D-57-80	[see caveat] Original: Newell on application, Newel on survey.
NP-152	Coxe, William	3 APR 1769	Northampton	Damascus, Wayne	400	A-76-16 C-78-213	(r14 JUL 1781)Lawerence Herbert/(r23 MAY 1792)John Tyler/[see caveat] Original: found
NP-153	Alexander, John	3 APR 1769	Berks	Nippenose, Lycoming	300	D-59-283 D-56-20 D-56-187 D-56-240 D-56-222 D-56-297 D-62-250 C-189-260	(r23 OCT 1788)Charles Stewart/James Reed Original: found

Table 6 - New Purchase Applications (1769-1773)

Number	Applicant	Date	Orig. Place	Later Place	Acres	Survey	Neighbors, Notes, etc.
NP-154	Barnes, Thomas Sr.	3 APR 1769	Berks	Augusta, Northumberland	300	C-7-230 C-21-192	(r22 APR 1782)John Lukens, Esq./widow McCormick Original: found
NP-155	Jones, Isaac	3 APR 1769	Berks	Chillisquaque Creek, Northumberland or Montour	300	D-6-54	Nathan Jones/(r17 MAR 1784)Samuel Wallis Original: found
NP-156	Gardner, Theophilus Jr.	3 APR 1769		Nippenose, Lycoming	300	D-56-77 D-56-202 D-57-299 C-135-103	(r12 AUG 1782)Blair McClanachan Original: found
NP-157	Beaver, Charles	3 APR 1769		Luzerne/ LD: Luzerne	300	X-196	William Webb Original: found
NP-158	Brown, Benjamin	3 APR 1769	Bald Eagle Creek	LD: Howard, Centre	300	C-83-235 A-34-12	(r & p14 MAR 1837)John Hall/James Gold/[patent H-37-46]/[see caveat] Original: found
NP-159	Brant, John	3 APR 1769	West Branch Susquehanna River	LD: Clinton/ Centre	300		Original: found
NP-160	Searle, James	3 APR 1769		Allegheny River, Westmoreland	300	D-6-35	(r9 AUG 1783)Samuel Wetherill, Jr./Elizabeth Grame Original: found
NP-161	Cochran, James	3 APR 1769	Berks	Turbot, Northumberland	300	C-23-283	(r31 AUG 1794) Original: found
NP-162	Cook, John	3 APR 1769		Union, Union	300	D-58-161 D-58-162 C-26-193	(r2 JUN 1812)John Cook Jr.(son of John Cook)/Col. Francis Original: found
NP-163	Ballmore, William	3 APR 1769	Berks	Limestone Run, Northumberland	300	L-155	(r23 FEB 1790)David Ireland Original: found

Table 6 - New Purchase Applications (1769-1773)

Number	Applicant	Date	Orig. Place	Later Place	Acres	Survey	Neighbors, Notes, etc.
NP-164	Magrath, John	3 APR 1769	Berks	Washington, Lycoming	300	D-57-33 D-57-253 D-57-297 D-56-89 D-56-98 D-56-120 D-56-115 D-56-263 D-56-271 D-56-155 D-56-292 D-55-69 D-55-99 D-55-52 B-6-14 D-60-223 D-62-286 D-62-297	(r17 AUG 1774)William Plunket, Esq. Original: found
NP-165	Foster, John Jr.	3 APR 1769	West Branch Susquehanna River	LD: Lycoming	300		Stephen Foster Original: found
NP-166	McRory, David	3 APR 1769		Allegheny, Armstrong	300	B-23-16	Original: found
NP-167	Montgomery, William	3 APR 1769	Berks	Washington, Lycoming	300	D-56-234 D-57-31 D-60-262 D-60-271 D-62-257 D-62-264 F-434	(r7 DEC 1781)/[see caveat] Original: Megamery on application, Montgomery on survey.
NP-168	Allen, Loveday	3 APR 1769	Cumberland - Bedford	St. Clair, Westmoreland/ LD: Ligonier, Westmoreland	300	H-489 C-28-249	(r21 DEC 1831)Alexander Craig Original: found
NP-169	Jones, Robert	3 APR 1769	Berks - Lycoming	Wayne, Clinton	300	D-55-79 D-56-86 D-62-222 A-22-89	(r5 SEP 1803)William Nowland Original: found

Table 6 - New Purchase Applications (1769-1773)

Number	Applicant	Date	Orig. Place	Later Place	Acres	Survey	Neighbors, Notes, etc.
NP-170	Miller, Henry	3 APR 1769	Berks - Union	two miles above Mahoning, Northumberland - Montour	300	C-197-205	(r12 DEC 1770)John Scull Original: found
NP-171	Gallahur, John	3 APR 1769	Berks	Clinton, Lycoming	300	D-57-254 D-60-210 A-10-61	(r3 APR 1770) Original: found. Galaher on survey, Gallagher on return.
NP-172	Barr, David	3 APR 1769		Hempfield, Westmoreland	300	D-57-275	[see caveat] Original: found
NP-173	Joice, John	3 APR 1769	Westmoreland	Thompsons Run, Allegheny	300	C-13-62	(r20 FEB 1794)John Barckley, Esq. Original: Signed
NP-174	McClain, Mathew	3 APR 1769	Bald Eagle Creek	LD: Clinton/ Centre	300		Original: found
NP-175	Hopkins, William Sr.	3 APR 1769	Berks - Northampton	Little Fishing Creek, Northumberland	300	A-74-203	William Cole, Sr./(r26 SEP 1800)John Biddle Original: found
NP-176	Espy, John	3 APR 1769	Northampton	Fishing Creek, Northumberland	300	A-8-195	Lazarus Stewart/(r13 FEB 1775)Josiah Espy Original: found
NP-177	Botts, John	3 APR 1769	Northumberland	Mahoning Creek, Montour	300	O-74	(r12 APR 1797)Samuel Wallis Original: found
NP-178	Boner, Robert	3 APR 1769	Cumberland	LD: Northumberland/ Montour	300		Nathan Jones Original: found
NP-179	Frank, Henry	3 APR 1769	East Branch Susquehanna River	LD: Wyoming	300		John Meyer Original: found
NP-180	Gist, Richard	3 APR 1769		Union & Dunbar, Fayette/ LD: Union & Dunbar, Fayette	300	D-57-268	Thomas Gist/Capt. Christopher Gist(by order of the Governor & Council of Virginia in 1752)/[see caveat] Original: Missing
NP-181	Kirk, Moses	3 APR 1769	Berks	Turbot, Northumberland	300	B-394 D-56-7	(r23 NOV 1796)William Kirk & James Kirk Original: found
NP-182	Fisher, William	3 APR 1769	Berks	Turbot, Northumberland	300	K-96	(r20 SEP 1774)/William Johnston Original: found
NP-183	Warder, Jeremiah Jr.	3 APR 1769		Muncy, Northumberland	300	K-18	James Alexander/(r24 MAR 1795)William Ellis Original: found
NP-184	Lowans, John	3 APR 1769		Fairfield, Lycoming	300	D-57-243	Samuel Purviance, Jr. Original: found

Table 6 - New Purchase Applications (1769-1773)

Number	Applicant	Date	Orig. Place	Later Place	Acres	Survey	Neighbors, Notes, etc.
NP-185	Pingley, Jonathan	3 APR 1769	Berks	White Deer, Union/ LD: Union	300	D-56-261 A-11-191 C-44-150	(r15 MAY 1794)Samuel Dale, Esq. Original: found
NP-186	Shank, John	3 APR 1769	Cumberland	Limestone Valley, Northumberland	300	A-19-28	(r5 MAY 1789)John Cox, Esq. Original: found
NP-187	Breckbill, Benjamin	3 APR 1769	West Branch Susquehanna River	LD: Lycoming	300		John Breckbill Original: found
NP-188	Claypoole, George	3 APR 1769	Berks	Chillisquaque, Northumberland	300	I-184	(r3 MAY 1810)Edward Burd/Henry Robinson/James Tilghman Original: found
NP-189	Diets, Michael	3 APR 1769	Berks	White Deer, Union	300	D-57-187 D-57-287 U-145	(r9 JAN 1815)John Hoffman Original: found
NP-190	Hoge, James	3 APR 1769	Stony Creek	LD: Somerset	300		Original: found
NP-191	Slack, Cornelius	3 APR 1769	Northampton	Mill Creek, Northumberland/ LD: Luzerne	300	A-224	Original: found
NP-192	Loghlan, James	3 APR 1769	Cumberland	Bald Eagle Creek, Northumberland	300	C-135-85	(r8 JUL 1782)Robert Morris, Esq./Bryan O'Hara Original: found
NP-193	Stewart, Daniel	3 APR 1769		Fairfield, Lycoming	300	D-57-244	Samuel Purviance Jr. Original: found
NP-194	Culbertson, Joseph Jr.	3 APR 1769	Blacklick Creek	LD: Indiana/ Cambria	300		Original: found
NP-195	Davis, John	3 APR 1769	Warriors Run	LD: Turbot, Northumberland	300		William Sims Original: found
NP-196	Little, Grace	3 APR 1769		Nippenose, Lycoming/ LD: Lycoming	300	D-57-245	Ralph Foster Original: found
NP-197	Grant, Adam	3 APR 1769	Westmoreland	Versailles, Allegheny	300	D-57-65 D-56-168 A-83-85	(r23 DEC 1811)William Shaw Original: found
NP-198	Jones John	3 APR 1769	Cumberland	Menallen, Fayette	300	A-44--135	(r28 JUN 1786) Original: found
NP-199	Hare, Emanuel	3 APR 1769	Lycoming Creek	LD: Lycoming	300		John Hare, Jr. Original: found

Table 6 - New Purchase Applications (1769-1773)

Number	Applicant	Date	Orig. Place	Later Place	Acres	Survey	Neighbors, Notes, etc.
NP-200	Robb, James	3 APR 1769		Muncy Creek Twp., Lycoming	300	D-56-270 D-60-194 D-55-75 D-55-53 D-57-24 D-57-281 D-57-296 C-2-290	(r9 SEP 1784)Henry Baker Original: Signed
NP-201	Heffelfinger, Martin	3 APR 1769	Berks	Buffalo, Union	300	D-57-263 D-57-276	[see caveat] Original: Missing
NP-202	Bare, John	3 APR 1769		Fairfield, Westmoreland	300	O-267 O-268	Thomas Woods/William McCune/John Woods/(r11 JUL 1805)John Elliott[name is John Barr on survey] Original: Signed
NP-203	McClure, Abdell	3 APR 1769		Unity, Westmoreland	300	B-1-233	(r31 MAR 1788) Original: Signed by John McClure
NP-204	Kreutter, Ludwig	3 APR 1769		East Branch Susquehanna River, Luzerne/ LD: Luzerne	300	F-233	Martin Kreider Original: found
NP-205	Matlack, Josiah	3 APR 1769	Berks	Buffalo, Union	300	D-55-34 D-55-35	["this is the same land of application No. 1646 to Jennet Forster which see."] Original: found
NP-206	Fleming, James	3 APR 1769	Berks	Buffalo, Union	300	D-56-145 A-57-173	John Penn/(r5 DEC 1785) Original: found
NP-207	Beckerton, Benjamin	3 APR 1769		Washington, Lycoming	300	D-56-112 D-57-8 D-57-26 C-9-182	(r20 JUN 1809)Edward Burd/Moor Trotter Original: found
NP-208	Death, James Jr.	3 APR 1769	Cumberland	Rush Run, Fayette	300	C-124-260 C-124-279	(r21 JAN 1800)John McConnell/(r1 MAR 1787)Aaron Hackney Original: found
NP-209	Flahavan, Catherine	3 APR 1769	Long Limestone Valley	LD: Centre	300		Ann Flahavan Original: found
NP-210	Jones, Richard	3 APR 1769	Berks - Northampton	Northumberland	300	E-27	Isaac Jones, Jr./(r17 MAR 1784)Samuel Wallis Original: found
NP-211	Perry, William	3 APR 1769		White Deer, Union	300	D-57-250	[see caveat] Original: found

Table 6 - New Purchase Applications (1769-1773)

Number	Applicant	Date	Orig. Place	Later Place	Acres	Survey	Neighbors, Notes, etc.
NP-212	Wright, John	3 APR 1769	Berks - Northumberland	Washington, Lycoming	300	D-56-121 D-56-132 D-57-10 D-62-291 C-112-58	(r6 APR 1770)John Lowden/[see caveat] Original: found
NP-213	Drell, Jacob	3 APR 1769		East Branch Susquehanna River, Luzerne	300	C-39-298	Jacob Shuler Original: found
NP-214	Foster, Margaret	3 APR 1769		Turbot, Northumberland	300	U-176	(r18 NOV 1776)William Bonham/William Gallagher Original: found
NP-215	Burbridge, Peter	3 APR 1769	Cumberland	Huntingdon, Westmoreland	300	C-31-249	(r8 MAR 1823)James Cowan & Joseph Cowan, administrators of John Thomas[NP-3446] Original: found
NP-216	Haines, Abraham	3 APR 1769	East Branch Susquehanna River	LD: Luzerne	300		Frederick Sager Original: found
NP-217	Moore, Samuel	3 APR 1769		Nippenose, Lycoming	300	D-57-251	Original: found
NP-218	Roger, Elias	3 APR 1769	Berks	West Buffalo, Union	300	D-56-295 D-56-296	George Kapp & Michael Kapp[same land as NP-1166 to Frederick Kapp]/[see caveat] Original: found
NP-219	Macklay, Charles	3 APR 1769		Franklin & North Huntingdon, Westmoreland	300	D-57-249	--- Tegard/Thomas Lyon Original: found
NP-220	Leadley, John	3 APR 1769	Berks	Augusta, Northumberland	250	M-219	(r13 MAY 1784)Nicholas Miller Original: found
NP-221	Kurtz, Henry	3 APR 1769		Point, Northumberland	300	C-64-210	Casper Graff/(r2 JUL 1796)Tench Francis, Jr. Original: found
NP-222	Seybert, George Henry	3 APR 1769	Northampton	near Wyoming, Luzerne/ LD: Hanover, Luzerne	300	X-141	George Wolf & John Wolf/Samuel Purviance, Jr. Original: found
NP-223	Emrick, John	3 APR 1769	Berks	Kelly, Union	300	D-57-36 D-57-37 D-56-221 C-146-226	Christopher Herrold/(r22 OCT 1771)W. Patterson, Esq. Original: found
NP-224	Robertson, John	3 APR 1769		Monongahela River, Allegheny	300	A-13-51	(r21 MAY 1795)/William McMahan Original: found

Table 6 - New Purchase Applications (1769-1773)

Number	Applicant	Date	Orig. Place	Later Place	Acres	Survey	Neighbors, Notes, etc.
NP-225	McConnell, James	3 APR 1769	Westmoreland	Conemaugh, Indiana	200	C-151-199 C-151-200 C-152-171 C-152-172	(r27 FEB 1822)Charles McComb/(r27 FEB 1822)William McComb/(r4 NOV 1828)Allen McComb Original: found
NP-226	Fisher, John	3 APR 1769	Berks	Kelly, Union/ LD: White Deer, Union	300	D-57-189 B-284 C-64-249 X-169 X-170 C-55-52	(r6 APR 1797)Michael Fisher/(r6 APR 1797)Henry Fisher/(r12 APR 1800)Powell Fisher/Michael Weylan Original: found
NP-227	Hillborn, Miles	3 APR 1769		Muncy Creek Twp., Lycoming	300	D-56-47 E-433 E-436 C-213-168	Richard Edwards/(r4 MAY 1822)heirs of Baltzer Stake/(r9 MAR 1833)William Clydes/[see caveat] Original: found
NP-228	Cox, Isaac	3 APR 1769		Washington, Lycoming	200	D-60-273 A-19-37	(r5 MAY 1789)John Cox, Esq./Eleanor Williams Original: found
NP-229	Reed, John	3 APR 1769	Cumberland	Forward, Allegheny/ LD: Elizabeth, Allegheny	300	D-87-72 S-100 A-16-74 A-16-75 B-18-83 B-18-84 C-94-282 C-191-87	(r17 JUN 1814)Lefford Thomson/(p10 FEB 1890)C. T. Paterson & J. K. Paterson & G. W. Paterson/(p10 FEB 1890)G. W. Paterson & W. W. O'Neil & W. D. O'Neil/(r9 APR 1838)James Kerr/--- Kelley Original: found
NP-230	Nafe, Michael	3 APR 1769	Berks	West Buffalo, Union	300	D-57-248	Original: found
NP-231	Maddox, Benjamin	3 APR 1769		Chillisquaque Creek, Northumberland or Montour/ LD: Northumberland/ Montour	300		John Crozer Original: found
NP-232	Robertson, Elizabeth	3 APR 1769	Cumberland	Centre/ LD: Lycoming	300		Daniel Robertson Original: found
NP-233	Vanbuskirk, Peter & Thomas Vanbuskirk & John Vanbuskirk	3 APR 1769	Fishing Creek	LD: Columbia	900		Original: found

Table 6 - New Purchase Applications (1769-1773)

Number	Applicant	Date	Orig. Place	Later Place	Acres	Survey	Neighbors, Notes, etc.
NP-234	Wolf, George	3 APR 1769	Northumberland	at or above Wyoming, Luzerne/ LD: Lackawanna, Luzerne	300	W-272	Samuel Purviance, Jr. Original: found
NP-235	Coats, Thomas	3 APR 1769	Berks	Muddy Run, Northumberland	300	C-78-247	Uriah Woolman/(r27 JUN 1782)Reuben Haines Original: found
NP-236	Creag, Alexander	3 APR 1769	Berks	Buffalo, Union	300	D-57-216 D-57-293 D-60-187 D-60-188 D-60-195 D-60-196 D-60-197 D-60-198 D-60-199 D-60-200 A-12-14 A-12-141 A-12-142	(r5 JAN 1775)Andrew Gibson & Ruth McCoskeey Original: found
NP-237	McKinney, William	3 APR 1769		East Branch Susquehanna River, Luzerne/ LD: Luzerne	200	A-232	Original: Signed "William McKenney"
NP-238	Shandy, Jacob	3 APR 1769	Hollowing Run	LD: Northumberland	200		Original: found
NP-239	Wirmly, John	3 APR 1769		East Branch Susquehanna River, Northumberland/ LD: Bradford	300	A-29-32	Christian Roher Original: found
NP-240	Harris, Margaret	3 APR 1769		Columbia/ LD: Columbia	300		Blanch Beaver Original: found
NP-241	Cook, Jacob (of Derry Township)	3 APR 1769	Northumberland	Monroe, Union/ LD: Buffalo, Union	300	D-20-55	(p19 JUN 1871)Philip Young Original: Signed by Robert Cook
NP-242	McClure, James	3 APR 1769		Huntingdon, Westmoreland	300	C-227-237	(r4 FEB 1847)H. Torrey & P. Torrey Original: Signed by John McClure

Table 6 - New Purchase Applications (1769-1773)

Number	Applicant	Date	Orig. Place	Later Place	Acres	Survey	Neighbors, Notes, etc.
NP-243	Shadden, James	3 APR 1769	Northumberland	Buffalo, Union	300	D-60-246 D-60-247 A-11-263 A-11-264 A-11-265	(r28 JUN 1774)James Young/Thomas McGuire, Esq./[see caveat] Original: Signed
NP-244	Edwards, Richard	3 APR 1769	Northampton	Muncy Creek Twp., Lycoming	300	C-38-4 C-213-168 C-213-5	Charles Lyon/(r4 MAY 1822)heirs of Baltzer Stake/(r9 MAR 1833)William Clyde Original: found
NP-245	McCullogh, Hugh	3 APR 1769		Mahoning, Northumberland/ LD: Columbia	300	A-32-198	Original: found
NP-246	Campbell, Robert Jr.	3 APR 1769	West Branch Susquehanna River	LD: Lycoming	300		Original: Signed
NP-247	Taylor, Valentine	3 APR 1769		East Branch Susquehanna River, Luzerne	300	A-12-117	Philip Suber/(r14 MAR 1775)John Gibson, Esq. Original: found
NP-248	Gibbon, Griffith	3 APR 1769	Cumberland	Bald Eagle Creek, Mifflin	300	C-115-47	(r5 FEB 1794)William Lamb/James Sharron/[see caveat] Original: Signed
NP-249	Hubley, John	3 APR 1769		Wilkins & Plum, Allegheny	300	D-62-84	Joseph Alston, Jr. Original: found
NP-250	Duncan, Isaac (in Philadelphia)	3 APR 1769	Berks	Chillisquaque Creek, Northumberland	300	A-39-219	(r18 APR 1770)Margaret Duncan/---Tilghman/John McCormick Original: found
NP-251	McCulluck, George	3 APR 1769	East Branch Susquehanna River	LD: Luzerne	300		Henry Neaff Original: found
NP-252	McCay, Neal	3 APR 1769	Berks	Buffalo, Union	300	D-57-247	William Leich/[see caveat] Original: Signed
NP-253	Campbell, James	3 APR 1769		Ligonier, Westmoreland	50	D-57-246	Original: found
NP-254	Hoge, John Sr.	3 APR 1769	Berks	Buffalo, Union	300	D-57-260	[see caveat] Original: found
NP-255	Steinmetz, Philip	3 APR 1769		LD: Lycoming	300		Charles Gemberling/John Loutermilk/Andrew Moore Original: found

Table 6 - New Purchase Applications (1769-1773)

Number	Applicant	Date	Orig. Place	Later Place	Acres	Survey	Neighbors, Notes, etc.
NP-256	Lowman, Martin	3 APR 1769	Washington	Hopewell, Beaver/ LD: South Beaver, Beaver	300	C-146-58 C-146-59 C-146-60	(r15 OCT 1838)A. McDowell/(r23 JAN 1839)Andrew McDowell/[see caveat] Original: found
NP-257	Whitmore, John Jr.	3 APR 1769	West Branch Susquehanna River	LD: Centre	300		John Whitmore Sr. Original: found
NP-258	Fullerton, John	3 APR 1769	Berks	Nippenose, Lycoming	300	D-57-252	Original: found
NP-259	Ulrick, George Jr.	3 APR 1769	Northumberland	Buffalo, Union	300	A-8-145	Jacob Gemberling/(r22 APR 1829) Original: found
NP-260	McAvoy, Charles	3 APR 1769	Cumberland	Sewickley Creek, Cumberland	300	A-70-60	(r15 FEB 1771)Joshua Archer/--- Proctor Original: found
NP-261	McClalin, John	3 APR 1769		Unity, Westmoreland	300	C-44-235	(r16 MAR 1791)Elias Davison/[see caveat] Original: Signed
NP-262	Morgan, Elizabeth	3 APR 1769	Lycoming Creek	LD: Lycoming	300		Original: found
NP-263	Harity, Cornelius	3 APR 1769	Braddock's Road	LD: Fayette	300		--- Gasst/[see caveat] Original: found
NP-264	Supplee, Jonathan	3 APR 1769	Berks	Nippenose, Lycoming	300	D-55-98 D-60-268 D-62-273 C-234-29	(r9 SEP 1774)Michael Troy, Esq. Original: found
NP-265	Bell, James	3 APR 1769	Berks	Washington, Lycoming/ LD: Washington, Northumberland	300	D-56-148 D-60-213 D-60-275 A-34-13 C-14-271	George Griffith/(r9 MAR 1853)John Bower & Charles Allen & William Piatt, administrators of Isaac Allen, Jr., deceased Original: found
NP-266	Laurey, Thomas	3 APR 1769	Berks	Buffalo, Union	200	D-56-207 D-57-12 D-57-13 D-57-14 D-57-15 D-57-16 D-57-17 D-60-201 W-114	(r9 SEP 1772)John Aurnt Original: found

Table 6 - New Purchase Applications (1769-1773)

Number	Applicant	Date	Orig. Place	Later Place	Acres	Survey	Neighbors, Notes, etc.
NP-267	Culp, Philip	3 APR 1769	Northumberland	Windham, Luzerne	300	H-157 D-17-67	Michael Wither/(r30 MAY 1839)Robert Williams Original: found
NP-268	Coale, William Sr.	3 APR 1769	Northampton	Fishing Creek, Northumberland	300	C-10-103	Gideon Preveal/(r24 APR 1789)James Bringhurst Original: found
NP-269	Habaker, George	3 APR 1769	Berks	Buffalo, Union	300	D-62-277 A-18-1	William Irwin/(r19 SEP 1785)William Irwin, Esq. Original: found
NP-270	Gasser, Philip	3 APR 1769	Berks	Lick Run, Union	300	C-223-81	(r24 FEB 1789)Jacob Weiss Original: found
NP-271	Gay, Samuel	3 APR 1769	Northumberland	Buffalo, Union	300	C-7-180	Henry Christ/(r24 JUN 1776)Peter Borhen Original: found
NP-272	Camel, John	3 APR 1769		Chillisquaque Creek, Montour/ LD: Columbia	300		John Gawen Original: found
NP-273	Brown, William	3 APR 1769	Berks - Northumberland	Chillisquaque Creek, Montour	300	C-179-24	(r15 JUN 1774)John Morrow Original: found
NP-274	Moore, Robert	3 APR 1769		Hopewell, Beaver	300	C-162-7	George Moore/(r15 JUL 1835)Benjamin McCormick & James McCormick Original: found
NP-275	Boner, Bernard	3 APR 1769	Cumberland - Berks	West Branch Susquehanna River, Northumberland	300	C-1-36	(r12 DEC 1772) Original: found
NP-276	Wheeler, Samuel	3 APR 1769		Washington, Lycoming	300	D-56-121 D-56-132 A-6-286	(r12 FEB 1770)Edward Shippen & Joseph Shippen Original: found
NP-277	Hinkson, John	3 APR 1769	Cumberland	Conemaugh River, Westmoreland	300	C-191-20	William McCune/John Woods/(r22 MAR 1831)James Peoples Original: found
NP-278	Coale, Philip	3 APR 1769	Cumberland	Stony Creek Twp., Somerset/ LD: Stony Creek, Somerset	300		William Coale, Jr. Original: found
NP-279	Smith, John	3 APR 1769	Berks - Northumberland	Fishing Creek, Columbia	300	C-44-85	(r13 MAY 1788)Margaret Dugan Original: found
NP-280	Jewell, George	3 APR 1769	Chillisquaque Creek	LD: Northumberland	300		John Trump Original: found

Table 6 - New Purchase Applications (1769-1773)

Number	Applicant	Date	Orig. Place	Later Place	Acres	Survey	Neighbors, Notes, etc.
NP-281	Jones, John Jr.	3 APR 1769	Berks	Chillisquaque Creek, Northumberland	300	F-41	Isaac Jones/(r15 JUL 1795)James Starr Original: found
NP-282	McConnel, James	3 APR 1769	Bedford	Fairfield, Westmoreland	300	A-38-199	(r28 MAR 1788)William Jack Esq. Original: found
NP-283	Smith, Devereux	3 APR 1769		Monongahela River, Allegheny/ LD: Allegheny	300	B-23-21	Thoms Bond, Jr./Samuel Semple/Col. Reed Original: Signed
NP-284	Willcox, William	3 APR 1769	Berks	Buffalo, Union	300	D-57-12 D-57-14	[same land as application NP-8666 to John Clin] Original: found
NP-285	Wright, Ellis	3 APR 1769	Berks - Northumberland	Chillisquaque, Montour	300	C-5-5	(r15 SEP 1805)John Allen & James Allen & Robert Allen & John Wilson Original: found
NP-286	Bickham, George	3 APR 1769	Muncy Hill	LD: Lycoming	300		Original: found
NP-287	Alexander, Frances	3 APR 1769	Chillisquaque Creek	LD: Northumberland	300		Original: found
NP-288	Overmire, George	3 APR 1769	Berks	Shamokin Creek, Northumberland	300	C-220-209	(r7 SEP1774)George Weyner Original: found
NP-289	Irison, Henry	3 APR 1769	White Deer Hole Creek		300		(r28 MAR 1832)James Irwin, executor of Martha Irwin, deceased/[see caveat] Original: found
NP-290	Boyle, William	3 APR 1769	Bedford	Elizabeth, Allegheny	300	D-62-189 C-173-91	Joseph Pearse/(r8 SEP 1790)Elisha Pearse Original: signed
NP-291	Patterson, William	3 APR 1769	Berks - Northumberland	Chillisquaque Creek, Montour	300	C-146-207	(r1 DEC 1769) Original: found
NP-292	Boor, Lawrence	3 APR 1769	Berks	Chillisquaque, Northumberland	300	X-193 C-16-103 C-16-194 C-153-210 C-42-169	(r8 MAY 1813)John Boyd & W. Wilson/(r28 DEC 1839)Peter Call/(r28 DEC 1839)Dennis Boay/(r8 APR 1840)Henry Magee/(r8 APR 1840)Dennis Call/Col. Francis/--- Montour/[see caveat] Original: found
NP-293	McCollem, Patrick	3 APR 1769	Cumberland	Mt. Pleasant, Westmoreland	300	D-57-258 D-57-259	Original: Signed
NP-294	Schneider, Martin	3 APR 1769	Cumberland	Conemaugh, Indiana	300	B-23-20	Michael Wirley/[see caveat] Original: found
NP-295	Duncan, William	3 APR 1769	Berks	White Deer, Union	300	D-60-243 C-173-175	(r25 APR 1793)Joseph Poak Original: found

Table 6 - New Purchase Applications (1769-1773)

Number	Applicant	Date	Orig. Place	Later Place	Acres	Survey	Neighbors, Notes, etc.
NP-296	Culbertson, Andrew	3 APR 1769	Berks	Buffalo, Union	300	D-56-62 D-56-63 D-56-64 D-56-65 D-56-71 D-56-72 D-56-73 C-39-300	(r23 NOV 1781)Stephen Duncan in trust for the heirs of William McCoskery Original: found
NP-297	Bell, Hamilton	3 APR 1769	Berks	Washington, Lycoming	300	D-56-156 D-56-159 D-56-285 D-57-6 D-57-197 D-62-184 A-70-46	(r19 JAN 1771)Francis Allison, D. D./[see caveat] Original: found
NP-298	Shee, Walter	3 APR 1769		Nippenose, Lycoming	300	D-57-299 D-57-300 D-56-6 D-56-222 D-62-279 A-8-106 D-13-266	John Malcom/(r10 FEB 1774)John Witmer, Jr. Original: found
NP-299	Hicks, Gilbert	3 APR 1769		Muncy Creek Twp., Lycoming/ LD: Lycoming	300	D-57-201 D-56-277 D-5-57 A-44-194 C-228-225 A-43-50	(warrant to accept 15 JAN 1849)--- Willets & --- Star/(warrant to accept 15 JAN 1849)John Vanderbill/(warrant to accept 15 JAN 1849)Charles Shoemaker/Burnet Richards Original: found
NP-300	Smith, Thomas	3 APR 1769	Cumberland	Howard, Centre/ LD: Howard, Centre	319	C-219-46 C-219-46 C-126-64	(p9 JAN 1870)Jacob Leather/(r31 MAR 1798)James Poe/Philip Gover Original: Missing
NP-301	Gillman, Martin	3 APR 1769		East Branch Susquehanna River, Luzerne	300	A-51-262	(r1 APR 1782)/Adolph Gilman Original: found
NP-302	Swisser, Cornelius	3 APR 1769	Berks	Northeast Branch Susquehanna River, Northumberland	300	A-6-287	(r16 MAR 1770)Edward Shippen & Joseph Shippen/[see caveat] Original: found

Table 6 - New Purchase Applications (1769-1773)

Number	Applicant	Date	Orig. Place	Later Place	Acres	Survey	Neighbors, Notes, etc.
NP-303	Smith, Richard Jr.	3 APR 1769	Berks	Washington, Lycoming	300	D-57-253	[see caveat] Original: found
NP-304	Irwin, Archibald	3 APR 1769	Bedford	Addison, Somerset	300	B-12-58 B-12-59	(r3 MAR 1815)George Herndbaugh/John Ourings Original: found
NP-305	Samuel, William	3 APR 1769	Cumberland	Spring, Centre	300	C-2-9	(r16 MAY 1812)William Alexander Original: Signed
NP-306	Hiltzsimer, Jacob	3 APR 1769	Cumberland	Clinton, Lycoming	300	D-57-254	Joseph Shute Original: found
NP-307	Leetch, William	3 APR 1769	West Branch Susquehanna River	LD: Union	300		Original: signed
NP-308	Boldwin, Elizabeth (of Backcreek, Frederick County, Virginia)	3 APR 1769		Greene, Washington	300	C-210-93	Rebecca Jenkins/(r21 SEP 1787)Elias Stones & wife/[see caveat] Original: Signed
NP-309	Holt, Mordicai	3 APR 1769		Chapman, Union/ LD: Union	300	D-57-257	Robert Iredell, Sr. Original: found
NP-310	McCurdy, Alexander	3 APR 1769	Berks	White Deer, Union	300	D-57-186 A-3-44	(r15 MAR 1773)Edward Shippen & Joseph Shippen Original: found
NP-311	Jenkins, William	3 APR 1769	Northumberland	Loyalsock Creek, Lycoming	300	A-14-32	Joseph Kendall/(r24 JUL 1812)William Rawle & Sarah Rawle & Buelah Howell Original: found
NP-312	Simeson, Samuel	3 APR 1769	Cumberland - Westmoreland	Sewickley Creek, Fayette	300	C-19-74	(r21 JUN 1787)Ephraim Blaine Original: found
NP-313	Crawford, James	3 APR 1769	Cumberland	Monongahela River, Bedford	300	C-23-124	(r16 NOV 1772) Original: found
NP-314	Clark, Joseph	3 APR 1769		Muncy, Lycoming	300	D-57-256	Original: Signed by John Clark
NP-315	Long, Richard	3 APR 1769		Unity or Ligonier, Westmoreland	300	D-57-230	--- Meyers/Joseph Irwin Original: found
NP-316	Morris, Samuel	3 APR 1769		Muncy, Northumberland	300	D-6-63	(r10 AUG 1784)Samuel Wallis Original: found
NP-317	Ryan, Michael	3 APR 1769	forks of the Susquehanna River	LD: Northumberland	300		Original: found

Table 6 - New Purchase Applications (1769-1773)

Number	Applicant	Date	Orig. Place	Later Place	Acres	Survey	Neighbors, Notes, etc.
NP-318	Morgan, Thomas	3 APR 1769		Columbia/ LD: Columbia	300		John Sprogle Original: found
NP-319	Burkholder, John	3 APR 1769	East Branch Susquehanna River	LD: Wyoming	300		Original: found
NP-320	Sheerer, John (of Peters Township, Cumberland County)	3 APR 1769		Rostraver, Westmoreland	300	B-18-135	--- Speers/Jehu Jones/(r 1797)William Sheerer/[see caveat] Original: found
NP-321	Jones, James Jr.	3 APR 1769		Turbot, Northumberland	300	M-215	Jehu Jones, Jr./(r17 JUN 1774)James McMahan Original: found
NP-322	Little, John	3 APR 1769		Plum, Allegheny	300	D-56-192 D-56-194 D-62-199 D-55-83 M-128	(r13 JUL 1781)/[patent P-1-14] Original: found
NP-323	Sanderson, George Sr.	3 APR 1769	Berks	Chillisquaque Creek, Northumberland	300	P-101 C-19-14	(r12 JAN 1787)Phineas Barber/(r6 MAY 1788)Joseph Coats/Mr. Tilghman Original: found
NP-324	Edge, Andrew	3 APR 1769	Berks	Buffalo, Union	300	D-55-97 A-49-95	(r11 DEC 1772) Original: found
NP-325	Stewart, Margaret	3 APR 1769		Unity, Westmoreland	300	D-57-229 C-217-141	[see caveat] Original: found
NP-326	Mitchell, Joshua	3 APR 1769	Northampton	Muncy, Northumberland	300	E-259	John Farmer/(r20 SEP 1794)Samuel Wallis/[see caveat] Original: found
NP-327	Cowperthwait, Joseph	3 APR 1769		West Branch Susquehanna River, Lycoming/ LD: Lycoming	300		Thomas Bonnell Original: found
NP-328	Coale, William Jr.	3 APR 1769	Cumberland	Stony Creek Twp., Somerset/ LD: Stony Creek, Somerset	300		Susanna Coale Original: found
NP-329	Montgomery, Hugh	3 APR 1769	Berks	Delaware Run, Northumberland	300	A-19-248 A-19-108	(r25 APR 1788)Matthew Correy Original: found
NP-330	Cahill, Daniel	3 APR 1769	Northumberland	Wapwallopen Creek, Luzerne	300	C-234-144	(r10 APR 1775)Robert Tayler Original: found

Table 6 - New Purchase Applications (1769-1773)

Number	Applicant	Date	Orig. Place	Later Place	Acres	Survey	Neighbors, Notes, etc.
NP-331	Robinson, John (son of George, of Sherman's Valley)	3 APR 1769	Northumberland	Patton, Centre	300	C-153-41 C-153-42 C-153-43	(r17 FEB 1803)Robert Moore Original: Signed
NP-332	Barnes, Elizabeth	3 APR 1769	Cumberland	LD: Somerset	300		Elizabeth Fisher Original: found
NP-333	Johnston, John	3 APR 1769	Cumberland - Northumberland	West Buffalo, Union	300	C-209-213 C-148-23 C-148-24	(r6 MAR 1815)John Speiglemeyer, Sr. & John Speiglemeyer, Jr./(r20 JAN 1822)William McClay Original: found
NP-334	Meanard, Jacob	3 APR 1769		East Branch Susquehanna River, Northumberland/ LD: Bradford	300	X-237	Frederick Meanard Original: found
NP-335	Roddy, Alexander	3 APR 1769	Northampton - Northumberland	Nescopeck, Luzerne	300	C-89-295	Bernard Bud/(r20 JAN 1789)George Irwin Original: found
NP-336	Worthington, John	3 APR 1769	Cumberland	Bald Eagle, Northumberland	300	D-6-55	Shipwith Cole/(r17 MAR 1784)Samuel Wallis/[see caveat] Original: found
NP-337	Hopkins, Garrard	3 APR 1769		LD: Columbia	300		Sarah Cole, Jr. Original: found
NP-338	Campbell, James Jr.	3 APR 1769	Bedford	Youghiogheny River, Fayette	300	A-72-62	(r3 FEB 1786)/[see caveat] Original: found
NP-339	Dickey, John	3 APR 1769	Cumberland	Unity, Westmoreland	300	E-344	William Longhery/James Barr/(r5 JUL 1797)Robert Smith Original: found
NP-340	Fucke alias Foulke, Jonas	3 APR 1769	Berks - Northumberland	Union, Union	300	D-62-230 C-148-95	(r7 MAY 1789)George Overmire/George Gabriel Original: found
NP-341	Seess, Henry	3 APR 1769	Berks	Buffalo, Union	300	D-56-127 D-56-128 D-56-129 D-56-130 F-155	(r14 OCT 1774)Edward Shippen & Joseph Shippen, Jr., Esq./Edward Bonsall Original: found
NP-342	Covien, Jeremiah	3 APR 1769	West Branch Susquehanna River	LD: Lycoming	300		Original: Corren on application
NP-343	Lownes, William	3 APR 1769	Northumberland	Bald Eagle, Centre/ LD: Nittany, Centre	300	A-33-268	Robert Trotter Original: found

Table 6 - New Purchase Applications (1769-1773)

Number	Applicant	Date	Orig. Place	Later Place	Acres	Survey	Neighbors, Notes, etc.
NP-344	Taylor, William	3 APR 1769	Berks	West Branch Susquehanna River, Centre/ LD: Clinton	300	W-254	Original: Signed
NP-345	Hoke, Benjamin	3 APR 1769	Monongahela River	LD: Washington	300		Original: found
NP-346	Jervis, Samuel	3 APR 1769	Berks	West Branch Susquehanna River, Lycoming	300	B-182	John Jarvis, Jr./(r6 JUL 1807)H. Drinker Original: found
NP-347	Campbell, William (of Cumberland County)	3 APR 1769		Muncy, Northumberland	300	A-55-154	(r8 JUN 1784)John Robb Original: Signed
NP-348	McClalin, Hugh	3 APR 1769	Bedford	Loyalhanna Creek, Westmoreland	300	C-39-190	(r30 OCT 1772)Elias Davison/[see caveat] Original: Signed
NP-349	Deihl, Adolph	3 APR 1769	Indian Creek between Wyalusing & Wyoming	LD: Wyoming	300		Thomas Heath Original: found
NP-350	Robb, David	3 APR 1769		Muncy, Lycoming	300	A-11-171	(r2 DEC 1808)/William Flemming/Frederick Martin Original: Signed
NP-351	Jewell, Robert	3 APR 1769	Berks	Buffalo, Union/ LD: Buffalo, Union	300	D-57-228	Original: found
NP-352	Burkholder, Jacob	3 APR 1769		east side Susquehanna River, Luzerne	300	C-222-272	(r9 AUG 1781)Joseph Wharton Original: found
NP-353	Cumings, James	3 APR 1769		Muncy, Lycoming	300	D-57-235	Original: signed
NP-354	Cord, James	3 APR 1769	Irwin's Run near Montour Creek	LD: Northumberland	300		Jas McMasen/George Irwin Original: found
NP-355	Crooks, Samuel	3 APR 1769	Northumberland	Nippenose, Lycoming	300	H-158 B-1-109	[included in warrant to George Johnston dated 8 APR 1811]/(p25 MAR 1870)George Johnston Original: found
NP-356	Pawling, Henry	3 APR 1769		Allegheny, Westmoreland	300	A-51-123	(r13 FEB 1815)Eleanor Johnston Original: Signed
NP-357	Todd, Nancy	3 APR 1769	Bald Eagle Creek	LD: Centre	300		Original: found

Table 6 - New Purchase Applications (1769-1773)

Number	Applicant	Date	Orig. Place	Later Place	Acres	Survey	Neighbors, Notes, etc.
NP-358	Bringman, Richard	3 APR 1769	Cumberland	Pitt, Westmoreland	300	C-104-69	William Bingman/(r17 MAY 1791)Wendel Keller Original: found
NP-359	Johnston, Philip	3 APR 1769		Luzerne	300	A-66-187	(r8 APR 1795)Joseph Scudder & Maria (his wife) Original: found
NP-360	Morris, Samuel Cad.	3 APR 1769		Augusta, Northumberland	300	N-256	(r5 SEP 1783)John Nixon & Alexander Forster Original: found
NP-361	Coale, Susannah	3 APR 1769	Cumberland	Stoneycreek, Somerset/ LD: Stoneycreek, Somerset	300		Margaret Gover Original: found
NP-362	Semple, Stell Jr.	3 APR 1769		Plum, Allegheny & Franklin, Westmoreland	300	D-57-79 D-62-85	Original: found
NP-363	Gray, William	3 APR 1769	Cumberland - Westmoreland	Washington, Armstrong	300	C-197-58	(r20 MAR 1818)S. Paul & Andrew Love Original: Signed
NP-364	Gurney, Henry Esq.	3 APR 1769	Bald Eagle Creek	LD: Clinton	300		John Ross Original: found
NP-365	Cunningham, Henry	3 APR 1769		Susquehanna River, Lycoming	300		Original: found
NP-366	Menges, John	3 APR 1769	East Branch Susquehanna River	LD: Luzerne	300		Conrad Keiger Original: found
NP-367	Barnes, John	3 APR 1769	Cumberland	LD: Somerset	300		Isabell Gorrell Original: found
NP-368	Kenley, Hannah	3 APR 1769	Northumberland	Briar Creek, Columbia/ LD: Columbia	300	D-46-92	Mary Jenkins, Jr. Original: found
NP-369	Wood, Jeremiah	3 APR 1769	Westmoreland	Pitt, Allegheny	200	D-56-182 A-13-94 A-13-95	Austin Pelley/(r27 MAR 1788)John Ferree Original: found
NP-370	Van Cleave, Chirneyance	3 APR 1769	Northumberland	East Branch Susquehanna River, Luzerne	300	K-25	John Parcel/(r22 AUG 1796)Dr. John Ewing Original: found
NP-371	Davis, George	3 APR 1769	Berks	Turbot, Northumberland	300	C-97	(r12 OCT 1774)William Cook, Esq. Original: found
NP-372	Moffit, Thomas	3 APR 1769		Wilkins, Allegheny	300	H-62-98	Original: found

Table 6 - New Purchase Applications (1769-1773)

Number	Applicant	Date	Orig. Place	Later Place	Acres	Survey	Neighbors, Notes, etc.
NP-373	Meeke, Robert	3 APR 1769	Bedford	Huntingdon, Westmoreland	200	C-195-35	(r4 MAR 1790)Thomas Robertson Original: found
NP-374	Crawford, William	3 APR 1769		Bullskin, Fayette	300	W-238	(r27 MAY 1795)William McCormick Original: found
NP-375	Mason, Hanah	3 APR 1769		Mahoning, Columbia/ LD: Columbia	300	X-235 X-236	Sarah Mason/[see caveat] Original: found
NP-376	Silkspinner, Joseph	3 APR 1769	Salt Lick Creek	LD: Clearfield	300		Daniel Stoie Original: found
NP-377	Stewart, James	3 APR 1769	two miles below "Lecomma" [Lycoming?]	LD: Lycoming	300		[see caveat] Original: found
NP-378	Byers, John	3 APR 1769		Washington, Westmoreland	300	D-68	(r4 MAR 1837)J. B. Alexander & T. Alexander & wife/--- Deyworthey Original: Signed
NP-379	McClure, William	3 APR 1769	Cumberland	Elizabeth, Allegheny	300	D-57-80 C-151-56	(r29 SEP 1789) Original: Signed by John McClure
NP-380	Culbertson, Joseph	3 APR 1769		Blacklick, Indiana	300	B-23-22	Alexander Culbertson Original: found
NP-381	Jones, Jehu Jr.	3 APR 1769		LD: Columbia	300		David Jones Original: found
NP-382	Perry, John	3 APR 1769	Bedford	Elizabeth, Allegheny	300	C-64-87 C-45-81 C-45-82	John Kyle/--- Dunlap/Robert McConnel/James Shannon/(r10 MAR 1829)Thomas Drenning/(r21 MAR 1831)Thomas Drennin Original: found
NP-383	Armitage, Benjamin	3 APR 1769		Washington, Westmoreland	300	C-2-50	(r8 OCT 1813)Francis Allison heirs/William Smith Original: found
NP-384	Robb, Robert	3 APR 1769	Stony Creek, Cumberland	LD: Somerset	300		John Robb Original: found
NP-385	Clark, William	3 APR 1769	Berks - Northumberland	East Branch Susquehanna River, Columbia	300	C-53-156	(r6 MAY 1793)/[see caveat] Original: Signed by John Clarke
NP-386	Hittner, George	3 APR 1769	Northumberland	Buffalo, Union	300	D-60-246 D-60-247	[the same land as application NP-2093 to John Beatty] Original: found
NP-387	Lutz, Frederick	3 APR 1769	Susquehanna River		300		Original: found

Table 6 - New Purchase Applications (1769-1773)

Number	Applicant	Date	Orig. Place	Later Place	Acres	Survey	Neighbors, Notes, etc.
NP-388	Cook, Robert (farmer)	3 APR 1769		Muncy Creek Twp., Lycoming/ LD: Lycoming	300	C-221-259 C-221-260	(r5 JUL 1870)Walter Officer Original: Signed
NP-389	Blaine, Alexander	3 APR 1769		Unity, Westmoreland/ LD: Unity, Westmoreland	300	B-1-65 B-1-66	William Proctor/[see caveat] Original: found
NP-390	Patterson, William (cooper)	3 APR 1769	Berks - Northampton	Fishing Creek, Northumberland	300	B-318	(r20 JAN 1789)G. Irwin/William Barton/Francis Stewart Original: found
NP-391	Feree, Joseph	3 APR 1769	Berks	Washington, Lycoming	300	C-143-62 C-143-180	(r6 JAN 1817)John Montgomery/John Ferree Original: found
NP-392	Troy, Mathew	3 APR 1769		Potter, Northumberland	300	W-255	Original: found
NP-393	McClure, David	3 APR 1769	Northampton	Greenwood, Columbia/ LD: Columbia	300	C-41-252 B-16-101 B-16-100 C-41-234	Samuel Power/(r21 DEC1825)Thomas Eves/(r7 FEB 1827)Chandler Eves/(r29 AUG 1832)Tomas Eves Original: Signed
NP-394	Boone, Samuel	3 APR 1769	Berks	Lycoming Creek, Northumberland	300	C-35-246	(r5 MAY 1789)John Cox, Esq. Original: found
NP-395	Huston, William	3 APR 1769	Youghiogheny River, Bedford	LD: Westmoreland	300	H-186	Zekiel Hickman/Joseph Huston/John Huston Original: found
NP-396	Gibbs, Samuel	3 APR 1769		Fairfield, Westmoreland	300	C-160-185	(r19 SEP 1796)John Phipps/John Hinkson Original: Signed
NP-397	McCollum, Patrick	3 APR 1769		Muncy, Lycoming	30\0	F-118	(r3 MAR 1812)Jacob Shoemaker/Thomas Robb Original: Signed
NP-398	Wilkins, John Sr.	3 APR 1769	Westmoreland	Turtle Creek, Allegheny	300	A-45-180	(r1 JUN 1801)heirs of William Dean Original: found
NP-399	Gillman, John	3 APR 1769	above Wyoming, East Branch Susquehanna River	LD: Bradford	300		John Martin Ackerman Original: found
NP-400	Faith, Thomas	3 APR 1769		Plum, Allegheny/ LD: Plum, Allegheny	300	A-39-86 C-124-101 C-106-72 C-106-73	(r16 MAY 1810)Thomas McDowell/(r10 MAR 1814)Christian Latchaw/(r9 MAR 1827)John King & Margaret King Original: Signed

Table 6 - New Purchase Applications (1769-1773)

Number	Applicant	Date	Orig. Place	Later Place	Acres	Survey	Neighbors, Notes, etc.
NP-401	Cowhawk, James	3 APR 1769		White Deer Valley, Lycoming	300	A-19-218	(r9 FEB 1818)Joseph Ball Original: found
NP-402	Seever, Frederick	3 APR 1769	Cumberland	Ligonier, Westmoreland	300	D-57-226 D-57-227	Andrew Boyer Original: found
NP-403	Wolfart, Philip	3 APR 1769	West Branch Susquehanna River	LD: Lycoming	200		Christopher Wolfart Original: found
NP-404	Smith, Hannah	3 APR 1769	Cumberland	Salem, Westmoreland	300	D-57-239 D-57-240	Joseph Hall Original: found
NP-405	Dunlany, Sharp	3 APR 1769		Chillisquaque, Northumberland	300	V-241	Benjamin Humphreys/(r22 JUN 1798)James Starr Original: found
NP-406	Rowan, Stewart Sr.	3 APR 1769		Conemaugh, Somerset	300	C-13-261 C-13-255	(r19 MAY 1824)Joseph Miller/(r13 MAR 1838)S. Berkley Original: found
NP-407	Sanderson, Francis	3 APR 1769	Berks	Chillisquaque Creek, Northumberland	300	C-170-240	(r17 SEP 1804)John Ritchey Original: found
NP-408	Barton, Richard Peters	3 APR 1769		Nippenose, Lycoming	300	D-57-298 D-62-299 D-55-87 D-55-59 D-56-157 D-56-240 A-59-67	(r6 MAR 1813)R. P. Barton/[Note on original: "The Revd. Mr. Peters is humbly requested to enter this location for his grandson & name sake"]/[see caveat] Original: found
NP-409	Sanderson, John	3 APR 1769	Peters Creek & Monongahela River	LD: Allegheny	300		Original: found
NP-410	McCormick, Hugh (in Middletown Township, Cumberland County)	3 APR 1769		Washington, Lycoming	300		(r21 APR 1831)Seth McCormick Original: Signed
NP-411	Hawkins, David	3 APR 1769	Bedford	Redstone Creek, Fayette	300	M-173	Adam Row/(r7 DEC 1787)John Matson Original: found
NP-412	Gorrell, Robert	3 APR 1769	Cumberland	Bald Eagle Creek, Centre	300	C-184-177	Oliver Gorrell/(r31 JUL 1820)Samuel Burge Rawle Original: found

Table 6 - New Purchase Applications (1769-1773)

Number	Applicant	Date	Orig. Place	Later Place	Acres	Survey	Neighbors, Notes, etc.
NP-413	Carson, Robert	3 APR 1769		North Huntingdon, Westmoreland	300	D-57-237	David Jackson Original: found
NP-414	Gover, Priscilla Sr.	3 APR 1769	Cumberland	Stoneycreek, Somerset/ LD: Columbia	300		Mary Gover Original: found
NP-415	Rankin, Thomas	3 APR 1769		Muncy Hill, Lycoming/ LD: Lycoming	300		John White Original: Signed
NP-416	Hunter, Samuel	3 APR 1769	Berks	Delaware Run, Northumberland	300	C-78-105	(r6 SEP 1774)Alexander Hunter Original: found
NP-417	Webster, Isaac	3 APR 1769	Berks	Wayne, Lycoming	300	D-56-24 D-56-149 D-62-259 A-22-115	Margaretta Talbout/(r11 APR 1770)Samuel Wallis Original: found
NP-418	Robinson, Jonathan (son of George, Esq., of Tyrone Township, Cumberland County)	3 APR 1769	Bald Eagle Creek	LD: Clinton	300		Alexander McDowell Original: Signed
NP-419	Heaton, Jean	3 APR 1769		Fairfield, Lycoming	300	D-57-234	John Lownes Original: found
NP-420	Slough, Jacob	3 APR 1769	Berks	East Branch Susquehanna River, Northumberland	200	C-197-189	(r10 SEP 1770) Original: Signed by Mathias Slough
NP-421	Reed, John	3 APR 1769	Berks	Chillisquaque Creek, Northumberland	300	C-152-24	(r11 NOV 1790)John Montgomery Original: found
NP-422	Palmer, George	3 APR 1769	Berks - Northumberland	Buffalo & Union, Union	300	D-57-228 D-57-293 D-56-69 D-56-70 C-112-114	(r13 MAY 1774)John Lee Original: found
NP-423	McGuire, Robert	3 APR 1769	Allegheny River below Crooked Creek	LD: Armstrong	300		Original: found
NP-424	Jervis, Charles	3 APR 1769		LD: Lycoming	300		John Jervis, Sr. Original: found

Table 6 - New Purchase Applications (1769-1773)

Number	Applicant	Date	Orig. Place	Later Place	Acres	Survey	Neighbors, Notes, etc.
NP-425	Heath, Thomas	3 APR 1769	Indian Creek & East Branch Susquehanna River	LD: Wyoming/ Bradford	300		Original: found
NP-426	Bauchman, Petter	3 APR 1769	Chillisquaque Creek	LD: Northumberland	300		Daniel Erisman Original: found
NP-427	Hill, Frederick (of Oley)	3 APR 1769	Berks	Augusta, Northumberland	300	H-161 H-486 C-21-192	Deitrick Mathew/(r26 MAY 1802)Jacob Conrad Original: found
NP-428	Burd, Edward	3 APR 1769		Kelly, Union	300	D-57-233	Original: found
NP-429	Smith, John Jr.	3 APR 1769	Cumberland	Lawrence, Clearfield	300	D-1-217	John Morgan/--- Shingle/(r28 MAR 1831)David Witmer Original: found
NP-430	Campbell, Robert	3 APR 1769		Muncy Creek Twp., Lycoming	300	D-57-19 D-57-201 C-228-224 C-228-223	(r15 JAN 1849)Jesse Willets/(r15 JAN 1849)John Vanderbilt Original: Signed
NP-431	Butler, Peirceval	3 APR 1769		Rostraver, Westmoreland	300	D-57-232	Conrad Winemiller Original: Signed
NP-432	Clogston, William	3 APR 1769	Bedford	Salem, Westmoreland	300	D-56-139 C-129-292 C-105-98 C-220-99 C-105-97	(r30 MAR 1816)Robert Marshall/(r27 JAN 1829)Jonathan Server/(r15 DEC 1837)William Johnston/George Patty Original: found
NP-433	Bayless, Samuel Sr.	3 APR 1769	Berks	Buffalo Creek, Northumberland	300	C-118-286	Thomas Boyle/(r23 AUG 1785)Samuel McClay Original: found
NP-434	Montgomery, Daniel	3 APR 1769	Berks	White Deer, Union	300	D-56-32 C-39-213	(r13 JAN 1773)Benjamin Dean Original: found
NP-435	Wilson, James	3 APR 1769		Derry, Westmoreland	300	C-57-57 C-157-190	James Barr/(r23 MAR 1785)John Patterson Original: found
NP-436	McCurdy, John	3 APR 1769		White Deer, Union	300	D-57-231	John Gregg Original: found

Table 6 - New Purchase Applications (1769-1773)

Number	Applicant	Date	Orig. Place	Later Place	Acres	Survey	Neighbors, Notes, etc.
NP-437	Dorsey, Benedict	3 APR 1769	White Hemp Creek & East Branch Susquehanna River, Northumberland or Berks		300		Original: found
NP-438	Lowden, Richard	3 APR 1769	Berks	Muncy, Lycoming/ LD: Lycoming	300	A-5-78 A-5-85 A-11-171	(r2 DEC 1808)David Robb Original: found
NP-439	Thompson, Thomas Jr.	3 APR 1769		Unity, Westmoreland	300	D-57-224 D-57-225	John Frazer/William Greer Original: found
NP-440	Hennessey, Mary	3 APR 1769	Northumberland	Fishing Creek, Columbia	300	C-179-27	(r5 OCT 1774)Dr. John Morgan Original: found
NP-441	McFarland, Andrew	3 APR 1769	Cumberland	LD: Westmoreland	300		John Sampson/Christopher Pharley Original: found
NP-442	Beale, William Jr.	3 APR 1769	Northumberland	Buffalo, Union	300	D-56-272 D-55-90 D-55-60 C-163-247	(r11 JAN 1775)Abel Rees Original: Signed
NP-443	McClure, William	3 APR 1769	Northampton	Little Fishing Creek, Columbia	300	B-238	Elizabeth McMean/(r12 APR 1800)John Eves Original: found
NP-444	Campbell, John	3 APR 1769	Cumberland	Stony Creek, Bedford	300	C-25-167	Francis Campbell/(r15 OCT 1785) Original: found
NP-445	Montgomery, John Jr.	3 APR 1769	Berks	Warrior Run, Northumberland	300	C-136-33	(r30 DEC 1769) Original: found
NP-446	Barr, James	3 APR 1769		Allegheny, Westmoreland	300	D-57-223	Robert Gibb/John Barr Original: Signed by James Barr & John Barr
NP-447	Ulrick, Stophel	3 APR 1769	Northumberland	Mahoning, Columbia	300	A-32-136	William Drewry Original: found
NP-448	Kerr, Robert	3 APR 1769	Northumberland	Muncy, Lycoming	300	B-1-13	(r7 MAY 1793)John Heap, Esq. Original: found
NP-449	Ogdon, Joseph	3 APR 1769	Berks	Derry, Northumberland/ LD: Columbia	300	A-36-9 A-44-115 A-40-270 C-10-181	(r6 JAN 1797)James Starr/(r22 MAR 1811)Marks John Biddle Original: found
NP-450	McCormick, Seth	3 APR 1769		Chillisquaque Creek, Northumberland	300	C-179-48	(r8 JUL 1774)/Col. Francis/[see caveat] Original: Signed by Seth McCormick and Hugh McCormick

Table 6 - New Purchase Applications (1769-1773)

Number	Applicant	Date	Orig. Place	Later Place	Acres	Survey	Neighbors, Notes, etc.
NP-451	Cooper, James	3 APR 1769	Berks	Chillisquaque Creek, Northumberland	300	M-216	(r24 SEP 1774)William Murray/[see caveat] Original: found
NP-452	Stricker, George	3 APR 1769	Berks - Cumberland	West Buffalo, Union	300	D-57-209 D-57-210	Frederick Kap Original: found
NP-453	Sherrack, Jacob Jr.	3 APR 1769	Berks - Northumberland	Buffalo, Union	300	C-163-255	(r15 DEC 1774)Thomas Rees Original: found
NP-454	Walker, David	3 APR 1769	Cumberland	Crooked Creek, Westmoreland	300	C-144-78	Original: found
NP-455	Sprogell, Ludowick	3 APR 1769	Northumberland	Bald Eagle, Union/ LD: Centre	300	X-142	[see caveat] Original: found
NP-456	McDonnal, Alexander	3 APR 1769	Northumberland	Mahoning, Montour	300	C-145-91	(r12 SEP 1812)John Montgomery/Col. Francis Original: Signed
NP-457	Pollock, James	3 APR 1769	Bedford	near Ligonier, Westmoreland	300	C-171-174	Robert Hannah/(r1 APR 1795) Original: found
NP-458	Jenkins, Rebecca	3 APR 1769		Monongahela River & White Clay Creek, Washington	300	C-218-261	(r15 MAY 1788)Lewis Williams/[see caveat] Original: Signed
NP-459	Miller, Edward	3 APR 1769	Berks	Mahoning, Northumberland	300	Y-43	James Chapmen/(r12 APR 1797)Samuel Wallis Original: found
NP-460	Bayless, Samuel Jr.	3 APR 1769	Cumberland - Berks	West Buffalo, Union	300	D-57-208	Original: found
NP-461	Myer, Jacob	3 APR 1769		East Branch Susquehanna River, Luzerne	300	C-222-271	(r9 AUG 1781)Joseph Wharton/Thomas Smith Original: found
NP-462	Hoofnagle, Peter	3 APR 1769		Derry, Westmoreland	300	D-57-207	--- Dogworthey Original: found
NP-463	Davis, John	3 APR 1769		Augusta, Northumberland	150	A-38-220	(r6 AUG 1783)Chalkley & Joseph James Original: found
NP-464	Willson, William	3 APR 1769		West Branch Susquehanna River, Lycoming/ LD: Lycoming	300		Joseph Cowperthwait Original: found
NP-465	Naftzger, John	3 APR 1769	Penns Creek, Cumberland	LD: Snyder	300		Michael Mentzer Original: found

Table 6 - New Purchase Applications (1769-1773)

Number	Applicant	Date	Orig. Place	Later Place	Acres	Survey	Neighbors, Notes, etc.
NP-466	Clock, Conrad	3 APR 1769		East Branch Susquehanna River, Luzerne/ LD: Luzerne	300	Z-49	Adam Clock Original: found
NP-467	Lowman, Ludwick	3 APR 1769		Fairfield, Westmoreland	300	D-57-206	Original: found
NP-468	Taylor, Mathew	3 APR 1769	Pine Creek	LD: Lycoming	300		Original: Signed by William Taylor
NP-469	Hopkins, Ann	3 APR 1769		LD: Columbia	300		Gerrard Hopkins Original: found
NP-470	Bond, Thomas Jr.	3 APR 1769		3.5 miles from Ft. Pitt, Allegheny	300	V-169	(r2 JAN 1788)Catharine Thompson/Col. Reed/Devereux Smith/Joseph Irwin Original: found
NP-471	Robinson, George Jr. (of Sherman's Valley, son of George, Esq.)	3 APR 1769	Mifflin	Potter, Centre/ LD: Potter, Centre	300	A-243	Original: signed
NP-472	Galbraith, Andrew	3 APR 1769	Cumberland	Sewickley Creek, Westmoreland	300	A-52-201	Samuel Simison/(r21 JUN 1787) Original: found
NP-473	Johns, Margaret	3 APR 1769	East Branch Susquehanna River, Berks or Northumberland	LD: Columbia	300		Original: found
NP-474	Dordes, Michael	3 APR 1769	Northumberland	White Deer Hole Creek, Union	300	A-44-94	Thomas Marshall/(r4 MAY 1810)Edward Burd Original: found
NP-475	Wilkins, Catherine	3 APR 1769		Pitt, Allegheny/ LD: Pitt, Allegheny	300	A-29-33	Ralph Starret Original: found
NP-476	James, John	3 APR 1769		Elizabeth, Allegheny	300	D-57-78	Original: found
NP-477	Simpson, James (of Cumberland County)	3 APR 1769	Cumberland	Blacklick, Indiana	300	D-57-220	William Rainey Original: found
NP-478	Simpson, Samuel	3 APR 1769	Northumberland	Spring, Centre/ LD: Spring, Centre	300	W-277 W-278 W-279	Original: found

Table 6 - New Purchase Applications (1769-1773)

Number	Applicant	Date	Orig. Place	Later Place	Acres	Survey	Neighbors, Notes, etc.
NP-479	Moore, John	3 APR 1769	Berks	Kelly, Union	300	D-56-90 D-56-91 D-56-94 D-56-145 D-56-232 D-60-280 D-60-274 C-220-267	(r18 JUN 1772)William Wilson/Mr. Ewing/Joseph Boughanan Original: found
NP-480	Yoner, Joseph	3 APR 1769	Buffalo Creek, West Branch Susquehanna River, adjoining Officers' survey	LD: Union/ [called Jacob in LD]	300		Original: found
NP-481	Coats, Linsey	3 APR 1769	Northumberland	Bald Eagle, Centre/ LD: Centre	300	G-459	Original: found
NP-482	Neil, William	3 APR 1769	Berks	Buffalo, Union	300	D-57-51 D-56-294 A-41-27	(r15 APR 1785)Edward Shippen & Joseph Shippen Original: found
NP-483	Gall, George	3 APR 1769	Berks	Buffalo, Union	300	D-57-247 C-23-128	(r11 MAY 1773)Adam Christ Original: found
NP-484	Hughes, Ellis	3 APR 1769	Northampton - Northumberland	Fishing Creek, Columbia	300	C-91-246 C-91-264	(r5 SEP 1788)Philip Kreamer, Esq. Original: found
NP-485	Stone, John	3 APR 1769	Chillisquaque Creek	LD: Montour	300		Original: found
NP-486	Alexander, James	3 APR 1769		Buffalo, Northumberland	300	C-87-170	(r19 JUN 1802)M. Holman/John Penn Original: found
NP-487	Barr, William	3 APR 1769		Quemahoning, Bedford	300	A-23-264	(r31 OCT 1788)/[see caveat] Original: Signed by William Barr and John Barr
NP-488	Huston, John	3 APR 1769		Tyrone, Fayette	300	D-57-218	William Huston Original: found
NP-489	Blessing, Michael	3 APR 1769	Berks	White Deer, Union	300	D-57-219	Jacob Blessing Original: found
NP-490	Clark, Robert	3 APR 1769		Bullskin, Fayette/ LD: Bullskin, Fayette	300	D-57-217	John Stevinson/Joseph Cree Original: found

Table 6 - New Purchase Applications (1769-1773)

Number	Applicant	Date	Orig. Place	Later Place	Acres	Survey	Neighbors, Notes, etc.
NP-491	Jervis, John Sr.	3 APR 1769		Muncy, Lycoming	300	D-56-141 D-60-278 B-1-20 B-1-21	(r6 SEP 1805)Henry Drinker Original: found
NP-492	Linn, Nathan Jr.	3 APR 1769	Bedford - Westmoreland	Washington, Fayette	300	D-62-202 C-112-65	(r4 NOV 1772)Andrew Linn Original: found
NP-493	Menoch, William	3 APR 1769	Bedford	Pitt, Allegheny	300	A-53-281 A-53-282 A-53-283 A-53-284 X-232 X-233 X-234	(r21 JUN 1809)Thomas Wilson & M. Jamison & Jane Taylor & Mary Donaldson Original: found
NP-494	Cantwell, Richard	3 APR 1769	Northampton	Muncy, Lycoming	300	E-419	John Jones/(r21 OCT 1785)Henry Thompson Original: found
NP-495	McClure, William	3 APR 1769	West Branch Montour Creek	LD: Montour	300		George Robinson, Esq. Original: Signed
NP-496	Beard, James (farmer)	3 APR 1769	Bedford	Huntingdon, Westmoreland	300	C-184-62	(r30 APR 1817)Martha Robinson, executor of James Robinson Original: found
NP-497	Rhoads, Samuel	3 APR 1769	"Koshicton", Northumberland	LD: Wayne	300		Andrew Allen Original: found
NP-498	Roddy, Alexander Jr.	3 APR 1769	East Branch Susquehanna River	LD: Luzerne	300		Original: found
NP-499	Suber, Philip	3 APR 1769		East Branch Susquehanna River, Luzerne	300	A-12-134	(r14 MAR 1775)John Gibson, Esq./Christopher Getzelman/--- Wickware Original: found
NP-500	Shinney, Lawrence	3 APR 1769	Berks	Mahoning Creek, Montour	30\0	C-197-191	(r16 MAY 1770)Edward Shippen & Joseph Shippen/John Toby/[see caveat] Original: Missing

Table 6 - New Purchase Applications (1769-1773)

Number	Applicant	Date	Orig. Place	Later Place	Acres	Survey	Neighbors, Notes, etc.
NP-501	Potter, John	3 APR 1769	Berks	White Deer, Union	300	D-62-231 D-62-232 D-62-233 D-62-234 D-62-235 D-62-236 D-62-237 D-62-238 C-146-224	(r21 JUN 1770)/James Potter Original: found
NP-502	Barnes, Thomas Jr.	3 APR 1769	Berks	Buffalo, Union/ LD: Union	200	D-57-216	Original: found
NP-503	Gilbert, Thomas	3 APR 1769	Cumberland - Berks	West Buffalo, Union	---	D-57-286 C-112-57	(r6 APR 1770)John Lowden Original: found
NP-504	Duncan, Matthew	3 APR 1769	Berks	Washington, Lycoming	300	D-55-91 C-130-139	(r25 JUL 1796)Thomas McCormick Original: found
NP-505	Paris, Peter	3 APR 1769	Chillisquaque Creek	LD: Turbot, Northumberland	300		Original: found
NP-506	McClure, John Sr.	3 APR 1769		Unity, Westmoreland	300	D-57-214	John Procter/William Greir Original: Signed
NP-507	Smith, Robert Jr.	3 APR 1769	Cumberland	Elizabeth, Allegheny	300	E-417	James Smith/(r10 JUN 1793)Mathew McKinney Original: found
NP-508	Willson, Martha	3 APR 1769	Berks - Northumberland	Mahoning, Montour	300	Y-41	(r12 APR 1797)Samuel Wallis/John Botts Original: found
NP-509	Rannels, John Esq.	3 APR 1769		Derry, Westmoreland/ LD: Derry, Westmoreland	300	D-56-150 D-62-35 C-173-24 C-57-271 D-25-186 C-57-288 C-173-23 C-57-287 D-90-169	(r2 JAN 1810)William Trindle/(r6 APR 1830)Samuel Moorehead/(p8 MAR 1870)Robert Foster/(p9 MAY 1917)John Siger & Samuel Siger/[patent H-78-212]/[see caveat] Original: found
NP-510	Doz, Martha	3 APR 1769		West Branch Susquehanna River, Northumberland/ LD: Lycoming/ Union	300	A-5-104	William Power/William Taylor Original: Signed

Table 6 - New Purchase Applications (1769-1773)

Number	Applicant	Date	Orig. Place	Later Place	Acres	Survey	Neighbors, Notes, etc.
NP-511	Mansfield, William	3 APR 1769	Berks	Buffalo, Union/ LD: Buffalo, Union	300	D-57-213	Original: found
NP-512	Harrison, James	3 APR 1769		German, Fayette	300	A-6-143	(r23 SEP 1801)Lawerance Rider & Peter Longnacker/Casper Edder/Michael Catt Original: Signed
NP-513	Black, John (weaver)	3 APR 1769	Berks	Augusta, Northumberland	300	C-1-40	(r9 MAY 1770) Original: found
NP-514	Gemberling, Charles	3 APR 1769	West Branch Susquehanna River	LD: Lycoming	300		Andrew Moore/John Lautermilk Original: found
NP-515	Blyth, Elizabeth	3 APR 1769	Berks	White Deer, Union	300	D-56-50 C-7-96 D-73-292 D-73-293 D-73-294 D-73-295 D-73-296	(r26 SEP 1774)/Margaret Blythe Original: signed
NP-516	Allen, James	3 APR 1769	Berks	Kelly, Union	300	D-60-280 D-56-90 C-136-37	(r9 FEB 1770)William McClosky/Mr. Ewing Original: found
NP-517	Preston, William	3 APR 1769		Strabane, Washington	300	B-9-125 B-9-194 B-9-124	(r27 JUL 1824)Thomas Morgan/(r26 FEB 1828)Alexander Murdock Original: found
NP-518	Clark, Robert Jr.	3 APR 1769	Berks	Turbot, Northumberland	200	C-7-92	(r31 AUG 1774)John Black Original: Signed by John Clark
NP-519	Haur, Christopher	3 APR 1769	Cumberland - Berks	Union, Union	300	D-57-211 D-57-212	George Albrecht Original: found
NP-520	Crawford, Valentine	3 APR 1769	Cumberland	Tyrone, Fayette	300	A-24-16	John Stephenson Original: found
NP-521	Worral, Benjamin	3 APR 1769	Berks	White Deer, Union	300	D-56-51 C-197-154	(r15 MAR 1773)Edward Shippen & Joseph Shippen/William McDowell/Alexander McCurdy Original: found
NP-522	Moore, David	3 APR 1769	Berks	Buffalo, Union	200	D-56-228 D-56-229 D-56-230 C-48-253	(r18 FEB 1790)James Forster Original: found

Table 6 - New Purchase Applications (1769-1773)

Number	Applicant	Date	Orig. Place	Later Place	Acres	Survey	Neighbors, Notes, etc.
NP-523	Harbidge, Edward	3 APR 1769		Center, Indiana	200	E-466 C-28-280 D-11-203	(r5 JUN 1833)Samuel Cummins & David Cummins/(r10 MAR 1834)John Wilson Original: found
NP-524	Fraizer, Joseph	3 APR 1769	Berks	White Deer, Union	300	D-57-40 D-57-26 D-57-27 D-57-28 A-48-226	(r13 FEB 1770)Benjamin Dean/Mr. Blythe Original: found
NP-525	McGuire, Charles	3 APR 1769	Cumberland - Westmoreland	Black Lick Creek, Indiana	300	C-123-289	(r14 MAY 1789)Robert Allison Original: found
NP-526	Gorrell, John	3 APR 1769	Berks	Chillisquaque Creek, Northumberland/ LD: Columbia	300	X-175	James Tilghman, Esq. Original: found
NP-527	McCune, William	3 APR 1769		Fairfield, Westmoreland	300	D-57-206 B-23-49 C-10-92	(r23 MAR 1789)David Brown/John Hinkson/Robert Hinkson/John Laughlin Original: Signed
NP-528	Blair, William	3 APR 1769		Point, Northumberland	300	D-57-205	Original: found
NP-529	Williams, Daniel Jr.	3 APR 1769		Mifflin, Allegheny	300	D-57-77	Original: Signed
NP-530	Sayre, Ezekiel	3 APR 1769	Rush Meadows, Northampton	LD: Bradford	300		Alphius Wickware Original: found
NP-531	Klugh, Charles	3 APR 1769	Northumberland	"Minamee", Luzerne/ LD: Luzerne	200	X-202	Original: found
NP-532	Anderson, William	3 APR 1769	Northampton	Northeast Branch Susquehanna River, Columbia	300	C-4-103	(r13 DEC 1837)John Achenbough Original: found
NP-533	Jones, Ann	3 APR 1769		Susquehanna River, Northumberland/ LD: Northumberland	300	A-32-134	Whitehead Jones Original: found
NP-534	Doughlas, Beniyah	3 APR 1769		Derry, Westmoreland	300	D-56-293 A-12-132 A-12-138	(r23 MAY 1816)James Wilson/John Pumrey Original: found

Table 6 - New Purchase Applications (1769-1773)

Number	Applicant	Date	Orig. Place	Later Place	Acres	Survey	Neighbors, Notes, etc.
NP-535	Kreutter (Kreider), Martin	3 APR 1769		East Branch Susquehanna River, Luzerne/ LD: Luzerne	300	X-201	John Wolff/George Wolff/George Henry Sybert Original: found
NP-536	Right, George	3 APR 1769		Franklin, Westmoreland	300	A-75-298	(r7 MAR 1789)William Thomas & Adam Briniegh/Col. Boquet's battleground Original: found
NP-537	Martin, Stoffel	3 APR 1769	Bald Eagle Creek	LD: Clinton/ Centre	300		Original: found
NP-538	Culbertson, Samuel Sr.	3 APR 1769		North Huntingdon, Westmoreland	300	C-26-216	(r17 DEC 1812) Original: found
NP-539	White, James	3 APR 1769	Margarets Creek	West Branch Susquehanna River, Northumberland	300	D-6-24	(r19 JUN 1783)/(p27 JUN 1783)/[patent P-1-44] Original: found
NP-540	Means, John	3 APR 1769		three miles above Ft. Augusta, Northumberland	100	M-330	(r8 APR 1774)Robert McBride Original: found
NP-541	Baldwin, Lydia	3 APR 1769		Monongahela River, Washington	300	C-79-91	(r18 APR 1792)John Guthry & Lydia (his wife) Original: Signed
NP-542	Cather, Robert	3 APR 1769	West Branch Susquehanna River	LD: Lycoming	300		Thomas Brown Original: found
NP-543	St. Clair, John Murray	3 APR 1769		Ligonier, Westmoreland/ LD: Ligonier, Westmoreland	300	D-55-73 D-55-74 D-56-231 C-83-225 C-83-226 C-222-81	(r19 JAN 1837)Frederick Harganot/(r11 MAR 1837)John Murry St. Clair/(r4 MAR 1841)T. McDowell & A. McClintock Original: found
NP-544	Crute, Rebecca	3 APR 1769	Allegheny Mountain near Stony Creek, Cumberland	LD: Somerset	300		William Clark Original: found
NP-545	McKay, Alexander	3 APR 1769		Unity, Westmoreland	300	A-50-19 D-70-233	(r17 MAR 1827)Richard Jackson/[see caveat] Original: found

Table 6 - New Purchase Applications (1769-1773)

Number	Applicant	Date	Orig. Place	Later Place	Acres	Survey	Neighbors, Notes, etc.
NP-546	Gibson, George	3 APR 1769		Loyalsock, Lycoming	300	D-56-44 E-138	Martin Stover/(r6 MAR 1794)Michael Ross Original: Signed
NP-547	Meckleroy, George	3 APR 1769	Shamokin Creek, Berks	LD: Northumberland	250	X-231	George Leadley Original: found
NP-548	Harrison, Robert	3 APR 1769		North Strabane, Washington	300	X-178 B-9-194 B-9-124 B-12-111 B-11-187	(r27 JUL 1824)Thomas Morgan/(r28 FEB 1828)Alexander Mendoch/(r5 SEP 1831)Robert Henderson/(r3 APR 1823)James Bunyan King/William Preston Original: found
NP-549	Fry, George	3 APR 1769		Howard, Centre	300	C-10-186	Benjamin Brown/Levi Hicks/[this tract patented to William Brown -- Apr 1811, see NP-1296]/[see caveat] Original: found
NP-550	Cummins, John	3 APR 1769		Conemaugh River, Bedford	300	M-176	(r17 APR 1788)Archibald McGuire/John Hinkson/John Woodson Original: Signed
NP-551	Farmer, John	3 APR 1769		Muncy Creek, Northampton	300	A-33-49 A-33-50	(r19 SEP 1794)William Ellis/Israel Jones/[see caveat] Original: found
NP-552	Miller, Jacob	3 APR 1769	Chillisquaque Creek		300		Original: found
NP-553	Preveal, Gideon	3 APR 1769		Little Fishing Creek, Northampton	300	D-181	(r24 APR 1769)James Bringhurst/John Jolly Original: found
NP-554	Irwin, Archibald	3 APR 1769		Mt. Pleasant, Westmoreland	300	D-57-190	Original: found
NP-555	Boos, John	3 APR 1769		Muncy Creek Twp., Lycoming	200	D-57-201	Original: found
NP-556	Gover, Ephriam	3 APR 1769	Cumberland	Boggs, Centre/ LD: Centre	300	A-57-79 H-163 C-20-69	(r28 JAN 1833)Henry Barnhart/(p25 NOV 1870)E. W. Sturdevant/Charles Worthington, Jr. Original: found
NP-557	Kerney, William	3 APR 1769	Westmoreland	Plum, Allegheny	300	C-128-31 C-128-30	(r30 JAN 1788)Adam Jacobs/(r2 MAR 1812)Jareus Clark (late Boyd)/Charles McGinnes/widow Meyers Original: found
NP-558	Goudie, James	3 APR 1769		Mt. Pleasant & Unity, Westmoreland	300	D-56-21 D-57-229 C-217-143	(r1 APR 1795)William Todd Original: found

Table 6 - New Purchase Applications (1769-1773)

Number	Applicant	Date	Orig. Place	Later Place	Acres	Survey	Neighbors, Notes, etc.
NP-559	Grimes, Mathew	3 APR 1769		Huntingdon, Westmoreland/ LD: Huntingdon, Westmoreland	---	D-46-96	Original: found
NP-560	Patterson, Galbraith	3 APR 1769	Berks	Kelly, Union	300	D-56-267 C-47-300 C-166-226 C-166-240	(r10 NOV 1812)John Frantz/(r10 APR 1828)William A. Patterson/[see caveat] Original: found
NP-561	Field, Mary	3 APR 1769		Nippenose, Lycoming	300	D-62-295 A-75-193	(r6 JAN 1787)Jasper Yeates, Esq./[see caveat] Original: found
NP-562	Forbes, Andrew	3 APR 1769		Sewickley Creek, Westmoreland/ LD: Westmoreland	300	X-171 D-46-100	[see caveat] Original: Signed
NP-563	Hoops, John Little	3 APR 1769	Berks	White Deer, Union/ LD: Union	300	D-57-219 H-162	[see NP-489] Original: Signed
NP-564	Jardon, Thomas	3 APR 1769	Berks	Buffalo, Union	300	B-267	(r14 DEC 1787)George Fry/--- Hammerly/[see caveat] Original: found
NP-565	Seber, Jacob	3 APR 1769		East Branch Susquehanna River, Luzerne/ LD: Luzerne	300		John Wabel Original: found
NP-566	Thomas, John	3 APR 1769	East Branch Susquehanna River	LD: Bradford	300		Valentine Taylor/--- Wickware Original: found
NP-567	Harrison, Benjamin	3 APR 1769	White Deer Hole Creek, Berks	LD: Lycoming	300		Rebecca Mitcheltree Original: found
NP-568	Ord, John Jr.	3 APR 1769	Berks	Union, Union/ LD: Buffalo, Union	300	D-57-211 D-57-212 A-38-60 C-123-121 C-123-156	(r31 MAY 1810)Martha Barber/(r13 MAR 1812)George Long Original: found
NP-569	Graham, Walter	3 APR 1769		St. Clair, Allegheny	300	D-57-76	Original: found
NP-570	Mears, Samuel	3 APR 1769		Unity, Westmoreland	300	D-57-203	Original: found

Table 6 - New Purchase Applications (1769-1773)

Number	Applicant	Date	Orig. Place	Later Place	Acres	Survey	Neighbors, Notes, etc.
NP-571	Clark, Robert Sr.	3 APR 1769	Northumberland	Fishing Creek, Columbia	300	Z-123	(r24 MAR 1774)Evan Owen Original: Signed by John Clark
NP-572	Eliot, John	3 APR 1769	Berks	Kelly, Union	---	D-57-39 D-56-253 D-56-254 C-146-223	(r29 MAY 1770)James Poak/James McConnell Original: Signed
NP-573	Jolley, John	3 APR 1769	Northampton	Little Fishing Creek, Northumberland - Columbia	300	D-180	(r24 APR 1789)James Bringhurst Original: found
NP-574	Ewa, Casper	3 APR 1769		Union, Union	300	D-57-198	George Ulrich, Jr. Original: found
NP-575	Yeates, Joseph	3 APR 1769		Monongahela River, Washington	300	A-32-137	[see caveat] Original: found
NP-576	Rich, John	3 APR 1769	Berks	Northumberland - Mahoning, Montour	300	Y-42	(r12 APR 1797)Samuel Wallis/John Botts Original: found
NP-577	Hutcheson, James	3 APR 1769	Northumberland	Bald Eagle, Centre/ LD: Centre	300	X-179	William Sims Original: found
NP-578	Paschall, Thomas	3 APR 1769	Northumberland	Bald Eagle, Centre/ LD: Damascus, Wayne/ Greene	300		James Hutchinson/S. Rhoads Original: found
NP-579	Perry, James	3 APR 1769	Bedford	Elizabeth, Allegheny	300	A-14-241 A-66-101	(r14 MAY 1804)/--- Maxwell Original: found
NP-580	Wright, John	3 APR 1769		Huntingdon & Hempfield, Westmoreland	300	A-61-112 C-46-138	(r24 SEP 1787)Robert Wilson/(r5 MAR 1799)Hugh Donaldson/Thomas Lyon/Capt. Thompson Original: found
NP-581	Perry, John	3 APR 1769		Washington, Lycoming	300	D-57-202	Jacob Blickendoffer Original: found
NP-582	Huling, Samuel	3 APR 1769	Berks	Kelly, Union	300	D-57-189	Original: found
NP-583	Bear, Benjamin	3 APR 1769		Susquehanna River, Luzerne	300	X-192	John Bear Original: found

Table 6 - New Purchase Applications (1769-1773)

Number	Applicant	Date	Orig. Place	Later Place	Acres	Survey	Neighbors, Notes, etc.
NP-584	McKee, Thomas	3 APR 1769		Moon, Allegheny	300		(r5 MAY 1795)James McKee/Capt. Henry Montour Original: found
NP-585	Lynn, David	3 APR 1769	Northumberland	Fishing Creek, Columbia	300	F-165	(r20 APR 1775)Edward Shippen & Joseph Shippen, Jr., Esq. Original: found
NP-586	Knight, Michael	3 APR 1769	Cumberland	Northumberland - Bald Eagle, Centre	300	A-77-95	(r27 OCT 1783)Samuel Wallis/John Mahaun Original: found
NP-587	McMurrey, Thomas	3 APR 1769		White Deer, Union	300	D-57-188	William Blythe Original: Signed
NP-588	McCroy, David	3 APR 1769	Westmoreland	Center, Indiana	300	B-7-94 B-7-74	[see warrant to Samuel Moorehead dated 24 JAN 1785, Westmoreland Co.]/(p26 APR 1844) Original: found
NP-589	Foster, William	3 APR 1769	Berks	East Branch Susquehanna River, Northumberland	300	C-48-48 D-46-80	(r5 NOV 1785)George Daugherty Original: found
NP-590	Duncan, Samuel	3 APR 1769		Derry, Westmoreland	300	D-60-259 D-62-294 A-9-166	(r14 JUL 1790)/John Campbell/Thomas Martin Original: found
NP-591	Guliford, Allen	3 APR 1769	Bald Eagle Creek	LD: Clinton/ Centre	300		James Sharon Original: signed
NP-592	Sprogle, John	3 APR 1769	Northumberland	Fishing Creek, Columbia	300	C-207-7	(r12 JUN 1789)Henry Singer & Jacob Growell/William Wilson Original: found
NP-593	Rose, David	3 APR 1769	Berks	Buffalo, Union	300	D-56-228 D-56-229	Jacob Croseyong/Richard Malone/[same land as NP-1339 to Nathaniel Lowry] Original: found
NP-594	Iredell, Charles	3 APR 1769	Berks	White Deer, Union	300	D-57-38 D-57-52 D-56-34 D-62-241 L-402	(r5 APR 1774)Jesse Lukens/Robert Iredell/[see caveat] Original: found
NP-595	Bradford, Margaret	3 APR 1769	Cumberland	Bald Eagle Creek, Centre/ LD: Centre	300		John George Bradford Original: found

Table 6 - New Purchase Applications (1769-1773)

Number	Applicant	Date	Orig. Place	Later Place	Acres	Survey	Neighbors, Notes, etc.
NP-596	Scott, Robert	3 APR 1769	West Branch Susquehanna River	LD: Clinton	300		Original: found
NP-597	Field, Sarah	3 APR 1769	Brushy Run branch of Bald Eagle Creek	LD: Centre	300		Original: found
NP-598	Smith, Robert	3 APR 1769		on road from Ft. Pitt to Ligonier, Westmoreland/ LD: Westmoreland	300	X-143	Original: found
NP-599	Reith, Jacob	3 APR 1769	Berks	Shamokin Creek, Northumberland	300	C-176-75	(r7 MAR 1775) Original: found
NP-600	Boggs, John	3 APR 1769	Standing Stone Creek	LD: Centre/ Huntingdon	300		Andrew Boggs/[see caveat] Original: Signed
NP-601	Rees, Mary	3 APR 1769	Berks	Chillisquaque Creek, Northumberland/ LD: Northumberland	300	X-126 C-179-48	Col. Francis/[see caveat] Original: found
NP-602	Robertson, Ephraim	3 APR 1769		White Deer, Union	300	D-57-187	William Blythe Original: found
NP-603	Jervis, Mary	3 APR 1769	Northumberland	Muncy Creek, Lycoming	300	E-28	Elizabeth Jervis, Sr./(r17 MAR 1784)Samuel Wallis Original: found
NP-604	McConal, Mathew	3 APR 1769	White Deer Hole Creek	LD: Lycoming	300		Original: Signed
NP-605	Diggs, Charles	3 APR 1769	Berks	Turbot, Northumberland	300	C-153-75	(r4 MAY 1803)John Montgomery Original: found
NP-606	Heyshan, William	3 APR 1769	Berks	White Deer, Union	300		Richard Footman Original: found
NP-607	West, Edward	3 APR 1769	East Branch Susquehanna River	LD: Columbia	300		Original: Signed by William West, Jr.
NP-608	Cathrall, Isaac	3 APR 1769		Rostraver, Westmoreland	300	D-57-200	Joseph Hill Original: found
NP-609	Keppele, Henry	3 APR 1769		Turbot, Northumberland	300	D-57-199	Michael Roger Original: found

Table 6 - New Purchase Applications (1769-1773)

Number	Applicant	Date	Orig. Place	Later Place	Acres	Survey	Neighbors, Notes, etc.
NP-610	Wetherhill, Joseph	3 APR 1769		North Branch Susquehanna River, Luzerne/ LD: Luzerne	300	W-271	Robert Hogg Original: Damaged - part missing
NP-611	Elder, Robert	3 APR 1769	Cumberland	LD: Somerset	300		Rebecca Crute Original: found
NP-612	Maurer, Nicholas	3 APR 1769	Berks	Washington, Lycoming	300	D-57-197	Hugh Kull/[see caveat] Original: found
NP-613	Shearer, William & Henry Shrihack	3 APR 1769		Luzerne, Fayette	600	B-17-64 B-17-66 A-88-32 A-88-33 B-17-65 B-17-67	(r3 FEB 1798)Robert Adams/(r8 MAR 1815)A. Porter/Stephen Fields/[see caveat] Original: found
NP-614	Litton, Martin	3 APR 1769	Cumberland	Nippenose, Lycoming	300	D-60-234 D-60-248 B-172	(r3 JUL 1807)Henry Drinker/John Litton Original: found
NP-615	Erb, Philip	3 APR 1769	Berks	Buffalo, Union	300	D-57-195 D-57-196	Original: found
NP-616	Walker, John	3 APR 1769	White Deer Creek at West Branch Susquehanna River	LD: Union	100		Original: Signed by William Walker
NP-617	West, William Jr.	3 APR 1769	Northumberland	Northeast Branch Susquehanna River, Luzerne	300	B-495	(r14 APR 1783)John M. Nesbitt Original: Signed
NP-618	Smallman, Thomas	3 APR 1769	Washington	Hopewell, Beaver/ LD: Hopewell, Beaver	300	C-146-29 W-273 W-274 W-275 W-276	(r15 OCT 1838)Andrew McDowell/Alexander McKee/[see caveat] Original: Signed
NP-619	Clark, John Jr.	3 APR 1769	East Branch Susquehanna River	LD: Columbia	250		Original: Signed
NP-620	Pumroy, John	3 APR 1769		Derry, Westmoreland	300	C-159-155	(r14 DEC 1804)/George Pumroy/Thomas Barr/John Leasure Original: found

Table 6 - New Purchase Applications (1769-1773)

Number	Applicant	Date	Orig. Place	Later Place	Acres	Survey	Neighbors, Notes, etc.
NP-621	Graham, John	3 APR 1769	Monongahela River	LD: Westmoreland/ Elizabeth, Allegheny	200		Original: found
NP-622	Latta, Moses	3 APR 1769		South Huntingdon, Westmoreland	300	C-82-80 C-87-216	(r10 JUL 1804 & 30 JUL 1803)James Hamilton/James Witherington Original: found
NP-623	Larimon, David	3 APR 1769	Washington	Monongahela River & Muddy Creek, Greene	300	C-35-238	(r19 FEB 1789)Oliver Crawford Original: found
NP-624	St. Clair, Daniel	3 APR 1769		Ligonier, Westmoreland	300	D-57-226 D-60-251 X-144	(r16 APR 1903)Elizabeth F. Denny heirs Original: found
NP-625	Doughton, John	3 APR 1769		Loyalsock, Lycoming & Pike, Clearfield	300	D-57-193 D-57-194	Original: found
NP-626	Chapman, James	3 APR 1769	Berks	Mahoning Creek, Montour	300	Y-40	(r12 APR 1797)Samuel Wallis/John Rich Original: found
NP-627	Murray, John	3 APR 1769		Loyalsock, Lycoming	300	D-57-192	Original: found
NP-628	Bishop, John	3 APR 1769	Cumberland	Youghiogheny River, Fayette	300	A-64-95	(r18 FEB 1782)General (George) Washington/Col. Washington Original: found
NP-629	Brown, Marth	3 APR 1769		Bald Eagle, Mifflin	300	C-219-46	(r31 MAR 1798)James Poe/[patent P-33-570] Original: found
NP-630	Lautermilk, Melchoir	3 APR 1769	West Branch Susquehanna River	LD: Northumberland	300		Original: found
NP-631	Coale, Sarah Sr.	3 APR 1769	Cumberland	Stoneycreek, Somerset/ LD: Stony Creek, Somerset	300		Margaret Coale Original: found
NP-632	Torrence, Hugh	3 APR 1769	Muncy Creek	LD: Lycoming	300		Original: found
NP-633	Walker, John	3 APR 1769	West Branch Susquehanna River	LD: Clinton	300		Original: Signed by William Walker
NP-634	Forster, John	3 APR 1769		Nippenose, Lycoming	300	D-57-34	Original: found

Table 6 - New Purchase Applications (1769-1773)

Number	Applicant	Date	Orig. Place	Later Place	Acres	Survey	Neighbors, Notes, etc.
NP-635	Dabsong, Joseph	3 APR 1769	Berks	Kelly, Union/ LD: Union	300	D-57-54 D-57-55	Mr. Hewing Original: found
NP-636	Riddle, John	3 APR 1769	Berks	Washington, Lycoming	300	D-57-33	William McEmory Original: found
NP-637	David, Enoch	3 APR 1769	Laurel Hill, Cumberland	LD: Fayette	300		Joseph Hunter/[see caveat] Original: found
NP-638	Hatfield, John	3 APR 1769	Berks	Nippenose, Lycoming	300	D-62-280 C-42-49	(r16 AUG 1838)T. Chambers Original: found
NP-639	Dillwyn, William	3 APR 1769		Muncy, Lycoming	300	D-56-122 A-2-203	(r22 APR 1809)Benjamin Courson Original: found
NP-640	Druckenmiller, Ludwig	3 APR 1769	Cumberland	Plum, Allegheny	300	D-62-96	Philip Weichel/Christian Wunder Original: found
NP-641	Roddy, James Jr.	3 APR 1769		Northeast Branch Susquehanna River, Luzerne	200		Original: found
NP-642	West, Francis	3 APR 1769		Northeast Branch Susquehanna River, Luzerne/ LD: Luzerne	100	A-29-34	Original: Signed by William West, Jr.
NP-643	Mitchell, Ross	3 APR 1769	Bald Eagle Creek	LD: Clinton/ Centre	300		James Mitchell Original: found
NP-644	Boyd, Samuel	3 APR 1769	Chillisquaque Creek		300		Original: found
NP-645	Elliott, Benjamin	3 APR 1769		Blacklick, Indiana	300	B-23-17 B-23-18	Original: found
NP-646	Eberly, George	3 APR 1769	Washington	Hopewell, Beaver	300	D-1-156	(r24 DEC 1830)James Marmock/Robert Moon Original: found
NP-647	Robinson, James	3 APR 1769	Berks	East Branch Susquehanna River, Northumberland	300	N-155	(r2 JUL 1773)Richard Robinson/[see caveat] Original: found
NP-648	Miller, George	3 APR 1769	Cumberland	West Buffalo, Union	150	D-57-53	Simon Merca/Christopher Man/George Esweiler Original: found
NP-649	Zorn, Christian	3 APR 1769		East Branch Susquehanna River, Luzerne	300	C-222-262	(r8 AUG 1781)Joseph Wharton/Jacob Waltman Original: found

Table 6 - New Purchase Applications (1769-1773)

Number	Applicant	Date	Orig. Place	Later Place	Acres	Survey	Neighbors, Notes, etc.
NP-650	Alen, William	3 APR 1769		North Huntingdon, Westmoreland/ LD: North Huntingdon, Westmoreland	300	D-57-48	[see caveat] Original: found
NP-651	Harding, Philip	3 APR 1769	Berks	Chillisquaque Creek, Northumberland	300	A-77-93	(r27 FEB 1800)A. Marks Biddle Original: found
NP-652	Baker, John	3 APR 1769		Unity, Westmoreland	300	D-57-63	John Proctor Original: found
NP-653	Pfeffer, Philip (of Heidelberg, Lancaster County)	3 APR 1769	Berks	Buffalo, Union	300	D-57-263	Jacob Gimberling/[same land as NP-201 to Martin Hefflefinger]/[see caveat] Original: found
NP-654	Meyer, John	3 APR 1769	East Branch Susquehanna River	LD: Bradford	300		John Flipson Original: found
NP-655	Frankson, John	3 APR 1769		Chartiers Creek, Washington	300	A-10-146	(r23 SEP 1788)John Bell/[patent P-14-280]/[see caveat] Original: found
NP-656	Smith, Thomas	3 APR 1769	Berks	White Deer, Union	200	D-57-52	Margaret Blyth Original: found
NP-657	Benham, William	3 APR 1769	Cumberland	Franklin, Westmoreland	300	D-57-47	Richard Buttler Original: found
NP-658	Rees, Hannah	3 APR 1769	Berks	Buffalo, Union	300	D-57-195 D-55-90 C-46-39	(r18 MAR 1814)Daniel Christ Original: found
NP-659	Moore, Thomas	3 APR 1769	Westmoreland	Wilkins, Allegheny	300	C-176-291 C-111-151 C-111-152	(r13 OCT 1832)Peter Parchment, Jr./(p14 MAY 1868)James Kelley/Daniel Elliott Original: found
NP-660	Starett, Ralph	3 APR 1769	Berks	Buffalo, Union	300	D-57-195 D-57-196	[same land as NP-615 to Philip Erb] Original: found
NP-661	Jewell, George	3 APR 1769	Berks	Mahoning Creek, Montour	300	A-6-269 A-6-290 C-135-148	(r12 DEC 1770)John Scull/(r2 OCT 1783)William Montgomery, Esq. Original: found
NP-662	Baker, William	3 APR 1769	Berks	Chillisquaque Creek, Northumberland	300		(r30 MAY 1795)Joseph Haines & Jonathan Haines, executors of Bartholomew Haines/Levi Hicks Original: found

Table 6 - New Purchase Applications (1769-1773)

Number	Applicant	Date	Orig. Place	Later Place	Acres	Survey	Neighbors, Notes, etc.
NP-663	Stephan, John	3 APR 1769		East Branch Susquehanna River, Luzerne/ LD: Luzerne	300	W-280	Henry Frank Original: found
NP-664	Hollingsworth, Jehu	3 APR 1769	Bedford	Wilkins, Allegheny/ LD: Wilkins, Allegheny	300	D-62-95 A-80 C-141-290 C-69-108	(r10 MAR 1852)John McCracken heirs/(r10 MAR 1852)David Gilliland heirs Original: Signed
NP-665	Dean, James	3 APR 1769	Buffalo Creek	LD: Union	300		William Winter Original: found
NP-666	Lands, Benjamin	3 APR 1769	Berks	Loyalsock Creek, Lycoming	300	A-39-206	(r18 APR 1770)Margaret Duncan Original: found
NP-667	Werner, Frederick	3 APR 1769		Huntingdon, Westmoreland	300	A-62-47 A-62-46	(r16 FEB 1787)Christopher Hays Original: found
NP-668	Stamp, Ann	3 APR 1769	Cumberland	LD: Luzerne	300		James Steel Original: found
NP-669	Gilbert, Michael Jr.	3 APR 1769	Berks	White Deer, Union	300	D-62-224 A-9-28	(r17 SEP 1772) Original: found
NP-670	Ward, Joseph	3 APR 1769	Berks	Buffalo, Union	300	D-57-51	Original: found
NP-671	Dillworth, James	3 APR 1769	Cumberland	Chest, Clearfield	300	D-57-61	Elizabeth Walter Original: found
NP-672	Beaver, William	3 APR 1769	Cumberland	Bald Eagle Creek, Centre/ LD: Centre	300		Samuel Willson Original: found
NP-673	Erwin, James	3 APR 1769	Cumberland	Findlay, Allegheny	300	D-57-75	James Crawford Original: found
NP-674	Baldwin, Thomas	3 APR 1769	West Branch Susquehanna River & Pine Creek	LD: Lycoming	300		Original: Signed
NP-675	Foster, Thomas Sr.	3 APR 1769	Berks	Buffalo, Union	300	D-62-276 D-62-283 D-55-33 D-55-34 D-55-35 D-55-43 C-176-114	(r3 JUN 1776)Thomas Rees Original: found

Table 6 - New Purchase Applications (1769-1773)

Number	Applicant	Date	Orig. Place	Later Place	Acres	Survey	Neighbors, Notes, etc.
NP-676	Johnston, James	3 APR 1769		East Huntingdon, Westmoreland	300	D-57-46	Moses Latta Original: found
NP-677	Pawling, John	3 APR 1769		Allegheny, Westmoreland	300	D-57-60	Original: Signed
NP-678	Duffield, John	3 APR 1769	White Deer Hole Creek	LD: Union	300		Original: found
NP-679	Withington, Peter	3 APR 1769		Loyalsock, Lycoming	300	D-57-32	Charles Biddle/Robert Galbraith Original: found
NP-680	Portter, John	3 APR 1769	Conemaugh River	LD: Indiana/ Westmoreland	300		Original: found
NP-681	Claypoole, James (of Philadelphia)	3 APR 1769		Fishing Creek branch of Bald Eagle Creek, Clinton	300	C-25-114	(r15 JAN 1784)Mathew Clarkson/Joseph Claypoole, Jr./[see caveat] Original: Signed
NP-682	Ralph, James	3 APR 1769	Cumberland	Rostraver, Westmoreland	300	A-48-56	(r1 SEP 1787)Eleanor Dehaus & John Dehaus & John Woods, Esq./James Burd/[see caveat] Original: found
NP-683	Harris, James	3 APR 1769	West Branch Susquehanna River	LD: Lycoming	300		Original: found
NP-684	Elliott, Thomas	3 APR 1769		Unity, Westmoreland	300	D-56-67 C-2-1	(r15 JAN 1812)Philip Ackerman Original: found
NP-685	Dyar, Alexander	3 APR 1769		Mifflin, Northumberland	300	E-339	(r12 AUG 1809)John Morgan & J. Simpson Original: found
NP-686	Habichar, George	3 APR 1769	Berks	Washington, Lycoming	300	D-57-31	Original: Signed
NP-687	Clark, James Jr.	3 APR 1769	Susquehanna River & Muncy Creek	LD: Lycoming	300		[see caveat] Original: Signed
NP-688	Gillispie, William	3 APR 1769		Turbot, Northumberland	300	A-51-263	(r1 APR 1782) Original: found
NP-689	Rennard, John	3 APR 1769	Chillisquaque Creek	LD: Northumberland/ Montour	300		Col. Francis/--- Montour Original: found
NP-690	Gorrell, Isabell	3 APR 1769	Cumberland	LD: Somerset/ Westmoreland	300		Martha Knight Original: found

Table 6 - New Purchase Applications (1769-1773)

Number	Applicant	Date	Orig. Place	Later Place	Acres	Survey	Neighbors, Notes, etc.
NP-691	Hill, Frederick	3 APR 1769		Augusta, Northumberland	300		(r26 MAY 1802)Jacob Conrad/Deitrick Mathew/[see NP-427] Original: found
NP-692	Morris, Anthony	3 APR 1769	Cumberland	Berks - Augusta, Northumberland	300	K-256	(r7 MAR 1832)Jane Clark/John Carmalt Original: found
NP-693	Sutten, John	3 APR 1769	Westmoreland	on Forbes Road, Allegheny	300	A-32-152	(r14 APR 1796)William Ward Burrows Original: Signed
NP-694	McGachey, Robert	3 APR 1769	Delaware Run & West Branch Susquehanna River	LD: Northumberland	300		Original: found
NP-695	McDowell, James, Jr.	3 APR 1769		Spring Hill & Georges, Fayette/ LD: Spring Hill & Georges, Fayette	---	A-52-196 B-4-21 B-4-22	(r13 JUN 1798)Charles Guffie/John Griffith Original: found
NP-696	Small, John	3 APR 1769		Huntingdon, Westmoreland	300	C-19-108	(r25 SEP 1787)William Beard/Robert Small Original: found
NP-697	Wallace, James	3 APR 1769		Blacklick, Indiana	300	A-29-35 A-29-36	William Rainey Carlisle/[see caveat] Original: found
NP-698	McDowell, William	3 APR 1769	Berks	White Deer, Union	300	D-56-226 D-56-227 C-197-155	(r15 MAR 1773)Edward Shippen & Joseph Shippen/Alexander McCurdy Original: found
NP-699	Smith, Jonathan Sr.	3 APR 1769	Bedford	Youghiogheny River, Westmoreland - Allegheny	200	A-5-302	(r24 NOV 1788)Robert Jameson & Mathew Jameson/Jose Ryles Original: found
NP-700	Pedan, John	3 APR 1769	Berks - Cumberland	Northumberland - Buffalo, Union	200	C-35-276	(r13 FEB 1790)John Clark Original: found
NP-701	Bonnell, Thomas	3 APR 1769		West Branch Susquehanna River, Lycoming/LD: Lycoming	300		Samuel Nicholas Original: found

Table 6 - New Purchase Applications (1769-1773)

Number	Applicant	Date	Orig. Place	Later Place	Acres	Survey	Neighbors, Notes, etc.
NP-702	Hammon, John	3 APR 1769		North East Branch Susquehanna River, Luzerne/LD: Luzerne	300	A-249	Original: found
NP-703	Dunlap, John	3 APR 1769	Berks	Limestone, Lycoming	300	A-75-184	(r7 OCT 1836)S. Stewart Original: Signed
NP-704	Sherack, John	3 APR 1769	Berks	West Buffalo, Union	300	D-68-238 A-21-280	(r23 DEC 1794)Jeremiah Parker/[see caveat] Original: found
NP-705	Butler, Thomas Jr.	3 APR 1769		North Huntingdon, Westmoreland	300	C-149-6 C-149-100	(r12 FEB 1816)James A. McGrew Original: Signed
NP-706	Smith, John	3 APR 1769		Augusta, Northumberland	300	D-6-169	Peter Boor/(r20 FEB 1811)Samuel Wright & James Wright Original: found
NP-707	Worthington, Mary	3 APR 1769		LD: Somerset	300		Ann Hopkins Original: found
NP-708	Smallman, Thomas	3 APR 1769		North Huntingdon, Westmoreland	300	D-57-48 W-281 C-160-106	Col. John Reed/(r15FEB 1797)John Probst Original: Signed
NP-709	Blane, Elinor	3 APR 1769		Wilkins, Allegheny	300	D-57-74	James Kelly/(w27 JUN 1786)E. McCollister Original: found
NP-710	Craike, Thomas	3 APR 1769		Augusta, Northumberland/ LD: Columbia	300	D-57-62	Original: found
NP-711	Armstrong, William, Jr.	3 APR 1769	Northumberland	White Deer, Union	300	D-55-58 D-55-59 A-11-190	William Gill/(r15 MAY 1794)Samuel Dale, Esq. Original: found
NP-712	McCawley, John	3 APR 1769	Berks	Chillisquaque Creek, , Northumberland	300	C-39-194	(r19 NOV 1772)John DeHaas Original: found
NP-713	Rairdon, Edward	3 APR 1769		Turbot, Northumberland	300	D-56-215 Q-12	John Stephens/Moses Kirk/(r21 JUN 1774)Cornelius Atkinson Original: found

Table 6 - New Purchase Applications (1769-1773)

Number	Applicant	Date	Orig. Place	Later Place	Acres	Survey	Neighbors, Notes, etc.
NP-714	Edwards, Richard	3 APR 1769	Berks	Kelly, Union	300	D-56-85 D-56-91 D-56-92 D-56-93 D-56-94 D-56-95 D-56-260 D-55-37 C-156-84 C-156-85	William Wishad/(r5 JUL 1823)Roan McClure/[see caveat] Original: found
NP-715	Johnston, Samuel	3 APR 1769		Northeast Branch Susquehanna River, Luzerne/ LD: Providence, Luzerne	300	M-513	Original: found
NP-716	Duncan, Daniel	3 APR 1769		Unity, Westmoreland	300	D-57-59	Abraham Bishure Original: found
NP-717	Crush, John	3 APR 1769		Hopewell & Moon, Beaver	300	B-23-19	Original: Signed
NP-718	Smith, Jacob	3 APR 1769	Cumberland	Buffalo, Union	300	D-57-45	Jacob Shaffer/Mathias Shaffer/Charles Shaffer Original: found
NP-719	Keyser, Conrad	3 APR 1769	Northumberland	Buffalo, Union	300	A-65-208	Mathias Krum/(r3 JUN 1773)Jacob Frick Original: found
NP-720	Hopkins, Susanna	3 APR 1769	Berks	Chillisquaque Creek, Northumberland	300	S-168	(r31 MAY 1796)Owen Biddle Original: found
NP-721	Stewart, Archibald	3 APR 1769		Northeast Branch Susquehanna River, Luzerne	300	A-11-83	(r5 MAR 1774) Original: found
NP-722	McDonnal, Alexander (son of Duncan McDonnel, of Derry Tonwship, Cumberland County)	3 APR 1769	Bald Eagle Creek	LD: Clinton/ Centre	300		Jonathan Robinson Original: Signed
NP-723	Gregg, John	3 APR 1769	Berks	White Deer, Union	300	D-57-30 C-44-151	[see caveat] Original: found

Table 6 - New Purchase Applications (1769-1773)

Number	Applicant	Date	Orig. Place	Later Place	Acres	Survey	Neighbors, Notes, etc.
NP-724	Hill, Joseph	3 APR 1769		LD: Columbia	300		Henry Paul, Jr. Original: found
NP-725	Crawford, Josiah	3 APR 1769	Cumberland	Bedford - Monongahela River, Fayette	300	C-23-125	(r16 NOV 1772) Original: found
NP-726	Breden, James	3 APR 1769	Chillisquaque Creek		300		[see caveat] Original: found
NP-727	Topham, Daniel	3 APR 1769		Turbot, Northumberland	300	A-69-248	John Smith/(r3 DEC 1811)James Wright & William Wright Original: found
NP-728	Hervey, John	3 APR 1769	Bedford	Derry, Westmoreland	300	C-35-211	James Gullerys(r11 APR 1786)Robert Crawford Original: found
NP-729	Horsely, Richard	3 APR 1769	Mounts Creek, Cumberland	LD: Fayette	300		Lewis Deval Original: found
NP-730	Marshall, Thomas	3 APR 1769		Washington, Lycoming	300	D-57-25	Caleb Hewett Original: found
NP-731	Allen, Samuel Jr.	3 APR 1769	Northumberland	West Branch Susquehanna River, Union	300	C-436	(r15 JUN 1797)Casper W. Haines & Josiah Matlack [Exrs. of Reuben Haines, deceased] Original: found
NP-732	Ward, Edward Sr.	3 APR 1769	Cumberland	Bald Eagle Creek, Centre/ LD: Clinton/ Centre	300		Margaret Bradford Original: found
NP-733	Buchanon, William	3 APR 1769	Berks	Buffalo, Union/ LD: Buffalo, Union	300	D-57-43 D-57-44 D-57-42	Original: found
NP-734	Nesbitt, John	3 APR 1769	Berks	Loyalsock, Lycoming	300	D-56-31 D-57-32 D-62-266 D-62-274 D-62-298 N-251	(r3 APR 1772) Original: found
NP-735	Smith, John	3 APR 1769	Berks	Buffalo, Union	300	D-56-71	[same land as NP-2336 to Peter Braght] Original: found
NP-736	Nicholson, William	3 APR 1769		East Branch Susquehanna River, Bradford	300	F-162	(r10 APR 1775)Archibald Stewert Original: found

Table 6 - New Purchase Applications (1769-1773)

Number	Applicant	Date	Orig. Place	Later Place	Acres	Survey	Neighbors, Notes, etc.
NP-737	Stringer, James	3 APR 1769		10 or 12 miles from Ft. Pitt, Allegheny	300	C-139-186	(r8 DEC 1807)William McCrea Original: Signed
NP-738	Lindsay, William Jr.	3 APR 1769		Huntingdon, Westmoreland	300	C-142-59	(r25 FEB 1799)Casper Merklin Original: found
NP-739	Crookes, Hendry	3 APR 1769		Augusta, Northumberland	100	T-276	(r23 FEB 1804) Original: found
NP-740	Harwickel, William	3 APR 1769	Berks	Kelly, Union	---	D-57-29	Mr. Ewing Original: found
NP-741	Smallman, Thomas	3 APR 1769		Pitt, Allegheny	300	H-98	Capt. William/Col. Reed/(r16 FEB 1811)James O'Harra Original: Signed
NP-742	Laird, Hugh	3 APR 1769	Berks	White Deer, Union	300	D-62-224 D-62-225	[same land as NP-2779 to Philip Kline] Original: found
NP-743	Williams, John	3 APR 1769		Mifflin, Allegheny	300	D-57-73	Original: found
NP-744	Beaver, Blanch	3 APR 1769		Little Fishing Creek, Columbia/ LD: Columbia	300		John Jolley Original: found
NP-745	McDowell, William Jr.	3 APR 1769		Unity, Westmoreland	300	D-56-57 D-60-255 B-23-68 C-136-48	Robert Bennefield/(r9 AUG 1770) Original: found
NP-746	Gregg, James	3 APR 1769	Muncy Creek	LD: Lycoming	300		John Kerr/James Douglas Original: Signed
NP-747	Wabel, John	3 APR 1769	East Branch Susquehanna River	LD: Wyoming/ Bradford	300		Bartholomew Brodhack Original: found
NP-748	Willson, Hugh	3 APR 1769	mouth of White Deer Creek	LD: Union	300		Original: Missing
NP-749	Riche, Mary	3 APR 1769	White Deer Hole Creek	LD: Lycoming	300		Sarah Riche Original: found
NP-750	Dixon, Joseph	3 APR 1769	Westmoreland	Blacklick, Indiana/ LD: Indiana/ Cambria	300	A-67-181	(r30 MAR 1870)Charles Campbell Original: Missing

Table 6 - New Purchase Applications (1769-1773)

Number	Applicant	Date	Orig. Place	Later Place	Acres	Survey	Neighbors, Notes, etc.
NP-751	Doudle, George	3 APR 1769		West Branch Muncy Creek, Lycoming/ LD: Lycoming	300		Original: found
NP-752	Gray, Thomas	3 APR 1769		Muncy Creek Twp., Lycoming	300	D-57-24	Frederick Martin Original: found
NP-753	Brinkhoff, Henry	3 APR 1769	Rush Meadow Creek, Northampton	LD: Wayne/ Bradford	300		Christopher Gaseman Original: Missing
NP-754	Maus, Phillip	3 APR 1769		Mahoning Creek, Montour	300	A-494 C-179-52	Morris Turner/Elijah Wickerson/(r10 AUG 1774) Original: found
NP-755	McDowell, Robert	3 APR 1769	Youghiogheny River	LD: Fayette	300		--- Sheart/Samuel McFarren Original: found
NP-756	McGlathry, Matthew	3 APR 1769		Augusta, Northumberland	300	N-258	Hugh Williamson/(r5 SEP 1783)John Nixon & Alexander Forster Original: found
NP-757	Clark, Jacob	3 APR 1769		Lawrence & Bradford, Clearfield	300	D-57-56	Original: found
NP-758	Segar, Christopher	3 APR 1769	"Mahoney Hill", north side Susquehanna River	LD: Montour	300		Original: found
NP-759	Corey, Daniel	3 APR 1769	Northampton	Waverly Borough, Lackawanna/ LD: Luzerne	300	H-159	Joseph Corey/(r20 JAN 1913)George E. Stevenson Original: found
NP-760	McKinzey, John	3 APR 1769		Blacklick, Indiana	300	D-56-160 A-83-233 D-28-162	(r8 AUG 1783)White Matlack Original: found
NP-761	Harris, Samuel	3 APR 1769	Northumberland	Fishing Creek branch of Bald Eagle Creek, Clinton	300	A-57-231	(r16 DEC 1772)Phillip Francis, Jr., Esq. Original: found
NP-762	Plumer, Mary	3 APR 1769	Berks	Turbot, Northumberland - Montour/ Turbot, LD: Northumberland	300	A-226	Original: found

Table 6 - New Purchase Applications (1769-1773)

Number	Applicant	Date	Orig. Place	Later Place	Acres	Survey	Neighbors, Notes, etc.
NP-763	Greer, James	3 APR 1769	Cumberland	Hempfield, Westmoreland	300	B-23-43	John Greer/James Boyle Original: found
NP-764	Moore, James (of Tyrone Township, Cumberland County)	3 APR 1769		Hempfield & Huntingdon, Westmoreland	300	D-57-58	Nathaniel Nilson Original: Signed
NP-765	Richards, Samuel	3 APR 1769		Washington & Clinton, Lycoming/ LD: Clinton, Lycoming	300	D-63-94 C-28-183 C-28-184 C-28-185 C-118-142	(r31 MAR 1831)Charles Low & Ann Low (his wife)/(r5 MAR 1831)Thomas Clark Original: found
NP-766	Duncan, William	3 APR 1769		Derry, Westmoreland	300	D-57-57	John Punroy/James Barr/John Pamer Original: found
NP-767	Bunn, Nicholas	3 APR 1769		Loyalsock, Lycoming	300	D-57-23	Original: found
NP-768	Cosselman, Wernet	3 APR 1769	East Branch Susquehanna River	LD: Wyoming	300		Henry Kling Original: found
NP-769	Piper, John	3 APR 1769	East Branch Bald Eagle Creek	LD: Centre	300		Original: Signed
NP-770	Armstrong, William (of Cumberland County, farmer)	3 APR 1769	Cumberland	Bedford - Unity, Westmoreland	300	A-38-213	(r23 MAR 1785)Lawrence Irwin Original: found
NP-771	Bear, Martin	3 APR 1769	East Branch Susquehanna River	LD: Luzerne/ Columbia/ Montour	300		Henry Grove Original: found
NP-772	Mitcheltree, Margaret	3 APR 1769	between Loyalsock & Lycoming Creeks	LD: Lycoming	300		Original: found
NP-773	Downey, John	3 APR 1769		Turbot, Northumberland	300	D-57-41	John Tenist Original: found
NP-774	Jones, Thomas	3 APR 1769	Cumberland	Westmoreland - Youghiogheny River, Fayette	300	E-19	John Paty/William Althoe/(r18 FEB 1782)Genl. Washington Original: found
NP-775	Pearson, Samuel	3 APR 1769	Berks	White Deer, Union	300	D-56-114 A-19-38	(r5 MAY 1789)John Cox, Esq./[see caveat] Original: found
NP-776	Ruthanburger, Adam	3 APR 1769	Northumberland	Muncy, Lycoming	300	A-16-139 A-16-140	(r11 JAN 1796)Samuel Wallis Original: found
NP-777	Harrison, John	3 APR 1769	Cumberland	Browns Run, Fayette	300	A-60-278	Casper Eder/Robert Harrison/(r7 APR 1787) Original: Signed

Table 6 - New Purchase Applications (1769-1773)

Number	Applicant	Date	Orig. Place	Later Place	Acres	Survey	Neighbors, Notes, etc.
NP-778	Hacket, Andrew	3 APR 1769	a mile from Bald Eagle Creek	LD: Centre	300		Original: found
NP-779	Wickersham, Elijah	3 APR 1769	Northumberland	Mahoning Creek, Montour	300	D-13-271	Maurice Turner/(r8 SEP 1773)Amos Wickersham Original: Signed by Maurice Turner
NP-780	Merryweather, Reuben	3 APR 1769	Berks	Kelly, Union	300		[same land as NP-2225 to Breeson Bowden] Original: found
NP-781	Dallam, Winston	3 APR 1769	Northumberland	Howard, Centre	300	A-79-295	Richard Dallam/(r6 OCT 1788)Eleanor Dehaas & John Dehaas Original: found
NP-782	Fullerton, George	3 APR 1769	Berks	West Branch Susquehanna River, Northumberland	300	A-58-230	(r3 APR 1772)Turbutt Francis, Esq. Original: found
NP-783	Ferry, Frederick	3 APR 1769		Ligonier - Ft. Pitt Road, Allegheny	300	B-273	(r12 MAR 1791)John Fance [or Ferry] Original: found
NP-784	Stephen, Andrew	3 APR 1769	Berks	White Deer, Union	300	D-57-26 D-57-27 D-57-28 D-57-40	Original: found
NP-785	Hess, Henry	3 APR 1769		"Lohawano" [Lackawanna?], about 4 miles from the mouth, Luzerne/ LD: Luzerne	300		Original: found
NP-786	Potter, James Jr.	3 APR 1769		Elizabeth, Allegheny/ LD: Elizabeth, Allegheny	300	D-57-72	Issac Martin Original: found
NP-787	Hare, Peter	3 APR 1769	Bald Eagle Creek	LD: Centre	300		Original: found
NP-788	Ryan, Daniel	3 APR 1769	Berks	Washington, Lycoming	300	C-42-16	(r9 JAN 1838)Daniel Caldwell/[see caveat] Original: found
NP-789	Barr, Robert	3 APR 1769	Bedford	Rostraver, Westmoreland	300	B-23-49 C-145	William McCune/Hugh Gibbs/(r26 MAR 1838)Paul Clark & William Clark Original: Signed by Robert Barr and John Barr

Table 6 - New Purchase Applications (1769-1773)

Number	Applicant	Date	Orig. Place	Later Place	Acres	Survey	Neighbors, Notes, etc.
NP-790	Carruthers, Rebecca	3 APR 1769		Huntingdon, Westmoreland	300	W-10	"where John Montgomery was shot"/(r5 MAY 1790)James Caruthers/[see caveat] Original: found
NP-791	Hannah, Robert	3 APR 1769		Hempfield, Westmoreland	300	C-207-119	Col. Wilkins/(r5 SEP 1826)John Steel Original: Signed
NP-792	Work, Jacob	3 APR 1769	Cumberland	Bedford - Jenner, Somerset	300	I-18	(r20DEC 1820)John B. Alexander Original: found
NP-793	Coale, Skipwith	3 APR 1769	Northumberland	Spring, Centre	300	N-210	Joseph Hopkins, Jr./(r27 OCT 1783)Samuel Wallis Original: found
NP-794	Simpson, Samuel	3 APR 1769	Northumberland	Spring, Centre	300	A-40-40	(r3 FEB 1784) Original: found
NP-795	Collins, Mary	3 APR 1769	Northumberland	Little Fishing Creek, Clinton	300	A-27-250	Stephen Collins/(r15 JUN 1802)John Bidde & Thomas Stewardson Original: found
NP-796	Jones, Isaac	3 APR 1769		Warrior Run, Northumberland	300	A-24-125	William Baskins/(r8 JAN 1773) Original: Signed
NP-797	Thompson, Robert (of Donegal Township, Lancaster County)	3 APR 1769	Bald Eagle Creek	LD: Centre	300		Original: Signed
NP-798	Latimer, Margaret	3 APR 1769		South side Youghiogheny River, Bedford	300	A-60-270	--- Saltman [called John Tollsman on survey]/--- Crawford/(r17 MAY 1787)Matthew Henderson/[applicant called Margaret Lattimore on survey] Original: found
NP-799	Hiltzheimer, Jacob	3 APR 1769	Northeast branch Susquehanna River	LD: Luzerne	300		Original: found
NP-800	Johnston, David	3 APR 1769	Berks	Northumberland - Hartley, Union	300	D-60-191 C-120-224	(r21 AUG 1787)William McClay, Esq. Original: found
NP-801	Stephenson, Rachel	3 APR 1769	Cumberland	Northumberland or Montour/ LD: Northumberland/ Montour	300		William Stephenson Original: found

Table 6 - New Purchase Applications (1769-1773)

Number	Applicant	Date	Orig. Place	Later Place	Acres	Survey	Neighbors, Notes, etc.
NP-802	Costor, John	3 APR 1769		Chillisquaque Creek, Northumberland/ LD: Northumberland	300		Joseph Gridley Original: found
NP-803	Calhoon, James	3 APR 1769		Huntingdon, Allegheny	300	V-88 C-173-29	Jane Thompson/(r23 NOV 1829)P. Meese, Jr. Original: found
NP-804	McMahon, James	3 APR 1769		Chillisquaque Creek, Columbia	300	C-116-218	James Murray/William Irwin/Thomas Flewitt/(r23 FEB 1790)/[see caveat] Original: found
NP-805	Breniman, Daniel	3 APR 1769		Loyalsock, Lycoming	300	D-57-22	Jacob Stoner Original: found
NP-806	Hambelton, Robert	3 APR 1769		Union, Fayette/ LD: Fayette	300	X-180 C-223-33 C-159-250	Josiah Rekas/(r5 SEP 1788)Samuel Work, Sr./(r18 MAR 1808)Isaac Philips Original: found
NP-807	Paul, Joseph	3 APR 1769			300		William Porter Original: found
NP-808	Horning, Peter	3 APR 1769	Northumberland	Buffalo, Union	300	C-163-253	(r15 DEC 1774)Thomas Reese Original: found
NP-809	McCoskry, Samuel Jr.	3 APR 1769	Berks	Chillisquaque Creek, Northumberland	300	A-39-216	Mr. Allens/Mr. Tilghman/(r23 JAN 1770)Issac Duncan Original: Signed by William McCoskry
NP-810	McKee, Alexander	3 APR 1769		South side Ohio River, Beaver/ LD: Beaver	300		Original: Signed
NP-811	Iredell, Robert Sr.	3 APR 1769	Berks	White Deer, Union	300	D-62-231	Abraham Lukens/[same land as NP-2778 to John Carmalt] Original: found
NP-812	Buchanon, John	3 APR 1769		Washington, Lycoming	300	D-57-21	Original: Signed
NP-813	Henry, William	3 APR 1769	Berks	Catawissa Town, Columbia	300	A-6-285	(r12 FEB 1770)Edward Shippen & Joseph Shippen Original: found
NP-814	Ehingeur, Daniel	3 APR 1769	Berks	Kelly, Union	300	D-57-39	Original: found
NP-815	Williamson, David	3 APR 1769	a branch of Chillisquaque Creek	LD: Northumberland	300		Original: found

Table 6 - New Purchase Applications (1769-1773)

Number	Applicant	Date	Orig. Place	Later Place	Acres	Survey	Neighbors, Notes, etc.
NP-816	Palmer, Thomas	3 APR 1769	Berks	Lower Augusta, Northumberland	150	C-157-159	(r17 JUL 1781)Major James Parr Original: found
NP-817	Cook, William (of Paxton)	3 APR 1769	Berks	White Deer, Union	300	D-57-38	Original: Signed by Robert Cook
NP-818	Hughes, Samuel	3 APR 1769		Washington, Lycoming	300	D-57-10	[see caveat] Original: found
NP-819	Springer, Josiah	3 APR 1769		Union, Fayette	300	D-62-170 C-91-236	(r5 MAY 1788)Jacob Knap Original: Signed
NP-820	Chambers, Ann	3 APR 1769	Berks	Kelly, Union	300	D-57-36 D-57-37	Original: found
NP-821	McCall, Michael	3 APR 1769	Chillisquaque Creek	LD: Chillisquaque, Northumberland/ Montour	300		Johanna Gale Original: found
NP-822	Alexander, David	3 APR 1769		Muncy Creek Twp., Lycoming	300	D-57-19	Original: found
NP-823	Roseberry, John, Michael Roseberry, & Philip Morris	3 APR 1769	Fishing Creek	LD: Columbia	900		Original: found
NP-824	Simpson, James	3 APR 1769	Berks	Buffalo, Union	300	D-57-35	Original: found
NP-825	Stewart, James Jr.	3 APR 1769	East Branch Susquehanna River	LD: Columbia	300		Original: A note on the original application reads "I deputize John Foster to take out a location in my name. Signed James Stewart, Juner."
NP-826	Montgomery, James	3 APR 1769		Pitt, Westmoreland	300	A-14-276	John Irwin/(r15 SEP 1789)Eli Coulter Original: found
NP-827	Brown, Elijah	3 APR 1769	five miles above the mouth of Wapwallopen Creek	LD: Luzerne	200		Original: Signed
NP-828	Wood, Abraham	3 APR 1769	Berks	Buffalo, Union	300	D-62-196 C-217-246	(r16 APR 1796)Stephen Toochman Original: found
NP-829	Grant, Alexander	3 APR 1769	8 miles above Ft. Augusta	LD: Northumberland	250		[see caveat] Original: found
NP-830	McCollogh, Samuel	3 APR 1769	Northeast Branch Susquehanna River	LD: Luzerne	300		Original: found
NP-831	Gibson, Hugh	3 APR 1769	Bald Eagle Creek	LD: Clinton	300		Dr. Allison Original: found

Table 6 - New Purchase Applications (1769-1773)

Number	Applicant	Date	Orig. Place	Later Place	Acres	Survey	Neighbors, Notes, etc.
NP-832	Campbell, Daniel	3 APR 1769		Loyalsock & Muncy, Lycoming	300	D-57-20	Joseph Champion Original: found
NP-833	Moote, Casper	3 APR 1769	Cumberland	Northumberland - Union, Union	300	D-63-99 A-18-238	(r23 APR 1773)Reuben Haines Original: found
NP-834	Espy, Josias	3 APR 1769	East Branch Susquehanna River & Fishing Creek	LD: Columbia	300		Original: A note on the original application reads "I deputize John Foster to take out a location in my name. Signed Josias Espy"
NP-835	Huling, John	3 APR 1769	Berks	Kelly, Union	300	D-56-278 D-56-279 D-56-280	James Warren/[see NP-1241 to George Blythe] Original: found
NP-836	Martin, Samuel	3 APR 1769	Berks	Turbot, Northumberland	300	D-60-261 M-333	Samuel Goudy/(r5 DEC 1774)John Miles Original: found
NP-837	Shannon, James	3 APR 1769		Elizabeth, Allegheny	300	D-57-71	John Shannon/[see caveat] Original: found
NP-838	Hamilton, James	3 APR 1769	Berks	Washington, Lycoming	300	D-57-6	Original: found
NP-839	Schwartz, Conrad	3 APR 1769		Wilkins, Allegheny	300	D-62-95	Casper Mickenfilder Original: found
NP-840	Morris, Phebe	3 APR 1769	West Branch Chillisquaque Creek	LD: Chillisquaque, Northumberland/ Montour	300		Mr. Allen Original: found
NP-841	Hubley, Adam	3 APR 1769		Northeast Branch Susquehanna River, Luzerne/ LD: Luzerne	300	A-36-12	Original: found
NP-842	Shoemaker, Thomas	3 APR 1769		Columbia/ LD: Columbia	300		Mary Willson Original: found
NP-843	Wall, Walter & James	3 APR 1769		Elizabeth, Allegheny/ LD: Elizabeth, Allegheny	300	D-62-99	Benjamin Aplegate Original: found
NP-844	Bowdon, Preeson	3 APR 1769			300		Hannah Willson Original: found

Table 6 - New Purchase Applications (1769-1773)

Number	Applicant	Date	Orig. Place	Later Place	Acres	Survey	Neighbors, Notes, etc.
NP-845	Wells, Mary	3 APR 1769		small branch of Youghiogheny River, Westmoreland	300	A-5-19	Peter Hodgson/James Pearson Original: found
NP-846	Lymson, William	3 APR 1769	North Branch Susquehanna River		300		--- McKee/(r14 NOV 1800)John Simpson Original: Out of order after NP-848
NP-847	Schaffner, Jacob	3 APR 1769	Cumberland	Berks - Buffalo, Union	300	D-57-42 D-57-44	[same land as NP-733 to William Buchanan] Original: Out of order after NP-848
NP-848	Pumroy, George	3 APR 1769		Derry, Westmoreland	300	A-69-78	John Pumroy/John Duncan/(r3 DEC 1787)John Pumroy Original: found
NP-849	Burkerk, Lorance	3 APR 1769	Cumberland	Versailles, Allegheny	300	D-62-94	Original: found
NP-850	Jarvis, Rebecca	3 APR 1769	Muncy Creek	LD: Lycoming	300		Mary Steele Original: found
NP-851	Power, William Jr.	3 APR 1769		Muncy Creek Twp., Lycoming	300	D-57-7	Original: found
NP-852	Hoofnagle, Peter	3 APR 1769		Washington, Lycoming	300	D-57-8	William Dunwich Original: found
NP-853	Bingman, William	3 APR 1769	Cumberland	Pitt, Westmoreland	300	C-104-69	Jacob Cuddy/(r17 MAY 1791)Wendel Keller Original: found
NP-854	Counselman, John	3 APR 1769		Wayne, Lycoming	300	A-23-19	(r28 JUL 1834)Thomas Chambers Original: found
NP-855	Harrison, Robert	3 APR 1769	Cumberland	German, Fayette	300	C-84-79	Gasper Edires/(r5 OCT 1784) Original: Signed
NP-856	Gibson, James	3 APR 1769	Berks	"Sinking Springs", Northumberland/ LD: Centre	300	H-487	Rev. Ewings Original: found
NP-857	Clark, Michael	3 APR 1769		White Deer Hole Creek, Lycoming	300		John Flahaven Original: found
NP-858	Riche, Grace	3 APR 1769	Cumberland	Bald Eagle Creek, Northumberland	300	E-134	(r9JUL 1782) Original: found
NP-859	Shoemaker, Jonathan	3 APR 1769		Columbia/ LD: Columbia	300		Cassander Wallis Original: found

Table 6 - New Purchase Applications (1769-1773)

Number	Applicant	Date	Orig. Place	Later Place	Acres	Survey	Neighbors, Notes, etc.
NP-860	Armstrong, Arthur	3 APR 1769	"Mud Lick including Buffalo Lick"		300		Original: Signed by Joseph Armstrong
NP-861	Hepburn, John Jr.	3 APR 1769	Berks	Derry, Columbia	300	C-131-32 C-115-20 C-131-32 C-131-33	Douty Gozin/(r25 APR 1793)John Linn/(r31 MAY 1817)Samuel Lowry Original: found
NP-862	Irvin, William	3 APR 1769	Cumberland	Elizabeth, Allegheny	300	C-172-125	(r 22 SEP 1788)Isaac Parr Original: found
NP-863	Butler, Thomas	3 APR 1769	Westmoreland	Tortoise Creek, Allegheny	300	C-130-218	William Evans/(r7 DEC 1795)Jeremiah Murray Original: Signed
NP-864	Polander, John Adam	3 APR 1769	Deep Run	LD: Lycoming	300		Original: found
NP-865	Armstrong, William Sr.	3 APR 1769	Northumberland	Washington, Lycoming	300	C-61-94 D-70-16 C-136-191	(r8 MAR 1815)R. Forsman/(r18 JAN 1833)Jacob McCurly Original: found
NP-866	Clin, John	3 APR 1769	Berks	Buffalo, Union/ LD: Union	300	D-57-12 D-57-13 D-57-14 D-57-15 D-57-16 D-57-17	Original: Signed
NP-867	Reese, Jacob	3 APR 1769	Berks	White Deer, Union	300	D-57-250 D-62-251 C-8-17	Ludwig Dar/Dietrick Reese/(r28 JAN 1773)Hawkins Boone Original: found
NP-868	James, Hugh	3 APR 1769	Berks	Muncy, Lycoming	300	D-57-234 D-57-243 D-57-244 D-56-146 Q-325	Samuel Purviance/(r6 DEC 1805)John Mckee Original: found
NP-869	Stiret, Charles	3 APR 1769		Hempfield, Westmoreland	300	C-150-24 C-209-166 C-209-180	(r18 APR 1810)William McKee, Jr./(r26 DEC 1814)John Stevenson Original: found
NP-870	Brown, Samuel	3 APR 1769		Lawrence & Bradford, Clearfield	300	D-57-56 D-56-106 C-139-143 C-139-142	(r9 NOV 1785)James Stewart/(r21 MAR 1807)J. B. McKean & James Miles Original: found
NP-871	Lehr, Henry	3 APR 1769	Berks	Buffalo, Union	300	D-57-11	Original: found

Table 6 - New Purchase Applications (1769-1773)

Number	Applicant	Date	Orig. Place	Later Place	Acres	Survey	Neighbors, Notes, etc.
NP-872	Bray, Andrew	3 APR 1769	Northampton	Lehigh River, Wyoming	300	B-560	(r13 FEB 1794)John M. Taylor Original: found
NP-873	McFadion, Thomas	3 APR 1769		Kelly, Union/ LD: Buffalo, Union	300	D-56-116 D-56-286 A-234 C-159-205	Rev. Ewing/(r9 MAY 1811)John Patterson/[see caveat] Original: found
NP-874	Leet, Isaac	3 APR 1769	Northeast Branch Susquehanna River	LD: Luzerne	100		Original: Signed by Daniel Leet
NP-875	Perry, Samuel	3 APR 1769		Elizabeth, Allegheny/ LD: Elizabeth, Allegheny	300	D-62-97	James Kelly/--- Smith Original: found
NP-876	Snivley, Barbara	3 APR 1769		Youghiogheny River, Allegheny/ LD: Allegheny	300		--- Pierce Original: found
NP-877	Kechlein, Peter	3 APR 1769		Lackawannock Creek, Luzerne/ LD: Luzerne	300		[see caveat] Original: found
NP-878	Klein, Philip	3 APR 1769	Northumberland	Sugarloaf, Luzerne	300	C-143-248	Jacob Seber/(r17 JUL 1781)John Nixon Original: found
NP-879	Spencer, Rowland	3 APR 1769	Berks	Chillisquaque Creek, Northumberland/ LD: Northumberland	300	W-282	John Gorrell Original: found
NP-880	Albright, George	3 APR 1769	Cumberland	Berks - Union, Union	300	D-62-218 D-62-219 A-70-77	John Mentzer/(r7 JUL 1774)/[see caveat] Original: found
NP-881	McDowell, James	3 APR 1769		Mt. Pleasant, Westmoreland	300	D-57-5	James Wetherinton Original: found
NP-882	Steel, Richard	3 APR 1769		Washington, Lycoming	300	D-57-10 D-60-185 D-60-226 D-62-291 C-91-182 C-86-31 C-91-162	James Caldwell/Hugh McCollester/(r19 JUN 1830)James Hammond/(r15 APR 1844)John Hunter Original: Signed

Table 6 - New Purchase Applications (1769-1773)

Number	Applicant	Date	Orig. Place	Later Place	Acres	Survey	Neighbors, Notes, etc.
NP-883	Neaf, Henry	3 APR 1769	East Branch Susquehanna River	LD: Luzerne	300		Casper Kohr Original: found
NP-884	Johnston, Robert	3 APR 1769	Berks	10 miles from Ft. Augusta, Northumberland	300	A-24-124	(r4 JAN 1773)Phillip Johnston Original: found
NP-885	Gelespey, John	3 APR 1769		Chillisquaque, Northumberland	300	C-71-188	John Blair/(r28 AUG 1801)William Gillespie heirs/[see caveat] Original: found
NP-886	Waltman, Jacob	3 APR 1769		East Branch Susquehanna River, Luzerne/ LD: Bradford	300	C-105-200	Original: found
NP-887	Miller, Martin	3 APR 1769	Cumberland	Berks - West Buffalo, Union	300	D-57-286	Original: found
NP-888	Baird, Richard	3 APR 1769		Unity, Westmoreland/ LD: Unity, Westmoreland	300	B-23-67	Original: found
NP-889	Mitchetree, Elizabeth	3 APR 1769		Muncy Creek Twp., Lycoming	300	D-57-296	Original: found
NP-890	Myer, Anna	3 APR 1769	Berks	Buffalo, Union	300	D-60-199	[same land as NP-1918 to John Blum] Original: found
NP-891	Margdant, Lawrence	3 APR 1769	West Branch Youghiogheny River, Cumberland	LD: Westmoreland	300		Jacob Bausman/--- Crawford Original: found
NP-892	Cathcart, Allen	3 APR 1769	Northumberland	Muncy, Lycoming	300	C-25-90	Mary Steel/(r17 MAR 1783)Stephen Collins Original: found
NP-893	Haly, John	3 APR 1769	Bald Eagle Creek	LD: Clinton	300		Henry Guiney Original: found
NP-894	Wiser, Jacob	3 APR 1769	Northumberland	East Branch Muncy Creek, Centre	300	A-5-20	Original: found
NP-895	Magaw, Robert	3 APR 1769	Limestone Valley	LD: Turbot, Northumberland	300		Original: found
NP-896	Taggart, Robert	3 APR 1769	mouth of Little Beaver Run	LD: Union	300		Original: found

Table 6 - New Purchase Applications (1769-1773)

Number	Applicant	Date	Orig. Place	Later Place	Acres	Survey	Neighbors, Notes, etc.
NP-897	Cavit, Thomas	3 APR 1769	Northumberland	Buffalo, Union	300	A-45-148	(r14 DEC 1787)John Rehrick/[see caveat] Original: found
NP-898	Brotherton, George	3 APR 1769	Westmoreland	Turtle Creek, Allegheny	300	C-35-181	widow Myers/(r12 MAR 1788)Henry Cotton Original: found
NP-899	Campbell, James	3 APR 1769	Westmoreland	Wilkins, Allegheny	300	K-309	(r6 JAN 1853)James Carothers Original: found
NP-900	Myer, Abraham	3 APR 1769		Unity & Ligonier, Westmoreland	300	D-57-288	--- Proctor Original: Signed
NP-901	Petterson, Samuel	3 APR 1769		Greene, Indiana	300	D-57-289 D-57-290	Original: found
NP-902	Mathew, Deedrick	3 APR 1769	Berks	Augusta, Northumberland	300	A-9-73 A-9-74	Harman Schneider/(r31 OCT 1803)Jonas Yocum Original: found
NP-903	Stephens, John	3 APR 1769	Berks	Washington, Lycoming	300	D-57-297	Thomas Forster, Jr./James Goudy Original: found
NP-904	Rudulph, Zebulon	3 APR 1769	Berks	Chillisquaque Creek, Northumberland	300	C-206-281 C-206-282	Mary Collins/(r12 APR 1800)James Starr Original: found
NP-905	Laughlin, Hugh	3 APR 1769		Limestone Valley, Northumberland	300	A-8-201	(r1 APR 1782)Rev. John Ewing Original: found
NP-906	Ramsey, John	3 APR 1769		Blacklick, Indiana	300	B-21-227	--- Letart Original: found
NP-907	Griffiths, George	3 APR 1769	White Deer Hole	LD: Lycoming/ Union	300		James Bell Original: found
NP-908	Stephen, Hugh	3 APR 1769		White Deer, Union	300	D-57-287	--- Blyth Original: found
NP-909	Greiter, Jacob	3 APR 1769	Cumberland	Long Limestone Valley, Northumberland	300	A-19-27	Michael Greiter/(r5 MAY 1789)John Cox, Esq. Original: found
NP-910	McNale, James	3 APR 1769	East Branch Susquehanna River opposite mouth of "Cottowassing" [Catawissa?]	LD: Columbia	300		Original: found
NP-911	Willson, Joseph Jr.	3 APR 1769	Cumberland	Bald Eagle Creek, Centre/ LD: Centre	300		Joseph Wilson, Sr. Original: found

Table 6 - New Purchase Applications (1769-1773)

Number	Applicant	Date	Orig. Place	Later Place	Acres	Survey	Neighbors, Notes, etc.
NP-912	Hunt, James	3 APR 1769	Cumberland	LD: Somerset	300		Catharine Hall Original: found
NP-913	Ewing, John	3 APR 1769	White Deer Hole Creek	LD: Lycoming [return says Menallen, Fayette]	300		(r26 MAR 1788 & p28 MAR 1788)William Haney/[Survey order for this application is filed with the regular applications for 1769 with the statement on the back "York. April 9th 1770. I do hereby certfie that the land for which this order is granted is taken by a prior application." (signed) Chas. Lukens] Original: found
NP-914	Thauly, George (of East Pennsborough Township, Cumberland County)	3 APR 1769	Washington	Monongahela River, Allegheny	300	C-157-206	(r8 DEC 1785)Paul Pierce Original: signed
NP-915	Hoover, Conrad	3 APR 1769	Berks	Muncy, Lycoming	300	K-19	Joshua Mitchell/(r24 MAR 1795)William Ellis Original: found
NP-916	Montgomery, John	3 APR 1769	Berks	Washington, Lycoming	300	D-56-120 D-56-234 D-56-271 D-60-209 C-143-166 C-143-180	(r6 JAN 1817)John Montgomery Original: found
NP-917	Whelin, Martin (farmer)	3 APR 1769	Bald Eagle Creek	LD: Clinton	300		Original: found
NP-918	McKee, James	3 APR 1769	Washington	Hopewell, Beaver	300	P-174	Alexander McKee/(r21 APR 1810) Original: Signed by A. McKee
NP-919	McElroy, Archibald	3 APR 1769	Chillisquaque Creek	LD: Montour	300		Original: found
NP-920	Craig, Joseph	3 APR 1769	Berks	Nippenose, Lycoming	300	D-57-298	Original: found
NP-921	Donnaldson, Hugh	3 APR 1769	Northampton	Northeast Branch Susquehanna River, Northumberland	300	D-13-269	(r13 JAN 1775)William West, Jr. Original: found
NP-922	Maxwell, Albert	3 APR 1769		Lewis, Northumberland	300	D-62-262 C-216-188 C-216-189	(r12 NOV 1851)Tweed Walts & John Tweed heirs Original: found

Table 6 - New Purchase Applications (1769-1773)

Number	Applicant	Date	Orig. Place	Later Place	Acres	Survey	Neighbors, Notes, etc.
NP-923	Johns, Kinsey	3 APR 1769		Nippenose, Lycoming	300	D-57-299	Original: found
NP-924	Tanner, George	3 APR 1769		Susquehanna River, Luzerne	300	A-24-137	Jacob Clock, Jr./(r19 APR 1782)James Johnston Original: found
NP-925	Guthery, James Jr.	3 APR 1769		Unity, Westmoreland	300	D-57-2	Original: found
NP-926	Beatey, Henry	3 APR 1769		North Huntingdon, Westmoreland	300	C-197-81	(r3 FEB 1820)James Park/[see caveat] Original: found
NP-927	Price, William	3 APR 1769		Youghiogheny River, Fayette	300	E-166	George Wallis/(r18 JAN 1799)Andrew Robinson Original: found
NP-928	Wood, John	3 APR 1769	Cumberland	Westmoreland - Kiskiminitas Creek, Indiana	300	C-117-92	John Hinkson/Thomas Woods/(r21 MAR 1806)Robert Leggat Original: Signed
NP-929	Jones, Francis	3 APR 1769	Berks	Chillisquaque Creek, Northumberland	300	D-519	John Gorrell/(r12 APR 1804)Mark Biddle Original: found
NP-930	Williams, William	3 APR 1769	between Monongahela & Youghiogheny Rivers	LD: Allegheny	300		Original: found
NP-931	Grebill, Peter	3 APR 1769		Nippenose, Lycoming	300	D-57-300	Original: found
NP-932	Brown, John	3 APR 1769		Nippenose, Lycoming	300	D-57-283	George Lauk Original: found
NP-933	Willson, Joseph Sr.	3 APR 1769	Cumberland	Bald Eagle Creek, Centre	300	A-2-169	John Wilson/(r31 JAN 1791)Job Packer Original: found
NP-934	Talbott, Margaret	3 APR 1769		Clinton/ LD: Clinton	300		Original: found
NP-935	Duncan, David	3 APR 1769		Derry, Westmoreland	300	A-22-79	Thomas Campbell/(r8 FEB 1797)William Dunlap Original: found
NP-936	Isherwood, George	3 APR 1769	Cumberland	Monongahela River, Allegheny	300	A-74-122	(r3 APR 1771) Original: found
NP-937	Sheaphard, Thomas	3 APR 1769		Pigeon Creek, Washington	300		(r1 MAR 1788 & p1 MAR 1788)Abraham Sheppard Original: found
NP-938	Huston, Samuel	3 APR 1769	Bald Eagle Creek	LD: Clinton/ Centre	300		Griffith Gibbon Original: Signed

Table 6 - New Purchase Applications (1769-1773)

Number	Applicant	Date	Orig. Place	Later Place	Acres	Survey	Neighbors, Notes, etc.
NP-939	Albrecht, Martin	3 APR 1769	Cumberland	Hartley, Union	300	D-57-295	Peter Cline Original: found
NP-940	Campbell, John	3 APR 1769		Loyalsock, Lycoming	300	D-57-282	Original: Signed
NP-941	Wilson, James	3 APR 1769	Cumberland	between Youghiogheny & Monongahela Rivers, Allegheny	300	Y-262	(r30 SEP 1788)Ann Wilson Original: found
NP-942	Mackenness, Thomas	3 APR 1769	Berks	Hartley, Union	300	D-62-284 C-166-92	(r6 JUL 1772) Original: found
NP-943	Duncan, Samuel Jr.	3 APR 1769		Derry, Westmoreland	300	C-138-178	Jacob Bower/(r13 JUN 1797)George Lazier Original: found
NP-944	Cox, William	3 APR 1769	White Deer Hole Creek	LD: Lycoming	300		Original: found
NP-945	Hutchins, Thomas	3 APR 1769		Pitt, Allegheny	300	D-62-93	Thomas Smallman Original: Signed
NP-946	Killcrest, Thomas	3 APR 1769		Turbot, Northumberland	300	D-56-190 A-45-133	(r18 APR 1788)Mungo Reed/[see caveat] Original: found
NP-947	Ennis, James Jr.	3 APR 1769	Berks	West Buffalo, Union	300	D-57-294	Mathew Grimes Original: found
NP-948	Ward, Martha	3 APR 1769	Westmoreland	Pitt, Allegheny	300	P-49	Alexander McGreeger/Capt. Thompson/James Royal/Richard McMahan/(r20 AUG 1787)Ephraim Blaine, Esq. Original: found
NP-949	Hopkins, William Jr.	3 APR 1769	Northampton	Fishing Creek, Columbia	300	P-17	William Hopkins, Sr./(r 25 SEP 1800)John Biddle Original: found
NP-950	Rees, Daniel	3 APR 1769	Northumberland	Buffalo, Union	300	C-49-175	(r29 AUG 1794)Joseph Fearon Original: Signed
NP-951	Duncan, Isaac Jr.	3 APR 1769	Berks	Buffalo, Union	300	D-57-293	Original: found
NP-952	Zigler, George	3 APR 1769	Bald Eagle Creek	LD: Clinton/ Centre	300		Original: found
NP-953	Okely, Silvanus	3 APR 1769		Tunkhannock Creek, Wyoming/ LD: Luzerne	300	X-154	David Rockman Original: found

Table 6 - New Purchase Applications (1769-1773)

Number	Applicant	Date	Orig. Place	Later Place	Acres	Survey	Neighbors, Notes, etc.
NP-954	Gemberling, Jacob	3 APR 1769	Berks	Buffalo, Union	300	D-57-291 D-57-292	Martin Heffelfinger/[see caveat] Original: found
NP-955	Irwin, Samuel	3 APR 1769	Cumberland	Salem, Westmoreland	300	M-244	(r10 NOV 1787)Mathew Miller Original: found
NP-956	Bowne, John	3 APR 1769		Northeast Branch Susquehanna River, Northumberland/ LD: Luzerne	300	H-156	Original: found
NP-957	Hopkins, Joseph Jr.	3 APR 1769	Northumberland	Spring, Centre/ LD: Spring, Centre	300	Q-269 C-20-68 X-181 X-182 X-183 C-233-219	Joseph Hopkins, Sr./(r28 JAN 1833)Henry Barnhart/(p25 NOV 1870)E. W. Sturdevant Original: found
NP-958	McClure, John Jr.	3 APR 1769		Lick Spring Branch of Sewickley Creek, Cumberland	300	C-136-42	William Proctor/Joseph Eagar/Arthur Harrow/(r JUN 1770) Original: Signed
NP-959	Doil, Samuel	3 APR 1769	Berks	Shamokin Creek, Northumberland	300	A-36-194	(r30 DEC 1774)William Winter Original: found
NP-960	Smith, Jacob	3 APR 1769		Pitt, Westmoreland	300	W-283	Original: found
NP-961	Forster, John Jr.	3 APR 1769	Warriors Run	LD: Northumberland	300		Original: found
NP-962	Litton, John	3 APR 1769	West Branch Susquehanna River		300		[see John Montgomery, NP-2413]/[see caveat] Original: found
NP-963	Messersmith, Valentine	3 APR 1769	Berks	Middle Chillisquaque Creek, Northumberland	300	C-44-92	John Allen, Esq./(r17 JUL 1788)Marrt Duncan Original: found
NP-964	McKee, William	3 APR 1769		Versailles, Allegheny	300	D-62-92	James McKee Original: found
NP-965	McCrea, Robert	3 APR 1769		Allegheny River, Westmoreland	300	A-38-188	(r7 DEC 1787)William Jack, Esq. Original: found

Table 6 - New Purchase Applications (1769-1773)

Number	Applicant	Date	Orig. Place	Later Place	Acres	Survey	Neighbors, Notes, etc.
NP-966	Morgan, Edward	3 APR 1769	Buffalo Swamp	LD: Union	300		Original: found
NP-967	Fisher, Stephen	3 APR 1769	Northumberland	Bald Eagle, Centre	300	C-87-240	Samuel McWilliams/(r29 AUG 1785)Lewis Karcher Original: found
NP-968	Rees, John	3 APR 1769	Berks	North Buffalo, Union	---	D-60-221 A-25-293 C-117-122 C-13-229	(r14 MAR 1806)Aaron Levy/(r6 FEB 1828)John Brickley/(r21 MAR 1839)J. L. Wright Original: found
NP-969	Shannon, Richard	3 APR 1769	Cumberland	Blacklick, Indiana/ LD: Blacklick, Indiana	300	D-56-273 D-56-274 D-56-58 A-29-57 C-1-206	Thomas Jameson/Frederick Rorer/(r15 JAN 1830)William Lintner Original: found
NP-970	Buckwalter, Abraham	3 APR 1769	Berks	Loyalsock Creek, Lycoming	300	A-39-220	Jacob Lands/(r18 APR 1770)Margaret Duncan Original: found
NP-971	Neisser, Augustine	3 APR 1769	above Nescopeck Falls on the Susquehanna River	LD: Luzerne	300		George Allen/Gabriel [an Indian] Original: found
NP-972	Shields, Edmond	3 APR 1769	North Branch Susquehanna River	LD: Columbia	300		Joseph Simons Original: found
NP-973	Byerley, Michael	3 APR 1769		Hempfield, Westmoreland	300	D-57-285	Joseph Bredy/[see caveat] Original: found
NP-974	Baldwin, Barshebe	3 APR 1769	Westmoreland	between Whiteley & Dunkard Creek, Greene	300	M-411	(r13 JUL 1790)William McCay & wife Original: Signed
NP-975	Eshelman, David	3 APR 1769	East Branch Susquehanna River	LD: Luzerne	300		Original: found
NP-976	Scott, James	3 APR 1769		Versailles, Allegheny	300	D-62-91	Capt. Thompson Original: found
NP-977	Peairs, Isaac	3 APR 1769	Cumberland	Redstone Creek, Fayette	300	C-157-252	Josiah Rickets/Samuel Lian/(r9 MAR 1786) Original: found

Table 6 - New Purchase Applications (1769-1773)

Number	Applicant	Date	Orig. Place	Later Place	Acres	Survey	Neighbors, Notes, etc.
NP-978	Frame, Nathan	3 APR 1769	Bedford	Reuben's Run, Redstone Settlement, Fayette	300	C-3-73	(r16 MAY 1796)Joseph Dungan Original: found
NP-979	Riche, Lydia	3 APR 1769	Berks	Loyalsock Creek, Lycoming	300	C-176-29	(r8 SEP 1770) Original: found
NP-980	Huntzecker, Samuel	3 APR 1769	Cumberland	Hartley, Union	300	D-57-284	Martin Albrecht Original: found
NP-981	Sayre, Samuel	3 APR 1769		Tunkhannock Creek, Wyoming	300	K-242	John Purcell/(r9 APR 1783)Ambrose Croker Original: found
NP-982	McMath, John	3 APR 1769		Hempfield, Westmoreland	300	A-77-171	(r28 APR 1788)William Elliot/[see caveat] Original: found
NP-983	Grojean, Jacob	3 APR 1769	Northumberland	Buffalo, Union	300	A-40-28	(r4 OCT 1784)Tetrick Struble Original: found
NP-984	Hughes, Thomas	3 APR 1769	Northumberland	Catawissa, Columbia	300	A-55-28	(r12 MAR 1811)William Hartman Original: found
NP-985	Smith, John	3 APR 1769	Cumberland	West Huntingdon, Westmoreland	300	C-133-80	Martha Brown/(r6 MAR 1786)William Marshall Original: found
NP-986	Parker, William	3 APR 1769		Unity, Westmoreland	300	D-57-3	Original: found
NP-987	Dobbs, Thomas	3 APR 1769		Versailles, Allegheny	300	D-57-65	Original: found
NP-988	Gay, William	3 APR 1769		Muncy Creek Twp., Lycoming	300	D-57-281	Robert Campbell Original: Signed
NP-989	Willson, Mary	3 APR 1769	Mahoning Creek	LD: Columbia	300		Martha Wilson Original: found
NP-990	Tuckness, Robert	3 APR 1769	Berks	Chillisquaque Creek, Northumberland	300	W-256	Zebulon Rudolph Original: found
NP-991	Eatten, James	3 APR 1769		Unity, Westmoreland	300	D-57-4	Original: found
NP-992	Ashton, Benjamin	3 APR 1769	Berks	Muncy, Lycoming	300	I-138	William Dillwyn/(r21 NOV 1807)Robert Coleman Original: found
NP-993	Fulten, William	3 APR 1769	Berks	White Deer, Union	300	D-56-50	[same land as NP-2122 to John Curry] Original: found

Table 6 - New Purchase Applications (1769-1773)

Number	Applicant	Date	Orig. Place	Later Place	Acres	Survey	Neighbors, Notes, etc.
NP-994	Whisler, Jacob	3 APR 1769		Limestone Valley, Centre/ LD: Centre	300		Benjamin Whitmore Original: found
NP-995	Walker, Mary	3 APR 1769	Nine Mile Run	LD: Westmoreland	300		Robert Read Original: found
NP-996	Myer, Isaac	3 APR 1769	Mahoning Creek	LD: Columbia	300		Original: found
NP-997	Weitzel, Paul Sr.	3 APR 1769		Loyalsock, Lycoming	300	D-56-35 T-107	George Gibson/(r27 MAR 1799)Thomas Grant Original: found
NP-998	Lonabergen, Michael	3 APR 1769		Jacob's Creek, Westmoreland	300	C-19-71	(r20 AUG 1787)Ephraim Blaine, Esq. Original: found
NP-999	Salmon, John	3 APR 1769	Northeast Branch Susquehanna River	LD: Luzerne	300		Original: found
NP-1000	Spoon, John	3 APR 1769		Fishing Creek, Columbia	300	A-40-39	(r31 JAN 1784)John Spohn & Michael Bright Original: missing
NP-1001	Adams, Halbert	3 APR 1769	Cumberland	Franklin, Fayette	300	D-56-119 C-11-102	Mr. Chamberly/--- Virgin/(r3 APR 1828)Jesse Arnold & Samuel Dunn Original: Missing
NP-1002	Culbertson, Samuel Jr.	3 APR 1769		Blacklick, Indiana	300	D-56-118	Original: found
NP-1003	Smith, Richard Jr.	3 APR 1769	Berks	Washington, Lycoming	300	D-56-120	Original: found
NP-1004	Grant, Daniel	3 APR 1769	Northampton	Wapwallopen Creek, Luzerne	300	A-258	(r9 APR 1783)George Campbell Original: found
NP-1005	Forster, Thomas Sr.	3 APR 1769	Berks	Warrior Run, Northumberland	300	A-58-223	(r1 AUG 1770) Original: found
NP-1006	Pidgeon, Conrad	3 APR 1769		Chillisquaque Creek, Northumberland or Montour/ LD: Northumberland	300		Benjamin Maddox Original: found
NP-1007	Cason, Joseph	3 APR 1769	Chillisquaque Creek	LD: Columbia	300		Original: found
NP-1008	Parker, Richard	3 APR 1769		Monongahela River, Fayette	300	C-133-15	(r15 SEP 1785)John McClure & William Fleming Original: found
NP-1009	Murray, Francis	3 APR 1769	Berks	Washington, Lycoming	300	D-56-115	Original: found

Table 6 - New Purchase Applications (1769-1773)

Number	Applicant	Date	Orig. Place	Later Place	Acres	Survey	Neighbors, Notes, etc.
NP-1010	Stewart, Lazarus	3 APR 1769	Northumberland	East Branch Susquehanna River, Columbia	300	C-215-97	(r31 MAR 1802)Mordecai Owen Original: A note on the original application reads: "I deputize John Foster to take out a location in my name. Signed Lazarus Stewart"
NP-1011	Smith, Mathew (of Paxton)	3 APR 1769	Northumberland	Washington & Jackson, Lycoming	300	E-85	(r26 MAR 1827)William H. Welsh Original: found
NP-1012	Steel, Mary	3 APR 1769	Northumberland	Muncy, Lycoming	300	C-25-91	(r17 MAR 1783)Stephen Collins Original: found
NP-1013	Wright, William	3 APR 1769		Plum, Allegheny	300	D-56-194	John Little Original: found
NP-1014	Simons, Joseph	3 APR 1769	North Branch Susquehanna River	LD: Columbia	300		Thomas Carpenter, Jr. Original: found
NP-1015	Galloway, Joseph	3 APR 1769	Berks	Turbot, Northumberland	300	B-196	(r19 MAR 1788)James Espey/Mr. Allen/Mr. Purviance/[see caveat] Original: found
NP-1016	Clark, Joseph Jr.	3 APR 1769		Lawrence & Bradford, Clearfield	300	D-56-106	Original: found
NP-1017	Wolf, Barney	3 APR 1769	Mahoning or Licking Creek	LD: Columbia	300		Original: found
NP-1018	McLaughlin, John	3 APR 1769	Berks	Warriors Run, Northumberland	300	O-210	(r3 MAY 1794)Jacob All & John Andree Original: found
NP-1019	Rinker, John	3 APR 1769	Chillisquaque Creek	LD: Montour	300		Original: found
NP-1020	Washington, John Augusta	3 APR 1769	Cumberland	Washington, Fayette	300	C-21-233	Col. Washington/(r17 MAR 1803)Thomas Cook/[see caveat] Original: found
NP-1021	Hall, Joseph	3 APR 1769	Cumberland	Salem, Westmoreland	300	D-56-101	Eliza Harrison Hall Original: found
NP-1022	Richardson, Isaac	3 APR 1769	Chillisquaque Creek	LD: Northumberland	300		Original: Signed
NP-1023	Halladay, James	3 APR 1769	Cumberland	four miles from Monongahela River, Westmoreland	300	A-67-61	(r17 OCT 1782)James Carroll Original: found
NP-1024	Power, Samuel Jr.	3 APR 1769	Bald Eagle Creek	LD: Clinton/ Centre	300		Original: Signed

Table 6 - New Purchase Applications (1769-1773)

Number	Applicant	Date	Orig. Place	Later Place	Acres	Survey	Neighbors, Notes, etc.
NP-1025	Blyth, Margaret	3 APR 1769		White Deer, Union	300	D-56-135 D-56-271 D-62-241 C-176-81	(r26 SEP 1774)John Reed Original: Signed
NP-1026	Morgan, David	3 APR 1769	Berks	Kelly, Union	300	D-56-116	Original: found
NP-1027	Logan, John	3 APR 1769	Berks	White Deer, Union	300	D-56-114	Original: found
NP-1028	Sprogel, John Ludwick	3 APR 1769	Berks	Turbot, Northumberland/ LD: Northumberland	300	D-56-113	John Sprogel Original: found
NP-1029	Wolff, John	3 APR 1769	Northumberland	near Wyoming, Luzerne/ LD: Luzerne	300	A-5-13	George Wolf/Samuel Purviance, Jr. Original: found
NP-1030	Findley, William Jr.	3 APR 1769		Plum, Allegheny	300	D-56-193	Benjamin Armitage Original: found
NP-1031	Lawrie, James	3 APR 1769	Northumberland	Muncy, Lycoming/ LD: Lycoming	300	A-5-86	Samuel Allison Original: found
NP-1032	Kendal, Joseph	3 APR 1769		Muncy, Lycoming/ LD: Lycoming	300		Whitehead Humphrey Original: found
NP-1033	Lafaver, Samuel	3 APR 1769		East Branch Susquehanna River, Luzerne	300	C-222-263	Jacob Burkholder/(r8 AUG 1781)Joseph Wharton Original: found
NP-1034	Bausman, William	3 APR 1769	Cumberland	Plum, Allegheny	300	D-64-129 A-2-170	(r15 MAR 1791)Nathaniel Pints/Col. Boquet Original: found
NP-1035	Gibson, William (of Cumberland County, surgeon)	3 APR 1769	Loyalhanna Creek, Cumberland	Loyalhanna Creek, Westmoreland	300		William Armstrong/(r22 SEP 1788)Issac Parr Original: found
NP-1036	Spicer, Jacob	3 APR 1769	Berks	Chillisquaque Creek, Northumberland/ LD: Northumberland	300	W-284 A-44-115	Robert Tuckness/(r6 JAN 1797)James Starr/(w28 DEC 1796) Original: found
NP-1037	Jackson, David	3 APR 1769	Cumberland	South Huntingdon, Westmoreland	300	D-56-102	Original: found

Table 6 - New Purchase Applications (1769-1773)

Number	Applicant	Date	Orig. Place	Later Place	Acres	Survey	Neighbors, Notes, etc.
NP-1038	Pearis, Joseph	3 APR 1769	Cumberland	branch of Youghiogheny River, Allegheny	300	C-161-288	(r27 MAY 1815) Original: Signed
NP-1039	Bradford, George	3 APR 1769		Centre/ LD: Centre	300		Original: found
NP-1040	Trotter, Moor	3 APR 1769		Washington, Lycoming	300	D-56-112	Edward Streeker Original: found
NP-1041	Lowrey, Alexander	3 APR 1769		Plum, Allegheny & Allegheny, Westmoreland	300	D-56-192	Original: Signed
NP-1042	Brodhack, Bartholamew	3 APR 1769	East Branch Susquehanna River	LD: Wyoming	300		Original: found
NP-1043	Wunder, Christopher	3 APR 1769	Cumberland	Turtle Creek, 23 miles from Ft. Pitt	300	C-144-121	William Rebets/Jacob Bausman/Benedict Garbell/(r18 OCT 1824)Jeremiah Murray Original: found
NP-1044	Shippen, Edward Sr.	3 APR 1769	Berks	Augusta, Northumberland	300	W-285 D-7-54 D-7-90 C-10-283	Joseph Shippen Jr./(r8 MAY 1810)Fredrick Weiser/(r7 SEP 1810)Phillip & Mary Weiser/(r6 DEC 1811)William Bartholomow Original: found
NP-1045	Webb, William	3 APR 1769	opposite mouth of White Hemp Creek, Berks or Northampton	LD: Luzerne	300		Original: found
NP-1046	Blaine, James Jr.	3 APR 1769		Plum, Allegheny	300	D-56-191	Original: found
NP-1047	Little, William	3 APR 1769	Berks	White Deer, Union	300	D-57-40-26	Adam King/William McCallister Original: Signed
NP-1048	Brison, John	3 APR 1769	Bedford	Westmoreland	300	D-9-251	(r29 SEP 1788)Thomas Young Original: found
NP-1049	Smith, William	3 APR 1769		Wyalusing Creek, Luzerne	300	W-286	Original: found
NP-1050	Harrison, Charles	3 APR 1769		North Branch Susquehanna River, Luzerne	300	B-228	(r20 AUG 1796)John Ewing Original: found
NP-1051	Frick, Philip	3 APR 1769		Washington, Lycoming	300	D-56-111	Original: found
NP-1052	Steel, Samuel	3 APR 1769		Donegal, Westmoreland	300	D-56-103	Mr. McLellan Original: found

Table 6 - New Purchase Applications (1769-1773)

Number	Applicant	Date	Orig. Place	Later Place	Acres	Survey	Neighbors, Notes, etc.
NP-1053	Johnston, John	3 APR 1769	Bedford	Redstone Creek, Fayette	300	C-193-248	(r31 MAR 1788)Samuel Stephen Original: found
NP-1054	Burd, John	3 APR 1769		Derry, Westmoreland	300	D-56-104	Original: found
NP-1055	O'Neil, Michael	3 APR 1769		Chartiers Creek, Allegheny/ LD: Allegheny	300	X-155	Original: found
NP-1056	Dixon, William	3 APR 1769		Derry, Westmoreland	300	I-179	(r17 DEC 1838)John Barnett Original: found
NP-1057	Peairs, George	3 APR 1769		North Union, Fayette	300	C-51-104 C-166-178 C-228-275	James Catumus/(r9 APR 1824)Gabrial D. Evans/(r3 OCT 1855)John Vance Original: Signed
NP-1058	Lebig, John	3 APR 1769		Nanticoke Creek, Northumberland	300	G-318	Henry Lebig/(r24 OCT 1782)Alex Power Original: found
NP-1059	Wilkens, Andrew	3 APR 1769	Bald Eagle Creek	LD: Centre	300		Original: found
NP-1060	Criner, Philip	3 APR 1769		Huntingdon, Westmoreland	300	C-48-235	(r28 SEP 1789)Robert Pulton Original: found
NP-1061	Cooper, Robert (son of Robert Cooper, of the City of Philadelphia, shoemaker)	3 APR 1769		Bald Eagle Town, Centre/ LD: Centre	300	Z-50	Original: Signed
NP-1062	Thomas, William Jr.	3 APR 1769		Salem, Westmoreland	300	D-57-280 D-57-279 D-70-233 D-13-101	(r28 AUG 1783) Original: Signed
NP-1063	Shriver, Henry	3 APR 1769	Chillisquaque Creek	LD: Northumberland	300		Daniel Topham Original: found
NP-1064	Darlin, Mathew	3 APR 1769	East Branch Susquehanna River	LD: Northumberland	300		Original: found
NP-1065	Foster, Thomas Sr.	3 APR 1769	West Branch Susquehanna River opposite Muncy Narrows		300		Original: found
NP-1066	Smith, Robert (son of Robert Smith)	3 APR 1769		Mt. Pleasant, Westmoreland	300	D-56-105	Original: found

Table 6 - New Purchase Applications (1769-1773)

Number	Applicant	Date	Orig. Place	Later Place	Acres	Survey	Neighbors, Notes, etc.
NP-1067	Rankin, John	3 APR 1769	West Branch Susquehanna River	LD: Union	300		William Blythe Original: Signed
NP-1068	Miller, Theobold	3 APR 1769		Bald Eagle, Northumberland/ LD: Centre	300	A-32-199	Original: found
NP-1069	Watts, James	3 APR 1769	Turbot		300		Original: found
NP-1070	McKeen, Thomas	3 APR 1769		Derry, Westmoreland	300	D-56-150	Original: found
NP-1071	Buck, Jacob	3 APR 1769	Berks	Fishing Creek, Northumberland	300	B-320	(r20 JAN 1789)George Irwin Original: found
NP-1072	Harris, Ann	3 APR 1769	Berks	Black Run, Union/ LD: Clinton	300	A-251	Joseph Harris Original: found
NP-1073	Simpson, Sarah	3 APR 1769	Berks	Buffalo, Union	300	D-56-124	[same land as NP-1574 to Casper Reed] Original: found
NP-1074	Cassey, Oliver	3 APR 1769		Turbot, Northumberland	300	C-85-272 C-85-279	John Allen/(r31 MAR 1814)Hugh Harrison Original: found
NP-1075	Allison, William Jr.	3 APR 1769	Westmoreland	Plum, Allegheny	300	C-89-13 D-2-12 D-2-13 D-2-14	(r10 OCT 1827)Archibald Bard/(r9 JAN 1843)Alexander Young Original: found
NP-1076	McCoskey, Samuel Sr.	3 APR 1769	White Deer Creek		300		Original: found
NP-1077	McPherson, John	3 APR 1769	Bedford	South Huntingdon, Westmoreland/ LD: South Huntingdon, Westmoreland	300	X-229 X-230 C-149-152 C-149-153 C-33-240	--- Koster/--- Dorsius/(r27 MAR 1840)John Nichols/(r18 FEB 1850)James Carothers heirs/(p4 NOV 1868)James Chambers Original: found
NP-1078	Wibbley, Jacob	3 APR 1769	Northampton	Muncy Creek, Northumberland	300	E-256	(r28 NOV 1787)Joseph J. Wallis Original: Signed
NP-1079	Breadin, James	3 APR 1769	Berks	Wayne, Lycoming	300	D-56-149	Original: Signed
NP-1080	Sisk, James	3 APR 1769	Chillisquaque Creek	LD: Northumberland/ Montour/ [Lisk in LD]	300		Jacob Raybolt/James Tilghman Original: found

Table 6 - New Purchase Applications (1769-1773)

Number	Applicant	Date	Orig. Place	Later Place	Acres	Survey	Neighbors, Notes, etc.
NP-1081	Pennybecker, Benjamin	3 APR 1769		Washington, Lycoming/ LD: Northumberland	300	D-56-148	Original: found
NP-1082	Hunter, Joseph	3 APR 1769		near Laurel Hill, Fayette/ LD: Somerset/ Fayette	300		[see caveat] Original: found
NP-1083	Beckerton, Joseph	3 APR 1769		Washington, Lycoming	300	D-56-147	Benjamin Beckerton Original: found
NP-1084	Galbraith, John	3 APR 1769		Chartiers, Washington	300	C-123-251	William Randall(r23 FEB 1789)Mosses Middlesworth Original: found
NP-1085	Grant, George	3 APR 1769		Muncy Creek Twp., Lycoming	300	D-56-61 D-56-57 A-51-261	(r6 MAR 1782)Thomas Grant Original: found
NP-1086	Cahell, Edmund	3 APR 1769	Bedford	Derry, Westmoreland	300	C-134-197 D-11-284 D-11-285 D-11-291	(r21 FEB 1806)Josiah Moorhead & John Moorhead/(r6 APR 1824)Peter Wallace Original: found
NP-1087	Fraser, James	3 APR 1769		Versailles, Allegheny	300	D-56-146 D-56-185	Original: found
NP-1088	Ryne, William	3 APR 1769	Spring Creek, Cumberland	LD: Centre	300		Samuel Purviance Original: found
NP-1089	Burtran, Moses	3 APR 1769		Fairfield, Lycoming	300		Samuel Purviance Original: found
NP-1090	Brown, Arthur	3 APR 1769	Black Creek, Bedford	LD: Luzerne	300		Original: Signed by William Brown, Carlisle
NP-1091	McSweeney, John	3 APR 1769	Bedford	Quemahoning Creek, Somerset	300	A-67-189	(r24 MAY 1784)Robert Morris, Esq. Original: Found
NP-1092	Beard, John	3 APR 1769		Wilkins & Plum, Allegheny	300	D-57-66 D-56-173 D-62-84 A-73-108	Matthew Elliott/Nicholas Dorran/(r23 OCT 1790)Richard Buttler Original: Signed
NP-1093	Warder, Jeremiah Jr.	3 APR 1769		Blacklick, Indiana/ LD: Blacklick, Indiana	300	D-56-160	Original: Signed

Table 6 - New Purchase Applications (1769-1773)

Number	Applicant	Date	Orig. Place	Later Place	Acres	Survey	Neighbors, Notes, etc.
NP-1094	Montgomery, Robert	3 APR 1769	Berks	Washington, Lycoming	300	D-56-159	Original: found
NP-1095	Alexander, James	3 APR 1769	Red Bank Run	LD: Union	300		Original: found
NP-1096	Kennard, Menon	3 APR 1769		LD: Washington, Lycoming	300		John Heaton Original: found
NP-1097	Brown, William	3 APR 1769		Loyalsock, Lycoming/ LD: Loyalsock, Lycoming	300	D-56-158	Original: Signed
NP-1098	Connolly, Francis	3 APR 1769	Berks	Black Run, Union	300	C-74-67	(r22 SEP 1790)Reuben Haines Original: found
NP-1099	Stephen, Alexander	3 APR 1769	Warriors Run	LD: Northumberland	300		Original: found
NP-1100	Flakingar, John	3 APR 1769		Buffalo Creek, Union	300	C-75-67	(r14 FEB 1788)John Harris Original: found
NP-1101	McNitt, Alexander	3 APR 1769	south side of Muncy Hill	LD: Clinton/ Centre	300		Original: Signed
NP-1102	Thompson, John	3 APR 1769		Turbot, Northumberland	300	C-55-141	(r31 JAN 1803)Conrad Fogleman Original: found
NP-1103	McKee, David	3 APR 1769		Versailles, Allegheny	300	D-56-165 H-10	Robert McKee/Thomas Mckee/(r4 NOV 1795)John Mckee Original: Signed
NP-1104	Fisher, James	3 APR 1769		Muncy Creek, Lycoming/ LD: Lycoming	300		Original: found
NP-1105	Rygart, Christopher	3 APR 1769	Cumberland	Boggs, Centre	300	X-127 X-128	Peter Graybill Original: found
NP-1106	McDonnall, Patrick	3 APR 1769	Muncy Creek	LD: Lycoming	300		Original: found
NP-1107	Leet, Isaac	3 APR 1769	Northampton	Shickshinny Creek, Luzerne	200	C-109-137	(r19 APR 1784)Jer Thatoher Original: Signed by Daniel Leet
NP-1108	Kelsoe, John	3 APR 1769		Chest Creek, Bedford	200	A-73-207	Charles Gough/(r11 MAY 1774)Robert Barclay Original: found
NP-1109	Palmer, John	3 APR 1769	Northumberland	Toby Creek, Clinton	300	D-26-284 D-26-285	(r17 AUG 1790)David Leamon/Jos. Watts Original: found
NP-1110	Boggs, John	3 APR 1769		Chartiers Creek, Allegheny	300	C-12-18 C-177-85	(r30 MAR 1785)/(r21 JAN 1809)John & Ephraim Morton/[see caveat] Original: Signed

Table 6 - New Purchase Applications (1769-1773)

Number	Applicant	Date	Orig. Place	Later Place	Acres	Survey	Neighbors, Notes, etc.
NP-1111	Miller, Frederick	3 APR 1769	Penns Creek	LD: Clinton	300		Frederick Albrecht/[see caveat] Original: found
NP-1112	Flemming, Susanna	3 APR 1769	Chartiers Creek, Cumberland	LD: Washington	300		Original: found
NP-1113	Burnet, Robert	3 APR 1769			300		Thomas Coats Original: found
NP-1114	Haberstick, Michael	3 APR 1769		Nippenose, Lycoming	300	D-56-157	Original: found
NP-1115	King, Robert	3 APR 1769	Berks	Washington, Lycoming	---	D-56-156	Original: found
NP-1116	Gillman, Adolph	3 APR 1769		East Branch Susquehanna River, Luzerne	300	A-37-269	Martin Kreider/(r1 APR 1782)Michel Shubard Original: found
NP-1117	McClure, William	3 APR 1769	West Branch Susquehanna River	LD: Lycoming	300		Original: found
NP-1118	Miller, Peter	3 APR 1769	Northampton	adjoining Stoke Manor, Luzerne/ LD: Luzerne	300	X-228	Original: found
NP-1119	Trotter, Robert	3 APR 1769	Berks	Washington, Lycoming	300	D-56-155	Original: found
NP-1120	McCoskey, William Jr.	3 APR 1769	Berks	Chillisquaque Creek, Northumberland	300	A-39-217	Mr. Allen/Mr. Tilghman/(r23 JAN 1770)Isaac Duncan Original: found
NP-1121	Brown, James	3 APR 1769		Liberty or Howard, Centre	300	C-149-237 C-188-281 C-188-282	James Samuel/(r17 JUN 1828)C. Nesselrode/(r5 OCT 1857)John Marsden Original: found
NP-1122	Clark, Jesse	3 APR 1769	Northampton	LD: Northumberland	300		Thomas Osburn Original: found
NP-1123	Garbel, Ephraim Benedict	3 APR 1769	Cumberland	North Huntingdon, Westmoreland	200	D-56-153 D-56-154	Anthonyn Walters/Andrew Byerly Original: found
NP-1123a	Garbel, Ephraim Benedict	3 APR 1769	Cumberland	Franklin, Westmoreland	100	D-56-153	Gen'l. Boquet Original: found
NP-1124	Flahavan, Roger	3 APR 1769		Trout Run, Centre		B-11	John Burns/(r9 JUL 1782)Margaret Duncan Original: found
NP-1125	Lamar, Marian	3 APR 1769	Cumberland	Buffalo Twp., Union	300	D-56-73	[same land as NP-2336 to Peter Bragth] Original: found

Table 6 - New Purchase Applications (1769-1773)

Number	Applicant	Date	Orig. Place	Later Place	Acres	Survey	Neighbors, Notes, etc.
NP-1126	Galbraith, Bartrem	3 APR 1769	Berks	above forks of Mahoning Creek, Montour	300	A-9-31	(r4 JUN 1773) Original: found
NP-1127	Robertson, Daniel	3 APR 1769	Cumberland	Centre/ LD: Centre	300		William Beaver Original: found
NP-1128	Clark, John	3 APR 1769	Muncy Creek	LD: Lycoming	300		Original: found
NP-1129	Jarvis, Susanna	3 APR 1769	at mouth of Fishing Creek, Berks or Northampton	LD: Columbia	300		Original: found
NP-1130	Kirlin, John	3 APR 1769	Berks	Augusta, Northumberland	300	D-57-62 C-189-185 C-189-191	(r21 FEB 1789)Casper Snyder Original: Signed
NP-1131	Brown, John	3 APR 1769	Chillisquaque Creek	LD: Montour	300		Original: found
NP-1132	Pierce, Joseph (of West Pennsborough Township, Cumberland County)	3 APR 1769	Washington	Chartiers Creek, Allegheny	300	C-157-220	Paul Pierce/(r8 DEC 1785)Paul Pierce Original: found
NP-1133	Markwrite, Stephen	3 APR 1769	Berks	Buffalo, Union	300	D-56-70	[same land as NP-2361 to Mary Allen] Original: found
NP-1134	Dixon, Samuel	3 APR 1769	Cumberland	Blacklick, Indiana	300	A-75-47	(r6 JUN 1832)Joseph Dickson & Gilles Doty & wife Original: found
NP-1135	Singer, John	3 APR 1769		Nippenose, Lycoming/ LD: Lycoming	300	D-56-152	[see caveat] Original: found
NP-1136	Thomas, John	3 APR 1769		North Huntingdon, Westmoreland	300	D-56-151	Joseph Brady Original: found
NP-1137	Wilts, Christian	3 APR 1769	Berks	Buffalo, Union	300	D-56-145	Rev. John Ewing Original: found
NP-1138	Davis, John	3 APR 1769	Northumberland	Muncy, Lycoming	300	X-241	(r17 MAR 1783)Stephen Collins Original: found
NP-1139	Hitchcock, John Jr.	3 APR 1769	Chillisquaque Creek	LD: Northumberland	300		John Letchworth/James Tilghman Original: found
NP-1140	Carruthers, James	3 APR 1769	Youghiogheny River	LD: Fayette	300		--- Crawford Original: found

Table 6 - New Purchase Applications (1769-1773)

Number	Applicant	Date	Orig. Place	Later Place	Acres	Survey	Neighbors, Notes, etc.
NP-1141	Salter, John	3 APR 1769	Berks	Limestone Run, Northumberland	200	A-38-214	Col. Francis/(r25 JUN 1784)James Jenkins Original: found
NP-1142	Brown, William	3 APR 1769	Northampton	Fishing Creek, Columbia	300	A-43-49	(r26 JUL 1781)Thomas Strawbridge Original: found
NP-1143	Gleaves, Isaac	3 APR 1769	Berks	Buffalo, Union	300	D-60-186	Robert Jewell/[same land as NP-1918 to John Blum] Original: found
NP-1144	Reay, George	3 APR 1769		Washington, Lycoming/ LD: Washington, Lycoming	150	D-56-144	Original: found
NP-1145	Cross, John	3 APR 1769	Northeast Branch Susquehanna River	LD: Point, Northumberland	300		Philip Dean Original: found
NP-1146	Forsith, Andrew	3 APR 1769		Turbot, Northumberland/ LD: Turbot, Northumberland	300		Henry Shriver Original: found
NP-1147	Commings, John	3 APR 1769		Columbia/ LD: Columbia	300		Richard Sattaford Original: found
NP-1148	Trump, John	3 APR 1769		Chillisquaque Creek, Northumberland/ LD: Northumberland	300		Peter Summers Original: found
NP-1149	Elliot, James	3 APR 1769		Wilkins, Allegheny	300	D-56-170	George Croghan Original: found
NP-1150	Smith, Thomas	3 APR 1769		Mifflin, Allegheny	300	D-57-73 D-57-77 M-408	Joseph Douglass/John Street/(r19 MAY 1786)John McClure Original: Signed
NP-1151	Murray, Francis	3 APR 1769		Pitt, Allegheny	300	D-56-169	Original: found
NP-1152	Weaver, George	3 APR 1769		Lawrence, Clearfield/ LD: Clearfield	300	D-56-143	Original: found
NP-1153	Sprogel, Ludwick	3 APR 1769		Hartley, Union	300	D-56-142	Original: found

Table 6 - New Purchase Applications (1769-1773)

Number	Applicant	Date	Orig. Place	Later Place	Acres	Survey	Neighbors, Notes, etc.
NP-1154	Clavoe, John	3 APR 1769	Northumberland	Madison, Columbia	300	D-46-67 D-46-68 C-108-13	(r4 MAR 1831)William Kitchen & J. Swisher Original: found
NP-1155	Freeman, John Jr.	3 APR 1769		Muncy, Lycoming	300	D-56-141	Original: found
NP-1156	Scott, Moses	3 APR 1769	Berks	Buffalo, Union	300	D-55-33 D-55-35	[same land as NP-1646 to Jennet Forster] Original: found
NP-1157	Greit, Bernard	3 APR 1769	Northampton	Tunkhannock Creek, Wyoming/ LD: Luzerne	300	D-46-95	John Lebig Original: found
NP-1158	Carmalt, Caleb	3 APR 1769	Cumberland	Union, Union	300	D-56-298	Original: found
NP-1159	White, John	3 APR 1769		Nippenose, Lycoming/ LD: Clinton	300	D-56-297	Original: Signed
NP-1160	Cooper, William	3 APR 1769	Berks	Turbot, Northumberland	300	M-217	William Murray/(r20 SEP 1774)William Murray Original: Signed by Alexander Murray
NP-1161	Campbell, Dugal	3 APR 1769		Jacobs Creek, Westmoreland	300	Q-314	Moses Lata/(r26 SEP 1787)David Hunter Original: found
NP-1162	Woolman, Uriah	3 APR 1769	Berks	Muddy Run, Northumberland	300	N-159	Israel Morris/(r28 JUN 1782)Reuben Haines Original: found
NP-1163	Crawford, John	3 APR 1769	Northumberland	Bald Eagle Creek, Centre/ LD: Centre	300	Z-51	Henry Quigley Original: found
NP-1164	Stephens, Even Sr.	3 APR 1769	Cumberland	Washington, Fayette	300	D-56-299 C-189-252	(p25 JUL 1788)E. Stephen Original: found
NP-1165	Lochery, William	3 APR 1769	Cumberland	Unity, Westmoreland	300	C-6-250 C-30-92 D-9-293 D-12-65 D-12-71 C-118-107 C-114-258	John Proctor/Capt. Lewis/William Proctor/(r25 FEB 1806)Joseph Campbell/(r19 OCT 1809)John Young/(r4 MAR 1819)George Smith/(r16 MAR 1831)John Boggert/(r7 FEB 1832)James Boggert Original: found
NP-1166	Kap, Frederick	3 APR 1769	Cumberland - Berks	West Buffalo, Union	300	D-56-295 D-56-296	Original: found
NP-1167	McMullin, Alexander	3 APR 1769	Cumberland	Pitt, Westmoreland	300	A-53-57	(r27 MAR 1788)Eli Coulter Original: found

Table 6 - New Purchase Applications (1769-1773)

Number	Applicant	Date	Orig. Place	Later Place	Acres	Survey	Neighbors, Notes, etc.
NP-1168	Armitage, James	3 APR 1769	Berks	Buffalo, Union/ LD: Buffalo, Union	300	D-56-294	Banance Person Original: found
NP-1169	Holt, Thomas	3 APR 1769	Bald Eagle Creek	LD: Centre	300		Adam Reigert Original: found
NP-1170	Reed, Isabella	3 APR 1769	Chillisquaque Creek	LD: Northumberland/ Montour	300		Mr. Allen Original: found
NP-1171	Thomas, Alexander	3 APR 1769		North Huntingdon & Hempfield, Westmoreland	300	D-56-151 A-29-48 C-11-33 C-11-34 C-11-35	Joseph Brady/(r15 MAR 1822)Martin Ashbaugh Original: found
NP-1172	Bear, John	3 APR 1769	Northumberland	Wyalusing Creek, Wyoming/ LD: Bradford	300	X-190	William Smith Original: found
NP-1173	Wilson, John	3 APR 1769	Berks	Buffalo, Union	300	D-57-13 D-57-12	[same land as NP-866 to John Clin] Original: Signed
NP-1174	Eppele, John	3 APR 1769	Bald Eagle Creek	LD: Centre	300		Original: found
NP-1175	Cory, Joseph	3 APR 1769	Northampton	Tunkhannock Creek, Wyoming	300	C-78-246	Ezekiel Sayre/(r27 JUN 1782)Capt. Mathew Henderson Original: found
NP-1176	Elliott, James	3 APR 1769	Westmoreland	on Kittanning Path, Indiana	300	A-87-187	(r18 APR 1799)John Evans & William Evans Original: found
NP-1177	Shank, Michael	3 APR 1769	Bald Eagle Creek	LD: Centre	300		Christopher Rygar Original: found
NP-1178	Robinson, Alexander	3 APR 1769	Cumberland	Limestone Creek, Northumberland	300	C-176-153	John Taylor/(r9 JUL 1782)Thomas Riche Original: found
NP-1179	Vance, Alexander	3 APR 1769	Cumberland	Tyrone, Fayette	300	A-10-186	(r25 FEB 1814)James Torrance Original: found
NP-1180	Dallam, Richard	3 APR 1769	Bald Eagle Creek, Cumberland	LD: Centre	300		John Dallam Original: found

Table 6 - New Purchase Applications (1769-1773)

Number	Applicant	Date	Orig. Place	Later Place	Acres	Survey	Neighbors, Notes, etc.
NP-1181	Chamberlin, John	3 APR 1769	Brushy Run in Redstone Settlement, Cumberland	LD: Fayette	300		Original: found
NP-1182	Duncan, John	3 APR 1769		Derry, Westmoreland	300	D-56-293	George Pumeroy/Alexander Barr/William Guthery Original: found
NP-1183	McEmery, William	3 APR 1769	Berks	Washington, Lycoming	300	D-56-292	William Coster Original: found
NP-1184	Miller, Jacob	3 APR 1769		White Deer, Union	300	D-56-291	Original: found
NP-1185	Tagart, Michael	3 APR 1769	Cumberland	Bullskin, Fayette	300	L-257	Lewis Devale/(r21 MAY 1793)James Keith, Exr. of Richard Stephenson Original: found
NP-1186	Connor, Roger	3 APR 1769		North Branch Susquehanna River, Luzerne/ LD: Huntingdon, Luzerne	300		John Farree Original: found
NP-1187	Morton, Robert	3 APR 1769	Laurence Creek, West Branch Susquehanna River	LD: Lycoming	300		Original: found
NP-1188	Long, Richard	3 APR 1769	Bald Eagle Creek	LD: Centre	300		Original: found
NP-1189	Lowers, Andrew	3 APR 1769	Cumberland	Blacklick, Indiana	300	A-33-266 A-33-267 A-33-280 D-56-87 D-56-88	Moses Stuart/Shedrick Muchnou [Muchmore]/[see caveat] Original: found
NP-1190	Sayre, Parson	3 APR 1769	Rush Meadow, Northampton	LD: Bradford	300		Ezekiel Sayre Original: found
NP-1191	Dicks, John	3 APR 1769	Northumberland	Sheshequin, Bradford	300	A-28-193	(r17 JUL 1854)Edward Spalding & Ann Spalding & John Snyder Original: found
NP-1192	Roberts, John	3 APR 1769	Laurel Hill, Cumberland	LD: Westmoreland	300		Enoch David/[see caveat] Original: found
NP-1193	Christy, William Jr.	3 APR 1769		Franklin, Westmoreland	300	C-35-242	Thomas Holtsland/(r30 MAR 1789)Eli Coulter Original: found

Table 6 - New Purchase Applications (1769-1773)

Number	Applicant	Date	Orig. Place	Later Place	Acres	Survey	Neighbors, Notes, etc.
NP-1194	Roberts, Margaret	3 APR 1769		LD: Wayne/ Greene	300		John Mauregnalt Original: found
NP-1195	Messersmith, John	3 APR 1769		Chillisquaque Creek, Northumberland	100	R-243	Col. Francis/(r26 MAY 1801)John Boyd Original: found
NP-1196	Vanhorne, Abram	3 APR 1769	East Branch Susquehanna River	LD: Luzerne	150		Original: signed
NP-1197	Stephen, Andrew	3 APR 1769	Berks	Washington, Lycoming	300	D-56-285	Original: found
NP-1198	Machan, Robert	3 APR 1769		Unity, Westmoreland	300	D-56-284	John Frazier/Thomas Thompson Jr. Original: found
NP-1199	Riche, Sarah	3 APR 1769	White Deer Hole Creek	LD: Lycoming	300		Thomas Riche Original: found
NP-1200	Galespie, Nathaniel	3 APR 1769	Berks	Buffalo Creek, Union	300	D-56-283	Stephen Porter Original: found
NP-1201	McCaskey, Alexander	3 APR 1769	Berks	White Deer, Union	300	D-56-261	Original: found
NP-1202	Gover, Cassandra	3 APR 1769		Stony Creek Twp., Somerset/ LD: Somerset	300		William Clark Original: found
NP-1203	Phile, Frederick	3 APR 1769	Westmoreland	Kiskiminitas River, Allegheny	300	C-157-197	James Searle/(r20 SEP 1784) Original: found
NP-1204	Shaffner, Charles	3 APR 1769	Cumberland - Berks	Buffalo, Union	300	D-56-281 D-56-282	Jacob Shafner Original: found
NP-1205	Willhelm, Jacob	3 APR 1769		East side Allegheny River, Westmoreland	300	D-56-262	Caleb Graydon Original: found
NP-1206	Trotter, Robert	3 APR 1769	Berks	Washington, Lycoming	300	D-56-263	Original: found
NP-1207	Thompson, James	3 APR 1769		Versailles, Allegheny	300	D-56-168	Original: found
NP-1208	Holmesing, John	3 APR 1769	White Deer Creek	LD: Lycoming	300		Original: found
NP-1209	Walton, Elizabeth	3 APR 1769	Cumberland - Clearfield	Muncy, Lycoming	300	D-56-264 D-56-265	Elizabeth Jarvis, Jr. Original: found
NP-1210	Robinson, John	3 APR 1769		White Deer, Union	300	C-141-51	(r17 DEC 1792)James McLaughlin/[see caveat] Original: found

Table 6 - New Purchase Applications (1769-1773)

Number	Applicant	Date	Orig. Place	Later Place	Acres	Survey	Neighbors, Notes, etc.
NP-1211	Coster, William	3 APR 1769	Berks	Washington, Lycoming	300	D-56-271	Original: found
NP-1212	Cummins, Charles	3 APR 1769		Fairfield, Westmoreland	300	D-64-105 D-490	John Hinkson/(r1 JUN 1811)James Brady Original: Signed
NP-1213	Hays, Robert	3 APR 1769	Cumberland - Westmoreland	Little Redstone Creek, Fayette	300	B-1-121	(r11 SEP 1783 & 26 MAR 1788)Dorsey Penticost, Esq. Original: found
NP-1214	Travis, John	3 APR 1769	Washington	Monongahela River, Allegheny	300	D-173	Bastian Frederick/Joseph Douglass/(r24 JAN 1788)William Butler Original: Signed
NP-1215	Myer, John	3 APR 1769		Buffalo, Union	300	D-56-272	Original: found
NP-1216	Douglas, Samuel	3 APR 1769		Blacklick, Indiana/ LD: Blacklick, Indiana	300	D-56-273 D-56-274	Original: found
NP-1217	Montgomery, David	3 APR 1769		Muncy, Lycoming	300	D-56-275	Original: found
NP-1218	McKiney, Alexander	3 APR 1769	Westmoreland	forks of Youghiogheny & Monongahela Rivers, Allegheny	300	D-56-184	Original: found
NP-1219	Starrit, Relph	3 APR 1769		Pitt, Allegheny	300	C-17-80 C-17-87	(r13 DEC 1805)James Blaine & Robert Blaine Original: found
NP-1220	Miller, Henry	3 APR 1769	Berks	Black Hole Creek, Union	300	C-39-221	(r29 APR 1773)Michel Diffenderfer Original: found
NP-1221	Parsons, Weldon	3 APR 1769		East Branch Bald Eagle Creek, Clinton/ LD: Clinton	300		William Knowls Original: found
NP-1222	Quigley, Chrisley	3 APR 1769		White Deer, Union	300	D-56-276	William Blyth Original: found
NP-1223	Eatton, John	3 APR 1769		Centre, Indiana	300	C-202-170 C-123-135 C-123-136	(r12 FEB 1806)David Sample/(r27 JAN 1812)John Lowry Original: found

Table 6 - New Purchase Applications (1769-1773)

Number	Applicant	Date	Orig. Place	Later Place	Acres	Survey	Neighbors, Notes, etc.
NP-1224	Gibbs, Robert	3 APR 1769	Bedford	West Wheatfield, Indiana	300	A-75-13	James McCurdy/Hugh Gibson/(r23 NOV 1830)F. Perian on warrant to Thomas Clark, guardian/[see C-191-1] Original: Signed
NP-1225	Erwin, Sarah	3 APR 1769		Findlay, Allegheny	300	D-56-167	James Erwin Original: found
NP-1226	Claypoole, James Jr.	3 APR 1769		Northeast Branch Susquehanna River, Luzerne/ LD: Salem, Luzerne	200		Original: found
NP-1227	Guy, Richard	3 APR 1769	Laurence Creek	LD: Lycoming	300		Original: found
NP-1228	Hall, Jacob	3 APR 1769	Berks	Kelly, Union	300		[same land as NP-2225 to Breeson Bawden] Original: found
NP-1229	Parrock, John	3 APR 1769	Northampton	Little Fishing Creek, Columbia	300	D-512	Isaac Stroude/(r3 MAR 1800 & 4 OCT 1800)Thomas Stewardson & John Biddle Original: found
NP-1230	Travers, Patrick	3 APR 1769	Margarets Creek, West Branch Susquehanna River	LD: Lycoming	300		Thomas Smith Original: found
NP-1231	Perkins, Ruben	3 APR 1769	Cumberland	Bald Eagle Creek, Centre/ LD: Centre	300	A-250	Thomas Smith Original: found
NP-1232	Harris, Joseph	3 APR 1769	Cumberland - Berks	Gregg, Union/ LD: Clinton	300	A-250	Original: found
NP-1233	Hazlehurst, Isaac	3 APR 1769	Berks	Limestone Branch, Northumberland	300	A-18-277	(r28 NOV 1771)Reuben Haines & Samuel Miles Original: found
NP-1234	Appelgate, Benjamin	3 APR 1769		Elizabeth, Allegheny/ LD: Elizabeth, Allegheny	300	Z-71 A-81-215	Original: found
NP-1235	Shaffer, Alexander	3 APR 1769	Berks	Kelly, Union	300		[same land as NP-1989 to Isaac Allen] Original: found
NP-1236	Kriteers, Andrew	3 APR 1769		Muncy Creek Twp., Lycoming	300	D-56-277	Original: found

Table 6 - New Purchase Applications (1769-1773)

Number	Applicant	Date	Orig. Place	Later Place	Acres	Survey	Neighbors, Notes, etc.
NP-1237	Armstrong, George	3 APR 1769	Westmoreland	Black Lick Creek, Indiana	300	A-5-283	(r11 NOV 1790)Samuel Dickson Original: Signed by Joseph Armstrong
NP-1238	Shute, Joseph	3 APR 1769	Cumberland	Washington, Lycoming	300	D-56-144 D-56-220 W-287	Samuel Richards/[see caveat] Original: found
NP-1239	Davis, David	3 APR 1769	Berks	Buffalo, Union	300	D-60-205 D-60-211 C-87-232	(r19 DEC 1803)Philip Hay Original: Signed
NP-1240	Reed, James	3 APR 1769	Red Bank Creek	LD: Armstrong	300		Thomas Rees Original: Signed
NP-1241	Blyth, George	3 APR 1769	Berks	Kelly, Union/ LD: Kelly, Union	300	D-56-278 D-56-260 D-56-279 D-56-280	Original: found
NP-1242	Vandunn, David	3 APR 1769	Northeast Branch Susquehanna River	LD: Luzerne	300		Original: found
NP-1243	Doz, Andrew	3 APR 1769	Berks	Muncy, Lycoming/ LD: Northumberland/ Union	300	F-228	Alexander Powers Original: Signed
NP-1244	Galoway, Alexander	3 APR 1769	Lowomen Creek	LD: Lycoming	300		Original: found
NP-1245	Long, Robert	3 APR 1769	Berks	Washington, Lycoming	300	N-87	(r15 APR 1785)Edward Shippen & Joseph Shippen, Esq. Original: found
NP-1246	Benham, Thomas	3 APR 1769	Cumberland	Franklin, Westmoreland	300	D-57-47 A-34-6 A-34-7 C-9-183 C-9-184	William Benham/Richard Battler/(r29 DEC 1796)John Botts/(r20 JUN 1809)Daniel Bloss Original: found
NP-1247	Carson, Samuel	3 APR 1769	Cumberland - Bedford	Sewickley Creek, Westmoreland/ LD: Westmoreland	300	Z-52	David Jackson Original: found
NP-1248	Minster, Charles	3 APR 1769	East Branch Susquehanna River	LD: Northumberland	300		Original: found

Table 6 - New Purchase Applications (1769-1773)

Number	Applicant	Date	Orig. Place	Later Place	Acres	Survey	Neighbors, Notes, etc.
NP-1249	Diggs, George	3 APR 1769	Berks	Kelly, Union/ LD: Union	300	D-56-280	Original: Missing
NP-1250	Harvey, James	3 APR 1769	Youghiogheny River	LD: Fayette/ Westmoreland	300		--- Stewart/Samuel McPherson Original: found
NP-1251	Mercer, Hugh	3 APR 1769	Cumberland	Youghiogheny River, Fayette	300	M-234	--- Stewart/--- McPherson/--- Dorsiris/--- Roston/(r26 FEB 1771) Original: found
NP-1252	Butler, Richard	3 APR 1769	Berks	adjoining Shamokin Hill, Northumberland	100	C-220-291	(r12 NOV 1772)John Wiggins Original: Signed
NP-1253	Polock, Oliver	3 APR 1769		Spring, Centre/ LD: Spring, Centre	300	A-34-37	Original: Missing
NP-1254	Carson, Samuel	3 APR 1769		Northeast Branch Susquehanna River, Luzerne/ LD: Luzerne	300		Original: found
NP-1255	Umsted, John	3 APR 1769		Buffalo, Union	300	A-5-92 C-94-108 A-5-93 C-94-107 A-31-97 C-180-42 D-2-38	(r12 FEB 1834)David Heinly/(r12 FEB 1834)John Heinly/(r13 FEB 1839)William Robinson & wife/(r6 MAR 1840)Jacob Young/[see caveat] Original: Signed
NP-1256	James, Martha	3 APR 1769	Berks	Limestone Run, Northumberland	300	C-49-265	(r5 JUL 1791)George Frey Original: found
NP-1257	Cuddy, Jacob	3 APR 1769	Cumberland	Westmoreland	300	C-10-75	Thomas Benham/(r9 OCT 1788)Dorcas Boyd Original: found
NP-1258	Paris, Peter Jr.	3 APR 1769	Chillisquaque Creek	LD: Turbot, Northumberland	200		Peter Paris [his father] Original: found
NP-1259	Edwards, Daniel	3 APR 1769	Laurel Hill, Cumberland	LD: Somerset	300		John Roberts/[see caveat] Original: found
NP-1260	Evans, William	3 APR 1769		Franklin, Westmoreland	300	Q-237	Thomas Butler, Sr./Philip Willisill/(r20 FEB 1794)John Barclay, Esq. Original: Signed
NP-1261	Dill, Robert	3 APR 1769	Cumberland	North Huntingdon, Westmoreland	300	I-336	(r10 AUG 1770) Original: found

Table 6 - New Purchase Applications (1769-1773)

Number	Applicant	Date	Orig. Place	Later Place	Acres	Survey	Neighbors, Notes, etc.
NP-1262	Bickman, Christopher	3 APR 1769	Berks	Susquehanna River, Northumberland	100	E-317	John Cox/(r15 OCT 1782)Charles Gough Original: found
NP-1263	Lauttenschleiger, George	3 APR 1769	West Branch Susquehanna River	LD: Lycoming	300		Michael Anders/[see caveat] Original: found
NP-1264	Grier, William	3 APR 1769		Unity, Westmoreland	300	D-56-284 A-52-203	John Proctor/(r10 AUG 1787) Original: found
NP-1265	Earl, David	3 APR 1769		Wayne, Lycoming	300	D-56-266	Original: found
NP-1266	Forster, John Sr.	3 APR 1769		Kelly, Union	300	D-56-267	[see caveat] Original: found
NP-1267	Gowdey, Samuel	3 APR 1769		Turbot, Northumberland	300	C-74-164	(r5 MAY 1791)Robert Hays Original: found
NP-1268	Nellson, Nathaniel	3 APR 1769		Hempfield, Westmoreland	300	D-56-268	Joseph Irwin Original: Signed
NP-1269	Scott, James Sr.	3 APR 1769	Lakeamack [Lycoming?] Creek, North side West Branch Susquehanna River	LD: Lycoming	300		Original: found
NP-1270	Sterrat, James	3 APR 1769		Muncy Creek Twp., Lycoming	300	D-56-270	Original: found
NP-1271	Tomson, Cornelius	3 APR 1769	Westmoreland	East side Monongahela River, Allegheny	300	Y-255	Walter Wall/(r21 NOV 1787) Original: found
NP-1272	Caldwell, James	3 APR 1769		Washington, Lycoming	300	D-56-269	Richard Steel Original: found
NP-1273	Botts, George	3 APR 1769	Berks	Buffalo Creek, Union	300	C-118-285	Samuel Bayloss, Sr./(r23 AUG 1785)Samuel McClay Original: found
NP-1274	Roberts, Richard	3 APR 1769	Berks	Muddy Run, Northumberland	300	N-156	Abraham Kintzing/(r28 JUN 1782)Reuben Haines Original: found
NP-1275	Sylverton, Benjamin	3 APR 1769	Berks	Turbot, Northumberland	300	C-21-269 C-21-270	Isaac Corso/(r13 SEP 1803)Daniel Caldwell Original: found

Table 6 - New Purchase Applications (1769-1773)

Number	Applicant	Date	Orig. Place	Later Place	Acres	Survey	Neighbors, Notes, etc.
NP-1276	Gridley, Joseph	3 APR 1769		Turbot, Northumberland/ LD: Northumberland	300		Andrew Forsythe Original: found
NP-1277	Knight, Hannah	3 APR 1769	Cumberland	Westmoreland/ LD: Somerset	300		John Green Original: found
NP-1278	Sprogell, John	3 APR 1769	Northampton	East Branch Fishing Creek, Columbia	300	C-25-102 C-25-103	(r20 DEC 1783)John Champ Original: found
NP-1279	Sympson, John	3 APR 1769	Berks	Washington, Lycoming	300	A-54-298	(r9 NOV 1816)William Gibson Original: found
NP-1280	Armstrong, Thomas	3 APR 1769	Muncy Creek	LD: Lycoming	300		Original: found
NP-1281	Scot, Moses	3 APR 1769		Franklin, Westmoreland & Versailles, Allegheny	300	D-56-166 D-56-180	Original: found
NP-1282	Hulings, Markus	3 APR 1769		Turbot, Northumberland	300	C-53-48	William Irwin/Richard Irwin/(r5 MAY 1791)John Coughran/[see caveat] Original: found
NP-1283	Morgan, John	3 APR 1769	Cumberland	above mouth of Clearfield Creek, Clearfield	300	D-3-272	Jacob Morgan, Jr./(r28 JUN 1808)Abram Witmer, Esq. Original: Signed by Jacob Morgan, Jr.
NP-1284	Humphreys, Richard	3 APR 1769	Northumberland	Muncy, Lycoming	300	C-93-143	Jeremiah Warder, Jr./(r19 SEP 1794)John Hall Original: found
NP-1285	Means, Hugh	3 APR 1769		West Buffalo, Union	300	D-56-250	Adam Torrence Original: Signed
NP-1286	Willson, Mathew	3 APR 1769	Bedford	Rostraver, Westmoreland	300	B-32	George Wotle/(r29 AUG 1785)Benjamin Davis Original: found
NP-1287	Mitchel, Joseph	3 APR 1769	Cumberland	Monongahela River 3 miles above Ten Mile Creek, Washington/ LD: Washington	300	X-227	Original: found
NP-1288	Buyvank, Peter	3 APR 1769		Washington, Lycoming	300	A-54-221	Samuel Boone/(r18 OCT 1810)James Cummins Original: found
NP-1289	Mitchell, James	3 APR 1769	Bald Eagle Creek	LD: Clinton/ Centre	300		Ross Mitchell Original: found

Table 6 - New Purchase Applications (1769-1773)

Number	Applicant	Date	Orig. Place	Later Place	Acres	Survey	Neighbors, Notes, etc.
NP-1290	Miller, Gustavus	3 APR 1769		Hempfield, Westmoreland	300	D-56-248 D-56-249	Nathaniel Nelson/Edward Higgins Original: found
NP-1291	Hall, John	3 APR 1769	Berks	West Branch Susquehanna River, Centre	300	C-192-53	Alexander McNitt/John McNitt/(r16 FEB 1786)John B. Smith, Esq. Original: found
NP-1292	Samuels, James	3 APR 1769	Mifflin	Liberty, Centre/ LD: Liberty, Centre	300	W-288 C-14-257 C-188-282 C-188-283	(r20 JAN 1853)Christian Bechtel/(r5 OCT 1857)John Marsden Original: found
NP-1293	Thompson, Samuel	3 APR 1769	Cumberland	Allegheny, Westmoreland	300	M-242	Aneas Mackay/(r31 AUG 1787)widow Mackey & children/[see caveat] Original: found
NP-1294	James, Martha	3 APR 1769	Berks	Muncy, Northumberland/ LD: Columbia	300	D-53-76 D-15-17	(r8 OCT 1795)Samuel Wallis Original: found
NP-1295	Trester, Michael	3 APR 1769	Berks	Hartley, Union	300	D-56-247	John Harris Original: found
NP-1296	Morton, James	3 APR 1769	Cumberland	Howard, Centre	300	C-10-185 C-10-186 C-10-187	(r15 APR 1811)William Brown Original: found
NP-1297	Reed, John	3 APR 1769		Versailles, Allegheny	300	D-56-166 C-131-17	Daniel Rees/(r13 JAN 1817)William Larimore & John Larimore Original: Signed
NP-1298	Crawford, William	3 APR 1769	Berks	White Deer, Union	300	D-56-246	Christian Quigley Original: found
NP-1299	Hunter, Joseph	3 APR 1769	Cumberland	East side Monongahela River, Fayette	300	B-11-96 B-11-79	Hugo Gilmore/(r2 JUN 1789)Robert Gordon Original: Signed
NP-1300	Casper, John	3 APR 1769	Berks	Kelly, Union	200	D-56-260	[see caveat] Original: found
NP-1301	Death, Edward	3 APR 1769	Cumberland	Luzerne, Fayette	300	D-56-259	Original: found
NP-1302	Poe, Thomas	3 APR 1769		North Huntingdon, Westmoreland	300	D-56-257 D-56-258	Original: found

Table 6 - New Purchase Applications (1769-1773)

Number	Applicant	Date	Orig. Place	Later Place	Acres	Survey	Neighbors, Notes, etc.
NP-1303	Schneider, George	3 APR 1769	forks of Fishing Creek, East Branch Susquehanna River	LD: Columbia	300		Original: found
NP-1304	Washington, Col. George	3 APR 1769	Cumberland - Westmoreland	Youghiogheny River, Fayette	300	A-64-96	(r18 FEB 1782) Original: found
NP-1305	Morison, James	3 APR 1769		Ligonier, Westmoreland	300	D-56-255 D-56-256	--- Limes Original: found
NP-1306	Hall, Elihu Jr.	3 APR 1769	Cumberland	LD: Somerset	300		Ruth Hunt Original: found
NP-1307	Shippen, Joseph Jr.	3 APR 1769		Augusta, Northumberland	300	A-466 D-7-90 C-43-65 B-17-186 C-178-299 C-178-300	(r7 SEP 1810)Philip Weiser & Mary Weiser/(1 APR 1817)Philip Denny/(r27 DEC 1821)John D. Ross/(r5 APR 1830)--- Baker & P. Shipman Original: found
NP-1308	Ashton, William	3 APR 1769		Kelly, Union/ LD: Kelly, Union	300	D-56-253 D-56-254	Mr. Ewing Original: found
NP-1309	Steel, James	3 APR 1769	Cumberland	LD: Luzerne	300		Jacob Hiltzeman Original: found
NP-1310	Trimble, Thomas	3 APR 1769	Berks	Buffalo, Union	300	D-60-198	Thomas McGuire/[same land as NP-1918 to John Blum] Original: Signed
NP-1311	Hare, John	3 APR 1769		Muncy, Lycoming	300	D-56-252	Abram Hare Original: found
NP-1312	Denny, William	3 APR 1769		Jefferson, Allegheny	300	D-56-179	Original: found
NP-1313	Barr, William Jr.	3 APR 1769	Bedford	Fairfield, Westmoreland	300	A-35-121	Hugh Gibson/Andrew Barr/(r14 MAR 1810)J. Updegraff Original: Signed by John Barr
NP-1314	Sharon, Samuel	3 APR 1769	Berks	Buffalo, Union	300	D-62-32	[same land as NP-2522 to Alexander Armstrong] Original: Signed
NP-1315	Forster, James Sr.	3 APR 1769		Muncy, Lycoming	300	D-56-245	Original: found
NP-1316	McClure, Denny	3 APR 1769		Franklin, Westmoreland	300	D-56-251	Original: Signed "John McClure in Cumberland."

Table 6 - New Purchase Applications (1769-1773)

Number	Applicant	Date	Orig. Place	Later Place	Acres	Survey	Neighbors, Notes, etc.
NP-1317	McClellan, James	3 APR 1769	Bedford	Unity, Westmoreland	300	C-116-271	(r10 MAY 1790) Original: found
NP-1318	Rowland, Evan	3 APR 1769		Huntingdon, Westmoreland	300	C-35-224	(r2 SEP 1788)Patrick Campbell Original: found
NP-1319	Brown, Thomas	3 APR 1769		West Branch Susquehanna River, Lycoming/ LD: Lycoming	300		Original: Signed by William Brown
NP-1320	Brown, Benjamin	3 APR 1769	Chillisquaque Creek	LD: Montour	300		Original: found
NP-1321	Cook, Edward	3 APR 1769		Huntingdon, Westmoreland	300	C-25-164	--- Claphan/(r7 FEB 1786)James Curnahans Original: found
NP-1322	Patterson, John	3 APR 1769		German, Fayette	300	C-172-27	Hugh Gilmore/(r19 MAY 1787)/[see caveat] Original: Signed
NP-1323	Pole, John	3 APR 1769	Rush Meadow, Northampton	LD: Northumberland	300		Adam Pole Original: found
NP-1324	Young, Aquilir	3 APR 1769	Bedford	Ligonier, Westmoreland	300	C-62-143 C-62-144 C-62-145	Samuel Shannon/Philip Harmon/George Cilts/(r11 MAR 1824)Abel Fisher & Matthias Fisher Original: found
NP-1325	Evalt, John	3 APR 1769		Unity, Westmoreland	300	D-56-243 D-56-244	--- Proctor/John Davis Original: found
NP-1326	McCalester, David	3 APR 1769		Allegheny, Cambria	300	D-56-242	John Miller Original: found
NP-1327	Green, John	3 APR 1769	Cumberland	Westmoreland/ LD: Westmoreland	300		Robert Elder Original: found
NP-1328	Gallahur, Thomas	3 APR 1769	Berks	Washington, Lycoming	300	D-56-241	Original: found
NP-1329	Nixon, Allen	3 APR 1769	Berks	Branch of Mahoning Creek, Montour/ LD: Columbia	300	X-157	Original: found
NP-1330	Yarnell, Mordicia	3 APR 1769	East Branch Susquehanna River, Forks of Fishing Creek		300		Original: found

Table 6 - New Purchase Applications (1769-1773)

Number	Applicant	Date	Orig. Place	Later Place	Acres	Survey	Neighbors, Notes, etc.
NP-1331	Shippen, Joseph W.	3 APR 1769		Northeast Branch Susquehanna River, Luzerne/ LD: Luzerne	300	W-289	Original: found
NP-1332	Badger, Susanna	3 APR 1769	Roaring Creek, West Branch Susquehanna River		300		John Rich Original: found
NP-1333	Elliot, Daniel	3 APR 1769		Pitt, Westmoreland	300	A-77-172	(r6 OCT 1786)William Elliott Original: found
NP-1334	Ratan, Josiah	3 APR 1769	Berks	West Buffalo, Union	300	D-63-71 D-63-72	[same land warranted to Thomas Paschal 25 AUG 1772] Original: found
NP-1335	Galloway, Samuel	3 APR 1769		Washington, Lycoming/ LD: Washington, Lycoming	300	D-56-144 D-56-220 C-72-146 C-86-131 C-86-132	(r9 FEB 1831)Isaac Allen/(r3 AUG 1831)A. L. Hay & Isabella Hay[his wife] Original: found
NP-1336	Small, James	3 APR 1769	Westmoreland	Plum, Allegheny & North Huntingdon, Westmoreland	300	C-38-6 C-38-7 C-38-15	Thomas Small/(r29 MAR 1832)Hugh Cavett Original: found
NP-1337	Baird, James	3 APR 1769		North Huntingdon, Westmoreland	300	C-71-123 C-71-124 C-71-125 C-71-126 C-20-136	--- Baird/"joining the place where Rough the body formerly lived"/(r27 OCT 1787)/(r13 APR 1797)James Guffee/[see caveat] Original: found
NP-1338	Hews, Josiah	3 APR 1769		between Pine & Lycoming Creeks, Lycoming/ LD: Northumberland/ Lycoming	300	A-36-13	Original: found
NP-1339	Lowrey, Nathaniel	3 APR 1769	Berks	Buffalo, Union	300	D-56-228 D-56-229 D-56-230	Original: found
NP-1340	Mitchel, Samuel	3 APR 1769	Berks	White Deer, Union	300	D-56-226 D-56-227	Original: Signed

Table 6 - New Purchase Applications (1769-1773)

Number	Applicant	Date	Orig. Place	Later Place	Acres	Survey	Neighbors, Notes, etc.
NP-1341	Ewing, George	3 APR 1769	Berks	Kelly, Union	300		[same land as NP-3489 to James Anderson]/[see caveat] Original: found
NP-1342	Stout, Benjamin Jr.	3 APR 1769		Nippenose, Lycoming	300	D-56-240	Original: found
NP-1343	Erwin, Robert	3 APR 1769		Salem, Westmoreland	300	D-56-238 D-56-239	Original: found
NP-1344	Folbert, John	3 APR 1769		Unity, Westmoreland	300	D-56-237	Original: found
NP-1345	Murray, John	3 APR 1769		Pitt, Allegheny	300	D-56-178	Original: found
NP-1346	Beatty, James	3 APR 1769		Plum, Allegheny/ LD: Plum, Allegheny	300	X-191 C-189-67 C-189-96 C-28-290	(r23 FEB 1826)John Reed/(25 FEB 1831)R. Clugstone Original: found
NP-1347	Knight, George	3 APR 1769		Bald Eagle, Centre	300	A-77-94	Michael Knight/(r27 OCT 1783)Samuel Wallis Original: found
NP-1348	Rowan, Charles	3 APR 1769		Unity, Westmoreland	300	B-23-65 B-23-66	Original: found
NP-1349	Johns, Nathan	3 APR 1769	Cumberland	LD: Stony Creek, Somerset	300		Sarah Coale, Sr. Original: found
NP-1350	Meninger, Theodorus	3 APR 1769		Muncy Creek Twp., Lycoming	300	D-56-236	Original: found
NP-1351	Quigley, James	3 APR 1769	six or seven miles from Fort Augusta	LD: Northumberland	300		Original: found
NP-1352	Kick, William	3 APR 1769		Muncy, Lycoming/ LD: Muncy, Lycoming	300	D-56-235	Original: found
NP-1353	Peairs, John	3 APR 1769		Elizabeth, Allegheny	300	D-56-171	--- Alexander Original: Signed
NP-1354	Codd, Nicholas	3 APR 1769	Berks	Washington, Lycoming	300	D-56-234	Francis Murphy Original: found
NP-1355	Cuddy, Henry	3 APR 1769		Hempfield & North Huntingdon, Westmoreland	300	D-56-233 D-64-111 C-75-72	--- Byerly/(r29 DEC 1787)Daniel Herhold Original: found

Table 6 - New Purchase Applications (1769-1773)

Number	Applicant	Date	Orig. Place	Later Place	Acres	Survey	Neighbors, Notes, etc.
NP-1356	Supplee, John	3 APR 1769	West Branch Susquehanna River	LD: Clinton	300		Original: found
NP-1357	Brown, John	3 APR 1769		Lawrence, Clearfield	300	D-62-246 A-18-202	(r9 NOV 1785)James Stewart/(r5 MAY 1807)Joseph B. McKean & Joseph Miles Original: found
NP-1358	Porter, William	3 APR 1769		Franklin, Westmoreland	300	A-4-60	(r28 MAR 1788)William Jack Original: found
NP-1359	Wither, Michael	3 APR 1769	Northampton	Windham, Luzerne/ LD: Windham, Luzerne	300	A-5-21 C-105-105	John Miller/(r19 APR 1841)P. B. Jennings Original: found
NP-1360	Alexander, James	3 APR 1769	Northampton	Muncy Creek, Lycoming	300	E-29	Conrad Hover/(r17 MAR 1784)Samuel Wallis Original: found
NP-1361	Wiser, Jane	3 APR 1769	East Branch Muncy Creek	LD: Lycoming	300		Jacob Wiser Original: found
NP-1362	Barr, Robert	3 APR 1769		Derry, Westmoreland	300	D-55-23 C-71-197 C-71-206	James Barr[his brother]/(r7 AUG 1801)William Gillson Original: found
NP-1363	Rownd, Samuel	3 APR 1769	Northampton	Southeast of Wyoming, Luzerne	300	D-6-20	(r23 JAN 1783)H. Williamson, Esq. Original: found
NP-1364	Neill, Henry	3 APR 1769		West Buffalo, Union	300	D-56-232	Rev. Mr. Ewing Original: found
NP-1365	Pobjay, James	3 APR 1769	Berks	Chillisquaque Creek, Montour	300	A-70-298	Col. Francis/(r14 DEC 1787)George Dougherty Original: found
NP-1366	Soler, Daniel	3 APR 1769		Ligonier, Westmoreland	300	D-56-231	Original: found
NP-1367	Reigert, Stophle	3 APR 1769		Bald Eagle, Centre	300	D-6-47	(r29 JUL 1784)John Whitmer, Jr. Original: found
NP-1368	Foulks, James	3 APR 1769	Berks	Chillisquaque, Northumberland	300	C-16-103 C-31-210	(r8 MAY 1813)John Boyd & William Wilson/(r13 FEB 1822)John Call/(r28 DEC 1839)Denis Bony/(r28 DEC 1839)Peter Call/(r8 APR 1840)Henry Man/(r8 APR 1840)Dennis Call Original: found
NP-1369	Ogelsvee, Jane	3 APR 1769	Berks	Chillisquaque Creek, Northumberland/ LD: Lycoming	300	W-66	Original: found

Table 6 - New Purchase Applications (1769-1773)

Number	Applicant	Date	Orig. Place	Later Place	Acres	Survey	Neighbors, Notes, etc.
NP-1370	McCausland, Alexander	3 APR 1769	Cumberland	Allegheny & Clearfield, Cambria	300	C-157-67	Alexander Stewert/(r24 MAY 1848)John T. Miles Original: found
NP-1371	Burd, Thomas	3 APR 1769		Crooked Creek, Armstrong/ LD: Armstrong	300	A-16-159	Original: found
NP-1372	Murray, Alexander	3 APR 1769	Chillisquaque Creek	LD: Northumberland	300		Robert Fowler Original: Signed
NP-1373	Taylor, Samuel	3 APR 1769		Fairfield, Westmoreland	300	D-56-225	John Cumming Original: found
NP-1374	Hays, Robart	3 APR 1769		between Turtle & Loyalhanna Creeks, Westmoreland	300	C-75-124	William Clogstone/(r1 APR 1788) Original: found
NP-1375	Loaf, James	3 APR 1769		Turbot, Northumberland	300	D-56-224	Original: Signed
NP-1376	Lugar, John	3 APR 1769	East Branch Susquehanna River	LD: Columbia	300		Original: found
NP-1377	Brown, William Jr.	3 APR 1769		Blacklick, Indiana	300	D-56-223 D-56-45 A-75-55	(r20 SEP 1787) Original: Signed by "William Brown, Carlisle."
NP-1378	Lauk, George	3 APR 1769		Nippenose, Lycoming	300	D-56-222	Original: found
NP-1379	Fleamons, Charles	3 APR 1769		Kelly, Union	200	D-56-221	Original: found
NP-1380	McNitt, William	3 APR 1769		Fairfield, Lycoming	300	D-56-210	Original: found
NP-1381	Whitman, Nathan	3 APR 1769		Pitt, Allegheny	300	D-56-177	John Friend Original: found
NP-1382	Patterson, John	3 APR 1769	Berks	Beaver Run branch of Chillisquaque Creek, Northumberland	300	C-146-208	(r1 DEC 1769) Original: found
NP-1383	Espey, George	3 APR 1769		East Branch Susquehanna River, Columbia	300	A-7-216	(r27 FEB 1784)Evan Owen/[see caveat] Original: found

Table 6 - New Purchase Applications (1769-1773)

Number	Applicant	Date	Orig. Place	Later Place	Acres	Survey	Neighbors, Notes, etc.
NP-1384	Sherer, John	3 APR 1769		Unity, Westmoreland	300	D-56-208 D-56-209	William Proctor Original: found
NP-1385	Glenn, Joseph	3 APR 1769	Berks	Buffalo, Union	150	D-56-207	James Par Original: found
NP-1386	Trester, Martin Jr.	3 APR 1769	Northumberland	Hartley, Union	300	C-55-200 C-191-11 C-191-12	(r4 AUG 1804)Henry Fisher/(r14 FEB 1831)Michael Peter/[see caveat] Original: found
NP-1387	Cooper, Robert (of the City of Philadelphia, shoemaker)	3 APR 1769		West Branch Susquehanna River, Lycoming/ LD: Lycoming	300		Original: Signed
NP-1388	Wikoff, John	3 APR 1769		Augusta, Northumberland	250	D-56-206	Original: found
NP-1389	Fisher, William Sr.	3 APR 1769		Luzerne/ LD: Luzerne	300	D-46-79	Charles Beever Original: found
NP-1390	Mason, Sarah	3 APR 1769		Turbot, Northumberland/ LD: Turbot, Northumberland	300	X-226	--- Mason/[see caveat] Original: found
NP-1391	Stuart, Mary	3 APR 1769		Washington, Lycoming	300	D-56-220	Original: found
NP-1392	Heath, Nathaniel	3 APR 1769		East Branch Susquehanna River, Luzerne/ LD: Luzerne	300	A-36-14	Thomas Heath, Jr. Original: found
NP-1393	Young, Ann	3 APR 1769	Cumberland	Jacobs Creek, Westmoreland	300	D-9-231	John Young/(r31 MAR 1772) Original: found
NP-1394	Early, John	3 APR 1769		Fayette County & South Huntingdon, Westmoreland	300	D-55-27 D-62-203 C-50-146	(r22 FEB 1771)Capt. William Thompson Original: found
NP-1395	Blaine, James Sr.	3 APR 1769		Pitt, Westmoreland	300	C-10-19	John Sampson/(r31 MAR 1788)Ephraim Blaine Original: found
NP-1396	Williamson, Hugh	3 APR 1769		East Branch Susquehanna River, Luzerne	300	E-25	Andrew Allen/(r23 JAN 1783) Original: found
NP-1397	Bull, John, Esq. (of Philadelphia County)	3 APR 1769		Chillisquaque Creek, Northumberland	300		--- Bridgins Original: Signed

Table 6 - New Purchase Applications (1769-1773)

Number	Applicant	Date	Orig. Place	Later Place	Acres	Survey	Neighbors, Notes, etc.
NP-1398	Rowan, Jean	3 APR 1769		Hempfield, Westmoreland	300	D-56-219	Original: found
NP-1399	Mease, James	3 APR 1769	Berks	West Buffalo, Union	300	D-56-218	Rev. John Ewing Original: found
NP-1400	Forster, Stephen	3 APR 1769		Muncy, Lycoming	300	D-56-217	James Forster, Sr. Original: found
NP-1401	Walker, Thomas	3 APR 1769	Cumberland	Monongahela River, Allegheny	300	A-85-99	(r21 FEB 1770)John Little Original: found
NP-1402	Wolfart, Christopher	3 APR 1769		Muncy, Lycoming	200	D-56-216	Original: found
NP-1403	Morris, Samuel	3 APR 1769		Loyalsock & Muncy, Lycoming	300	D-15-65	(r11 JAN 1796)Samuel Wallis Original: found
NP-1404	Neeper, Joseph	3 APR 1769	West Branch Susquehanna River	LD: Lycoming	300		Jane Ogilvie Original: found
NP-1405	Martin, Aberhood	3 APR 1769	Bald Eagle Creek	LD: Clinton/ Centre	300		James Crompton Original: found
NP-1406	Hess, Abraham	3 APR 1769	West Branch Susquehanna River		300		(r4 MAR 1789)Adam Dreisback Original: found
NP-1407	Jameson, David	3 APR 1769		East of Allegheny River, Westmoreland	300	A-71-263	Frederick Philes/(r18 JUL 1774) Original: found
NP-1408	Coffie, James	3 APR 1769		LD: Turbot, Northumberland	300		Preeson Bowdin Original: found
NP-1409	Burd, James	3 APR 1769		Pitt, Allegheny	300	D-56-176	Original: found
NP-1410	Palmer, Thomas	3 APR 1769	Berks	Northeast Branch Susquehanna River, Northumberland	50	C-146-296	(r7 MAR 1774)Jesse Lukens Original: found
NP-1411	Rodger, James	3 APR 1769	Cumberland	Centre, Indiana	300	A-69-30	(r18 JAN 1851)William Earhart Original: found
NP-1412	Beatty, William Jr.	3 APR 1769	Bedford	Sewickley Creek, Westmoreland	---	A-68-224	(r17 JUN 1789)Mathew Dill & James Dill Original: found

Table 6 - New Purchase Applications (1769-1773)

Number	Applicant	Date	Orig. Place	Later Place	Acres	Survey	Neighbors, Notes, etc.
NP-1413	Warnock, James	3 APR 1769		Turbot, Northumberland/ LD: Northumberland	300	D-56-215	Original: found
NP-1414	Hoke, George	3 APR 1769		Chapman, Union	---	D-56-214	William Blyth Original: found
NP-1415	Care, William	3 APR 1769		Waddles Creek & Buffalo Creek, Armstrong	300	C-124-169	Thomas Elliott/Alexander Sanderson/(r20 JUN 1815)Nicholas Lyon Original: found
NP-1416	Steel, Rebechah	3 APR 1769	Berks or Northampton	East Branch Susquehanna River, Columbia/ LD: Columbia	300	A-29-55	Original: found
NP-1417	McMullon, John	3 APR 1769	Winemillers Run	Rostraver, Westmoreland/ LD: Rostraver, Westmoreland	300	X-225	Original: found
NP-1418	Footman, Richard	3 APR 1769		Hartley, Union	300	D-56-213	Original: found
NP-1419	Rowan, Mary	3 APR 1769		Unity, Westmoreland	300		Original: found
NP-1420	Letchworth, John	3 APR 1769		Chillisquaque Creek, Northumberland/ LD: Northumberland	300		John Coster Original: found
NP-1421	Cochrin, Samuel	3 APR 1769	Laurel Run two miles from Loyalsock	LD: Lycoming	300		Original: found
NP-1422	Barr, James	3 APR 1769		Derry, Westmoreland	300	D-55-23 A-29-139 C-71-206	David Duncan/(r14 MAY 1796) Original: found
NP-1423	Gorrell, Oliver	3 APR 1769	Cumberland	Bedford - Marsh Creek, Centre	300	C-184-176	(r31 JUL 1820)Samuel Burge Rawle Original: found

Table 6 - New Purchase Applications (1769-1773)

Number	Applicant	Date	Orig. Place	Later Place	Acres	Survey	Neighbors, Notes, etc.
NP-1424	Hall, John	3 APR 1769	Berks	Kelly, Union	300	D-56-287 D-57-39 D-60-224 D-60-225 D-60-231 F-186	Richard Edwards/(r12 JAN 1792)Rev. William Smith, D. D. Original: found
NP-1425	Lindsey, David	3 APR 1769	Luzerne	Standing Stone, Bradford	300	C-93-36	(r12 FEB 1794)Adam Hoops Original: found
NP-1426	Morton, John	3 APR 1769	Northampton	Little Fishing Creek, Columbia	300	D-495	Moses Hewes/(r25 JUN 1796)Owen Biddle Original: found
NP-1427	Tzorn, Christian	3 APR 1769	Susquehanna River opposite Margarets Creek	LD: Lycoming	300		Original: found
NP-1428	Jacobs, Benjamin Jr.	3 APR 1769		Muncy Creek Twp., Lycoming	300	D-56-212	Joshua Beale/"French Margaret's Town" Original: Signed
NP-1429	Ferree, John	3 APR 1769		Bald Eagle, Lycoming	300	D-56-211	Original: found
NP-1430	Burnes, Bernhard	3 APR 1769	Cumberland	West Huntingdon, Westmoreland/ LD: North Huntingdon, Westmoreland	300	X-189	(r7 APR 1825)Joseph Thompson Original: found
NP-1431	Andrews, John	3 APR 1769		Frankstown, Huntingdon	300	P-139	(r28 JAN 1833)Charles Smith/[see caveat] Original: found
NP-1432	Hopkins, Samuel Jr.	3 APR 1769	Cumberland	Northumberland - Bald Eagle, Centre/ LD: Centre	300	A-36-15	Original: found
NP-1433	Guthrey, William	3 APR 1769		Derry, Westmoreland	300	A-58-183	Robert Bar/(r4 MAR 1799) Original: found
NP-1434	Clugston, William	3 APR 1769		Elizabeth, Allegheny/ LD: Elizabeth, Allegheny	300	D-56-175	James Kelley Original: found
NP-1435	Paty, George	3 APR 1769		Hempfield, Westmoreland	300	C-159-122 C-159-123	William Brotherton/(r2 FEB 1804) Original: found
NP-1436	Masden, Thomas	3 APR 1769	Westmoreland	Monongahela River, Allegheny	300	X-52	(r17 MAY 1804)Jacob Ferree Original: Signed

Table 6 - New Purchase Applications (1769-1773)

Number	Applicant	Date	Orig. Place	Later Place	Acres	Survey	Neighbors, Notes, etc.
NP-1437	Norcross, William	3 APR 1769	White Deer Hole Creek	LD: Lycoming	300		[see caveat] Original: found
NP-1438	Patton, John	3 APR 1769	Northumberland	Nanticoke Creek, Luzerne/ LD: Luzerne	300	X-162	Original: found
NP-1439	Coale, Samuel	3 APR 1769	Bald Eagle Creek, Cumberland	LD: Centre	300		[see caveat] Original: found
NP-1440	Humphreys, Benjamin	3 APR 1769	Berks	Derry, Northumberland	300	A-36-9 V-241 Z-69 C-10-181	Joseph Ogden/(r22 JUN 1798)James Star/(22 MAR 1811)Marko John Biddle Original: found
NP-1441	Gover, Philip	3 APR 1769	Cumberland	Northumberland - Bald Eagle Creek, Centre/ LD: Centre	300	H-164 C-5-161 A-22-22	Ephraim Gover/(r16 AUG 1810)Philip Antes Original: found
NP-1442	Wilkins, John Jr.	3 APR 1769		Unity, Westmoreland	300	A-29-37	William Fergerson Original: found
NP-1443	Wickware, Alpheus	3 APR 1769	Rush Meadows, Northampton	LD: Bradford	300		John Wickware Original: found
NP-1444	Chambers, James	3 APR 1769		Muncy, Lycoming	300	D-56-205	Original: found
NP-1445	Hindman, James	3 APR 1769		North Huntingdon, Westmoreland	300	D-56-204	Philip Criner Original: found
NP-1446	Carpenter, Thomas Jr.	3 APR 1769	North Branch Susquehanna River	LD: Columbia	300		John Noarth Original: found
NP-1447	Rennalls, John, Esq.	3 APR 1769		Loyalhanna, Westmoreland	300	A-11-291	(r3 APR 1789)Samuel Findley Original: found
NP-1448	Latta, William	3 APR 1769	Bedford	Westmoreland - Monongahela River, Fayette	200	C-157-202	Joseph Holladay/(r4 APR 1785)John Patterson Original: found
NP-1449	Pollock, John	3 APR 1769		Pitt & Wilkins, Allegheny	300	D-56-182 L-361	Auston Putty/(p14 MAY 1868)James Kelly Original: found
NP-1450	Gable, Abraham	3 APR 1769		Pitt, Westmoreland	300	A-11-148	(r9 MAR 1810)Michael Coon Original: Signed

Table 6 - New Purchase Applications (1769-1773)

Number	Applicant	Date	Orig. Place	Later Place	Acres	Survey	Neighbors, Notes, etc.
NP-1451	Pollock, Charles	3 APR 1769	Berks	Chillisquaque Creek, Northumberland/ LD: Northumberland	300	X-163	[see caveat] Original: found
NP-1452	McCoskry, William Sr.	3 APR 1769	Berks	Buffalo, Union	300	D-57-12 D-57-15 D-57-16	[same land as NP-866 to John Clin] Original: found
NP-1453	Miller, George	3 APR 1769	Northampton	Nanticoke Creek, Luzerne/ LD: Luzerne	300	X-224	Peter Miller Original: found
NP-1454	Lautermilk, John Jr.	3 APR 1769	West Branch Susquehanna River	LD: Lycoming	300		Andrew Moore Original: found
NP-1455	Risk, Charles (of Philadelphia)	3 APR 1769		West Branch Susquehanna River, Lycoming	300		Original: Signed
NP-1456	McClure, James	3 APR 1769	East Branch Susquehanna River	LD: Columbia	300		Original: found
NP-1457	Morris, Israel	3 APR 1769	Berks	Muddy Creek, Northumberland	300	C-289	Richard Roberts/(r28 JUN 1782)Reuben Hains Original: found
NP-1458	Allee, Abraham Jr.	3 APR 1769		Nippenose, Lycoming	300	D-56-202	Walter Snee Original: found
NP-1459	Colemore, Conrad	3 APR 1769		Unity, Westmoreland	300	C-22	(r21 SEP 1785) Original: found
NP-1460	Murdock, William	3 APR 1769	Berks	Union, Union	150	D-56-201	Original: found
NP-1461	Wiggins, John	3 APR 1769		Turbot, Northumberland	300	D-56-190	Original: found
NP-1462	Green, Michael	3 APR 1769	Berks	Buffalo, Union	300	A-3-45 D-55-34 D-55-43 D-60-266 D-62-276 D-62-283	Christopher Parris/(r23 APR 1773)Edward Shippen & Joseph Shippen Original: found
NP-1463	Carnahan, James	3 APR 1769		Huntingdon, Westmoreland	300	C-49-298 C-49-300	--- Saltman/(r25 JUN 1791)Andrew Findley/[see caveat] Original: found

Table 6 - New Purchase Applications (1769-1773)

Number	Applicant	Date	Orig. Place	Later Place	Acres	Survey	Neighbors, Notes, etc.
NP-1464	Porter, Stephen	3 APR 1769	Berks	Buffalo, Union/ LD: Buffalo, Union	300	D-56-189	Original: found
NP-1465	Barnhill, John	3 APR 1769		Muncy Creek Twp., Lycoming	300	D-56-188	Original: found
NP-1466	Gardner, Archibald	3 APR 1769		Nippenose, Lycoming	300	D-56-187	Original: found
NP-1467	Shaaf, George	3 APR 1769	Berks	Limestone Run, Northumberland	300	M-214	(r25 JAN 1774)William McWilliams Original: found
NP-1468	Alexander, John	3 APR 1769		Muncy Creek Twp., Lycoming	300	D-56-186	Original: found
NP-1469	Robinson, Aaron	3 APR 1769		Uniontown, Fayette	300	A-46-173	Phillon Scot/Aaron Jenkins/(r17 MAR 1786)James Galagher Original: found
NP-1470	Row, John	3 APR 1769	Cumberland	Northumberland - Haines, Centre	250	C-125-197	George Row/(r15 JAN 1811)Jacob Hosterman Original: found
NP-1471	Martin, Hugh	3 APR 1769		Hempfield, Westmoreland	300	C-120-237	--- Stockbiger/Samuel Willson/Joseph Eager/(r25 SEP 1787) Original: found
NP-1472	Templeton, John	3 APR 1769	Cumberland	Buffalo, Union	300	C-116-221	(r28 JUN 1792)John Lowdon Original: found
NP-1473	Alen, James	3 APR 1769	Westmoreland	Plum, Allegheny	300	A-42-50	(r8 MAY 1806)Robert Johnston Original: found
NP-1474	Hare, Christian	3 APR 1769	West Branch Susquehanna River	LD: Lycoming	300		Original: found
NP-1475	Graydon, Caleb	3 APR 1769		Allegheny, Westmoreland	300	D-64-102 D-46-93	Original: found
NP-1476	Carson, Joseph	3 APR 1769	Berks	Nippenose, Lycoming	300	D-56-200	Francis Harris Original: found
NP-1477	Longane, William	3 APR 1769	at or near mouth of Conemaugh or Twolick Creek	LD: Indiana/ Armstrong	300		Original: found
NP-1478	Robinson, Henry	3 APR 1769	Chillisquaque Creek	LD: Chillisquaque, Northumberland/ Montour	300		George Jewell Original: found

Table 6 - New Purchase Applications (1769-1773)

Number	Applicant	Date	Orig. Place	Later Place	Acres	Survey	Neighbors, Notes, etc.
NP-1479	Morris, Joseph	3 APR 1769		one mile above mouth of Wyalusing Creek, Luzerne	300	A-12-113	(r14 MAR 1775)John Gibson, Esq. Original: found
NP-1480	Eshleman, Benjamin	3 APR 1769		East Branch Susquehanna River, Luzerne	300	C-222-275	Jacob Meanard/(r9 AUG 1781)Joseph Wharton Original: found
NP-1481	Mathews, James	3 APR 1769	Fishing Creek	LD: Columbia	400		Original: found
NP-1482	McCormick, James	3 APR 1769	Northumberland	Kelly, Union/ LD: Union	300	X-223 A-46-263 C-14-148	Mr. Ewing/(r16 MAY 1818)Thomas Johnston/(r12 FEB 1852)Samuel Burkheimer Original: Signed by Hugh McCormick
NP-1483	Lindsay, Samuel	3 APR 1769		Elizabeth, Allegheny	300	D-56-174	James Potter Original: found
NP-1484	Davis, Owen	3 APR 1769	Bedford	Georges Creek, Fayette	300	C-48-81	(r15 MAR 1786) Original: Signed
NP-1485	Gardner, Alexander	3 APR 1769		Nippenose, Lycoming	300	C-135-102	Thomas Gardner, Jr./(r12 AUG 1782)Blair McClenachan Original: found
NP-1486	Thompson, George	3 APR 1769		Versailles, Allegheny	300	D-64-126 A-32-254	John Frazier/William Powell/(r2 JAN 1788)/(r9 FEB 1811)John Perry/[see caveat] Original: found
NP-1487	Palmer, Thomas	3 APR 1769	Shamokin Creek		100		Original: found
NP-1488	Hays, Moses	3 APR 1769	Fishing Creek	LD: Columbia	300		Alexander McClintock Original: found
NP-1489	Collins, Stephen	3 APR 1769	Northumberland	Little Fishing Creek, Columbia	300	A-27-249	Susanna Hopkins/(r16 JUN 1802)John Biddle & Thomas Steardson Original: found
NP-1490	Miller, James	3 APR 1769	Warriors Run, Berks	LD: Northumberland	300		Original: found
NP-1491	Johns, Elizabeth	3 APR 1769	Berks	Hemlock, Columbia	300	C-17-30	(r26 FEB 1805)Elishu Barton Original: found
NP-1492	Cash, Caleb	3 APR 1769	Berks	West Branch Susquehanna River, Northumberland	300	C-192-52	David McClure/(r16 FEB 1786)John B. Smith Original: Signed
NP-1493	Ross, John Esq.	3 APR 1769	Bald Eagle Creek	LD: Clinton	300		Original: found

Table 6 - New Purchase Applications (1769-1773)

Number	Applicant	Date	Orig. Place	Later Place	Acres	Survey	Neighbors, Notes, etc.
NP-1494	Clugston, John	3 APR 1769	Muddy Creek 1.5 miles from Buffalo Lick	LD: Northumberland	300		Original: found
NP-1495	Harris, Francis	3 APR 1769	Berks	Nippenose, Lycoming	300	D-56-199	Original: found
NP-1496	Arnold, Lawrence	3 APR 1769		Turbot, Northumberland/ LD: Turbot, Northumberland	300	D-56-198	Original: found
NP-1497	Poe, Mary	3 APR 1769		in Sewickley Manor, Westmoreland	300	D-56-196	Original: found
NP-1498	Guthery, William Jr.	3 APR 1769		Unity, Westmoreland	300	D-56-195	Original: found
NP-1499	Yearly, Mary	3 APR 1769	Cumberland	Howard, Centre	300	C-91-204 C-91-205 C-14-170 C-14-171	(r21 OCT 1845)Jesse Hall/(r8 APR 1852)Ephraim Banks Original: found
NP-1500	Wolfart, Michael	3 APR 1769	Berks	Delaware Run, Northumberland	300	D-55-38 A-34-175	(r1 NOV 1810)John Jacobs Original: Missing
NP-1501	Gardner, Margaret	3 APR 1769		White Deer, Union	300	D-56-163	Original: found
NP-1502	Buck, Barnard	3 APR 1769	Northeast Branch Susquehanna River at Bohemia Creek	LD: Luzerne	300		Original: found
NP-1503	Barkley, Mary (widow)	3 APR 1769	Monongahela River near Redstone Creek	LD: Fayette	300		--- McClean Original: found
NP-1504	Long, Isaac	3 APR 1769	Muddy Creek below the Buffalo Lick	LD: Union	300		Original: found
NP-1505	Findley, John	3 APR 1769		Plum, Armstrong	300	A-14-35	John Lattamor/Tohog [probably an Indian]/(r4 DEC 1812)David Ralston heirs Original: found
NP-1506	McConnell, Francis	3 APR 1769		Blacklick, Indiana/ LD: Blacklick, Indiana	300	A-233 A-73-3	(p20 JUN 1870)Archibald S. Pattison Original: found

Table 6 - New Purchase Applications (1769-1773)

Number	Applicant	Date	Orig. Place	Later Place	Acres	Survey	Neighbors, Notes, etc.
NP-1507	Donne, John	3 APR 1769	Peters Creek [empties into Monongahela River]	LD: Snowden, Allegheny	300		Benjamin Cockendall/James Kelly Original: found
NP-1508	Allen, Samuel	3 APR 1769	Mahoning, Northeast Branch Susquehanna River	LD: Montour	300		Original: found
NP-1509	McMachen, William	3 APR 1769	Washington	Monongahela River, Allegheny	300	H-122	Richard McMachen/(r15 APR 1789)Henry Heth/[patent P-13-531] Original: found
NP-1510	Elliot, Barbara	3 APR 1769		Salem, Westmoreland	300	A-87-119	James Elliott/(r22 SEP 1788)James Ferguson Original: found
NP-1511	Latta, John	3 APR 1769	Cumberland	Crooked Creek, Indiana	300	A-85-229	Tohogo [probably an Indian] Original: found
NP-1512	White, William	3 APR 1769	West Branch Susquehanna River	LD: Lycoming	300		Hugh McCallister/Hugh Gibson Original: Signed
NP-1513	Allison, Samuel	3 APR 1769		Muncy Creek Twp., Lycoming	300	D-62-278 K-20	Joseph Smith/(r25 MAR 1795)William Ellis Original: found
NP-1514	Martin, William	3 APR 1769		Unity, Westmoreland	300	D-66-162	Original: found
NP-1515	Hutchison, John	3 APR 1769		Turbot, Northumberland	200	D-56-161	Original: found
NP-1516	Davis, John Jr.	3 APR 1769	Cumberland	Unity, Westmoreland	300	C-151-95	(r7 AUG 1788)James Mckee Original: Signed
NP-1517	Pearson, Samuel	3 APR 1769		Augusta, Northumberland	300	L-325 C-53-144	(r3 APR 1793)William Clark/(r5 AUG 1831)Peter Keffer Original: Signed
NP-1518	Middleton, Edward	3 APR 1769	Berks	Buffalo, Union	300	D-56-127 D-56-128 D-56-129	Original: found
NP-1519	Newswanger, David	3 APR 1769		"Three Islands", Susquehanna River, Luzerne/ LD: Clinton	300	A-245	(p6 APR 1937)Merton Vanderpool/[patent H-79-278] Original: found
NP-1520	Fouts, Andrew	3 APR 1769		Union, Fayette/ LD: Union, Fayette	300	D-56-130	Philip Shutes/Aron Jenkins Original: found

Table 6 - New Purchase Applications (1769-1773)

Number	Applicant	Date	Orig. Place	Later Place	Acres	Survey	Neighbors, Notes, etc.
NP-1521	Wallis, Sarah	3 APR 1769	Northumberland	Little Fishing Creek, Columbia	300	D-520	(r27 FEB 1800 & 4 OCT 1800)John Biddle & Thomas Stewardson Original: found
NP-1522	Roger, Michael	3 APR 1769		Turbot, Northumberland	300	A-45-126 C-119-96 C-119-97	(r8 APR 1833)U. Hopkins/(r16 JAN 1840)George Lilley Original: found
NP-1523	Parker, Joseph	3 APR 1769		Muncy, Lycoming	300	A-3-214	Richard Humphreys/(r21 NOV 1807)Robert Coleman Original: found
NP-1524	Schneider, Harman	3 APR 1769		Augusta, Northumberland	300	A-14-285 C-24-292	John Kirling/(r30 NOV 1789)John Cearlin/(r27 FEB 1797)John Cearlin alias Kerlin Original: found
NP-1525	Dixon, James	3 APR 1769		Warriors Run, Northumberland	300	C-53-262	(r24 SEP 1788)Robert Galbreath Original: found
NP-1526	Vanmeter, Abraham	3 APR 1769	Cumberland	Monongahela River on Muddy Creek Branch, Greene/ LD: Cumberland, Greene	300	X-121	Jacob Vanmeter Original: found
NP-1527	Starrett, John	3 APR 1769	West Branch Susquehanna River below Margarets Creek	LD: Northumberland/ Lycoming/ Clinton	300		Original: Signed
NP-1528	Gill, William	3 APR 1769	Berks	West Branch Susquehanna River, Union/ LD: Union	300	D-46-94	Original: found
NP-1529	Ballard, John	3 APR 1769	Northampton	Rush Meadows, Wyoming/ LD: Wyoming	300		Samuel Sayer Original: found
NP-1530	Sloan, John	3 APR 1769	Cumberland	Huntingdon, Westmoreland	300	C-116-28 C-116-8	(r23 APR 1788)Benjamin Lodge Original: found
NP-1531	McNutt, Jeams	3 APR 1769		Muncy Creek Twp., Lycoming	300	D-56-126	Original: found
NP-1532	Johnson, James	3 APR 1769	Berks	Buffalo, Union/ LD: Union	300	D-56-140	Original: found
NP-1533	Singer, Casper	3 APR 1769	Forks of Chartiers Creek	LD: Washington	300		Original: found

Table 6 - New Purchase Applications (1769-1773)

Number	Applicant	Date	Orig. Place	Later Place	Acres	Survey	Neighbors, Notes, etc.
NP-1534	Sutherland, Thomas	3 APR 1769	Northumberland	Buffalo, Union/ LD: Union	300	W-290 W-291 W-292 A-22-270	(r28 SEP 1792)/(r22 OCT 1792)George Cooper/(r4 APR 1797)Hugh Beaty/[see caveat] Original: found
NP-1535	Brown, William	3 APR 1769		Salem, Westmoreland/ LD: Salem, Westmoreland	300	D-56-139	Original: found
NP-1536	Row, Martin Sr.	3 APR 1769	two miles from Buffalo Run, Cumberland	LD: Potter, Centre	300		George Row Original: found
NP-1537	Hover, James	3 APR 1769		Allegheny, Westmoreland	300	D-56-138	Original: found
NP-1538	Hagener, Peter	3 APR 1769		Plum, Allegheny	300	D-56-173	James Hannah Original: found
NP-1539	McCorkle, William	3 APR 1769	Berks	White Deer, Union	200	D-55-42 A-76-279	(r3 DEC 1796)David Lenox & Abraham Lukens, Executors of John Lukens, deceased Original: found
NP-1540	Nailor, Ralph (innholder)	3 APR 1769	Cumberland	Boggs, Centre/ LD: Boggs, Centre	300	X-158 X-159	Original: found
NP-1541	Cash, Thomas	3 APR 1769	Berks	West Branch Susquehanna River, Northumberland	300	C-192-51	(r16 FEB 1786)John B. Smith Original: Signed
NP-1542	Osborn, Thomas	3 APR 1769	West Branch Susquehanna River	LD: Luzerne	300		Original: found
NP-1543	McCarter, Thomas	3 APR 1769		Washington, Lycoming	300	D-56-137	Original: found
NP-1544	Burns, John	3 APR 1769	Cumberland	Bald Eagle - Frankstown Road, Northumberland	300	B-30	Alexander Robinson/(r9 JUL 1782)Margert Duncan Original: found
NP-1545	Freeman, Benjamin	3 APR 1769	Berks	Delaware Run, Northumberland	250	A-57-208	(r25 MAY 1774)John Freeman, Jr. Original: found
NP-1546	Cathrall, Benjamin	3 APR 1769		Rostraver, Westmoreland	300	D-56-136	James Cathrall Original: found

Table 6 - New Purchase Applications (1769-1773)

Number	Applicant	Date	Orig. Place	Later Place	Acres	Survey	Neighbors, Notes, etc.
NP-1547	Stopher, Jacob	3 APR 1769		St. Clair, Allegheny	300	D-56-172	Original: found
NP-1548	Henry, John	3 APR 1769	West Branch Susquehanna River	LD: Northumberland	300		Original: found
NP-1549	McClelan, John Jr.	3 APR 1769		Kelly, Union	300		Parson Ewing/[same land as NP-2225 to Breeson Bowden] Original: found
NP-1550	Remely, Frederick	3 APR 1769	East Branch Susquehanna River	LD: Luzerne	300		Peter Albright Original: found
NP-1551	Jewell, Robert	3 APR 1769	Berks	Turbot, Northumberland	300	D-56-113 C-207-171 C-207-164 B-18-195	John Sprogle/(r21 APR 1827)James Sloat Original: found
NP-1552	Maurignault, John	3 APR 1769		Greene/ LD: Damascus/ Wayne; Greene	300		Hanna Rhoads Original: found
NP-1553	Walker, John	3 APR 1769		Armstrong, Indiana	300	D-13-176	(r13 APR 1827)Robert Walker & Alexander Walker Original: found
NP-1554	Brownholtz, Francis	3 APR 1769	North Branch Susquehanna River		300		Original: found
NP-1555	Whitmore, Benjamin	3 APR 1769	Long Limestone Valley, south of West Branch Susquehanna River	LD: Centre	300		John Whitmore, Jr. Original: found
NP-1556	Wallrad, Adolph	3 APR 1769		East Branch Susquehanna River, Luzerne/ LD: Wyoming	300	A-29-38	Conrad Pickert Original: found
NP-1557	Pusey, William	3 APR 1769	Cumberland	White Deer, Union	300	D-56-135	Original: found
NP-1558	Young, Peter	3 APR 1769		LD: Westmoreland	300		Benjamin Cathrall Original: found

Table 6 - New Purchase Applications (1769-1773)

Number	Applicant	Date	Orig. Place	Later Place	Acres	Survey	Neighbors, Notes, etc.
NP-1559	Patterson, Samuel	3 APR 1769	Bedford	Monongahela River, Fayette	300	B-18-21	John Patterson/Hugh Gilman/(r26 JUL 1785)John Patterson, Jr. Original: Signed
NP-1560	Foster, Lovia	3 APR 1769		Turbot, Northumberland	300	C-133-269	(r31 OCT 1811)David McGuire/[see caveat] Original: found
NP-1561	Snivley, Elizabeth	3 APR 1769		LD: Allegheny	300		James Kelley Original: found
NP-1562	Miller, Johannes	3 APR 1769		West Buffalo, Union	300	D-55-80 C-39-200	(r11 DEC 1772)Phillip Diehl Original: found
NP-1563	Randles, William	3 APR 1769		Chartiers Creek, Washington	300	A-83-82 A-73-119 A-73-120	(r22 MAR 1788)David Hoge, Esq. Original: found
NP-1564	Bussard, John	3 APR 1769	East Branch Susquehanna River five miles above Ft. Augusta		300		Original: found
NP-1565	McCoskry, Elizabeth Jr.	3 APR 1769		White Deer, Union	300	D-56-134	William Blyth Original: found
NP-1566	Kuhn, Ludwig	3 APR 1769	Northampton	Nescopeck Creek, Luzerne	300	N-252	John Wolf/George Wolf/George Henry Seybert/Samuel Purviance, Jr./(r17 JUL 1781)John Nixon Original: found
NP-1567	Franklin, George (of the City of Philadelphia)	3 APR 1769		Allegheny, Westmoreland	300	D-56-133	Original: found
NP-1568	Morris, John (cooper)	3 APR 1769	East Branch Susquehanna River & Beaver Creek	LD: Luzerne	300		Original: found
NP-1569	Hopkins, Joseph Sr.	3 APR 1769	Cumberland	Northumberland - Boggs, Centre	300	C-195-169 C-195-170 C-195-196 C-195-110	(p18 APR 1887)Daniel Rhoades/[patent H-74-631] Original: found
NP-1570	Mitcheltree, Rebecca	3 APR 1769	Berks	Washington, Lycoming	300	D-56-131	Original: found
NP-1571	Deaney, William Sr.	3 APR 1769		Washington, Lycoming	300	D-56-131	Original: found

Table 6 - New Purchase Applications (1769-1773)

Number	Applicant	Date	Orig. Place	Later Place	Acres	Survey	Neighbors, Notes, etc.
NP-1572	Derr, George	3 APR 1769		West Branch Susquehanna River & Red Bank Creek, Lycoming/ LD: Armstrong	300		Ludwig Derr/"Old Hans" Original: found
NP-1573	Nicholas, Samuel	3 APR 1769		West Branch Susquehanna River & Pine Creek, Lycoming/ LD: Lycoming	300		Original: found
NP-1574	Reed, Casper Sr.	3 APR 1769	Berks	Buffalo, Union/ LD: Buffalo, Union	300	D-56-124 D-56-125	Original: found
NP-1575	Dillwyn, William	3 APR 1769	Berks	Northumberland - Muncy, Lycoming	300	D-56-122 D-56-123	Original: found
NP-1576	Holdbrook, Edward	3 APR 1769	Berks	Northumberland - Kelly, Union	300	C-166-239	(r9 APR 1828)William A. Patterson Original: found
NP-1577	Graham, William	3 APR 1769		Turbot, Northumberland	300	A-51-124 C-42-119 C-143-96 C-42-127	James Johnston, Jr./(r26 APR 1814)John Jacoby/(r18 MAR 1817)Robert McKee/(r24 JUN 1839)William Clyde Original: found
NP-1578	Ryan, John	3 APR 1769		Versailles, Allegheny	300	D-56-165	Original: found
NP-1579	Bell, John	3 APR 1769	East Branch Susquehanna River & Mill Creek	LD: Luzerne	300		Original: found
NP-1580	Blank, Adam	3 APR 1769	East Branch Susquehanna River & Wyalusing Creek	LD: Bradford	300		Phillip Klein Original: found
NP-1581	Elliot, Robert	3 APR 1769		Fairfield, Westmoreland	300	D-46-98	(r5 OCT 1790)Paul Clark Original: found
NP-1582	McCune, James	3 APR 1769		Pitt & Wilkins, Allegheny	300	D-56-182	John McKee Original: found

Table 6 - New Purchase Applications (1769-1773)

Number	Applicant	Date	Orig. Place	Later Place	Acres	Survey	Neighbors, Notes, etc.
NP-1583	Rowan, Stewart Jr.	3 APR 1769	Cumberland	Quemahoning, Somerset	300	D-17-297	(r14 FEB 1803)John Wilkins Original: found
NP-1584	Cochran, James	3 APR 1769	Berks	Union, Union	300	D-167 D-56-201 D-60-238	(r3 MAY 1791)James Bevaird Original: found
NP-1585	Pollex, Robert	3 APR 1769	Cumberland	Franklin, Fayette	300	C-74-265 C-74-266	John Bougs/Alexander Pollex/Robert Ross/(r18 APR 1792)John Hamilton/[see caveat] Original: found
NP-1586	McCullough, Joseph	3 APR 1769		Washington, Lycoming	300	D-56-121	Original: found
NP-1587	Brown, Mathew	3 APR 1769	on road from Ft. Augusta to Ft. Hunter		200		Original: Signed
NP-1588	Nicholas, Samuel	3 APR 1769		West Branch Susquehanna River & Pine Creek, Lycoming	300		Original: found
NP-1589	Taylor, Frederick	3 APR 1769	Berks	Turbot, Northumberland	300	C-215-269 D-9-61 C-215-268 C-106-298 C-151-269 C-215-268 C-215-267	(r6 FEB 1822)D. Weaver/(r6 FEB 1822)J. Kehr/(r6 FEB 1822)D. Montgomery/(r30 MAY 1822)Frederick Taylor & William Taylor Original: found
NP-1590	Brown, William Sr.	3 APR 1769		Derry, Westmoreland	300	D-56-110	Original: Signed "William Brown, Carlisle."
NP-1591	St. Clair, Elizabeth	3 APR 1769		Ligonier, Westmoreland	300	C-94-6	(r5 OCT 1835)Robert Graham Original: found
NP-1592	Snowden, John	3 APR 1769	Berks	Donegal, Westmoreland/ LD: Clinton	300		Original: found
NP-1593	Stephenson, William	3 APR 1769	Cumberland	LD: Northumberland/ Montour	300		William Paress Original: found
NP-1594	Reed, John	3 APR 1769		Fairfield, Westmoreland	300	D-56-109	Original: found
NP-1595	Sheaphard, William	3 APR 1769	Cumberland	Union, Fayette	300	D-56-108	Ezekiel Johnston Original: found

Table 6 - New Purchase Applications (1769-1773)

Number	Applicant	Date	Orig. Place	Later Place	Acres	Survey	Neighbors, Notes, etc.
NP-1596	Hopkins, Samuel Sr.	3 APR 1769	Cumberland	LD: Centre	300		Francis Dallam, Jr. Original: found
NP-1597	Miller, Mathias	3 APR 1769	Fishing Creek	LD: Columbia	300		William Ledlies/John Rinker/Ephraim Bloom Original: found
NP-1598	West, Jacob & Thomas Force & Martinus Martinea	3 APR 1769	Corkins Brook	LD: Luzerne	300 acres each		Original: found
NP-1599	Leashure, John	3 APR 1769		Derry, Westmoreland	300	D-56-107	John Pumroy/Thomas Campbell Original: found
NP-1600	Culbertson, Alexander	3 APR 1769		Blacklick, Indiana	300	D-56-181 D-56-183	Original: found
NP-1601	Hunter, Ephraim	3 APR 1769		Unity, Westmoreland	300	D-55-21	Capr. Proctor Original: Signed
NP-1602	McClure, David	3 APR 1769	Fishing Creek below Cherry Tree Bottom	LD: Columbia	300		Original: found
NP-1603	Clark, John Sr.	3 APR 1769	East Branch Susquehanna River	LD: Northumberland	300		Original: Signed
NP-1604	McConnel, Alexander	3 APR 1769	Bedford	Menallen, Fayette	300	A-61-9	Mr. Cox/(r26 JAN 1775)Rev. James Finley Original: found
NP-1605	Conley, Neal	3 APR 1769	Northumberland	White Deer, Union	300	D-62-239 C-125-162	William Croker/(r2 MAY 1812)Richard Hartshorn Original: found
NP-1606	Mease, John	3 APR 1769	Berks	Kelly, Union	300	D-56-85 D-56-94	Rev. John Ewing/[same land as NP-2368 to Thomas Beatty] Original: found
NP-1607	McConnell, Robert	3 APR 1769		Rostraver, Westmoreland	300	C-123-244 C-123-243	(r8 JAN 1789)Benjamin Davis Original: found
NP-1608	Linn, Andrew	3 APR 1769	Cumberland	Redstone Settlement, Fayette	300	C-75-156	John Wiseman/(r6 JUN 1788)Margaret Hulton Original: found
NP-1609	Smith, Robert	3 APR 1769	Northumberland	Bald Eagle, Centre	300	B-8-45	(r12 JUL 1784)Peter Victor Dorsy & A. Goddard Original: found
NP-1610	Graymes, Michael	3 APR 1769		Hempfield, Westmoreland	300	D-55-22	Original: found
NP-1611	Smith, Robert Jr.	3 APR 1769		Crooked Creek, Indiana	300		Samuel Findley/(r18 JAN 1815 & p19 JAN 1815)Bejamin Walker Original: found

Table 6 - New Purchase Applications (1769-1773)

Number	Applicant	Date	Orig. Place	Later Place	Acres	Survey	Neighbors, Notes, etc.
NP-1612	Rohrer, John	3 APR 1769		East Branch Susquehanna River, Luzerne/ LD: Luzerne	300		Original: found
NP-1613	McClure, Alexander	3 APR 1769		Fishing Creek, Columbia	300	C-212-27	(r11 MAY 1773)Thomas Minssell Original: found
NP-1614	Cooper, Adam	3 APR 1769		Turbot, Northumberland	300	A-35-175	James McMachan/(r15 JUN 1774)James Murray/[see caveat] Original: found
NP-1615	Hoape, Rudolph	3 APR 1769		East Branch Susquehanna River, Luzerne/ LD: Tuscarora, Bradford	300	A-247	Original: found
NP-1616	Riche, John	3 APR 1769	West Branch Susquehanna River on Red Bank or Roaring Creek	LD: Clearfield	300		Original: found
NP-1617	Hall, Richard	3 APR 1769	Cumberland	LD: Somerset	300		Elisha Hall Jr. Original: found
NP-1618	North, John	3 APR 1769	North Branch Susquehanna River at Fishing Creek	LD: Columbia	300		Original: found
NP-1619	Gurhery, James Sr.	3 APR 1769		Unity, Westmoreland	300	C-79-63 C-79-71	(r7 DEC 1791) Original: found
NP-1620	Fangle, John	3 APR 1769	Berks	Kelly, Union	300		Mr. Ewing/[same land as NP-2225 to Reeson Bowden] Original: found
NP-1621	Eshleman, Benjamin Jr.	3 APR 1769		East Branch Susquehanna River, Northumberland/ LD: Bradford	300	H-153	Benjamin Eshleman Original: found
NP-1622	Renicks, Henry	3 APR 1769	East Branch Susquehanna River	LD: Luzerne/ Columbia	100		Original: found

Table 6 - New Purchase Applications (1769-1773)

Number	Applicant	Date	Orig. Place	Later Place	Acres	Survey	Neighbors, Notes, etc.
NP-1623	Orbey, Jacob	3 APR 1769		Fishing Creek, Columbia	300	A-39-100	(r7 MAR 1811)Lawrence Miller Original: found
NP-1624	Whislor, Christian	3 APR 1769	Long Limestone Valley south of West Branch Susquehanna River	LD: Centre	300		Jacob Whisler Original: found
NP-1625	Barclay, Mary (of Philadelphia)	3 APR 1769	Washington	Robinson, Allegheny	300	B-14-188 D-38-149	Capt. Alexander McKee/Robert Barclay/(r10 APR 1862)James McKnight Original: found
NP-1626	Porter, Alexander	3 APR 1769		Derry, Westmoreland	300	D-55-23	John Palmer/Nicholas Shufler/Robert Noetz Original: found
NP-1627	Conner, Thomas	3 APR 1769		Lawrence & Bradford, Clearfield	300	D-55-24	Original: found
NP-1628	Freeman, Charles	3 APR 1769		Turbot, Northumberland/ LD: Turbot, Northumberland	300	D-55-25	Original: found
NP-1629	Alexander, Hugh	3 APR 1769	West Branch Chillisquaque Creek	LD: Northumberland/ Montour	300		George Robinson Original: found
NP-1630	Barr, Alexander	3 APR 1769		Derry, Westmoreland	300	C-211-258 C-134-193 C-17-82 C-40-39 C-211-257	William Guthery/(r4 FEB 1806)Uriah Maston/(r4 FEB 1806)John Barr/(r29 DEC 1808)John Craig & wife/(r10 APR 1834)Robert Thompson & wife Original: found
NP-1631	Willson, Thomas	3 APR 1769	Berks	Buffalo Creek, Union	300	A-75-38	(r5 DEC 1774)William Irwin Original: found
NP-1632	Ball, William	3 APR 1769	North Branch Susquehanna River	LD: Clearfield/ [Baugh in LD]	300		Original: found
NP-1633	Campbell, James	3 APR 1769		Bradford, Clearfield	300	D-55-31	Original: Signed
NP-1634	Troy, Michael	3 APR 1769		Potter, Centre	300	W-257	Original: found

Table 6 - New Purchase Applications (1769-1773)

Number	Applicant	Date	Orig. Place	Later Place	Acres	Survey	Neighbors, Notes, etc.
NP-1635	Scott, James Jr.	3 APR 1769		Lawrence Creek & West Branch Susquehanna River, Lycoming/ LD: Lycoming	300		Original: found
NP-1636	Campbell, Francis	3 APR 1769	Cumberland	Quemahoning, Somerset	300	C-1-131	(r10 MAY 1809)Joseph Bereke Original: found
NP-1637	McKee, John	3 APR 1769		Pitt, Allegheny/ LD: Pitt, Allegheny	250	X-222	William Elliott/Capt. Thompson Original: found
NP-1638	Jones, Whitehead	3 APR 1769	Northumberland	Fishing Creek, Columbia	300	A-23-86	Edward Wells/(r26 MAR 1795)Margaret Duncan Original: found
NP-1639	Cammer, Ludwick	3 APR 1769		Franklin, Westmoreland	300	D-55-32	Original: found
NP-1640	Hinkson, Robert	3 APR 1769		West Wheatfield, Indiana/ LD: Wheatfield, Indiana	300	C-118-95 C-118-96 C-4-30 C-92-204	James McCurdy/Thomas Woods/(r20 JAN 1830)William Liggit/(r12 MAR 1834)John B. Alexander/(p26 JUL 1870)James W. Vanhorn Original: Signed
NP-1641	Hollingsworth, Levi	3 APR 1769	Fishing Creek	LD: Columbia	300		Susanna Jarvis Original: found
NP-1642	Hogg, Robert	3 APR 1769	Northampton	Northumberland - North Branch Susquehanna River, Luzerne/ LD: Luzerne	300	A-248	I. Witherhill Original: found
NP-1643	Richards, William	3 APR 1769		White Deer, Union/ LD: White Deer, Union	200	D-56-276 E-409 C-131-185 C-140-256	(r8 DEC 1825)Joseph Long/(r26 MAR 1831)John McGinnis/(r13 NOV 1856)F. Dersham Original: found
NP-1644	Morgan, David	3 APR 1769	Sewickley Old Town	LD: Westmoreland	300		William Morgan Original: Signed by Jacob Morgan, Jr.
NP-1645	Hibert, Joseph	3 APR 1769		Chillisquaque Creek, Montour/ LD: Montour	300		Nathan Bonsall Original: found
NP-1646	Forster, Jennet	3 APR 1769	Berks	Buffalo, Union	300	D-55-34 D-55-35	Original: found

Table 6 - New Purchase Applications (1769-1773)

Number	Applicant	Date	Orig. Place	Later Place	Acres	Survey	Neighbors, Notes, etc.
NP-1647	Hughes, Evan	3 APR 1769	Northumberland	East of Mahoning Creek, Luzerne & Columbia	300	T-76	[see caveat] Original: found
NP-1648	Truman, Thomas	3 APR 1769		Blacklick, Indiana	200	D-56-181 D-56-183 A-14-10 D-6-172	(r22 MAR 1811)Peter Wallace/(r18 JAN 1812)Peter Wallace Original: found
NP-1649	Sandwith, Mary	3 APR 1769	near North Branch Susquehanna River	LD: Lycoming	300		Original: found
NP-1650	Zigler, George	3 APR 1769	Berks	White Deer, Union	300	D-62-231	Elizabeth Blyth/[same land as NP-2778 to John Carmalt] Original: found
NP-1651	Ryerson, George	3 APR 1769	Northeast Branch Susquehanna River	LD: Luzerne	300		Original: found
NP-1652	Dallam, Francis Jr.	3 APR 1769	Cumberland	LD: Centre	300		Francis Dallas, Sr. Original: found
NP-1653	Smith, John	3 APR 1769		Pitt, Allegheny	300	D-55-81	Original: found
NP-1654	Elliot, Benjamin	3 APR 1769		Fairfield, Westmoreland/ LD: Montour	300	D-55-36	Robert Elliot Original: found
NP-1655	Wishard, William	3 APR 1769		Kelly, Union	300	D-55-37	Rev. Ewing Original: found
NP-1656	Baum, Christian	3 APR 1769	Cumberland	Derry, Westmoreland	300	C-21-300	Anthony Allman/Henry Strauch/(r8 MAR 1804)James Crow Original: found
NP-1657	West, Francis	3 APR 1769		Northeast Branch Susquehanna River, Luzerne/ LD: Luzerne	200	A-5-22	Original: Signed by William West, Jr.
NP-1658	Carpenter, Elizabeth	3 APR 1769	Muncy Creek	LD: Lycoming	300		Ann Foutz Original: found

Table 6 - New Purchase Applications (1769-1773)

Number	Applicant	Date	Orig. Place	Later Place	Acres	Survey	Neighbors, Notes, etc.
NP-1659	Thompson, James	3 APR 1769	West Branch Susquehanna River	LD: Lycoming	300		James White Original: found
NP-1660	Hillands, James	3 APR 1769	Bald Eagle Creek	LD: Centre	300		William Samuel Original: Signed
NP-1661	Smith, Thomas	3 APR 1769		East Branch Susquehanna River, Northumberland/ LD: Bradford	300	A-51-72	Original: found
NP-1662	Bausman, Lawrance	3 APR 1769	Cumberland	Wilkins, Allegheny	300	D-55-70	George Croghan Original: found
NP-1663	Watkins, William	3 APR 1769	Bedford	Cheat River, Fayette	200	C-109-15	John Morgan/(r23 JUN 1789)Jehu John Original: found
NP-1664	Dallam, John	3 APR 1769	on path from Bald Eagle Town to Frankstown, Cumberland	LD: Centre	300		--- Baynton & --- Wharton Original: found
NP-1665	Smith, Samuel	3 APR 1769	Lycoming Creek	LD: Lycoming	300		Original: found
NP-1666	Gabriel, George	3 APR 1769		Bald Eagle - Frankstown Road, Northumberland	300	A-19-42	(r5 MAY 1789)John Cox, Esq./[see caveat] Original: found
NP-1667	Pidgen, John	3 APR 1769		Chillisquaque Creek, Northumberland or Montour/ LD: Northumberland	300		Conrad Pidgeon Original: found
NP-1668	Boyer, Christopher	3 APR 1769	Berks	Delaware Run, Northumberland	300	D-55-38	Henry Keppele Original: found
NP-1669	Leonhart, Phillip	3 APR 1769	Bald Eagle Creek	LD: Clinton/ Centre	300		John McDonnall Original: found

Table 6 - New Purchase Applications (1769-1773)

Number	Applicant	Date	Orig. Place	Later Place	Acres	Survey	Neighbors, Notes, etc.
NP-1670	Steinbrecher, Frederick	3 APR 1769	Cumberland	North Huntingdon, Westmoreland & Wilkins, Allegheny/ LD: South Huntingdon, Westmoreland	250	D-55-39 D-55-40	Original: found
NP-1671	Birgeman, John	3 APR 1769	Chillisquaque Creek		300		James Tilghman Original: found
NP-1672	Allison, John	3 APR 1769	Bedford	Salem, Westmoreland	300	C-206-105	(r21 FEB 1799)John Shields Original: found
NP-1673	Goz, Graft	3 APR 1769		Unity, Westmoreland	300	D-55-26 D-55-50	Philip Baltimore Original: found
NP-1674	Bossert, Andrew	3 APR 1769			300		Christopher Boyer Original: found
NP-1675	Altman, John Peter	3 APR 1769	Cumberland	Westmoreland - Conemaugh River, Indiana	300	A-75-41	John Brand/Anthony Altman/(r12 JAN 1789) Original: found
NP-1676	Boyle, John	3 APR 1769	Montours Run		300		Original: found
NP-1677	Smith, William Sr. (of Peters Township [now Franklin County])	3 APR 1769		South Huntingdon, Westmoreland & Fayette	300	D-55-27	Original: found
NP-1678	Wallis, Cassandra	3 APR 1769		LD: Columbia/ Montour	300		Martha Wilson Original: found
NP-1679	Smith, Jonathan Jr.	3 APR 1769		Mt. Pleasant, Westmoreland	300	D-56-105 C-129-284	Robert Smith, Jr./(r6 MAR 1816)Oliver Mitchell & Thomas Mitchell Original: found
NP-1680	McGuire, Philip & Robert	3 APR 1769		Conemaugh, Indiana	600	D-55-28	Original: found
NP-1681	Campbell, Landslet	3 APR 1769	Bald Eagle Creek	LD: Centre	300		Original: Signed
NP-1682	Burd, Thomas	3 APR 1769		Kittanning, Armstrong/ LD: Kittanning, Armstrong	300	D-55-29	Benjamin Suttan Original: found

Table 6 - New Purchase Applications (1769-1773)

Number	Applicant	Date	Orig. Place	Later Place	Acres	Survey	Neighbors, Notes, etc.
NP-1683	Campbell, Charles	3 APR 1769	Cumberland	Johnstown City, Cambria	300	A-20-266	(r24 APR 1788)James McClinachan/[in Johnstown City] Original: found
NP-1684	Culbertson, Robert Jr.	3 APR 1769		North Huntingdon, Westmoreland	300	D-55-30	James Kernahan Original: found
NP-1685	Kirkpatrick, John	3 APR 1769	East Branch Susquehanna River	LD: Luzerne	300		Original: found
NP-1686	Pumroy, George Sr.	3 APR 1769	Cumberland	Westmoreland - Blacklick Creek, Indiana	300	A-78-247	(r7 JAN 1774)Andrew Walker Original: Signed by John Pumroy
NP-1687	Carr, James	3 APR 1769		Derry, Westmoreland	300	D-55-41	Original: found
NP-1688	Grant, Thomas	3 APR 1769	Berks	Augusta, Northumberland	300	A-50-173	(r24 MAR 1788)/[see caveat] Original: found
NP-1689	Stevenson, John	3 APR 1769	Cumberland	Westmoreland - Centre, Indiana	300	A-29-56 D-90-232 D-90-233	Original: found
NP-1690	Gaddis, Thomas	3 APR 1769	Cumberland	Union & Georges, Fayette	300	B-10-169	(r6 JUN 1788) Original: found
NP-1691	McFarren, Samuel	3 APR 1769	Youghiogheny River	LD: Fayette	300		James Harvey Original: found
NP-1692	Davis, David	3 APR 1769	Berks	Delaware Run, Northumberland	300	A-19-107	Jacob Stoute/[see NP-329 to Hugh Montgomery]/(r21 APR 1788)Mathew Corry Original: found
NP-1693	Webster, John Lee	3 APR 1769	Berks	Wayne, Lycoming	300	D-56-266 D-62-259 D-7-260	Francis Wallis/(r11 APR 1770)Samuel Wallis [on Berks County warrant] Original: found
NP-1694	McDowell, Robert (son of James)	3 APR 1769	Peters Creek & Monongahela River	LD: Allegheny	300		John Downe/Samuel Allen Original: found
NP-1695	Blessing, Jacob	3 APR 1769	Berks	White Deer, Union	300	D-55-42	Phillip Kline Original: found
NP-1696	Jones, Isaac Jr.	3 APR 1769		Muncy, Lycoming	300	D-56-264 U-21	Mary Jervis/(r6 SEP 1805)H. Drinker Original: found

Table 6 - New Purchase Applications (1769-1773)

Number	Applicant	Date	Orig. Place	Later Place	Acres	Survey	Neighbors, Notes, etc.
NP-1697	Paress, William	3 APR 1769	Cumberland	LD: Northumberland/ Montour	300		Robert Bonner Original: found
NP-1698	Kerr, James	3 APR 1769	near Muncy Creek	LD: Lycoming	300		[see caveat] Original: Signed
NP-1699	Paris, Christopher	3 APR 1769		Buffalo, Union	300	D-55-43	Rev. John Ewing Original: found
NP-1700	Peters, John	3 APR 1769		Montour/ LD: Montour	300		Jacob Spicer Original: found
NP-1701	Boyd, Andrew	3 APR 1769	Monongahela River	LD: Washington/ Allegheny	300		Original: found
NP-1702	Row, George	3 APR 1769	Cumberland	Northumberland - Potter, Centre	300	C-223-57	(r1 NOV 1788)David Weaver Original: found
NP-1703	Bull, Thomas (of Philadelphia County)	3 APR 1769	Berks	Turbot, Northumberland	300	C-200-246 C-200-260	(r19 FEB 1811)David Shannon Original: Signed
NP-1704	Lofflin, William	3 APR 1769		Nippenose, Lycoming	300	D-60-234 B-118	(r6 SEP 1805)H. Drinker Original: found
NP-1705	Douglas, William	3 APR 1769	Cumberland	South Huntingdon, Westmoreland	300	D-55-44	Original: found
NP-1706	Caruthers, John	3 APR 1769		Elizabeth, Allegheny	300	D-55-51 D-55-52 C-72-133	--- Saltman/(r2 JUL 1830)Jesse Greer Original: found
NP-1707	Beels, Joshua	3 APR 1769		Muncy Creek Twp., Lycoming	300	D-55-45	John Jacob, Jr./French Margaret Original: The original numbered NP-1707 is NP-1805. NP-1707 not found.
NP-1708	Jones, Nathan	3 APR 1769	Berks	Chillisquaque Creek, Northumberland	300	B-453	Francis Jones/(r29 JAN 1796)Thomas Lightfoot Original: found
NP-1709	Culbertson, Robert	3 APR 1769		Blacklick, Indiana	300	D-55-53 D-55-54	Original: found
NP-1710	Hinckel, Lodick	3 APR 1769		North Huntingdon, Westmoreland/ LD: North Huntingdon, Westmoreland	300	D-46-91	--- Crawford/[see C-72-78] Original: Signed

Table 6 - New Purchase Applications (1769-1773)

Number	Applicant	Date	Orig. Place	Later Place	Acres	Survey	Neighbors, Notes, etc.
NP-1711	Irwin, Thomas	3 APR 1769		Unity, Westmoreland/ LD: Unity, Westmoreland	300	D-55-55	John Frazer Original: found
NP-1712	Quigley, Henry Sr.	3 APR 1769		Hartley, Union	300	D-55-56	Original: found
NP-1713	Trester, Martin	3 APR 1769	Berks	Hartley, Union	300	D-56-247 A-13-24	John Hains/Mr. Matlack/(r3 MAY 1811)Nicholas Wyerbaugher Original: found
NP-1714	Jameson, Thomas	3 APR 1769		Blacklick, Indiana	300	D-57-220 C-129-140 D-28-203	(r23 SEP 1786)John McCready Original: found
NP-1715	Spencer, Richard	3 APR 1769		Chillisquaque Creek, Northumberland or Montour/ LD: Northumberland/ Montour	300		Turbutt Francis Original: found
NP-1716	Brown, George	3 APR 1769		Youghiogheny River, Bedford/ LD: Fayette	300	H-185	Alexander Bolden Original: found
NP-1717	Foster, Andrew	3 APR 1769		Muncy, Lycoming	300	D-55-57	Original: found
NP-1718	McDonald, Duncan	3 APR 1769	Fishing Creek	LD: Columbia	300		Original: Signed
NP-1719	Wood, Henry	3 APR 1769	Washington	Monongahela River, Allegheny	300	B-435	(r17 APR 1789)Conrad Loutherback/]patent P-15-5] Original: found
NP-1720	Hodge, William	3 APR 1769	Cumberland	Susquehanna, Cambria	300	C-83-257 C-83-258	Alexander Stuart/(r24 APR 1787)Robert Allison, Esq. Original: found
NP-1721	Chambers, David	3 APR 1769	Northumberland	Northeast Branch Susquehanna River, Columbia	200	D-12-250	(r24 APR 1787)Penrose Wiley Original: found
NP-1722	Flipson, Nicholas	3 APR 1769	East Branch Susquehanna River	LD: Wyoming	300		George Tanner Original: found
NP-1723	Rockman, David	3 APR 1769	Rush Meadows, Northampton	LD: Bradford	300		Jesse Clark Original: found

Table 6 - New Purchase Applications (1769-1773)

Number	Applicant	Date	Orig. Place	Later Place	Acres	Survey	Neighbors, Notes, etc.
NP-1724	Forster, Ralph	3 APR 1769	Northumberland	Nippenose, Lycoming	300	A-28-74	(r3 MAY 1831)Henry Antis/[see caveat] Original: found
NP-1725	Yeates, Jasper	3 APR 1769		Pitt, Allegheny	300	D-55-64	James Hannah Original: found
NP-1726	Rankan, William	3 APR 1769		Huntingdon, Westmoreland	300	C-126-16	(r31 MAR 1788)Benjamin Lord Original: found
NP-1727	Knieble, Frederick	3 APR 1769	Northumberland	White Deer, Union	300	D-55-58 D-55-59	George Zigler/(r31 MAR 1788)Benjamin Lord Original: found
NP-1728	Porter, Mary	3 APR 1769		Unity, Westmoreland	300	D-55-46	--- Proctor Original: found
NP-1729	Christ, George	3 APR 1769	Berks	West Buffalo, Union	300	D-55-47	Adam Christ Original: found
NP-1730	Champion, James	3 APR 1769		Loyalsock, Lycoming	300	D-55-48	Original: found
NP-1731	Creigh, Thomas	3 APR 1769	Cumberland	Unity & Salem, Westmoreland	300	D-46-84 C-189-86 C-90-198 C-90-209 C-59-179	(r6 MAY 1824)E. A. Robinson, Esq./(r26 FEB 1827)Adam Hickenlooper/(r16 MAR 1831)Michael Frantz, Sr. Original: Signed
NP-1732	Shank, Michael Jr.	3 APR 1769	Cumberland	Trout Run, Centre	300	A-19-29	John Shank, Jr./(r5 MAY 1789)John Cox, Esq. Original: found
NP-1733	Iredell, Robert Jr.	3 APR 1769	Berks	White Deer, Union/ LD: Union	300	D-57-30 E-218	Daniel Ryan/[application NP-723 to John Gregg]/[see caveat] Original: found
NP-1734	Hewitt, Thomas	3 APR 1769		Turbot, Northumberland	300	C-78-123	John Murray/James McNachon/(r20 SEP 1774) Original: found
NP-1735	Smith, Henry	3 APR 1769		Point, Northumberland/ LD: Northumberland	300	D-55-49	Original: found
NP-1736	Pusey, William	3 APR 1769	White Flint Creek, Cumberland	LD: Union	300		Original: found
NP-1737	Small, Robert	3 APR 1769		North Huntingdon, Westmoreland/ LD: Huntingdon, Westmoreland	300	D-60-218 A-29-54	Original: found

Table 6 - New Purchase Applications (1769-1773)

Number	Applicant	Date	Orig. Place	Later Place	Acres	Survey	Neighbors, Notes, etc.
NP-1738	McIntosh, David	3 APR 1769	Berks	Kelly, Union	300		--- Hamersly/[same land as NP-2225 to Breeson Bawden] Original: found
NP-1739	Blaine, Patrick	3 APR 1769		Wilkins & Plum, Allegheny	300	D-64-104 A-2-259	(r28 APR 1788)William Elliott Original: found
NP-1740	Scott, Abram	3 APR 1769	Berks	Augusta, Northumberland	300	E-354	(r15 OCT 1782)Charles Gough Original: found
NP-1741	Franklinberry, Joseph	3 APR 1769	Berks	White Deer, Union/ LD: Buffalo, Union	300	D-56-247 C-88-54 C-230-81 C-88-53	(p13 OCT 1873)Dewald Sanders/(p13 OCT 1873)Jacob Heinley Original: found
NP-1742	Reading, Richard	3 APR 1769	Susquehanna River opposite Isle of Cue	LD: Lycoming	200		Original: found
NP-1743	Spence, Andrew	3 APR 1769	Mahoning, East Branch Susquehanna River	LD: Montour	300		Original: found
NP-1744	Conn, Robert	3 APR 1769		Shamokin, Northumberland	300	E-136	(r9 MAR 1790)Isaac Richardson/[see caveat] Original: found
NP-1745	Gibson, Hugh	3 APR 1769	White Deer Hole Creek	LD: Lycoming	300		Hugh McCallester/William White Original: Signed
NP-1746	Meanard, Frederick	3 APR 1769	Northumberland	East Branch Susquehanna River, Bradford/ LD: Luzerne	300	A-235	John Wirmly Original: found
NP-1747	Calhoon, John	3 APR 1769		Unity, Westmoreland	300	D-55-61 D-55-62	--- Baltimore Original: found
NP-1748	Scully, John	3 APR 1769	Berks	Nippenose, Lycoming	300	D-55-63	Original: found
NP-1749	Barton, Joseph	3 APR 1769	Cumberland	Washington, Westmoreland	300	D-55-65	Original: found
NP-1750	Husband, William	3 APR 1769	Cumberland	Berks - Black Run, Northumberland	300	C-341	Thomas Wallis/(r23 SEP 1790)Reuben Haines Original: found
NP-1751	Allee, John	3 APR 1769		Hepburn, Lycoming	300	D-55-71	Richard Cantwell Original: found

Table 6 - New Purchase Applications (1769-1773)

Number	Applicant	Date	Orig. Place	Later Place	Acres	Survey	Neighbors, Notes, etc.
NP-1752	Owings, John	3 APR 1769		White Lick Creek, Greene/ LD: Greene	300		Original: found
NP-1753	Watson, Thomas	3 APR 1769		Turbot, Northumberland	300	D-55-72	Original: found
NP-1754	Potter, James	3 APR 1769	Northumberland	West Buffalo, Union	300	C-125-214	(r7 MAR 1811)Charles Hall, Esq. Original: found
NP-1755	Stimble, Isaac	3 APR 1769		Ligonier, Westmoreland	300	D-55-73 D-55-74	William McKinzey/John Campbell Original: found
NP-1756	Kricker, Adam	3 APR 1769		Muncy Creek Twp., Lycoming	300	D-55-75	Original: found
NP-1757	Johns, Margaret	3 APR 1769	East Branch Susquehanna River below Catawissa Creek, Berks or Northampton	LD: Columbia	300		Original: found
NP-1758	Kearny, William	3 APR 1769		Hempfield, Westmoreland	300	A-2-258	John McMath/(r28 APR 1788)William Elliott/[see caveat] Original: found
NP-1759	Baird, Thomas	3 APR 1769		South Huntingdon, Westmoreland	300	D-11-158 D-11-159	Arthur Lindsey/(r20 DEC 1836)T. Hanna/(r21 DEC 1836)Paul Warden Original: found
NP-1760	Eatten, James	3 APR 1769		1 mile west of Kittanning Path, Indiana	300	C-65-58	--- Barr/(r30 MAR 1789 & p 31 MAR 1789)/[patent P-13-535] Original: found
NP-1761	Blane, Robert	3 APR 1769	West Branch Susquehanna River four miles above Shamokin		300		[same land as NP-1918 to John Blum] Original: found
NP-1762	Mengies, George	3 APR 1769		West Buffalo, Union	300	D-55-76	Original: found
NP-1763	Irwin, Joseph	3 APR 1769	Cumberland	LD: Pitt, Allegheny	300	F-239 C-145-288 BB-1-24	Edward Smith/James Royal/Casper Toubson/(r1 JAN 1814)W. Duncan & Jacob Negley/(p11 JUL 1872)Samuel Lightner [patent H-70-460]/(p19 FEB 1886)Jerome B. Anjer [patent H-74-573] Original: Signed
NP-1764	Harris, David Jr.	3 APR 1769	Northumberland	Buffalo, Union	300	C-531	(r10 FEB 1802)Samuel Maclay Original: found

Table 6 - New Purchase Applications (1769-1773)

Number	Applicant	Date	Orig. Place	Later Place	Acres	Survey	Neighbors, Notes, etc.
NP-1765	Ewing, Alexander	3 APR 1769	Berks	Buffalo, Union	300	D-60-187	[same land as NP-1918 to John Blum] Original: Missing
NP-1766	Christy, Thomas	3 APR 1769		Pitt, Westmoreland	300	D-46-83	William Christy/[see caveat] Original: found
NP-1767	Robb, Thomas	3 APR 1769	Northumberland	Muncy Creek Twp., Lycoming	300	C-119-164	John Ren/(r22 MAR 1843)E. G. Lyon & H. Ulsh/[see caveat] Original: Signed
NP-1768	Pearce, Thomas	3 APR 1769	Cumberland	Bedford - Monongahela River, Fayette	300	L-415	(r4 JUN 1788)Andrew Lynn Original: found
NP-1769	Shippen, Edward Jr.	3 APR 1769		Augusta, Northumberland	300	F-131 D-7-90 C-26-155 C-178-299 C-178-300	Edward Shippen, Sr./(r7 SEP 1810)Philip Weiser & Mary Weiser/(r11 JAN 1812)Peter Conrad/(r15 APR 1830)C. Raker & Peter Sassaman Original: found
NP-1770	Cathcort, William	3 APR 1769	West Branch Susquehanna River	LD: Union	300		William Blyth Original: found
NP-1771	Wallis, Grace	3 APR 1769	Northampton & Berks	Chillisquaque Creek, Columbia	300	D-491	(r3 MAR 1800 & 4 OCT 1800)John Biddle & Thomas Stewardson Original: found
NP-1771a	Brenner, James	-----	Berks	Buffalo, Union	---	C-8-2 D-56-99 D-56-100 D-56-189 D-56-124 D-56-125 D-56-140 D-57-213	[entered after NP-3853 in register] Original: found
NP-1772	Alexander, Joseph	3 APR 1769		Elizabeth, Allegheny	300	D-55-78	Joseph Pearson Original: Signed
NP-1773	White, Charles	3 APR 1769	Berks	Lycoming - Wayne, Clinton	300	D-55-79	--- Patterson Original: found
NP-1774	Knight, Giles Jr.	3 APR 1769		Muncy, Lycoming	300	E-54 D-56-252 D-60-263 D-62-292	Giles Knight Sr./(r20 SEP 1794)Samuel Wallis Original: found

Table 6 - New Purchase Applications (1769-1773)

Number	Applicant	Date	Orig. Place	Later Place	Acres	Survey	Neighbors, Notes, etc.
NP-1775	Crooks, William	3 APR 1769		Northeast Branch Susquehanna River, Luzerne	300	C-11-83	(r20 APR 1824)Stephen Arnold Original: found
NP-1776	Robison, James	3 APR 1769		West Bethlehem, Washington	300	C-219-27	(r26 APR 1798)Alexander Swan/[see caveat] Original: found
NP-1777	Colhoon, John	3 APR 1769	Berks	Northumberland - Muncy, Lycoming	300	A-4-168	(r6 JAN 1802)Jerushia Robb & John Robb & Mary Robb Original: found
NP-1778	Miller, Vight	3 APR 1769		East Branch Susquehanna River, Luzerne	300	C-222-254	Jacob Meyer/(r8 AUG 1781)Joseph Wharton Original: found
NP-1779	Talbott, John	3 APR 1769	Cumberland	LD: West Buffalo, Union	300		Ann Coale Original: found
NP-1780	Claypole, Joseph Jr. (of Philadelphia)	3 APR 1769	Berks	Bald Eagle Creek, Centre	300	C-15	Samuel Power/(r15 JAN 1784)Mathew Clarkson Original: Signed
NP-1781	Hartley, Henry	3 APR 1769	Westmoreland	Turtle Creek, Allegheny	300	C-13-61	Christian Wonder/John Sutton/(r20 FEB 1794)John Barclay, Esq. Original: Signed
NP-1782	Mentzer, Michael	3 APR 1769	Cumberland	West Buffalo, Union	300	D-55-80	Martin Albrecht Original: found
NP-1783	Pharley, Christopher	3 APR 1769	Cumberland	Hempfield, Westmoreland	300	A-52-148	John Sampson/(r3 JUN 1803)Margaret Deney & Jacob Rugh & Jacob Frantz Original: found
NP-1784	Todd, William	3 APR 1769		Turbot, Northumberland	300	D-56-198 C-213-7	[see Northumberland warrant D-40 to Michael Doutel] Original: Signed
NP-1785	Vaneken, Aaron	3 APR 1769	Berks	White Deer, Union	300	D-56-227	[same land as NP-1340 to Samuel Mitchell] Original: found
NP-1786	Clock, Adam	3 APR 1769		East Branch Susquehanna River, Luzerne	300	C-157-161	Christian Welckley/(r21 DEC 1781)Henry Roatt [Pratt] & Solomon Marache [March] Original: found
NP-1787	Irwin, Richard	3 APR 1769	Berks	Chillisquaque Creek, Northumberland/ LD: Northumberland	300	C-179-48	Markus Hulings/George Enon/[see caveat] Original: found

Table 6 - New Purchase Applications (1769-1773)

Number	Applicant	Date	Orig. Place	Later Place	Acres	Survey	Neighbors, Notes, etc.
NP-1788	McMotry, John	3 APR 1769	Berks	White Deer, Union	300	D-62-231	William Blyth/[same land as NP-2778 to John Carmalt] Original: found
NP-1789	Shuler, Jacob	3 APR 1769		East Branch Susquehanna River, Luzerne	300	E-15	Peter Ney/(r8 AUG 1781)Joseph Wharton Original: found
NP-1790	Stoner, John	3 APR 1769		East Branch Susquehanna River, Luzerne	300	C-222-265	Jacob Whitmore/(r8 AUG 1781)Joseph Wharton Original: found
NP-1791	Morgan, John	3 APR 1769	near Sewickley	LD: Westmoreland	300		David Morgan Original: Signed by Jacob Morgan, Jr.
NP-1792	Weed, Elijah	3 APR 1769	Berks	Northeast Branch Susquehanna River, Northumberland	300	M-222	(r2 JUL 1785)Dr. John Morgan/[see caveat] Original: found
NP-1793	Athel, William	3 APR 1769	Cumberland	Youghiogheny River, Westmoreland	300	A-64-93	Col. Washington/(r18 FEB 1782)Gen. George Washington Original: found
NP-1794	Hare, John Jr.	3 APR 1769		Loyalsock, Lycoming/ LD: Montour	300	D-55-66	Original: found
NP-1795	Stuart, Charles	3 APR 1769	Montour Creek & Pine Run, Berks	LD: Montour	300		Alexander Hunter Original: found
NP-1796	Masden, John (of West Pennsborough, Cumberland County)	3 APR 1769	Westmoreland	Chartiers Creek, Washington	300	A-87-57 A-87-58	(r5 MAR 1782)Dr. Edward Hand Original: found
NP-1797	Bailey, Robert (of Philadelphia)	3 APR 1769	Washington	Robinson, Allegheny	300	B-14-188 C-171-49 D-13-126 D-38-149	Capt. Alexander McKee/David Scott/(r11 MAR 1799)Edward Price/(r12 MAY 1826)John Wilson/[see NP-1625] Original: found
NP-1798	Stroud, Isaac	3 APR 1769	Northampton	Little Fishing Creek, Columbia	300	D-513	William Hopkins, Jr./(r1 MAR 1800 & 4 OCT 1800)John Biddle & Thomas Stewardson Original: found
NP-1799	Beaty, Mary	3 APR 1769	Bedford	Derry, Westmoreland	300	C-150-2	Shedrick Machmoore/(r14 MAR 1810)A. Maxwell Original: found

Table 6 - New Purchase Applications (1769-1773)

Number	Applicant	Date	Orig. Place	Later Place	Acres	Survey	Neighbors, Notes, etc.
NP-1800	McAlister, William	3 APR 1769	Berks	White Deer, Union	300	D-62-231	William Blyth/David Morton/[same land as NP-2778 to William Carmalt] Original: Signed
NP-1801	Wells, Jane	3 APR 1769	Berks	Buffalo, Union	300		[same land as NP-1918 to John Blum] Original: found
NP-1802	Travis, Robert	3 APR 1769		Versailles, Allegheny	300	D-55-82	John McKee Original: Signed
NP-1803	Conrad, Jacob (of Oley)	3 APR 1769	Berks	Augusta, Northumberland/ LD: Augusta, Northumberland	300	F-232 C-61	Frederick Hill/(r23 AUG 1813) Original: found
NP-1804	Neisbite, William	3 APR 1769		Hempfield, Westmoreland	300	F-230 D-55-67	Robert Laughlin/Barnet Cunningham Original: Signed
NP-1805	Elliott, Jean Jr. (of Path Valley, Cumberland County)	3 APR 1769	Cumberland	Crooked Creek, Armstrong	300	C-35-209	(r29 SEP 1788)Alexander Craig Original: Original filed as NP-1707
NP-1806	Strubel, Christopher	3 APR 1769	East Branch Susquehanna River below Wyalusing	LD: Wyoming/ Bradford	300		Thomas Heath Original: found
NP-1807	Stephens, David Sr.	3 APR 1769	Cumberland	Berks - Brush Run Branch of Penns Creek, Northumberland/ LD: Union	300	A-29-53	[see caveat] Original: found
NP-1808	Robinson, Andrew	3 APR 1769	West Branch Susquehanna River	LD: Lycoming	300		Robert Morris Original: found
NP-1809	McNaul, Joseph	3 APR 1769	Bedford	Youghiogheny River, Westmoreland	300	C-84-100	Alexander Dunlap/Robert McConnell/John Perry/John Reig/(r10 APR 1786)Charles Hanah Original: found
NP-1810	Musser, Joseph	3 APR 1769	Berks	first falls above Ft. Augusta, Northumberland	300	C-197-187	David Eshelman/(r10 SEP 1770)Mathias Slough Original: found
NP-1811	Robinson, Isabella (widow)	3 APR 1769		Shamokin, Northumberland	300	C-209-16 C-209-17	(r10 APR 1783)John Simpson Original: found
NP-1812	Yoner, John	3 APR 1769		Franklin, Westmoreland	300	D-55-68	Original: found

Table 6 - New Purchase Applications (1769-1773)

Number	Applicant	Date	Orig. Place	Later Place	Acres	Survey	Neighbors, Notes, etc.
NP-1813	Pollox, Alexander	3 APR 1769		Franklin, Fayette	300	C-74-267	Robert Pollox/John Bouga/(r18 APR 1792)Joseph Huston Original: found
NP-1814	Todd, William	3 APR 1769	Bald Eagle Creek	LD: Clinton	300		Original: found
NP-1815	Young, Jacob	3 APR 1769	Berks	Black Hole Creek, Lycoming	300	C-39-222	(r29 APR 1773)Micheal Diffenderfer Original: found
NP-1816	Cumings, Samuel	3 APR 1769	Berks	Washington, Lycoming	300	D-55-69	Robert Taylor Original: Signed by James Cumings
NP-1817	Fockler, George	3 APR 1769	Cumberland	Northumberland - Buffalo, Union	300	C-135-71	John Brock/--- Reyer/(r8 MAY 1782)William Macklay, Esq. Original: Signed
NP-1818	Henderson, Daniel	3 APR 1769	Berks	Buffalo, Union	300	D-55-77	Mr. Ewing Original: found
NP-1819	Stewart, Andrew	3 APR 1769	Nippenose Creek	LD: Lycoming	300		Original: found
NP-1820	Thompson, John	3 APR 1769		Monongahela River, Washington/ LD: Washington	300	A-29-47	Hugh Read/[see caveat] Original: found
NP-1821	Worthington, Charles Jr.	3 APR 1769	Cumberland	Bald Eagle Creek, Centre/ LD: Centre	300		Joseph Hopkins Sr. Original: found
NP-1822	Thauley, George Jr.	3 APR 1769		Allegheny, Westmoreland & Plum, Allegheny	300	D-55-83 D-55-84	Original: Missing
NP-1823	Galbraith, Robert	3 APR 1769	Berks	Loyalsock, Lycoming	300	D-62-298 A-9-283	(r25 MAY 1772)Turbutt Francis, Esq. Original: found
NP-1824	Flahaven, John	3 APR 1769		Washington, Lycoming	300	D-55-91	Original: found
NP-1825	Kling, Ludwig	3 APR 1769		Tunkhannock Creek, Northumberland	300	C-7-231	John George Baur/(r22 APR 1782)William Brown Original: found
NP-1826	Forgeson, William Jr.	3 APR 1769		Unity, Westmoreland	300	D-55-92 D-55-93	Original: found

Table 6 - New Purchase Applications (1769-1773)

Number	Applicant	Date	Orig. Place	Later Place	Acres	Survey	Neighbors, Notes, etc.
NP-1827	Albright, Peter	3 APR 1769	Tunkhannock Creek & East Branch Susquehanna River	LD: Wyoming	300		Original: found
NP-1828	Douglass, Joseph	3 APR 1769		Mifflin, Allegheny	300	D-55-85	John Travis/Phillip Whitesell/Thomas Smith Original: Signed
NP-1829	Lemon, Thomas	3 APR 1769	West Branch Susquehanna River	LD: Buffalo, Union	300		William Blyth Original: found
NP-1830	Springer, Nathan	3 APR 1769		Redstone Creek, Fayette	300	D-60-207 C-44-67	(r5 MAY 1788)Ephraim Douglass, Esq. Original: Signed
NP-1831	Smith, Thomas	3 APR 1769	Bedford	Allegheny, Cambria	300	Q-88	Alexander Stuart/(r11 JUL 1837)Patrick Mullen Original: found
NP-1832	Kelly, William	3 APR 1769	Northampton	Northumberland - Tunkhannock Creek, Wyoming	300	A-24-138	Robert Wood/(r19 APR 1782)James Johnston Original: found
NP-1833	Osburn, Thomas	3 APR 1769	Northampton	Northumberland - Tunkhannock Creek, Wyoming/ LD: Luzerne	300	X-156	John Ballard Original: found
NP-1834	Kinney, Jacobus, Peter, & John	3 APR 1769	Fishing Creek	LD: Columbia	900		Original: found
NP-1835	Johnson, David	3 APR 1769	Northampton	Northeast Branch Susquehanna River, Northumberland	300	N-246	(r14 APR 1783)John K. Nesbitt Original: found
NP-1836	Black, William	3 APR 1769		Muncy Creek Twp., Lycoming	300	D-55-94	Original: found
NP-1837	Gibons, James	3 APR 1769	Long Limestone Valley	LD: Centre	300		Peter Light Original: found
NP-1838	Taylor, John (merchant)	3 APR 1769	Northumberland	Long Limestone Valley, Centre & Blair	300	C-176-154	(r9 JUL 1782)Thomas Riche Original: found
NP-1839	Pearson, James	3 APR 1769	Cumberland	North Huntingdon, Westmoreland	300	N-214	(r24 APR 1807)George Morgan Original: found

Table 6 - New Purchase Applications (1769-1773)

Number	Applicant	Date	Orig. Place	Later Place	Acres	Survey	Neighbors, Notes, etc.
NP-1840	Rowan, John	3 APR 1769		Unity, Westmoreland	300	D-55-95	Original: found
NP-1841	Gemberling, Paul (of Heydelberg, Lancaster County)	3 APR 1769	Berks	Buffalo, Union	300	D-57-291	Martin Heffelfinger/[same land as NP-954 to Jacob Gemberling] Original: found
NP-1842	Gilmore, David	3 APR 1769	Berks	White Deer, Union	300	D-62-231	Elizabeth Blyth/[same land as NP-2778 to John Carmalt] Original: found
NP-1843	Menoch, James	3 APR 1769	Chillisquaque Creek	LD: Northumberland	300		Richard Irwin Original: found
NP-1844	Thomas, John Jr.	3 APR 1769		Unity & Hempfield, Westmoreland	300	D-55-96	Original: found
NP-1845	Porter, Stephen	3 APR 1769		Buffalo, Union	300	D-55-97	Original: found
NP-1846	Huff, Edmond	3 APR 1769		Nippenose, Lycoming	300	D-55-98	Original: found
NP-1847	Beatty, John Sr.	3 APR 1769		Hempfield, Westmoreland	300	C-35-215	James Beatty/(r6 AUG 1788)John Concle Original: found
NP-1848	Heaton, John	3 APR 1769	Berks	Washington, Lycoming	300	D-55-99	Richard Smith, Jr. Original: found
NP-1849	Sheaphard, David	3 APR 1769	Cumberland	Pigeon Creek, Washington	300	C-193-258 C-193-259	David Walsh/(r28 MAR 1788)Jacob Spright Original: found
NP-1850	Lindsay, James	3 APR 1769		Huntingdon, Westmoreland	300	C-144-190 C-144-201	(r10 APR 1827)Benjamin Miller Original: found
NP-1851	Wilkin, Mathew	3 APR 1769		Brush Run, Centre/ LD: Centre	300		Original: found
NP-1852	Murray, Alexander	3 APR 1769		Tyrone, Fayette & Unity, Westmoreland	300	D-55-86 D-55-100	Robert Adams/Mr. Wells Original: Signed
NP-1853	McLees, James	3 APR 1769	Northumberland	Mahoning, Columbia/ LD: Columbia	300	X-221	Original: found
NP-1854	Smith, Forten	3 APR 1769	Westmoreland	Indiana	300	A-71-262	David Jameson/(r18 JUL 1774)Dr. David Jameson Original: found
NP-1855	Jarvis, Elizabeth Jr.	3 APR 1769	Cumberland	Pike, Clearfield	300	A-32-131	Original: found

Table 6 - New Purchase Applications (1769-1773)

Number	Applicant	Date	Orig. Place	Later Place	Acres	Survey	Neighbors, Notes, etc.
NP-1856	Hudnot, Joseph	3 APR 1769		Buffalo, Union	300	D-60-266 D-60-276 C-39-228	(r22 OCT 1773)Ludowick Derr Original: found
NP-1857	Hill, George	3 APR 1769		Nippenose, Lycoming	300	D-55-87	John Brown Original: found
NP-1858	Shaffer, Henry	3 APR 1769	Berks	Kelly, Union	300	D-56-85 D-56-93	Alexander Shaffer/[same land as NP-2368 to Thomas Beatty] Original: found
NP-1859	Devall, Lewis	3 APR 1769	Cumberland	Bullskin, Fayette	300	D-55-88	Original: found
NP-1860	Parr, James	3 APR 1769	Northumberland	Buffalo, Union	300	B-260	(r6 SEP 1784)Isaac Franks Original: found
NP-1861	Richardson, Edward	3 APR 1769		Muncy, Lycoming	300	D-55-89	Original: Signed by Joseph Richardson
NP-1862	Fisher, Thomas	3 APR 1769		Augusta, Northumberland	300	K-101	(r5 SEP 1783)John Nixon & Alex Foster Original: found
NP-1863	Moore, John	3 APR 1769	Berks	Buffalo, Union	300	D-55-90	John Willson Original: Signed
NP-1864	Blaine, Ephraim	3 APR 1769		Hempfield, Westmoreland	300	D-56-219 D-62-187 D-64-213 C-12-175 D-45-13	(r25 APR 1786)/[see caveat] Original: found
NP-1865	Kirney, Richard	3 APR 1769		Heidlers Run, Westmoreland/ LD: Allegheny	300	A-253	Original: found
NP-1866	Snivly, Sarah	3 APR 1769	Whiteley Creek	LD: Greene	300		Original: found
NP-1867	Elliott, William	3 APR 1769		Derry, Westmoreland	300	D-60-181	Original: Signed
NP-1868	Bell, George	3 APR 1769	West Branch Susquehanna River opposite mouth of Pine Creek	LD: Lycoming/ Clinton	300		Original: found
NP-1869	Dunlap, Alexander	3 APR 1769		Elizabeth, Allegheny	300	D-55-51 C-135-188	Joseph McNaw/John Perry/ John Kyle/(r29 JUL 1784)Thomas Morton, Esq. Original: found

Table 6 - New Purchase Applications (1769-1773)

Number	Applicant	Date	Orig. Place	Later Place	Acres	Survey	Neighbors, Notes, etc.
NP-1870	Lebig, Henry	3 APR 1769	Northampton	Rush Meadows, Luzerne	300	A-371	Henry Pole/(r24 OCT 1782)Alexander Power Original: found
NP-1871	Gasselman, Christopher	3 APR 1769	Northampton	Rush Meadow, Luzerne	300	A-12-135	(r14 MAR 1775)John Gibson, Esq. Original: found
NP-1872	McKee, James	3 APR 1769		East Huntingdon, Westmoreland/ LD: Westmoreland	300	D-60-219 C-190-289 B-8-27 C-190-290 B-8-26	(p23 JUN 1870)Michael Reiff/(p23 JUN 1870)David Robinson/(p16 OCT 1878)William R. Byers Original: found
NP-1873	Culbertson, Samuel	3 APR 1769		Blacklick, Indiana	300	D-60-182 D-60-183	Original: found
NP-1874	McGuire, Thomas	3 APR 1769	Berks	Buffalo, Union	300	D-60-200	[same land as NP-1918 to John Blum] Original: found
NP-1875	Warner, Joseph	3 APR 1769	opposite Muncy Hill, Cumberland	LD: Lycoming	300		Original: found
NP-1876	Smith, Thomas	3 APR 1769		Unity, Westmoreland	300	D-55-62 C-192-214	--- Proctor/(r18 AUG 1786) Original: found
NP-1877	Fouts, Ann	3 APR 1769	Muncy Creek	LD: Lycoming	300		Original: found
NP-1878	McHenry, Mathew	3 APR 1769		Loyalsock, Lycoming	300	D-60-184	Original: found
NP-1879	Clark, Joseph	3 APR 1769		East of Allegheny River, Indiana	300	A-71-261	Forten Smith/(r18 JUL 1774)Dr. David Jameson Original: found
NP-1880	Mauhaun, William	3 APR 1769	Berks	Point, Northumberland	300	D-55-49 B-282	Richard Spencer/(r16 JUL 1794)Hugh Ferguson, Jr. Original: found
NP-1881	Irwin, William	3 APR 1769		Chillisquaque, Northumberland	300	D-76 C-46-269 D-77	James McMahon/George Irwin/Marcus Hulings/(r11 SEP 1807)James Durham/(r7 APR 1825)James Armstrong, executor of John Pollock, deceased Original: found
NP-1882	Hynes, Andrew	3 APR 1769	Monongahela River	LD: Fayette	300		Original: found
NP-1883	Erwin, Edward	3 APR 1769	Berks	Washington, Lycoming	300	D-60-185	John Buchanon Original: found

Table 6 - New Purchase Applications (1769-1773)

Number	Applicant	Date	Orig. Place	Later Place	Acres	Survey	Neighbors, Notes, etc.
NP-1884	Harris, Thomas	3 APR 1769		one mile below old Bald Eagle Town, Centre/ LD: Centre	300		Original: found
NP-1885	Smith, John	3 APR 1769		Plum, Armstrong	300	C-198-278	(r10 MAR 1828)James Mitchell Original: found
NP-1886	Shute, Sarah	3 APR 1769	Northumberland	Little Fishing Creek, Columbia	300	V-145	John Morton/(r25 JUN 1796)Owen Biddle Original: found
NP-1887	Latimer, George	3 APR 1769	Bald Eagle Creek	LD: Centre	300		Original: found
NP-1888	Brand, John	3 APR 1769	Cumberland	Westmoreland - Altmans Run, Indiana	300	A-48-49	Anthony Altman/(r19 MAR 1788)Frederick Rohrer Original: found
NP-1889	McCord, William	3 APR 1769	Chillisquaque Creek	LD: Northumberland	300		Original: found
NP-1890	Good, Henry	3 APR 1769	Long Limestone Valley	LD: Centre	300		John Manderbach Original: found
NP-1891	McGachey, John	3 APR 1769	North Branch Susquehanna River 7 miles from Ft. Augusta	LD: Northumberland	300		Original: found
NP-1892	Robinson, Mathew	3 APR 1769	Berks	Buffalo, Union	300	D-57-12 D-57-17	[same land as NP-866 to John Clin] Original: found
NP-1893	Stevenson, John	3 APR 1769		Altmans Run, Indiana	300	C-144-45 C-144-270	(r2 APR 1788)William McFarland Original: found
NP-1894	Barnes, Thomas Jr.	3 APR 1769	Northeast Branch Susquehanna River	LD: Montour	100		Original: found
NP-1895	Sherack, Christian	3 APR 1769		West Buffalo, Union	300	D-57-248 A-29-52 C-61-17	(r6 MAR 1813)William Forster & John Forster Original: found
NP-1896	Mahaun, John	3 APR 1769	Cumberland	Bald Eagle Creek, Centre/ LD: Centre	300		Rubin Perkins Original: found
NP-1897	Taylor, William	3 APR 1769	Delaware Run	LD: Northumberland	300		Original: found
NP-1898	Barclay, Alexander	3 APR 1769	Cumberland	Chest Creek, Bedford - Cambria	300	A-73-206	Alexander Stuart/(r10 MAY 1774)Robert Barclay Original: found

Table 6 - New Purchase Applications (1769-1773)

Number	Applicant	Date	Orig. Place	Later Place	Acres	Survey	Neighbors, Notes, etc.
NP-1899	Taylor, William	3 APR 1769	Muncy Creek	LD: Lycoming	300		Original: Signed
NP-1900	Wilkin, Robert Jr.	3 APR 1769	Brush Run	LD: Centre	300		[see caveat] Original: found
NP-1901	Cook, John	3 APR 1769	Jacobs Creek near Braddocks Road	LD: Fayette	300		Original: found
NP-1902	Bringham, John	3 APR 1769	Cumberland	Pigeon Creek, Washington/ LD: Washington	300		Andrew Martin Original: found
NP-1903	Pedens, Hugh	3 APR 1769	Berks	Hartley, Union	300	D-60-191	Original: found
NP-1904	Moore, John	3 APR 1769	Bald Eagle Creek	LD: Centre	300		Thomas Harris Original: found
NP-1905	Brotherton, William	3 APR 1769		Salem & Unity, Westmoreland	300	C-49-212	(r5 DEC 1794)William Frame Original: found
NP-1906	Humphreys, Whitehead	3 APR 1769		Muncy, Lycoming	300	D-60-193	Joshua Humphries Original: found
NP-1907	Makin, William	3 APR 1769	Northeast Branch Susquehanna River	LD: Luzerne	300		Original: found
NP-1908	Boyd, Samuel	3 APR 1769	Monongahela River	LD: Pitt, Allegheny	300		Jasper Yeates Original: found
NP-1909	Cunningham, Barnet	3 APR 1769		Hempfield, Westmoreland	300	D-70-231 D-70-232 D-70-233 D-70-293 C-192-116	William Neisbite/Nathaniel Nelson/(r9 MAY 1786)William Shaw Original: Signed
NP-1910	Hall, William	3 APR 1769		Muncy Creek Twp., Lycoming	300	D-60-194	Original: found
NP-1911	Willson, Thomas Esq.	3 APR 1769		Northeast Branch Susquehanna River, Lycoming/ LD: Columbia	300		William Brown Original: found
NP-1912	Silver, Gersham	3 APR 1769	Cumberland	Berks - Kelly, Union	300	D-57-37	[same land as NP-820 to Ann Chambers] Original: found
NP-1913	Harrison, William	3 APR 1769		German, Fayette	300	C-127-237	(r7 DEC 1797)John Mason Original: Signed

Table 6 - New Purchase Applications (1769-1773)

Number	Applicant	Date	Orig. Place	Later Place	Acres	Survey	Neighbors, Notes, etc.
NP-1914	Nelson, George	3 APR 1769	Berks	Turbot, Northumberland	300	A-18-278	Isaac Hazelhurst/(r28 NOV 1771)Reuben Haines & Samuel Miles Original: found
NP-1915	Palmer, John	3 APR 1769		Bradford & Boggs, Clearfield	300	H-445	(r9 JUN 1830)Charles Smith & Benjamin R. Morgan/[see caveat] Original: found
NP-1916	Fooks, Paul	3 APR 1769		North Strabane, Washington	300	F-237 B-12-111 B-12-112 C-150-136	David Evans/(r5 SEP 1831)Robert Henderson/(r4 NOV 1863)Eben McClellandon Original: found
NP-1917	Ferree, John	3 APR 1769		Northeast Branch Susquehanna River 4 miles from Ft. Augusta, Northumberland	300	C-135-34	John Cross/(12 DEC 1782)White Matlack & Phillip Frick Original: found
NP-1918	Blum, John	3 APR 1769	Berks	Buffalo, Union	300	D-60-200 D-60-186 D-60-187 D-60-188 D-60-195 D-60-196 D-60-197 D-60-198	Original: found
NP-1919	Colder, Joseph	3 APR 1769		Buffalo, Union	300	D-60-208	Original: found
NP-1920	Jenkins, Mary Jr.	3 APR 1769	Northumberland	Fishing Creek, Columbia	300	C-148-149	(r29 NOV 1785)Evan Owen Original: found
NP-1921	Walker, William	3 APR 1769		Point, Northumberland	200	D-60-189	Original: Signed
NP-1922	Coale, Sarah Jr.	3 APR 1769		Columbia/ LD: Columbia	300		Margaret Harris Original: found
NP-1923	Sharon, James	3 APR 1769		Spring, Centre	300	C-85-230	(r18 SEP 1815)Charles Huston, Esq./[see caveat] Original: Signed
NP-1924	Butler, William	3 APR 1769	Youghiogheny River	LD: Fayette	300		Adam Douglas Original: Signed
NP-1925	Wilson, John	3 APR 1769		Lawrence, Clearfield	300	D-60-190	Original: found

Table 6 - New Purchase Applications (1769-1773)

Number	Applicant	Date	Orig. Place	Later Place	Acres	Survey	Neighbors, Notes, etc.
NP-1926	Kishler, Samuel	3 APR 1769	Berks	Buffalo, Union	100	D-60-201	Original: found
NP-1927	Murray, John	3 APR 1769	Berks	Kelly, Union	300	D-56-254	John Hall/[same land as NP-1308 to William Ashton] Original: found
NP-1928	Death, James Sr.	3 APR 1769	Dunlap Creek in Redstone Settlement, Cumberland		300		(r6 DEC 1787) Original: found
NP-1929	Sweger, John	3 APR 1769		Mifflin, Allegheny	300	D-60-202	Original: Signed
NP-1930	Barr, Jacob	3 APR 1769	West Branch Susquehanna River	LD: Centre	300		Original: found
NP-1931	Young, Mathias	3 APR 1769	Cumberland	Wilkins, Allegheny	300	D-60-203	William Bausman Original: found
NP-1932	Miller, John (of Strasburg)	3 APR 1769		East Branch Susquehanna River, Luzerne/ LD: Luzerne	300	X-220 C-105-105	(r19 APR 1841)P. B. Jennings Original: found
NP-1933	Jonson, James Sr.	3 APR 1769	Berks	West Buffalo, Union	300	D-55-47 C-138-62	(r2 MAR 1796)John Lowdon/[see caveat] Original: found
NP-1934	Neff, Abram	3 APR 1769	Northeast Branch Susquehanna River	LD: Columbia	300		John Hoofnagle/"Old Nutimus" Original: found
NP-1935	Dobbins, Thomas	3 APR 1769	Berks	West Branch Susquehanna River, Centre/ LD: Lycoming/ Union	300	D-46-99	[see caveat] Original: Signed
NP-1936	Young, John	3 APR 1769		Jacobs Creek, Bedford	300	D-9-224	Thomas Green/(r31 MAR 1772) Original: found
NP-1937	Wilkin, William	3 APR 1769		Pitt, Westmoreland/ LD: North Huntingdon, Westmoreland	300	A-29-39	Original: found
NP-1938	Webster, Ann	3 APR 1769	Fishing Creek	LD: Columbia	300		Original: found

Table 6 - New Purchase Applications (1769-1773)

Number	Applicant	Date	Orig. Place	Later Place	Acres	Survey	Neighbors, Notes, etc.
NP-1939	Linn, Nathan	3 APR 1769		Monongahela River & Pike Run, Washington	300	C-89-231	(r22 FEB 1785)Robert Jackman Original: found
NP-1940	Kenley, William	3 APR 1769	East Branch Susquehanna River	LD: Luzerne	300		Original: found
NP-1941	Jones, Lewis	3 APR 1769		Chillisquaque Creek, Northumberland	300	M-218	William Maughan/(r20 SEP 1776)Robert Martin Original: found
NP-1942	Vanhorne, Thomas	3 APR 1769	East Branch Susquehanna River	LD: Luzerne	300		Original: found
NP-1943	Hains, Adam	3 APR 1769	West Branch Susquehanna River 5 miles above Buffalo Creek	LD: Union	200		Original: Signed
NP-1944	Shever, Philip	3 APR 1769	West Branch Susquehanna River 4 miles above Buffalo Creek	LD: Northumberland	300		Original: found
NP-1945	Armstrong, John	3 APR 1769	Berks	Buffalo, Union	300	D-60-205 D-60-211	Original: Signed by Joseph Armstrong
NP-1946	Peoples, Robert	3 APR 1769		Washington, Lycoming	300	D-60-212	Original: Signed
NP-1947	Lemon, Margaret	3 APR 1769		Washington, Lycoming/ LD: Northumberland	300	D-60-213	Original: found
NP-1948	Tholey, William	3 APR 1769	Washington	Saw Mill Run, Allegheny	300	D-13-107	(r18 APR 1785)Daniel Elliott Original: Signed
NP-1949	Metzner, John Dieterick	3 APR 1769		Point, Northumberland	300	C-144-43	Casper Graff/Henry Kurtz/(r31 MAR 1788) Original: found
NP-1950	Earl, Edward	3 APR 1769		White Deer, Union	300	D-60-214	Original: found
NP-1951	Waddell, James	3 APR 1769	Westmoreland	Blacklick Creek, Indiana	300	C-109-295	(r13 DEC 1787)James Lawson Original: found

Table 6 - New Purchase Applications (1769-1773)

Number	Applicant	Date	Orig. Place	Later Place	Acres	Survey	Neighbors, Notes, etc.
NP-1952	Work, James	3 APR 1769	Northumberland	Northeast Branch Susquehanna River, Columbia	300	L-153	Robert Glenn/(r9 DEC 1785)George Irwin Original: found
NP-1953	Long, John	3 APR 1769	Red Bank Creek	LD: Armstrong	300		Original: Signed
NP-1954	Robinson, George Esq.	3 APR 1769	Chillisquaque Creek	LD: Montour	300		James Tilghman, Esq./William McClure Original: Signed
NP-1955	Johnston, Elizabeth	3 APR 1769		Hempfield, Westmoreland	300	C-12-25	(r30 MAR 1785)John Boggs & Eliza Boggs Original: found
NP-1956	Gibson, Thomas	3 APR 1769		Buffalo, Union	300	D-60-215	Original: found
NP-1957	McCormick, Elizabeth	3 APR 1769		White Deer, Union	300	D-60-216	Original: found
NP-1958	Dean, Philip	3 APR 1769		Point, Northumberland	300	D-60-217	Original: found
NP-1959	Moore, John (of Tyrone)	3 APR 1769		Huntingdon, Westmoreland	300	D-60-218	Original: Signed "John Moor"
NP-1960	Carrothars, Armstrong	3 APR 1769		Hempfield, Westmoreland/ LD: Hempfield, Westmoreland	300	D-60-219	Original: found
NP-1961	Montgomery, Robert	3 APR 1769	Berks	Buffalo, Union	300		[same land as NP-2336 to Peter Bragth] Original: found
NP-1962	Hutchison, Alexander	3 APR 1769		Unity & Hempfield, Westmoreland	300	D-60-220 D-60-206	Original: found
NP-1963	Dun, James	3 APR 1769	Crooked Creek two miles below old Kittanning Town	LD: Armstrong	300		Original: found
NP-1964	McVay, James	3 APR 1769	Cumberland	Ft. Pitt Road, Westmoreland	300	B-268	(r31 MAR 1788)Charles Foreman Original: found
NP-1965	Jervis, Elizabeth Sr.	3 APR 1769		Muncy, Lycoming	300	O-214	Samuel Jarvis/(r6 SEP 1805)H. Drinker Original: found
NP-1966	Lukens, Abraham	3 APR 1769	Berks	White Deer, Union	300	D-56-50 D-73-295	John Palmer/[same land as NP-2122 to John Currie] Original: found

Table 6 - New Purchase Applications (1769-1773)

Number	Applicant	Date	Orig. Place	Later Place	Acres	Survey	Neighbors, Notes, etc.
NP-1967	Hannah, James	3 APR 1769	Monongahela River	LD: Pitt, Allegheny	300		James Burd Original: found
NP-1968	Robinson, Edward	3 APR 1769		Redstone Creek, Fayette	300	D-60-207	Isack Meeks/Aaron Robinson Original: found
NP-1969	Evans, David	3 APR 1769		North Strabane, Washington	300	F-238 B-9-124 B-12-111 B-12-112 C-150-135	Robert Harrison/(r26 FEB 1828)Alexander Murdock/(r5 SEP 1863)Robert Harrison/(r4 NOV 1863)Ebenezer MCClelland Original: found
NP-1970	O'Hara, Bryan	3 APR 1769		Bald Eagle Creek, Centre	300	C-135-84	William Hussey/(r8 JUL 1782)Robert Morris, Esq. Original: found
NP-1971	Crane, John	3 APR 1769		Washington, Lycoming	300	D-60-209	Original: Signed
NP-1972	Brewton, Robert	3 APR 1769		Clinton, Lycoming	300	D-60-210	Joseph Shute Original: found
NP-1973	Kap, Michael George	3 APR 1769	Cumberland	West Buffalo, Berks - Union	300	D-60-221	George Stricker/Frederick Kap Original: found
NP-1974	Humphreys, Joshua	3 APR 1769		Muncy, Lycoming	300	D-60-193 E-425	Joseph Parker/(r28 MAR 1833)I. White Original: found
NP-1975	Clark, William	3 APR 1769	Cumberland	Stony Creek Twp., Somerset/ LD: Stony Creek, Somerset	300		Original: found
NP-1976	Willson, John	3 APR 1769	Cumberland	Northumberland - Bald Eagle, Clinton	300	A-74-276	George Knight/(r27 OCT 1783)Samuel Wallis Original: found
NP-1977	Smith, Joseph	3 APR 1769	Northumberland	Muncy, Lycoming	300	B-218	(r19 SEP 1794)William Ellison Original: found
NP-1978	Lowman, George	3 APR 1769	West Branch Susquehanna River	LD: Buffalo, Union	300		William Blyth Original: found
NP-1979	Smith, James	3 APR 1769		Monongahela River, Allegheny	300		--- Applegate Original: found
NP-1980	McDowel, William	3 APR 1769		Blacklick, Indiana	300	A-32-186 A-32-200	Original: found

Table 6 - New Purchase Applications (1769-1773)

Number	Applicant	Date	Orig. Place	Later Place	Acres	Survey	Neighbors, Notes, etc.
NP-1981	McWilliams, Samuel	3 APR 1769		Howard, Centre/ LD: Howard, Centre	300	F-397 C-22-83	(r5 OCT 1857)Jacob Brickley/(r5 OCT 1857)David Bechtle/[see caveat] Original: found
NP-1982	Atkinson, Welton	3 APR 1769	Chillisquaque Creek	LD: Howard, Centre	300		Original: found
NP-1983	Sprogle, John	3 APR 1769		Turbot, Northumberland	300	C-207-163 C-207-165 C-207-173 B-18-195 C-207-147	(r21 APR 1827)James Sloat Original: found
NP-1984	Chambers, Joseph	3 APR 1769		Watson, Lycoming	300	C-1-291 C-39-223	(r29 APR 1773)M. Diffenderfer Original: found
NP-1985	Piper, William (sergeant)	3 APR 1769		Fairfield, Westmoreland	300	A-3-287	Capt. Sinclair/John Palmer/Alexander Johnson/(r1 APR 1790)William Piper Original: found
NP-1986	Frazer, David	3 APR 1769		Northeast Branch Susquehanna River, Luzerne	300	B-231	(r22 AUG 1796)Dr. John Ewing Original: found
NP-1987	Roberts, Hugh Sr.	3 APR 1769		Muddy Run, Northumberland	300	C-315	Robert Roberts/(r28 JAN 1782)Ruben Haines Original: found
NP-1988	Campbell, Robert Sr.	3 APR 1769		Washington, Lycoming	300	D-60-223	Original: Signed
NP-1989	Allen, Isaac	3 APR 1769	Berks	Kelly, Union	300	D-60-224 D-60-225 D-60-231 D-60-232	Rev. Mr. Ewing Original: found
NP-1990	Stoute, Jacob	3 APR 1769		Turbot, Northumberland	300	D-56-96 B-184	John Thompson/(r25 SEP 1790)James Durham Original: found
NP-1991	Irwin, Francis	3 APR 1769		Turbot, Northumberland	300	A-40-23	(r27 OCT 1783)Thomas Strawbridge/[see caveat] Original: found
NP-1992	Baldwin, Francis (of Black Creek, Frederick County, Virginia)	3 APR 1769	Big White Clay Creek & Monongahela River	LD: Greene	300		Original: Signed
NP-1993	Power, Alexander	3 APR 1769		Muncy, Lycoming	300	O-48	William McNitt/(r19 AUG 1774) Original: found

Table 6 - New Purchase Applications (1769-1773)

Number	Applicant	Date	Orig. Place	Later Place	Acres	Survey	Neighbors, Notes, etc.
NP-1994	Campbell, George (attorney)	3 APR 1769	Westmoreland	Plum Creek, Allegheny/ LD: Allegheny/ Armstrong	300	D-46-82	James Letarts [an Indian] Original: found
NP-1995	Irwin, John	3 APR 1769	Limestone Run	LD: Montour	300		John Ferguson/[see caveat] Original: found
NP-1996	Mitchell, Alexander	3 APR 1769		Muddy Creek & Monongahela River, Greene/ LD: Greene	300	X-219	Original: found
NP-1997	Sturgeon, Robert	3 APR 1769	West Branch Susquehanna River	LD: Northumberland	300		Original: found
NP-1998	Ewing, Thomas	3 APR 1769		Union, Union	300	D-60-233	Original: found
NP-1999	Robinson, David	3 APR 1769		White Deer Hole Creek, Lycoming/ LD: Lycoming	300		[see caveat] Original: found
NP-2000	Cuddy, James	3 APR 1769		Hempfield, Westmoreland	300	C-10-88	Henry Cuddy/(r6 MAR 1789)Christian Baum Original: found
NP-2001	Jervis, John Jr.	3 APR 1769		West Branch Susquehanna River 1.5 miles above Muncy Creek, Lycoming	300	B-171	Charles Jervis/(r3 JUL 1807)Henry Drinker Original: found
NP-2002	Volans, Joseph	3 APR 1769	adjoining Kennard Manor	West Branch Susquehanna, Lycoming	300		Menor Kennard/(r3 JUL 1807)Henry Drinker Original: found
NP-2003	Sloan, David	3 APR 1769		Unity, Westmoreland	200	D-60-255 C-109 B-23-68 C-192-48	(r16 NOV 1789)George Clark/[see NP-22, 3627, 3626, & 745]/[see caveat] Original: found
NP-2004	Hess, Samuel	3 APR 1769		Nippenose, Lycoming	200	D-60-234	Eberhart Gruber Original: found
NP-2005	Henton, George	3 APR 1769		Kelly, Union	300	D-60-235 D-60-236	John Hulings Original: found
NP-2006	Winter, William	3 APR 1769		Buffalo, Union/ LD: Union	300	A-29-40	Original: found

Table 6 - New Purchase Applications (1769-1773)

Number	Applicant	Date	Orig. Place	Later Place	Acres	Survey	Neighbors, Notes, etc.
NP-2007	Roddy, John	3 APR 1769		East Branch Susquehanna River, Luzerne	300	B-319	Adam Hubly/(r20 JAN 1789)George Irwin Original: found
NP-2008	Murray, Samuel	3 APR 1769		White Deer, Union	300	D-60-237	Original: found
NP-2009	Byrd, William	3 APR 1769		Buffalo, Union	300	D-60-238	Original: found
NP-2010	Gardner, Margaret	3 APR 1769	Berks	White Deer, Union	300	D-56-50 D-73-293	[same land as NP-2122 to John Currie] Original: found
NP-2011	Newale, William	3 APR 1769	Berks	Nippenose, Lycoming	300	D-60-239	Original: found
NP-2012	Fisher, Samuel Jr.	3 APR 1769	Chillisquaque Creek	LD: Northumberland	300		Alexander Murray/[see caveat] Original: Signed by Alexander Murray
NP-2013	Vernon, Henry	3 APR 1769	Cumberland	Hempfield, Westmoreland	300	D-60-240	James McVay Original: found
NP-2014	Grame, Elizabeth	3 APR 1769	Westmoreland	Allegheny River, Armstrong	300	D-6-34	James Young/(r9 AUG 1783)Samuel Wetherill, Jr. Original: found
NP-2015	Moore, James	3 APR 1769	Berks	Washington, Lycoming	300	D-60-226	William White Original: Signed
NP-2016	Keiger, Ignacias	3 APR 1769		Catawissa Creek, Columbia/ LD: Northumberland	300	X-200	George Minges Original: found
NP-2017	Ryne, George Jr.	3 APR 1769	Cumberland	West Buffalo, Union	300	D-56-250 C-146-253	(r14 AUG 1772)Thomas Pashall Original: found
NP-2018	Tedmarsh, Richard	3 APR 1769		Derry, Northumberland	300	A-36-9 D-507	Sarah Shale/(r25 JUN 1796)Owen Biddle Original: found
NP-2019	Williams, Eleanor	3 APR 1769	White Deer Hole Creek	LD: Lycoming	300		John Bayard Original: Signed
NP-2020	McCulley, Robert	3 APR 1769	Berks	Point, Northumberland	300	A-19-287 C-37-90	--- McAllen/(r30 JAN 1816)Alexander Colt Original: Signed
NP-2021	Bratton, Philip	3 APR 1769		Elizabeth, Allegheny/ LD: Elizabeth, Allegheny	300	D-60-227	Original: found
NP-2022	Duncan, Thomas	3 APR 1769		Hempfield, Westmoreland	300	D-60-228 D-60-229	James Guthry/James Moore Original: found

Table 6 - New Purchase Applications (1769-1773)

Number	Applicant	Date	Orig. Place	Later Place	Acres	Survey	Neighbors, Notes, etc.
NP-2023	Martin, Andrew	3 APR 1769	Pigeon Creek, Cumberland	LD: Washington	300		David Shepherd Original: found
NP-2024	Wilkins, Thomas	3 APR 1769		Blacklick, Indiana	300	D-60-182 M-134 A-77-32 C-114-221	Moses Stewart/(r28 Apr 1830)Abner Willits/(r3 MAR 1837)Daniel Lintner/[see caveat] Original: found
NP-2025	Rush, William	3 APR 1769	Berks	Kelly, Union	300	D-60-232	Robert Tagart/[same land as NP-1989 to Isaac Allen] Original: found
NP-2026	Morgan, John	3 APR 1769		Hartley, Union	300	D-60-230	Lodwig Sprogell Original: found
NP-2027	Atkison, Cornealious	3 APR 1769		Limestone Run, Northumberland	300	A-57-209	(r15 SEP 1774)Jacob Fulmer/[see caveat] Original: found
NP-2028	Hoff, George (of Heidleberg)	3 APR 1769		on Susquehanna River at Wyoming, Luzerne	300	A-51-264	(r8 MAY 1782)William Gray Original: found
NP-2029	Warner, Joseph	3 APR 1769	Northumberland	Little Fishing Creek, Columbia	300	D-465	John Perroch/(r5 APR 1796)Owen Biddle Original: found
NP-2030	Burd, Benjamin	3 APR 1769		Conemaugh, Indiana	300	D-60-241 D-60-242	Original: Missing
NP-2031	Garven, John	3 APR 1769		Chillisquaque Creek, Northumberland or Montour/ LD: Northumberland/ Montour	300		Jacob Hibert Original: found
NP-2032	Lippencott, William	3 APR 1769	Northumberland	1.5 miles above Muncy Creek, Lycoming	300	E-30	Richard Jones/(r17 MAR 1784)Samuel Wallis Original: found
NP-2033	Welckle, Christian	3 APR 1769	East Branch Susquehanna River	LD: Wyoming/ Bradford	300		Adam Black Original: found
NP-2034	Miller, Lawrence	3 APR 1769	Berks	White Deer, Union	300	D-60-243	Original: found
NP-2035	Glass, John	3 APR 1769		Ligonier, Westmoreland/ LD: Ligonier, Westmoreland	300	C-175-257 C-22-223 C-175-256 C-175-257	(r25 OCT 1864)Henry Brenizer/(r25 OCT 1864)James Meneher [patent H-60-177] Original: Signed

Table 6 - New Purchase Applications (1769-1773)

Number	Applicant	Date	Orig. Place	Later Place	Acres	Survey	Neighbors, Notes, etc.
NP-2036	Smith, John (fuller)	3 APR 1769		Franklin, Westmoreland	300	D-56-180 D-64-140 D-49	(r3 NOV 1790)William Allison, Jr. Original: found
NP-2037	Annis, John	3 APR 1769	Mahoning or Licking Creek	LD: Montour	300		Original: found
NP-2038	Smith, Nathaniel	3 APR 1769	West Branch Susquehanna River	LD: Lycoming	300		Mathew Scott Original: found
NP-2039	Trapnall, Benjamin	3 APR 1769	Cumberland	Union, Union	300	D-60-244	Joseph Jacobs/Owen Evens/George Evens/[see caveat] Original: found
NP-2040	Lawrence, Robert	3 APR 1769	Northumberland	Nippenose Creek, Lycoming	300	A-69-143	Mary Fields/(r4 DEC 1783)Thomas Riche Original: found
NP-2041	Hannah, James	3 APR 1769	Cumberland	Ligonier, Westmoreland	300	C-46-11 C-29-229 C-29-131 C-29-230 C-29-231	Lt. St. Clair/(r11 FEB 1814)Joseph Clifford & Thomas Clifford/(r10 JAN 1829)Joseph Clifford/(r22 JAN 1829)Thomas Clifford Original: Signed
NP-2042	Volen alias Eolen, Joseph	3 APR 1769		Ligonier, Westmoreland	300	D-60-245	Original: found
NP-2043	McKinney, John	3 APR 1769		Northeast Branch Susquehanna River, Luzerne	300	A-11-84	James Shaw/(r5 MAR 1774)Archibald Stewart Original: found
NP-2044	Willson, Hannah	3 APR 1769		Turbot, Northumberland	300	D-60-252	Original: found
NP-2045	Eyman, Christian	3 APR 1769		Centre/ LD: Centre	300		Jacob Eyman Original: found
NP-2046	Kintzing, Abraham	3 APR 1769		Muddy Run, Northumberland	300	C-316	Hugh Roberts, Jr./(r28 JUN 1782)Reuben Haines Original: found
NP-2047	Price, John	3 APR 1769		Allegheny, Cambria	300	A-44-85	--- Hart/(r5 MAY 1810)D. R. Barton Original: found
NP-2048	Raybolt, Jacob	3 APR 1769		Chillisquaque, Northumberland/ LD: Northumberland	300		John Pidgeon Original: found

Table 6 - New Purchase Applications (1769-1773)

Number	Applicant	Date	Orig. Place	Later Place	Acres	Survey	Neighbors, Notes, etc.
NP-2049	Cramphon, Peter	3 APR 1769		Chillisquaque, Northumberland	300	C-41-172 C-31-190 C-26-33	(r 1 JUN 1815)Thomas Dugan & Henry Cline/(r13 FEB 1822)John Call/(r28 DEC 1839)Dennis Bony/(r28 DEC 1840)Peter Call Original: found
NP-2050	Parcel, John	3 APR 1769	Northampton	Northumberland - Tunkhannock Creek, Wyoming	300	T-285	John Wickware/(r21 JUN 1783)Chris Galley Original: found
NP-2051	Menges, George	3 APR 1769	Northumberland	Catawissa Creek, Columbia	300	C-234-44	(r17 FEB 1775)Abram Tooly Original: found
NP-2052	Smith, William (fuller)	3 APR 1769		Hempfield, Westmoreland	300	D-60-253	Robert Laughlin/Joseph Irwin Original: found
NP-2053	Glasgow, Ezekiel	3 APR 1769	West Branch Susquehanna River & Beaver Creek	LD: Union	300		Original: found
NP-2054	Potter, Isabella	3 APR 1769	Bald Eagle Creek	LD: Centre	300		Joseph Chambers Original: found
NP-2055	Morris, Cadwalader	3 APR 1769	Cedar Run south of West Branch Susquehanna River	LD: Centre	300		Original: found
NP-2056	McLone, Richard	3 APR 1769	Berks	West Buffalo, Union/ LD: Union	300	D-56-295 D-56-296 A-32-187 A-14-16 C-117-122 C-24-51 C-215-169	John Lowden/(r14 MAR 1806)Aaron Levy/(r28 JAN 1812)George Rausch/(r5 DEC 1828)John Beeber/(r9 MAR 1830)James Thompson Original: found
NP-2057	Gover, Mary	3 APR 1769	Cumberland	Stony Creek Twp., Somerset/ LD: Columbia	300		Casandia Gover Original: found
NP-2058	Donnellan, Thomas	3 APR 1769		Pike, Clearfield/ LD: Clearfield	300	D-60-254	(2 MAY 1833)Henry Keppeler Original: found
NP-2059	Cahill, Thomas	3 APR 1769	Westmoreland	Conemaugh River, Indiana	300	C-151-119	(r2 OCT 1788)William Moorhead Original: found
NP-2060	Harper, Henry	3 APR 1769	Berks	Kelly, Union	300	D-56-85 D-56-91	Rev. John Ewing/[same land as NP-2368 to Thomas Beatty] Original: found
NP-2061	Ewing, Alexander	3 APR 1769		LD: Union	200		William Ewing [his brother] Original: Signed

Table 6 - New Purchase Applications (1769-1773)

Number	Applicant	Date	Orig. Place	Later Place	Acres	Survey	Neighbors, Notes, etc.
NP-2062	Streeker, Edward	3 APR 1769	White Deer Hole Creek	LD: Lycoming	300		Thomas Snowden Original: found
NP-2063	Hays, William	3 APR 1769	Berks	Union, Union	300	D-57-211 D-57-212	John Hays, Jr./[same land as NP-519 to Christian Hauer] Original: found
NP-2064	Nesbit, Thomas	3 APR 1769	Bald Eagle Creek	LD: Centre	300		Original: found
NP-2065	Duncan, Stephen Sr.	3 APR 1769	Pine Creek & West Branch Susquehanna River	LD: Lycoming	300		Original: found
NP-2066	Richards, Burnet	3 APR 1769		Muncy Creek Twp., Lycoming	300	C-185-127	William Richards/(r29 JAN 1807)Jacob Hill Original: found
NP-2067	Sipes, Charels	3 APR 1769		Elizabeth, Allegheny/ LD: Elizabeth, Allegheny	200	C-147-64 C-147-65	(p13 APR 1870)Alexander R. McClure & William A. McClure Original: found
NP-2068	Moore, William & John	3 APR 1769		Unity, Westmoreland	600	D-60-255	Original: found
NP-2069	Pole, Henry	3 APR 1769	Rush Meadows, Northampton	LD: Northumberland	300		John Pole Original: found
NP-2070	Manderbarch, John	3 APR 1769	Long Limestone Valley	LD: Centre	300		Jacob Greiter Original: found
NP-2071	Gray, John	3 APR 1769	Westmoreland	Allegheny River, Allegheny	300	C-10-22	(r2 APR 1788)Ephraim Blaine Original: found
NP-2072	Winter, John	3 APR 1769	Berks	West Buffalo, Union	300	D-57-209 D-57-210	[same land as NP-452 to George Stricker] Original: found
NP-2073	Roddy, Josiah	3 APR 1769	Northeast Branch Susquehanna River	LD: Luzerne	300		Original: found
NP-2074	Mourer, Jacob	3 APR 1769	Mahanoy Creek	LD: Columbia/ Montour	300		Original: found
NP-2075	Leet, Daniel	3 APR 1769	Northeast Branch Susquehanna River below Sunbury Manor	LD: Northumberland	200		Original: Signed
NP-2076	Galbraith, Josiah	3 APR 1769		Chillisquaque Creek, Northumberland	300	A-9-32	(r8 JUN 1773)/[see caveat] Original: found

Table 6 - New Purchase Applications (1769-1773)

Number	Applicant	Date	Orig. Place	Later Place	Acres	Survey	Neighbors, Notes, etc.
NP-2077	Armstrong, James	3 APR 1769		Loyalhanna Creek, Westmoreland	300	C-228-38	[also a warrant dated 28 MAR 1786 to John Shields] Original: Signed by Joseph Armstrong
NP-2078	Couder, John	3 APR 1769		Elizabeth, Allegheny/ LD: Elizabeth, Allegheny	300	D-60-256	Original: Signed
NP-2079	Cook, William	3 APR 1769		Union, Union	300	D-57-104 D-60-244 C-116-76 C-116-77 A-40-77	(r9 APR 1790)William Leech/(r11 NOV 1801)Samuel Templeton Original: found
NP-2080	Hunt, Peter	3 APR 1769		East Branch Susquehanna River, Luzerne/ LD: Wyoming	300	U-53 U-54	Adolph Walradon Original: found
NP-2081	Smith, Richard	3 APR 1769		Union, Luzerne/ LD: Luzerne	300	W-293	Original: found
NP-2082	Beale, William Sr.	3 APR 1769		Muncy Creek Twp., Lycoming	300	D-60-257	French Margaret Original: Signed
NP-2083	Newell, William	3 APR 1769		Huntingdon, Westmoreland	300	A-51-142	Col. Clapham/(r20 MAY 1796)John Gardener Original: found
NP-2084	Old, John	3 APR 1769		Chillisquaque Creek, Montour/ LD: Montour	300		Ellis Wright Original: found
NP-2085	Willson, Robert	3 APR 1769	Berks	Buffalo, Union	300	D-56-228 D-56-230	[same land as NP-1339 to Nathaniel Loury] Original: found
NP-2086	Campbell, Donald	3 APR 1769		Derry, Westmoreland	300	D-60-258 D-60-259	Samuel Duncan/--- McKee Original: found
NP-2087	Findley, Samuel	3 APR 1769		Kittanning Twp., Armstrong	300	C-231-148	James Dun/(r29 APR 1841)Beaton Smith Original: found
NP-2088	McCalister, James Jr.	3 APR 1769		Ligonier, Westmoreland	300	D-60-260	Original: found
NP-2089	Held, Lodowick	3 APR 1769	Cumberland	Buffalo, Union	250	D-62-15	John Archert/[same land as NP-3744 to Christian Ewig] Original: found
NP-2090	Schriver, John	3 APR 1769	West Branch Susquehanna River	LD: Lycoming	300		Original: found

Table 6 - New Purchase Applications (1769-1773)

Number	Applicant	Date	Orig. Place	Later Place	Acres	Survey	Neighbors, Notes, etc.
NP-2091	Grady, Norry	3 APR 1769		Allegheny, Westmoreland	300	C-104-245 C-31-244 C-104-244	George Plinge/(r15 JAN 1823)George I. Crawford/(r8 APR 1851)Peter Kaple & John Kaple Original: found
NP-2092	Derr, George Leonard	3 APR 1769	Susquehanna River & Dog Run	LD: Clarion/ Allegheny/ Armstrong	300		Ludwig Derr Original: found
NP-2093	Beaty, John	3 APR 1769	Northumberland	Buffalo, Union	300	D-60-246 D-60-247	[see caveat] Original: found
NP-2094	Hicks, William	3 APR 1769	Northumberland	Buffalo Valley, Union/ LD: Union	300	K-364	Original: found
NP-2095	Landes, Jacob	3 APR 1769	Northumberland	Penns Creek, Union	300	I-335	John Harris/(r19 APR 1770)William Duncan Original: found
NP-2096	Armstrong, William	3 APR 1769	Dog Run 3 miles from West Branch Susquehanna River	LD: Northumberland/ Lycoming/ Union	300		Original: Signed
NP-2097	Bready, John (son of Joseph)	3 APR 1769		North Huntingdon, Westmoreland	300	D-62-271 C-218-226	(r31 MAR 1788)Micheal Walthower Original: found
NP-2098	Riche, Thomas	3 APR 1769	White Deer Hole Creek	LD: Lycoming	300		Michael Clark Original: found
NP-2099	Gruber, Eberhart	3 APR 1769		Nippenose, Lycoming	200	D-60-248	Original: found
NP-2100	Savoise, Jacob	3 APR 1769		Buffalo, Union	200	D-62-220 D-62-206	[same land as NP-2814 to Joseph Allen] Original: found
NP-2101	Kling, Henry	3 APR 1769	Northumberland	Tunkhannock Creek, Wyoming	300	C-7-55	Ludwig Kling/(r22 APR 1782)William Brown Original: found
NP-2102	Fisher, James	3 APR 1769		Chillisquaque Creek, Northumberland/ LD: Northumberland	300		Benjamin Sherman Original: found
NP-2103	Hughes, Henry	3 APR 1769	Chillisquaque Creek	LD: Northumberland	300		Original: found

Table 6 - New Purchase Applications (1769-1773)

Number	Applicant	Date	Orig. Place	Later Place	Acres	Survey	Neighbors, Notes, etc.
NP-2104	Campbell, Thomas	3 APR 1769		Derry, Westmoreland	300	D-56-150 D-62-35 C-53-263 C-53-264	Alexander Johnston/James Wilson/(r29 SEP 1788)Charles Gibson/[see caveat] Original: found
NP-2105	Hutchinson, William	3 APR 1769		Susquehanna, Cambria/ LD: Allegheny, Cambria	300	D-60-249	Original: found
NP-2106	Gray, James	3 APR 1769		Muncy Creek Twp., Lycoming	300	D-60-250	Original: found
NP-2107	Boyls, Henry	3 APR 1769		Redstone Creek, Fayette	300	B-2-143	Samuel Lyon/Isaac Pear/(r9 MAR 1786)James Finley/[see caveat] Original: Signed
NP-2108	Thompson, Anthony	3 APR 1769		Pitt, Westmoreland	300	C-48-222	Thomas Gibson/(r6 AUG 1788)John Fence [or Ferree] Original: found
NP-2109	Shakespear, Samuel	3 APR 1769		Kelly, Union	300		[same land as NP-1989 to Isaac Allen] Original: found
NP-2110	Levers, Robert	3 APR 1769		Loyalsock, Lycoming	300	D-73-281	Original: found
NP-2111	Lems, Christopher	3 APR 1769		Ligonier, Westmoreland	300	D-73-282 D-73-283	Original: found
NP-2112	Bright, Jacob	3 APR 1769	East Branch Susquehanna River near Fishing Creek	LD: Columbia	300		Original: found
NP-2113	Maghen, Robert	3 APR 1769	Berks	Buffalo, Union	300		[same land as NP-2336 to Peter Bragth] Original: found
NP-2114	Morgan, William	3 APR 1769		Pucketa Creek, Allegheny/ LD: Plum, Allegheny	300	D-73-284	Original: Signed by Jacob Morgan, Jr.
NP-2115	Hill, John	3 APR 1769		Plum, Allegheny	300	D-73-285	Original: Signed
NP-2116	Jacobs, John Sr. (of Providence Township, Philadelphia County)	3 APR 1769		Washington, Lycoming/ LD: Northumberland	200	D-56-78	--- Bond Original: Signed
NP-2117	Dunwoody, John	3 APR 1769		Washington, Lycoming	300	D-62-252 D-70-15	(r17 SEP 1792)Reuben Haines Original: found

Table 6 - New Purchase Applications (1769-1773)

Number	Applicant	Date	Orig. Place	Later Place	Acres	Survey	Neighbors, Notes, etc.
NP-2118	Moroson, Robert	3 APR 1769	Berks	Kelly, Union	300		Parson Ewing/[same land as NP-2225 to Breeson Bawden] Original: found
NP-2119	Harkness, William Jr.	3 APR 1769	Berks	White Deer, Union	300	D-56-51 D-73-291	William McCallister Original: found
NP-2120	Elliott, Daniel	3 APR 1769		Saw Mill Run, Washington	300	D-62-83 A-12-15	(r18 APR 1785) Original: Signed
NP-2121	McDowell, Mary	3 APR 1769		Hempfield, Westmoreland	300	M-174	(r5 APR 1788) Original: found
NP-2122	Currie, John	3 APR 1769	Berks	White Deer, Union	300	D-56-50 D-73-292 D-73-293 D-73-294 D-73-295 D-73-296	Mordecai Holt Original: found
NP-2123	Yung, Abram	3 APR 1769	Bald Eagle Creek	LD: Centre	300		Original: found
NP-2124	Little, John (of Lancaster)	3 APR 1769	Larry Creek & West Branch Susquehanna River	LD: Lycoming	300		Original: found
NP-2125	McCallister, Ester	3 APR 1769	Plum Creek at Kittanning Path	LD: Armstrong	300		Original: found
NP-2126	Hoyladay, Thomas	3 APR 1769		South Huntingdon, Westmoreland	300	Z-63 Z-65 Z-66 C-206-87	(r15 FEB 1799)Thomas Shields/[see caveat] Original: found
NP-2127	Paul, Henry Jr.	3 APR 1769		LD: Somerset	300		Joseph Paul Original: found
NP-2128	Pimm, William	3 APR 1769		Versailles, Allegheny	300	D-73-297	Original: found
NP-2129	Power, James	3 APR 1769		Loyalsock, Lycoming	300	D-56-49	Original: Signed
NP-2130	Pollock, Thomas	3 APR 1769	Bedford	Pitt & Wilkins, Allegheny	300	D-56-182 A-83-189	Austin Piety/(r30 SEP 1788)Hugh Alexander Original: found

Table 6 - New Purchase Applications (1769-1773)

Number	Applicant	Date	Orig. Place	Later Place	Acres	Survey	Neighbors, Notes, etc.
NP-2131	Elliott, Isaac	3 APR 1769	3 or 4 miles above Fishing Creek, North Branch Susquehanna River	LD: Columbia	300		Original: found
NP-2132	Cahill, Edmund Jr.	3 APR 1769		Unity, Westmoreland	300	M-422	(r7 APR 1788)Robert McConoughy Original: found
NP-2133	Leet, Daniel	3 APR 1769	Susquehanna River near Old Nanticoke Town	LD: Luzerne	100		Original: Signed
NP-2134	Hammersleys, Jacob	3 APR 1769	Turbot, Northumberland	Columbia	300	I-370	(r29 APR 1796)John Donaldson Original: Signed
NP-2135	Ackels, William	3 APR 1769	Montours Hill, Forks of Susquehanna River	LD: Montour	300		James McCord Original: found
NP-2136	Hening, David	3 APR 1769		Elizabeth, Allegheny	300	D-73-298	--- Saltman Original: found
NP-2137	Eastburne, Robert	3 APR 1769	Mahanoy Creek	LD: Luzerne	300		Original: found
NP-2138	McDonnall, Archibald (shoemaker; son of Duncan McDonnall of Derry Township)	3 APR 1769	South Branch Buffalo Creek		300		John McDowell Original: Signed
NP-2139	Deimer, James	3 APR 1769	Northumberland	Fishing Creek, Columbia	300	C-48-34	(r6 JAN 1784) Original: found
NP-2140	Boyd, Robert	3 APR 1769	West Branch Susquehanna River	LD: Allegheny	300		John Little Original: found
NP-2141	Smith, John	3 APR 1769	Westmoreland	Four Mile Run, Allegheny	300	A-10-299	James Royal/James Reed/Nicholas Dorran/(r14 JUN 1787)Joseph Lewis Finley Original: Signed
NP-2142	Piper, William Jr.	3 APR 1769	Bald Eagle Creek		300		Original: Signed by James Piper
NP-2143	Grimbes, James	3 APR 1769		Nippenose, Lycoming	300	D-56-48	Original: found

Table 6 - New Purchase Applications (1769-1773)

Number	Applicant	Date	Orig. Place	Later Place	Acres	Survey	Neighbors, Notes, etc.
NP-2144	Brown, John	3 APR 1769	Chillisquaque Creek		300		Original: found
NP-2145	Sinckler, Samuel Jr.	3 APR 1769		Allegheny, Washington	300	C-223-26	Benjamin Kirkindoll/(r19 SEP 1788)Samuel Wallis Original: found
NP-2146	Smith, John	3 APR 1769	Berks	Buffalo, Union	300	D-57-12 D-57-18	[same land as NP-866 to John Cline] Original: found
NP-2147	King, John	3 APR 1769		Allegheny, Westmoreland	300	C-143-94	Norry Grady/(r8 MAR 1817)John Morgan heirs Original: found
NP-2148	Zeigler, Frederick	3 APR 1769		Bald Eagle, Centre	300	C-1-175	Ludwig Zeigler/(r21 MAY 1813)James Miles & Joseph B. McKean Original: found
NP-2149	Beattey, William	3 APR 1769		Patton, Allegheny	300	D-58-258 B-16-20 B-5-64	John Johnston/(r16 FEB 1864)Samuel Beaty/(r27 JAN 1864)William Beaty & Robert Beaty & J. R. Beaty & Margaret Welty Original: found
NP-2150	Fisher, William Jr.	3 APR 1769		LD: Augusta, Northumberland	300		James Fisher Original: found
NP-2151	Fisher, James	3 APR 1769		Augusta, Northumberland	300	N-259	Benedict Dorsey/(r5 SEP 1783)John Nixon & Alexander Forster Original: found
NP-2152	Ewing, Christian	3 APR 1769	Northumberland	Buffalo, Union	300	C-203-176	--- Allen/(r12 JUN 1810)John Swinford Original: found
NP-2153	Bunner, Rudolph	3 APR 1769		White Deer Hole Creek, Union	300	D-203	Henry Pontius/(r31 JAN 1784)Micheal Bright Original: found
NP-2154	Musser, Peter	3 APR 1769		Muncy Creek Twp., Lycoming	300	D-506	(r18 MAR 1816)John Beaver Original: found
NP-2155	Simpson, Joseph	3 APR 1769		Union, Union	300	D-60-233 K-114	(r15 JUN 1795)Michael Fought Original: found
NP-2156	Gale, Johannes	3 APR 1769	Chillisquaque Creek	LD: Montour	300		John Rennard Original: found
NP-2157	Rebman, Michael	3 APR 1769	Cumberland	Berks - Union, Union	300	D-58-161 D-58-162	[same land was warranted on 11 FEB 1771 to Levi Hollingsworth] Original: found
NP-2158	Tolbert, Jeremiah	3 APR 1769		East Branch Susquehanna River, Luzerne/ LD: Bradford	300	W-258	(p6 APR 1937)Merton Vanderpool [patent H-79-272] Original: found

Table 6 - New Purchase Applications (1769-1773)

Number	Applicant	Date	Orig. Place	Later Place	Acres	Survey	Neighbors, Notes, etc.
NP-2159	Mitcheltree, Rebecca	3 APR 1769		Muncy Creek Twp., Lycoming	300	D-56-47	[see caveat] Original: found
NP-2160	Supplee, David	3 APR 1769		Limestone, Lycoming/ LD: Limestone, Lycoming	300	W-294 W-295 C-186-178	Original: found
NP-2161	Johnston, William	3 APR 1769		Patton, Allegheny	300	C-98-84	Martha McCrea/(r19 FEB 1866)William Johnston Original: found
NP-2162	McCalmont, Thomas	3 APR 1769	Cumberland	Mt. Pleasant, Westmoreland	300	D-56-46	Original: Signed
NP-2163	Coale, Margaret	3 APR 1769	Cumberland	Stony Creek Twp., Somerset/ LD: Stony Creek, Somerset	300		Phillip Coale Original: found
NP-2164	McKee, Hugh	3 APR 1769		Huntingdon, Westmoreland	300	C-116-209	James McKee/(r8 SEP 1791)George Lattimore/[see caveat] Original: found
NP-2165	Werly, Michael	3 APR 1769	Cumberland	Westmoreland - Conemaugh River near Blacklick, Indiana	300	C-223-44	Henry Kunkle/(r29 SEP 1788)Hugh Wilson & Thomas Wilson Original: found
NP-2166	Heath, Thomas Jr.	3 APR 1769		East Branch Susquehanna River, Luzerne/ LD: Wyoming	300	A-36-16	Thomas Heath, Sr. Original: found
NP-2167	Rennick, William	3 APR 1769		Mahoning, Northumberland	300	X-129 A-45-160 C-145-12	(r29 JAN 1811 & 27 JAN 1812)Daniel Montgomery Original: found
NP-2168	Strauch, Henry	3 APR 1769	Cumberland	Conemaugh River, Westmoreland - Indiana	300	A-89-297	Anthony Altman/(r24 JUL 1789)Abraham Sherian Original: found
NP-2169	Kuhn, Frederick	3 APR 1769	Cumberland	Versailles, Allegheny	300	D-60-192	Original: found
NP-2170	Ramsey, Robert	3 APR 1769		Armstrong	300	C-29-89	Thomas Taylor/(r18 Jun 1825)Alexander Craig Original: found

Table 6 - New Purchase Applications (1769-1773)

Number	Applicant	Date	Orig. Place	Later Place	Acres	Survey	Neighbors, Notes, etc.
NP-2171	Tredwell, James	3 APR 1769	Northeast Branch Susquehanna River	LD: Columbia	300		Original: found
NP-2172	Hulings, Markus Sr.	3 APR 1769		Turbot, Northumberland	300	A-65-209	Alexander Monroe/(r18 APR 1782)Michael Fulmer Original: found
NP-2173	Prather, Henry	3 APR 1769		Plum, Allegheny	300	D-73-299	Original: Signed
NP-2174	McMullen, James Jr.	3 APR 1769		Quemahoning Creek, Somerset	300	D-456	(r3 MAY 1797)Charles Boyle, Jr. Original: found
NP-2175	Burn, Peter (of Lebanon)	3 APR 1769		Penn, Union	300	A-34-14 C-178-265	(r8 JAN 1830)John Ritter Original: found
NP-2176	Hamilton, Robert	3 APR 1769		Buffalo, Union	150	D-56-60	Original: found
NP-2177	Carether, James	3 APR 1769	West Branch Susquehanna River above Pine Creek	LD: Clinton	300		Original: found
NP-2178	Lyon, Thomas	3 APR 1769		Hempfield, Westmoreland	300	A-19-50	Capt. Charles Edminston/John Wright/(28 MAR 1788)Eli. Coulter Original: found
NP-2179	Scott, Samuel	3 APR 1769	East Branch Susquehanna River	LD: Columbia	300		Original: found
NP-2180	Armstrong, Joseph	3 APR 1769		Derry, Westmoreland/ LD: Derry, Westmoreland	300	D-62-190 V-180 C-41-33 C-32-193 C-210-259 C-17-226	(r4 MAR 1812)Thomas Dunlap [patent H-8-104]/(r19 MAY 1836)Joseph Chapman [patent H-35-571]/(r23 FEB 1838)John Stouffer [patent H-39-54]/(r11 OCT 1844)James Bradley [patent H-45-258]/(r14 FEB 1845)James Foster [patent H-45-315] Original: Signed
NP-2181	McCullough, David	3 APR 1769	Northeast Branch Susquehanna River	LD: Luzerne	300		Original: found

Table 6 - New Purchase Applications (1769-1773)

Number	Applicant	Date	Orig. Place	Later Place	Acres	Survey	Neighbors, Notes, etc.
NP-2182	Mickenfelder, Casper	3 APR 1769		Wilkins, Allegheny/ LD: Westmoreland	300	R-295 C-231-305 B-17-37 B-21-109	Jehu Hollingsworth/(r27 JUL 1852)Thomas McMasters & heirs of John McMasters [patent H-50-161]/(p29 AUG 1905)P. W. Schornagle/(p14 JUN 1909)Maria E. Sharpnack/(p11 OCT 1909)Matilda J. Snyder Original: found
NP-2183	Thomas, Ann	3 APR 1769	Northumberland	Mahoning Creek, Montour	300	W-259	Original: found
NP-2184	Crampton, James	3 APR 1769	Bald Eagle Creek	LD: Centre	300		Joseph Poultney Original: found
NP-2185	Potts, Rachel	3 APR 1769		Nippenose, Lycoming	300	D-56-59	Joseph Carson Original: found
NP-2186	Roberts, William	3 APR 1769	Crooked Creek near Allegheny River	LD: Armstrong	300		Original: found
NP-2187	Henderson, John	3 APR 1769		Youghiogheny River, Fayette	300	A-21-302	William McMacken/(r11 MAY 1785)Isaac Mason, Esq. Original: found
NP-2188	Harris, Samuel Jr.	3 APR 1769	Cumberland	West Branch Susquehanna River, Lycoming	300	A-16-128	(r28 APR 1796)Robert Richey Original: found
NP-2189	Morgan, Jacob Jr.	3 APR 1769		Chincleclamuse Old Town, Clearfield	300	A-78-95	(r22 DEC 1806)Abraham Witmer Original: Signed
NP-2190	Jones, John	3 APR 1769		Hepburn, Lycoming	300	D-55-71 C-109-161	Nawalegan [probably an Indian]/(r21 OCT 1785)John Lukens, Esq. Original: found
NP-2191	Dorsius, John	3 APR 1769		South Huntingdon, Westmoreland/ LD: South Huntingdon, Westmoreland	300	E-219 B-11-227	W. Kostor/--- Stewart/(r2 MAR 1833)Thomas Morgan/(r27 MAR 1840)John Nichols/(p19 MAR 1873)John Carthers Original: found
NP-2192	Beattey, Robert (doctor)	3 APR 1769		Franklin, Fayette	300	D-56-58 C-16-195	Joseph Snivly/(r17 AUG 1814)Archibald Bard Original: found
NP-2193	Johnston, James Jr.	3 APR 1769	Mifflin	Bald Eagle, Centre	300	A-3-109	Mathew Johnston/(r2 APR 1794) Original: found
NP-2194	Pole, Adam	3 APR 1769	Rush Meadows, Northampton	LD: Northumberland	300		--- Vancleave Original: found

Table 6 - New Purchase Applications (1769-1773)

Number	Applicant	Date	Orig. Place	Later Place	Acres	Survey	Neighbors, Notes, etc.
NP-2195	Duncan, Stephen	3 APR 1769		Derry, Westmoreland	300	D-56-56 D-56-57	Samuel Slone Original: found
NP-2196	Harris, William	3 APR 1769	Northumberland	Bald Eagle Creek, Clinton	300	Z-204	(r16 DEC 1772)Phillip Francis, Jr. Original: found
NP-2197	Dennis, Jean	3 APR 1769	Cumberland	Berks - White Deer, Union	300	D-56-50 D-73-292	William Pussey/[same land as NP-2122 to John Currie] Original: found
NP-2198	Finney, Richard	3 APR 1769		Susquehanna, Cambria	300	C-83-138	(r22 MAY 1837)George Glass Original: found
NP-2199	Gasser, John	3 APR 1769	Northumberland	Penn, Snyder	300	C-219-30	Phillip Gasser/(r15 FEB 1798)Christopher Shible Original: found
NP-2200	Hall, Elizabeth Harrison	3 APR 1769	Cumberland	Hempfield, Westmoreland/ LD: Ligonier, Westmoreland	300	H-491	Loveday Allen Original: found
NP-2201	Silver, Jane	3 APR 1769		Washington, Westmoreland	300	D-56-55	--- Warren Original: found
NP-2202	Gebhart, Peter	3 APR 1769		Muncy, Lycoming	200	D-56-54	Christopher Wolfart Original: found
NP-2203	Luce, Benjamin	3 APR 1769		Northeast Branch Susquehanna River, Luzerne	300	C-84-77	(r22 JUN 1784)Thomas Hartley, Esq. Original: found
NP-2204	Zeller, John	3 APR 1769		Union, Union	300	D-59-197 D-6-204	(r7 MAY 1789)Fredrick Wise Original: Signed
NP-2205	Tenist, John	3 APR 1769		Warriors Run, Northumberland	300	I-449	(r5 DEC 1774)Josiah Espey Original: found
NP-2206	Penrose, Joseph	3 APR 1769	Fishing Creek & East Branch Susquehanna River	LD: Columbia	300		Original: found
NP-2207	Grove, David	3 APR 1769	White Deer Hole Creek	LD: Lycoming	300		Original: found
NP-2208	Gorrell, William	3 APR 1769	Cumberland	Northumberland - Bald Eagle Creek, Centre	300	B-16	Jeremiah Sheradine/(r15 OCT 1784)Jacob Dowde & Michael Dowde Original: found

Table 6 - New Purchase Applications (1769-1773)

Number	Applicant	Date	Orig. Place	Later Place	Acres	Survey	Neighbors, Notes, etc.
NP-2209	Jones, James	3 APR 1769	Cumberland	Howard, Centre	300	X-205 A-51-133 A-68-281	Zacharia Allen/(r12 AUG 1816)James Crawford/(r5 APR 1856)Irwin Thomas/[see caveat] Original: found
NP-2210	McBride, Francis	3 APR 1769		Turbot, Northumberland	300	C-67-41 C-67-42	Richard Irwin/Makus Huling/(r8 MAR 1811)Paul Geddis Original: found
NP-2211	Graham, William	3 APR 1769	Cumberland	Salem, Westmoreland/ LD: Westmoreland	300	X-176	Original: Signed
NP-2212	Brannon, Patrick	3 APR 1769		Muncy Creek Twp., Lycoming	300	D-56-53	Original: found
NP-2213	Pierce, Paul (of West Pennsborough Township, Cumberland County)	3 APR 1769		Cecil, Washington/ LD: Cecil, Washington	300	C-173-45 C-86-73 C-86-64	--- Pierce/(r6 OCT 1829)James Moore/(r31 JAN 1831)Robert Hill Original: Signed
NP-2214	Peoples, George	3 APR 1769	White Deer Hole Creek	LD: Lycoming	300		Original: Signed
NP-2215	McCausland, Alexander	3 APR 1769		Armstrong, Indiana/ LD: Armstrong	300	D-64-178 D-64-179 X-218	John Latta/John Finley/Tohogod [probably an Indian] Original: found
NP-2216	Culbertson, John	3 APR 1769	Northumberland	White Deer Hole Creek, Union	300	C-347	(r17 DEC 1792)Ruben Haines Original: found
NP-2217	Shannon, John	3 APR 1769		Rostraver, Westmoreland	300	N-109	John Kyle/John Perry/Samuel Bigert/(r16 MAR 1789)John Mitchell & Thomas Mitchell/(r16 MAR 1789)Samuel Holliday Original: found
NP-2218	Holmes, James	3 APR 1769		Washington, Lycoming	300	D-56-52	Original: found
NP-2219	Harris, Robert	3 APR 1769	Berks	White Deer, Union	300	D-56-51	--- Hammersly/Thomas Jardon Original: found
NP-2220	Muchmore, Jonathan	3 APR 1769		Blacklick, Indiana	300	D-56-223 D-56-45	[see caveat] Original: found
NP-2221	Mitchell, William (in Philadelphia)	3 APR 1769	Berks	Buffalo, Union	300	D-56-128 D-56-129	[same land as NP-1518 to Edward Middleton] Original: found
NP-2222	Stuart, Moses	3 APR 1769		Blacklick, Indiana	300	D-56-87 D-56-88 O-103	Richard Shannon/Nathan Young/(r7 APR 1788) Original: found

Table 6 - New Purchase Applications (1769-1773)

Number	Applicant	Date	Orig. Place	Later Place	Acres	Survey	Neighbors, Notes, etc.
NP-2223	Henry, William	3 APR 1769		Loyalsock, Lycoming	300	D-56-44	Paul Weitzel Original: found
NP-2224	Wallis, Thomas	3 APR 1769	Cumberland	Black Run, Union	300	E-262	Joseph Jacob Wallis/(r23 SEP 1790)Ruben Haines Original: found
NP-2225	Bawden, Preeson	3 APR 1769	Berks	Kelly, Union	300	D-56-26 D-56-27 D-56-28 D-56-29 D-56-30 D-56-39 D-56-40 D-56-41 D-56-42 D-56-43	Mr. Ewing Original: found
NP-2226	Hunter, William	3 APR 1769	Westmoreland	Youghiogheny River, Fayette	300	G-483	--- Studebaker/(r28 MAR 1804)Robert Smith Original: found
NP-2227	Bounjure, Andrew	3 APR 1769		Ligonier, Westmoreland	300	A-34-180	James Black/John Simon/Alexander Jonson/(r20 APR 1809)William Irwin Original: found
NP-2228	McLaughlin, James	3 APR 1769	Berks	White Deer, Union	300	D-57-40 D-57-28	[same land as NP-784 to Andrew Stevens]/[see caveat] Original: found
NP-2229	Shram, Henry	3 APR 1769		Buffalo, Union	300	D-56-99 D-56-100	[same land as NP-2384 to Philip Rogers] Original: found
NP-2230	Gist, Thomas	3 APR 1769		Union & Dunbar, Fayette/ LD: Union & Dunbar, Fayette	300	D-56-38	[settled by Capt. Christopher Gist in 1752 under Virginia]/[see caveat] Original: found
NP-2231	Knight, Joseph	3 APR 1769		LD: Fairfield, Westmoreland	300		Samuel Taylor Original: found
NP-2232	Barton, William	3 APR 1769		Fishing Creek, Columbia/ LD: Columbia	300		Original: found
NP-2233	Mitcheltree, John	3 APR 1769	Berks	Buffalo, Union	300	D-56-63	[same land as NP-2336 to Peter Bragth] Original: found

Table 6 - New Purchase Applications (1769-1773)

Number	Applicant	Date	Orig. Place	Later Place	Acres	Survey	Neighbors, Notes, etc.
NP-2234	Bray, John	3 APR 1769	on road from Wyoming Manor at a place called "Shades of Death"	LD: Luzerne	300		Original: found
NP-2235	Jones, Joseph	3 APR 1769		Turbot, Northumberland	300	A-463	Josiah Hewses/(r16 MAR 1775)Archibald Irwin Original: found
NP-2236	Whitehill, Robert	3 APR 1769		Madison, Columbia	300	C-51-106 C-41-220 C-41-221	(r21 DEC 1825)Chandler Eves/(r2 APR 1831)Milton Eves & Ezra Eves Original: found
NP-2237	Thompson, Robert	3 APR 1769		Elizabeth, Allegheny	300	A-47-27 B-6-221 B-6-222	Samuel Sinckler/(r10 FEB 1791)George Mockler/(r14 JUN 1836)William L. McClure Original: found
NP-2238	Ellis, Daniel	3 APR 1769	Chillisquaque Creek	LD: Montour	300		Original: found
NP-2239	Helm, Benjamin	3 APR 1769	Northumberland	West Branch Susquehanna River, Lycoming	300	A-51-273	(r9 AUG 1781)William Govet, Esq. Original: found
NP-2240	Irwin, Lawrence (of Cumberland County)	3 APR 1769		Unity, Westmoreland	100	D-64-143 A-45-83	(r11 DEC 1787)David Rankin Original: found
NP-2241	Hunter, Alexander	3 APR 1769	Northumberland	Chillisquaque Creek, Montour	300	A-19-30 A-19-31	James Pobjea/(r30 APR 1789)"Corporation for ye Releif of Poore and distressed Presbeterian Ministers" Original: found
NP-2242	Barber, Robert	3 APR 1769	Susquehanna River 3 miles from mouth of Bald Eagle Creek, Cumberland	LD: Clinton	300		Original: Signed
NP-2243	Steel, Rebecca	3 APR 1769	Northampton or Berks	Augusta, Northumberland - Columbia	300	M-50	(r7 APR 1791)John Lee Original: found
NP-2244	Fowler, Robert	3 APR 1769		Turbot, Northumberland	300	C-141-39	William Johnston/(r27 OCT 1792)Alexander Murray/[see caveat] Original: found
NP-2245	Kuntz, Jacob	3 APR 1769	Northumberland	Buffalo, Union	300	C-166-27	--- Blyth/(r8 JUL 1773)John Musser Original: found
NP-2246	McBath, James	3 APR 1769		Hartley, Union	300	D-56-142 C-188-219	(r21 FEB 1792)John Resnor Original: found

Table 6 - New Purchase Applications (1769-1773)

Number	Applicant	Date	Orig. Place	Later Place	Acres	Survey	Neighbors, Notes, etc.
NP-2247	Sutton, Benjamin	3 APR 1769		Donegal, Westmoreland	300	D-56-37	Original: found
NP-2248	Weaver, Henry	3 APR 1769	West Branch Susquehanna River	LD: Clinton	300		Bejamin Breckbill Original: found
NP-2249	Bayard, John	3 APR 1769		Washington, Lycoming	300	D-56-36	Cornelius Cox Original: found
NP-2250	Pugh, Henry	3 APR 1769		Loyalsock, Lycoming	300	D-56-35	Original: Missing
NP-2251	Lebb, Stoffer	3 APR 1769	Northumberland	White Deer, Union	300	D-55-58 D-55-59	George Zeiger/[same land as NP-1727 to Frederick Kneible] Original: found
NP-2252	Sheaphard, John	3 APR 1769	South Branch Pigeon Creek, Cumberland	Pigeon Creek, Washington	300		Thomas Shepard/(r & p1 MAR 1788)Abraham Sheaphard Original: found
NP-2253	Gollespey, William	3 APR 1769	West Branch Mahanoy Creek	LD: Montour	300		Original: found
NP-2254	George, John	3 APR 1769	Northeast Branch Susquehanna River	LD: Montour	200		Original: found
NP-2255	Jones, David	3 APR 1769	Northumberland	Chillisquaque Creek, Montour	300	C-78-262	Lewis Jones/(r28 MAY 1782)Nathan Haines Original: found
NP-2256	Worthington, Edward	3 APR 1769	Bald Eagle Creek	LD: Clinton/ Centre	300		Original: found
NP-2257	Johns, Mary	3 APR 1769	Cumberland	Berks - White Deer, Union	300	D-56-34	Original: found
NP-2258	Smith, Joseph	3 APR 1769		Nippenose, Lycoming	300	D-56-33	Original: found
NP-2259	Seger, Frederick	3 APR 1769	East Branch Susquehanna River	LD: Luzerne	300		Original: found
NP-2260	Kugger, Stoffer	3 APR 1769	between Holland Run & Mahoning Hill on Susquehanna River	LD: Luzerne	300		Original: found
NP-2261	Scott, Mathew	3 APR 1769	West Branch	LD: Lycoming	300		James Harris Original: found

Table 6 - New Purchase Applications (1769-1773)

Number	Applicant	Date	Orig. Place	Later Place	Acres	Survey	Neighbors, Notes, etc.
NP-2262	Hewitt, Caleb	3 APR 1769	White Deer Hole Creek	LD: Lycoming	300		Joseph McCulloough Original: found
NP-2263	Gibson, James	3 APR 1769		White Deer, Union	300	D-56-32	William Blyth Original: Signed
NP-2264	Irwin, Robert	3 APR 1769		Dunbar, Fayette	300	C-185-42	George Paul/(r11 FEB 1807)James Rodgers Original: found
NP-2265	Morris, Robert	3 APR 1769	Berks	Loyalsock, Lycoming	300	D-56-31 D-57-32	Original: found
NP-2266	Whitmore, John	3 APR 1769		Long Limestone Valley, Centre/ LD: Centre	300		Christopher Teines Original: found
NP-2267	Brown, William	3 APR 1769	Youghiogheny River	LD: Somerset/ Fayette/ Westmoreland	300		Joshua Martin Original: found
NP-2268	Ewing, Robert	3 APR 1769	Northumberland	Buffalo, Union	300	C-65-43	(r31 JAN 1789)Rev. John Ewing & Jacob Ewing & Patrick Ewing Original: found
NP-2269	Snively, Jacob Jr.	3 APR 1769	Bedford	Redstone Creek, Fayette	300	C-53-57	Mary Barclay (widow)/(r6 JUN 1791)William Colvin & Thomas Colvin Original: found
NP-2270	Craford, John	3 APR 1769		Mahoning, Northumberland	300	A-82-238	Thomas Hewett/(r22 APR 1785)John Alexander Original: found
NP-2271	Crooks, William	3 APR 1769		Rush, Northumberland	300	C-56-2 C-32-281 C-83-97 C-69-162 C-32-280 C-32-281	(r5 JUL 1838)William Depuy/(r26 MAR 1845)Ebenezer Greenough/(r26 AUG 1862)Benjamin Gearhart/(r26 AUG 1862)William Depuey Original: found
NP-2272	Rees, Thomas Jr.	3 APR 1769	Berks	White Deer, Union	300	D-57-40 D-57-27	Elizabeth Blythe/[same land as NP-784 to Andrew Stevens] Original: Signed
NP-2273	McFadden, John	3 APR 1769	Berks	Warriors Run, Northumberland	300	C-136-47	(r2 AUG 1770) Original: found
NP-2274	Myre, Elizabeth	3 APR 1769	Lycoming	Wayne, Clinton/ LD: Clinton	300	D-56-24	Original: found
NP-2275	Croker, William	3 APR 1769		White Deer, Union	300	D-56-291 C-125-181	Evan Vale/(r1 MAY 1812)Richard Hartshorne Original: found
NP-2276	Fudle, Abraham	3 APR 1769	Muncy Creek	LD: Lycoming	300		Original: found

Table 6 - New Purchase Applications (1769-1773)

Number	Applicant	Date	Orig. Place	Later Place	Acres	Survey	Neighbors, Notes, etc.
NP-2277	Boyle, Thomas	3 APR 1769	Cumberland	Northumberland - Buffalo Creek, Union	300	C-109-149	(r23 AUG 1785)John Lowden Original: found
NP-2278	Wells, Edward	3 APR 1769	Northumberland	Briar Creek, Columbia	300	A-29-27	Hannah Kenly Original: found
NP-2279	Keney, Joseph	3 APR 1769		Elizabeth, Allegheny	150	B-7-80 B-7-193	Mathew Wilson/(r1 APR 1802)Robert Smith Original: found
NP-2280	Reed, Elizabeth	3 APR 1769	Northumberland	head of Lick Run, Union/ LD: Union/ Snyder	300	A-242	[see caveat] Original: Signed by John Reed
NP-2281	Wallis, Joseph Jacob	3 APR 1769	Cumberland	Black Run, Northumberland - Union	300	C-74-129	(r22 SEP 1790)Ruben Haines Original: found
NP-2282	Same, John	3 APR 1769	Cumberland	Tyrone, Fayette	300	D-56-23	John Stephenson Original: found
NP-2283	Douglass, Adam Jr.	3 APR 1769		Franklin, Westmoreland	300	C-584	Jacob Zennit/(r2 DEC 1802)John Young, Esq. [patent P-48-159] Original: Signed
NP-2284	Toblor, George	3 APR 1769		Chartiers, Washington	300	A-58-299	Paul Pierce/(r14 AUG 1787)John Wilkins & Charles Wilkins Original: found
NP-2285	Whitehead, Robert	3 APR 1769		LD: Columbia	300		Thomas Shoemaker Original: found
NP-2286	Shower, George	3 APR 1769	West Branch Susquehanna River	LD: Lycoming	100		Original: found
NP-2287	Campbell, Thomas	3 APR 1769		Unity, Westmoreland	300	D-56-21	Original: found
NP-2288	Meyer, Henry	3 APR 1769	Cumberland	Hartley, Union	300	D-56-10	John Harris Original: found
NP-2289	Duning, James	3 APR 1769		Quemahoning, Somerset	300	D-17-298	(r15 FEB 1803)John Wilkins Original: found
NP-2290	Coale, Ann	3 APR 1769		West Buffalo, Union/ LD: West Buffalo, Union	300	D-56-9	James Dilworth Original: found
NP-2291	Rubley, Jacob	3 APR 1769	Long Limestone Valley	LD: Centre	300		Christopher Whislor Original: found
NP-2292	Rinker, John	3 APR 1769		LD: Columbia	300		William Ledlie Original: found

Table 6 - New Purchase Applications (1769-1773)

Number	Applicant	Date	Orig. Place	Later Place	Acres	Survey	Neighbors, Notes, etc.
NP-2293	McClure, John	3 APR 1769	East Branch Susquehanna River	LD: Northumberland	300		John Bell Original: found
NP-2294	Jervis, Elizabeth Jr.	3 APR 1769		Chest, Clearfield	300	D-56-8	Original: found
NP-2295	Coner, Patrick	3 APR 1769	White Deer Hole Creek		300		["Note: - This place taken by a prior location & relocation No. 385 in the name of John Ewing."]/[On the back of a survey order dated 3 APR 1769, filed with the regular applications for the letter "C" for 1769 is the following statement: April 9th 1770. "I do hereby certifie that the land for which this order is granted is taken by prior applications or application." (signed by) Chas. Lukens] Original: found
NP-2296	Flahaven, Ann	3 APR 1769	Long Limestone Valley	LD: Centre	300		Rodger Flagavan/[see caveat] Original: found
NP-2297	Turner, Maurice	3 APR 1769	Berks	Mahoning Creek, Montour	300	W-260	Original: Signed
NP-2298	Robison, Thomas	3 APR 1769		Turbot, Northumberland/ LD: Northumberland	300	D-56-7	Original: found
NP-2299	Roberts, Robert	3 APR 1769		Turbot, Northumberland	300	N-154	Joseph Jones/(r28 JUN 1782)Ruben Haines Original: found
NP-2300	Pettit, Charles	3 APR 1769	West Branch Susquehanna River 3 miles from Ft. Augusta	LD: Northumberland	300		Original: found
NP-2301	Dowell, Grace	3 APR 1769		Fairfield, Lycoming	300	D-55-89 A-39-208	(r8 SEP 1770) Original: found
NP-2302	Ryerson, Martin Jr.	3 APR 1769	Northeast Branch Susquehanna River	LD: Luzerne	200		George Ryerson Original: found
NP-2303	Hunter, Hugh	3 APR 1769		Pitt, Westmoreland/ LD: Wilkins, Allegheny	300	A-5-202	William Powell/John McMull/[see caveat] Original: Signed
NP-2304	Smith, Adam	3 APR 1769	Penns Creek, Cumberland		300	C-202-138	(r4 SEP 1805)Phillip Swaim Original: found

Table 6 - New Purchase Applications (1769-1773)

Number	Applicant	Date	Orig. Place	Later Place	Acres	Survey	Neighbors, Notes, etc.
NP-2305	Allison, Francis Jr.	3 APR 1769		Youghiogheny River, Westmoreland	300	Q-42	(r14 FEB 1783)/[see caveat] Original: found
NP-2306	Walker, John	3 APR 1769		Crooked Creek, Armstrong	300	A-63-248 A-63-249	(r20 NOV 1809)Thomas Hamilton Original: found
NP-2307	Bartram, William	3 APR 1769		Nippenose, Lycoming	300	D-56-6	Original: found
NP-2308	Gover, Margaret	3 APR 1769	Cumberland	Stony Creek Twp., Somerset/ LD: Columbia	300		Prisella Gover Original: found
NP-2309	Crawford, John	3 APR 1769		Youghiogheny River, Fayette	300	C-25-290	(r9 JAN 1787)Edward Cook, Esq. Original: found
NP-2310	More, Andrew	3 APR 1769	three miles above Rush Creek on West Branch Susquehanna River	LD: Lycoming	300		Original: found
NP-2311	Cochran, William	3 APR 1769	Cumberland	Whitethorn Creek, Westmoreland/ LD: Unity, Westmoreland	300	H-97	Original: Signed
NP-2312	Gorell, John	3 APR 1769	Chillisquaque Creek	LD: Columbia/ Montour	300		James Tilghman, Esq. Original: found
NP-2313	Maxwell, Andrew	3 APR 1769	Warriors Run 4 miles from Susquehanna River		300		Original: found
NP-2314	Hare, Christian Jr.	3 APR 1769	Northumberland	West Branch Susquehanna River, Lycoming	300	C-39-215	Christian Hare, Sr./(r5 FEB 1773)David Duncan Original: found
NP-2315	Lattimer, George (farmer)	3 APR 1769	Winemillers Run & road to Fort Burd	LD: Fayette/ Westmoreland	300		Burd Clapham Original: found
NP-2316	Taylor, Robert	3 APR 1769		East Branch Susquehanna River 6 miles below Tunkhannock Creek, Luzerne	300	B-230 C-57-125	(r22 AUG 1796)Dr. John Ewing/(r18 FEB 1808)John Ewing Original: found

Table 6 - New Purchase Applications (1769-1773)

Number	Applicant	Date	Orig. Place	Later Place	Acres	Survey	Neighbors, Notes, etc.
NP-2317	McCormick, John	3 APR 1769	Chillisquaque Creek	LD: Northumberland/ Montour	300		Mr. Tilghman Original: Signed by Hugh McCormick
NP-2318	Goz, Philip	3 APR 1769		Loyalhanna, Westmoreland	300	S-66	Dr. Smith/(r17 OCT 1788)Daniel St. Clair Original: found
NP-2319	Breadin, William	3 APR 1769		Nippenose, Lycoming	300	D-56-20	Original: found
NP-2320	Jones, Jamime	3 APR 1769	Cumberland	LD: Somerset	300		John Barnes Original: found
NP-2321	Reed, Robert	3 APR 1769		Ligonier, Westmoreland	300	X-130 X-131 C-3-270 A-6-129 C-198-1 C-225-73	(r18 DEC 1801)Robert Reed, Jr./(r20 OCT 1858)Daniel Agnew/(r26 APR 1865)George Reed/(r26 APR 1892)George J. Sickles Original: found
NP-2322	Franklin, James	3 APR 1769	Penns Creek opposite mouth of Spring Creek, Cumberland	LD: Snyder	300		Original: found
NP-2323	Caruthers, Samuel	3 APR 1769	Chillisquaque Creek	LD: Montour	300		Original: found
NP-2324	Hoge, Jonathan	3 APR 1769		White Deer, Union	300	D-52-129	Original: found
NP-2325	Crozer, John	3 APR 1769	Chillisquaque Creek	LD: Northumberland	300		John Camel Original: found
NP-2326	Silvers, Francis	3 APR 1769		Northumberland or Montour/ LD: Armstrong	300		--- Weinn Original: found
NP-2327	Maclure, James	3 APR 1769		Fairfield, Lycoming	300	D-52-130	Original: found
NP-2328	Gordon, Thomas	3 APR 1769		Muncy Creek Twp., Lycoming	300	D-56-61	Original: found
NP-2329	Chesney, William	3 APR 1769	Northumberland	Buffalo, Union	300	C-152-115	(r10 MAY 1790)Alexander McGready Original: found

Table 6 - New Purchase Applications (1769-1773)

Number	Applicant	Date	Orig. Place	Later Place	Acres	Survey	Neighbors, Notes, etc.
NP-2330	Lowden, James	3 APR 1769		West Buffalo, Union	300	A-33-270 C-61-135 C-52-288 C-207-92 D-8-227 D-8-228	(r24 OCT 1815 & 22 MAR 1812)Jacob Fries/(r28 MAR 1826)Mary Speigelmoyer/(r9 JAN 1829)Jacob Zerbe/(r10 MAR 1836)John Yon Original: found
NP-2331	Koster, William	3 APR 1769		South Huntingdon, Westmoreland/ LD: South Huntingdon, Westmoreland	300	F-368	(r2 MAR 1833)Thomas Morgan Original: found
NP-2332	Oiller, Philip Jacob (of Philadelphia City)	3 APR 1769	where Plum Creek empties into Crooked Creek	LD: Armstrong/ [Jacob Philip in LD]	300		Original: found
NP-2333	Mentzer, John	3 APR 1769	Penns Creek, Cumberland	LD: Snyder	300		Samuel Huntzecker Original: found
NP-2334	Gay, Samuel	3 APR 1769	Muncy Creek	LD: Lycoming	300		John Heron/James Greag Original: found
NP-2335	Harrison, William	3 APR 1769		Northeast Branch Susquehanna River, Luzerne	300	F-197 Z-67	(r5 FEB 1794)Archibald Stewart Original: found
NP-2336	Bragth, Peter	3 APR 1769	Berks	Buffalo, Union	300	D-56-62 D-56-63 D-56-64 D-56-65 D-56-71 D-56-72 D-56-73	Original: found
NP-2337	Irvin, Mathew (of the City of Philadelphia, merchant)	3 APR 1769	Cumberland	Derry, Westmoreland	300	D-56-74	William Irwin Original: found
NP-2338	Keiger, Conrad	3 APR 1769	East Branch Susquehanna River	LD: Luzerne	300		Original: found
NP-2339	Carmalt, John	3 APR 1769	Cumberland	White Deer, Union	300	D-56-75	Original: found

Table 6 - New Purchase Applications (1769-1773)

Number	Applicant	Date	Orig. Place	Later Place	Acres	Survey	Neighbors, Notes, etc.
NP-2340	Taggart, Robert	3 APR 1769	Berks	Kelly, Union	300	D-56-85 D-56-92	[same land as NP-2368 to Thomas Beatty] Original: found
NP-2341	Christ, Adam	3 APR 1769		West Buffalo, Union	300	D-56-76	Original: found
NP-2342	Martin, William	3 APR 1769	Bedford	Sewickley Creek, Westmoreland/ LD: Westmoreland	300	A-236	John Sherer Original: found
NP-2343	Scott, John	3 APR 1769	Lycoming Creek	LD: Lycoming	300		Original: found
NP-2344	McCormick, Thomas	3 APR 1769		Loyalsock, Lycoming	300	D-56-78	Original: Signed by Hugh McCormick
NP-2345	Wallis, Francis	3 APR 1769	Cumberland	Berks - West Branch Susquehanna River, Northumberland	300	A-85-279	(r11 APR 1770)Samuel Wallis Original: found
NP-2346	Craig, James	3 APR 1769	Berks	Kelly, Union	300	D-56-43	[same land as NP-2225 to Beeson Bowden] Original: found
NP-2347	Pollock, Adam	3 APR 1769	Montour Creek, Berks	LD: Northumberland/ Montour	300		Original: found
NP-2348	Polock, James	3 APR 1769		Nippenose, Lycoming	300	D-56-77	Original: found
NP-2349	McKee, John	3 APR 1769		Allegheny, Westmoreland	300	D-56-79	Original: found
NP-2350	Derr, Ludwick	3 APR 1769	West Branch Susquehanna River at Dog Run	LD: Clarion/ Allegheny/ Armstrong	300		George Derr Original: found
NP-2351	Wilson, William	3 APR 1769	Berks	Buffalo, Union	300	D-56-281	[same land as NP-1204 to Charles Shafner] Original: Signed
NP-2352	Smith, James Jr. (son of Robert)	3 APR 1769		South Huntingdon, Westmoreland	300	D-55-44 C-157-245	Col. Clapham/William Newell/(r4 MAR 1786)James Perry Original: found
NP-2353	Rowan, David	3 APR 1769		Unity, Westmoreland	300	D-56-66	Original: found

Table 6 - New Purchase Applications (1769-1773)

Number	Applicant	Date	Orig. Place	Later Place	Acres	Survey	Neighbors, Notes, etc.
NP-2354	Freeman, William	3 APR 1769		Delaware, Northumberland	250	A-57-207	Benjamin Freeman/(r25 MAY 1774)John Freeman, Jr. Original: found
NP-2355	Manning, Richard	3 APR 1769	Cumberland	Northumberland - Buffalo, Union	300	A-42-201 A-42-202	(r15 OCT 1782)Robert Tate Original: found
NP-2356	Joy, Daniel	3 APR 1769		Nippenose Valley, Lycoming/ LD: Lycoming	300	X-206	Charles Ryor Original: Missing
NP-2357	Sheerer, Timothy	3 APR 1769		Unity, Westmoreland	300	D-56-76	Original: found
NP-2358	McCay, John	3 APR 1769		Augusta, Northumberland	200	B-497	(r5 SEP 1783)John Nixon & Alexander Forster Original: found
NP-2359	McMean, Elizabeth	3 APR 1769		Greenwood, Columbia	300	C-41-232 B-16-101 B-16-100 C-41-233 C-41-234 C-41-235	(21 DEC 1825)Thomas Eves/(r7 FEB 1827)Charles Eves/(r29 AUG 1832)T. Eves Original: found
NP-2360	Jacobs, John Jr.	3 APR 1769		Muncy Creek Twp., Lycoming/ LD: Lycoming	300	D-56-68	William Beale, Sr./French Margaret [an Indian] Original: Signed
NP-2361	Allen, Mary	3 APR 1769		Buffalo, Union	300	D-56-69 D-56-70	Nerdoine Elsworth Original: found
NP-2362	Blickenstoffer, Jacob	3 APR 1769		Washington, Lycoming	300	D-56-81	Peter Hoofnagle Original: found
NP-2363	Bell, Margaret	3 APR 1769		Turbot, Northumberland	300	C-69-262 D-9-53 D-9-54	(r3 MAR 1807)Joseph Hutchinson/(r13 OCT 1819)James Watson Original: found
NP-2364	Grimes, Mathew	3 APR 1769		Delaware, Northumberland	300	D-56-82	Edward Middleton Original: found
NP-2365	Seaton, Thomas	3 APR 1769		Ligonier, Westmoreland	300	D-56-83	James Hill Original: found
NP-2366	Iredell, Abraham	3 APR 1769	West Branch Susquehanna River	LD: Union	300		Charles Iredell/Mr. Ewing Original: found
NP-2367	Farree, John	3 APR 1769		North Huntingdon, Westmoreland	300	D-56-84	Original: found

Table 6 - New Purchase Applications (1769-1773)

Number	Applicant	Date	Orig. Place	Later Place	Acres	Survey	Neighbors, Notes, etc.
NP-2368	Beatty, Thomas	3 APR 1769	Berks	Kelly, Union	300	D-56-85 D-56-91 D-56-92 D-56-93 D-56-94 D-56-95	Mr. Young Original: found
NP-2369	Duffield, John	3 APR 1769	Northumberland	Roaring Creek, Columbia/ LD: Luzerne	300	F-230	[see caveat] Original: found
NP-2370	Burnet, Timothy	3 APR 1769		Versailles, Allegheny	300	D-57-65 D-56-168 A-76-259	(r17 JUN 1789)Dorcus Boyd [patent P-15-86] Original: found
NP-2371	Grove, Henry	3 APR 1769	Northumberland	East Branch Susquehanna River, Columbia	300	F-399	Joseph Musser/(r25 JUL 1774)Nicholas Reitenaur Original: found
NP-2372	Renicks, Jean	3 APR 1769	Susquehanna River at Mathenac Hill	LD: Centre	300		Original: found
NP-2373	Gallacher, William	3 APR 1769		Delaware, Northumberland	300	D-56-96	John Stephens Original: found
NP-2374	Hall, Elihu	3 APR 1769	Cumberland	LD: Somerset	300		Elizabeth Barns Original: found
NP-2375	Wood, William	3 APR 1769	Laurel Hill on Roaring Run	LD: Somerset	300		Original: found
NP-2376	Johns, Elizabeth	3 APR 1769	Berks or Northampton	Nescopeck Falls, Columbia	300	A-67-122	(r9 APR 1783)Evan Owen Original: found
NP-2377	McClintock, Abram	3 APR 1769	Briar Run, North Branch Susquehanna River	LD: Columbia	300		Original: Signed
NP-2378	Thompson, William	3 APR 1769		Versailles, Allegheny	300	D-56-97	Original: found
NP-2379	White, George	3 APR 1769	Berks	Washington, Lycoming	300	D-56-98	Original: Signed
NP-2380	Dorsey, Benedict	3 APR 1769	White Hemp Creek, Northampton or Berks		300		Original: found

Table 6 - New Purchase Applications (1769-1773)

Number	Applicant	Date	Orig. Place	Later Place	Acres	Survey	Neighbors, Notes, etc.
NP-2381	Evans, John	3 APR 1769	Northeast Branch Susquehanna River	LD: Hanover, Luzerne	300		John Fry Original: found
NP-2382	Greg, John	3 APR 1769		Buffalo, Union	200	D-62-206 D-62-207	[same land as NP-2814 to Joseph Allen] Original: found
NP-2383	Burd, James	3 APR 1769		Allegheny, Armstrong/ LD: Armstrong	300	D-64-31	Original: found
NP-2384	Rogers, Philip	3 APR 1769		Buffalo, Union	300	D-56-99 D-56-100	Original: found
NP-2385	Bausman, Jacob	3 APR 1769	Youghiogheny River	LD: Fayette	300		--- Crawford/[see caveat] Original: found
NP-2386	Greenfield, John	3 APR 1769	Berks	Lycoming - Wayne, Clinton	300	D-56-86	Original: found
NP-2387	Wallace, Richard	3 APR 1769		Allegheny, Armstrong	300	D-33-95 D-9-117 D-12-39 D-9-117	(r26 APR 1814)Joseph Wilson/(r28 NOV 1818)Davis Shields Original: found
NP-2388	Etswiler, George	3 APR 1769		West Buffalo, Union/ LD: Union	300	H-154 C-128-11 C-61-26 D-2-227	James McKoy/Jacob Rotten/(r28 JAN 1812)David Kaufman/(r6 MAR 1813)William Forster & John Forster/(r21 JUN 1815)James Wright & William Wright Original: Signed
NP-2389	Ewing, William	3 APR 1769		Northeast Branch Susquehanna River, Northumberland	300		(r5 DEC 1785 & p6 DEC 1785)James McLees/[patent P-4-171]/[see caveat] Original: found
NP-2390	Brown, George	3 APR 1769	Cumberland	Blacklick, Indiana	300	D-56-87	Original: Signed by William Brown, Carlisle
NP-2391	Erwin, George	3 APR 1769		Turbot, Northumberland	300	A-71-100	William Irwin/Richard Irwin/(r20 SEP 1774)/[see caveat] Original: found
NP-2392	McClintock, Alexander	3 APR 1769	mouth of Fishing Creek, Northeast Branch Susquehanna River	LD: Columbia	300		Original: found
NP-2393	Taylor, Thomas	3 APR 1769		Derry, Westmoreland	300	A-11-103 A-11-121	James Wilson/(r30 MAR 1789)Charles Beard Original: found

Table 6 - New Purchase Applications (1769-1773)

Number	Applicant	Date	Orig. Place	Later Place	Acres	Survey	Neighbors, Notes, etc.
NP-2394	Eairl, John	3 APR 1769		Peters, Washington	300	G-163	(r2 JAN 1788)Catherine Thompson Original: found
NP-2395	Davison, Elias	3 APR 1769		Elizabeth, Allegheny/ LD: Elizabeth, Allegheny	300	D-62-197 A-66-122	[caveated by Henry Leming on warrant dated 18 JUL 1786] Original: Signed
NP-2396	Wise, Frederick	3 APR 1769	Berks	Buffalo, Union	300	D-57-42 D-57-43	[same land as NP-733 to William Buchanan] Original: Signed
NP-2397	Miller, John	3 APR 1769	Cumberland	Howard, Centre/ LD: Centre	300	X-217 C-91-205 A-48-23 C-14-170	Mary Yearly/(r21 OCT 1845)Jesse Hall/(r19 FEB 1846)John Harris & William Harris/(r8 APR 1852)Ephraim Banks Original: found
NP-2398	Mackey, John	3 APR 1769		West Buffalo, Union	300	D-57-272 D-62-272 D-17-167	George Ickawee/Richard Melone/(r21 MAR 1839)Thomas L. Wright Original: found
NP-2399	Fry, John	3 APR 1769	Berks	Washington, Lycoming	300	D-56-89	Peter Hoocher Original: found
NP-2400	McClure, Jonathan	3 APR 1769	Northampton	Fishing Creek, Columbia	300	C-212-28	(r11 MAY 1773)Thomas Minshell Original: found
NP-2401	Murray, Thomas	3 APR 1769		Turbot, Northumberland	300	C-166-33	James Murray/(r15 JUN 1774) Original: Signed by Alexander Murray
NP-2402	Poultney, Benjamin	3 APR 1769	Berks	Kelly, Union	300	D-56-90	Rev. Ewing Original: found
NP-2403	Drewry, William	3 APR 1769		Turbot, Northumberland	300	D-60-261	Original: found
NP-2404	Britebough, Christopher	3 APR 1769	Berks	Washington, Lycoming	300	D-60-262	Phillip Britebough Original: found
NP-2405	Vanmeter, Jacob	3 APR 1769	Cumberland	Muddy Creek, Greene/ LD: Greene	300	X-122	Original: found
NP-2406	Cumings, William	3 APR 1769		Muncy, Lycoming	300	D-60-263	Original: Signed by James Cumings
NP-2407	Armstrong, James Jr.	3 APR 1769		Conemaugh, Indiana/ LD: Conemaugh, Indiana	300	D-60-264 D-60-265	George Armstrong Original: Signed by Joseph Armstrong
NP-2408	Burns, Peter	3 APR 1769		Limestone, Northumberland	300	I-329	(r14 JUL 1786)Phillip Davis/[see caveat] Original: found

Table 6 - New Purchase Applications (1769-1773)

Number	Applicant	Date	Orig. Place	Later Place	Acres	Survey	Neighbors, Notes, etc.
NP-2409	Bonsal, Edward	3 APR 1769		Buffalo, Union	300	D-62-206 D-62-207 A-41-28	(r15 APR 1785)Edward Shippen, Esq. & Joseph Shippen, Esq. Original: found
NP-2410	Talbot, Margaret	3 APR 1769		West Branch Susquehanna River, Union	300	A-22-236	(r1 AUG 1820)Samuel B. Rawle Original: found
NP-2411	Urie, Thomas	3 APR 1769		Versailles, Allegheny	300	A-71-250	(r6 FEB 1771)/[patent AA-11-506] Original: found
NP-2412	Fearis, Bernard	3 APR 1769	Berks	Washington, Lycoming	300	D-60-271	Original: found
NP-2413	Montgomery, John Jr.	3 APR 1769	Berks	Nippenose, Lycoming/ LD: Lycoming	300	D-56-152 C-202-274 C-202-275	(p14 AUG 1871)Charles Stewart & William H. Gibson/[see caveat] Original: found
NP-2414	Biard, David	3 APR 1769		Derry & Unity, Westmoreland	300	M-131	(r1 APR 1788)Jeremiah Lochrey Original: found
NP-2415	McKee, James (carpenter)	3 APR 1769	Cumberland	Bullskin, Fayette	300	D-60-272	Original: found
NP-2416	Blane, William	3 APR 1769	East Branch Susquehanna River above Shamokin		300		Original: found
NP-2417	Elsworth, VerDine	3 APR 1769	Berks	Buffalo, Union	300	D-60-188	[same land as NP-1918 to John Blum] Original: found
NP-2418	Dunwick, William	3 APR 1769		Washington, Lycoming	300	D-60-273	Samuel Wheeler Original: found
NP-2419	Huston, Joseph	3 APR 1769		Tyrone, Fayette/ LD: Westmoreland	300	A-36-17 D-57-218	William Huston Original: found
NP-2420	Calwell, David	3 APR 1769		Monongahela River, Allegheny	300	A-88-250	(r27 AUG 1816)George Roush Original: found
NP-2421	Blair, John	3 APR 1769	Berks	Kelly, Union	300	D-60-274	Original: found
NP-2422	Field, Lydia	3 APR 1769	Red Bank Creek	LD: Northumberland	300		--- Blyth Original: found
NP-2423	Haines, William	3 APR 1769	Red Creek south of East Branch Susquehanna River	LD: Luzerne/ Columbia	200		Original: found

Table 6 - New Purchase Applications (1769-1773)

Number	Applicant	Date	Orig. Place	Later Place	Acres	Survey	Neighbors, Notes, etc.
NP-2424	Wallace, Robert	3 APR 1769	West Branch Susquehanna River opposite Loyalsock Creek	LD: Lycoming	300		Original: found
NP-2425	Smith, Jacob	3 APR 1769		Washington, Lycoming/ LD: Washington, Lycoming	300	D-60-275	Original: found
NP-2426	McMullen, James	3 APR 1769		Buffalo, Union	100	D-60-276	Col. Francis/Gov. Penn Original: found
NP-2427	Garber, Michael	3 APR 1769	Northumberland	Turbot, Columbia	300	D-57-199 C-124-136 C-124-137	(r20 OCT 1814)James Lemmon Original: Signed
NP-2428	Clark, Joseph	3 APR 1769		Lawrence & Bradford, Clearfield	300	D-60-277	Original: found
NP-2429	Lindsay, Arthur	3 APR 1769		Youghiogheny River, Westmoreland	300	C-193-288	Thomas Baird/(r15 FEB 1787)Jacob Smith Original: found
NP-2430	Jenkins, Aaron (of Frederick County, Virginia)	3 APR 1769		Redstone Creek, Fayette	300	B-5-68	Philip Shute/(r12 NOV 1787)James Rankin Original: signed
NP-2431	Hepburn, James	3 APR 1769		Muncy, Lycoming	300	D-60-278	Original: found
NP-2432	McMeans, William	3 APR 1769		Buffalo, Union	300	D-60-279	Original: found
NP-2433	Cox, John Jr.	3 APR 1769	Berks	Kelly, Union	300	D-56-42	Mr. Ewing/[same land as NP-2225 to Breeson Bowden] Original: Signed
NP-2434	Perry, David	3 APR 1769		Rostraver, Westmoreland/ LD: Rostraver, Westmoreland	300	X-164 C-168-212	John McKean Original: found
NP-2435	Jervis, Susannah	3 APR 1769	Fishing Creek, East Branch Susquehanna River, Northampton or Berks	LD: Columbia	300		Original: found

Table 6 - New Purchase Applications (1769-1773)

Number	Applicant	Date	Orig. Place	Later Place	Acres	Survey	Neighbors, Notes, etc.
NP-2436	Bond, Samuel	3 APR 1769	East Branch Susquehanna River	LD: Salem, Luzerne	300		Original: Signed
NP-2437	Supplee, Peter	3 APR 1769	Berks	Nippenose, Lycoming	---	C-45-118	(r20 JUN 1832)Martha Duncan, Exr. of Thomas Duncan, deceased Original: found
NP-2438	Gardner, Elizabeth	3 APR 1769		Turbot, Northumberland	300	A-10-84	[see caveat] Original: found
NP-2439	Hunter, George	3 APR 1769		Augusta, Northumberland	300	E-410	(r20 FEB 1812)Abraham Julicks Original: found
NP-2440	Bauer, John George	3 APR 1769	East Branch Susquehanna River between Wyalusing & Wyoming	LD: Washington, Lycoming	300		Jacob Weaver Original: found
NP-2441	Beale, David (the younger)	3 APR 1769	Berks	Kelly, Union	300	D-60-280	Original: Signed
NP-2442	Martin, James	3 APR 1769		Huntingdon, Westmoreland	300	C-144-190 R-99 R-100	(r11 APR 1797) Original: found
NP-2443	Wetherington, Alexander	3 APR 1769		Buffalo, Union	300	D-60-266	Col. Francis Original: found
NP-2444	Martin, Jesse	3 APR 1769		Washington, Fayette	300	D-60-267	Original: found
NP-2445	Virgin, Joshua	3 APR 1769		Turbot, Northumberland	300	A-78-140	(r18 DEC 1772) Original: found
NP-2446	Reigart, Adam	3 APR 1769	Bald Eagle Creek	LD: Centre	300		Original: found
NP-2447	Jones, Thomas	3 APR 1769	West Branch Lehigh River	LD: Luzerne	300		Original: found
NP-2448	Hews, Moses	3 APR 1769	Northumberland	Little Fishing Creek, Columbia	300	V-146	Joseph Ogden/(r25 JUN 1796)Owen Biddle Original: found
NP-2449	Smith, Charles	3 APR 1769	Huntingdon	Lawrence, Clearfield	300	D-17-152	(r10 JUN 1803)Abraham Witmer Original: found
NP-2450	Quigley, Henry Jr.	3 APR 1769	West Branch Susquehanna River	LD: Lycoming/ Union	300		Original: found
NP-2451	Malcolm, John	3 APR 1769		Nippenose, Lycoming	300	D-60-268	Archibald Gardner Original: found

Table 6 - New Purchase Applications (1769-1773)

Number	Applicant	Date	Orig. Place	Later Place	Acres	Survey	Neighbors, Notes, etc.
NP-2452	Thornhill, Joseph	3 APR 1769	Chillisquaque Creek	LD: Northumberland/ Montour	300		Original: found
NP-2453	Crawford, Moses	3 APR 1769	Cumberland	head of Elk Run, Fayette	300	C-10-141	Jeremiah Vergin/(r25 SEP 1789)Andrew Byers Original: found
NP-2454	Wade, Evan	3 APR 1769		White Deer, Union	300	D-60-214 C-125-182	(r2 MAY 1812)Richard Hartshorne Original: found
NP-2455	Clarke, George	3 APR 1769	Cumberland	Washington, Fayette	300	D-60-269	Original: found
NP-2456	Cummings, Edward (of Providence, Philadelphia County)	3 APR 1769	West Branch Susquehanna River	LD: Clinton	300		Original: Signed
NP-2457	Gearick, George	3 APR 1769		Point, Northumberland	100	C-166-142 C-166-232	(r24 DEC 1822)J & J Paul/(r25 APR 1827)Joseph B. Priestly Original: found
NP-2458	Davison, Hugh	3 APR 1769		Rostraver, Westmoreland	300	C-48-21	(r30 AUG 1783) Original: Signed
NP-2459	Rhoads, Samuel Jr.	3 APR 1769		Greene/ LD: Bradford	300		Thomas Paschall Original: found
NP-2460	Starrett, Mathew	3 APR 1769		Wilkins, Allegheny	300	D-62-198	Original: found
NP-2461	Celly, Charles	3 APR 1769		Hempfield, Westmoreland	300	D-60-270	Original: found
NP-2462	Alkison, Charles	3 APR 1769		Turbot, Northumberland	300	C-97-46	(r13 JUN 1809)Joseph Hutchinson Original: found
NP-2463	Fulton, Robert	3 APR 1769		Buffalo, Union	300	D-62-181	Original: found
NP-2464	Pikly, Phoelix	3 APR 1769		Loyalsock Creek, Lycoming	300	A-39-207	Abraham Buckwalter/(r18 APR 1770)Margaret Duncan Original: found
NP-2465	Stoner, Jacob	3 APR 1769	Lycoming Creek	LD: Lycoming	300		Original: found
NP-2466	White, Hugh	3 APR 1769		Unity, Westmoreland	300	D-62-182	Original: found
NP-2467	Donnely, Matica	3 APR 1769		Allegheny, Westmoreland	200	D-56-79 D-56-80 D-56-133 M-421	(r1 APR 1788)John Moore, Esq. Original: Signed

Table 6 - New Purchase Applications (1769-1773)

Number	Applicant	Date	Orig. Place	Later Place	Acres	Survey	Neighbors, Notes, etc.
NP-2468	Miller, John	3 APR 1769	Brush Run	LD: Westmoreland	300		Original: found
NP-2469	Porter, James	3 APR 1769	Berks	Buffalo, Union	300	D-57-12 D-57-16	[same land as NP-866 to John Clin] Original: found
NP-2470	Willson, Andrew	3 APR 1769	Mingo Run, Muncy Creek	LD: Lycoming	300		Original: found
NP-2471	Zimmerman, Bernard	3 APR 1769		Turbot, Northumberland	300	D-62-183	Michael Wolfart Original: found
NP-2472	McMullen, Thomas Sr.	3 APR 1769		Huntingdon, Westmoreland	300	C-195-78 C-195-79 C-195-80	(r23 SEP 1790)John Robertson Original: found
NP-2473	McMurtree, William	3 APR 1769		Washington, Lycoming	300	D-62-184	Original: found
NP-2474	Baxter, George	3 APR 1769	West Branch Susquehanna River	LD: Lycoming	300		Nathaniel Smith Original: found
NP-2475	Sherman, Benjamin	3 APR 1769	Chillisquaque Creek	LD: Northumberland/ Montour	300		Michael McCall Original: found
NP-2476	Hopkins, Samuel Jr.	3 APR 1769	Cumberland	Northumberland - Fishing Creek, Centre or Clinton	300	C-120-214	(r16 AUG 1787)Benjamin Morgan Original: found
NP-2477	Brotherton, James	3 APR 1769		Salem, Westmoreland	300	D-257-279 D-257-280 I-496	(r1 APR 1788)John Gourty Original: found
NP-2478	Krum, Matthias	3 APR 1769		West Buffalo, Union	300	D-62-185	Original: found
NP-2479	Allen, Samuel Sr.	3 APR 1769	Chillisquaque Creek	LD: Northumberland	300		Original: found
NP-2480	Sturges, Daniel	3 APR 1769	Cumberland	Huntingdon, Westmoreland/ LD: Huntingdon, Westmoreland	300	W-296	Original: found
NP-2481	Alricks, Harmanus	3 APR 1769	Northumberland	Catawissa, Columbia	300	C-188-133	(r3 MAY 1794)William Rittenhouse Original: found

Table 6 - New Purchase Applications (1769-1773)

Number	Applicant	Date	Orig. Place	Later Place	Acres	Survey	Neighbors, Notes, etc.
NP-2482	Kohr, Casper	3 APR 1769	East Branch Susquehanna River & Fall Creek	LD: Northumberland	300		Original: found
NP-2483	Wallace, John	3 APR 1769		Unity, Westmoreland	300	D-62-191 D-62-192	Abraham Lesher Original: found
NP-2484	Cox, Cornelius	3 APR 1769		Washington, Lycoming	300	D-62-193	William Cox Original: Signed
NP-2485	Watts, Frederick	3 APR 1769		Turbot, Northumberland	300	D-13-221	(r24 JAN 1775) Original: found
NP-2486	Harris, John Jr.	3 APR 1769	Northumberland	Fishing Creek branch of Bald Eagle Creek, Clinton	300	Z-203	(r16 DEC 1772)Phillip Francis, Esq. Original: found
NP-2487	Goudey, James	3 APR 1769		Clinton, Lycoming	300	C-1-59	(r18 JAN 1773)John Backhouse Original: found
NP-2488	Montgomery, Rebecca	3 APR 1769	Berks	Washington, Lycoming	300	D-62-194	Original: found
NP-2489	Snively, Jacob	3 APR 1769		Redstone, Allegheny	300	D-56-25 B-21-228	Adam Rowe/--- Jennings/--- Keigart/[see caveat] Original: found
NP-2490	Lyon, Charles	3 APR 1769		LD: Lycoming	300		James Laura Original: found
NP-2491	McConnell, Adam (son of Robert)	3 APR 1769	Bedford	Monongahela River, Allegheny	300	C-134-128	Godfrey Waggoner/(r30 MAR 1805) Original: found
NP-2492	Crastin, John (of Cumberland County)	3 APR 1769		Allegheny, Westmoreland	300	D-62-195	Original: found
NP-2493	Dunlap, William	3 APR 1769		Derry, Westmoreland	300	C-119-280	(r14 FEB 1804)William Moorehead & Hugh Hamilton Original: found
NP-2494	Kunkle, Henry	3 APR 1769	Cumberland	Westmoreland - Conemaugh River, Indiana	300	A-38-129	Anthony Altman/Henry Straugh/Christian Baum/(r19 MAR 1788)Frederick Rohrer Original: found
NP-2495	Henry, John	3 APR 1769	Fishing Creek	LD: Columbia	300		Original: found
NP-2496	Graham, Richard	3 APR 1769		Hempfield, Westmoreland	300	C-58-264	(r5 FEB 1771) Original: found
NP-2497	McMachen, William (smith)	3 APR 1769		Youghiogheny River, Fayette	300	A-21-207	William Thompson/(r20 DEC 1787)Isaac Meason, Esq. Original: found

Table 6 - New Purchase Applications (1769-1773)

Number	Applicant	Date	Orig. Place	Later Place	Acres	Survey	Neighbors, Notes, etc.
NP-2498	Smith, William (of Conecockeague)	3 APR 1769		Plum, Allegheny	300	D-62-199	Original: found
NP-2499	Pennybecker, Dorrick	3 APR 1769	Berks	Buffalo, Union	300	D-62-196	Original: Missing
NP-2500	Paul, Abram	3 APR 1769		Turbot, Northumberland	300	K-115	(r4 MAY 1825 & p5 May 1825)Adam Fulmer & Thomas Pollock/[patent H-23-233] Original: Missing
NP-2501	Chambers, Robert	3 APR 1769		Elizabeth, Allegheny/ LD: Elizabeth, Allegheny	300	D-62-200	Jesse Martin/[covered by warrant to Moses Devoir dated 7 JAN 1788]/(p27 FEB 1830)Moses Devoir [patent H-27-489] Original: Missing
NP-2502	Kilcreest, John	3 APR 1769		Turbot, Northumberland	300	C-123-282	Lovia Forster/(r7 MAY 1789)David McGuire/[see caveat] Original: found
NP-2503	Furster, Peter	3 APR 1769		Mahoning Gap, Northumberland	300	B-281	(r20 MAY 1795)George Furster Original: found
NP-2504	Lindsay, Mary	3 APR 1769		Derry, Westmoreland	300	D-62-190	Original: found
NP-2505	Parks, Able	3 APR 1769		Derry, Westmoreland	300	D-62-290	Original: found
NP-2506	Ney, Peter	3 APR 1769		East Branch Susquehanna River, Luzerne	300	C-191-109	(r6 NOV 1835)William Patterson heirs Original: found
NP-2507	Zeller, Peter	3 APR 1769		West Buffalo, Union/ LD: Buffalo, Union	300	A-32-138 C-209-153 C-180-262 C-180-263	(r19 AUG 1814)John Seebold/(r3 MAY 1837)William Rishel Original: Signed by John Zeller
NP-2508	Baird, Isaac	3 APR 1769	Cumberland	branch of Sewickley Creek, Westmoreland	300	C-1-25	(r1 SEP 1770) Original: found
NP-2509	Irvine, William	3 APR 1769		West Buffalo, Union	300	D-55-77 D-137	Col. Francis/(r7 FEB 1793)William Ball, Jr. & Isabell Ball [his wife] Original: found
NP-2510	Lowdon, John	3 APR 1769	Northumberland	West Buffalo, Union	300	D-6-144	(r16 OCT 1811)S. Witmer/[see caveat] Original: found
NP-2511	Shaffner, Mathias	3 APR 1769	Cumberland	Buffalo, Union	300	D-62-21	Jacob Shaffner/Charles Shaffner Original: found

Table 6 - New Purchase Applications (1769-1773)

Number	Applicant	Date	Orig. Place	Later Place	Acres	Survey	Neighbors, Notes, etc.
NP-2512	Harminson, John	3 APR 1769	East Branch Susquehanna River	LD: Luzerne	200		Original: found
NP-2513	Wallace, John	3 APR 1769		Kelly, Union	300	D-62-22	John Ewing Original: found
NP-2514	McKnight, Robert	3 APR 1769		West Buffalo, Union	300	D-62-23	Rev. John Ewing Original: found
NP-2515	Maclellan, Alexander	3 APR 1769		Donegal, Westmoreland	300	A-32-188	[see Westmoreland warrant #55 to John Ewing] Original: found
NP-2516	Little, Jane	3 APR 1769		Loyalsock & Hepburn, Lycoming/ LD: Lycoming	300	D-63-98 F-227	Original: found
NP-2517	Wells, John	3 APR 1769	Northumberland	Muncy, Lycoming	300	A-5-86	Miles Hilburn Original: found
NP-2518	Irvine, Alexander	3 APR 1769		Unity???White Deer Hole Creek, Westmoreland	300	D-55-95 B-23-35	Original: found
NP-2519	Grove, Jacob	3 APR 1769	Northumberland	Washington, Lycoming	300	C-219-125	(r29 JUL 1797)Salome Shingle Original: found
NP-2520	Koocher, Peter	3 APR 1769		Hartley, Lycoming	300	D-62-24	Robert Trotter Original: found
NP-2521	Ewings, William	3 APR 1769		Union	200	D-62-24 D-62-25	Original: found
NP-2522	Armstrong, Alexander	3 APR 1769	Berks	Buffalo, Union	300	D-62-31 D-62-32	Original: Signed
NP-2523	Brown, John	3 APR 1769	Bald Eagle Creek	LD: Centre	300		Original: found
NP-2524	Carruthers, Rebaca	3 APR 1769	West Branch Susquehanna River, Red Bank Run	LD: Armstrong	300		Original: found
NP-2525	Logane, James	3 APR 1769	Berks	White Deer, Union	300	D-62-231	[same land as NP-2778 to John Carmalt] Original: found
NP-2526	Semple, Robert	3 APR 1769		North Huntingdon, Westmoreland	300	C-168-204	(r8 OCT 1788)Daniel Roberdeau, Esq. Original: found

Table 6 - New Purchase Applications (1769-1773)

Number	Applicant	Date	Orig. Place	Later Place	Acres	Survey	Neighbors, Notes, etc.
NP-2527	Christy, William	3 APR 1769		Pitt, Allegheny/ LD: Pitt, Allegheny	300	B-21-76	Original: found
NP-2528	Waddle, Samuel	3 APR 1769		between Conemaugh River & Blacklick Creek, Indiana	300	A-5-104 A-5-23	Original: found
NP-2529	Piper, James	3 APR 1769		Muncy, Lycoming	300	D-62-33	Original: Signed
NP-2530	Pryor, Charles	3 APR 1769		Nippenose, Lycoming/ LD: Nippenose, Lycoming	300	X-165	Daniel Jay Original: found
NP-2531	Baird, John	3 APR 1769		Derry, Westmoreland	300	D-62-34	Original: found
NP-2532	Snowden, Thomas	3 APR 1769		Washington, Lycoming	300	D-62-36	Original: found
NP-2533	Paty, John	3 APR 1769	Westmoreland	Youghiogheny River, Fayette	300	A-64-94	Col. Washington/(r18 FEB 1782)Gen'l. Washington Original: found
NP-2534	Clark, James Sr.	3 APR 1769		Muncy Creek Twp., Lycoming	300	D-62-37	Original: Signed
NP-2535	Preater, Henry	3 APR 1769		North Huntingdon, Westmoreland & Plum, Allegheny	300	C-38-15	[in right of Thomas Small]/[see NP-1336] Original: found
NP-2536	Tredwell, James	3 APR 1769		Nanticoke Creek, Luzerne/ LD: Luzerne	300	W-261	Original: found
NP-2537	Johnston, William	3 APR 1769		Chillisquaque Creek, Northumberland	300	L-152	William Murray/(r20 SEP 1774)/[see caveat] Original: found
NP-2538	Kintner, Jacob	3 APR 1769		Northeast Branch Susquehanna River, Luzerne	300	C-152	(r20 APR 1824)William Corney & William Jane Original: found
NP-2539	Silvers, James	3 APR 1769		Salem, Westmoreland	300	D-62-38	Original: found

Table 6 - New Purchase Applications (1769-1773)

Number	Applicant	Date	Orig. Place	Later Place	Acres	Survey	Neighbors, Notes, etc.
NP-2540	Gilespie, Stephen	3 APR 1769	Northumberland	Mahoning Creek, Montour/ LD: Columbia	300	H-165	Original: found
NP-2541	Galloway, James	3 APR 1769		Unity, Westmoreland	300	D-62-39	Capt. John Proctor/James Furgeson Original: found
NP-2542	Ackerman, John Martin	3 APR 1769	East Branch Susquehanna River above Wyoming	LD: Bradford	300		Martin Gilman Original: found
NP-2543	Fry, John	3 APR 1769	Northeast Branch Susquehanna River	LD: Montour	300		Original: found
NP-2544	Corsa, Isaac	3 APR 1769		Warriors Run, Northumberland	300	C-83	(r15 NOV 1771)Cornelius Cox Original: found
NP-2545	Zigler, Ludwick	3 APR 1769	Bald Eagle Creek	LD: Clinton/ Centre	300		George Zigler Original: found
NP-2546	Bull, Joseph	3 APR 1769		Warriors Run, Northumberland	300	A-7-284	(r15 NOV 1771)Cornelius Cox/[see caveat] Original: found
NP-2547	Summers, Peter	3 APR 1769		Chillisquaque Creek, Northumberland/ LD: Northumberland	300		James Fisher Original: found
NP-2548	Thompson, William	3 APR 1769		South Huntingdon , Westmoreland	300	C-120-266	(r5 OCT 1787)John Miller Original: found
NP-2549	Musser, Martin	3 APR 1769		Delaware, Northumberland	300	C-112-130	(r14 DEC 1774)John Lytle Original: found
NP-2550	Britebough, Philip	3 APR 1769		Washington, Lycoming/ LD: Washington, Lycoming	300	D-62-40	John Cran Original: found
NP-2551	Gray, Isaac	3 APR 1769		Loyalsock, Lycoming	300	D-15-71	Samuel Morris/(r11 JAN 1796)Samuel Wallis/(w2 SEP 1795) Original: found
NP-2552	Carter, Jacob	3 APR 1769		Buffalo, Union	300	D-62-26	Original: found
NP-2553	Smith, Moses	3 APR 1769		Tyrone & Bullskin, Fayette	300	D-62-27	Original: found

Table 6 - New Purchase Applications (1769-1773)

Number	Applicant	Date	Orig. Place	Later Place	Acres	Survey	Neighbors, Notes, etc.
NP-2554	McCrea, James Mease	3 APR 1769		Bedford	300		Original: found
NP-2555	Gallaugher, William	3 APR 1769		Buffalo, Union	300	D-62-14	Mr. Ewing/[same land as NP-3744 to Christian Ewig] Original: found
NP-2556	Correy, Laughlin	3 APR 1769	Chillisquaque Creek	LD: Columbia	300		Original: found
NP-2557	Neeper, John	3 APR 1769		Loyalsock, Lycoming	300	D-62-281	Joseph McIntire Original: found
NP-2558	Knight, Giles Sr.	3 APR 1769		Muncy Creek Twp., Lycoming	300	E-350	(r12 SEP 1811)M. Ross Original: found
NP-2559	Hussey, William	3 APR 1769		Bald Eagle Creek, Centre	300	C-135-86	Cathrine Flehaven/(r8 JUL 1782)Robert Morris, Esq. Original: found
NP-2560	Wickware, John	3 APR 1769	Rush Meadows, East Branch Susquehanna River	LD: Bradford	300		Original: found
NP-2561	Bonsall, Nathan	3 APR 1769		Chillisquaque Creek, Montour	300		Col. Francis Original: found
NP-2562	Irvin, Margaret	3 APR 1769		North Huntingdon, Westmoreland	300	D-62-282	Original: found
NP-2563	Slough, Mathias	3 APR 1769	East Branch Susquehanna River & Nescopeck Creek	LD: Luzerne	300		Original: Signed
NP-2564	Morris, Samuel	3 APR 1769	Cedar Run, West Branch Susquehanna River	LD: Centre	300		Original: found
NP-2565	Moon, Jacob	3 APR 1769	Berks	Buffalo, Union	300	D-62-283	Original: found
NP-2566	Brown, Alexander	3 APR 1769	Pine Creek & West Branch Susquehanna River	LD: Lycoming	300		Original: Signed by William Brown

Table 6 - New Purchase Applications (1769-1773)

Number	Applicant	Date	Orig. Place	Later Place	Acres	Survey	Neighbors, Notes, etc.
NP-2567	Findlay, William (farmer)	3 APR 1769		Blacklick, Indiana/ LD: Indiana	300	A-85-159	Shedrick Muchmore/(p28 JAN 1870)Archibald S. Pattison Original: found
NP-2568	Parker, Mary	3 APR 1769		Derry, Westmoreland	300	C-83-186 C-61-281 C-68-121 C-83-185	(r25 JAN 1814 & 2 FEB 1822)Thomas Gallagher/(r3 APR 1838)J. Gallagher Original: found
NP-2569	Harvey, William	3 APR 1769	Berks	Hartley, Union	300	D-62-284	Original: found
NP-2570	Duncan, James	3 APR 1769		Mahoning Creek, Montour/ LD: Luzerne	300	F-236	Original: found
NP-2571	Reed, Hamilton	3 APR 1769		White Deer, Union	300	D-62-285	Original: found
NP-2572	McCollister, Hugh	3 APR 1769		Washington, Lycoming	300	D-62-291	Original: found
NP-2573	Sprogel, John	3 APR 1769		Muncy, Lycoming	300	D-62-292	Original: Signed
NP-2574	Siewright, George	3 APR 1769	Northeast Branch Susquehanna River at Mahoning	LD: Luzerne	300		Original: found
NP-2575	Stapler, Stephen	3 APR 1769		Loyalsock & Hepburn, Lycoming	300	D-63-98 C-176-152	(r9 JUL 1782)Thomas Riche Original: found
NP-2576	McNutt, John	3 APR 1769	Northumberland	Centre - Bald Eagle Creek, Clinton/ LD: Centre	300	A-32-189	Samuel Power Original: found
NP-2577	Queen, Daniel	3 APR 1769		Unity, Westmoreland	300	D-62-293 D-62-294	Original: Signed
NP-2578	Reese, Catharine	3 APR 1769		Buffalo, Union/ LD: Buffalo, Union	300	D-62-260 C-187-89 C-187-90 C-129-19 C-76-274	(r13 JUN 1831)Jacob Renchler/(r11 FEB 1834)R. Loury/(p27 JUN 1870)George Hirsh Original: found

Table 6 - New Purchase Applications (1769-1773)

Number	Applicant	Date	Orig. Place	Later Place	Acres	Survey	Neighbors, Notes, etc.
NP-2579	Grant, Alexander	3 APR 1769		Northeast Branch Susquehanna River, Northumberland	50	A-11-77	(r12 JAN 1775)Jacob Schauffner Original: found
NP-2580	Slack, Abraham	3 APR 1769	Northampton	near Nanticoke, Luzerne	300	B-496 C-143-265	(r14 APR 1783)John M. Nesbitt Original: found
NP-2581	Davison, John	3 APR 1769	Fishing Creek, North Branch Susquehanna River	LD: Columbia	300		Original: Signed
NP-2582	Waddell, William	3 APR 1769	Bedford	Loyalhanna Creek, Westmoreland	300	C-144-44	(r1 APR 1788)John M. Ready Original: found
NP-2583	Nidok, Christian	3 APR 1769	Mahanoy Creek, Berks	LD: Columbia	300		Original: found
NP-2584	Alston, Joseph Jr.	3 APR 1769		Wilkins, Allegheny	300	B-23-1	Original: found
NP-2585	Caghel, Isaac	3 APR 1769		Derry, Westmoreland	300	C-53-16	(r23 SEP 1790)Abraham Cahill Original: found
NP-2586	Sampson, John	3 APR 1769		Franklin, Westmoreland	300	A-41-50	(r3 MAR 1783)Dan Roberdeau, Esq. Original: found
NP-2587	Hoover, John	3 APR 1769	Warriors Run	LD: Northumberland	300		Stophel Ulrich/William Drewry Original: found
NP-2588	Holodey, John Jr.	3 APR 1769	Bald Eagle Creek	LD: Centre/ [Holden in LD]	200		Original: found
NP-2589	Keagy, Abraham	3 APR 1769	East Branch Susquehanna River	LD: Luzerne	300		Martin Bear Original: found
NP-2590	Ewing, Rachel	3 APR 1769		Mahoning, Montour/ LD: Luzerne	300	F-235	Original: found
NP-2591	Chambers, Joseph	3 APR 1769	Bald Eagle Creek	LD: Centre	300		Original: found
NP-2592	Smith, Peter	3 APR 1769		Hempfield, Westmoreland/ LD: Westmoreland	300	A-29-51	Boston Frederick Original: found

Table 6 - New Purchase Applications (1769-1773)

Number	Applicant	Date	Orig. Place	Later Place	Acres	Survey	Neighbors, Notes, etc.
NP-2593	Miller, James	3 APR 1769	Mill Creek	LD: Luzerne	150		Original: found
NP-2594	Grant, Alexander	3 APR 1769		Augusta, Northumberland	300	C-157-172	(r26 APR 1782)--- Parr & --- Roes Original: Signed
NP-2595	Yearl, John	3 APR 1769		Versailles, Allegheny & North Huntingdon, Westmoreland	300	C-29-104 C-29-105 C-220-114 115	(r20 MAR 1826)John Cavitt/(r27 FEB 1829)John Stewert Original: found
NP-2596	Shaffer, Nicholas	3 APR 1769	Northumberland	Catawissa, Columbia	300	A-18-290 O-217	(r2 MAR 1789)George Hughes/[see caveat] Original: found
NP-2597	Field, Robert	3 APR 1769		Nippenose, Lycoming	300	D-62-295	Original: found
NP-2598	Lasher, Abraham	3 APR 1769		Unity, Westmoreland	300	D-57-267 C-109-294	(r12 DEC 1787)/[see caveat] Original: found
NP-2599	Cochran, John	3 APR 1769		Salem, Westmoreland	300	D-62-296	Original: found
NP-2600	Snively, John	3 APR 1769	Cumberland	Youghiogheny River, Fayette	300	A-82-137	--- Virgin/--- Pearsall/(r25 JAN 1786)Andrew Arnold Original: found
NP-2601	Pickert, Conrad	3 APR 1769		East Branch Susquehanna River, Luzerne/ LD: Luzerne	300	X-166	Josiah Heath Original: found
NP-2602	Touch, Thomas	3 APR 1769		Fishing Creek, Columbia	300	A-228	Original: found
NP-2603	Hutchison, Joseph	3 APR 1769	Berks	Washington, Lycoming	300	D-62-297	Original: found
NP-2604	McCallister, James	3 APR 1769		on Ligonier - Kittanning path, Armstrong	300	A-13-282	(r10 JUN 1791)Andrew Sharp Original: found
NP-2605	Hazlehurst, Isaac	3 APR 1769	Columbia	Derry, Montour	300	C-543	(r11 DEC 1827)John Morrison Original: found
NP-2606	Meeks, Isack	3 APR 1769	Cumberland	branch of Redstone Creek, Fayette	300	C-1-83	John Davey/(r20 JUL 1773)Thomas Brownfield Original: found

Table 6 - New Purchase Applications (1769-1773)

Number	Applicant	Date	Orig. Place	Later Place	Acres	Survey	Neighbors, Notes, etc.
NP-2607	Munro, Donald	3 APR 1769	Cumberland	East Branch Monongahela River, Allegheny	300	B-1-105	Robert Tompson/(r21 DEC 1787)Samuel Mackey & Stephen Bayard & Elizabeth Bayard [his wife] Original: found
NP-2608	Preator, Henry	3 APR 1769		Versailles & Plum, Allegheny	300	D-62-186	Col. Read Original: found
NP-2609	Morris, Hannah	3 APR 1769	Chillisquaque Creek	LD: Northumberland	300		Original: found
NP-2610	Thomas, George Jr.	3 APR 1769		Forbes Road, Westmoreland	300	C-234-171	Robert Laughlin/(r23 MAR 1786)John Thomas Original: Signed
NP-2611	Stover, Martin	3 APR 1769	Berks	Loyalsock, Lycoming	300	D-62-298	Original: Signed
NP-2612	Campbell, George	3 APR 1769		near Mahoning, Montour/ LD: Montour	200		George Sievright Original: found
NP-2613	Knowles, William	3 APR 1769	Bald Eagle Creek	LD: Clinton/ Centre	300		Weldon Parsons Original: found
NP-2614	Allison, Robert	3 APR 1769		Conemaugh River, Westmoreland	300	C-12-108	(r9 FEB 1786)James Beard Original: found
NP-2615	Richards, Samuel	3 APR 1769		Washington, Lycoming/ LD: Lycoming	300	D-56-220 X-132	Original: found
NP-2616	Morris, John	3 APR 1769	Cedar Run, West Branch Susquehanna River	LD: Centre	300		Original: found
NP-2617	Blaine, Rebecka	3 APR 1769		Huntingdon, Westmoreland	300	D-57-249 D-62-282 D-64-213 A-55-223	Ephraim Blaine/(r25 APR 1786) Original: found
NP-2618	Ritchey, John	3 APR 1769		Wilkins & Plum, Allegheny	300	D-64-104 C-232-145 C-232-151	(r4 DEC 1811)Emanuel Stotler Original: found
NP-2619	Eyman, Jacob	3 APR 1769		LD: Centre	300		Christian Been Original: found
NP-2620	Murray, Alexander	3 APR 1769	Berks	Nippenose, Lycoming	300	A-37-126	John Kelso/(r14 MAY 1816)Joseph Clark Original: found

Table 6 - New Purchase Applications (1769-1773)

Number	Applicant	Date	Orig. Place	Later Place	Acres	Survey	Neighbors, Notes, etc.
NP-2621	Stephen, Ann	3 APR 1769		Nippenose, Lycoming	300	D-62-299	Original: found
NP-2622	Yost, Peter	3 APR 1769	West Branch Susquehanna River	LD: Clinton/ Centre	300		Original: found
NP-2623	Rudolph, Adam	3 APR 1769	East Branch Susquehanna River above Wyoming	LD: Luzerne	300		Martin Akerman/John Wolf Original: found
NP-2624	Miller, Thomas	3 APR 1769	Holland Run	LD: Centre	60		George Gabriel Original: found
NP-2625	Lidlie, William	3 APR 1769	Fishing Creek	LD: Columbia	300		Original: found
NP-2626	Waddell, Francis	3 APR 1769		Blacklick, Indiana/ LD: Blacklick, Indiana	300	A-5-7 A-5-8 A-5-9 C-51-270 C-41-214 A-5-110 C-118-84 C-119-250 C-128-99 C-161-22	Joseph Armstrong/John Culbertsun/James Armstrong/(r7 JUN 1828)John Loughry/(r23 MAR 1829)D. Earhart/(r28 MAR 1831)William Earhart/(r15 FEB 1849)John Loughry/(p4 OCT 1864)William Laurence/(p2 SEP 1875)Francis McConnell Original: found
NP-2627	Hodgson, Peter	3 APR 1769		North Huntingdon, Westmoreland	300	N-213	James Pearson/(r24 APR 1807)George Morgan Original: found
NP-2628	Baskins, William	3 APR 1769		Turbot, Northumberland	300	C-75-102	(r24 MAR 1788)Thomas Hamilton Original: Signed
NP-2629	McColester, Archibald Jr.	3 APR 1769		Hempfield, Westmoreland	300	D-62-300	Original: found
NP-2630	Taylor, Robert	3 APR 1769	Berks	Washington, Lycoming	300	D-62-286	Original: Signed by William Taylor
NP-2631	Douglass, William	3 APR 1769		Ligonier, Westmoreland/ LD: Ligonier, Westmoreland	300	D-62-287 D-62-288	Original: found
NP-2632	Hare, Abraham	3 APR 1769		Muncy Creek, Lycoming	300	D-62-289	Original: found

Table 6 - New Purchase Applications (1769-1773)

Number	Applicant	Date	Orig. Place	Later Place	Acres	Survey	Neighbors, Notes, etc.
NP-2633	Hoff, Thomas	3 APR 1769		Howard, Centre	300	A-44-292	John Miller/(r19 FEB 1846)John Harris & William Harris Original: found
NP-2634	Beaty, James Sr.	3 APR 1769		Huntingdon, Westmoreland/ LD: Westmoreland	300	D-62-261 D-55-40	John Beatty Original: found
NP-2635	Sims, William	3 APR 1769		Turbot, Northumberland	300	D-62-262	Original: found
NP-2636	Johnston, Thomas	3 APR 1769	Bald Eagle Creek	LD: Centre	300		[see caveat] Original: found
NP-2637	Houston, Jane	3 APR 1769	Berks	Chillisquaque Creek, Montour/ LD: Columbia	300	D-55-103	James Pobjea/Col. Francis Original: found
NP-2638	Montgomery, Hugh	3 APR 1769		Huntingdon, Westmoreland	300	C-151-92	(r5 AUG 1788)Samuel Mann Original: found
NP-2639	Louch, Elizabeth	3 APR 1769	Brushy Creek branch of Bald Eagle Creek	LD: Centre	300		Original: found
NP-2640	Galley, James	3 APR 1769	Northumberland	White Deer, Union	300	B-23-32	[see Northumberland warrant #291] Original: found
NP-2641	Rees, Thomas	3 APR 1769	Chillisquaque Creek	LD: Northumberland	300		Col. Francis Original: found
NP-2642	Harwick, Anthony	3 APR 1769	North Branch Moony Creek	LD: Lycoming	300		Original: found
NP-2643	Killcrese, Robert	3 APR 1769	Berks	Washington, Lycoming	300	D-62-263	Original: found
NP-2644	Murphy, Francis	3 APR 1769		Washington, Lycoming	300	D-62-264	B. Fearis Original: found
NP-2645	Jack, Patrick	3 APR 1769	Bald Eagle Creek	LD: Centre	300		Original: found
NP-2646	Lea, Rebecca	3 APR 1769		Loyalsock, Lycoming	300	D-62-265	Original: found
NP-2647	Rohrer, Christian	3 APR 1769	Northumberland	East Branch Susquehanna River, Bradford or Luzerne/ LD: Luzerne/ Bradford	300	X-133	Original: found

Table 6 - New Purchase Applications (1769-1773)

Number	Applicant	Date	Orig. Place	Later Place	Acres	Survey	Neighbors, Notes, etc.
NP-2648	McCurday, James	3 APR 1769		West Wheatfield, Indiana	300	C-84-202	Robert Gibb/Robert Hinkson/(r7 DEC 1785)Henry Hise Original: signed
NP-2649	Johnstone, Jadiah	3 APR 1769		Redstone Creek, Fayette	300	C-193-247	John Johnston/(r1 APR 1788)Samuel Stephens Original: found
NP-2650	McConnell, William (son of Robert)	3 APR 1769		Elizabeth, Allegheny	300	Y-250	Andrew McMeans/(r16 DEC 1811)George Shields Original: found
NP-2651	Hews, Josiah	3 APR 1769		West Branch Susquehanna River, Lycoming/ LD: Lycoming	300	A-36-18	Original: found
NP-2652	Grame, Thomas	3 APR 1769	Bedford	Jacobs Creek, Fayette	300	D-9-225	Ann Fitzgerald/(r31 MAR 1772)James Young, Esq. Original: found
NP-2653	Plenge, George	3 APR 1769		Allegheny, Westmoreland	300	X-167 C-31-243 C-29-128 C-20-198 C-104-243 C-17-251	(r15 JAN 1823)George T. Crawford/(r21 DEC 1826)Robert Culbertson/(r18 OCT 1837)Thomas Boyd/(r8 APR 1851)Peter Kaple & John Kaple/(r18 OCT 1851)George Bovard Original: found
NP-2654	Sproat, David	3 APR 1769	North Branch Susquehanna River	LD: Luzerne	300		Original: found
NP-2655	Steel, William	3 APR 1769	White Deer Creek & Susquehanna River	LD: Union	300		William Blyth Original: found
NP-2656	Bready, Joseph	3 APR 1769		North Huntingdon, Westmoreland	300	D-62-271	Original: found
NP-2657	Baskins, James	3 APR 1769		Turbot, Northumberland	300	D-57-41	(r19 MAR 1788)James Espy/[see caveat] Original: found
NP-2658	Baird, William	3 APR 1769		Plum & Versailles, Allegheny	300	B-23-2	Original: found
NP-2659	Yearly, Thomas	3 APR 1769		West Buffalo, Union	300	D-62-272	Original: found

Table 6 - New Purchase Applications (1769-1773)

Number	Applicant	Date	Orig. Place	Later Place	Acres	Survey	Neighbors, Notes, etc.
NP-2660	Rawle, John Jr.	3 APR 1769	Northumberland	Wyoming - Tunkhannock Creek, Lackawanna	300	A-64-90	Sylvanus Okeley/(r22 APR 1782)--- White & --- Roberts Original: found
NP-2661	Pearce, Elisha	3 APR 1769		Redstone Creek, Fayette	300	C-173-63	John Johnston/(r12 JUN 1789) Original: found
NP-2662	Wallace, Peter	3 APR 1769		Ligonier, Westmoreland	300	C-37-224	(r20 MAR 1817)Nicolas Chapman Original: found
NP-2663	Muchmore, Shedrick	3 APR 1769		Ligonier, Westmoreland	300	F-242	(r21 MAR 1866)Mary E. Darlington/[see caveat] Original: found
NP-2664	Robeson, Richard	3 APR 1769		Nippenose, Lycoming	300	D-62-273	Original: found
NP-2665	Maus, Frederick (living in the City of Phildelphia)	3 APR 1769	Berks	Mahoning Creek, Montour	300	C-179-34	Phillip Maus/(r10 AUG 1774) Original: found
NP-2666	Askey, Robert	3 APR 1769	Fishing Creek	LD: Columbia	300		Original: Signed by Thomas Askey
NP-2667	Biddle, Charles	3 APR 1769	Berks	Loyalsock, Lycoming	300	D-62-274	Original: found
NP-2668	Dixon, John	3 APR 1769		Derry, Westmoreland	300	B-23-33 B-23-34	Original: found
NP-2669	Patton, Richard	3 APR 1769		Nanticoke Creek, Luzerne/ LD: Luzerne	300	A-34-38	Original: found
NP-2670	Dwire, Thomas	3 APR 1769	Berks	Chillisquaque Creek, Montour/ LD: Columbia	300	H-485	Jane Houston Original: found
NP-2671	Andres, Michael	3 APR 1769	Flint Creek, West Branch Susquehanna River	LD: Lycoming/ Union	300		Theobold Miller Original: found
NP-2672	Hudson, John	3 APR 1769		Allegheny, Cambria	300	A-44-91	--- Hart/John Price/(r5 MAY 1810)D. R. Barton Original: found
NP-2673	Davison, James	3 APR 1769	Westmoreland	Indiana	300	C-44-236	(r16 MAR 1791)Elias Davison Original: Signed
NP-2674	Rannels, John Jr.	3 APR 1769		Fairfield, Westmoreland	300	P-151 C-215-205 C-215-212	(r12 FEB 1831)T. Trimble/(12 FEB 1831)T. Trimble Original: found

Table 6 - New Purchase Applications (1769-1773)

Number	Applicant	Date	Orig. Place	Later Place	Acres	Survey	Neighbors, Notes, etc.
NP-2675	Beeler, Christopher	3 APR 1769	Cumberland	Tyrone, Fayette/ LD: Tyrone, Fayette	300	D-62-275	Joseph Beeler Original: found
NP-2676	Floyd, William	3 APR 1769		West Branch Susquehanna River, Northumberland/ LD: Centre	300	D-46-73	Original: found
NP-2677	Scot, David	3 APR 1769		Chartiers, Allegheny	300	C-52-222	Capt. Alexander McKee/(r1 JAN 1816)William Findley, Esq. Original: found
NP-2678	Weiser, John & John Creme	3 APR 1769	Muncy Creek	LD: Lycoming	300		Original: found
NP-2679	Ray, Thomas	3 APR 1769		Plum & Wilkins, Allegheny & Westmoreland	300	D-62-187 B-23-3	Original: found
NP-2680	Rees, Able	3 APR 1769	Berks	West Buffalo, Union	300	D-57-294 C-96-182	(r13 APR 1804)Peter Jordan Original: found
NP-2681	Sharron, William Jr.	3 APR 1769		Spring, Centre/ LD: Spring, Centre	300	X-145 X-146 X-147 C-211-250 C-101-2	James Sharon/(r17 APR 1835)William A. Thomas/(r5 DEC 1837)S. C. Harris Original: Signed
NP-2682	Bright, Michael	3 APR 1769	East Branch Susquehanna River	LD: Columbia	300		Original: found
NP-2683	Reed, Joseph	3 APR 1769	Berks	Buffalo, Lycoming	300	D-62-276	Original: found
NP-2684	Beatty, Johnston	3 APR 1769		Plum, Allegheny	300	A-44-281 A-44-282 A-44-283	(r13 MAR 1839)S. Cunningham/(r15 JUN 1839)William Highby Original: found
NP-2685	Russell, William	3 APR 1769		Derry, Westmoreland	300	D-62-290 D-60-259 A-85-236	(r7 DEC 1818)Peter Wallace Original: found
NP-2686	Johnston, John	3 APR 1769		North Huntingdon, Westmoreland	300	A-52-132 C-144-253	(r3 JAN 1828)S. Mayes Original: found
NP-2687	Horning, Mickel	3 APR 1769		Buffalo, Union	200	D-62-277	Original: found

Table 6 - New Purchase Applications (1769-1773)

Number	Applicant	Date	Orig. Place	Later Place	Acres	Survey	Neighbors, Notes, etc.
NP-2688	Hoover, George	3 APR 1769		Muncy Creek Twp., Lycoming	300	D-62-278	Original: found
NP-2689	Hughes, Thomas	3 APR 1769	Northumberland	Fishing Creek, Columbia	300	O-31	(r17 SEP 1779)Evan Owen Original: found
NP-2690	Fine, John	3 APR 1769	Northumberland	Black Hole Creek, Lycoming	300	G-385	Benjamin Helm/(r9 AUG 1781)William Govert, Esq. Original: found
NP-2691	Heath, Josiah	3 APR 1769		East Branch Susquehanna River, Luzerne/ LD: Wyoming	300	Z-68	Thomas Heath Original: found
NP-2692	Hunter, John	3 APR 1769		Nippenose, Lycoming	300	D-62-279	Original: found
NP-2693	Neeper, William	3 APR 1769	West Branch Susquehanna River 3 miles above Lycoming Creek	LD: Lycoming	300		Thomas Brown Original: found
NP-2694	Reed, Mungo	3 APR 1769	Catawissa Creek	LD: Columbia	50		Original: Signed
NP-2695	Yost, Jacob	3 APR 1769		Nippenose, Lycoming	300	D-62-280	Original: found
NP-2696	Montgomery, Jane	3 APR 1769		Hartley, Union	300	D-60-230 C-152-59	(r15 MAR 1791)Samuel McClay, Esq. Original: found
NP-2697	Burn, Christian	3 APR 1769	branch of Penns Creek	LD: Centre	300		Peter Burn Original: found
NP-2698	Shute, Joseph	3 APR 1769	Berks	Loyalsock, Lycoming	300	D-62-266	Original: found
NP-2699	Simpson, Andrew	3 APR 1769	Cumberland	Conemaugh, Indiana/ LD: Conemaugh, Indiana	300	A-14-273 A-14-274 A-31-264 C-204-146	(r29 SEP 1789)William Crawford/(r20 MAR 1817)J. Smith & John Robinson Original: found
NP-2700	Summers, Martin (of Philadelphia)	3 APR 1769	Cumberland	Penn, Union/ LD: Penn, Snyder	300	D-62-267	Original: found
NP-2701	Reed, Robert	3 APR 1769		Derry, Westmoreland	300	D-62-268	John Palmer/William Guthery Original: found
NP-2702	Irwin, James	3 APR 1769		Hempfield, Westmoreland	300	C-11-56	(r24 FEB 1824)Benjamin Allsworth/[see caveat] Original: found

Table 6 - New Purchase Applications (1769-1773)

Number	Applicant	Date	Orig. Place	Later Place	Acres	Survey	Neighbors, Notes, etc.
NP-2703	Christy, Thomas Jr.	3 APR 1769		Chartiers Creek, Allegheny	300	C-61-221	--- Grenow/John Irwin/Andrew Robinson/(r15 FEB 1813)James Glenn Original: found
NP-2704	Askey, James	3 APR 1769		Unity, Westmoreland	300	D-62-269 D-62-270	John Frazer Original: Signed by Thomas Askey
NP-2705	Wainwright, John	3 APR 1769		Mill Creek Branch of Loyalhanna Creek, Westmoreland	300	A-29-28	Original: found
NP-2706	Clark, John Sr.	3 APR 1769	East Branch Susquehanna River at Fishing Creek	LD: Columbia	200		Original: Signed
NP-2707	Smith, Peter	3 APR 1769	Red Bank Creek	LD: Clarion/ Allegheny/ Armstrong	300		Ludwig Derr Original: found
NP-2708	Thomas, John	3 APR 1769		Nippenose, Lycoming	300	D-62-250	Neetimis [an Indian] Original: found
NP-2709	Ralins, Edward	3 APR 1769	Cumberland	Muddy Creek, Greene/ LD: Cumberland, Greene	300	X-134	Jacob Vonmeter Original: found
NP-2710	Baird, Samuel	3 APR 1769		Derry, Westmoreland	300	C-17-106	Catanian Path/(r10 MAR 1806)John Baird/[see caveat] Original: found
NP-2711	Dennis, Jean	3 APR 1769	Cumberland	Berks - White Deer, Union	300	D-56-50	William Pusey/[same land as NP-2122 to John Currie] Original: found
NP-2712	Blecker, Peter	3 APR 1769	Northumberland	Centre or Bald Eagle, Clinton	300	A-34-15	Original: found
NP-2713	Neil, William	3 APR 1769	Berks	White Deer, Union	300	D-62-241	Original: found
NP-2714	Elliott, Jean	3 APR 1769		Quemahoning, Somerset	300	C-176-179	Skagoe [an Indian]/(r24 AUG 1784)John Rhoads Original: found
NP-2715	Kelso, William	3 APR 1769	Warriors Run	LD: Turbot, Northumberland	300		Original: found

Table 6 - New Purchase Applications (1769-1773)

Number	Applicant	Date	Orig. Place	Later Place	Acres	Survey	Neighbors, Notes, etc.
NP-2716	Prather, Thomas	3 APR 1769		Plum, Allegheny	200	B-23-4	Original: Signed
NP-2717	Morris, Anthony	3 APR 1769		Augusta, Northumberland	250	C-143-275	(r5 SEP 1788)John Nixon & Alexander Foster Original: found
NP-2718	Herold, Peter	3 APR 1769		White Deer, Union	300	A-35-73 A-35-74 C-133-184	(r10 JAN 1811)Thomas McGuire/(r20 JUN 1814)Jesse Yocum Original: found
NP-2719	Rhoads, Hannah	3 APR 1769		Greene/ LD: Wayne	300		Samuel Rhoads, Jr. Original: found
NP-2720	Boren, Peter	3 APR 1769	Berks	Kelly, Union	300	D-62-242	Original: found
NP-2721	Achert, John	3 APR 1769	Cumberland	Buffalo, Union	250	D-62-243	Original: found
NP-2722	Row, Martin Jr.	3 APR 1769	Cumberland	Penn, Northumberland	300	B-13-221	George Row/(r6 JUL 1784)Phillip Moyer Original: found
NP-2723	Schneider, Abraham	3 APR 1769		Kelly, Union	300	D-62-244	Original: Signed in German script (on back) by Christian Schneideer
NP-2724	Sharon, Hugh	3 APR 1769		White Deer, Union	300	D-62-223 A-64-88	(r26 JUN 1782)John Weitzell Original: Signed
NP-2725	McKinzey, William	3 APR 1769		Donegal, Westmoreland	300	C-29-73	Philip Harmon/Thomas Campbell/(r4 FEB 1825)Thomas Campbell Original: found
NP-2726	Mackey, William	3 APR 1769		Muncy Creek Twp., Lycoming	300	D-62-245	Original: found
NP-2727	Wallis, Francis	3 APR 1769		White Deer, Union	300	D-62-251	Original: found
NP-2728	Beatty, John	3 APR 1769	Berks	Buffalo, Union	300	D-56-72	[same land as NP-2336 to Peter Bragth] Original: found
NP-2729	Creigh, John	3 APR 1769		Loyalsock, Lycoming	300	D-62-252	Robert Long Original: Signed
NP-2730	Macmurtry, David	3 APR 1769		Kelly, Union	300	D-62-253	George Blyth Original: found
NP-2731	Beatty, Henry Jr.	3 APR 1769		North Huntingdon, Westmoreland	300	D-62-254	[see caveat] Original: found
NP-2732	Blare, John	3 APR 1769	Northumberland	Buffalo, Union	300	C-7-89	John Golespy/(r16 AUG 1774) Original: found
NP-2733	Zimmerman, Stovel	3 APR 1769	Muncy Creek	LD: Lycoming	300		Original: found

Table 6 - New Purchase Applications (1769-1773)

Number	Applicant	Date	Orig. Place	Later Place	Acres	Survey	Neighbors, Notes, etc.
NP-2734	Robins, Teackle	3 APR 1769		Washington, Lycoming/ LD: Lycoming	300	D-56-241 D-62-194 D-62-255	Original: found
NP-2735	Mitchele, William	3 APR 1769	Berks	Washington, Lycoming	200	D-62-256	Original: found
NP-2736	St. Clair, Arthur	3 APR 1769		Ligonier, Westmoreland/ LD: Westmoreland	300	Q-103	(p8 MAR 1870)Elizabeth F. Denny Original: found
NP-2737	Hill, Mager	3 APR 1769		Mt. Pleasant, Westmoreland	300	D-62-257 D-62-258	William Proctor Original: found
NP-2738	Brown, James	3 APR 1769		Wayne, Lycoming		D-62-259	Original: Signed by William Brown
NP-2739	McCroskey, Samuel	3 APR 1769		Youghiogheny River, Westmoreland	300	M-233	Hugh Mercer/(r26 FEB 1771)Hugh Mercer [of Fredericksburg, VA] Original: found
NP-2740	Altman, Anthony	3 APR 1769	Cumberland	Conemaugh River below Blacklick Creek, Indiana	300	C-75-151	(r6 AUG 1788)John Herrold Original: found
NP-2741	Johnston, Robert (farmer)	3 APR 1769		Dirty Camp Run, Allegheny	300	A-38-191	William Beatty/(r2 MAR 1789) Original: found
NP-2742	Chapman, George	3 APR 1769		Buffalo, Union	300	D-62-260	Original: Signed
NP-2743	Walsh, David	3 APR 1769	Cumberland	Pigeon Creek, Washington/ LD: Washington	300	A-29-26	Original: found
NP-2744	Campbell, William	3 APR 1769		Lawrence, Clearfield	300	D-62-246	Original: found
NP-2745	McClintock, John	3 APR 1769	Briar Run, North Branch Susquehanna River	LD: Columbia	300		Original: found
NP-2746	Sweger, George	3 APR 1769		Derry, Westmoreland	300	D-62-247	Original: Signed
NP-2747	Gebhart, Henry	3 APR 1769		Muncy, Lycoming	200	D-62-248	Phlillip Wolfart Original: found
NP-2748	Johnston, John Sr.	3 APR 1769		Pitt, Allegheny	300	B-23-5	Mr. Elliot Original: found

Table 6 - New Purchase Applications (1769-1773)

Number	Applicant	Date	Orig. Place	Later Place	Acres	Survey	Neighbors, Notes, etc.
NP-2749	Jenkins, Mary	3 APR 1769	Fishing Creek	LD: Columbia	300		Original: found
NP-2750	Young, John	3 APR 1769		Ligonier, Westmoreland	300	D-62-249	Original: found
NP-2751	Hays, John Jr.	3 APR 1769	Berks	Union, Union	300	D-62-230	Original: found
NP-2752	Scott, Samuel	3 APR 1769	Sewickley Creek	South Huntingdon, Westmoreland	300	C-191-36 C-191-14	Capt,. Thompson/(r9 MAR 1831)William Pinkerton & Thomas Robertson Original: found
NP-2753	McCallister, John Jr.	3 APR 1769		Salem, Westmoreland	300	M-175	Mr. Mackey/(r10 APR 1788)John Moore, Esq. Original: found
NP-2754	Bloom, Ephraim	3 APR 1769	Fishing Creek	LD: Columbia	300		John Rinker/William Lidlie Original: found
NP-2755	Breden, Nathaniel	3 APR 1769	Northumberland	Mahoning Creek, Montour	300	C-176-72	(r27 OCT 1772)William Ross Original: found
NP-2756	McLees, William	3 APR 1769		White Deer, Union	300	D-62-229	Original: found
NP-2757	Schneider, Jacob	3 APR 1769		White Deer, Union	300	C-134-146 C-134-147 C-134-144 C-134-145	Abraham Schneider/(r17 JUN 1805)William Nassey Original: found
NP-2758	Weaver, Jacob	3 APR 1769	between Wyalusing & Wyoming	LD: Bradford	300		John Stephens Original: found
NP-2759	Johnston, Martha	3 APR 1769	Northumberland	Bald Eagle, Centre or Clinton	300	C-109-140	Thomas Johnston/(r16 JUL 1784)Robert Lylbuin Original: found
NP-2760	Johnston, Dr. Robert	3 APR 1769		Ligonier, Westmoreland	300	D-62-228	Boston Frederick Original: found
NP-2761	Menoch, William	3 APR 1769	Bedford	Pitt, Allegheny	300	A-53-281 A-53-282 A-53-283 A-53-284 X-232 X-233 X-234	(r21 JUN 1809)Thomas Wilson & M. Jamison & Mary Donaldson/(r21 JUN 1809)Matthew Jamison & Jane Taylor/(r21 JUN 1809)Thomas Wilson/(r21 JUN 1809)Matthew Jamison & Mary Donaldson Original: found
NP-2762	White, James	3 APR 1769		North Huntingdon, Westmoreland	300	D-62-227	Original: found

Table 6 - New Purchase Applications (1769-1773)

Number	Applicant	Date	Orig. Place	Later Place	Acres	Survey	Neighbors, Notes, etc.
NP-2763	Yost, Daniel	3 APR 1769	Berks	Nippenose, Lycoming	300	D-62-226	Original: found
NP-2764	Kelso, Thomas	3 APR 1769		Loyalsock, Lycoming	300	D-62-240	Original: found
NP-2765	Sympson, John (of Hanover)	3 APR 1769	Berks	Union, Union	300	D-62-219	[same land as NP-2816 to Samuel Shanks] Original: found
NP-2766	Corbett, John	3 APR 1769		White Deer, Union	300	D-62-239	Original: Signed
NP-2767	Caldwell, Thomas	3 APR 1769		Pitt & Hempfield, Westmoreland	300	A-77-175 A-77-178	(r15 JUN 1790)William Elliott/[see caveat] Original: found
NP-2768	Fitzgerald, Ann	3 APR 1769	Westmoreland	Youghiogheny River, Fayette	300	M-235	Samuel McCrosky/(r26 FEB 1771)Hugh Mercer [of Fredericksburg, VA] Original: found
NP-2769	Knox, Susanna	3 APR 1769		Blacklick, Indiana	200	B-23-23 B-23-47	Samuel Dickson/[see NP-2796] Original: found
NP-2770	Pickel, Henry	3 APR 1769	Berks	Buffalo, Union	300	D-56-127 D-56-129	[same land as NP-1518 to Edward Middleton]/[see NP-341] Original: found
NP-2771	Miller, John	3 APR 1769	Wyoming, Northampton	LD: Luzerne	300		George Miller Original: Missing
NP-2772	Perry, William Sr.	3 APR 1769		Sewickley Creek, Westmoreland	300	C-151-137	(r7 NOV 1788)Hugh Mitchell & Charles Mitchell Original: found
NP-2773	Clock, Jacob Jr.	3 APR 1769		East side Susquehanna River, Luzerne/ LD: Luzerne	300	Z-53	Conrad Clock Original: found
NP-2774	Krammer, Daniel	3 APR 1769		West Buffalo, Union	300	D-62-238	Original: found
NP-2775	Johnston, John Jr.	3 APR 1769		Plum, Allegheny/ LD: Plum, Allegheny	300	P-43 C-230-69 C-156-75	(r3 DEC 1823)H. Morrison/(fees paid7 NOV 1873)George M. Bowman/(p23 DEC 1873)William Spangler Original: found
NP-2776	Price, Lewis	3 APR 1769	Northeast Branch	LD: Columbia	200		Hugh McCullough Original: found
NP-2777	Leadly, George	3 APR 1769		Augusta, Northumberland/ LD: Shamokin, Northumberland	250	A-5-87 A-5-88	Samuel Davis/[see caveat] Original: found

Table 6 - New Purchase Applications (1769-1773)

Number	Applicant	Date	Orig. Place	Later Place	Acres	Survey	Neighbors, Notes, etc.
NP-2778	Carmalt, John	3 APR 1769	Berks	White Deer, Union	300	D-62-231 D-62-232 D-62-233 D-62-234 D-62-235 D-62-236 D-62-237	Jean Dennis Original: found
NP-2779	Klein, Philip	3 APR 1769	Berks	White Deer Creek, Union	300	D-62-224 D-62-225	Jacob Miller Original: Missing
NP-2780	Herold, Christopher	3 APR 1769		White Deer, Union	300	D-62-223	Original: Missing
NP-2781	Davis, Samuel	3 APR 1769		Augusta, Northumberland	250	L-293	Lawrence Kelly/(r5 JAN 1784)Law Keene Original: found
NP-2782	Weyland, George	3 APR 1769	at head of Sinking Spring at Chickelamis' Old Town	White Deer, Northumberland/ LD: White Deer, Union	300	W-269	Jacob Weyland/Chickelamis [an Indian]/[see caveat] Original: found
NP-2783	Harris, John	4 APR 1769		Hartley, Union/ LD: Hartley, Union	300	C-62-222 D-59-194 A-36-19 C-62-221 C-62-223	Edward Lee/John Turner/William Donan/Andrew Smith/(r20 NOV 1827)John Foster/[see caveat] Original: found
NP-2784	Rhoads, John Jr.	3 APR 1769	East Branch Susquehanna River	LD: Columbia	200		Robert Peters Original: Signed. With NP-2785.
NP-2785	Dodson, Richard	3 APR 1769	West Branch Susquehanna River	LD: Lycoming	200		Robert Peter/John Rhoads Original: Signed. With NP-2784.
NP-2786	Dodson, Samuel	3 APR 1769	East Branch Susquehanna River 7 miles below Nescopeck	LD: Columbia	200		Original: Signed
NP-2787	Rhoads, John Sr.	3 APR 1769	Robert Peter's Creek, 17 miles above Shamokin	LD: Columbia	200		Robert Peters Original: Signed
NP-2788	Glass, William (of Carlisle)	3 APR 1769	Lycoming	Bald Eagle, Clinton	300	D-56-211 C-131-79	Dr. Allison/(r23 JAN 1819)David Lush/[see caveat] Original: Signed
NP-2789	Carson, Samuel Jr. (of Philadelphia)	3 APR 1769	Bald Eagle Creek	LD: Centre	300		Original: Signed

Table 6 - New Purchase Applications (1769-1773)

Number	Applicant	Date	Orig. Place	Later Place	Acres	Survey	Neighbors, Notes, etc.
NP-2790	Armstrong, Frances	3 APR 1769		LD: Centre	300		Original: Signed
NP-2791	Vandecrift, Christopher	3 APR 1769	Bald Eagle Creek	LD: Centre	300		Original: Signed
NP-2792	Carson, Samuel Sr. (of Philadelphia)	3 APR 1769	Berks	Lycoming - Wayne, Clinton	300	D-62-222	Dr. Ewing Original: Signed
NP-2793	Vance, John	3 APR 1769		Salem, Westmoreland	300	A-21-143 A-21-144	Original: found
NP-2794	McConnall, James	3 APR 1769	Berks	Kelly, Lycoming (Union)	300	D-57-55	Barney Parson/[same land as NP-635 to Joseph Dobson] Original: found
NP-2795	Thompson, Alexander	3 APR 1769		Crabtree Run, Westmoreland	300	C-193-272	William McCutchen/James McCutchen/(r7 APR 1788)Moses Shaw Original: found
NP-2796	Bradford, Thomas	3 APR 1769		East Huntingdon, Westmoreland	300	D-62-221	Original: Signed
NP-2797	McCutchen, William	3 APR 1769		Salem, Westmoreland	300	D-57-279 D-57-280 C-140-150 A-69-196 A-69-197	Alexander Thompson/(r31 JAN 1814)Samuel McCutchen/(r4 NOV 1822)M. Kepple heirs Original: found
NP-2798	Miller, William	3 APR 1769		Derry, Westmoreland/ LD: Westmoreland	300	A-32-190 A-3-200	[see caveat] Original: found
NP-2799	Fleming, John (of New London)	3 APR 1769		Washington, Westmoreland	300	C-135-261	(r28 DEC 1814)A. McBrier Original: found
NP-2800	McCullough, James Jr.	3 APR 1769	West Branch Susquehanna River above McTowers Creek	LD: Northumberland/ Lycoming	300		Original: found
NP-2801	Lesley, William	3 APR 1769		Wilkins, Allegheny	300	D-60-203 C-148-89	(r30 MAR 1790)James O'Harra Original: found
NP-2802	McCully, George	3 APR 1769		Plum Creek, Allegheny	300	A-24-38	Richard Buttler/(r1 JUN 1789)Richard Buttler Original: found
NP-2803	McCully, Robert	4 APR 1769		Franklin, Westmoreland	300	D-62-210	Richard Buttler Original: found

Table 6 - New Purchase Applications (1769-1773)

Number	Applicant	Date	Orig. Place	Later Place	Acres	Survey	Neighbors, Notes, etc.
NP-2804	Chambers, James	4 APR 1769		Plum & Wilkins, Allegheny	300	B-23-6	Robert George Original: found
NP-2805	McCully, Hugh	4 APR 1769		Wilkins, Allegheny	300	D-60-203 C-148-88	Richard Butler/(r30 MAR 1790)James O'Harra Original: found
NP-2806	George, Robert	4 APR 1769		Plum, Allegheny	300	C-6-144	(r25 OCT 1790)Richard Buttler Original: found
NP-2807	Forguson, William (near Carlisle)	4 APR 1769		Unity, Westmoreland	300	D-62-208 D-62-209	Original: found
NP-2808	Hunter, James (of East Pennboro Township, Cumberland County)	5 APR 1769	Westmoreland	14 Mile Run, Allegheny	300	D-57-64 C-88-5	(r6 MAY 1790) Original: Signed
NP-2809	McDowell, Andrew	5 APR 1769		Fairfield, Westmoreland	300	Q-86	(r2 MAR 1837)John Blair Original: Signed
NP-2810	Cochran, Charles	5 APR 1769		Chillisquaque, Northumberland/ LD: Turbot, Northumberland	300	L-54 C-21-281	Jacob Hemerly/(r10 FEB 1804) Original: found
NP-2811	Leef, Henry	5 APR 1769	Northumberland	Buffalo, Union	300	C-84-28	John Harris/(r7 MAR 1811)Paul Fisher/[see caveat] Original: found
NP-2812	Colhoon, Andrew	5 APR 1769	Northumberland	Buffalo, Union	300	C-6-223	James McConnell/(r23 MAY 1791)Wendal Baker Original: found
NP-2813	Colhoon, Robert	5 APR 1769		Buffalo Valley, Union	300	C-102-133	Andrew Calhoon/(r4 FEB 1773)Jacob Keen Original: found
NP-2814	Alen, Joseph	5 APR 1769		Buffalo, Union	300	D-62-220 D-62-206 D-62-207	Original: found
NP-2815	Wargintin, Peter	5 APR 1769		Holland Run, Northumberland	300	C-50-285	(r11 FEB 1788)Dr. John Ewing Original: found
NP-2816	Shank, Samuel	5 APR 1769	Berks	Union, Union	300	D-62-218 D-62-219	--- Harris Original: found
NP-2817	Van Meter, Frederick	5 APR 1769	White Deer Creek	LD: Union	300		Original: found
NP-2818	Kylle, Samuel Jr.	5 APR 1769		Elizabeth, Allegheny	300	Z-242	James Smith/John Shanon/John Perry/(r23 SEP 1791)James Wilson Original: found

Table 6 - New Purchase Applications (1769-1773)

Number	Applicant	Date	Orig. Place	Later Place	Acres	Survey	Neighbors, Notes, etc.
NP-2819	Kyll, William	5 APR 1769		Elizabeth, Allegheny	300	D-62-188	William McConnell Original: found
NP-2820	Kyll, John	5 APR 1769		Elizabeth, Allegheny	300	Y-252	(r7 APR 1834)James Scott Original: found
NP-2821	McColman, Nicholas	5 APR 1769		Huntingdon, Westmoreland	300	C-234-160	(r2 JAN 1788)Cathrine Thompson Original: found
NP-2822	McConnell, Alexander	5 APR 1769		Huntingdon, Westmoreland	300	A-19-118	(r8 DEC 1787)Eli Coulter Original: found
NP-2823	Kyll, Joseph	5 APR 1769		Elizabeth, Allegheny	300	D-62-189	John Work Original: found
NP-2824	Work, John Jr.	5 APR 1769		Elizabeth, Allegheny	300	C-125-243	James Smith/John Kyll/(r13 MAY 1811)Matthew Henderson Original: found
NP-2825	McCrerry, Robert	5 APR 1769		Unity, Westmoreland	300	D-62-216 D-62-217	Original: Signed
NP-2826	Baker, Peter	5 APR 1769		Hempfield, Allegheny	300	A-34-102 A-34-103 A-34-104	(r31 DEC 1787)executors of William Thompson, deceased Original: found
NP-2827	Moore, John	5 APR 1769		Unity, Westmoreland	300	D-62-214 D-62-215	Original: found
NP-2828	McCreery, Andrew	5 APR 1769		Hempfield, Westmoreland	300	D-62-213	Original: Signed
NP-2829	Cox, Joseph	5 APR 1769		German, Fayette	300	D-62-212	Original: found
NP-2830	Rayl, William	5 APR 1769		Menallen, Fayette	300	D-62-211	John Hamilton/Ralph Hickenbottom Original: Signed
NP-2831	Wilson, James	5 APR 1769		Buffalo, Union	300	D-62-205	Original: Signed
NP-2832	McKee, John	5 APR 1769		Pitt, Westmoreland	300	A-61-225	John Carter/William McManemy(r16 JUN 1787) Original: found
NP-2833	McKee, Robert	5 APR 1769		Versailles, Allegheny	300	D-56-165 P-285	David McKee/(r16 APR 1829)Robert Sinclair Original: found
NP-2834	McKee, Thomas	5 APR 1769		Versailles, Allegheny/ LD: Allegheny	300	P-209	David McKee/James Tamson/[see NP-3339 for survey] Original: Signed by David McKee
NP-2835	Crawford, Effe	5 APR 1769	Monongahela River a mile from Georges Creek	LD: Greene	300		Original: Signed by William Crawford

Table 6 - New Purchase Applications (1769-1773)

Number	Applicant	Date	Orig. Place	Later Place	Acres	Survey	Neighbors, Notes, etc.
NP-2836	Stephenson, James	5 APR 1769	Youghiogheny River	LD: Fayette	300		John Riggs Original: found
NP-2837	Peal, William	5 APR 1769		South Huntingdon, Westmoreland	300	D-62-204	Joseph Beeler Original: found
NP-2838	Benat, William	5 APR 1769		Youghiogheny River, Fayette/ LD: Tyrone & Bullskin, Fayette	300		John Stephenson Original: found
NP-2839	Bell, Robert	5 APR 1769		Franklin, Fayette/ LD: Dunbar, Fayette	300	A-34-16	Original: found
NP-2840	Beeler, Joseph	5 APR 1769		South Huntingdon, Westmoreland	300	D-62-203	Original: found
NP-2841	Linn, Andrew	5 APR 1769	Bedford	Westmoreland - Washington, Fayette	300	D-62-201 D-62-202	Original: found
NP-2842	Lynn, James	5 APR 1769		Little Redstone Creek, Fayette	300	C-74-268	(r19 APR 1792)Margaret Hutton Original: found
NP-2843	Thompson, Nace	5 APR 1769		Dunlap Creek, Fayette	300	B-1-150	(r17 MAR 1783)Phillip Tanner Original: found
NP-2844	Petters, William	5 APR 1769		Monongahela River, Washington	300	I-508	(r27 JAN 1787)Neal Gillespie Original: found
NP-2845	Battom, Thomas	5 APR 1769		Springhill, Fayette	300	C-12-80	(r15 MAR 1786) Original: found
NP-2846	Johnston, William	5 APR 1769	Monongahela River below Georges Creek	LD: Monongahela, Greene	300		Effe Crawford Original: found
NP-2847	Linn, William	5 APR 1769		Monongahela River half a mile below Little Redstone Creek, Fayette	300	C-33-82	(r8 SEP 1796)Edward Cook, Esq. Original: found
NP-2848	Sweet, Benjamin	5 APR 1769		Spears Run, Westmoreland	300	A-10-313	(r14 NOV 1787)James Finley Original: found
NP-2849	Kellum, Phinis	5 APR 1769	Washington	Ten Mile Creek, Greene	300	D-151	(r25 JUL 1792)H. H. Brackenridge/[see caveat] Original: found

Table 6 - New Purchase Applications (1769-1773)

Number	Applicant	Date	Orig. Place	Later Place	Acres	Survey	Neighbors, Notes, etc.
NP-2850	Swearingan, Thomas Jr.	5 APR 1769		Union, Fayette	300	D-62-170	Original: found
NP-2851	Linn, Andrew Jr.	5 APR 1769		Redstone Creek, Fayette	300	B-4-217	(r29 MAR 1787) Original: found
NP-2852	Swearingan, Vann	5 APR 1769		Jefferson, Fayette	300	C-157-152 C-157-151 C-157-153	(r1 NOV 1809 & r30 JUL 1850)L. Merchand Original: found
NP-2853	Swearingan, Thomas Jr.	5 APR 1769		Monongahela Creek, Washington	300	A-15-247	(r27 FEB 1790) Original: found
NP-2854	Logan, Charles (of Cumberland County)	6 APR 1769	Youghiogheny River, Cumberland	LD: Westmoreland	300		--- Crawford Original: Signed
NP-2855	Campbell, William	6 APR 1769	Monongahela River 2.5 miles below Dunkard Creek	LD: Nicholson, Greene	300		Original: Signed with a mark "D" by Daniel Campbell
NP-2856	Campbell, Margaret	6 APR 1769	Monongahela River	LD: Nicholson, Greene	300		"Old" Gilmore Original: Signed with a mark "D" by Daniel Campbell
NP-2857	Byers, David	6 APR 1769		North Huntingdon, Westmoreland	300	D-70-128	Samuel Simison/Col. Clapham/--- Sinclair Original: found
NP-2858	McGregor, Alexander	6 APR 1769		Pitt, Westmoreland	300	C-144-40	(r27 MAR 1788)Robert McFarlane Original: found
NP-2859	Hyser, Thomas	6 APR 1769		Chartiers Creek, Washington	300	A-11-97 A-11-98	(r22 OCT 1788)Ephraim Blaine, Esq./[see caveat] Original: found
NP-2860	Byers, James Jr.	6 APR 1769	Washington	Monongahela River, Allegheny	300	D-200	(r24 DEC 1784)Ephraim Blaine, Esq./[see NP-3116]/[see caveat] Original: found
NP-2861	Austin, Nicholas	7 APR 1769	Northeast Branch Susquehanna River, a half mile above Roaring Creek	LD: Montour	300		Original: Signed by Benjamin Austin

Table 6 - New Purchase Applications (1769-1773)

Number	Applicant	Date	Orig. Place	Later Place	Acres	Survey	Neighbors, Notes, etc.
NP-2862	Ellicott, Joseph	7 APR 1769	Kiskiminitas Creek (Conemaugh River), Cumberland	LD: Armstrong	300		Thomas Austin Original: found
NP-2863	Cadwalader, Isaac	7 APR 1769		North Branch Susquehanna River, Northumberland above Ft. Augusta	300	C-143-207	(r12 NOV 1771)Alexander Nelson [of New York] Original: found
NP-2864	Knight, Joshua	7 APR 1769	Cumberland	Armstrong, Indiana	300	M-135	Jacob Paul/(r20 APR 1797)David Lenox Original: found
NP-2865	Cain, John	7 APR 1769	Northumberland	Sugar Valley, Centre	300	A-14-25	Mathew Conrad/(r15 NOV 1804)George Morgan Original: found
NP-2866	Tyson, Joseph	7 APR 1769	Northumberland	Sugar Valley, Centre	300	A-14-13	(r15 NOV 1804)George Morgan Original: found
NP-2867	Thomas, Enoch	7 APR 1769	Berks	Mahoning Creek, Montour	300	A-29-46	[see caveat] Original: found
NP-2869	Dugan, Clement Jr.	7 APR 1769	Delaware River		300		[Joining his fathers land] Original: found
NP-2870	Doyl, Edward	7 APR 1769	Northumberland	Sugar Valley, Centre	300	A-14-27	Joseph Tyson/(r15 NOV 1804)George Morgan Original: found
NP-2871	Robers, Lewis	7 APR 1769	Fishing Creek, North Branch Susquehanna River	LD: Columbia	300		Original: found
NP-2872	Lippingcott, Jacob	7 APR 1769	Fishing Creek	LD: Columbia	300		Original: found
NP-2873	Davis, Samuel	7 APR 1769		Turbot, Northumberland	300	D-70-143	Original: found
NP-2874	Dungan, Elias	7 APR 1769	North Branch Susquehanna River	LD: Columbia	300		Jeremiah Dungan [his brother] Original: found
NP-2875	Lloyd, Lewis	7 APR 1769	Northumberland	Sugar Valley, Centre	300	A-14-28	John Cain/(r15 NOV 1804)George Morgan Original: found
NP-2876	Roberts, John (of Milford, Bucks County)	7 APR 1769	Northumberland	Sugar Valley, Centre	300	A-14-29	Lewis Lloyd/(r15 NOV 1804)George Morgan Original: found

Table 6 - New Purchase Applications (1769-1773)

Number	Applicant	Date	Orig. Place	Later Place	Acres	Survey	Neighbors, Notes, etc.
NP-2877	Tyson, Rynear	7 APR 1769	Northumberland	Sugar Valley, Centre	300	A-14-30	(r15 NOV 1804)George Morgan Original: found
NP-2878	Austin, Thomas	7 APR 1769	Kiskiminitas Creek, Cumberland	LD: Allegheny, Westmoreland/ Armstrong	300		Benjamin Austin [his brother]/[see caveat] Original: found
NP-2879	Austin, Benjamin	7 APR 1769	Kiskiminitas Creek, Cumberland	LD: Allegheny, Westmoreland/ Armstrong	300		--- Warren/[see caveat] Original: found
NP-2880	Paul, Jacob	7 APR 1769	Cumberland	Armstrong, Indiana	300	C-138-165 C-138-166	(r20 APR 1797)David Lenox Original: found
NP-2881	Roberts, Charles	7 APR 1769	West Branch Fishing Creek	LD: Columbia	300		Jacob Lippencott Original: found
NP-2882	Dungan, Clement Sr.	7 APR 1769	Delaware River opposite Mongape		300		Original: found
NP-2883	Cain, Charles	7 APR 1769	North Branch Susquehanna River	LD: Columbia	300		Lewis Roberts Original: found
NP-2884	Solovan, Dennis	7 APR 1769	Berks	Shamokin, Northumberland	300	C-68-47 C-68-48	(r18 MAR 1818)Ebenezer Greenough Original: found
NP-2885	Cunrad, Mathew	7 APR 1769		Sugar Valley, Centre	300	A-14-26	Rynear Tyson/(r15 NOV 1804)George Morgan Original: found
NP-2886	Dungan, Jeremiah	7 APR 1769	North Branch Susquehanna River 10 miles above Fishing Creek	LD: Columbia	300		Noutimape [an Indian] Original: found
NP-2887	Logan, Daniel	7 APR 1769	West Branch Fishing Creek	LD: Columbia	300		Charles Roberts Original: found
NP-2888	Austin, Joseph	7 APR 1769	Berks	Shamokin, Northumberland	300	C-87-33	Dennis Solovans/(r1 AUG 1799)executors of Reuben Haines Original: found
NP-2889	Trautner, George	7 APR 1769		Unity, Westmoreland	300	D-70-242	Original: With NP-2890
NP-2890	Trautner, John	7 APR 1769		Derry, Columbia	300	W-262 W-263	Mr. Tilghman Original: With NP-2889
NP-2891	Bower, John George	7 APR 1769		Little Shamokin Creek, Northumberland	300	C-162-71	(r8 JAN 1773)John Musser Original: With NP-2892

Table 6 - New Purchase Applications (1769-1773)

Number	Applicant	Date	Orig. Place	Later Place	Acres	Survey	Neighbors, Notes, etc.
NP-2892	Benetsh, Lorentz	7 APR 1769	Shamokin Creek	LD: Columbia	300		John George Bower Original: With NP-2891
NP-2893	Campbell, John Jr.	7 APR 1769		Ligonier, Westmoreland	300	C-47-70	Thomas Jameson/James Elliott/Isaac Stimble/Samuel Shannon/(r21 MAR 1866)Mary C. Darlington Original: Signed with a mark "+"
NP-2894	Campbell, Daniel	7 APR 1769	east side Laurel Hill	LD: Somerset	300		--- Rogers Original: Signed with a mark "+" by John Campbell
NP-2895	Hendricks, James Sr.	7 APR 1769	Chartiers Creek	LD: Washington	300		Original: Includes a letter signed by applicant. With NP-2896 & 2897
NP-2896	Scholfield, George	7 APR 1769		Quemahoning, Somerset/ LD: Quemahoning, Somerset	300	C-22-25 C-147-132 C-147-133	Francis Campbell/(r6 MAY 1856)John Bowman/(p18 JUL 1870)Noah J. Miller Original: found
NP-2897	Dougal, Samuel	7 APR 1769		Quemahoning, Somerset	300	E-408	Keichne Pawling/George Scholfield/(r1 FEB 1839)D. Barnhart Original: found
NP-2898	Hain, Henry Adam	7 APR 1769	Rush Meadows, East Branch Susquehanna River	LD: Bradford	300		John Blaze Original: With NP-2899
NP-2899	Pauli, Christopher	7 APR 1769	Northumberland	Rush Meadows, East Branch Susquehanna River, Wyoming	300	C-7-56	Henry Adam Haine/(r22 APR 1782)William Brown Original: With NP-2898
NP-2900	Hain, Henry	7 APR 1769	Rush Meadows, East Branch Susquehanna River	LD: Bradford	300		John Wickware Original: found
NP-2901	Blaze, John	7 APR 1769	Rush Meadows, East Branch Susquehanna River	LD: Bradford	300		Michael Schimick Original: found
NP-2902	Schinick, Michael	7 APR 1769	Rush Meadows, above Wyalusing	LD: Bradford	300		John Wickware Original: found
NP-2903	Thompson, James	7 APR 1769	Cumberland	Quemahoning, Somerset	300	A-3-7	(r21 JAN 11800)David Holly Original: With NP-2904 - 2920

Table 6 - New Purchase Applications (1769-1773)

Number	Applicant	Date	Orig. Place	Later Place	Acres	Survey	Neighbors, Notes, etc.
NP-2904	Campbell, George	7 APR 1769	Cumberland	Blacklick, Indiana	300	A-23-24 C-113-209	(r13 MAR 1813)Samuel Riddle/(r27 JAN 1854)William Latemer & Tobias Banker/John Robinson Original: found
NP-2905	Thompson, John	7 APR 1769		Stoneycreek, Somerset/ LD: Somerset	300		Original: found
NP-2906	Christy, Thomas	7 APR 1769	Cumberland	Flat Run, Somerset/ LD: Somerset	300		John Thompson Original: found
NP-2907	Maunsel, William	7 APR 1769	Cumberland	Quemahoning, Somerset	300	A-3-24	(r21 JAN 1800)David Holly Original: found
NP-2908	Heath, William	7 APR 1769	Cumberland	LD: Quemahoning, Somerset	300		William Maunsel Original: found
NP-2909	Dougherty, James	7 APR 1769	Cumberland	Conemaugh, Cambria	300	A-20-280	(r8 AUG 1849)William E. Smith Original: found
NP-2910	Sinnett, Jacob	7 APR 1769	Cumberland	Jenner, Somerset/ LD: Somerset	300	A-31-128 C-122-148 C-221-172	James Dougherty/(r10 JAN 1845)Christopher Keim/(r20 MAY 1870)William A. Griffith Original: found
NP-2911	Husk, Jacob	7 APR 1769	Cumberland	Fairfield, Westmoreland	300	D-70-127	Original: found
NP-2912	Dalton, James	7 APR 1769	Cumberland	Conemaugh, Cambria/ LD: Cambria	300	D-70-116	Jacob Sinnet Original: found
NP-2913	Gurty, James	7 APR 1769	Cumberland	Fairfield, Westmoreland - Indiana	300	D-70-126	Jacob Husk Original: found
NP-2914	Dougherty, Cornelius	7 APR 1769	Cumberland	Conemaugh, Cambria/ LD: Conemaugh, Cambria	300	D-70-117	James Girty Original: found
NP-2915	Ormsby, John	7 APR 1769	Cumberland	Fairfield, Westmoreland	300	D-70-125	Original: found
NP-2916	Sinclair, Samuel	7 APR 1769	Cumberland	Fairfield, Westmoreland	300	D-70-139	John Ormsby Original: found
NP-2917	Burbige, Thomas	7 APR 1769	Cumberland	Conemaugh, Cambria	300	M-202	(r17 SEP 1794)William McNutt Original: found

Table 6 - New Purchase Applications (1769-1773)

Number	Applicant	Date	Orig. Place	Later Place	Acres	Survey	Neighbors, Notes, etc.
NP-2918	Doran, Nicholas	7 APR 1769	Cumberland	Brothers Valley Twp., Somerset	300	B-417	(r24 OCT 1837)Abraham Kerns Original: found
NP-2919	Flaherty, Patrick	7 APR 1769	Cumberland	Jenner, Somerset	300	A-1-223	Nicholas Donar/(r13 FEB 1837)George Graham [attorney] Original: found
NP-2920	McMannamy, William	7 APR 1769	Cumberland	Jenner, Somerset	300	C-59-171	Patrick Flaherty/(r13 JUN 1831)Coleman Fisher Original: found
NP-2921	Prentice, John	7 APR 1769	Cumberland	Turtle Creek, Westmoreland - Allegheny	300	C-7-202	(r4 MAR 1782)William Ball, Esq. Original: With NP-2922 - 2929
NP-2922	Roberts, Thomas	7 APR 1769	Cumberland	Versailles, Allegheny	300	C-169-112 C-169-113	(r27 MAR 1843)Davis S. McKee [patent H-44-408] Original: found
NP-2923	Collins, Thomas	7 APR 1769	Cumberland	Brush Run, Allegheny	300	C-117-284	--- Small/(r16 JUL 1792)Joseph Mather & Charles Vanderen & Thomas Smith, executors of John Vanderen, deceased Original: found
NP-2924	Whitner, John	7 APR 1769	Cumberland	North Huntingdon, Westmoreland	300	A-2-85	(r12 JAN 1853)George W. Stevens & Charles Potts, executors of Stacy Potts, deceased/[see caveat] Original: found
NP-2925	Black, Symon	7 APR 1769	Cumberland	Brush Creek, Westmoreland/ LD: Indiana	300	H-177	[see caveat] Original: found
NP-2926	Rhodes, John	7 APR 1769	Cumberland	Ft. Pitt - Ligonier road, Westmoreland	300	C-7-201	(r4 MAR 1782)William Ball, Esq. Original: found
NP-2927	Sympson, Hugh	7 APR 1769	Cumberland	Pitt, Westmoreland	300	A-45-97	(r5 APR 1788)Thomas Ross Original: found
NP-2928	Davis, Elias	7 APR 1769	Cumberland	Turtle Creek, Westmoreland	300	D-239	(r4 MAR 1782)William Ball, Esq. Original: found
NP-2929	Cowen, William	7 APR 1769	Cumberland	Ft. Pitt-Ligonier road, Westmoreland	300	C-7-224	(r4 MAR 1782)William Ball, Esq. Original: found
NP-2930	Campbell, John	7 APR 1769	Elk Run & Beaver Run, Cumberland	LD: Somerset	300		Original: With NP-2931 - 2953

Table 6 - New Purchase Applications (1769-1773)

Number	Applicant	Date	Orig. Place	Later Place	Acres	Survey	Neighbors, Notes, etc.
NP-2931	Higgins, John	7 APR 1769	Elk Run, Allegheny Mountains, Cumberland	LD: Somerset	300		John Campbell Original: found
NP-2932	Jackes, Richard	7 APR 1769	Elk Run, Allegheny Mountains, Cumberland	LD: Somerset	300		John Higgens Original: found
NP-2933	Logston, Edward	7 APR 1769	Beaver Run & Buffalo Run, Allegheny Mountains Cumberland	LD: Somerset	300		John Campbell Original: found
NP-2934	Ormsby, Oliver	7 APR 1769	Buffalo Run, Allegheny Mountains, Cumberland	LD: Somerset	300		Edward Logston Original: found
NP-2935	Campbell, James	7 APR 1769	Buffalo Run, Allegheny Mountains, Cumberland	LD: Somerset	300		Oliver Ormsby Original: found
NP-2936	Higgins, Michael	7 APR 1769	Buffalo Run, Allegheny Mountains, Cumberland	LD: Somerset	300		James Campbell Original: found
NP-2937	McCallister, Aeneas	7 APR 1769	Buffalo Run, Allegheny Mountains, Cumberland	LD: Somerset	300		Michael Higgins Original: found
NP-2938	Erwin, Isaac	7 APR 1769	Beaver Run, Allegheny Mountains, Cumberland		300		Edward Logston Original: found
NP-2939	Douglass, Ephraim	7 APR 1769	Beaver Run, Allegheny Mountains, Cumberland		300		Issac Irwin Original: found

Table 6 - New Purchase Applications (1769-1773)

Number	Applicant	Date	Orig. Place	Later Place	Acres	Survey	Neighbors, Notes, etc.
NP-2940	Christy, William	7 APR 1769	Beaver Run, Allegheny Mountains, Cumberland		300		Ephraim Douglas Original: found
NP-2941	Murry, William	7 APR 1769	Beaver Run, Allegheny Mountains, Cumberland	LD: Somerset	300		William Christy Original: found
NP-2942	Murry, Francis	7 APR 1769	Beaver Run, Allegheny Mountains, Cumberland	LD: Somerset	300		William Murray Original: found
NP-2943	Henry, Moses	7 APR 1769	Ft. Pitt road, Allegheny Mountains	LD: Somerset	300		Samuel Wallace/John Miller Original: found
NP-2944	Milligan, James	7 APR 1769	Ft. Pitt road, Allegheny Mountains, Cumberland	LD: Somerset	300		Samuel Wallace Original: found
NP-2945	Hall, Richard	7 APR 1769	Shade Run, Allegheny Mountains, Cumberland	LD: Somerset	300		Original: found
NP-2946	Hall, David	7 APR 1769	Cumberland	Shade, Somerset	300	C-83-143	John Miller/(r9 AUG 1837)James Gohn Original: found
NP-2947	Cochran, John	7 APR 1769	Shade Run, Allegheny Mountains, Cumberland	LD: Somerset	300		Original: found
NP-2948	Mitchel, Thomas	7 APR 1769	Cumberland	Quemahoning, Somerset	300	C-84-167	John Miller/(r30 APR 1785)John Hazelwood Original: found
NP-2949	Kelly, James	7 APR 1769	Cumberland	Quemahoning, Somerset	300	C-84-168	John Miller/Thomas Mitchell/(r30 APR 1785)John Hazelwood Original: found
NP-2950	Miller, John	7 APR 1769	Cumberland	Allegheny, Cambria/ LD: Allegheny, Cambria	300	D-70-118	Allen McClean Original: found
NP-2951	Robinson, John	7 APR 1769	Cumberland	Jenner, Somerset	300	A-70-143	(r26 MAR 1836)Abraham Hershberger Original: found

Table 6 - New Purchase Applications (1769-1773)

Number	Applicant	Date	Orig. Place	Later Place	Acres	Survey	Neighbors, Notes, etc.
NP-2952	Rutherford, Thomas	7 APR 1769	Stony Creek, Allegheny Mountains, Cumberland	LD: Somerset	300		Original: found
NP-2953	Wood, Thomas	7 APR 1769		Quemahoning, Somerset	300	A-11-127	(r11 FEB 1836)Fredrick Walker Original: found
NP-2954	Reyer, Stufel	7 APR 1769		Augusta, Northumberland	300	C-135-143	George Tayney/(r29 AUG 1783)William McClay, Esq./[see caveat] Original: With NP-2955
NP-2955	Knable, George	7 APR 1769		Augusta, Northumberland	300	C-127-294	Stufel Reyer/(r1 FEB 1797)William Maclay, Esq./[see caveat] Original: With NP-2954
NP-2956	Knable, Herman	7 APR 1769		Augusta, Northumberland	300	C-129-175	(r12 JAN 1787)William Maclay, Esq./[see caveat] Original: found
NP-2957	Kunggel, Jacob	7 APR 1769	Shamokin Creek	LD: Northumberland	300		George Mikell Groff Original: found
NP-2958	Tayney, George	7 APR 1769	Shamokin Creek	LD: Northumberland	300		Jacob Kunggel Original: found
NP-2959	Burgerd, Mickell	7 APR 1769		Augusta, Northumberland	300	C-499	(r14 MAR 1774)George Miller Original: With NP-2960
NP-2960	Croff, Mickell George	7 APR 1769		Augusta, Northumberland	300	F-149	Mickell Burgerd/(r30 DEC 1772)David Shakespear Original: With NP-2959
NP-2961	Stevenson, James (of Philadelphia)	7 APR 1769	Northumberland	Mahoning Creek, Montour	300	C-209-12	(r9 JUL 1783)John Stille Original: found
NP-2962	Milligan, James	7 APR 1769		Donegal, Westmoreland	300	C-207-30	(r17 OCT 1788)Arthur St. Clair, Esq. Original: With NP-2963-2968
NP-2963	Wharton, Thomas Jr.	7 APR 1769		Unity, Westmoreland	300	D-70-136	Original: found
NP-2964	Moore, William	7 APR 1769		Ligonier, Westmoreland	300	D-70-137 D-70-138	[see caveat] Original: found
NP-2965	Montgomery, Robert	7 APR 1769		Ligonier, Westmoreland		D-70-135	Original: found
NP-2966	Wharton, James	7 APR 1769		Salem, Westmoreland	300	A-55-25	(r1 FEB 1811)Matthew Jack Original: found
NP-2967	Story, Enoch	7 APR 1769		Salem, Westmoreland	300	C-200-252	James Wharton/(r1 FEB 1811)Mathew Jack Original: found

Table 6 - New Purchase Applications (1769-1773)

Number	Applicant	Date	Orig. Place	Later Place	Acres	Survey	Neighbors, Notes, etc.
NP-2968	Story, Thomas	7 APR 1769		Hempfield, Westmoreland	300	D-70-134	Enoch Story Original: found
NP-2969	Grant, John	7 APR 1769		Unity, Westmoreland	300	D-55-62 D-62-293 D-62-294 C-207-56	Arthur St. Clair/(r17 Oct 1788)Daniel St. Clair/[see caveat] Original: found
NP-2970	Dicas, Thomas	7 APR 1769		Pitt, Allegheny	300	D-70-100	--- Sly/--- Ryan Original: found
NP-2971	Holtz, Thomas	7 APR 1769		Huntingdon, Westmoreland	300	D-70-133	Original: found
NP-2972	McEwen, Phillip	7 APR 1769		Versailles, Allegheny	300	D-70-280	Original: found
NP-2973	Stephenson, Hugh	7 APR 1769		North Huntingdon, Westmoreland/ LD: East Huntingdon, Westmoreland	300	D-70-130 D-70-132	Original: found
NP-2974	Worthington, James	7 APR 1769	Westmoreland	Tyrone, Fayette & Huntingdon, Westmoreland	300	M-423 M-424	(r30 MAY 1788)Issac Mason Original: found
NP-2975	Doyl, Edward	7 APR 1769		East Huntingdon, Westmoreland & Bullskin, Fayette/ LD: Bullskin, Fayette	300	D-70-106 D-70-129	John Stephenson Original: found
NP-2976	Hatfield, Adam	7 APR 1769		Mt. Pleasant, Westmoreland & Bullskin, Fayette	300	A-16-211	(r28 NOV 1787)Issac Meason, Esq. Original: found
NP-2977	Baldin, John	7 APR 1769		Huntingdon, Westmoreland	300	C-151-89	Hugh Stephenson/(r5 SEP 1788)Issac Meason, Esq. Original: found
NP-2978	McCarmick, James	7 APR 1769		Jacobs Creek, Westmoreland & Fayette	300	C-53-219	Edward Boyle/(r16 MAY 1788)Samuel Glasgow Original: found
NP-2979	Stephenson, Marcus	7 APR 1769		East Huntingdon, Westmoreland	300	D-70-131	Original: found

Table 6 - New Purchase Applications (1769-1773)

Number	Applicant	Date	Orig. Place	Later Place	Acres	Survey	Neighbors, Notes, etc.
NP-2980	Holes, William	7 APR 1769		Tyrone, Fayette	300	A-21-288	James Worthington/(r15 MAR 1786)Issac Meason, Esq. Original: found
NP-2981	Worthington, Robert Jr.	7 APR 1769		Mt. Pleasant, Westmoreland	300	C-151-76	(r9 JUN 1788)Issac Meason, Esq./[see caveat] Original: found
NP-2982	Worthington, Robert Sr.	7 APR 1769		Mt. Pleasant, Westmoreland	300	C-34-22	Robert Worthington, Jr./(r25 SEP 1787)Ralph Cherry Original: found
NP-2983	McDonald, Angus	8 APR 1769		Dunlap Creek, Fayette	300	C-53-52 C-53-53	(r9 JUL 1791)Rees Cadwalder/[see caveat] Original: found
NP-2984	Fouts, Leonard	8 APR 1769	Cumberland	Buffalo, Union	150	D-70-144	Original: With NP-2985-2990
NP-2985	Inglish, James	8 APR 1769		Kelly, Union	150	D-70-150	Original: found
NP-2986	Fouts, John Jr.	8 APR 1769		Buffalo, Union	150	D-70-151	James Inglish Original: found
NP-2987	Gruber, Everhart	8 APR 1769	Berks	Buffalo, Union	100	D-56-300	Leonard Fouts Original: found
NP-2988	Inglish, James	8 APR 1769	Berks	Kelly, Union	150	D-56-85 D-56-95	John Fouts/[same land as NP-2368 to Thomas Beatty] Original: found
NP-2989	Fouts, George	8 APR 1769	Cumberland	Kelly, Union	100	D-56-286	Original: found
NP-2990	Fouts, John Jr.	8 APR 1769	Cumberland	Berks - Kelly, Union	50	D-56-287	Original: found
NP-2991	Nicely, Jacob	8 APR 1769	Stony Creek, Allegheny Mountains, Cumberland	LD: Somerset	300		Original: With NP-2992-2996
NP-2992	Black, Samuel	8 APR 1769	Bright Creek, Allegheny Mountains, Cumberland	LD: Westmoreland/ Armstrong	300		Samuel Blacks Original: found
NP-2992a	Witzel, Phillip	8 APR 1769	Bright Creek, Allegheny Mountains, Cumberland	LD: Armstrong	300		Phillip Wiseman Original: found

Table 6 - New Purchase Applications (1769-1773)

Number	Applicant	Date	Orig. Place	Later Place	Acres	Survey	Neighbors, Notes, etc.
NP-2993	Wiseman, Phillip	8 APR 1769	Bright Creek, Allegheny Mountains, Cumberland	LD: Armstrong/ Westmoreland	300		Samuel Black Original: found
NP-2994	Castleman, Jacob	8 APR 1769	Conemaugh River, Cumberland	LD: Cambria	300		Original: found
NP-2995	Neifly, Frederick	8 APR 1769	Cumberland	Jenner, Somerset	300	C-13-156	(r9 APR 1836)John A. Blooget Original: found
NP-2996	Sheets, Frederick	8 APR 1769	Cumberland	Quemahoning, Somerset	300	A-1-224	(r13 FEB 1837)George Graham, Jr. Original: found
NP-2997	Craig, George	8 APR 1769		Clearfield & Allegheny, Cambria/ LD: Allegheny, Cambria	300	Z-55 Z-56 C-98-280	Josiah Rees/(p29 OCT 1870)Elizabeth Kratzer Original: With NP-2998 & 2999
NP-2998	Wilson, Robert	8 APR 1769		Chest, Clearfield/ LD: Clearfield	300	D-56-290	Original: found
NP-2999	Gamwell, Henry	8 APR 1769		Cheat, Clearfield/ LD: Clearfield	300	D-56-288	Robert Wilson Original: found
NP-3000	Tush, George	8 APR 1769		Pike, Clearfield	300	A-23-18	(r28 MAY 1834)A. Custard Original: found
NP-3001	Rees, Josiah	8 APR 1769		Clearfield Creek, Clearfield	300	A-37-125	William McDonald/(r11 APR 1816)Joseph Clark Original: found
NP-3002	McDonald, William	8 APR 1769		Allegheny, Cambria	300	C-144-206	(r18 JUN 1827)H. J. McGuire & James Maloney Original: found
NP-3003	Graff, George	8 APR 1769		Chest, Clearfield/ LD: Clearfield	300	D-56-289	Original: With NP-3004-3006
NP-3004	West, William	8 APR 1769		Chest, Clearfield	300	D-70-294	William Hodge Original: found
NP-3005	Williams, Humphry	8 APR 1769		Pike, Clearfield	300	C-91-181	William West/(r3 APR 1844)Joseph Hoover & Samuel Caldwell Original: found

Table 6 - New Purchase Applications (1769-1773)

Number	Applicant	Date	Orig. Place	Later Place	Acres	Survey	Neighbors, Notes, etc.
NP-3006	Magaw, Samuel	8 APR 1769		Centre & Bradford Twp., Clearfield/ LD: Clearfield	300	D-58-290	Original: found
NP-3007	Byerly, Andreas	10 APR 1769		Hempfield, Westmoreland	300	D-70-283 D-70-284	Original: With NP-3008
NP-3008	Byerly, Francis	10 APR 1769		Hempfield, Westmoreland	300	D-9-107	(r16 DEC 1818)A. Wagle Original: found
NP-3009	Burens, Samuel	10 APR 1769		Monongahela River, Fayette/ LD: Fayette	300		Samuel Lindsay Original: With NP-3010
NP-3010	Lindsay, Samuel	10 APR 1769		Monongahela River, Fayette/ LD: Fayette	300		Samuel Burens Original: found
NP-3011	Morhead, Thomas	10 APR 1769		East Huntingdon, Westmoreland	300	D-70-290 D-70-291	Original: found
NP-3012	Beally, Elizabeth	10 APR 1769		Unity, Westmoreland	300	D-70-292 D-70-293	Original: found
NP-3013	Lovegrove, Margaret	11 APR 1769		Buffalo, Union/ LD: Union	300	D-70-295	Richard Peters Original: found
NP-3014	Dunlap, Edward	11 APR 1769	Northumberland	Susquehanna River, Columbia	300	Z-285	(r18 JUN 1795)Abraham Miller Original: found
NP-3015	Reynolds, David	11 APR 1769	Northumberland	Susquehanna River, Columbia	300	A-470	(r25 FEB 1782)Ann Rose Original: Signed
NP-3016	Martin, James	11 APR 1769	Northumberland	Nanticoke Creek, Luzerne/ LD: Luzerne	200	X-216	Original: found
NP-3017	Seber, Severinus	11 APR 1769		between Wyalusing & Wyoming, Luzerne/ LD: Exeter, Luzerne	300	X-148	Original: found

Table 6 - New Purchase Applications (1769-1773)

Number	Applicant	Date	Orig. Place	Later Place	Acres	Survey	Neighbors, Notes, etc.
NP-3018	Newton, Ambrose	11 APR 1769	Westmoreland	four miles east of Ft. Pitt, Allegheny	300	C-164-116	widow Girty/Joseph Arden/James Royal/John Maggee/(r7 DEC 1787)Robert Neill Original: Signed
NP-3019	Elliott, William	11 APR 1769	Westmoreland	Pitt, Allegheny	300	A-12-10	Daniel Elliott/(r6 OCT 1786)/[see caveat] Original: Signed
NP-3020	Evans, Henry	11 APR 1769		Plum, Allegheny	300	D-70-91	Original: Signed
NP-3021	Elliott, James (Indian trader)	11 APR 1769	Cumberland	Pitt, Allegheny	300	C-41-247	(r14 JAN 1835)Juliet Sample Original: Signed
NP-3022	Elliott, Robert	11 APR 1769	Cumberland	Pitt, Allegheny	300	D-56-177 D-70-296	William Elliott/Capt. Thompson Original: Signed
NP-3023	Hoult, Charles	11 APR 1769	Cumberland	South Huntingdon, Westmoreland	300	D-70-297	Conrad Winemiller Original: Signed
NP-3024	Cawlley, John	11 APR 1769		Plum & Wilkins, Allegheny	300	D-64-104 C-44-68	John Hoults/(r6 MAY 1788)Ephraim Douglass Original: Signed
NP-3025	Douglass, Adam Sr.	11 APR 1769		Elizabeth, Allegheny	200	D-70-298	William Butler/William Saltsman/Anthony Walter Original: Signed
NP-3026	Tate, Benjamin	11 APR 1769		Wilkins, Allegheny & Hempfield, Westmoreland/ LD: Allegheny	100	D-70-285 D-70-299	Original: Signed
NP-3027	Elliott, Jane	11 APR 1769	Cumberland	Hempfield, Westmoreland	300	A-77-174	(r10 JAN 1789)William Elliott/[see caveat] Original: Signed
NP-3028	Sample, Samuel	11 APR 1769		Pitt, Allegheny	150	A-13-248	Jordan Styger/Col. John Reed/(r12 DEC 1789) Original: Signed
NP-3029	Memminger, Thomas (the son of Theodore Memminger)	11 APR 1769		Hartley, Union	300	D-70-286	Original: Signed by Thomas and Theodore Memminger

Table 6 - New Purchase Applications (1769-1773)

Number	Applicant	Date	Orig. Place	Later Place	Acres	Survey	Neighbors, Notes, etc.
NP-3030	Fiscus, Charles Jr.	11 APR 1769		Unity, Westmoreland	300	D-62-208 D-62-209 C-62-84	Jerhard Fiscus/Samuel Hook/(17 NOV 1820)J. Fiscus & H. Furry Original: found
NP-3031	Fiscus, Gerhard	11 APR 1769		Mt. Pleasant, Westmoreland	300	C-228-174	George Stockberger/Rube Sckinner/(r24 APR 1807)John Wills Original: found
NP-3032	Fiscus, Abraham Jr.	11 APR 1769		Mt. Pleasant, Westmoreland	300	C-62-109 C-62-110 D-46-78	Samuel Hook, Jr./(r11 FEB 1823)A. Fiscus Original: found
NP-3033	Stockberger, Michael	12 APR 1769		Unity, Westmoreland	300	D-70-287 D-70-288	Simon Sorrel Original: found
NP-3034	Carnahan, John	12 APR 1769	Berks	Kelly, Union	200		[same land as NP-2225 to Breeson Bawden] Original: Signed
NP-3035	Sinkler, John	12 APR 1769	Elm Creek	LD: Somerset	150		Original: Signed
NP-3036	Reaborn, John	12 APR 1769	Wolfs Creek	LD: Somerset	300		Original: found
NP-3037	Miller, James	12 APR 1769	Elk Creek	LD: Somerset	300		--- Downing Original: found
NP-3038	Sinkler, James	12 APR 1769		LD: Somerset	300		William Tice Original: found
NP-3039	Sinkler, William Jr.	12 APR 1769		LD: Somerset	300		--- Casselman Original: found
NP-3040	Sinkler, William Sr.	12 APR 1769		Elk Lick, Somerset	300	C-138-92	Andrew Hendrickson/Benjamin Rogers/(r6 JUN 1796)Peter Livergood Original: found
NP-3041	Sinkler, John	12 APR 1769	Bedford	Elk Lick, Somerset/ LD: Somerset	150		--- Casselman Original: found
NP-3042	Lyons, Joseph	12 APR 1769	Bedford	Great Road, 22 miles from Ft. Pitt, Westmoreland	300	C-10-20	Thomas Lyon/Jacob Jewell/(r31 MAR 1788)Edward Byram Original: Signed

Table 6 - New Purchase Applications (1769-1773)

Number	Applicant	Date	Orig. Place	Later Place	Acres	Survey	Neighbors, Notes, etc.
NP-3043	Schub, Henry	13 APR 1769	East Branch Susquehanna River	LD: Bradford	300		Christian Pauli Original: found
NP-3044	Russell, Andrew	13 APR 1769	Berks	Turbot, Columbia	300	A-16-92	(r2 MAR 1815)Samuel Russell & John Russell & Patrick Russell [sons of Andrew Russell, deceased] Original: Signed
NP-3045	Galbreath, John	13 APR 1769		North Huntingdon, Westmoreland	300	D-70-289	Samuel Simeson Original: found
NP-3046	Brownfield, John	13 APR 1769	Bedford	Monongahela River, Allegheny	300	M-406	Capt. Thompson/John McKee/(r27 FEB 1772)John McKee [patent AA-13-49]/[see caveat] Original: found
NP-3047	Jameson, William	13 APR 1769		Ligonier, Westmoreland/ LD: Ligonier, Westmoreland	300	A-32-133	Original: found
NP-3048	Cofman, Michael	13 APR 1769		Donegal, Westmoreland/ LD: Donegal, Westmoreland	300	Z-61 C-178-148	Philemon Askins/Thomas Pitton/Thomas Campbell/(r16 OCT 1827)Jacob Roodman Original: found
NP-3049	Laughlin, John	13 APR 1769	Bedford	Sewickley Creek, Westmoreland/ LD: Westmoreland	300	A-5-89	Original: found
NP-3050	Laughlin, James	13 APR 1769		Donegal, Westmoreland	300	D-70-156	Original: Signed
NP-3051	Laughlin, Alexander	13 APR 1769		Hempfield, Westmoreland	300	D-70-154 D-70-155	Robert Laughlin Original: found
NP-3052	Laughlin, Robert Sr.	13 APR 1769		Unity, Westmoreland	300	C-10-96	(r6 APR 1789)Charles Brookens Original: found

Table 6 - New Purchase Applications (1769-1773)

Number	Applicant	Date	Orig. Place	Later Place	Acres	Survey	Neighbors, Notes, etc.
NP-3053	Laughlin, Hugh	13 APR 1769		Ligonier - Ft. Pitt road, Westmoreland/ LD: Ligonier, Westmoreland	300	A-33-279	Robert Laughlin/Alexander Laughier/[see caveat] Original: found
NP-3054	Laughlin, Robert Jr.	13 APR 1769		Unity, Westmoreland/ LD: Ligonier, Westmoreland	300	A-257	Original: found
NP-3055	Joder, Michael	13 APR 1769	East Branch Susquehanna River	LD: Bradford	300		Henry Shaub/Christian Pauli Original: found
NP-3056	Glen, John	14 APR 1769		Washington, Westmoreland	300	C-63-232	(r3 NOV 1826) Original: found
NP-3057	Glen, Hugh	14 APR 1769		Plum, Allegheny	300	D-70-115	Original: found
NP-3058	Glen, James	14 APR 1769		Washington, Westmoreland	300	C-63-232	(r3 NOV 1826)John Glenn Original: found
NP-3059	Sinkler (Sinclair), Samuel	14 APR 1769		Rostraver, Westmoreland	300	P-10 R-95	(r16 MAR 1789) Original: found
NP-3060	Moore, Moses (son of John)	14 APR 1769	between Crooked & Plum Creeks	LD: Armstrong	300		Original: With NP-3061 & 3062. Signed by Moses & John Moore
NP-3061	Ewing, John (pedlar)	14 APR 1769	Westmoreland	branch of Conemaugh River, Armstrong	300	C-222-248	(r26 JUL 1781)John Wilson Original: Signed
NP-3062	Willson, John (pedlar)	14 APR 1769		Squirrel Hill, Armstrong	300	C-222-247	(r26 JUL 1781) Original: Signed
NP-3063	Sills, William	17 APR 1769	Monongahela River near Peters Creek	LD: Allegheny	300		Thomas McCasky Original: found
NP-3064	Linnes, James	17 APR 1769		Fallowfield, Washington	300	A-5-306	William Nowland/(r17 JAN 1808)Daniel Depuy, Esq. Original: found

Table 6 - New Purchase Applications (1769-1773)

Number	Applicant	Date	Orig. Place	Later Place	Acres	Survey	Neighbors, Notes, etc.
NP-3065	McClasky, Thomas	17 APR 1769		Pigeon Creek, Washington	300	A-5-306	(r10 JUN 1805)Daniel Depuy, Esq. Original: found
NP-3066	Nowland, William	17 APR 1769		Fallowfield, Washington	300	U-23	(r10 JUN 1805)Daniel Depuy, Esq. Original: found
NP-3067	Powell, William	17 APR 1769		Wilkins, Allegheny	300	S-20 C-167-163 C-14-300	(r26 MAY 1853)John Parchment/(r22 JUN 1853)Allen Brown Original: found
NP-3068	White, James	17 APR 1769		Wilkins, Allegheny	300	D-70-114	William Powell Original: found
NP-3069	Morgan, David	17 APR 1769		Spring Hill, Fayette	300	C-123-257	(r4 MAR 1789) Original: With NP-3070-3088
NP-3070	Griffey, John	17 APR 1769		Georges, Fayette	300	C-75-224	(r27 MAR 1789)Joseph Hunt Original: found
NP-3071	Conn, George	17 APR 1769	Bedford	Georges Creek, Fayette	300	C-53-154	(r27 MAY 1793) Original: found
NP-3072	Ashcraft, Ichabud	17 APR 1769	Cumberland	Georges Creek, Fayette	300	A-83-173	(r28 MAR 1788) Original: found
NP-3073	McDonnell, John	17 APR 1769		Georges, Fayette	300	F-95 C-215-123 A-48-89	(r29 SEP 1803)John Springer & Jacob Springer/(r29 SEP 1803)James Downard Original: found
NP-3074	Allen, William Jr.	17 APR 1769		Georges Creek, Fayette	300	S-114-8 K-64 C-114-28	(r8 JUN 1793)Randolph Freeman/(r8 JUN 1797)Jacob Kyle Original: found
NP-3075	Froman, Jacob	17 APR 1769		Monongahela River & Maple Run, Washington	300	C-18	(r27 DEC 1784)Fredrick Cooper Original: found
NP-3076	Froman, Paul Sr.	17 APR 1769		Youghiogheny River near Maryland line, Fayette	300	C-223-29	(r22 SEP 1788)Arthur Watson Original: found

Table 6 - New Purchase Applications (1769-1773)

Number	Applicant	Date	Orig. Place	Later Place	Acres	Survey	Neighbors, Notes, etc.
NP-3077	Ulmar, Frederick	17 APR 1769		Youghiogheny River, Somerset	300	I-443	(r10 JAN 1798)Peter Everly Original: found
NP-3078	Spears, Jacob	17 APR 1769		Youghiogheny River, Somerset	300	C-233-29	(r31 OCT 1817)P. D. Smith Original: found
NP-3079	Froman, Paul Jr.	17 APR 1769		Monongahela River & Pigeon Creek, Washington	300	Y-238	(r23 MAY 1785) Original: found
NP-3080	Hardin, William	17 APR 1769		Georges Creek, Fayette	300	A-51-296	(r20 JUN 1785)Jacob Goms Original: found
NP-3081	Hardin, John Jr.	17 APR 1769		Georges Creek, Fayette	300	B-12-179	William Hardin/(r18 SEP 1788) Original: found
NP-3082	Hardin, John	17 APR 1769		Spring Hill, Fayette	300	C-53-218	(r7 MAY 1788)Charles Griffin Original: found
NP-3083	Hardin, Martin	17 APR 1769		Spring Hill, Fayette	300	B-3-141	William Hardin/John Hardin, Jr./(r5 JUN 1804)Joshua Brown Original: found
NP-3084	Hardin, Mark	17 APR 1769		Spring Hill, Fayette/ LD: Spring Hill, Fayette	300	C-54-298 C-54-299 C-54-299 C-72-201	John Hardin/(r22 MAR 1836)William Griffith, deceased/(p6 MAY 1869)William P. Griffin/[see caveat] Original: found
NP-3085	Hardin, Benjamin	17 APR 1769		Spring Hill, Fayette	300	A-18-214	Mark Hardin/(r4 JUN 1804)Joshua Brown Original: found
NP-3086	Hardin, Susanah	17 APR 1769		Spring Hill, Fayette	300	D-70-119	[see caveat] Original: found
NP-3087	Comes, Joseph	17 APR 1769		Spring Hill, Fayette	300	D-46-81 C-182-286 C-143-86 C-143-87 C-64-16	(r16 FEB 1790)James Sutton/(r22 MAR 1817)Sarah Masterson/(r23 DEC 1825)Samuel Davis Original: found
NP-3088	Neall, James	17 APR 1769		Spring Hill, Fayette	300	C-143-284	(r26 SEP 1785) Original: found

Table 6 - New Purchase Applications (1769-1773)

Number	Applicant	Date	Orig. Place	Later Place	Acres	Survey	Neighbors, Notes, etc.
NP-3089	Spears, Henry	17 APR 1769	Westmoreland	Monongahela River, Fayette	300	N-83	(r17 JUN 1784)Benjamin Fry & Regina Spears Original: With NP-3090-3094
NP-3090	Crist, Nicholas	17 APR 1769		Monongahela River, Washington	300	C-16	(r17 JUN 1784) Original: found
NP-3091	Frye, William	17 APR 1769		Monongahela River, Washington	300	B-26	(r26 AUG 1785)Abraham Fry Original: found
NP-3092	Brinton, Joseph	17 APR 1769	Monongahela River	LD: Washington/ Greene/ Allegheny	300		Original: found
NP-3093	Thorn, Robert	17 APR 1769		Luzerne, Fayette	300	B-23-23	Original: found
NP-3094	Resoner, Peter	17 APR 1769		Rostraver, Westmoreland/ LD: Fayette	300	H-126 B-18-135	(r11 APR 1797)William Sherer/[see caveat] Original: found
NP-3095	Dixon, Samuel (formerly of Conocheague Creek Town)	17 APR 1769		Blacklick, Indiana	300	D-64-173 D-64-174 A-21-163	(r30 JAN 1797)Peter Rugh Original: With NP-3096-3101.
NP-3096	Dixon, John (Brother of Samuel)	17 APR 1769		Blacklick, Indiana	300	B-23-31 C-37-256	(r14 APR 1838)Joseph Dixon Original: found
NP-3097	Miller, Samuel (of Conocheague)	17 APR 1769	Blacklick Creek	LD: Indiana/ Cambria	300		Original:. Signed
NP-3098	Taylor, Thomas (of Conocheague)	17 APR 1769		Hattenbaugh's Run, Westmoreland	300	A-78-196	(r15 SEP 1789)John Gibson/[see caveat] Original: found
NP-3099	Taylor, Richard (of Near Carlisle)	17 APR 1769		Blacklick, Indiana	300	C-223-93	(r14 MAR 1789)John Wray Original: found
NP-3100	Miller, Samuel James (of Above Shippensburg, yeoman)	17 APR 1769		Blacklick, Indiana	300	D-70-107 D-70-108	Original: found

Table 6 - New Purchase Applications (1769-1773)

Number	Applicant	Date	Orig. Place	Later Place	Acres	Survey	Neighbors, Notes, etc.
NP-3101	Caughel, Thomas (yeoman)	17 APR 1769		Blacklick, Indiana	300	K-169	(r22 SEP 1788)Charles Campbell Original: found
NP-3102	Hunter, James (of Philadelphia, merchant)	19 APR 1769	Westmoreland	Youghiogheny River, Fayette	300	C-84-25	Col. Washington/John Persall/John Pitts/(r8 SEP 1783) Original: With NP-3103
NP-3103	Hunter, Eleanor	19 APR 1769		Youghiogheny River, Fayette	300	C-84-22	John Persall & John Pitts/(r8 SEP 1783)James Hunter & Elizabeth Hunter [his wife] Original: found
NP-3104	McKeen, Hugh	19 APR 1769		East Huntingdon, Westmoreland	300	C-90-164	(r29 SEP 1826)John Hunter & Rosana Hunter [his wife] Original: found
NP-3105	Thorn, William	19 APR 1769		East Huntingdon, Westmoreland	300	C-194-267 C-194-279 C-194-280	Hugh McKean/(r7 DEC 1838)W. Rankin Original: Signed
NP-3106	Schub, Abraham	19 APR 1769	East Branch Susquehanna River	LD: Bradford	300		Henry Shaub/Michael Ioder Original: With NP-3107-3110
NP-3107	Meyer, Martin	19 APR 1769	East Branch Susquehanna River	LD: Bradford	300		Abraham Shub Original: found
NP-3108	Sober, John	19 APR 1769	East Branch Susquehanna River	LD: Bradford	300		Martin Meyer Original: found
NP-3109	Keppel, Andrew	19 APR 1769	East Branch Susquehanna River	LD: Bradford	300		John Sober Original: found
NP-3110	Gressman, Adam	19 APR 1769		East Branch Susquehanna River, Luzerne	300	A-12-116	Andrew Kepple/(r14 MAR 1775)John Gibson, Esq. Original: found
NP-3111	Furgeson, Robert	20 APR 1769	East Branch Susquehanna River near Rush Meadows	LD: Bradford	300		Henry Hain Original: With NP-3112
NP-3112	Furgeson, James	20 APR 1769		Tunkhannock Creek, Wyoming	300	A-24-136	Robert Furgeson/(r19 APR 1782)James Johnston Original: found
NP-3113	Urguhart, Eneas	20 APR 1769		Two Mile Run, Allegheny	300	D-70-113	Original: found

Table 6 - New Purchase Applications (1769-1773)

Number	Applicant	Date	Orig. Place	Later Place	Acres	Survey	Neighbors, Notes, etc.
NP-3114	Wright, Henry	20 APR 1769		Fayette, Allegheny/ LD: Fayette, Allegheny	300	C-29-189 C-29-197	Lewis Fredrick/(r21 APR 1828)Christian Cowan Original: found
NP-3115	Dunn, John	20 APR 1769		Wilkins, Allegheny/ LD: Wilkins, Allegheny	300	D-70-111 D-70-112	John Frazer/Peter Rollettor/Conrad Winemiller/William Elliott Original: found
NP-3116	Ross, Alexander	20 APR 1769		Washington & Allegheny	300	D-199	[adjudged to James Byers on NP-2860 by Property Board on 1 SEP 1783]/[see caveat] Original: found
NP-3117	Marks, Levy	20 APR 1769	Monongahela River	LD: Westmoreland/ Washington	300		Janet Pendergrass Original: found
NP-3118	Levy, Levy Andrew Jr.	20 APR 1769		Hempfield & North Huntingdon, Westmoreland	300	D-70-145	Joseph Simons Original: found
NP-3119	Simon, Moses	20 APR 1769		Franklin & North Huntingdon, Westmoreland	300	D-70-158	William Tygarden Original: found
NP-3120	Tygarden, William Sr.	20 APR 1769		Franklin & North Huntingdon, Westmoreland	300	D-62-282 D-64-213 C-215-166 C-215-167 C-215-168 C-215-180	Andrew Byerly/(r8 MAR 1830)Aaron Teagarden heirs Original: found
NP-3121	Simon, Joseph	20 APR 1769		Nine Mile Run, Westmoreland	300	G-226 C-194-51	David Franks/(r23 JAN 1795) Original: found
NP-3122	Levy, Levy Andrew Sr.	20 APR 1769		Franklin, Westmoreland	300	S-239	David Franks/(r19 APR 1788)Cathrine Thompson Original: found
NP-3123	Franks, David	20 APR 1769		Wilkins, Allegheny	300	G-209	John Metcalf/(r3 JAN 1829)James Ross Original: found
NP-3124	Boreman, John	20 APR 1769		Pitt, Allegheny	300	D-56-169 S-238	David Franks/(r25 MAY 1790) Original: found

Table 6 - New Purchase Applications (1769-1773)

Number	Applicant	Date	Orig. Place	Later Place	Acres	Survey	Neighbors, Notes, etc.
NP-3125	Hogeland, Benjamin	20 APR 1769		Quemahoning, Somerset/ LD: Quemahoning, Somerset	300	A-5-214 C-210-137 D-3-208 C-147-125	(r5 APR 1838)John Shaeffer/(r20 MAY 1858)E. Wakeland/(p13 JUL 1870)Noah J. Miller Original: found
NP-3126	Franks, Abraham	20 APR 1769		Redstone Creek, Washington/ LD: Washington	300	W-65	Indian Peter [an Indian] Original: found
NP-3127	Thompson, Thomas	20 APR 1769		East Huntingdon, Westmoreland	300	D-62-221 P-401	(r11 MAY 1785)George Swan Original: found
NP-3128	Innis, Robert	20 APR 1769		Chartiers Creek/ LD: Washington/ Allegheny	300	A-252	Indian Peters [an Indian] Original: found
NP-3129	Marks, Henry	20 APR 1769		Elizabeth, Allegheny/ LD: Elizabeth, Allegheny	300	D-70-110	James Thompson Original: found
NP-3130	England, George	20 APR 1769		Monongahela River, Allegheny	300	M-407	Alexander Ross/William Thompson/[adjudged to John Brownfield's assignee John McKee; see NP-3046]/[see caveat] Original: found
NP-3131	Price, Richard	20 APR 1769		Monongahela River, 7 miles from Ft. Pitt, Allegheny	300	M-410	John McCallister/(r27 NOV 1788)Andrew McFarlan Original: found
NP-3132	Wells, Cowley	20 APR 1769		Allegheny, Westmoreland	300	D-70-157 D-70-158	[part returned on NP-2653 and NP-15] Original: found
NP-3133	Reading, Philip Rev.	21 APR 1769		Susquehanna, Cambria	300	C-17-163	(r11 FEB 1842)James Byrne Original: With NP-3134-3135 Signed
NP-3134	Reading, Philip Jr.	21 APR 1769		Susquehanna, Cambria	300	C-20-62 C-20-63	Rev. Philip Reading/(r16 MAR 1836)Emericus Bender Original: found
NP-3135	Reading, Catharine Anne	21 APR 1769		Susquehanna, Cambria/ LD: Carroll, Cambria	300	A-25-163 C-233-185	Phillip Reading, Jr./(p19 SEP 1870)Peter Shira/(p18 FEB 1901)Harry White Original: found

Table 6 - New Purchase Applications (1769-1773)

Number	Applicant	Date	Orig. Place	Later Place	Acres	Survey	Neighbors, Notes, etc.
NP-3136	Craig, Robert	21 APR 1769	Washington	Chartiers Creek, Allegheny	300	F-181	John Stewart/(r6 AUG 1787)Edward Shippen & Joseph Shippen, Jr., Esq. Original: found
NP-3137	Mackey, John	21 APR 1769	Washington	Chartiers Creek, Allegheny	300	F-179	Robert Craig/(r6 AUG 1787)Edward Shippen & Joseph Shippen, Jr. [patent P-11-65] Original: found
NP-3138	Street, John	21 APR 1769	Washington	Chartiers Creek, Allegheny	300	D-7-92 C-177-53 D-7-85	John Mackey/(r27 SEP 1808)John Morton & Ephraim Morton/(r14 JUL 1810)Samuel Wilson/[see caveat] Original: found
NP-3139	Frederick, Sebastian	21 APR 1769		Mifflin, Allegheny	300	D-55-85 A-89-29 A-87-149 A-87-286	John McCallister/(r19 MAR 1789)Alexander Lowery, Esq. Original: Missing
NP-3140	Painter, Peter	21 APR 1769	Washington	Chartiers Creek, Allegheny	300	C-164-105	William Christy/Henry Miller/(r10 APR 1788)John Nevill Original: Missing
NP-3141	Derr, Henry	21 APR 1769		St. Clair, Allegheny	200	D-70-104	Peter Rowletter/Thomas Street Original: Missing
NP-3142	Weitzell, Peter	21 APR 1769	Westmoreland	Wilkins, Allegheny/ LD: Wilkins, Allegheny	300	A-5-11 C-224-47 C-126-168	Mr. Frazer/Peter Roletter/(r22 JUN 1839)James Stewart/(p15 JUL 1871)Henry Lloyd Original: With NP-3143-3144 Signed by "Pilips Weitzel"
NP-3143	Weitzell, Jacob	21 APR 1769		Washington - Dickinson, Allegheny	300	A-87-147	--- McCallister/(r16 MAR 1798)James Whitacre Original: found
NP-3144	Weitzell, John	21 APR 1769		Wilkins, Allegheny	300	D-70-103	--- Kelly Original: found
NP-3145	Toupe, Jacob	21 APR 1769		near Pittsburgh, Allegheny/ LD: Pitt, Allegheny	300	P-242	Christian Lims, Esq./Capt. William Thompson/Alexander McGruger/James Royal/George Sly/Casper Troupe Original: found
NP-3146	Toup, Casper Sr.	21 APR 1769		near Pittsburgh, Allegheny	300	E-293	Col. George Croughen, Esq./Chritian Lims, Esq./Jacob Tups, Jr./(r18 NOV 1793)Conrad Winebidder Original: found

Table 6 - New Purchase Applications (1769-1773)

Number	Applicant	Date	Orig. Place	Later Place	Acres	Survey	Neighbors, Notes, etc.
NP-3147	Hoops, Robert	21 APR 1769	Delaware River, Northampton	LD: Pike	300		Andrew Allen Original: found
NP-3148	Allison, William	24 APR 1769	Redstone Creek	LD: Franklin, Fayette	300		Original: found
NP-3149	Allison, Robert (of Letterkenny)	24 APR 1769		Franklin, Fayette/ LD: Franklin, Fayette	300	D-70-105	Original: found
NP-3150	Mitchel, Charles	24 APR 1769	Redstone Creek	LD: Fayette	300		Original: found
NP-3151	McCallister, John	24 APR 1769		Mifflin, Allegheny	300	D-70-102	Original: With NP-3152
NP-3152	McCallister, Eneas	24 APR 1769		Mifflin, Allegheny	300	D-57-73 D-57-77 X-215	John McCallister Original: found
NP-3153	Sam, Adam	24 APR 1769		Huntingdon, Westmoreland	300	C-210-21	William Saltman/Col. Clapham/(r18 APR 1787) Original: With NP-3154
NP-3154	Wolf, Rynard	24 APR 1769		Huntingdon, Westmoreland	300	W-128	Adam Sam/(r29 DEC 1787)William McGrew Original: found
NP-3155	Saam, Frederick	24 APR 1769		Huntingdon, Westmoreland	300	C-210-22	Col. Clapham/John Frey/[see Adam Sam's survey on NP-3153] Original: found
NP-3156	Jacob, William	24 APR 1769		Washington, Fayette	300	D-60-267 A-40-247	(r30 JAN 1789)Samuel Jackson Original: Missing
NP-3157	Campbell, Dougal (of Allentown, Northampton County, joiner)	24 APR 1769		Wilkins, Allegheny	300	D-70-101	George Croghan/--- Bossman Original: With NP-3158 Signed
NP-3158	Kerley, John (of Allentown)	24 APR 1769		Wilkins, Allegheny	300	D-70-80	--- Campbell/Col. George Croghan Original: found
NP-3159	Kerr, William	24 APR 1769	Cumberland	Centre, Indiana	300	C-121-46	(r29 MAR 1822)B. Odair & J. Agey Original: found

Table 6 - New Purchase Applications (1769-1773)

Number	Applicant	Date	Orig. Place	Later Place	Acres	Survey	Neighbors, Notes, etc.
NP-3160	Collier, John	24 APR 1769	Cumberland	Allegheny, Armstrong	300	C-189-80	(r25 APR 1827)James Ross Original: found
NP-3161	Elder, John	24 APR 1769	Cumberland	Gilpin, Armstrong	300	D-46-97	Original: found
NP-3162	Rennick, James	24 APR 1769	Cumberland	Bethel, Armstrong	300	C-65-157	(r11 JAN 1803)Thomas Gallagher/[see caveat] Original: found
NP-3163	Steel, John	24 APR 1769	Cumberland	Crooked Run, Armstrong	300	C-37-88	(r22 DEC 1815)P. Clingansmith Original: found
NP-3164	Campbell, William	24 APR 1769	Centre	Bald Eagle, Clinton	300	A-23-168	(r6 JAN 1813)Alexander Robertson & Margraet Robertson [his wife] Original: With NP-3165 Signed Francis Campbell
NP-3165	Campbell, John	24 APR 1769		Bald Eagle Creek, Clinton/ LD: Colebrook, Clinton	300		Original: found
NP-3166	Mahan, David	24 APR 1769	Bald Eagle Creek	LD: Clinton/ Centre	300		Original: found
NP-3167	Perry, Robert	24 APR 1769	Whitely Creek	LD: Greene	300		Charles Burcome/[see caveat] Original: found
NP-3168	Perry, Samuel	24 APR 1769		Dunbar, Fayette/ LD: Tyrone, Fayette	300	X-168 C-33-147	(r14 FEB 1846)Thomas Craig Original: found
NP-3169	Perry, John	24 APR 1769		Dunbar, Fayette	300	C-29-152 C-152-239 B-14-160	(r16 OCT 1827)David Cathcart/(r27 MAY 1829)Alexander McCalland/(r4 NOV 1864)Mary Meason Original: found
NP-3170	McCleane, Andrew (of Shippensburg, skinner)	26 APR 1769		Ligonier, Westmoreland	300	D-70-123 D-70-124	Robert Laughlin Original: Signed.
NP-3171	Steigel, Henry William	27 APR 1769		Washington, Lycoming	300	D-70-141	Original: With NP-3172

Table 6 - New Purchase Applications (1769-1773)

Number	Applicant	Date	Orig. Place	Later Place	Acres	Survey	Neighbors, Notes, etc.
NP-3172	Ege, George	27 APR 1769		Wayne, Lycoming	300	D-70-140	Original: found
NP-3173	Rice, John	27 APR 1769		Chapman, Union	300	D-70-153	William Blyth Original: found
NP-3174	Tomkin, Thomas	27 APR 1769		Briar Creek Twp., Columbia	300	A-38-47	(r21 SEP 1810)Edward Burd Original: found
NP-3175	Cannon, William	27 APR 1769		Briar Creek, Columbia	300	C-210-80	(r6 AUG 1787)Edward Shippen & Joseph Shippen Jr. Esq. Original: With NP-3176-3177
NP-3176	Sneider, Simon	27 APR 1769		Briar Creek, Columbia	300	F-180	William Cannon/(r27 JUL 1787)Edward Shippen & Joseph Shippen, Jr., Esq. Original: found
NP-3177	Griem, Garret	27 APR 1769	Northumberland	Briar Creek, Columbia	300	D-91	Simon Sneider/(r5 JUL 1797)Anthony Adam Original: found
NP-3178	Lesher, George	27 APR 1769		Briar Creek, Columbia	300	C-193-244	Garret Griem/(r19 MAR 1788)Edward Shippen & Joseph Shippen Original: With NP-3179-3181
NP-3179	King, Daniel	27 APR 1769	Northumberland	Briar Creek, Columbia	300	F-63	(r26 JUN 1797)Edward Shippen & Joseph Shippen Jr. Original: found
NP-3180	Guy, John	27 APR 1769	Northumberland	Briar Creek, Columbia	300	A-38-59	Daniel King/(r4 MAY 1810)Edward Burd Original: found
NP-3181	McGannon, Michael	27 APR 1769	Northumberland	Briar Creek, Columbia	300	F-57	(r26 JUN 1797)Edward Shippen & Joseph Shippen Original: found
NP-3182	Breidebach, Michael	27 APR 1769		Chapman, Union/ LD: Fayette	100	D-70-152	George Herold/George Bower Original: Signed With NP-3183
NP-3183	Whitmore, Peter (of Lebanon)	27 APR 1769	Northumberland	Middle Creek, Union - Snyder	300	A-48-66	(r6 NOV 1787)Abraham Raiguee Original: found
NP-3184	Bratt, Andrew	1 MAY 1769	East Branch Susquehanna River	LD: Wyoming	300		Thomas Heath Original: found

Table 6 - New Purchase Applications (1769-1773)

Number	Applicant	Date	Orig. Place	Later Place	Acres	Survey	Neighbors, Notes, etc.
NP-3185	Berringer, Nicholas	1 MAY 1769	East Branch Susquehanna River	LD: Bradford	300		James Furgeson Original: found
NP-3186	Campbell, Cleary (of Juniata)	5 MAY 1769		Blacklick Creek, Indiana	300	D-70-109	Original: With NP-3187-3188
NP-3187	Long, Cookson (of Lurgan Township, [now Franklin County], yeoman)	5 MAY 1769		Walker, Centre	300	C-86-213 C-94-131 C-141-257 C-141-259	(r24 FEB 1820)John Irvine/(r9 JAN 1835)John Hay/(r14 JUL 1851)Hugh McManegal Original: found
NP-3188	Long, John (of Juniatta, silversmith)	5 MAY 1769	West Branch Susquehanna River	LD: Clinton	300		Cleary Campbell Original: Signed
NP-3189	McKibbins, James Sr. (of Lurgan, yeoman)	5 MAY 1769		Centre, Centre	300	N-141	(r1 MAY)William McKibben & Archibald Allison Original: With NP-3190-3191
NP-3190	McKibbins, Joseph Jr. (of Lurgan, yeoman)	5 MAY 1769		Bald Eagle, Centre	300	C-145-69	John McKibbins/(r17 JUL 1812)Joseph McKibbin Original: found
NP-3191	McKibbins, James Jr. (of Lurgan, yeoman)	5 MAY 1769		Bald Eagle, Centre	300	C-218-7 C-17-250 C-145-69	Joseph Mckibbin/(r22 OCT 1851)William Swanzey & H. Swanzey/(r22 OCT 1851)Jesse Beck & Nathan Beck/(r17 JUL 1812)Joseph McKibbin Original: found
NP-3192	Long, Ann (of Hopewell)	5 MAY 1769		Walker, Centre/ LD: Walker, Centre	300	D-33-53 C-213-131 C-213-125	(r22 APR 1812)Samuel Weakley & Thomas Campbell/(r7 FEB 1822)William Smith Original: found
NP-3193	Long, George (of Lurgan, yeoman)	5 MAY 1769	West Branch Susquehanna River	LD: Clinton	300		Original: found
NP-3194	Pollock, Mary (of Carlisle)	5 MAY 1769	Lycoming	Nittany Valley, Centre	300	C-160-154	(r24 JUN 1796)James Pollock Original: found
NP-3195	Mahan, Alexander (of Lurgan, yeoman)	5 MAY 1769	Muncy Hill	LD: Clinton/ Centre	300		Original: found
NP-3196	Campbell, Thomas (of New Castle County)	5 MAY 1769	Bald Eagle Creek	LD: Centre	300		Original: found
NP-3197	Stafford, James	8 MAY 1769		Hempfield, Westmoreland	300	D-56-268 D-70-121 D-70-122	Joseph Erwin/Robert Laughlin Original: found

Table 6 - New Purchase Applications (1769-1773)

Number	Applicant	Date	Orig. Place	Later Place	Acres	Survey	Neighbors, Notes, etc.
NP-3198	Christy, John	8 MAY 1769		Shamokin Creek, Northumberland	300	C-78-115	Chillaway [an Indian](r7 SEP 1774)Reuben Haines Original: With NP-3199-3200
NP-3199	Treat, Samuel	8 MAY 1769		Shamokin Creek, Northumberland	300	C-78-113	John Christy/(r7 SEP 1774)Reuben Haines Original: found
NP-3200	Clark, John	8 MAY 1769		Shamokin Creek, Northumberland	300	C-78-114	Samuel Treat/(r7 SEP 1774)Reuben Haines Original: found
NP-3201	Mitchell, Robert	9 MAY 1769		Pitt, Allegheny/ LD: Pitt, Allegheny	300	X-210	John Donne Original: With NP-3202-3207
NP-3202	McDowal, Thomas	9 MAY 1769		South Huntingdon, Westmoreland	300	D-70-120	James Thompson Original: found
NP-3203	Howcroft, Thomas	9 MAY 1769		East Huntingdon, Westmoreland	300	D-70-149	Hugh Bay Original: found
NP-3204	Hoult, William	9 MAY 1769		East Huntingdon, Westmoreland	300	D-70-148	Thomas McDowell/Thomas Howcroft Original: found
NP-3205	Mitchell, John	9 MAY 1769		Pitt, Allegheny	300	D-55-64 D-56-176 D-56-178 E-69	Col. James Burd/(r27 JAN 1800)John Woods, Esq. Original: found
NP-3206	Hoye, Andrew	9 MAY 1769		Plum, Allegheny/ LD: North Huntingdon, Westmoreland	300	A-36-20	Aneas McKay/[see caveat] Original: found
NP-3207	Tate, Benjamin	9 MAY 1769	Washington	Monongahela River, Allegheny	300	D-201	Alexander Ross/George England/(r8 MAR 1784)William Bousman, Esq. Original: found
NP-3208	Campbell, John	9 MAY 1769	Cumberland	Fayette, Allegheny	300	A-28-194	(r28 FEB 1804)J. Beard Original: With NP-3209-3210
NP-3209	Fleming, David	9 MAY 1769		St. Clair, Allegheny	300	C-177-53 D-7-85 D-7-91	(r27 SEP 1808)John Morton & E. Morton/(r14 JUL 1810)Samuel G. Wilson/[see caveat] Original: found
NP-3210	Dunfield, Frederick	9 MAY 1769	Cumberland	Mifflin, Allegheny	300	D-70-81	Original: found

Table 6 - New Purchase Applications (1769-1773)

Number	Applicant	Date	Orig. Place	Later Place	Acres	Survey	Neighbors, Notes, etc.
NP-3211	Henry, Moses	9 MAY 1769	Cumberland	Pitt, Allegheny	300	D-70-83	Maj. Murray Original: found
NP-3212	Milligan, James	9 MAY 1769	Cumberland	Peebles, Allegheny	300	A-57-128 B-1-123 A-57-129	Charles McClure/(r4 AUG 1851)Dalmont Jones [patent H-48-262]/(p12 APR 1786) Original: Signed
NP-3213	McClure, Charles	9 MAY 1769	Cumberland	Burrell, Westmoreland - Armstrong	300	C-183-88	(r1 FEB 1812)William Ross Original: Signed
NP-3214	Kelly, James	9 MAY 1769	Cumberland	Plum, Allegheny	300	D-70-82 C-172-87	James Fleming/(27 MAR 1788)John Parker Original: Signed
NP-3215	Hamilton, Robert	9 MAY 1769	Chummumimis Run, Cumberland	LD: Peebles, Allegheny	300		James Milligan/Charles McClure Original: Signed
NP-3216	Fleming, James	9 MAY 1769	Cumberland	Plum, Allegheny/ LD: Plum, Allegheny	300	D-70-84	Original: Signed
NP-3217	Scott, William (of Donegal)	13 MAY 1769		Bald Eagle, Centre/ LD: Centre	300	H-78	Original: found
NP-3218	Scott, John (of Donegal)	13 MAY 1769	Bald Eagle Creek	LD: Centre	300		[see caveat] Original: found
NP-3219	Diehl, Godfrey	13 MAY 1769	on road from Easton to Wyoming		300		Original: found
NP-3220	Rodney, John (of Sussex County)	13 MAY 1769		Wheatfield, Clearfield	300	B-594	(r6 APR 1841)Samuel Thomas Original: Missisng
NP-3221	Anderson, Thomas	13 MAY 1769	Northeast Branch Susquehanna River	LD: Bradford	300		Original: found
NP-3222	Anderson, Alexander	13 MAY 1769		Plymouth, Luzerne	300	P-90	William Anderson/Isaac Stille/(r3 MAR 1823)Martha Wilson Original: found
NP-3223	Anderson, William	13 MAY 1769	Northeast Branch Susquehanna River	LD: Bradford	300		Isaac Stille Original: Signed
NP-3224	Elder, Mary	13 MAY 1769	Cumberland	Crooked Creek, Indiana	300	I-445	(r13 MAR 1811)Robert Elder Original: found

Table 6 - New Purchase Applications (1769-1773)

Number	Applicant	Date	Orig. Place	Later Place	Acres	Survey	Neighbors, Notes, etc.
NP-3225	Elder, Robert	13 MAY 1769	Cumberland	Plum Creek, Indiana	300	C-50-298	(r9 APR 1788)Joshua Elder Original: found
NP-3226	Cowden, William	13 MAY 1769	Cumberland	Westmoreland - Crooked Creek, Armstrong	300	Q-249	(r23 APR 1805) Original: found
NP-3227	Elder, John	13 MAY 1769	Cumberland	Conemaugh, Indiana	300	C-60-231 C-60-239	(r26 OCT 1814)Thomas Elder/[see caveat] Original: found
NP-3228	McGery, Clemens	13 MAY 1769		Mt. Pleasant & Unity, Westmoreland	300	D-70-146 D-70-147	Original: found
NP-3229	Miller, Mathew	13 MAY 1769		Sewickley Creek, Westmoreland/ LD: Westmoreland	300	A-237	Archibald McKee Original: found
NP-3230	Brown, William	13 MAY 1769		Hempfield, Westmoreland	300	C-39-67	Nathaniel Nelson/Joseph Morrison/Isaac Miller/(r8 DEC 1787)/[see caveat] Original: found
NP-3231	Miller, Samuel	13 MAY 1769		Little Sewickley Creek, Westmoreland	300	C-136-38	John Brown/Nathaniel Nelson/(r12 MAR 1770) Original: found
NP-3232	Polke, Edmond	13 MAY 1769	Washington	Muddy Run, Greene	300	A-11-24	John Swons, Jr./(r30 SEP 1788)Charles Anderson Original: Signed
NP-3233	Merrill, Joseph	17 MAY 1769	Northeast Branch Susquehanna River	LD: Luzerne	150		[see caveat] Original: found
NP-3234	Hill, John	17 MAY 1769	Northeast Branch Susquehanna River	LD: Northumberland	300		Original: found
NP-3235	Martin, John	17 MAY 1769		Pitt, Allegheny	300	D-70-90	Capt. Anguish McDonald/Josiah Crawford Original: Signed by Thomas Martin
NP-3236	Martin, Thomas	17 MAY 1769		Washington, Fayette	300	C-93-4	William Dane/Moses Browd/(r28 AUG 1793)Margaret Hutton Original: found

Table 6 - New Purchase Applications (1769-1773)

Number	Applicant	Date	Orig. Place	Later Place	Acres	Survey	Neighbors, Notes, etc.
NP-3237	Martin, Samuel	17 MAY 1769		Washington, Fayette	300	C-25-118	William Lines/William Crocket/David Welsh/(r27 DEC 1784)Edward Cook, Esq. Original: found
NP-3238	Martin, Samuel (of Allen Township, Cumberland County, yeoman)	17 MAY 1769		Monongahela River, Greene/ LD: Washington	300	X-214	Henry Horoble/Andrew Martin Original: found
NP-3239	Martin, Samuel Sr. (of Allen Township, Cumberland County, weaver)	17 MAY 1769		Rostraver, Westmoreland & Washington, Fayette	300	C-141-40	Alexander Bolins/Alexander Boten/(r30 OCT 1792)Thomas Moorhead/[see caveat] Original: found
NP-3240	Miller, Peter	17 MAY 1769		Point, Northumberland/ LD: Turbot, Northumberland	1000	D-62-119 A-238 C-78-248 D-25-93	(r28 JUN 1782)Reuben Haines/(r25 APR 1795)William Rawle, Esq. & Susannah Pater & Frederick Beatis, executors of Peter Miller, deceased Original: found
NP-3241	Bunsure, John	19 MAY 1769		Ligonier, Westmoreland	300	A-34-17	Henry Slaughter/Fredrick Sever Original: Signed
NP-3242	Martin, Thomas	19 MAY 1769		Armstrong, Indiana	300	C-204-123	Thomas Jemison/(r8 JAN 1817)George Scott Original: Signed
NP-3243	Laveor, Daniel	19 MAY 1769		Mill Creek, Westmoreland/ LD: Ligonier, Westmoreland	300	A-33-269	McCall Coffman/Robert Laughlin/James Elliott Original: Signed
NP-3244	Laveor, John Jacob	19 MAY 1769		Donegal, Westmoreland	300	C-53-280	(r3 APR 1789)Andrew Galbreath & John Galbreath Original: found
NP-3245	McCleery, William	20 MAY 1769		Union, Fayette	300	D-70-269	[see caveat] Original: Signed
NP-3246	McCleery, Isabella	20 MAY 1769		Union, Fayette	300	B-13-61 B-13-62	Capt. Brownfield/(r20 NOV 1788)Thomas Kindle/[see caveat] Original: Signed
NP-3247	Hervey, William Sr.	20 MAY 1769		Mt. Pleasant, Westmoreland	300	D-70-267	--- Nicholas/Capt. William Thompson Original: With NP-3248

Table 6 - New Purchase Applications (1769-1773)

Number	Applicant	Date	Orig. Place	Later Place	Acres	Survey	Neighbors, Notes, etc.
NP-3248	Brice, James	20 MAY 1769		Mt. Pleasant, Westmoreland	300	D-70-265 D-70-266	William Hervey Original: found
NP-3249	Hervey, John	20 MAY 1769		Elizabeth, Allegheny	300	D-70-279	Samuel Kyle's sons Original: With NP-3250
NP-3250	Hervey, William	20 MAY 1769		Elizabeth, Westmoreland & Allegheny	300	D-70-278	John Hervey Original: found
NP-3251	Lyon, Samuel Sr.	20 MAY 1769		Hempfield, Westmoreland	300	D-70-276 D-70-277	William Perry/James Baird/Capt. Thompson Original: found
NP-3252	Ashbridge, William	20 MAY 1769	Youghiogheny River	LD: Fayette	300		Alexander Dunlap Original: found
NP-3253	Alison, Benjamin	20 MAY 1769	Northumberland	Bald Eagle Creek, Centre	300	Q-37	French John/Dr. Allison/(r31 MAY 1782) Original: Signed by Francis Alison
NP-3254	Neely, Charles	22 MAY 1769		Unity, Westmoreland	300	D-70-275	Josiah Campbell Original: found
NP-3255	Reef, John	23 MAY 1769		Maple Creek, Washington	300	C-189-179	(r7 JAN 1789)Henry Spear Original: With NP-3256-3258
NP-3256	Rice, Ezeriah	23 MAY 1769	tributary of Monongahela River	LD: Washington/ Allegheny	300		Original: found
NP-3257	Smith, William (son of William, formerly magistrate)	23 MAY 1769		Rostraver, Westmoreland	300	C-21-219	(r15 FEB 1803)Edward Cook Original: found
NP-3258	Stuart, Mary	23 MAY 1769	Merggo Creek	LD: Washington	300		James Colvin Original: found
NP-3259	Hutchison, John	23 MAY 1769		Hempfield, Westmoreland	300	D-60-21 D-70-274	William Wilson Original: found
NP-3260	Rankin, William	23 MAY 1769		Nottingham, Washington	300	C-35-155	Robert Newell, Jr./(r10 NOV 1787)James Chambers Original: found

Table 6 - New Purchase Applications (1769-1773)

Number	Applicant	Date	Orig. Place	Later Place	Acres	Survey	Neighbors, Notes, etc.
NP-3261	Allmen, John	23 MAY 1769		Chartiers Creek, Washington	300	S-161	(r2 APR 1798)Alexander Spears Original: With NP-3262
NP-3262	McDowell, Thomas	23 MAY 1769		LD: Washington	300		John Allman Original: found
NP-3263	Young, William	23 MAY 1769		Chartiers Creek, Washington	300	R-298 A-67-137	Mathew Willson/Thomas McDowell/(r23 1788)Joseph Wherry/[see caveat] Original: found
NP-3264	Young, Alexander	23 MAY 1769		Hempfield, Westmoreland	300	A-9-205	(r7 AUG 1788)William Young/[see caveat] Original: found
NP-3265	McDowell, Agnes	23 MAY 1769		Hempfield, Westmoreland	300	D-70-273	Original: found
NP-3266	McDowell, Elizabeth	23 MAY 1769		North Huntingdon, Westmoreland/ LD: Westmoreland	300	D-70-272	Col. Chapham Original: found
NP-3267	Evans, William	23 MAY 1769		Centre, Indiana	300	E-181	Robert Huston/(r15 DEC 1812)John Ross Original: Signed
NP-3268	Willson, John	23 MAY 1769		Hempfield, Westmoreland	300	A-31-143 C-31-144 C-90-287	(r20 MAY 1828)Peter Herold/(r23 MAR 1830)John Young Original: found
NP-3269	Willson, William Jr.	23 MAY 1769	West Branch Chartiers Creek	LD: Allegheny	300		Original: found
NP-3270	Willson, Isaac	23 MAY 1769		Huntingdon, Westmoreland	300	D-56-258 D-70-268	Original: found
NP-3271	Willson, William Sr.	23 MAY 1769	East Branch Chartiers Creek	LD: Allegheny	300		Original: found
NP-3272	Wilson, Elizabeth	23 MAY 1769		South Huntingdon, Westmoreland	300	D-1-74 D-1-75	--- Proctor/(r25 FEB 1833) Original: found

Table 6 - New Purchase Applications (1769-1773)

Number	Applicant	Date	Orig. Place	Later Place	Acres	Survey	Neighbors, Notes, etc.
NP-3273	Hunter, Robert	23 MAY 1769		Hempfield & North Huntingdon, Westmoreland	300	D-70-271	Original: found
NP-3274	Willson, Matthew	23 MAY 1769	West Branch Chartiers Creek	LD: Allegheny	300		Original: found
NP-3275	Hunter, David	23 MAY 1769		North Huntingdon, Westmoreland	300	D-55-30 W-11	(r14 SEP 1790)Deborah Blackburn Original: found
NP-3276	Milner, Edward	23 MAY 1769	Cumberland	Washington, Lycoming	300	D-56-137 C-44-151	(r23 MAY 1794)John Donaldson, Esq. Original: found
NP-3277	Dunn, Thomas	23 MAY 1769	Moshannon Creek	LD: Clinton	300		Original: With NP-3278-3280
NP-3278	Swales, John	23 MAY 1769		Moshannon Creek, Clearfield/ LD: Clearfield	300		Thomas Dunn Original: found
NP-3279	Hess, Nicholas	23 MAY 1769		Chest, Clearfield	300	D-70-264 D-70-270	Original: found
NP-3280	Braithwaite, Thomas	23 MAY 1769	West Branch Susquehanna River	Frankstown, Huntingdon/ LD: Cambria	300	A-34-18	[see caveat] Original: found
NP-3281	McDowell, James Jr.	23 MAY 1769		Monongahela River, Washington	300	A-89-240	(r17 DEC 1793)Nathan Dailey Original: found
NP-3282	Willson, John	23 MAY 1769	Westmoreland	Rostraver, Allegheny	300	D-56-184 A-14-130	John Kyle/(8 OCT 1790)Robert Smith Original: found
NP-3283	Smith, Jonathan Jr.	23 MAY 1769	Monongahela River between Pigeon Creek & Mingo Creek	LD: Washington	300		Original: found
NP-3284	Willson, Isaac	23 MAY 1769		Monongahela River, Washington	300	A-77-35	(r13 FEB 1794)Cornelius Wayground Original: found

Table 6 - New Purchase Applications (1769-1773)

Number	Applicant	Date	Orig. Place	Later Place	Acres	Survey	Neighbors, Notes, etc.
NP-3285	Sipes, Charles	23 MAY 1769		Nottingham, Washington	300	C-93-33	James McDowell, Jr./(r6 DEC 1800)James Logan Original: found
NP-3286	Willson, William	23 MAY 1769		Pigeon Creek, Washington	300	C-205-187	(r16 MAY 1794)Christopher Stucker/[see caveat] Original: found
NP-3287	King, John	23 MAY 1769	Washington	Monongahela River, Allegheny	300	A-85-250	Richard McMahan/Benjamin Cockendal/(r18 SEP 1787)John McElhenry Original: found
NP-3288	Baird, George	23 MAY 1769		Mt. Pleasant, Westmoreland	300	D-15-49	Robert Peoples/William Furguson/(r26 NOV 1795)John Wolfart Original: found
NP-3289	Kenneday, William	24 MAY 1769	West Branch Susquehanna River	LD: Lycoming/ Clinton	300		Original: With NP-3290
NP-3290	Russell, Robert	24 MAY 1769	Muncy Hill	LD: Clinton	300		Original: Signed
NP-3291	Hall, David	26 MAY 1769	Cumberland	Westmoreland - Kiskiminitas Old Town, Allegheny	150	D-70-263	John Montgomery/Alexander Stuart/[see caveat] Original: With NP-3292
NP-3292	Hall, David	26 MAY 1769	Cumberland	Washington, Westmoreland/ LD: Washington, Westmoreland	100	A-36-6	Original: found
NP-3293	Caruther, John	26 MAY 1769	Montour Creek	LD: Northumberland	100		Col. Francis Original: found
NP-3294	Howey, William	26 MAY 1769		South Huntingdon, Westmoreland	300	C-107-1 C-107-2	William Martin/(r19 DEC 1814)Cathrine Howe & John Millikin Original: found
NP-3295	Flenicken, James	27 MAY 1769		Muddy Run, Greene/ LD: Greene	150	F-240	Original: With NP-3296-3300
NP-3296	Flenicken, James	27 MAY 1769		Cumberland, Greene/ LD: Greene	150	X-172 X-173	(p17 NOV 1899)Allen P. Dickey & Thomas S. Crago/[see caveat] Original: found

Table 6 - New Purchase Applications (1769-1773)

Number	Applicant	Date	Orig. Place	Later Place	Acres	Survey	Neighbors, Notes, etc.
NP-3297	Kennedy, John (of Peters Township)	27 MAY 1769	Washington	Muddy Creek, Greene/ LD: Cumberland, Greene	300		Original: Signed
NP-3298	Flenicken, James (son of John)	27 MAY 1769	Washington	Muddy Creek, Greene	300	A-10-308	(r24 SEP 1787) Original: found
NP-3299	Armstrong, John	27 MAY 1769		Cumberland, Greene	300	D-82	(r27 JAN 1814) Original: found
NP-3300	Kennedy, David (of Antrim Township, Cumberland County, son of David Kennedy)	27 MAY 1769		Monongahela River, Greene	300	C-35-47	(r5 APR 1815)David Bell Original: found
NP-3301	Wilson, Samuel	27 MAY 1769		Mt. Pleasant, Westmoreland	300	C-79-152 C-79-150	John McCelen/John McDonald/Edward Husk/(r14 MAR 1796)Nathaniel Hurst/[see caveat] Original: found
NP-3302	Brown, John Jr.	30 MAY 1769		Hempfield, Westmoreland	300	C-8-280	Rodge McBride/William Wilson/(r17 SEP 1794)/[patent P-23-267] Original: found
NP-3303	Campbell, John (formerly of the Path Valley)	30 MAY 1769		Hempfield, Westmoreland/ LD: Westmoreland	300	Z-57 Z-58 Z-59 Z-60 C-221-23	James Dorough/John Brown, Jr./(r10 MAY 1808)John M. Stake/[see caveat] Original: found
NP-3304	Miller, Abraham	30 MAY 1769	West Branch Susquehanna River, near Buffalo Creek, Cumberland	LD: Union	200		Mr. Smith Original: With NP-3305 Signed
NP-3305	Crows, Andrew	30 MAY 1769	Shamokin Creek	LD: Hempfield, Westmoreland	300		Original: found
NP-3306	Smith, Phillip	1 JUN 1769		Georges Creek, Fayette	300	C-215-3	(r26 JUN 1801)S. Smith Original: With NP-3307-3308
NP-3307	Smith, Henry	1 JUN 1769		Menallen, Fayette	300	C-168-202	(r9 JUN 1788)John Rogers Original: found

Table 6 - New Purchase Applications (1769-1773)

Number	Applicant	Date	Orig. Place	Later Place	Acres	Survey	Neighbors, Notes, etc.
NP-3308	Smith, Nicholas	1 JUN 1769		Menallen, Fayette	300	C-189-213	Henry Smith/(r26 MAR 1789) Original: found
NP-3309	Mike, Christopher (of Hunterdon, Jersey)	2 JUN 1769		Kingston, Luzerne/ LD: Kingston, Luzerne	300		Original: found
NP-3310	Lemly, Jacob (of Sussex County)	2 JUN 1769	Northumberland	Mill Creek & Lackawanna Creek, Luzerne	300	C-143-271	Mr. Allen/(r14 APR 1783)John M. Nesbit Original: found
NP-3311	Savage, Patrick (of Hunterdon)	2 JUN 1769		Luzerne/ LD: Luzerne	300	A-29-45	Phillip Johnston Original: found
NP-3312	Anderson, John	2 JUN 1769	at mouth of Tuscarora Creek	LD: Wyoming	150		Original: With NP-3313-3315
NP-3313	Anderson, John	2 JUN 1769	Tuscarora Creek	LD: Wyoming	150		Original: found
NP-3314	Anderson, John	2 JUN 1769	Susquehanna River	LD: Bradford	200		Original: found
NP-3315	Jennings, John	2 JUN 1769		East Branch Susquehanna River, Luzerne	1000	C-9-201 A-67-97	(29 SEP 1812)Eleazer Blackman/(r25 SEP 1809)Samuel Bowman Original: found
NP-3316	Baumgartner, George	3 JUN 1769		Monongahela River at Ten Mile Run, Washington	300	A-32-149	(r1 APR 1796) Original: With NP-337-3319
NP-3317	Baumgartner, Frederick	3 JUN 1769		Ten Mile Run, Washington/ LD: Washington	300	D-45-12 A-34-19 D-45-11	John Thoughtes/(r31 DEC 1798)Henry Enoch [on VA certificate]/(p2 JAN 1799)/[patent P-35-88] Original: found
NP-3318	Hop, Everhard	3 JUN 1769		Ten Mile Run, Washington	300	C-75-142	George Baumgartner/(r15 MAY 1788) Original: found
NP-3319	Hop, John	3 JUN 1769		Ten Mile Run, Washington	100	A-60-258	(r3 FEB 1797)George Teegarden Original: found
NP-3320	Hunter, Mary	5 JUN 1769	Cumberland	Youghiogheny River, Westmoreland	300	A-27-183	(r10 AUG 1770) Original: Signed by James Hunter
NP-3321	Scott, John	7 JUN 1769	Susquehanna River below Manahannunk Island	LD: Luzerne	300		Mr. Allen Original: With NP-3322-3325

Table 6 - New Purchase Applications (1769-1773)

Number	Applicant	Date	Orig. Place	Later Place	Acres	Survey	Neighbors, Notes, etc.
NP-3322	Scott, Amos	7 JUN 1769	Susquehanna River 3 miles above Manahannunk Island	LD: Luzerne	300		Mr. Allen Original: found
NP-3323	Hays, Thomas	7 JUN 1769		Susquehanna River at Manahannunk Island, Luzerne	300	N-241	(r14 APR 1783)John M. Nesbit Original: found
NP-3324	Hays, Andrew	7 JUN 1769	Nanticoke Creek	LD: Luzerne	300		Original: found
NP-3325	Simson, James	7 JUN 1769		Nanticoke Creek, Luzerne/ LD: Luzerne	300	A-225	Original: found
NP-3326	Munday, Baniah	8 JUN 1769	mouth of Catawissa Creek	LD: Columbia	200		Original: With NP-3327
NP-3327	Munday, Joshua	8 JUN 1769	Susquehanna River five miles above Fishing Creek	LD: Columbia	200		Original: found
NP-3328	King, John	12 JUN 1769		Kings Valley, Columbia or Luzerne	300	C-102-87	(r6 FEB 1770)/[see caveat] Original: With NP-3329-3331
NP-3329	Young, Lazarus	12 JUN 1769	Northeast Branch Susquehanna River & Fishing Creek	LD: Columbia	300		John King/[see caveat] Original: found
NP-3330	King, Lydia	12 JUN 1769		Kings Valley, Columbia or Luzerne	300	C-112-292	Lazarus Young/(r7 MAR 1776)Samuel Miles, Esq./[see caveat] Original: found
NP-3331	Young, Robert	12 JUN 1769	Northeast Branch Susquehanna River & Fishing Creek	LD: Columbia	300		Lydia King/[see caveat] Original: found
NP-3332	King, Cornelius	12 JUN 1769		Kings Valley, Columbia or Luzerne	300	C-112-294	Robert Young/(r8 MAR 1776)Samuel Miles, Esq./[see caveat] Original: With NP-3333

Table 6 - New Purchase Applications (1769-1773)

Number	Applicant	Date	Orig. Place	Later Place	Acres	Survey	Neighbors, Notes, etc.
NP-3333	Young, William	12 JUN 1769	Northeast Branch Susquehanna River & Fishing Creek	LD: Columbia	300		Cornelius King/[see caveat] Original: Signed by Lazarus Young
NP-3334	McClure, James	12 JUN 1769	Fishing Creek, East Branch Susquehanna River	LD: Columbia	300		Original: found
NP-3335	Kelly, John	12 JUN 1769	Berks	Kelly, Union	300	D-57-233 D-62-244 C-104-12	(r10 FEB 1796) Original: Signed by Andrew Kelly
NP-3336	Kelly, William	12 JUN 1769	Northumberland	Buffalo, Union	300	C-7-89	John Buchannon/(r10 AUG 1774)Thomas Black Original: Signed
NP-3337	Miller, John	13 JUN 1769	road to Ft. Pitt, 5 miles from Stony Creek	LD: Somerset	300		Original: found
NP-3338	Wells, Samuel Jr.	13 JUN 1769		Dunbar, Fayette	300	D-70-260	Samuel Wells, Sr. Original: found
NP-3339	Keiser, Peter	13 JUN 1769		Versailles, Allegheny	300	P-286	Jacob Zeinnot/--- McKee Original: Signed
NP-3340	Batersby, Timothy	13 JUN 1769		Huntingdon, Westmoreland	300	C-109-275 C-109-274	John Ross/William Irwin/(r26 SEP 1787)Benjamin Lodge Original: found
NP-3341	Braton, George	13 JUN 1769	Cumberland	East Huntingdon, Westmoreland & Bullskin, Fayette/ LD: Fayette	300	D-70-261 D-70-262	Original: found
NP-3342	Waugh, Robert	13 JUN 1769		Pitt, Westmoreland	300	A-57-129 A-57-131	James Milliken/Simeon Girty/James Bird/(r12 APR 1786)James Milliken [patent P-4-507] Original: found
NP-3343	McIlvaine, Andrew	13 JUN 1769		Bullskin, Fayette	300	D-70-249	Original: found

Table 6 - New Purchase Applications (1769-1773)

Number	Applicant	Date	Orig. Place	Later Place	Acres	Survey	Neighbors, Notes, etc.
NP-3344	Zeinnet, Jacob Jr.	13 JUN 1769		McKeesport & Versailles Twp., Allegheny/ LD: Versailles, Allegheny	300	D-56-165 X-137 X-138 X-139 C-8-63 B-11-5 B-9-239 C-161-170 C-6-84 B-19-76 C-128-244 B-20-127 B-20-176	John Zinnet/(p13 MAY 1891)McKeesport & Bessemer R. R. Co. [patent H-75-38]/(p5 APR 1899)Alonzo Inskeep & John Guice & Charles M. Bailey & William D. Chisholm [patent H-75-475]/(p18 MAY 1900)Catherine Soles [patent H-75-611]/(p7 JUN 1904)Jane E. Mars [patent H-76-386]/(p15 JUL 1892)Nannie M. Weddell [patent H-75-114]/(p25 MAR 1903)Mary Shaw & Margaret Stewart [patent H-76-260]/(p25 MAR 1903)Locust Grove Land Co. [patent H-76-259]/(p9 JUL 1906)Joseph A. Herron [patent H-77-201]/(p25 SEP 1907)Alice K. McIntyre [patent H-77-270] Original: Signed
NP-3345	McFarlington, James	13 JUN 1769		North Huntingdon, Westmoreland	300	D-70-259	Original: found
NP-3346	Hand, Edward	13 JUN 1769		Chartiers Creek, Allegheny	300	C-74-185	Eaneas Mackay/Samuel Young(r16 JUN 1791)/[see caveat] Original: found
NP-3347	Sample, John	13 JUN 1769		Chartiers Creek, Allegheny/ LD: Robinson, Allegheny	300	A-31-121	Andrew Robinson/Lewis Frederick Original: found
NP-3348	Bay, Hugh	13 JUN 1769		East Huntingdon, Westmoreland	300	D-70-247	Original: found
NP-3349	Cherry, Ralph	13 JUN 1769		Sewickley & Brush Creeks, Westmoreland	300	C-34-42	(r25 SEP 1787) Original: found
NP-3350	Horible, Barnabas	13 JUN 1769	Huntingdon	Long Ridge, branch of Youghiogheny River, Westmoreland - Allegheny/ LD: Westmoreland	300	A-36-7 A-36-8	Original: found

Table 6 - New Purchase Applications (1769-1773)

Number	Applicant	Date	Orig. Place	Later Place	Acres	Survey	Neighbors, Notes, etc.
NP-3351	McCuffog, Robert	13 JUN 1769		Huntingdon, Westmoreland/ LD: Huntingdon, Westmoreland	300	A-239	Johnston Smith/John Stevenson Original: found
NP-3352	Lyon, Samuel Jr.	13 JUN 1769		Redstone Creek, Fayette	300	A-23-139 A-23-140 B-2-143	James Cothamas/(r9 MAR 1786)James Finley/[see caveat] Original: Signed
NP-3353	Girty, Simon	13 JUN 1769		Pitt, Allegheny	300	D-70-248	Mary Girty/James Reed/Thomas Gibson Original: Signed
NP-3354	Bratten, Adam	13 JUN 1769		Huntingdon, Westmoreland	300	C-164-136	Capt. Thompson/(r16 JUN 1789)John Neil [patent P-15-78] Original: found
NP-3355	Bargamot, John	13 JUN 1769		North Huntingdon, Westmoreland/ LD: North Huntingdon, Westmoreland	300	F-241 D-12-168 C-226-263	(r9 OCT 1820)Robert Stewart/(r7 APR 1825)Joseph Thompson Original: found
NP-3356	Young, Adam	13 JUN 1769		Pike Run, Washington	150	C-89-230	Isaac William/Peter Young/(r22 FEB 1785)Robert Jackman Original: found
NP-3357	Penticost, Dorsey	13 JUN 1769		Rostraver, Westmoreland	300	I-338	(r24 JUL 1787)Cumberland Dugan/[see caveat] Original: found
NP-3358	Meek, Joshua	13 JUN 1769		East Huntingdon, Westmoreland	300	D-70-246	Original: found
NP-3359	Davison, Lewis	13 JUN 1769		Versailles, Allegheny	300	D-70-245	Capt. Thompson Original: found
NP-3360	McFigart, Charles	13 JUN 1769		North Branch Sewickley Creek, Westmoreland	300	A-83-187	Benjamin Brunston/(r5 AUG 1788)Anthony Alteman Original: found
NP-3361	Street, William	13 JUN 1769		Chartiers Creek, Allegheny/ LD: Upper St. Clair, Allegheny	200	X-149	Robert Bell/John Ronno/John Erwin Original: found
NP-3362	Powell, John	13 JUN 1769	Westmoreland	Pitt, Allegheny	100	B-600	(r30 NOV 1795)Michael Zimmerman Original: found

Table 6 - New Purchase Applications (1769-1773)

Number	Applicant	Date	Orig. Place	Later Place	Acres	Survey	Neighbors, Notes, etc.
NP-3363	McFarlane, James	13 JUN 1769	Cumberland	Chartiers Creek, Westmoreland - Allegheny	300	M-409	(r27 NOV 1788) Original: found
NP-3364	Barnabas, Christopher	13 JUN 1769		Sewickley Creek, Westmoreland	300	A-86-96	Benjamin Brunston/(r4 MAY 1798)John Peter Alteman Original: found
NP-3365	Miers, James	13 JUN 1769		Pitt, Westmoreland	300	C-89-278	(r30 JUL 1788)Adam Jacoby Original: found
NP-3366	Husk, John	13 JUN 1769		Greene, Greene	300	B-45-64 C-64-60 C-64-61	(r30 JAN 1830)Mathew Donaway Original: found
NP-3367	Milliken, James	13 JUN 1769	six miles east of Ft. Pitt	Peebles, Allegheny/ LD: Pitt, Allegheny	200	A-60-101 A-60-102	James Beaty/James Reed/John Carter/[returned on two Allegheny County warrants:] (w1 APR 1845)Walter Forward/(r22 JAN 1873)John S. Bruner/(w23 JAN 1846 & r25 MAR 1846)William Craig Original: found
NP-3368	Meirs, Martha (widow)	13 JUN 1769		Plum, Allegheny	300	D-64-141 C-120-253	James Meirs/(r8 DEC 1787)Eleazer Myers/[patent P-11-449] Original: found
NP-3369	Greenbury, Thomas	13 JUN 1769		North Huntingdon, Westmoreland	300	D-70-258	James McFarlington Original: found
NP-3370	Powel, Eliazer	13 JUN 1769	Westmoreland	Huntingdon, Allegheny	300	C-116-199	(r19 JAN 1792)Daniel Leap/[patent P-18-333] Original: found
NP-3371	Holliday, James	13 JUN 1769		South Huntingdon, Westmoreland	300	Z-64 Z-65 Z-66 C-206-86	William Butler/(r15 FEB 1799)Thomas Shields/[see caveat] Original: found
NP-3372	Williams, Isaac	13 JUN 1769	Cumberland	Monongahela River, Washington	300	B-15	John Williams/(r1 OCT 1784)Joshua Dixon Original: found
NP-3373	Tramel, Ezekiel	13 JUN 1769		Hickman Run, Fayette/ LD: Westmoreland	300	A-229	Josiah Wallace/Ezekiel Hickman Original: found
NP-3374	Nichols, John Sr.	13 JUN 1769		Tyrone, Fayette	300	D-70-257	Capt. Thompson/Johnston Smith/John Stephenson Original: found

Table 6 - New Purchase Applications (1769-1773)

Number	Applicant	Date	Orig. Place	Later Place	Acres	Survey	Neighbors, Notes, etc.
NP-3375	Wells, Samuel Sr.	13 JUN 1769		Tyrone, Fayette	300	A-21-291	Capt. Thompson/(r11 SEP 1790)Abraham Stauffer Original: found
NP-3376	Husk, Nathaniel	13 JUN 1769		Hempfield, Westmoreland	300	D-64-124 M-132	(r6 AUG 1788)Christopher Lavengair Original: found
NP-3377	Young, Adam	13 JUN 1769		Fallowfield, Washington	200	C-43-183	Henry Swort/Ebenezer Bruster/(r14 JAN 1822)Alexander C. Donaldson Original: found
NP-3378	Presser, Henry	13 JUN 1769		Monongahela River, Washington	300	A-64-228	George Corn/John Williams/(r21 DEC 1774)Joseph Allen Original: found
NP-3379	Swort, Henry	13 JUN 1769		Monongahela River, Washington	300	K-31	Peter Hank & Adam Young/(r22 APR 1788)James Ellis Original: found
NP-3380	Hank, Peter	13 JUN 1769	Westmoreland	Monongahela River, Washington	300	C-40-162	Henry Swort/(r3 JUL 1810)James Cook Original: found
NP-3381	Nicholas, John	13 JUN 1769		Mt. Pleasant, Westmoreland	300	C-210-27	Jacob Swany/(r5 MAY 1787)William Shrater/[see caveat] Original: found
NP-3382	Harrison, Battle	13 JUN 1769		Youghiogheny River, Fayette	300	C-144-64	Lawrence Harrison, Jr./(r18 APR 1788)William Miller/[see caveat] Original: found
NP-3383	Brooks, William	13 JUN 1769	Westmoreland	Braddocks Road, Fayette	300	C-7-222	Capt. Charles Edmonstone/(r18 FEB 1782)Gen'l. Washington Original: found
NP-3384	Lynn, William	13 JUN 1769	Little Redstone Creek	LD: Fayette	300		Original: found
NP-3385	Harrison, Lawrence, Jr.	13 JUN 1769		Youghiogheny River, Fayette	300	D-6-69 D-6-70	Benjamin Harrison/(r19 APR 1785)George Wallace Original: found
NP-3386	O'Harra, Arthur	13 JUN 1769		Unity, Westmoreland	300	D-70-255 D-70-256	John Davey Original: found
NP-3387	Anderson, John	13 JUN 1769		branch of Sewickley Creek, Westmoreland/ LD: Westmoreland	300	Z-70	[see caveat] Original: found

Table 6 - New Purchase Applications (1769-1773)

Number	Applicant	Date	Orig. Place	Later Place	Acres	Survey	Neighbors, Notes, etc.
NP-3388	Wilson, Edward	13 JUN 1769	Cumberland	Sewickley Creek, Westmoreland	300	A-5-12	Nathaniel Nelson Original: found
NP-3389	McGuffog, Joseph	13 JUN 1769		East Huntingdon, Westmoreland	300	D-70-254	Capt. Thompson Original: found
NP-3390	Smith, James	13 JUN 1769		Dunbar, Fayette	300	D-70-253	Original: found
NP-3391	Milliken, George	13 JUN 1769		Pitt, Allegheny	250	D-70-252	Thomas Gibson/Simeon Girty/Robert Waugh Original: found
NP-3392	Gibson, Thomas	13 JUN 1769		Pitt & Wilkins, Allegheny/ LD: Pitt & Wilkins, Allegheny	300	D-56-169 W-70 A-5-193 D-33-297 B-1-94	(r3 MAR 1826)John Reed/(r28 APR 1854)Boyle Irwin/(p12 MAR 1941)Dominick Corsale & Kathryn Corsale/[patent H-79-366] Original: found
NP-3393	Simon, Andrew	13 JUN 1769		Versailles, Allegheny	200	D-70-251	Capt. William Thompson Original: found
NP-3394	Jack, Samuel	13 JUN 1769		Chartiers Creek, Allegheny	300	A-85-182	John Stewert/Joseph Crosswell/Christian Miller/(r27 FEB 1807)Gillston George Original: Signed
NP-3395	Troop, William	13 JUN 1769		Pitt, Allegheny	200	B-7-107	Mary Girty/Col. Bird/(r7 MAY 1785)Charles Duke Original: Signed
NP-3396	Miers, Eleazer	13 JUN 1769		Pitt, Westmoreland/ LD: Allegheny	300	X-213	Jacob Bowsman Original: found
NP-3397	Girty, George	13 JUN 1769		Pitt, Allegheny	300	D-70-250	James Reed/Simon Girty Original: found
NP-3398	Barret, Nathaniel	13 JUN 1769		South Fork of Mounts Creek, Fayette	300	A-59-56	(r13 MAY 1784)Phillip Tanner Original: found
NP-3399	Simpson, Thomas	13 JUN 1769		Hempfield, Westmoreland/ LD: Hempfield, Westmoreland	300	C-221-83 C-221-81 C-221-82 C-221-84 C-221-85 B-18-209	Thomas Thompson/John Nicholason/(r18 JAN 1813)Mathias Moyer/(r11 APR 1831)James Simpson/(p1 APR 1870)Daniel Mitchell/(p8 APR 1870)William Simpson Original: found
NP-3400	McGines, Charles	13 JUN 1769		Pitt & Hempfield, Westmoreland	100	M-416	Aunges McCay/(r18 APR 1786) Original: found

Table 6 - New Purchase Applications (1769-1773)

Number	Applicant	Date	Orig. Place	Later Place	Acres	Survey	Neighbors, Notes, etc.
NP-3401	McIlvane, James	13 JUN 1769		Jacobs Creek & Meeks Run, Allegheny	300	C-176-51	Joashua Meeks/(r11 JAN 1771)William Robinson Original: found
NP-3402	McHenry, Joseph	13 JUN 1769		South Huntingdon, Westmoreland & Tyrone, Fayette	300	D-70-240 D-70-243	Joseph Huston Original: found
NP-3403	Arden, Joseph	13 JUN 1769	Cumberland	four miles east of Ft. Pitt, Westmoreland/ LD: Pitt, Allegheny	200	X-15 C-28-198 C-153-165	Devereux Smith/James Ryal/Mr. Ambrose Newton/(p16 JUN 1800)James Chadwick[patent H-272-362]/(p16 OCT 1839)William Moore[patent H-41-333] Original: Signed
NP-3404	Touseman, John	13 JUN 1769		Elizabeth, Allegheny	300	B-124	John Fry/(r16 FEB 1814)Anthony Drevox Original: found
NP-3405	Flitcher, James	13 JUN 1769		Unity, Westmoreland	300	D-62-269 D-62-270 C-125-191	William Proctor/(r26 JAN 1811)Samuel Hunter Original: found
NP-3406	Davey, John	13 JUN 1769		Mt. Pleasant, Westmoreland	300	A-75-299	(r17 MAR 1789)William Todd, Esq. Original: found
NP-3407	Smelserer, John	13 JUN 1769		Pitt, Allegheny	200	D-70-241	John Carter Original: Signed
NP-3408	Bumstick, William	13 JUN 1769	Westmoreland	Ligonier - Ft. Pitt Road, Allegheny	300	A-12-231	--- Medcalf/(r28 MAR 1788)Thomas Shields/[patent P-14-70] Original: found
NP-3409	Flatcher, Thomas	13 JUN 1769		Unity, Westmoreland	300	D-70-242 D-70-244 C-48-255	William Proctor/(r4 MAR 1790) Original: found
NP-3410	McCoyne, James	13 JUN 1769		Ligonier, Westmoreland	300	D-70-229	William McKinzy Original: found
NP-3411	McKee, James	13 JUN 1769		Plum, Allegheny	200	D-70-92	Eneas McCoy/widow Myer Original: found
NP-3412	Smellser, Peter	13 JUN 1769		Pitt & Wilkins, Allegheny/ LD: Pitt, Allegheny	200	D-70-228 D-56-169 C-17-191 D-33-297	Thomas Gibson/James Reed/John Boyle Original: found
NP-3413	McKee, Thomas	13 JUN 1769		Hempfield, Westmoreland	300	D-70-227	Original: found

Table 6 - New Purchase Applications (1769-1773)

Number	Applicant	Date	Orig. Place	Later Place	Acres	Survey	Neighbors, Notes, etc.
NP-3414	Mansfield, Joseph	13 JUN 1769		Ligonier, Westmoreland & Dunbar, Fayette	300	D-70-225 D-70-226	John Fisher/[name is Manfield and Mawfield on surveys] Original: found
NP-3415	Dunstable, Christian	13 JUN 1769		Huntingdon, Westmoreland	300	C-194-281	(r3 JUL 1795)John Shanon Original: found
NP-3416	Stewart, Thomas	13 JUN 1769		Chartiers Creek, Allegheny/ LD: St. Clair, Allegheny	300	A-222	Samuel Black Original: found
NP-3417	Stewart, John	13 JUN 1769		Tyrone, Fayette	300	C-210-96	Ezekial Tramel/(r2 OCT 1787) Original: found
NP-3418	Stewart, John	13 JUN 1769		North Huntingdon, Westmoreland	300	C-172-78 B-16-36	--- Crawford/(r17 DEC 1787)George Baird, Esq. Original: found
NP-3419	McFadian, Archibald	13 JUN 1769		Pitt, Westmoreland	300	C-193-260	William Bumstick/William Powell/(r28 MAR 1788)Thomas Shields/[patent P-14-69]/[see caveat] Original: found
NP-3420	Robinson, William	13 JUN 1769		Mt. Pleasant, Westmoreland	300	D-70-239	Original: found
NP-3421	Hickman, Ezekiel	13 JUN 1769		Mt. Pleasant, Westmoreland	300	D-70-238	Original: found
NP-3422	Brunston, Benjamin	13 JUN 1769		Hempfield, Westmoreland	300	D-70-237	Original: found
NP-3423	McMenimy, William	13 JUN 1769		Pitt, Allegheny	200	D-70-236	Fredrick Ferry/John McKee/Mary Girty/Deveroux Smith/James Royle Original: Signed
NP-3424	Gregory, Gustavus	13 JUN 1769		Hempfield, Westmoreland/ LD: Hempfield, Westmoreland	200	D-70-235	Original: found
NP-3425	Allen, Robert	13 JUN 1769		St. Clair, Allegheny	300	D-70-93	Original: found
NP-3426	Dewit, Ezekiel	13 JUN 1769		Fallowfield & Allen, Washington/ LD: Washington	300	H-166	Peter Hinks Original: found

Table 6 - New Purchase Applications (1769-1773)

Number	Applicant	Date	Orig. Place	Later Place	Acres	Survey	Neighbors, Notes, etc.
NP-3427	McFarlane, Andrew	13 JUN 1769		Monongahela River, Washington	300	C-93-32	John Cox/(r23 MAY 1785) Original: found
NP-3428	McDonnel, Martin	13 JUN 1769		Mt. Pleasant, Westmoreland	300	D-55-100 C-53-203	Hugh Bays/(r7 MAR 1787)James Guthry Original: found
NP-3429	Spencer, Thomas	13 JUN 1769	Peters Creek, Cumberland	LD: Allegheny	300		Original: found
NP-3430	Zeinnet, John	13 JUN 1769		Versailles, Allegheny	300	D-70-94	Robert Travirs/Jacob Zeinnet, Jr. Original: Signed
NP-3431	McNavare, William	13 JUN 1769		Mt. Pleasant, Westmoreland	300	D-70-234	John Ross Original: found
NP-3432	Proctor, William (son of John)	13 JUN 1769		Unity, Westmoreland	300	D-55-60 D-55-46 C-47-257 C-199-147 D-55-46 C-80-84 C-152-195 C-152-196	William Proctor, Sr./(r8 JAN 1812)David Fletcher/(r6 MAR 1812)George Smith/(r10 FEB 1819)H. Hamilton/(r9 FEB 1829)Robert McGrogan heirs and wife Original: found
NP-3433	Jurdan, John	13 JUN 1769		Hempfield or Unity, Westmoreland	300	D-56-66 D-70-231 D-70-232 D-70-233	Original: found
NP-3434	Drumfield, Hercules	13 JUN 1769		Mt. Pleasant, Westmoreland	300	D-57-190 C-40-211	--- Thompson/(r2 NOV 1810)Alexander Crig & J. Simpson & J. Parr Original: found
NP-3435	Swanzy, Robert	13 JUN 1769		Derry, Westmoreland	300	D-56-110 Q-136	(r3 JUN 1795)William Allison Original: found
NP-3436	Swanzy, James	13 JUN 1769		Loyalhanna Creek, Westmoreland	300	A-52-114	(r1 MAR 1805)William Dickson Original: found
NP-3437	Drinker, Theophilus	13 JUN 1769		Hempfield, Westmoreland	300	D-70-230	Original: found
NP-3438	Lyon, Samuel	13 JUN 1769		North Union, Fayette/ LD: Union, Fayette	300	A-5-90 A-47-189 A-47-192	Thomas Gross/Isaac Pierer/(r9 OCT 1844)Joseph Pennock/(r11 JUN 1864)Isaac Woods Original: Signed
NP-3439	Martin, John	13 JUN 1769		Plum, Allegheny	300	D-56-191 C-129-278	Thomas Small/Eneas Mackay/James McMillian/(r1 MAR 1816)John McGraw Original: found

Table 6 - New Purchase Applications (1769-1773)

Number	Applicant	Date	Orig. Place	Later Place	Acres	Survey	Neighbors, Notes, etc.
NP-3440	Littlehead, Peter	13 JUN 1769		Salem, Westmoreland	300	C-218-228	Robert Laughlin/William Burbridge/(r1 APR 1788)James Westbay Original: found
NP-3441	Harrison, Laurence	13 JUN 1769		Dunbar, Fayette/ LD: Dunbar, Fayette/ Mt. Pleasant, Westmoreland	300	E-217 C-31-49 C-195-275 C-88-253	Cap. William Crawford/(r12 APR 1854)---Blackstone & --- Davidson/(p16 FEB 1874)Cyrus D. Robinson/(p10 APR 1899)H. C. Frick Coke Company[patent H-75-476]/(w15 OCT 1785)Thomas Moore Original: found
NP-3442	Cline, George	13 JUN 1769	Cumberland	Donegal, Westmoreland	300	Z-62	Phillip Askew Original: found
NP-3443	Butterage, Henry	13 JUN 1769		Hempfield, Westmoreland	300	D-70-224	Alexander Laughlin Original: found
NP-3444	Martin, Andrew	13 JUN 1769		Monongahela River, Washington & Allegheny/ LD: Washington	300	X-212	William Peter/Samuel Martin Original: found
NP-3445	Thomas, Gerrard	14 JUN 1769		North Huntingdon, Westmoreland	300	A-37-26 A-37-40	Anthony Walter/Adam Saum/(r17 DEC 1801)Bernhard Thomas & Garret Thomas Original: With NP-3446-3448. Signed in German script "Gerhart Thomas"
NP-3446	Thomas, John	14 JUN 1769	Cumberland	Huntingdon, Westmoreland	300	C-31-250	Gerrard Thomas/(r8 MAR 1823)James Cowen & Joseph Cowen Original: found
NP-3447	Milliron, Jacob	14 JUN 1769		North Huntingdon, Westmoreland	300	D-70-223	John Thomas Original: found
NP-3448	Milliron, John Jr.	14 JUN 1769		North Huntingdon, Westmoreland	300	D-70-222	Jacob Miliron Original: found
NP-3449	Irvin, George	14 JUN 1769		Elizabeth, Allegheny	300	D-70-96	William Butler/ --- Hoalland Original: With NP-3450
NP-3450	Irwin, Robert	14 JUN 1769		Elizabeth, Allegheny	300	D-70-95	William Butler/--- Kulland Original: found
NP-3451	Hunter, James Jr.	14 JUN 1769	Youghiogheny River	LD: Washington	300		Joseph Hunter Original: found
NP-3452	Gudgion, Andrew	14 JUN 1769	Westmoreland	Luzerne, Fayette	300	B-4-94	Hans Coke/Josiah Crawford/(r10 JUN 1788) Original: found

Table 6 - New Purchase Applications (1769-1773)

Number	Applicant	Date	Orig. Place	Later Place	Acres	Survey	Neighbors, Notes, etc.
NP-3453	Sweringham, Van	14 JUN 1769	Monongahela River	LD: Fayette	150		John Wisman Original: found
NP-3454	Nailor, William Jr.	14 JUN 1769	Braddocks Road	LD: Allegheny	300		James Thompson Original: found
NP-3455	Beeson, Henry	14 JUN 1769		Union, Fayette	300	A-49-155 A-54-21 Z-142 A-49-155	Thomas Douthel/John Henthorn/(r26 MAR 1788)Jacob Beeson/(r23 FEB 1790)William Campbell Original: found
NP-3456	Brownfield, Charles	14 JUN 1769		Union, Fayette/ LD: Fayette	300	H-178 C-10-71 A-49-143 C-234-167	Thomas Brownfield/(r22 SEP 1788)Benjamin Brownfield/(r26 MAY 1807)Isaac Sutton/(r23 FEB 1786)George Troutman Original: found
NP-3457	Burkem, Charles	14 JUN 1769		Georges Creek, Fayette	300	A-21-105	(r26 JUL 1796)Phillip Rodgres Original: found
NP-3458	Perkins, John	14 JUN 1769		Luzerne, Fayette	300	A-54-85	(r19 JUN 1801)James William Original: Missing
NP-3459	Jennens (Jennings), David	14 JUN 1769		Redstone Creek, Fayette	300	C-109-24	John Henthorn/(r18 APR 1792) Original: found
NP-3460	Peters, John	14 JUN 1769	mouth of Dunlap Creek	LD: Redstone, Fayette	100		Maj. McCullock/John Venble/Hans Moore Original: found
NP-3461	Myers, George	14 JUN 1769		Franklin, Westmoreland	300	D-70-221	James Death/Stuphel Cooke Original: found
NP-3462	Brownfield, Edward	14 JUN 1769		Georges, Fayette	300	B-1-67 C-128-277 C-7-264	Thomas Head/(r12 MAR 1802)Stephen Mackey/(r21 FEB 1816)Mary White & B. Brownfield Original: found
NP-3463	McCoy, James	14 JUN 1769		Union & Menallen, Fayette	300	C-120-218 C-129-141 C-120-238	Thomas Brumfit/Thomas Douthit/Isaac Suttin/(r25 SEP 1787) Original: found
NP-3464	Crooks, Richard	14 JUN 1769		Union, Fayette	300	C-149-20	(r9 FEB 1816)L. C. McClean & S. McClean Original: found
NP-3465	Stewart, James	14 JUN 1769		Union, Fayette	300	I-431	Phillip Shoot/John Davis/(r8 MAY 1850)Henry W. Beeson/(r14 JAN 1852)Samuel Evans Original: found
NP-3466	Grundy, George	14 JUN 1769		Redstone Creek, Fayette	300	C-172-107	(r30 JUN 1788)John Patrick/[see caveat] Original: found
NP-3467	McCartney, Nathaniel	14 JUN 1769		Union & Menallen, Fayette	300	C-129-141	(r25 SEP 1786) Original: found

Table 6 - New Purchase Applications (1769-1773)

Number	Applicant	Date	Orig. Place	Later Place	Acres	Survey	Neighbors, Notes, etc.
NP-3468	Brownfield, Thomas	14 JUN 1769		Georges Creek, Fayette	300	C-12-109	Thomas Aday/Charles Brownfield/(r17 MAR 1786) Original: found
NP-3469	Watson, John	14 JUN 1769		Redstone Creek, Fayette	300	D-6-109	(r9 NOV 1785) Original: found
NP-3470	Brown, Adam	14 JUN 1769		Redstone Creek, Fayette	300	C-12-111	Morris Brown/Benjamin Jennens/(r17 MAR 1786) Original: found
NP-3471	Henthorn, James	14 JUN 1769		Union, Fayette/ LD: Fayette	300	I-176 C-152-75	John Henthorn/Adam McCarty/(r6 JUN 1791)Samuel McCady/(r9 MAR 1864)Hannah Barton Original: found
NP-3472	Waller, John	14 JUN 1769		Union, Fayette	300	D-56-130 A-21-145 C-35-200 A-88-208 C-132-171 D-27-8 C-46-46 C-112-22	Phillip Shoot/Thomas Douthill/(r5 JUN 1788)William Clark/(r8 SEP 1796)Benjamin Evy/(r3 OCT 1809)Samuel Miner & Isaac Miner/(r15 APR 1814)Samuel Clark/(r25 OCT 1846)E. Hoover Original: found
NP-3473	Brown, Maunie	14 JUN 1769		Dunlop Creek, Fayette	300	C-12-98	Adam Brown/Richard Crooks/William Downard/(r1 FEB 1786)Maunus Brown Original: found
NP-3474	Hambleton, John	14 JUN 1769		Dunlop Creek, Fayette	300	B-5-97	(r11 APR 1788)Mary Catharine Hite & Sarah Hite Original: found
NP-3475	Grundy, William	14 JUN 1769		Georges, Fayette	200	C-149-282	Thomas Hadder/(r16 DEC 1829)William Nixon/[see caveat] Original: found
NP-3476	Colvin, William	14 JUN 1769		Washington, Fayette	300	C-48-162	Van Swerington/(r8 JAN 1787)William Forsyth Original: found
NP-3477	Harbert, Michael	14 JUN 1769		Unity, Westmoreland	300	D-70-209	[see caveat] Original: found
NP-3478	Stevenson, Robert	14 JUN 1769		Franklin, Fayette	300	D-70-207	Col. Washington/John Persal/James Hunter Original: found
NP-3479	Laugling, Robert	14 JUN 1769		Ligonier, Westmoreland	300	D-70-208	Original: found
NP-3480	Higinbotham, Ralph	14 JUN 1769		Redstone Creek, Fayette	150	D-70-206	Original: found

Table 6 - New Purchase Applications (1769-1773)

Number	Applicant	Date	Orig. Place	Later Place	Acres	Survey	Neighbors, Notes, etc.
NP-3481	Shute, Phillip	14 JUN 1769		Union, Fayette	300	L-149 B-5-199 B-5-215	John Waller/James Stewart/(r28 DEC 1815)J. Jackson Original: found
NP-3482	Waller, Richard	14 JUN 1769		Union, Fayette	300	C-161-213 C-53-39 C-161-212	James Frenches/(r11 MAR 1791)Charles Clinton/(r4 FEB 1813)A. Parker Original: Missing
NP-3483	Downard, William	14 JUN 1769		Browns Creek, Fayette	300	B-2-161	Maneses Brown/Richard Crooks/(r27 AUG 1793)Jacob Downard Original: found
NP-3484	Douthit, Thomas	14 JUN 1769		Redstone Creek, Fayette	300	C-5-227	James McCoy/Henry Beeson/John Waller/(r10 AUG 1786)Henry Beeson Original: found
NP-3485	Henthorn, John	14 JUN 1769		Redstone Creek, Fayette	300	B-14-113 B-14-114	David Jennens/James Henthorn/(r16 MAY 1796)Mary Henthorn & John Henthorn Original: Missing
NP-3486	Joans, Thomas	14 JUN 1769		Elizabeth, Allegheny	300	D-70-97	--- Kelly Original: Signed
NP-3487	Creigh, Mary	14 JUN 1769		Elizabeth, Allegheny	300	D-70-205 A-61-221 A-17-99 C-191-88 C-113-218 A-59-187	James Kelly/(r25 FEB 1834)A. McClure/(r25 FEB 1834)John Phillips/(r24 OCT 1850)Joseph Linch/(20 MAR 1851)John Edmondson Original: Signed by John Creigh
NP-3488	Boland, Alexander	14 JUN 1769		Washington, Fayette	300	C-193-276	(r10 APR 1788)Van Swearingen Original: found
NP-3489	Anderson, James Jr.	14 JUN 1769	Berks	Kelly, Union	300	D-70-218 D-70-219 A-40-86	[see caveat] Original: found
NP-3490	Lodge, Jonathan Jr.	14 JUN 1769	Berks	Chillisquaque, Northumberland	300	N-44	James Tilghman/(r26 MAR 1807)William Tilghman Original: With NP-3491
NP-3491	Lodge, Benjamin Sr.	14 JUN 1769	Berks	Chillisquaque, Northumberland/ LD: Northumberland	300	A-254	Mr. Tilghman/Mr. Allen/Mr. Purviance Original: found
NP-3492	Norris, Robert	14 JUN 1769	Berks	Turbot, Northumberland	300	D-56-123 C-152-24	Joseph Galloway/John Reed/(r11 NOV 1790)John Montgomery Original: With NP-3493

Table 6 - New Purchase Applications (1769-1773)

Number	Applicant	Date	Orig. Place	Later Place	Acres	Survey	Neighbors, Notes, etc.
NP-3493	Davidson, John	14 JUN 1769	Berks	Chillisquaque, Northumberland	300	C-35-285	Charles Diggs/John Patterson/(r16 APR 1790)Robert Cavins & John McGown Original: found
NP-3494	Zantzinger, Paul	14 JUN 1769	Northumberland	Chillisquaque, Montour	300	C-128-265	William Patterson/(r5 MAR 1802)Charles McClung Original: With NP-3495-3498
NP-3495	Lodge, Benjamin Jr.	14 JUN 1769	Columbia	Derry, Montour/ LD: Derry, Columbia	300	A-32-192	Paul Zantzinger Original: found
NP-3496	Gelaspy, Michael	14 JUN 1769	Berks	Derry, Northumberland - Montour	300	A-9-129 A-9-130	Bartram Galbreath/Mr. Allen/(r21 APR 1788)William Gilmore/(r8 JAN 1811)Andrew Clark Original: found
NP-3497	Steward, William	14 JUN 1769	Berks	Derry, Montour	300	T-299	John Hepburn/Samuel Hepburn/William Baker/(r30 MAY 1795)Samuel Maun Original: found
NP-3498	Magruder, John	14 JUN 1769	Columbia	Derry, Montour	300	C-143-127 C-143-128	William McCrosky/Samuel Caruthers/(r2 JUL 1817)Joseph Miller, deceased executors Original: found
NP-3499	Rogers, John	14 JUN 1769	Berks	Northumberland - Derry, Montour	300	C-159-151	John Hepburn/Samuel Hepburn/(r17 SEP 1804)William Pegg Original: found
NP-3500	Jones, Benjamin	14 JUN 1769	Berks	Chillisquaque, Northumberland	300	D-191	John Patterson/(r26 APR 1786)John Buyers, Esq. Original: With NP-3501-3503
NP-3501	Jones, John Jr.	14 JUN 1769	Berks	Turbot, Northumberland	300	L-151	John Reed/(r7 DEC 1774)Benjamin Jones Original: found
NP-3502	Boon, Hawkins	14 JUN 1769	Berks	Turbot, Northumberland	300	C-127-264 C-127-246	John Reed/(r21 NOV 1796)James McClurg Original: found
NP-3503	Galloway, John	14 JUN 1769	Northumberland	opposite Ft. Augusta, Union	50	C-74-119	(r23 SEP 1790)Ruben Haines Original: found
NP-3504	Kelly, Andrew	14 JUN 1769	Berks	Kelly, Union	200	D-70-218 D-70-219 V-220 V-221	Thomas McGuire/(r25 OCT 1802)John Johnston & William Johnston/[see caveat] Original: Signed
NP-3505	King, Thomas	15 JUN 1769		Marsh Creek Branch of Bald Eagle Creek, Centre	300	L-460	(r6 JUN 1855)John Liggit Original: found

Table 6 - New Purchase Applications (1769-1773)

Number	Applicant	Date	Orig. Place	Later Place	Acres	Survey	Neighbors, Notes, etc.
NP-3506	Lasher, Leonard	15 JUN 1769	Berks	Roaring Creek, Columbia/ LD: Columbia	200	X-204	Original: With NP-3507
NP-3507	Ensminger, Frederick	15 JUN 1769	Berks	Roaring Creek, Columbia/ LD: Luzerne/ Bradford	300	H-484	Leonard Lasher Original: found
NP-3508	Kuykindall, Benjamin	17 JUN 1769		Peters Creek & Monongahela River, Allegheny	300	C-104-46	(r10 FEB 1791)Sarah Kirkindall & Moses Kirkindall/[see caveat] Original: With NP-3509-3513
NP-3509	Kuykindall, Moses	17 JUN 1769	Washington	Jefferson, Allegheny	300	A-5-303	Benjamin Kuykindall/(r26 DEC 1822)J. Gromly Original: found
NP-3510	Dacker, John Jr.	17 JUN 1769	Washington	Peters Creek & Monongahela River, Allegheny/ LD: Mifflin, Allegheny	300	X-199	Original: found
NP-3511	Decker, Jacob	17 JUN 1769	Washington	Monongahela River, Allegheny	300	C-193-262	John Decker/(r4 APR 1788)Samuel Sinclair Original: found
NP-3512	Miller, John	17 JUN 1769	Washington	Peters Creek & Monongahela River, Allegheny/ LD: Washington	300	X-211	Original: found
NP-3513	Pettit, Joshua	17 JUN 1769		Elizabeth, Allegheny	300	D-70-98	Mr. McCoy Original: found
NP-3514	Davis, Samuel	19 JUN 1769	Berks	West Buffalo, Union	300	D-55-47 C-138-63	Capt. I. Irwin/(r2 MAR 1796)John Lowden/[see caveat] Original: Signed
NP-3515	Winters, William	19 JUN 1769		Turbot, Northumberland	300	D-70-217	Col. Francis Original: found
NP-3516	Hunter, Joseph Jr.	19 JUN 1769		Chartiers Creek, Washington	300	A-77-180	Abram Hunter/(r22 MAR 1788)John Hoge & William Hoge Original: With NP-3517-3518 Signed
NP-3517	Hunter, Abram	19 JUN 1769		Chartiers Creek, Washington	300	A-77-179	Joseph Hunter, Jr./Catfish [a Delaware Indian]/(r22 MAR 1788)John Hoge & William Hoge Original: found

Table 6 - New Purchase Applications (1769-1773)

Number	Applicant	Date	Orig. Place	Later Place	Acres	Survey	Neighbors, Notes, etc.
NP-3518	Hunter, Martha	19 JUN 1769		branch of Chartiers Creek, Washington	300	C-75-101	Joseph Hunter, Jr./(r22 MAR 1788)John Hoge & William Hoge Original: found
NP-3519	McFall, Thomas	20 JUN 1769	Berks	Muncy Creek, Lycoming	300	C-227-152	David Robb/(r24 FEB 1800)David Robb Original: Signed
NP-3520	Robb, Susanna	20 JUN 1769	Mingo Run, Berks	LD: Lycoming	300		[see caveat] Original: found
NP-3521	Robb, Mathew	20 JUN 1769	Berks	Wolf Run, Muncy Creek, Northumberland -Lycoming	300	C-7-70	(r15 OCT 1782)Samuel Bayles Original: Signed by John Robb
NP-3522	Wells, Richard	23 JUN 1769		Brothers Valley, Somerset	300	C-114-69 C-114-104 C-114-105	(r14 MAR 1799)Abraham Kimmel/(r19 FEB 1801)David Kimmel Original: With NP-3523-3524
NP-3523	Wells, James	23 JUN 1769		Mt. Pleasant, Westmoreland	300	D-70-215 D-70-216	Original: found
NP-3524	Wells, George	23 JUN 1769		Stony Creek, Somerset	300	B-10-115	John Rhodes/(r9 FEB 1775)Abraham Cable Original: found
NP-3525	McClintock, Alexander	23 JUN 1769		Hempfield, Westmoreland	300	D-70-214	Joseph Brownlee/Archibald McKee Original: found
NP-3526	Torrance, James	23 JUN 1769		Hempfield, Westmoreland/ LD: Hempfield, Westmoreland	300	D-70-213	William Nesbit/Barnet Cuningham Original: found
NP-3527	Hanna, John	23 JUN 1769	Cumberland	Donegal, Westmoreland	300	D-64-185 C-20-82 C-20-83	(r7 JAN 1833) Original: found
NP-3528	Brownlee, Joseph	23 JUN 1769		Hempfield, Westmoreland	300	A-86-258	Alexander McClintock/Samuel Miller/William Brownlee/(r12 FEB 1800)James Guthrie, Esq./[see caveat] Original: found
NP-3529	Gray, William	23 JUN 1769	Cumberland	Donegal, Westmoreland/ LD: Donegal, Westmoreland	300	C-63-294 C-27-210 D-17-171	(r20 APR 1829)David Williams/(r7 MAR 1839)R. Williams/(p8 FEB 1870)George Barnhart Original: found
NP-3530	Galt, William	23 JUN 1769	Cumberland	Fairfield, Westmoreland	300	C-157-166	(r24 APR 1783)Alexander Powers Original: found
NP-3531	Alexander, William, Jr.	23 JUN 1769	Cumberland	Donegal, Westmoreland	300	D-62-10 C-96-255	(r14 JUL 1808)Mathew Jack Original: found

Table 6 - New Purchase Applications (1769-1773)

Number	Applicant	Date	Orig. Place	Later Place	Acres	Survey	Neighbors, Notes, etc.
NP-3532	Galt, Margaret	23 JUN 1769	Cumberland	Donegal, Westmoreland	300	D-70-212	Original: found
NP-3533	Hanna, Robert (farmer)	23 JUN 1769	Salt Creek, Cumberland	LD: Donegal, Westmoreland	300		Original: found
NP-3534	Hanna, Robert (blacksmith)	23 JUN 1769	Cumberland	Fairfield, Westmoreland/ LD: Donegal, Westmoreland	300	C-79-263	(r6 APR 1797)Thomas Hamilton Original: found
NP-3535	McKee, Easter	23 JUN 1769	Cumberland	Saltlick, Fayette	300	C-80-126	Champin [possibly an Indian]/(r1 SEP 1819)John Hazelton Original: found
NP-3536	Hannah, Elizabeth	23 JUN 1769	Cumberland	Donegal, Westmoreland	300	D-70-211	Original: found
NP-3537	Shanon, Samuel (farmer)	23 JUN 1769	Cumberland	Champion Run, Fayette/ LD: Westmoreland	300	X-150	Original: found
NP-3538	Shanon, Elizabeth	23 JUN 1769	Cumberland	Bullskin, Fayette	300	C-135-276 C-224-11	(r2 FEB 1815)James Muir Original: found
NP-3539	Alexander, Thomas	23 JUN 1769	Cumberland	Donegal, Westmoreland	300	D-46-85	Original: found
NP-3540	Dougherty, Barnard	23 JUN 1769	Cumberland	Quemahoning, Somerset	300	C-1-251	John St. Clair/John Brady/(r30 MAR 1809)Michael Zimmerman Original: found
NP-3541	McCormick, Mary	23 JUN 1769		Chillisquaque, Northumberland	300	D-33-6	Alexander Morris/(r24 MAR 1813)John Wilson Original: found
NP-3542	Duncan, Margaret	23 JUN 1769	Northumberland	Fishing Creek Twp., Columbia	300	C-135-113	Isaac Duncan/(r7 OCT 1782)John McKim & wife Original: Signed by William Duncan
NP-3543	St. Clair, Arthur	23 JUN 1769		Unity, Westmoreland	300	D-55-62 D-62-293 D-62-294 C-207-56	Col. Reed/(r17 OCT 1788)Daniel St. Clair Original: With NP-3544. Signed
NP-3544	Rorer, Frederick	23 JUN 1769		Fairfield, Westmoreland	300	D-57-226 D-57-227 B-1-61	Capt. St. Clair/(p15 DEC 1902)Elizabeth F. Denny heirs[patent H-76-216] Original: found
NP-3545	Missinner, Adam	23 JUN 1769	West Branch Susquehanna River	LD: Luzerne	200		Original: Signed with a mark
NP-3546	Nilson, George	24 JUN 1769		Hempfield, Westmoreland	300	D-70-204	Original: found

Table 6 - New Purchase Applications (1769-1773)

Number	Applicant	Date	Orig. Place	Later Place	Acres	Survey	Neighbors, Notes, etc.
NP-3547	Nellson, Alexander	24 JUN 1769		Hempfield, Westmoreland	300	C-14-80	George Nelson/(r3 FEB 1803)Jacob Buergy Original: found
NP-3548	Jones, John	24 JUN 1769		Mifflin, Allegheny	300	C-216-50	David McKee/Thomas Gray/(r24 MAR 1832)Alexander Snodgrass Original: found
NP-3549	McKee, David Jr.	24 JUN 1769		Mifflin, Allegheny/ LD: Mifflin, Allegheny	300	A-34-21 A-34-22 B-1-79 D-90-37	Andrew Simons/John Jones/(r4 MAR 1912)Duquesne & McKeesport Land Company [patent H-78-98] Original: found
NP-3550	Gray, Joseph	24 JUN 1769		Mifflin, Allegheny	300	C-58-270	Thomas Gray/(r 27 FEB 1772) Original: Signed
NP-3551	Gray, John	24 JUN 1769		Mifflin, Allegheny	300	C-37-210	David McKee/(r17 JUN 1817)E. Cunningham & A. Snodgrass Original: Signed
NP-3552	Gray, Thomas	24 JUN 1769		Mifflin, Allegheny	300	D-70-99	David McKee/John Gray Original: found
NP-3553	Gray, Andrew	24 JUN 1769		Mifflin, Allegheny	300	I-509	Joseph Gray/David Mckee/(r15 NOV 1771) Original: Signed
NP-3554	Kore, Thomas	26 JUN 1769	Cumberland	Huntingdon, Westmoreland	300	D-70-203	Original: With NP-3555-3556
NP-3555	Dombalt, Frederick	26 JUN 1769	Cumberland	South Huntingdon, Westmoreland	300	D-70-202	Original: found
NP-3556	Bantze, Ludwick	26 JUN 1769	Cumberland	North Huntingdon, Westmoreland	300	D-70-200 D-70-201	Original: found
NP-3557	Martin, Samuel Jr.	26 JUN 1769	Northumberland	Middle East Branch Chillisquaque Creek, Montour/ LD: Montour	300	D-60-261 C-146-207	William Patterson, Esq. Original: Signed
NP-3558	Mertain, Mathew	26 JUN 1769	Chillisquaque Creek	LD: Montour	300		Alexander Murray Original: Signed
NP-3559	Lindsay, Samuel	26 JUN 1769	Middle East Branch Chillisquaque Creek	LD: Montour	300		William Patterson, Esq. Original: Signed

Table 6 - New Purchase Applications (1769-1773)

Number	Applicant	Date	Orig. Place	Later Place	Acres	Survey	Neighbors, Notes, etc.
NP-3560	Lyon, William	27 JUN 1769		Hempfield, Westmoreland	300	C-123-62	Capt. Thompson/(r14 MAR 1811)James Carlisle & Elizabeth Carlisle [late Elizabeth Lyon] Original: Signed
NP-3561	Lyon, Thomas Jr.	27 JUN 1769		North Huntingdon, Westmoreland & Versailles, Allegheny	300	D-70-188 D-70-189	John Reed Original: Signed by William Lyon
NP-3562	Kinkead, John Jr.	27 JUN 1769		Peters, Washington-Allegheny	300	B-21	(r9 NOV 1784)John Douglass, Esq. Original: found
NP-3563	Rivington, Peter	27 JUN 1769		Hemlock, Columbia or Montour	300	F-503 C-53-34 C-211-149 C-161-256 C-119-56	(r16 FEB 1791)Andrew Clark/(r8 SEP 1845)Jacob Rishel/(r11 MAR 1814)David Philips/(r26 Sep 1838)James Longhead Original: With NP-3564-3565
NP-3564	Reyer, Godfrey	27 JUN 1769		Columbia - Hemlock, Montour	300	C-84-50 C-125-2 C-125-3	Peter Rivington/(r8 MAR 1784)Rudolph Haines/(r22 MAY 1810)Sarah Harriot & John Seckler & Hannah Seckler [his wife] & Thomas Boyer & Mary Boyer [his wife] Original: found
NP-3565	Beckley, William	27 JUN 1769		Columbia - Hemlock, Montour	300	C-78-112	Peter Rivington/(r22 JUN 1774)Jacob Haines Original: found
NP-3566	McAfee, Joshua	27 JUN 1769	Northumberland	Shamokin, Snyder	100	C-69-207	(r28 MAR 1816)Nancy Hunter & Mary Scott Original: found
NP-3567	Haddy, Thomas Sr.	27 JUN 1769	Cumberland	Wittle Creek, Fayette	300	A-83-169	Thomas Brumfield/Edward Brumfield/Charles Burkcom/(r9 JUN 1788)George Troutman Original: found
NP-3568	Campbell, James	27 JUN 1769		Georges Creek, Fayette	300	C-118-225	William Hardin/John Swearingham/(r31 JAN 1785)Aaron Moore Original: Signed
NP-3569	Haddy, Thomas Jr.	27 JUN 1769		Georges, Fayette	300	D-13-67 C-162-190 C-162-161	Thomas Haddy, Sr./William Allen/(r23 JAN 1823)I. Wynn/(r22 NOV 1847)F. H. Oliphant Original: Missing
NP-3570	Rice, John	27 JUN 1769		Wharton, Fayette	100	C-168-239 C-168-240	(r23 JUL 1788)John Rice Original: Missing

Table 6 - New Purchase Applications (1769-1773)

Number	Applicant	Date	Orig. Place	Later Place	Acres	Survey	Neighbors, Notes, etc.
NP-3571	Bowsman, Andrew	27 JUN 1769		Mifflin, Allegheny	300	A-89-38 A-87-293 A-89-27 A-87-281 A-88-258	Boston Fredericks/(r4 APR 1826)Thomas Hays/(r16 APR 1829)Dr. Calhoon/(r13 DEC 1837)S. Ferguson/(r1 APR 1845)Alexander McClure Original: Signed in German script by Jacob Baussman
NP-3572	Eckhard, Jacob	27 JUN 1769	Cumberland	Perry, Union	300	C-83-171 C-83-172 C-83-170 C-83-169	Michael Motz/Andrew Wittemoyer/(r3 MAR 1809)Tobias Zeller/(r13 DEC 1821)Samuel Shedle/(r20 FEB 1838)John Garman Original: Signed
NP-3573	Ripley, William	27 JUN 1769		Bethlehem, Washington	300	C-171	(r25 FEB 1808)Noah Cook Original: found
NP-3574	Ripy, Samuel (son of William)	27 JUN 1769		Amwell, Washington	300	C-171 S-249	(r25 FEB 1808)Nathan McGriffin Original: found
NP-3575	Dean, Benjamin	28 JUN 1769		Limestone Run, Northumberland	300	B-27	Samuel Allen, Sr./(r23 NOV 1781)Stephen Duncan in trust for the heirs of William McKoskey Original: Signed
NP-3576	Foulke, Judah	28 JUN 1769		Catawissa Creek, Columbia	300	C-7-203	(r4 MAR 1782)William Ball, Esq. Original: With NP-3577-3579
NP-3577	Wirt, Joseph	28 JUN 1769		Catawissa Creek, Columbia	300	D-240	Judah Foulk/(r26 FEB 1782)William Ball, Esq. Original: found
NP-3578	Sheed, William	28 JUN 1769		Catawissa Creek, Columbia	300	A-413	Joseph Wirt/(r4 MAR 1782)William Ball, Esq. Original: found
NP-3579	Hibberd, Hezekiah	28 JUN 1769		Catawissa Creek, Columbia	300	D-237	William Sheed/(r27 FEB 1782)William Ball, Esq./[adjoining NP-3578 & NP-3580] Original: found
NP-3580	Dilworth, Jonathan	28 JUN 1769	Berks	Catawissa Creek, Columbia	300	C-7-204	Hezekiah Hubbert/(r4 MAR 1782)William Ball, Esq. Original: With NP-3581
NP-3581	Stuber, Frederick	28 JUN 1769		Catawissa Creek, Columbia	300	C-93-230	Jonathan Dillworth/(r5 MAR 1795)John Hilborn Original: found
NP-3582	Bolter, Hannah	1 JUL 1769		Chillisquaque Creek, Columbia	300	C-1-20	George Sanderson, Sr./Samuel Hepburn/John Hepburn/(r19 JAN 1770) Original: found
NP-3583	McCollock, John	3 JUL 1769	Cumberland	Menallen, Fayette	300	C-12-93	(r24 FEB 1786)Thomas Brown Original: found

Table 6 - New Purchase Applications (1769-1773)

Number	Applicant	Date	Orig. Place	Later Place	Acres	Survey	Neighbors, Notes, etc.
NP-3584	Zane, Silas	3 JUL 1769	Cumberland	Monongahela River, Greene/ LD: Washington	300	X-136	Ebenezer Zane Original: found
NP-3585	Coxe, James	3 JUL 1769	Cumberland	between Georges & Jacobs Creeks, Fayette	300	A-37-63	(r28 OCT 1785)Richard Stephens Original: found
NP-3586	Zane, Ebenezer	3 JUL 1769	Cumberland	Monongahela River, Greene/ LD: Washington	300	X-135	Silas Zane Original: found
NP-3587	Hulme, Robert	3 JUL 1769	Cumberland	Henry Clay, Fayette	300	C-222-215	(r11 JUL 1836)Andrew Stewart Original: found
NP-3588	Biddle, Clement	3 JUL 1769	Cumberland	Pike Run, Washington & Greene	300	C-7-209	John Biddle/(r12 OCT 1781) Original: found
NP-3589	Biddle, John	3 JUL 1769	Cumberland	Pike Run, Washington	300	M-113	(r18 APR 1798)Benjamin Loxley Original: found
NP-3590	Loxley, Benjamin	3 JUL 1769	Cumberland	Monongahela River, Westmoreland-Fayette	300	C-108-240	John McCollack/(r18 APR 1798) Original: found
NP-3591	McCollack, Samuel	3 JUL 1769	Cumberland	Menallen, Fayette	300	X-33	John McCollack/(r24 FEB 1786)Thomas Brown Original: found
NP-3592	Ashbee, Stephen	3 JUL 1769	Cumberland	Jacobs Creek, Fayette	300	B-7-58	(r14 AUG 1770)John Vanderver Original: found
NP-3593	Farrow, Alexander	3 JUL 1769	Cumberland	Jacobs Creek, Fayette	300	C-146-231	(r27 JUL 1770)John Paul Original: found
NP-3594	Ashbee, Thomas	3 JUL 1769	Cumberland	Georges Creek, Fayette	300	C-146-225	(r27 JUL 1770)John Paul Original: found
NP-3595	Cottral, Andrew	3 JUL 1769	Cumberland	mouth of Georges Creek, Fayette	300	D-6-128	George Cottral/(r17 SEP 1785)John Wilson Original: found
NP-3596	Vanderien, John	3 JUL 1769		Pigeon Creek, Washington	300	A-71-240	--- McCullough/(r7 SEP 1770)/[see caveat] Original: found
NP-3597	Gray, William	3 JUL 1769		Pigeon Creek, Washington	300	A-79-22 A-79-23	--- McCullough/(r16 MAY 1799)Benjamin Loxley/(r18 SEP 1811)S. Clark Original: found
NP-3598	McDowell, Nathan (of Peters Township)	4 JUL 1769		Strabane, Washington	300	A-86-78 A-86-79	(r20 DEC 1790)Henry Taylor, Esq. Original: With NP-3599

Table 6 - New Purchase Applications (1769-1773)

Number	Applicant	Date	Orig. Place	Later Place	Acres	Survey	Neighbors, Notes, etc.
NP-3599	McDowell, Molley (of Peters Township)	4 JUL 1769		Chartiers Creek, Washington	300	D-26-289	Nathan McDowell/(r20 DEC 1790)John White/[see caveat] Original: found
NP-3600	McDermont, James	5 JUL 1769		Turbot, Northumberland/ LD: Turbot, Northumberland	300	C-55-199 C-45-88 A-44-212 A-44-234 A-45-121	(r28 FEb 1806)Lazarus Finney/(r23 MAY 1831)George Doyle/(p4 MAR 1831)C. Riddles & S. Riddles, administrators of C. Riddles, deceased Original: found
NP-3601	Campbell, Alexander	5 JUL 1769		Chillisquaque Creek, Northumberland	300		Ellinor Pollock/(r28 APR 1796 & p4 MAY 1796)Alexander Pollock/[patent P-29-20] Original: found
NP-3602	Steel, Ephraim	5 JUL 1769		Anthony, Montour/ LD: Derry, Columbia	300	C-135-250 C-43-216 C-51-149 C-43-217 C-43-225	Alexander Campbell/(r23 AUG 1814)Barnard McGee/(r9 APR 1828)C. Ellis/(r15 SEP 1864)Andrew Ellis heirs Original: found
NP-3603	Street, Mary	5 JUL 1769		Turbot, Northumberland/ LD: Turbot, Northumberland	300	X-151 X-152 X-153	Joseph Allison/[see caveat] Original: found
NP-3604	Pollock, Ellinor	5 JUL 1769		Chillisquaque Creek, Northumberland	300	I-17	(r13 NOV 1790)James Armstrong & Elenor Armstrong (his wife) Original: found
NP-3605	Allison, Joseph	5 JUL 1769		Turbot, Northumberland	300	C-184-46	(r6 MAR 1817)Samuel Russel & John Russel & Patrick K. Russel[sons of Andrew Russel, deceased]/[see caveat] Original: found
NP-3606	Pollock, Agnes	5 JUL 1769		Chillisquaque Creek & Warriors Run, Northumberland	300	A-14-37	James McDermont/(r28 FEB 1800) Original: found
NP-3607	Peace, Daniel	5 JUL 1769		Turbot, Northumberland/ LD: Turbot, Northumberland	300	A-5-91 C-208-280 C-2-5	James McDermont/(r18 MAR 1811)Richard Vanderhoof/(r3 FEB 1812)Anthony Armstrong Original: found
NP-3608	Patterson, Charles	5 JUL 1769		Turbot, Northumberland	300	C-202-156 C-144-175 C-144-176	Mr. Galloway/Mr. Petterson/(r25 NOV 1805)John Stahl/(r31 JAN 1827)William Montgomery Original: found

Table 6 - New Purchase Applications (1769-1773)

Number	Applicant	Date	Orig. Place	Later Place	Acres	Survey	Neighbors, Notes, etc.
NP-3609	Scull, Benjamin	5 JUL 1769		Turbot, Northumberland	300	C-55-222	(r28 FEB 1806)Lazarus Finney Original: found
NP-3610	McNeal, Robert	5 JUL 1769		Turbot, Northumberland	300	D-70-187	Original: found
NP-3611	McKinly, Henry	5 JUL 1769		Turbot, Northumberland	300	C-125-93 C-125-94	Charles Patterson/(r25 NOV 1805)John Stahl/(r30 OCT 1811)D. Hunter Original: found
NP-3612	Love, John	5 JUL 1769		Chillisquaque, Northumberland	300	A-29-235 A-29-236 A-29-237	William Irwin/Marcus Hullings/John Gillaspy/(r29 OCT 1811)John Painter Original: found
NP-3613	Patterson, Esther	5 JUL 1769		Augusta, Northumberland	300	O-44	(r6 JAN 1775) Original: With NP-3614-3615
NP-3614	Louden, Sarah	5 JUL 1769	Berks	Point, Northumberland	300	C-112-68	(r6 JUL 1770) Original: found
NP-3615	Boone, Samuel	5 JUL 1769		Turbot, Northumberland/ LD: Turbot, Columbia	300	X-187 X-188 A-1-30	[see caveat] Original: found
NP-3616	McKee, Robert	7 JUL 1769		Hempfield, Westmoreland	200	D-60-270 C-120-258	Archibald McKee/James Darrigh/(r25 SEP 1787)/[see caveat] Original: Signed
NP-3617	Dalrymple, James	7 JUL 1769		Hempfield, Westmoreland	300	D-70-185 D-70-186	[see caveat] Original: found
NP-3618	McKee, Samuel Jr.	7 JUL 1769		Hempfield, Westmoreland	200	C-120-236	James Darugh/Joseph Morrison/(r25 SEP 1787) Original: Signed
NP-3619	McKee, Archibald	7 JUL 1769		Hempfield, Westmoreland	200	D-60-270 A-10-137	Roger McBride/(r5 AUG 1783)William Beass Original: Signed by Samuel McKee
NP-3620	Hamilton, Robert (of Sherman's Valley)	8 JUL 1769		Chartiers Creek, Washington	300	A-72-210	(r4 APR 1792)James Ross, Esq. Original: Signed
NP-3621	Hamilton, Thomas (of Sherman's Valley)	8 JUL 1769		Chartiers Creek, Washington	300	A-69-142	Thomas Rankin/(r4 APR 1792)James Ross, Esq. Original: Signed
NP-3622	Rankin, James (son of William)	8 JUL 1769		Redstone Creek, Fayette	200	B-5-69	Richard Walter/Charles Lingly/(r12 NOV 1787)Hugh Rankin Original: found
NP-3623	Rankin, Thomas (of Sherman's Valley)	8 JUL 1769		Chartiers Creek, Washington	300	A-69-141	Robert Hamilton/(r4 APR 1792)James Ross, Esq. Original: found

Table 6 - New Purchase Applications (1769-1773)

Number	Applicant	Date	Orig. Place	Later Place	Acres	Survey	Neighbors, Notes, etc.
NP-3624	Rankin, William (of Sherman's Valley)	8 JUL 1769		Redstone Creek, Fayette	300	B-5-67	James Catterman/James Pinack/Richard Walor/(r13 NOV 1787) Original: found
NP-3625	Marshal, Michael (of Sherman's Valley)	8 JUL 1769		Strabane, Washington	300	A-34-46 A-34-47 A-34-48 A-34-49 C-173-37 C-156-281	(r24 FEB 1830)D. Moore/(r8 MAR 1833)James Orr/(r4 MAY 1835)David Quail Original: found
NP-3626	Mitchell, Charles Sr.	8 JUL 1769	Bedford	Unity, Westmoreland	300	D-60-255 M-178 B-23-68	William Allison/(r24 SEP 1789)Elizabeth Mitchell Original: Signed by William Mitchell
NP-3627	Allison, William	8 JUL 1769		Unity, Westmoreland	300	D-60-255 D-23-68	Charles Mitchell/Joseph Campbell/Samuel Sloan/William Mitchell/(r20 MAR 1811)John Sloan Original: found
NP-3628	Mitchel, William	8 JUL 1769		Loyalhanna, Westmoreland	250	A-60-140	William Allison/Jacob Wise/(r6 DEC 1809)Joseph Balbridge Original: found
NP-3629	Mitchel, Charles Jr.	8 JUL 1769		Derry, Westmoreland	300	D-70-198 D-70-199	Original: found
NP-3630	Beatty, Mary Jr.	10 JUL 1769		North Huntingdon, Westmoreland	300	D-70-197	James Small Original: found
NP-3631	Beatty, Robert	10 JUL 1769	Westmoreland	Turtle Creek, Allegheny	300	M-426	John Sampson/(r29 NOV 1788)Francis McFarland & James McFarland Original: found
NP-3632	Parr, Andrew (near Shippensburg)	10 JUL 1769		Fairfield, Westmoreland	300	A-48-14 C-24-14 C-59-94	(r12 DEC 1827)William Barr executors/(r8 MAY 1829)Alexander W. Foster Original: found
NP-3633	Paul, James	10 JUL 1769		Tyrone, Fayette	300	C-172-132 C-172-133	George Paul, Sr./(r2 OCT 1788) Original: found
NP-3634	Willey, Hugh	10 JUL 1769	Westmoreland	Conemaugh River, Indiana	300	A-42-211	(r13 DEC 1787)William Todd, Esq. Original: found
NP-3635	Paul, George Sr.	10 JUL 1769		Franklin, Fayette	300	B-17-56	(r21 NOV 1788) Original: found
NP-3636	Paul, George Jr.	10 JUL 1769		Union, Fayette	300	D-59-249 C-53-274 C-53-273	Charles Lindsay/(r26 FEB 1789)John Gaddis Original: found

Table 6 - New Purchase Applications (1769-1773)

Number	Applicant	Date	Orig. Place	Later Place	Acres	Survey	Neighbors, Notes, etc.
NP-3637	Gay, James (near Shippensburg, weaver)	10 JUL 1769		Ligonier, Westmoreland	300	D-70-196	John Pawmer[Palmer on survey]/Richard Shannon Original: found
NP-3638	McGuire, Robert (near Shippensburg)	11 JUL 1769		Armstrong, Indiana	300	D-70-194 D-70-195	Original: found
NP-3639	Jameson, Ann	11 JUL 1769	Westmoreland	Crooked Creek, Armstrong	300	C-173-51	(r23 FEB 1789)James Patterson Original: found
NP-3640	Allen, John	12 JUL 1769	Cumberland	Hempfield, Westmoreland	300	D-70-193	Joseph Burrows Original: Signed
NP-3641	Burrows, Joshua	12 JUL 1769	Cumberland	North Huntingdon, Westmoreland	300	X-185	Thomas McKamisk/John Sampson Original: Signed
NP-3642	Burrows, Joseph	12 JUL 1769		Fayette, Allegheny/ LD: Fayette, Allegheny	300	D-70-85	Samuel Jack Original: found
NP-3643	Elliott, Samuel	12 JUL 1769		North Huntingdon, Westmoreland	300	A-51-299	John Sampson/(r28 SEP 1787)Michael Gratz/[see caveat] Original: Signed
NP-3644	Elliott, John	12 JUL 1769		North Huntingdon, Westmoreland	300	A-51-298	William Elliott/James McCrey/(r28 SEP 1787)Michael Gratz/[see caveat] Original: Signed
NP-3645	Sherrerd, John	12 JUL 1769		Muncy Creek Twp., Lycoming	300	D-70-192	William Richards Original: found
NP-3646	Kinny, John	17 JUL 1769		East Branch Susquehanna River, Luzerne	300	A-12-133	(r14 MAR 1775)John Gibson, Esq. Original: found
NP-3647	Morris, Jonathan Ford	17 JUL 1769	Northumberland	opposite Standing Stone, Bradford	300	C-534	(r30 MAY 1795)Samuel Meredith Original: Signed
NP-3648	King, John	17 JUL 1769		East Branch Susquehanna River, Luzerne	300	B-20	(r30 APR 1785)Peter Dehavent & Adam Hubley Original: found
NP-3649	Katterly, Andrew	19 JUL 1769	Berks	Mahoning Creek, Northumberland	300	C-115-60	George Adam Stump/Godfrey Lefler/(r7 MAY 1794)Henry Latcha Original: found
NP-3650	Fletcher, Alexander (of Lancaster County)	20 JUL 1769	Northumberland	North Branch Susquehanna River, Luzerne	300	C-50-82	(r4 JUN 1801)Thomas Craig Original: found

Table 6 - New Purchase Applications (1769-1773)

Number	Applicant	Date	Orig. Place	Later Place	Acres	Survey	Neighbors, Notes, etc.
NP-3651	Fiscus, John	20 JUL 1769		Mt. Pleasant & Unity, Westmoreland/ LD: Mt. Pleasant, Westmoreland	300	H-490 A-59-98 D-14-36	Gerhart Fiscus/(r30 APR 1810)George Buzzard/(r23 DEC 1839)John Weaver & Joseph Cramer Original: Signed
NP-3652	Lee, Robert	24 JUL 1769	west end of Muncy Hill	LD: Lycoming	300		Original: Signed by John Lee
NP-3653	Fall, Alexander	24 JUL 1769	Northumberland	Buffalo, Union	300	C-167-17	James Shannon/(r12 NOV 1774)Henry Pockle Original: found
NP-3654	Moore, John	24 JUL 1769		Buffalo, Union	20	C-112-115	John Lee/(r14 MAY 1774)John Lee Original: found
NP-3655	Wilson, Jeams [James]	24 JUL 1769		Buffalo, Union	300	W-267 W-268 C-191-46	John Wilson/(r1 APR 1833)Jane Penny Original: found
NP-3656	Straugh, Henry (of Greenwich Township, Berks County, miller)	25 JUL 1769		South Huntingdon, Westmoreland/ LD: South Huntingdon, Westmoreland	300	D-70-191	Original: found
NP-3657	Uhre, Vendle	25 JUL 1769		Sewickley Creek, Westmoreland	300	C-220-289	John Brown/Daniel Nelson/Peter Uhri [his father]/(r8 JUN 1773)Jacob Welcker Original: Signed
NP-3658	Uhre, Peter	25 JUL 1769		Hempfield, Westmoreland	300	C-144-57	John Brown/Samuel Miller/(r9 APR 1788)Dewalt Mecklin Original: Signed
NP-3659	Waterson, James	25 JUL 1769		Hempfield, Westmoreland	300	C-123-268	Robert Miller/John Rotery/(r6 MAR 1789)Peter Miller Original: Signed
NP-3660	Williams, Daniel	25 JUL 1769		Hempfield, Westmoreland	300	D-70-190 E-282	Peter Kore/Peter Oldman/(r29 DEC 1787) Original: found
NP-3661	Irwin, Robert	25 JUL 1769		North Huntingdon, Westmoreland	300	C-168-205	Thomas Lyons/(r8 OCT 1788)Daniel Roberdeau, Esq. Original: With NP-3662-3665
NP-3662	Irwin, Robert Jr.	25 JUL 1769		North Huntingdon, Westmoreland	300	D-70-184	Col. Clapham Original: found
NP-3663	Irwin, John (Indian trader)	25 JUL 1769		Pitt, Westmoreland	300		Thomas Lyons/[see NP-3668]/[see caveat] Original: found

Table 6 - New Purchase Applications (1769-1773)

Number	Applicant	Date	Orig. Place	Later Place	Acres	Survey	Neighbors, Notes, etc.
NP-3664	Guthrey, Archibald	25 JUL 1769		Hempfield, Westmoreland	300	C-89-273	Joseph Bready/(r31 MAR 1788)John Irwin, Esq. Original: found
NP-3665	Irwin, James	25 JUL 1769		North Huntingdon, Westmoreland	300	D-70-183	John Irwin/Christopher Rudebaugh Original: found
NP-3666	Knox, James	25 JUL 1769		Fairfield, Westmoreland	300	C-135-263 C-135-264 C-135-262	(r27 DEC 1814)John McKoy[McCoy]/(r27 DEC 1814)David McKoy[McCoy] Original: With NP-3667 Signed
NP-3667	Knox, George	25 JUL 1769		Fairfield, Westmoreland/ LD: Fairfield, Westmoreland	300	D-64-157 D-64-158	James Knox Original: Signed
NP-3668	Irwin, John	25 JUL 1769		Pitt, Westmoreland	300	A-2-116 A-2-117	Joseph Bready/William Elliott/(r19 MAR 1791)/[see caveat] Original: Missing
NP-3669	Connelly, Philip	25 JUL 1769		St. Clair, Allegheny	300	D-70-86	Peter Romters/John Bell Original: Missing
NP-3670	Compass, James	25 JUL 1769		Robinson, Washington	300	L-154	(r7 DEC 1787)John Erwin, Esq. Original: found
NP-3671	Lungan, William A.	25 JUL 1769		Robinson, Washington	300	C-19-85	(r4 SEP 1787)Ephraim Blaine, Esq./[see caveat] Original: found
NP-3672	Irwin, John	25 JUL 1769		Fayette, Allegheny	300	D-70-87	Original: found
NP-3673	Callender, Robert	25 JUL 1769		Big Beaver Creek, Beaver/ LD: Beaver	300	B-21-77	(p5 SEP 1787)Ephraim Blain, Esq./[see caveat] Original: found
NP-3674	Elliott, John	25 JUL 1769		Smith, Washington	300	A-58-291	--- Moris/--- Eberly/--- Crush/(r8 DEC 1787)William Wilson Original: found
NP-3675	Gibson, John	25 JUL 1769		Findlay, Allegheny	300	D-70-88	--- Moris/--- Eberly/--- Crush Original: found
NP-3677	Dougherty, Cornelius	25 JUL 1769	Washington	Raccoon Creek, Allegheny	300	C-50-77	John Irwin/(r7 SEP 1801)Robert Callender Original: found
NP-3678	Lake, Thomas	25 JUL 1769		mouth of Tuscarora Creek, Luzerne	300	K-11	(r31 JAN 1789)Rev. John Ewing Original: found
NP-3679	Maxwell, John	25 JUL 1769	Fishing Creek	LD: Columbia	300		Original: found

Table 6 - New Purchase Applications (1769-1773)

Number	Applicant	Date	Orig. Place	Later Place	Acres	Survey	Neighbors, Notes, etc.
NP-3680	Riffer, Henry	25 JUL 1769		Franklin, Westmoreland	200	A-37-62	(r12 JAN 1785)John Shryack Original: found
NP-3681	Bittel, George	25 JUL 1769		Donegal, Westmoreland	300	D-70-182	Benjamin Sitton/Capt. Thompson Original: With NP-3682-3685
NP-3682	Tumbald, Frederick	25 JUL 1769		Donegal, Westmoreland	300	D-70-180 D-70-181	George Bittle/Capt. Thompson Original: found
NP-3683	Bettel, George Jr.	25 JUL 1769		Donegal, Westmoreland	300	D-62-9	Andrew Baucher/Capt. Thompson Original: found
NP-3684	Tumbald, Frederick Jr.	25 JUL 1769		Salt Lick, Fayette	300	C-224-5 C-224-11	George Bettel/Capt. Thompson/(r14 MAR 1839)William Stull Original: found
NP-3685	Tumbald, Abram	25 JUL 1769		Bullskin, Fayette/ LD: Saltlick, Fayette	300	D-62-8 C-224-11	Capt. Thompson Original: found
NP-3686	Thesh, Mathias	25 JUL 1769		Hempfield, Westmoreland	300	D-62-7	Nicholas Bierly/David Morshed Original: found
NP-3687	Heil, Walter	25 JUL 1769		Hempfield & North Huntingdon, Westmoreland	200	D-56-233 D-57-58 C-35-214	--- Delap/David Loud/(r6 AUG 1788)Joseph Cost Original: With NP-3688
NP-3688	Kenson, Henry	25 JUL 1769		Fairfield, Westmoreland	300	D-62-6	John Miller Original: found
NP-3689	Fussleman, Philip	27 JUL 1769		Hempfield, Westmoreland	300	A-75-296 A-75-297	Henry Baush/Daniel Williams/Christian Barr/Anthony Altman/(r6 MAR 1789)Christian Truby, Esq. Original: found
NP-3690	Rodgers, Samuel (of Lebanon)	28 JUL 1769		Sugar Loaf, Luzerne	300	C-46-45	(r6 APR 1814)R. Counyngham Original: found
NP-3691	Anderson, John (of Lebanon)	28 JUL 1769	Northumberland	between Lackawanna River & Mill Creek, Luzerne	300	C-143-272	(r14 APR 1783)John M. Nesbitt Original: found
NP-3692	Beavers, Joseph	28 JUL 1769		Tunkhannock Creek, Luzerne	300	C-95-17	(r15 JUL 1797)John Hale, Esq. Original: found
NP-3693	Fleming, Thomas	28 JUL 1769		Tunkhannock Creek, Luzerne/ LD: Luzerne	300	H-160	Original: found

Table 6 - New Purchase Applications (1769-1773)

Number	Applicant	Date	Orig. Place	Later Place	Acres	Survey	Neighbors, Notes, etc.
NP-3694	Drumond, Alexander	28 JUL 1769		Chartiers Creek, Allegheny/ LD: Robinson, Allegheny	300	H-167	Andrew Robinson/[see caveat] Original: found
NP-3695	Cunningham, James	28 JUL 1769		Mansfield Borough & Scott Twp., Allegheny/ LD: Upper St. Clair, Allegheny	200	B-19-91 D-46-69	William Street/William Richmond/(p11 DEC 1874)R. F. Smith [patent H-73-117]/(p11 DEC 1874)M. B. Brown [patent H-73-116]/(p11 DEC 1874)John Gormly[patent H-73-114]/([11 DEC 1874)Josh Stephenson [patent H-73-115]/[see caveat] Original: found
NP-3696	Fout, Philip	29 JUL 1769	Cumberland	Henry Clay, Fayette/ LD: Henry Clay, Fayette	300	D-62-20	Original: found
NP-3697	Peeples, Robert Jr.	29 JUL 1769		Muncy Creek Twp., Lycoming	300	D-62-19	Robert McConaughy/James Kerr/[see caveat] Original: Signed
NP-3698	Gillespy, George	3 AUG 1769		Turbot, Northumberland	300	A-9-131	James Gillespy/John Gillespy/(r6 FEB 1811)D. Carson Original: found
NP-3699	Gillespy, James	3 AUG 1769		Turbot, Northumberland	300	C-61-227 C-61-228	John Blair/George Gillespy/(r30 NOV 1812)John Gillespy Original: found
NP-3700	Thatcher, Daniel	3 AUG 1769		Nescopeck Creek, Luzerne	300	K-235	(r24 APR 1775)Isaac Cox Original: Signed by Jeremiah Thatcher
NP-3701	Fourman, John	3 AUG 1769		Sugar Loaf, Luzerne	200	N-242	Daniel Thatcher/(r24 APR 1775)John Maxwell Nesbitt Original: found
NP-3702	Stephenson, Samuel	3 AUG 1769		Sugar Loaf, Luzerne	200	E-438	Daniel Thatcher/(r24 APR 1775)Isaac Cox Original: found
NP-3703	Clark, Jesse	3 AUG 1769		Sugar Loaf, Luzerne/ LD: Sugarloaf, Luzerne	300	D-46-66 C-113-67 C-22-118	Daniel Thatcher/(r23 JUN 1859)William Kisner/(r28 SEP 1859)William Beessel Original: found
NP-3704	Thatcher, Edward	3 AUG 1769		Sugar Loaf, Luzerne	300	N-245	Daniel Thatcher/(r24 APR 1775)John Maxwell Nesbitt Original: found
NP-3705	Roat, John	3 AUG 1769		Sugar Loaf, Luzerne	150	D-209	Daniel Thatcher/(r24 APR 1775)John Boyle Original: found

Table 6 - New Purchase Applications (1769-1773)

Number	Applicant	Date	Orig. Place	Later Place	Acres	Survey	Neighbors, Notes, etc.
NP-3706	Austin, Mary	3 AUG 1769		Nittany Valley, Centre - Clinton	300	C-102-126	John Fame/(r3 FEB 1773)Henry Keppell, Jr. Original: With NP-3707. Signed by Joseph Austin
NP-3707	Comley, Rachel	3 AUG 1769	Northumberland	Bald Eagle, Centre	300	C-102-125	Mary Austin/(r3 FEB 1773)Henry Keppell, Jr. Original: found
NP-3708	Austin, Susannah	3 AUG 1769		Bald Eagle, Centre	300	C-102-124	Rachel Comly/(r3 FEB 1773)Henry Keppell, Jr. Original: With NP-3709. Signed by Joseph Austin
NP-3709	Lippingcott, Elizabeth	3 AUG 1769	Northumberland	Bald Eagle, Centre	300	C-102-123	Susanna Austin/(r3 FEB 1773)Henry Keppell, Jr. Original: found
NP-3710	Moore, William	4 AUG 1769		Unity, Westmoreland	300	C-144-179	(r26 FEB 1827)James Maxwell Original: found
NP-3711	Seely, Sylvanus	4 AUG 1769		Dyberry, Wayne	300	C-228-43	(r14 NOV 1820) Original: Signed by Samuel Seely
NP-3712	Seely, Jane	4 AUG 1769		Lackawaxen River, Wayne	300	C-142-173	Peter Deckert/(r25 MAR 1836)James Manning Original: Signed by Samuel Seely
NP-3713	Hesser, Frederick	4 AUG 1769	Lackawanna River	LD: Luzerne/ [name in LD is Wesser]	300		John Seely Original: found
NP-3714	Priser, John	4 AUG 1769	Lackawanna River	LD: Luzerne	300		Frederick Hesser Original: found
NP-3715	Peterman, Jacob	4 AUG 1769	Lackawanna River	LD: Luzerne	300		Isaac Sayler Original: found
NP-3716	Reader, Jacob	4 AUG 1769	Lackawanna River	LD: Luzerne	300		John Seely Original: found
NP-3717	Seely, John (of New York)	4 AUG 1769	Lackawanna River	LD: Luzerne	300		Hans Vanates Original: found
NP-3718	Sayler, Isaac	4 AUG 1769	Lackawanna River	LD: Luzerne	300		John Priser Original: found
NP-3719	McBride, Roger	4 AUG 1769		Hempfield, Westmoreland	300	C-62-18	--- Venlore/John Brown/William Nelson Original: With NP-3720
NP-3720	Crutis, George	4 AUG 1769		Hempfield, Westmoreland	300	C-217-286 C-217-287	Roger McBride/(r27 FEB 1797)John Turner Original: found
NP-3721	Morton, Japheth	4 AUG 1769	Berks	Buffalo, Union	200	D-57-35 C-135-253 C-135-254	James Brenner/(r29 SEP 1814)/[see caveat] Original: Signed by Edward Morton

Table 6 - New Purchase Applications (1769-1773)

Number	Applicant	Date	Orig. Place	Later Place	Acres	Survey	Neighbors, Notes, etc.
NP-3722	Theobald, Prior	9 AUG 1769	Cumberland	Mt. Pleasant & Huntingdon, Westmoreland	300	C-220-123	Charles Edmondson, Esq./(r16 APR 1829)Jesse Swan Original: found
NP-3723	Anderson, Thomas	9 AUG 1769		between Loyalhanna Creek & Conemaugh River, Westmoreland	300	A-81-201	James Cooper/(r6 OCT 1787) Original: With NP-3724
NP-3724	Elder, Hannah	9 AUG 1769		between Loyalhanna Creek & Conemaugh River, Westmoreland	300	C-50-278	Thomas Anderson/(r5 OCT 1787) Original: found
NP-3725	Anderson, Joshua	9 AUG 1769		Derry, Westmoreland	300	A-81-98	Hannah Elder/(r5 FEB 1801)John Anderson & Charles Anderson Original: With NP-3726 Signed by Thomas Anderson
NP-3726	Anderson, Robert	9 AUG 1769		Derry, Westmoreland	300	C-180-38 C-180-36 C-180-37 C-4-33	Joshua Anderson/(r13 MAR 1834)Thomas Anderson/(r23 JAN 1839)James Rodgers & S. M. Porter Original: found
NP-3727	Cooper, James	9 AUG 1769		between Loyalhanna Creek & Conemaugh River, Westmoreland	300	A-82-170	(r6 OCT 1787)Thomas Anderson Original: found
NP-3728	Rogers, Phillip (of East Nantmeal Township, Chester County)	9 AUG 1769		Monongahela River, Fayette	300	B-1-110 B-1-122	(r12 MAR 1788)William Kitcham Original: Signed
NP-3729	McConnall, James (son of William McConnall, of Peters Township, Cumberland County)	9 AUG 1769		Elizabeth, Allegheny	300	D-70-89	--- Kelly Original: found

Table 6 - New Purchase Applications (1769-1773)

Number	Applicant	Date	Orig. Place	Later Place	Acres	Survey	Neighbors, Notes, etc.
NP-3730	Davis, Azariah (of Peters Township, Cumberland County)	9 AUG 1769		Rostraver, Westmoreland	300	A-45-84	(r15 JAN 1788)Andrew Robinson Original: found
NP-3731	Chew, Benjamin Esq.	10 AUG 1769		Fishing Creek Twp., Columbia	5000	B-21-110 B-21-111 B-21-112 K-327 BB-1-21	(r21 MAR 1796)/(r29 OCT 1799) Original: found
NP-3732	McNair, Robert	19 AUG 1769		Shamokin Creek, Northumberland/ LD: Northumberland	300	X-209	Edward Shippen/Joseph Shippen, Esq. Original: With NP-3733
NP-3733	McNair, John	19 AUG 1769		Shamokin Creek, Northumberland		C-96-93	Robert McNair/(r11 AUG 1796)Jeremiah Jackson Original: found
NP-3734	Cannon, Samuel	19 AUG 1769	Tunkhannock Creek	LD: Wyoming	300		Original: With NP-3735
NP-3735	Ogden, Gilbert	19 AUG 1769	Tunkhannock Creek	LD: Luzerne	300		Original: found
NP-3736	Hollingsworth, Hannah	21 AUG 1769		Nippenose, Lycoming	300	D-62-17	John Harris [on NP-74] Original: With NP-3737
NP-3737	Olar, Philip	21 AUG 1769		Nippenose, Lycoming	300	D-62-16	Hannah Hollingsworth Original: found
NP-3738	Taylor, Benjamin	21 AUG 1769		Chillisquaque, Northumberland	300	W-264 W-265 C-141-243	(r2 APR 1851)John Murray Original: found
NP-3739	Slusher, Thomas	21 AUG 1769	Susquehanna River	LD: Northumberland/ Montour	300		Benjamin Taylor Original: found
NP-3740	Berckman, Charles	21 AUG 1769	Berks	Buffalo, Union	200	D-55-90 Q-230	Andrew Edge/(r24 FEB 1802)Henry Aurandt Original: found
NP-3741	Musser, John	21 AUG 1769		Point, Northumberland	200	D-60-189 C-136-41	Sarah Lowden/(r6 JUN 1770)John Musser & James Davis Original: found

Table 6 - New Purchase Applications (1769-1773)

Number	Applicant	Date	Orig. Place	Later Place	Acres	Survey	Neighbors, Notes, etc.
NP-3742	Murdock, Mary	21 AUG 1769		Turbot, Northumberland	300	C-23-43	Robert Armstrong/(r24 MAY 1822)J. Bryson Original: found
NP-3743	Johnston, Joseph (mariner, of Hunterdon County, Kingwood [Twp., NJ])	22 AUG 1769	Northumberland	Susquehanna River 3 miles below Nescopeck, Luzerne	300	C-176-140	(r25 FEB 1782)Ann Rose Original: found
NP-3744	Ewig, Christian	23 AUG 1769	Union	Buffalo, Snyder	300	D-62-13 D-62-14 D-62-15	Gov. Penn/Ludwig Derr Original: With NP-3745-3746
NP-3745	Ewig, Adam	23 AUG 1769	Cumberland or Berks	Penn, Snyder	300	A-44-213	Dr. William Smith/David Herbster/Dr. Gay/(r12 AUG 1831)W. Rooper Original: found
NP-3746	Ewig, Philip	23 AUG 1769	Cumberland	Buffalo, Snyder	300	D-56-272 C-91-286	Ludwig Derr/Christian Ewig/John Wilson/(r31 JUL 1789)David Kennedy, Esq. Original: found
NP-3747	Neil, Thomas	24 AUG 1769	Northumberland	Nescopeck Falls Susquehanna River, Luzerne/ LD: Luzerne	300	X-160 X-161	William Webb Original: found
NP-3748	Patterson, Alexander	24 AUG 1769		Susquehanna River, Luzerne	300	C-176-70	William McKinney/(r4 MAY 1775)Deetrick Rees Original: found
NP-3749	Grandin, Philip	24 AUG 1769		North Branch Susquehanna River, Columbia	300	N-263	(r14 FEB 1772)John Maxwell Nesbitt Original: found
NP-3750	Smith, Samuel & William Smith (sons of John Smith, carpenter at Fort Pitt)	24 AUG 1769		North Huntingdon, Westmoreland	300	D-62-12	Original: found
NP-3751	Nana, William	26 AUG 1769		Washington, Lycoming/ LD: Washington, Lycoming	300	D-63-82 A-244 C-140-125 C-178-134	David Duncan/(r29 OCT 1813)Robert Martin/(r30 MAY 1829)David Reed/[called William Hanna in the caveat]/[see caveat] Original: With NP-3751-3757. Signed by Levi Stephens
NP-3752	Casner, George	26 AUG 1769		White Deer, Union	300	A-40-67	William Nana/(r21 MAY 1808)Conrad Tinbrock & Abraham Tinbrock Original: found

Table 6 - New Purchase Applications (1769-1773)

Number	Applicant	Date	Orig. Place	Later Place	Acres	Survey	Neighbors, Notes, etc.
NP-3753	Stephens, Mary	26 AUG 1769		Washington, Lycoming	300	D-60-212 C-9-85	David Duncan/(r18 APR 1808)William Bell/[see caveat] Original: found
NP-3754	Stephens, Rachel	26 AUG 1769		Washington, Lycoming	300	D-60-212 D-63-97 D-464	Mary Stephens/(r18 APR 1808)William Bell Original: found
NP-3755	Stephens, Elizabeth	26 AUG 1769	south branch White Deer Hole Creek	LD: Lycoming	300		William McKroskey Original: found
NP-3756	Stephens, Sarah	26 AUG 1769		Washington, Lycoming/ LD: Lycoming	300	D-62-11	Elizabeth Stephens Original: found
NP-3757	Evers, Jonathan	26 AUG 1769		Bald Eagle, Centre	300	C-154-237 C-154-238	Joseph Augustus/(r29 APR 1795)William Miller Original: found
NP-3758	Taylor, Jonathan	26 AUG 1769		Washington, Lycoming	300	D-56-111 C-91-80 C-91-81	Sarah Stephens/(r10 NOV 1840)Jacob Hess Original: With NP-3759-3760
NP-3759	Taylor, Joseph	26 AUG 1769	Northumberland	White Deer, Union	300	C-221-24	Jonathan Taylor/(r21 MAY 1808)Jacob Snyder Original: found
NP-3760	Taylor, Morris	26 AUG 1769		White Deer Hole Valley, Lycoming	300	A-19-219	Edward Shippen, Esq./(r9 FEB 1818)Joseph Bell Original: found
NP-3761	Robertson, John	26 AUG 1769	Beech Creek	LD: Centre	300		Michael Troy/Capt. Piper/Lt. Wiggant Original: With NP-3762
NP-3762	Robertson, Sarah	26 AUG 1769	Beech Creek	LD: Centre	300		Michael Troy Original: found
NP-3763	McCollock, Samuel	26 AUG 1769		Monongahela River, Washington	300	E-565	George McCollock/(r17 APR 1788)George Passmore Original: found
NP-3764	Calvin, Vincent	26 AUG 1769		Pigeon Creek, Washington	300	C-35-187	(r28 MAR 1788)/[on judgement of Board of Property]/[see caveat] Original: found
NP-3765	Thomas, Thomas	26 AUG 1769		Chartiers Creek, Allegheny/ LD: Allegheny	300	A-230	[see NP-3767] Original: found

Table 6 - New Purchase Applications (1769-1773)

Number	Applicant	Date	Orig. Place	Later Place	Acres	Survey	Neighbors, Notes, etc.
NP-3766	Thomas, Jeremiah (son of Philip Thomas)	26 AUG 1769		Chartiers Creek, Allegheny/ LD: Upper St. Clair, Allegheny	300	W-266	Philip Thomas Original: found
NP-3767	Thomas, Phillip	26 AUG 1769		St. Clair, Allegheny	300	D-62-28	Thomas Thomas Original: found
NP-3768	Hammond, Nathan	26 AUG 1769		Monongahela River, Washington	300	A-5-292 C-8-54 D-38-206	(r6 MAY 1796)Thomas Heslip Original: found
NP-3769	Spiere, Jacob	26 AUG 1769	Monongahela River & Pigeon Creek	LD: Washington	300		Original: found
NP-3770	McCollock, George	26 AUG 1769		Monongahela River, Washington	300	A-61-142	Peter Young/(r3 APR 1773)Samuel Dickson Original: found
NP-3771	Reily, Phillip	26 AUG 1769		Monongahela River, Washington/ LD: Washington	300	A-227	Original: found
NP-3772	Zenes, Jonathan	26 AUG 1769		Pike Run, Washington	300	F-20	William Zenes/(r18 MAR 1795)Daniel Shively Original: found
NP-3773	Drenning, Jacob	26 AUG 1769	Monongahela River	LD: Allegheny	300		Original: found
NP-3774	Furman, Joseph	26 AUG 1769		Monongahela River, Washington	300	C-16-279	(r23 JAN 1796)Vincent Colvin Original: found
NP-3775	Erwin, Arthur	26 AUG 1769		Fallowfield, Washington/ LD: Washington/ Allegheny	300	F-244	Ezekiel Dewitt/William Frye/(p1 AUG 1904)John S. Rogers [patent H-76-400] Original: found
NP-3776	Calvin, James	26 AUG 1769		mouth of Mingo Creek, Washington	300	C-93-34	(r12 MAY 1787)Elisha Teeters/[see caveat] Original: found
NP-3777	Black, David	26 AUG 1769		St. Clair, Allegheny	300	D-62-30	Original: found

Table 6 - New Purchase Applications (1769-1773)

Number	Applicant	Date	Orig. Place	Later Place	Acres	Survey	Neighbors, Notes, etc.
NP-3778	Calvin, Stephen	26 AUG 1769		Monongahela River, Washington/ LD: Washington/ Greene	300	F-229	Original: found
NP-3779	Decker, Joseph	26 AUG 1769		Monongahela River, Washington	300	H-169	(r12 MAR 1788)Daniel Vanoorhis Original: found
NP-3780	Decker, Moses	26 AUG 1769		Pigeon Creek, Washington/ LD: Washington/ Allegheny	300	H-168	John Decker/Stephen Calvin Original: found
NP-3781	Decker, Tobias	26 AUG 1769		Pigeon Creek, Washington/ LD: Washington	300	H-170	John Decker/Abram Decker Original: found
NP-3782	Decker, John	26 AUG 1769		Monongahela River, Washington	300	A-33-265	(r4 NOV 1795)Andrew McFarland Original: found
NP-3783	Decker, Abraham	26 AUG 1769		Fallowfield, Washington	300	A-5-298	John Decker/Paul Froman/(r11 MAY 1796)Joseph Parkinson Original: found
NP-3784	Craig, Isaac	28 AUG 1769		Fallowfield, Washington	300	C-35-154	Mr. Ozean/(r6 OCT 1787) Original: Signed
NP-3785	Althouse, Isaiah	28 AUG 1769		Buffalo, Union	300	D-60-279 A-78-126	(r13 DEC 1774)Henry Vandike/[see caveat] Original: found
NP-3786	Parsons, Barnabus	28 AUG 1769	Cumberland	Kelly, Union	300	D-62-253 C-89-267	James McConnel/(r19 OCT 1787)Henry Iddings Original: found
NP-3787	Gray, William (of Kent County)	28 AUG 1769		Northeast Branch Susquehanna River, Columbia	300	N-264	(r14 FEB 1772)John M. Nesbitt Original: found
NP-3788	Tharp, William (of Maryland)	28 AUG 1769		Northeast Branch Susquehanna River, Columbia	300	B-492	(r14 FEB 1772)John M. Nesbitt Original: found

Table 6 - New Purchase Applications (1769-1773)

Number	Applicant	Date	Orig. Place	Later Place	Acres	Survey	Neighbors, Notes, etc.
NP-3789	Whitley, Michael	29 AUG 1769	1.5 miles from path from Ft. Augusta to Muncy Hill	LD: Northumberland	300		Original: found
NP-3790	Rice, Joseph	29 AUG 1769		Turbot, Northumberland	300	D-56-161 A-72-79	Benjamin Freeman/William Freeman/(r25 MAY 1774)John Freeman, Jr. Original: found
NP-3791	Randell, James (of Sherman's Valley, yeoman)	29 AUG 1769		near Northeast Branch Susquehanna River, Luzerne	300	D-89-313	Francis West/(r17 AUG 1773)William West, Jr. Original: found
NP-3792	West, Ann (spinster)	29 AUG 1769		Northeast Branch Susquehanna River, Northumberland or Montour	300	D-13-275	John Field/(r13 JAN 1775)William West, Jr. Original: found
NP-3793	Francis, Turbutt	29 AUG 1769		Northampton or Montour/ LD: Columbia	300		Connosque [an Indian]/John Thompson [a Delaware Indian] Original: found
NP-3794	McClannegan, Blair	31 AUG 1769	south of Bald Eagle Mountain	LD: Centre	300		Original: With NP-3795-3799
NP-3795	Charleton, Thomas	31 AUG 1769	Lycoming	branch of Fishing Creek, Centre - Clinton	300	C-198-232	Blair McClenegan/(r17 JUN 1796)Thomas Stewardson Original: found
NP-3796	Donaldson, Hugh	31 AUG 1769	branch of Fishing Creek	Centre - Clinton/ LD: Centre	300		Thomas Charleton Original: found
NP-3797	Whealin, Richard	31 AUG 1769	branch of Fishing Creek	Centre - Clinton/ LD: Centre	300		Hugh Donaldson Original: found
NP-3798	Kennedy, Robert	31 AUG 1769		Fishing Creek, Centre - Clinton	300	C-82-48	(r2 MAY 1804)John Hopkins & John Cox Original: found
NP-3799	Kennedy, Thomas	31 AUG 1769		Fishing Creek, Centre - Clinton	300	C-82-69	Robert Kennedy/(r3 MAY 1804)John Hopkins & John Cox Original: found

Table 6 - New Purchase Applications (1769-1773)

Number	Applicant	Date	Orig. Place	Later Place	Acres	Survey	Neighbors, Notes, etc.
NP-3800	Smith, Philip	31 AUG 1769		Fishing Creek, Centre - Clinton	300	C-82-57	Thomas Kennedy/(r3 MAY 1804)John Hopkins & John Cox Original: With NP-3801-3804
NP-3801	Purdon, John	31 AUG 1769		Centre, Centre	300	C-21-173	(r11 JAN 1802)Cornelius Cox, Esq. Original: found
NP-3802	Porter, Andrew	31 AUG 1769		Centre, Centre	300	C-21-172	John Purdon/(r11 JAN 1802)Cornelius Cox, Esq. Original: found
NP-3803	Dougherty, Dennis	31 AUG 1769	Lycoming	Centre, Centre	300	S-117	(r15 JUN 1796)Thomas Stewardson Original: found
NP-3804	Dougan, John	31 AUG 1769		Walker, Centre	300	C-144-154	(r15 MAY 1826)Alexander McEwen Original: found
NP-3805	Carroll, Timothy	31 AUG 1769		Walker, Centre	300	C-144-155	(r15 MAY 1826)Alexander McEwen Original: With NP-3806-3809
NP-3806	Badge, Thomas	31 AUG 1769		Centre, Centre	300	C-21-174	Timothy Carroll/(r11 JAN 1802)Cornelius Cox, Esq. Original: found
NP-3807	Bray, George	31 AUG 1769	Lycoming	Fishing Creek, Centre	300	C-198-233	Thomas Badge/(r17 JUN 1796)Thomas Stewardson Original: found
NP-3808	Sheredin, John	31 AUG 1769	Lycoming	Fishing Creek, Centre	300	C-198-234	George Brays/(r17 JUN 1796)Thomas Stewardson Original: found
NP-3809	Casson, Joseph	31 AUG 1769	Lycoming	Fishing Creek, Centre	300	F-23	John Sheredin/(r15 JUN 1796)Thomas Stewardson Original: found
NP-3810	Dougherty, Margaret	31 AUG 1769	Lycoming	branch of Fishing Creek, Centre	300	C-198-225	Jane Kirk/(r16 JUN 1796)Thomas Stewardson Original: With 3811-3815
NP-3811	Dougherty, Patrick	31 AUG 1769	Lycoming	branch of Fishing Creek, Centre	300	C-198-224	(r16 JUN 1796)Thomas Stewardson Original: found
NP-3812	Snowdon, John Jr. (of Philadelphia)	31 AUG 1769	Lick Run south of Bald Eagle Mountain	LD: Union	300		James Armitage Original: found

Table 6 - New Purchase Applications (1769-1773)

Number	Applicant	Date	Orig. Place	Later Place	Acres	Survey	Neighbors, Notes, etc.
NP-3813	Smith, John	31 AUG 1769	Lick Run south of Bald Eagle Mountain	LD: Union	300		John Snowdon Original: found
NP-3814	Travers, Patrick	31 AUG 1769		below Spring Creek Gap, Bald Eagle Mountain, Centre	300	C-82-58	(r2 MAY 1804)John Hopkins & John Cox Original: found
NP-3815	Burns, James	31 AUG 1769		branch of Fishing Creek, Centre	300	C-82-70	(r2 MAY 1804)John Hopkins & John Cox Original: found
NP-3816	Cooke, James	31 AUG 1769	south of Bald Eagle Mountain	LD: Clinton/ Centre	300		Jane Potts Original: With NP-3817-3821
NP-3817	McGlathery, John	31 AUG 1769	south of Bald Eagle Mountain	LD: Centre	300		James Cooke Original: found
NP-3818	Potts, Margaret	31 AUG 1769	Northumberland	south of Bald Eagle Mountain, Centre - Clinton	300	A-11-252	John McGlathery/(r17 SEP 1781)Jasper Yeates, Esq. Original: found
NP-3819	Eaken, Andrew	31 AUG 1769	Lycoming	Lick Run, Centre - Clinton	300	C-198-223	(r16 JUN 1796)Thomas Stewardson Original: found
NP-3820	Moore, William	31 AUG 1769	Lycoming	Lick Run, Centre - Clinton	300	C-198-231	Robert Allison/(r16 JUN 1796)Thomas Stewardson Original: found
NP-3821	Kirk, Jane	31 AUG 1769	Lycoming	Lick Run, Centre - Clinton	300	C-198-222	William Moore/(r16 JUN 1796)Thomas Stewardson Original: found
NP-3822	Potts, Jane	31 AUG 1769	Lycoming	Fishing Creek, Centre - Clinton	300	C-198-221	(r16 JUN 1796)Thomas Stewardson Original: With NP-3823-3825
NP-3823	Troy, Rachel	31 AUG 1769	Lycoming	Fishing Creek, Centre	300	C-82-49	Jane Potts/(r2 MAY 1804)John Hopkins & John Cox Original: found
NP-3824	George, William	31 AUG 1769		south of Bald Eagle Mountain, Centre/ LD: Clinton/ Centre	300		Rachel Troy Original: found

Table 6 - New Purchase Applications (1769-1773)

Number	Applicant	Date	Orig. Place	Later Place	Acres	Survey	Neighbors, Notes, etc.
NP-3825	Willson, Joseph	31 AUG 1769	south of Bald Eagle Mountain	LD: Centre	300		William George Original: found
NP-3826	Burns, Patrick	31 AUG 1769	Northumberland	south of Bald Eagle Mountain, Lycoming-Clinton	300	A-11-250	(r17 SEP 1781)Jasper Yeates Original: found
NP-3827	Rice, Patrick	31 AUG 1769	Northumberland	south of Bald Eagle Mountain, Lycoming-Clinton	300	A-11-251	Patrick Burns/(r17 SEP 1781)Jasper Yeates Original: found
NP-3828	Moore, John	31 AUG 1769		south of Bald Eagle Mountain, Clinton/ LD: Wayne, Clinton	300		Thomas Scully Original: found
NP-3829	Boner, Barnabas	31 AUG 1769	Lycoming	Nippenose Valley, Centre - Clinton	300	C-138-110 C-138-111	(r15 AUG 1796)Ludwig Lauman Original: found
NP-3830	Whitly, Sarah	31 AUG 1769	Lycoming	head of Nippenose Valley, Centre - Clinton/ LD: Lycoming	300	A-5-25	Barnabas Boner Original: found
NP-3831	Scully, Thomas	31 AUG 1769	Lycoming	south of Bald Eagle Mountain, Centre - Clinton/ LD: Clinton	300	X-98	Thomas Turner Original: found
NP-3832	Turner, Thomas	31 AUG 1769		south of Bald Eagle Mountain, Clinton/ LD: Clinton	300		Patrick Rice Original: found
NP-3833	Sherswood, William	31 AUG 1769	east end Fishing Creek Valley	LD: Centre	300		Michael Troy Original: found
NP-3834	Sherswood, James	31 AUG 1769	Fishing Creek Valley	LD: Centre	300		Michael Troy/[see caveat] Original: found
NP-3835	Karcher, Catharine (of Philadelphia, spinster)	31 AUG 1769		Buffalo, Union	300	D-63-86 A-8-142	Maj. DeHaas/(r17 APR 1793)Christopher Johnston Original: Signed by Ludwig Karcher

Table 6 - New Purchase Applications (1769-1773)

Number	Applicant	Date	Orig. Place	Later Place	Acres	Survey	Neighbors, Notes, etc.
NP-3836	Smith, David	31 AUG 1769	Cumberland	Moon, Allegheny	300	D-62-29	Thomas McKee Original: found
NP-3837	Stewart, Andrew	31 AUG 1769	Cumberland	Robinson, Allegheny	300	B-7-41 B-7-42	Alexander McKee/(r1 JUN 1837)James McKee Original: found
NP-3838	Wikoff, Peter	31 AUG 1769	north of West Branch Susquehanna River, Berks	LD: Lycoming	300		Thomas Gilcrease Original: found
NP-3839	Armstrong, Robert	31 AUG 1769		Turbot, Northumberland	300	C-154-104	--- Howsche/Alexander Steen/(r5 MAY 1794)George McKee & Robert McKee/[see caveat] Original: With NP-3840-3841
NP-3840	Bayux, Thomas	31 AUG 1769		Turbot, Northumberland	300	D-62-5	Original: found
NP-3841	Van Devourt, Peter	31 AUG 1769		Turbot, Northumberland	300	X-123 X-124 X-125 C-199-262	Thomas Bayax/(r22 FEB 1813)William Stratten Original: found
NP-3842	Rhea, John	31 AUG 1769	Catawissa Creek, Northampton & Berks	LD: Columbia	300		Original: With NP-3843
NP-3843	Bayns, Robert	31 AUG 1769	3.5 miles from Northeast Branch Susquehanna River, Northampton & Berks	LD: Lycoming	300		John Cox, Jr. Original: found
NP-3844	Eyre, Severn	31 AUG 1769	headwaters of Fishing Creek south of Bald Eagle Mountain	LD: Clinton/ Centre	300		Original: found
NP-3845	Spencer, John	5 SEP 1769		Mahoning, Northumberland	300	C-210-110 C-210-121 C-210-122	(r25 JAN 1785)William Wilson, Esq./(r17 DEC 1787) Original: Missing
NP-3846	Wilson, James	5 SEP 1769		Point, Northumberland	300	D-57-205 D-62-119 C-82-123	(r13 MAR 1805)Susanna Hunter [widow] Original: found

Table 6 - New Purchase Applications (1769-1773)

Number	Applicant	Date	Orig. Place	Later Place	Acres	Survey	Neighbors, Notes, etc.
NP-3847	Calhoon, George	5 SEP 1769		Point, Northumberland	300	C-53-59	Robert McCully/(r10 AUG 1791)William Cook, Esq./[see caveat] Original: found
NP-3848	Weeks, Joseph	5 SEP 1769	White Deer Hole Creek	LD: Lycoming	300		Original: found
NP-3849	Sunderland, Joseph	5 SEP 1769	Black Run above White Deer Hole Creek	LD: Lycoming	300		Original: Missing
NP-3850	Ewing, John	17 APR 1770		Menallen, Fayette	300	A-57-141	James Wilson/(r26 MAR 1788)William Haney Original: found
NP-3851	Conner, Patrick	17 APR 1770		McKibbins Run, Fayette	300	C-65-88	John Moore/James Willson/Robert Gilmous/(r8 MAR 1791)John Ewing Original: found
NP-3852	Montour, Andrew	--------		Fairfax, Lycoming	880	D-62-240 D-43-33 D-56-210 D-57-20 D-57-282 W-253	(r17 JUN 1785)Peter Zachary Floyd Original: Missing
NP-3852a	Jennings, John	16 DEC 1773		Pine Creek, Northumberland	1000		--- Vancleve/[relocation in lieu of NP-3315, allowed by the Governor's special order] Original: Missing
NP-3853	Crawford, Hugh	22 JAN 1768		Union, Fayette	---	B-5-199 B-5-215	William Peters [aka Redstone Peter, an Indian]/(r28 DEC 1815)John Jackson/(r28 DEC 1815)Philip Shute [NP-3481] Original: Missing

Instructions for Using the Phonetic Cross Reference Section

In the preparation of this book, the spelling of surnames found in the original documents has been retained. Because many of the names were written phonetically, there is considerable variation in their spellings. To make it easier to locate these spelling variants, the following two sections use the Daitch-Mokotoff (D-M) coding system to identify possible variations in spelling. Since the spellings used in the documents were sometimes quite different than the spelling that the persons themselves may have used, considerable latitude should be used in searching for individual surnames.

The following two sections contain all of the surnames found in this volume. To use the Phonetic Cross Reference, first look up the surname in the first section of the cross reference (Daitch-Mokotoff Code Index). Some surnames will have more than one D-M Code. You should check each D-M Code listed. If the name you are looking for is not listed, select a name that is listed that is similar to the one you are searching for. Then use the D-M code listed for that name and find that D-M code in the second section of the cross reference (Daitch-Mokotoff Phonetic Cross Reference). Scan the names around that D-M code for possible spelling variants. The spelling variants identified can then be looked up in the alphabetical index at the end of the book.

Name	Code
Achenbough	046705
Achenbough	056705
Achert	049300
Achert	059300
Ackels	045840
Ackels	058400
Ackerman	045966
Ackerman	059660
Acre	049000
Acre	059000
Adam	036000
Adams	036400
Aday	030000
Agey	050000
Agnew	056700
Aiken	056000
Aitkin	035600
Akerman	059660
Albrecht	087943
Albrecht	087953
Albright	087953
Alen	086000
Ales	084000
Alexander	085463
Alison	084600
Alkison	085460
All	080000
Allee	080000
Allen	086000
Allens	086400
Allison	084600
Allman	086600
Allmen	086600
Allsworth	084793
Alricks	089454
Alricks	089540
Alston	084360
Alteman	083660
Althoe	083000
Althouse	083040
Altman	083660
Alward	087930
Alwood	087030
Anders	063400
Anders	063940
Anderson	063460
Anderson	063946
Andree	063900
Andres	063940
Andrews	063974
Anjer	061900
Anjer	064900
Annis	064000
Antes	063400
Antis	063400
Aplegate	078530
Appelgate	078530
Appleby	078700
Applegate	078530
Archer	094900
Archer	095900
Archert	094930
Archert	095930
Arden	093600
Armitage	096350
Armstrong	096439
Arnold	096830
Ashbaugh	047500
Ashbee	047000
Ashbridge	047935
Ashcraft	044973
Ashcraft	045973
Ashton	043600
Askew	045700
Askey	045000
Askins	045640
Athel	038000
Atkinson	035646
Atkison	035460
Auchmuty	046300
Auchmuty	056300
Augustus	054340
Aurandt	096300
Aurnt	096300
Austin	043600
Backhouse	745504
Backhouse	755040
Backus	745400
Backus	754000
Badge	735000
Badger	735900
Bailey	780000
Baird	793000
Baker	759000
Balbridge	787935
Baldin	783600
Baldwin	783760
Bale	780000
Ball	780000
Ballard	789300
Ballmore	786900
Baltimore	783690
Banfield	767830
Banker	765900
Banks	765400
Bantze	764000
Bar	790000
Barber	797900
Barckley	794580
Barckley	795800
Barclay	794800
Barclay	795800
Bard	793000
Bare	790000
Bargamot	795630
Barkley	795800
Barnabas	796740
Barnes	796400
Barnett	796300
Barnhart	796593
Barnhill	796580
Barns	796400
Barr	790000
Barret	793000
Bartholomow	793867
Barton	793600
Bartram	793960
Baskins	745640
Batersby	734700
Batersby	739470
Batt	730000
Battler	738900
Battom	736000
Baucher	749000
Baucher	759000
Bauchman	746600
Bauchman	756600
Bauer	719000
Baum	760000
Baumgartner	765936
Baur	790000
Baush	740000
Bausman	746600
Baussman	746600
Bawden	773600
Baxter	754390
Bay	700000
Bayard	719300
Bayax	715400
Bayers	714000
Bayers	719400
Bayles	784000
Bayless	784000
Bayloss	784000
Bayns	764000
Baynton	763600
Bays	740000
Bayux	715400
Beale	780000
Beally	780000
Bear	790000
Beard	793000
Beason	746000
Beass	740000
Beatey	730000
Beatis	734000
Beattey	730000
Beatty	730000

Name	Code
Beaty	730000
Beaver	779000
Beavers	774000
Beavers	779400
Bechtel	743800
Bechtel	753800
Bechtle	743800
Bechtle	753800
Beck	745000
Beck	750000
Beckerton	745936
Beckerton	759360
Beckley	745800
Beckley	758000
Bee	700000
Beeber	779000
Beeler	789000
Beels	784000
Been	760000
Beeson	746000
Beessel	748000
Beever	779000
Bell	780000
Benat	763000
Bender	763900
Benetsh	764000
Benham	765600
Bennefield	767830
Bennett	763000
Benninger	766590
Bentley	763800
Berckman	794566
Berckman	795660
Bereke	795000
Berkley	795800
Berringer	796590
Bettel	738000
Bevaird	779300
Beyerly	719800
Biard	793000
Bickham	745560
Bickham	755600
Bickman	745660
Bickman	756600
Bidde	730000
Biddle	738000
Bierly	798000
Bigert	759300
Bingman	765660
Birch	794000
Birch	795000
Bird	793000
Birgeman	795660
Bishop	747000
Bishure	749000
Bittel	738000
Bittle	738000
Black	784500
Black	785000
Blackburn	784579
Blackburn	785796
Blackman	784566
Blackman	785660
Blacks	784540
Blacks	785400
Blackstone	784543
Blackstone	785436
Blain	786000
Blaine	786000
Blair	789000
Blane	786000
Blank	786500
Blare	789000
Blaze	784000
Bleakley	785800
Blecker	784590
Blecker	785900
Blessing	784650
Blickendoffer	784563
Blickendoffer	785637
Blickenstoffer	784564
Blickenstoffer	785643
Blooget	780530
Bloom	780600
Bloss	784000
Blum	786000
Blyth	783000
Blythe	783000
Boay	700000
Boggert	759300
Boggs	754000
Boland	786300
Bolden	783600
Boldwin	783760
Bolen	786000
Bolins	786400
Bolter	783900
Bond	763000
Boner	769000
Bonham	765600
Bonnell	768000
Bonner	769000
Bonsal	764800
Bonsall	764800
Bony	760000
Boon	706000
Boone	706000
Boor	709000
Boos	704000
Boquet	753000
Boreman	796600
Boren	796000
Borhen	795600
Bossert	749300
Bossman	746600
Boten	736000
Botts	740000
Boucher	704900
Boucher	705900
Boude	703000
Bouga	705000
Boughanan	705660
Bougs	705400
Bounjure	706190
Bounjure	706490
Bouquet	705300
Bousman	704660
Bovard	779300
Bowden	773600
Bowdin	773600
Bowdon	773600
Bower	779000
Bowman	776600
Bowne	776000
Bowsman	774660
Boyd	730000
Boyer	719000
Boyle	780000
Boyles	784000
Boyls	784000
Bracken	794560
Bracken	795600
Brackenridge	794569
Brackenridge	795693
Bradford	793793
Bradley	793800
Brady	793000
Braght	795300
Bragth	795300
Braithwaite	793730
Brand	796300
Brandon	796360
Brannon	796600
Brant	796300
Bratain	793600
Braton	793600
Bratt	793000
Bratten	793600
Brattin	793600
Bratton	793600
Bray	790000
Brays	794000
Breadin	793600
Bready	793000
Breckbill	794578
Breckbill	795780
Breckenridge	794569
Breckenridge	795693

Name	Code
Breden	793600
Bredy	793000
Breidebach	793740
Breidebach	793750
Breniman	796660
Brenizer	796490
Brenner	796900
Brewton	797360
Brice	794000
Brice	795000
Brickley	794580
Brickley	795800
Bridgins	793564
Bright	795300
Brillinger	798659
Briney	796000
Bringham	796560
Bringhurst	796543
Bringhurst	796594
Bringman	796566
Briniegh	796500
Brinigh	796500
Briniman	796660
Brinker	796590
Brinkhoff	796570
Brinton	796360
Brison	794600
Britebough	793705
Brittain	793600
Brock	794500
Brock	795000
Brodhack	793545
Brodhack	793550
Brookens	790564
Brooks	790540
Brotherntin	793963
Brotherton	793936
Browd	797300
Brown	797600
Brownfield	797678
Brownholtz	797658
Brownlee	797680
Bruce	794000
Bruce	795000
Brumfield	796783
Brumfit	796730
Bruner	796900
Brunston	796436
Bruster	794390
Bryan	796000
Bryson	794600
Buchanan	746600
Buchanan	756600
Buchannon	746600
Buchannon	756600
Buchanon	746600
Buchanon	756600
Bucher	749000
Bucher	759000
Buck	745000
Buck	750000
Buckwalter	745783
Buckwalter	757839
Bud	730000
Budd	730000
Buergy	795000
Bull	780000
Bumstick	764345
Bumstick	764350
Bunkhoff	765700
Bunn	760000
Bunner	769000
Bunsure	764900
Burbige	797500
Burbridge	797935
Burcome	794600
Burcome	795600
Burd	793000
Burens	796400
Burgerd	795930
Burk	795000
Burkcom	795460
Burkcom	795560
Burkem	795600
Burkerk	795950
Burkham	795600
Burkheimer	795690
Burkholder	795839
Burn	796000
Burnes	796400
Burnet	796300
Burns	796400
Burrows	797400
Burtran	793960
Bussard	749300
Butler	738900
Butterage	739500
Buttler	738900
Buyers	714000
Buyers	719400
Buyvank	776500
Buzzard	749300
Byerley	798000
Byerly	798000
Byers	740000
Byers	794000
Byram	796000
Byrd	793000
Byrne	796000
Cable	478000
Cable	578000
Cadwalader	437839
Cadwalader	537839
Cadwalder	437839
Cadwalder	537839
Cadwallader	437839
Cadwallader	537839
Caghel	458000
Caghel	558000
Cahell	458000
Cahell	558000
Cahill	458000
Cahill	558000
Cain	460000
Cain	560000
Caldwell	483780
Caldwell	583780
Calendar	486390
Calendar	586390
Calhoon	485060
Calhoon	585060
Call	480000
Call	580000
Callahan	485600
Callahan	585600
Callender	486390
Callender	586390
Calvin	487600
Calvin	587600
Calwell	487800
Calwell	587800
Calyton	483600
Calyton	583600
Camel	468000
Camel	568000
Cammer	469000
Cammer	569000
Campbell	467800
Campbell	567800
Campble	467800
Campble	567800
Cannon	466000
Cannon	566000
Canon	466000
Canon	566000
Cantwell	463780
Cantwell	563780
Care	490000
Care	590000
Carether	493900
Carether	593900
Carlisle	498480
Carlisle	598480
Carmalt	496830
Carmalt	596830
Carmichael	496480
Carmichael	496580
Carmichael	596480

Name	Code
Clavoe	587000
Claypole	487800
Claypole	587800
Claypoole	487080
Claypoole	587080
Clayton	483600
Clayton	583600
Clifford	487930
Clifford	587930
Clin	486000
Clin	586000
Cline	486000
Cline	586000
Clingansmith	486564
Clingansmith	586564
Clinton	486360
Clinton	586360
Clock	484500
Clock	485000
Clock	584500
Clock	585000
Clogston	485436
Clogston	585436
Clogstone	485436
Clogstone	585436
Clugston	485436
Clugston	585436
Clugstone	485436
Clugstone	585436
Clyde	483000
Clyde	583000
Clydes	483400
Clydes	583400
Clymer	486900
Clymer	586900
Coale	408000
Coale	508000
Coats	404000
Coats	504000
Cochran	449600
Cochran	459600
Cochran	549600
Cochran	559600
Cochrin	449600
Cochrin	459600
Cochrin	549600
Cochrin	559600
Cockendal	445638
Cockendal	456380
Cockendal	545638
Cockendal	556380
Cockendall	445638
Cockendall	456380
Cockendall	545638
Cockendall	556380
Codd	430000
Codd	530000
Coffie	470000
Coffie	570000
Coffman	476600
Coffman	576600
Cofman	476600
Cofman	576600
Coke	450000
Coke	550000
Colder	483900
Colder	583900
Cole	480000
Cole	580000
Coleman	486600
Coleman	586600
Colemore	486900
Colemore	586900
Colhoon	485060
Colhoon	585060
Collier	489000
Collier	589000
Collins	486400
Collins	586400
Colt	483000
Colt	583000
Colvin	487600
Colvin	587600
Comes	464000
Comes	564000
Comley	468000
Comley	568000
Comly	468000
Comly	568000
Commings	466540
Commings	566540
Compass	467400
Compass	567400
Concle	464800
Concle	465800
Concle	564800
Concle	565800
Condy	463000
Condy	563000
Coner	469000
Coner	569000
Conley	468000
Conley	568000
Conn	460000
Conn	560000
Connally	468000
Connally	568000
Connelly	468000
Connelly	568000
Conner	469000
Conner	569000
Connolly	468000
Connolly	568000
Connor	469000
Connor	569000
Connosque	464500
Connosque	564500
Conrad	469300
Conrad	569300
Cook	405000
Cook	505000
Cooke	405000
Cooke	505000
Coon	406000
Coon	506000
Cooper	407900
Cooper	507900
Copper	479000
Copper	579000
Corbett	497300
Corbett	597300
Cord	493000
Cord	593000
Corey	490000
Corey	590000
Corn	496000
Corn	596000
Corney	496000
Corney	596000
Corren	496000
Corren	596000
Correy	490000
Correy	590000
Corry	490000
Corry	590000
Corsa	440000
Corsa	494000
Corsa	540000
Corsa	594000
Corsale	448000
Corsale	494800
Corsale	548000
Corsale	594800
Corso	440000
Corso	494000
Corso	540000
Corso	594000
Cory	490000
Cory	590000
Cosselman	448660
Cosselman	548660
Cost	443000
Cost	543000
Coster	443900
Coster	543900
Costor	443900
Costor	543900
Cothamas	436400

Name	Code
Cothamas	536400
Cotton	436000
Cotton	536000
Cottral	439800
Cottral	539800
Couder	403900
Couder	503900
Coughran	405960
Coughran	505960
Coulter	408390
Coulter	508390
Counselman	406486
Counselman	506486
Counyngham	406656
Counyngham	506656
Courson	404600
Courson	409460
Courson	504600
Courson	509460
Covde	473000
Covde	573000
Covien	476000
Covien	576000
Covode	473000
Covode	573000
Cowan	476000
Cowan	576000
Cowden	473600
Cowden	573600
Cowen	476000
Cowen	576000
Cowhawk	475750
Cowhawk	575750
Cowperthwait	479373
Cowperthwait	579373
Cox	454000
Cox	554000
Coxe	454000
Coxe	554000
Coxs	454400
Coxs	554400
Craford	497930
Craford	597930
Crafts	497400
Crafts	597400
Crago	495000
Crago	595000
Craig	495000
Craig	595000
Craike	495000
Craike	595000
Cramer	496900
Cramer	596900
Cramphon	496760
Cramphon	596760
Crampton	496736
Crampton	596736
Cran	496000
Cran	596000
Crane	496000
Crane	596000
Crastin	494360
Crastin	594360
Crawford	497930
Crawford	597930
Creag	495000
Creag	595000
Cree	490000
Cree	590000
Creigh	495000
Creigh	595000
Creme	496000
Creme	596000
Crider	493900
Crider	593900
Crig	495000
Crig	595000
Criner	496900
Criner	596900
Crist	494300
Crist	594300
Crocket	494530
Crocket	495300
Crocket	594530
Crocket	595300
Croff	497000
Croff	597000
Crogham	495600
Crogham	595600
Croghan	495600
Croghan	595600
Croker	495900
Croker	595900
Crompton	496736
Crompton	596736
Crookes	490540
Crookes	590540
Crooks	490540
Crooks	590540
Croseyong	494165
Croseyong	594165
Cross	494000
Cross	594000
Crosswell	494780
Crosswell	594780
Croughen	490560
Croughen	590560
Crow	497000
Crow	597000
Crows	497400
Crows	597400
Crozer	494900
Crozer	594900
Crush	494000
Crush	594000
Crute	493000
Crute	593000
Crutis	493400
Crutis	593400
Cuddy	430000
Cuddy	530000
Culbertson	487946
Culbertson	587946
Culbertsun	487946
Culbertsun	587946
Culp	487000
Culp	587000
Cumings	466540
Cumings	566540
Cumming	466500
Cumming	566500
Cummings	466540
Cummings	566540
Cummins	466400
Cummins	566400
Cumpton	467360
Cumpton	567360
Cuningham	466560
Cuningham	566560
Cunningham	466560
Cunningham	566560
Cunrad	469300
Cunrad	569300
Curnahans	496564
Curnahans	596564
Currie	490000
Currie	590000
Curry	490000
Curry	590000
Custard	443930
Custard	543930
Cuthbert	437930
Cuthbert	537930
Dabsong	374650
Dacker	345900
Dacker	359000
Dailey	380000
Daitch	340000
Dale	380000
Dallam	386000
Dallas	384000
Dalrymple	389678
Dalton	383600
Dane	360000
Daniels	368400
Dar	390000
Darlin	398600
Darlington	398653

Name	Code
Darrigh	395000
Darugh	395000
Daugherty	359300
Davey	370000
David	373000
Davidson	374600
Davis	374000
Davison	374600
Dean	360000
Deaney	360000
Death	330000
Decker	345900
Decker	359000
Deckert	345930
Deckert	359300
Dehaas	354000
DeHaas	354000
Dehaas	354000
Dehaus	354000
Dehavent	357630
Deihl	380000
Deimer	369000
Delap	387000
Deney	360000
Dennis	364000
Denny	360000
DeNormandie	369663
Depuey	370000
Depuy	370000
Derr	390000
Dersham	345600
Dersham	394560
Deval	378000
Devale	378000
Devall	378000
Devoir	379000
Dewit	373000
Dewitt	373000
Deyworthey	379300
Dicas	344000
Dicas	354000
Dick	345000
Dick	350000
Dickey	345000
Dickey	350000
Dicks	345400
Dicks	354000
Dickson	345460
Dickson	354600
Diehl	380000
Diets	340000
Diffenderfer	376397
Diggs	354000
Dill	380000
Dillworth	387930
Dillwyn	387600
Dilworth	387930
Dixon	354600
Dobbins	376400
Dobbs	374000
Dobson	374600
Dodson	346000
Dogworthey	357930
Doil	380000
Dombalt	367830
Donaldson	368460
Donan	366000
Donar	369000
Donaway	367000
Donnaldson	368460
Donne	360000
Donnellan	368600
Donnely	368000
Doran	396000
Dordes	393400
Dorough	390500
Dorran	396000
Dorsey	340000
Dorsey	394000
Dorsiris	349400
Dorsiris	394940
Dorsius	344000
Dorsius	394400
Dorsy	340000
Dorsy	394000
Doty	330000
Doudle	303800
Dougal	305800
Dougan	305600
Dougherty	305930
Doughlas	305840
Doughton	305360
Douglas	305840
Douglass	305840
Doutel	303800
Douthel	303800
Douthill	303800
Douthit	303300
Dowde	373000
Dowdle	373800
Dowell	378000
Downard	376930
Downe	376000
Downey	376000
Downing	376650
Downs	376400
Doyl	380000
Doyle	380000
Doz	340000
Dreisback	394745
Dreisback	394750
Drell	398000
Drennin	396600
Drenning	396650
Drevox	397540
Drewry	397900
Drinker	396590
Druckenmiller	394566
Druckenmiller	395668
Drumfield	396783
Drummond	396630
Drumond	396630
Duff	370000
Duffield	378300
Dugan	356000
Duke	350000
Dumars	364000
Dumars	369400
Dun	360000
Duncan	364600
Duncan	365600
Dunfield	367830
Dungan	365600
Duning	366500
Dunlaney	368600
Dunlany	368600
Dunlap	368700
Dunn	360000
Dunrumple	369678
Dunstable	364378
Dunwich	367400
Dunwich	367500
Dunwick	367450
Dunwick	367500
Dunwoody	367030
Durham	395600
Dushane	346000
Dwire	379000
Dyar	390000
Eagar	059000
Eager	059000
Eairl	098000
Eaken	056000
Eaker	059000
Earhart	095930
Earl	098000
Early	098000
Eastburne	043796
Eatten	036000
Eatton	036000
Eberly	079800
Eby	070000
Eckhard	045593
Eckhard	055930
Edder	039000
Eder	039000
Edge	035000
Edires	039400

Name	Code
Edminston	036643
Edmondson	036646
Edmonstone	036643
Edmunson	036646
Edwards	037940
Ege	050000
Ehingeur	056590
Elder	083900
Eliot	083000
Ellicott	084300
Ellicott	085300
Elliot	083000
Elliott	083000
Ellis	084000
Ellison	084600
Elsworth	084793
Emrick	069450
Emrick	069500
England	065863
Ennis	064000
Enoch	064000
Enoch	065000
Enon	066000
Ensminger	064665
Eolen	086000
Eppele	078000
Erb	097000
Erisman	094660
Erwin	097600
Eshelman	048660
Eshleman	048660
Espey	047000
Espy	047000
Essweiler	047890
Esweiler	047890
Etswiler	047890
Evalt	078300
Evans	076400
Evens	076400
Everhart	079593
Everit	079300
Everly	079800
Evers	074000
Evers	079400
Eves	074000
Evy	070000
Ewa	070000
Ewalt	078300
Ewig	075000
Ewing	076500
Ewings	076540
Eyman	066000
Eyre	090000
Fague	750000
Faith	730000
Fall	780000
Fame	760000
Fance	764000
Fance	765000
Fangle	765800
Faree	790000
Farmer	796900
Farree	790000
Farrow	797000
Feagley	758000
Fearis	794000
Fearon	796000
Fence	764000
Fence	765000
Feree	790000
Fergerson	795460
Fergerson	795946
Ferguson	795460
Ferree	790000
Ferry	790000
Field	783000
Fields	784000
Findlay	763800
Findley	763800
Fine	760000
Finley	768000
Finney	760000
Fiscus	744000
Fisher	749000
Fitzgerald	745983
Fitzsimons	746640
Flagavan	785760
Flahavan	785760
Flahaven	785760
Flaherty	785930
Flakingar	785659
Flatcher	784900
Fleamons	786640
Flehaven	785760
Fleming	786650
Flemming	786650
Flenegan	786560
Flenicken	786456
Flenicken	786560
Fletcher	784900
Flewitt	787300
Flipson	787460
Flitcher	784900
Floyd	783000
Fockler	745890
Fockler	758900
Fogleman	758660
Folbert	787930
Fooks	705400
Footman	703660
Forbes	797400
Force	794000
Force	795000
Foreman	796600
Forgeson	795460
Forguson	795460
Forsith	743000
Forsith	794300
Forsman	746600
Forsman	794660
Forster	743900
Forster	794390
Forsyth	743000
Forsyth	794300
Forsythe	743000
Forsythe	794300
Forward	797930
Foster	743900
Fought	705300
Foulk	708500
Foulke	708500
Foulks	708540
Foullew	708700
Fourman	709660
Fout	703000
Fouts	704000
Foutz	704000
Fowler	778900
Fox	754000
Fraizer	794900
Frame	796000
Francis	796440
Francis	796540
Frank	796500
Franklin	796586
Franklinberry	796586
Franks	796540
Frankson	796546
Frantz	796400
Fraser	794900
Frazer	794900
Frazier	794900
Frederick	793945
Frederick	793950
Fredericks	793945
Fredericks	793954
Fredrick	793945
Fredrick	793950
Freeman	796600
Frenches	796440
Frenches	796540
Frey	790000
Frick	794500
Frick	795000
Friend	796300
Fries	794000
Fritchman	794660
Froman	796600

Name	Code
Fruit	793000
Fry	790000
Frye	790000
Fucke	745000
Fucke	750000
Fudle	738000
Fullerton	789360
Fulmer	786900
Fulten	783600
Fulthy	783000
Fulton	783600
Furgeson	795460
Furguson	795460
Furman	796600
Furry	790000
Furster	743900
Furster	794390
Fussleman	748660
Gable	578000
Gabriel	579800
Gaddis	534000
Galagher	585900
Galaher	585900
Galbraith	587930
Galbreath	587930
Gale	580000
Galespie	584700
Gall	580000
Gallacher	584900
Gallacher	585900
Gallagher	585900
Gallahur	585900
Gallaugher	585900
Galley	580000
Galloway	587000
Galoway	587000
Galt	583000
Gamble	567800
Gamwell	567800
Garbel	597800
Garbell	597800
Garber	597900
Gardener	593690
Gardner	593690
Garland	598630
Garman	596600
Garven	597600
Gaseman	546600
Gasselman	548660
Gasser	549000
Gasst	544300
Gawen	576000
Gay	500000
Gearhart	595930
Gearick	594500
Gearick	595000
Gebhart	575930
Geddis	534000
Gelaspy	584700
Gelespey	584700
Gemberling	567986
George	595000
Getzelman	548660
Gibb	570000
Gibbon	576000
Gibbons	576400
Gibbs	574000
Gibons	576400
Gibson	574600
Giffen	576000
Gilbert	587930
Gilcrease	584940
Gilcrease	585940
Gilcreast	584943
Gilcreast	585943
Gilespie	584700
Gilfillen	587860
Gill	580000
Gillaspy	584700
Gillespie	584700
Gillespy	584700
Gilliland	588630
Gillispie	584700
Gillman	586600
Gillson	584600
Gilman	586600
Gilmer	586900
Gilmore	586900
Gilmous	586040
Gilpin	587600
Gimberling	567986
Girty	593000
Gist	543000
Glasgow	584570
Glass	584000
Gleaves	587400
Glen	586000
Glenn	586000
Goddard	539300
Godshalk	548500
Gohn	560000
Gold	583000
Golespy	584700
Gollespey	584700
Goms	564000
Gonsalus	564840
Gonzales	564840
Good	503000
Gordon	593600
Gorell	598000
Gormly	596800
Gorrell	598000
Goudey	503000
Goudie	503000
Goudy	503000
Gough	505000
Gourty	509300
Gover	579000
Govert	579300
Govet	573000
Gowdey	573000
Goz	540000
Gozin	546000
Grady	593000
Graff	597000
Graham	595600
Grame	596000
Grandin	596360
Grant	596300
Gratz	594000
Gray	590000
Graybill	597800
Graydon	593600
Graymes	596400
Greag	595000
Grebill	597800
Green	596000
Greenbury	596790
Greenfield	596783
Greenough	596050
Greer	599000
Greg	595000
Gregg	595000
Gregory	595900
Greir	599000
Greit	593000
Greiter	593900
Grenow	596700
Gressman	594660
Gridley	593800
Griem	596000
Grier	599000
Griffey	597000
Griffin	597600
Griffith	597300
Griffiths	597340
Grimbes	596740
Grimes	596400
Groff	597000
Grojean	591600
Gromly	596800
Gross	594000
Grove	597000
Growell	597800
Gruber	597900
Grundy	596300
Gudgion	535600
Guffee	570000

Name	Code
Guffie	570000
Guice	540000
Guice	550000
Guiney	560000
Guliford	587930
Gurhery	595900
Gurney	596000
Gurty	593000
Guthery	539000
Guthrey	539000
Guthrie	539000
Guthry	539000
Guy	500000
Guyer	519000
Habaker	575900
Haberstick	574345
Haberstick	574350
Haberstick	579434
Haberstick	579435
Habichar	574900
Habichar	575900
Hacket	545300
Hacket	553000
Hackney	545600
Hackney	556000
Hadder	539000
Haddy	530000
Hagener	556900
Hain	560000
Haine	560000
Haines	564000
Hains	564000
Hale	580000
Hall	580000
Halladay	583000
Haly	580000
Hambelton	567836
Hambleton	567836
Hambright	567953
Hamersly	564800
Hamersly	569480
Hamilton	568360
Hammerly	569800
Hammersleys	564840
Hammersleys	569484
Hammersly	564800
Hammersly	569480
Hammon	566000
Hammond	566300
Hanah	560000
Hand	563000
Haney	560000
Hank	565000
Hanna	560000
Hannah	560000
Hans	564000
Harbert	597930
Harbet	597300
Harbidge	597350
Hardin	593600
Harding	593650
Hare	590000
Harety	593000
Harganot	595630
Harington	596536
Harity	593000
Harkness	595640
Harminson	596646
Harmon	596600
Harper	597900
Harriot	593000
Harris	594000
Harrison	594600
Harrow	597000
Hart	593000
Hartley	593800
Hartman	593660
Hartshorn	549600
Hartshorn	594960
Hartshorne	549600
Hartshorne	594960
Harvey	597000
Harwick	597450
Harwick	597500
Harwickel	597458
Harwickel	597580
Hatfield	537830
Hauer	519000
Haur	590000
Havelitch	578400
Haverliny	579860
Hawkins	575640
Hay	500000
Hays	540000
Hazelhurst	548543
Hazelhurst	548594
Hazelton	548360
Hazelwood	548703
Hazlehurst	548543
Hazlehurst	548594
Head	530000
Heap	570000
Heath	530000
Heaton	536000
Heer	590000
Heffelfinger	578765
Hefflefinger	578765
Heil	580000
Heinley	568000
Heinly	568000
Heiser	549000
Held	583000
Helm	586000
Hemerly	569800
Henderson	563460
Henderson	563946
Hendricks	563945
Hendricks	563954
Hendrickson	563945
Hendrickson	563954
Hendrix	563954
Hening	566500
Hennessey	564000
Henry	569000
Henthorn	563960
Henton	563600
Hepburn	579600
Herbert	597930
Herbster	597439
Herhold	595830
Herndbaugh	596375
Herold	598300
Heron	596000
Herrold	598300
Herron	596000
Hershberger	547959
Hershberger	594795
Hervey	597000
Heslip	548700
Hess	540000
Hesser	549000
Heth	530000
Hewes	574000
Hewett	573000
Hewing	576500
Hewitt	573000
Hews	574000
Hewses	574400
Heyshan	546000
Hibberd	579300
Hibert	579300
Hice	540000
Hice	550000
Hickenbottom	545673
Hickenbottom	556736
Hickenlooper	545680
Hickenlooper	556807
Hickman	545660
Hickman	556600
Hickock	545450
Hickock	545500
Hickock	554500
Hickock	555000
Hicks	545400
Hicks	554000
Hiester	543900
Higgens	556400
Higgins	556400

Name	Code	Name	Code	Name	Code
Highby	557000	Hook	505000	Hussey	540000
Higinbotham	556736	Hoops	507400	Huston	543600
Hilborn	587960	Hoover	507900	Hutcheson	544600
Hilburn	587960	Hop	570000	Hutchings	546540
Hill	580000	Hopkins	575640	Hutchins	546400
Hillands	586400	Horbach	597400	Hutchinson	546460
Hillborn	587960	Horbach	597500	Hutchison	544600
Hillsborough	584790	Horible	597800	Huthy	530000
Hiltzeman	584660	Horning	596650	Hutton	536000
Hiltzheimer	584569	Horoble	597800	Hyle	580000
Hiltzsimer	584690	Horsely	548000	Hynes	564000
Hinckel	564580	Horsely	594800	Hyse	540000
Hinckel	565800	Hosterman	543966	Hyser	549000
Hindman	563660	Hoult	508300	Ickawee	045700
Hinks	565400	Hoults	508400	Ickawee	057000
Hinkson	565460	Houseker	504590	Iddings	036540
Hirsh	540000	Housseggor	504590	Inglish	065840
Hirsh	594000	Houston	504360	Innis	064000
Hise	540000	Hover	579000	Inskeep	064570
Hitchcock	544450	Howcroft	574973	Ioder	139000
Hitchcock	544500	Howcroft	575973	Iredell	093800
Hitchcock	545450	Howe	570000	Ireland	098630
Hitchcock	545500	Howell	578000	Irisen	094600
Hite	530000	Howey	570000	Irison	094600
Hittner	536900	Howsche	574000	Irvin	097600
Hoalland	508630	Hoy	500000	Irvine	097600
Hoape	507000	Hoye	510000	Irwin	097600
Hockley	545800	Hoyladay	583000	Isherwood	049703
Hockley	558000	Hubbert	579300	Jack	145000
Hodge	535000	Hubley	578000	Jack	150000
Hodgson	535460	Hubly	578000	Jack	445000
Hoff	570000	Hudnot	536300	Jack	450000
Hoffman	576600	Hudson	546000	Jackes	145400
Hoge	550000	Huff	570000	Jackes	154000
Hogeland	558630	Huffnagle	576580	Jackes	445400
Hogg	550000	Hughes	554000	Jackes	454000
Hoke	550000	Huling	586500	Jackman	145660
Hokes	554000	Hulings	586540	Jackman	156600
Holdbrook	583790	Hullings	586540	Jackman	445660
Holes	584000	Hulme	586000	Jackman	456600
Holladay	583000	Hulton	583600	Jackson	145460
Holliday	583000	Humphrey	567900	Jackson	154600
Hollingsworth	586547	Humphreys	567940	Jackson	445460
Hollingworth	586579	Humphries	567940	Jackson	454600
Holly	580000	Hunsicker	564459	Jacob	147000
Holman	586600	Hunsicker	564590	Jacob	157000
Holmes	586400	Hunt	563000	Jacob	447000
Holmesing	586465	Hunter	563900	Jacob	457000
Holodey	583000	Huntzecker	564459	Jacobs	147400
Holt	583000	Huntzecker	564590	Jacobs	157400
Holtsland	584863	Huntzicker	564459	Jacobs	447400
Holtz	584000	Huntzicker	564590	Jacobs	457400
Hoocher	504900	Hurst	543000	Jacoby	147000
Hoocher	505900	Hurst	594300	Jacoby	157000
Hooder	503900	Husband	547630	Jacoby	447000
Hoofnagle	507658	Husk	545000	Jacoby	457000

Name	Code
James	164000
James	464000
Jameson	164600
Jameson	464600
Jamison	164600
Jamison	464600
Jane	160000
Jane	460000
Jardon	193600
Jardon	493600
Jarvis	197400
Jarvis	497400
Jay	100000
Jay	400000
Jemison	164600
Jemison	464600
Jenkins	165640
Jenkins	465640
Jennens	166400
Jennens	466400
Jennings	166540
Jennings	466540
Jervis	197400
Jervis	497400
Jewell	178000
Jewell	478000
Joans	106400
Joans	406400
Joder	139000
Joder	439000
John	160000
John	460000
Johns	164000
Johns	464000
Johnson	164600
Johnson	464600
Johnston	164360
Johnston	464360
Johnstone	164360
Johnstone	464360
Joice	140000
Joice	150000
Joice	440000
Joice	450000
Jolley	180000
Jolley	480000
Jolly	180000
Jolly	480000
Jones	164000
Jones	464000
Jonson	164600
Jonson	464600
Jordan	193600
Jordan	493600
Joy	100000
Joy	400000
Julicks	184540
Julicks	185400
Julicks	484540
Julicks	485400
Jurdan	193600
Jurdan	493600
Justice	143400
Justice	143500
Justice	443400
Justice	443500
Kade	530000
Kap	570000
Kaple	578000
Kapp	570000
Karcher	594900
Karcher	595900
Katterly	539800
Kaufman	576600
Keagy	550000
Kearney	596000
Kearny	596000
Kechlein	548600
Kechlein	558600
Kechline	548600
Kechline	558600
Keen	560000
Keene	560000
Keester	543900
Keffer	579000
Kehr	590000
Keigart	559300
Keiger	559000
Keim	560000
Keiser	549000
Keith	530000
Keller	589000
Kelley	580000
Kellum	586000
Kelly	580000
Kelso	584000
Kelsoe	584000
Kendal	563800
Kendall	563800
Kendrick	563945
Kendrick	563950
Keney	560000
Kenley	568000
Kenly	568000
Kennard	569300
Kenneday	563000
Kennedy	563000
Kenson	564600
Keppel	578000
Keppele	578000
Keppeler	578900
Keppell	578000
Kepple	578000
Kerley	598000
Kerlin	598600
Kern	596000
Kernahan	596560
Kerney	596000
Kerns	596400
Kerr	590000
Kessler	548900
Keyser	549000
Kick	545000
Kick	550000
Kilcreest	584943
Kilcreest	585943
Kilcriest	584943
Kilcriest	585943
Kilcrist	584943
Kilcrist	585943
Killcrese	584940
Killcrese	585940
Killcrest	584943
Killcrest	585943
Killum	586000
Kimmel	568000
Kindle	563800
King	565000
Kingsberry	565479
Kinkead	565300
Kinney	560000
Kinny	560000
Kintner	563690
Kintzing	564650
Kirk	595000
Kirkbride	595793
Kirkindall	595638
Kirkindoll	595638
Kirkpatrick	595739
Kirlin	598600
Kirling	598650
Kirney	596000
Kishler	548900
Kisner	546900
Kissinger	546590
Kitcham	546000
Kitchen	546000
Klein	586000
Kline	586000
Kling	586500
Klugh	585000
Knable	567800
Knap	567000
Kneible	567800
Knieble	567800
Knight	565300
Knoble	567800
Knowles	567840

Name	Code
Knowls	567840
Knox	565400
Kohr	590000
Koocher	504900
Koocher	505900
Kore	590000
Koster	543900
Kostor	543900
Krammer	596900
Kratzer	594900
Kreamer	596900
Kreider	593900
Kreutter	593900
Kricker	594590
Kricker	595900
Kriteers	593400
Kriteers	593940
Krum	596000
Kugger	559000
Kuhn	560000
Kull	580000
Kulland	586300
Kunckle	564580
Kunckle	565800
Kunggel	565800
Kunkle	565800
Kuntz	564000
Kurtz	594000
Kuykendale	556380
Kuykindall	556380
Kyle	580000
Kyll	580000
Kylle	580000
Lafaver	877900
Laird	893000
Lake	850000
Lamar	869000
Lamb	867000
Landes	863400
Landislyer	863489
Lands	864000
Laning	866500
Larimon	896600
Larimore	896900
Lasher	849000
Lata	830000
Latcha	840000
Latchaw	847000
Latemer	836900
Latimer	836900
Latta	830000
Lattamor	836900
Lattimer	836900
Lattimore	836900
Laughier	859000
Laughlin	858600
Laughman	856600
Laugling	858650
Lauk	850000
Lauman	866000
Laura	890000
Laurence	896400
Laurence	896500
Laurey	890000
Lautenslager	836485
Lautensliger	836485
Lautermilk	839685
Lauttenschleiger	836485
Lavengair	876590
Laveor	879000
Lawrence	879640
Lawrence	879650
Lawrie	879000
Lawson	874600
Lazier	849000
Lea	800000
Leadley	838000
Leadly	838000
Leamon	866000
Leap	870000
Leashure	849000
Leasure	849000
Leather	839000
Lebb	870000
Lebig	875000
Ledlie	838000
Ledlies	838400
Lee	800000
Leech	840000
Leech	850000
Leef	870000
Lees	840000
Leet	830000
Leetch	840000
Lefever	877900
Lefler	878900
Leggat	853000
Lehr	890000
Leich	840000
Leich	850000
Leming	866500
Lemly	868000
Lemmon	866000
Lemon	866000
Lems	864000
Lenox	865400
Leonhart	865930
Lesher	849000
Lesley	848000
Letart	839300
Letarts	839400
Letchworth	847930
Levers	874000
Levers	879400
Levy	870000
Lewis	874000
Leyninger	866590
Lian	860000
Lidlie	838000
Ligat	853000
Liggit	853000
Light	853000
Lightcap	854700
Lightfoot	853703
Lightner	853690
Lilley	880000
Limes	864000
Lims	864000
Linch	864000
Linch	865000
Lindsay	864000
Lindsey	864000
Lines	864000
Lingly	865800
Linn	860000
Linnes	864000
Lintner	863690
Lippencott	876430
Lippencott	876530
Lippingcott	876543
Lippingcott	876553
Little	838000
Littlehead	838530
Litton	836000
Livergood	879503
Lloyd	830000
Loaf	807000
Lochery	849000
Lochery	859000
Lochrey	849000
Lochrey	859000
Lochry	849000
Lochry	859000
Lockry	845900
Lockry	859000
Lodge	835000
Lofflin	878600
Logan	856000
Logane	856000
Loghlan	858600
Logston	854360
Lonabergen	867956
Long	865000
Longane	865600
Longe	865000
Longhead	865300
Longhery	865900
Longnacker	865645

Name	Code
Longnacker	865659
Loning	866500
Lord	893000
Louch	804000
Louch	805000
Loud	803000
Louden	803600
Loughry	805900
Loury	809000
Loutermilk	803968
Loutherback	803974
Loutherback	803975
Love	870000
Lovegrove	875970
Lovengier	876590
Low	870000
Lowans	876400
Lowden	873600
Lowdon	873600
Lowers	874000
Lowers	879400
Lowery	879000
Lowman	876600
Lownes	876400
Lowrey	879000
Lowry	879000
Loxley	854800
Luce	840000
Luce	850000
Lugar	859000
Lukens	856400
Lungan	865600
Lush	840000
Lute	830000
Lutz	840000
Lylbuin	887600
Lymson	864600
Lynn	860000
Lyon	860000
Lyons	864000
Lytle	838000
Mabben	676000
Machan	646000
Machan	656000
Machmoore	646090
Machmoore	656090
MacKay	645000
Mackay	645000
MacKay	650000
Mackay	650000
Mackenness	645640
Mackenness	656400
MacKey	645000
Mackey	645000
MacKey	650000
Mackey	650000
Macklay	645800
Macklay	658000
Maclay	648000
Maclay	658000
Maclellan	648860
Maclellan	658860
Maclure	648900
Maclure	658900
Macmurtry	646939
Macmurtry	656939
Maddox	635400
Magaw	657000
Magee	650000
Maggee	650000
Maghen	656000
Magrath	659300
Magruder	659390
Maguire	659000
Mahan	656000
Mahaun	656000
Makin	656000
Malcolm	684860
Malcolm	685860
Malcom	684600
Malcom	685600
Malone	686000
Maloney	686000
Man	660000
Manderbach	663974
Manderbach	663975
Manderbarch	663979
Manfield	667830
Mann	660000
Manning	666500
Mansfield	664783
Marache	694000
Marache	695000
March	694000
March	695000
Marchant	694630
Marchant	695630
Margaret	695930
Margdant	695363
Marks	695400
Markwrite	695793
Marmock	696450
Marmock	696500
Marrion	696000
Mars	640000
Mars	694000
Marsden	643600
Marsden	694360
Marshal	645800
Marshal	694580
Marshall	645800
Marshall	694580
Martin	693600
Martinea	693600
Masden	643600
Mason	646000
Masters	643400
Masters	643940
Masterson	643460
Masterson	643946
Maston	643600
Mather	639000
Mathew	637000
Mathews	637400
Mathiot	633000
Matlack	638450
Matlack	638500
Matson	646000
Matthews	637400
Mauer	619000
Maughan	656000
Mauhan	656000
Mauhaun	656000
Maun	660000
Maunsel	664800
Mauregnalt	695683
Maurer	699000
Maurignault	695683
Maus	640000
Mawfield	678300
Maxwell	654780
Mayes	614000
McAfee	647000
McAfee	657000
McAlister	648439
McAlister	658439
McAllen	648600
McAllen	658600
McAllester	648439
McAllester	658439
McAvoy	647000
McAvoy	657000
McBath	647300
McBath	657300
McBeth	647300
McBeth	657300
McBride	647930
McBride	657930
McBrier	647990
McBrier	657990
McCady	643000
McCady	653000
McCalester	648439
McCalester	658439
McCalister	648439
McCalister	658439
McCall	648000
McCall	658000

Name	Code
McCalland	648630
McCalland	658630
McCallester	648439
McCallester	658439
McCallister	648439
McCallister	658439
McCalmont	648663
McCalmont	658663
McCanahey	646500
McCanahey	656500
McCarmick	649645
McCarmick	649650
McCarmick	659645
McCarmick	659650
McCarter	649390
McCarter	659390
McCartney	649360
McCartney	659360
McCarty	649300
McCarty	659300
McCaskey	644500
McCaskey	654500
McCasky	644500
McCasky	654500
McCausland	644863
McCausland	654863
McCawley	647800
McCawley	657800
McCay	640000
McCay	650000
McCelen	648600
McCelen	658600
McClain	648600
McClain	658600
McClalin	648860
McClalin	658860
McClanachan	648646
McClanachan	648656
McClanachan	658646
McClanachan	658656
McClannegan	648656
McClannegan	658656
McClasky	648450
McClasky	658450
McClay	648000
McClay	658000
McClean	648600
McClean	658600
McCleane	648600
McCleane	658600
McCleery	648900
McCleery	658900
McClelan	648860
McClelan	658860
McClellan	648860
McClellan	658860
MCClelland	648863
MCClelland	658863
McClellandon	648863
McClellandon	658863
McClenachan	648646
McClenachan	648656
McClenachan	658646
McClenachan	658656
McClenegan	648656
McClenegan	658656
McClinachan	648646
McClinachan	648656
McClinachan	658646
McClinachan	658656
McClintock	648634
McClintock	648635
McClintock	658634
McClintock	658635
McClosky	648450
McClosky	658450
McClung	648650
McClung	658650
McClure	648900
McClure	658900
McClurg	648950
McClurg	658950
McClurgh	648950
McClurgh	658950
McColester	648439
McColester	658439
McCollack	648450
McCollack	648500
McCollack	658450
McCollack	658500
McCollem	648600
McCollem	658600
McCollester	648439
McCollester	658439
McCollister	648439
McCollister	658439
McCollock	648450
McCollock	648500
McCollock	658450
McCollock	658500
McCollogh	648500
McCollogh	658500
McCollum	648600
McCollum	658600
McColman	648660
McColman	658660
McComb	646700
McComb	656700
McConal	646800
McConal	656800
McConaughy	646500
McConaughy	656500
McConnall	646800
McConnall	656800
McConnel	646800
McConnel	656800
McConnell	646800
McConnell	656800
McConoughy	646050
McConoughy	656050
McCord	649300
McCord	659300
McCorely	649800
McCorely	659800
McCorkle	649580
McCorkle	659580
McCormick	649645
McCormick	649650
McCormick	659645
McCormick	659650
McCoron	649600
McCoron	659600
McCoskeey	644500
McCoskeey	654500
McCoskery	644590
McCoskery	654590
McCoskey	644500
McCoskey	654500
McCoskry	644590
McCoskry	654590
McCoy	640000
McCoy	650000
McCoyne	646000
McCoyne	656000
McCracken	649456
McCracken	649560
McCracken	659456
McCracken	659560
McCrea	649000
McCrea	659000
McCready	649300
McCready	659300
McCreary	649900
McCreary	659900
McCreery	649900
McCreery	659900
McCrerry	649900
McCrerry	659900
McCrey	649000
McCrey	659000
McCroskey	649450
McCroskey	659450
McCrosky	649450
McCrosky	659450
McCroy	649000
McCroy	659000
McCuffog	647500
McCuffog	657500

Name	Code
McCulley	648000
McCulley	658000
McCullock	648450
McCullock	648500
McCullock	658450
McCullock	658500
McCullogh	648500
McCullogh	658500
McCulloough	648005
McCulloough	658005
McCullough	648050
McCullough	658050
McCulluck	648450
McCulluck	648500
McCulluck	658450
McCulluck	658500
McCully	648000
McCully	658000
McCune	646000
McCune	656000
McCurday	649300
McCurday	659300
McCurdy	649300
McCurdy	659300
McCurly	649800
McCurly	659800
McCutchen	644600
McCutchen	654600
McDermont	643966
McDermont	653966
McDonald	643683
McDonald	653683
McDonnal	643680
McDonnal	653680
McDonnall	643680
McDonnall	653680
McDonnel	643680
McDonnel	653680
McDonnell	643680
McDonnell	653680
McDowal	643780
McDowal	653780
McDowel	643780
McDowel	653780
McDowell	643780
McDowell	653780
McElhenry	648569
McElhenry	658569
McElroy	648900
McElroy	658900
McEmery	646900
McEmery	656900
McEmory	646900
McEmory	656900
McEwen	647600
McEwen	657600
McFadden	647360
McFadden	657360
McFaddion	647360
McFaddion	657360
McFaden	647360
McFaden	657360
McFadian	647360
McFadian	657360
McFadion	647360
McFadion	657360
McFall	647800
McFall	657800
McFarlan	647986
McFarlan	657986
McFarland	647986
McFarland	657986
McFarlane	647986
McFarlane	657986
McFarlington	647986
McFarlington	657986
McFarren	647960
McFarren	657960
McFigart	647593
McFigart	657593
McGachey	645400
McGachey	645500
McGachey	655400
McGachey	655500
McGahan	645560
McGahan	655560
McGannon	645660
McGannon	655660
McGee	645000
McGee	655000
McGery	645900
McGery	655900
McGines	645640
McGines	655640
McGinnes	645640
McGinnes	655640
McGinnis	645640
McGinnis	655640
McGlathery	645839
McGlathery	655839
McGlathry	645839
McGlathry	655839
McGlaughlin	645858
McGlaughlin	655858
McGown	645760
McGown	655760
McGraw	645970
McGraw	655970
McGready	645930
McGready	655930
McGreegar	645959
McGreegar	655959
McGreeger	645959
McGreeger	655959
McGregor	645959
McGregor	655959
McGrew	645970
McGrew	655970
McGriffin	645976
McGriffin	655976
McGrogan	645956
McGrogan	655956
McGruger	645959
McGruger	655959
McGuffog	645750
McGuffog	655750
McGuire	645900
McGuire	655900
McHenry	646900
McHenry	656900
McIlvaine	648760
McIlvaine	658760
McIlvane	648760
McIlvane	658760
McIntire	646390
McIntire	656390
McIntosh	646340
McIntosh	656340
McIntyre	646390
McIntyre	656390
McKachney	645460
McKachney	645560
McKachney	654600
McKachney	655600
McKamisk	645645
McKamisk	656450
McKay	645000
McKay	650000
McKean	645600
McKean	656000
McKee	645000
Mckee	645000
McKee	645000
Mckee	645000
McKee	645000
Mckee	645000
McKee	645000
Mckee	645000
McKee	645000
McKee	650000
Mckee	650000
McKee	650000
Mckee	650000
McKee	650000
Mckee	650000
McKee	650000
Mckee	650000
McKee	650000

Name	Code
McKeen	645600
McKeen	656000
McKenney	645600
McKenney	656000
McKessen	645460
McKessen	654600
McKibben	645760
McKibben	657600
McKibbin	645760
Mckibbin	645760
McKibbin	645760
McKibbin	657600
Mckibbin	657600
McKibbin	657600
McKibbins	645764
McKibbins	657640
McKim	645600
McKim	656000
McKiney	645600
McKiney	656000
McKinly	645680
McKinly	656800
McKinney	645600
McKinney	656000
McKinzey	645640
McKinzey	656400
McKinzy	645640
McKinzy	656400
McKnight	645653
McKnight	656530
McKoskey	645450
McKoskey	654500
McKown	645760
McKown	657600
McKoy	645000
McKoy	650000
McKroskey	645945
McKroskey	659450
McLaughlin	648586
McLaughlin	658586
McLees	648400
McLees	658400
McLellan	648860
McLellan	658860
McLone	648600
McLone	658600
McMachan	646460
McMachan	646560
McMachan	656460
McMachan	656560
McMachen	646460
McMachen	646560
McMachen	656460
McMachen	656560
McMacken	646456
McMacken	646560
McMacken	656456
McMacken	656560
McMahan	646560
McMahan	656560
McMahon	646560
McMahon	656560
McManegal	646658
McManegal	656658
McMannamy	646660
McMannamy	656660
McMasen	646460
McMasen	656460
McMasters	646434
McMasters	646439
McMasters	656434
McMasters	656439
McMath	646300
McMath	656300
McMean	646600
McMean	656600
McMeans	646640
McMeans	656640
McMeen	646600
McMeen	656600
McMenimy	646660
McMenimy	656660
McMillian	646860
McMillian	656860
McMotry	646390
McMotry	656390
McMull	646800
McMull	656800
McMullen	646860
McMullen	656860
McMullin	646860
McMullin	656860
McMullon	646860
McMullon	656860
McMurray	646900
McMurray	656900
McMurrey	646900
McMurrey	656900
McMurtree	646939
McMurtree	656939
McNachon	646460
McNachon	646560
McNachon	656460
McNachon	656560
McNair	646900
McNair	656900
McNale	646800
McNale	656800
McNaul	646800
McNaul	656800
McNavare	646790
McNavare	656790
McNaw	646700
McNaw	656700
McNeal	646800
McNeal	656800
McNitt	646300
McNitt	656300
McNutt	646300
McNutt	656300
McPherson	647460
McPherson	647946
McPherson	657460
McPherson	657946
McRory	649900
McRory	659900
McSweeney	647600
McVay	647000
McVay	657000
McWilliams	647864
McWilliams	657864
Meanard	669300
Means	664000
Mears	640000
Mears	694000
Mease	640000
Meason	646000
Meckleroy	645890
Meckleroy	658900
Mecklin	645860
Mecklin	658600
Medcalf	634870
Medcalf	635870
Meek	650000
Meeke	650000
Meeks	654000
Megamery	656900
Meginness	656400
Meirs	640000
Meirs	694000
Melone	686000
Memminger	666590
Mendoch	663400
Mendoch	663500
Meneher	665900
Menges	665400
Mengies	665400
Meninger	666590
Menoch	664000
Menoch	665000
Mentzer	664900
Merca	694000
Merca	695000
Mercer	694900
Mercer	695900
Merchand	694630
Merchand	695630
Merchant	694630

Name	Code
Merchant	695630
Meredith	693300
Merklin	695860
Merrill	698000
Merryweather	697390
Mertain	693600
Messersmith	644630
Messersmith	649463
Metcalf	648700
Metzner	646900
Meyer	619000
Meyers	614000
Meyers	619400
Michael	648000
Michael	658000
Mickenfelder	645678
Mickenfelder	656783
Mickenfilder	645678
Mickenfilder	656783
Middlesworth	638479
Middleton	638360
Miers	640000
Miers	694000
Mifflin	678600
Mike	650000
Miles	684000
Miliron	689600
Miller	689000
Milligan	685600
Milliken	685600
Millikin	685600
Milliron	689600
Millison	684600
Milner	686900
Miner	669000
Minges	665400
Minshell	664800
Minssell	664800
Minster	664390
Mirca	694000
Mirca	695000
Misser	649000
Missinner	646900
Mitchel	648000
Mitchele	648000
Mitchell	648000
Mitcheltree	648390
Mitchetree	643900
Mockler	645890
Mockler	658900
Moffit	673000
Mokotoff	653700
Monckton	664536
Monckton	665360
Monroe	669000
Montgomery	663569
Montour	663090
Moodie	603000
Moon	606000
Moor	609000
Moore	609000
Moorehead	609530
Moorhead	609530
Moote	603000
More	690000
Morgan	695600
Morhead	695300
Moris	694000
Morison	694600
Moroson	694600
Morris	694000
Morrison	694600
Morrow	697000
Morshed	645300
Morshed	694530
Morton	693600
Motz	640000
Mourer	609900
Moyer	619000
Muchmore	646900
Muchmore	656900
Muchnou	646000
Muchnou	656000
Muhlenberg	686795
Muir	690000
Mullen	686000
Mulligan	685600
Munday	663000
Munger	665900
Munro	669000
Murdock	693450
Murdock	693500
Murphy	697000
Murray	690000
Murry	690000
Musser	649000
Myer	690000
Myers	640000
Myers	694000
Myler	689000
Myre	690000
Nafe	670000
Naftzger	674590
Nagle	658000
Nailor	689000
Nana	660000
Nassey	640000
Nawalegan	678560
Neaf	670000
Neaff	670000
Neall	680000
Nearson	646000
Nearson	694600
Neave	670000
Neeland	686300
Neely	680000
Neeper	679000
Neetimis	636400
Neff	670000
Negley	658000
Neifly	678000
Neil	680000
Neill	680000
Neisbite	647300
Neisser	649000
Nellson	684600
Nelson	684600
Nesbit	647300
Nesbitt	647300
Nesselrode	648930
Nevill	678000
Newale	678000
Newel	678000
Newell	678000
Newswanger	674765
Newton	673600
Ney	600000
Nice	640000
Nice	650000
Nicely	648000
Nicely	658000
Nicholas	648400
Nicholas	658400
Nicholason	648460
Nicholason	658460
Nichols	648400
Nichols	658400
Nicholson	648460
Nicholson	658460
Nidok	635000
Nilson	684600
Nixon	654600
Noarth	609300
Noetz	604000
Norcross	694940
Norcross	695940
Norris	694000
North	693000
Noutimape	603670
Nowland	678630
Nutimus	636400
Odair	039000
Officer	074900
Officer	075900
Ogden	053600
Ogdon	053600
Ogelsvee	058470
Ogilvie	058700

Name	Code
O'Hara	059000
O'Harra	059000
Oiller	089000
Okeley	058000
Okely	058000
Olar	089000
Old	083000
Oldman	083660
Oliphant	087630
O'Neil	068000
Orbey	097000
Ord	093000
Ormsby	096470
Orr	090000
Osborn	047960
Osburn	047960
Ourings	096540
Ovenshire	076490
Overfield	079783
Overmire	079690
Owen	076000
Owings	076540
Ozean	046000
Packer	745900
Packer	759000
Painter	763900
Palmer	786900
Pamer	769000
Par	790000
Parcel	794800
Parcel	795800
Parchment	794663
Parchment	795663
Paress	794000
Paris	794000
Park	795000
Parker	795900
Parkinson	795646
Parks	795400
Parr	790000
Parris	794000
Parrock	794500
Parrock	795000
Parson	746000
Parson	794600
Parsons	746400
Parsons	794640
Paschal	748000
Paschall	748000
Pashall	748000
Passmore	746900
Pater	739000
Paterson	734600
Paterson	739460
Path	730000
Patrick	739450
Patrick	739500
Patterson	734600
Patterson	739460
Pattison	734600
Patton	736000
Patty	730000
Paty	730000
Paul	780000
Pauli	780000
Pauling	786500
Pawling	778650
Pawmer	776900
Peace	740000
Peace	750000
Peairs	740000
Peairs	794000
Peal	780000
Pear	790000
Pearce	794000
Pearce	795000
Pearis	794000
Pearsall	748000
Pearsall	794800
Pearse	740000
Pearse	794000
Pearson	746000
Pearson	794600
Pedan	736000
Pedens	736400
Peeples	778400
Pegg	750000
Pelley	780000
Pendergrass	763959
Penn	760000
Pennock	764500
Pennock	765000
Penny	760000
Pennybecker	767459
Pennybecker	767590
Penrose	769400
Penticost	763443
Penticost	763543
Peoples	778400
Perian	796000
Perkins	795640
Perroch	794000
Perroch	795000
Perry	790000
Perryman	796600
Persal	748000
Persal	794800
Persall	748000
Persall	794800
Persian	746000
Persian	794600
Person	746000
Person	794600
Peter	739000
Peterman	739660
Peters	734000
Peters	739400
Petters	734000
Petters	739400
Petterson	734600
Petterson	739460
Pettit	733000
Pfeffer	779000
Pharley	798000
Phile	780000
Philes	784000
Philips	787400
Phillips	787400
Phipps	774000
Physick	744500
Physick	745000
Piatt	730000
Pickel	745800
Pickel	758000
Pickert	745930
Pickert	759300
Pidgen	735600
Pidgeon	735600
Pierce	794000
Pierce	795000
Pierer	799000
Piety	730000
Pikly	758000
Pimm	760000
Pinack	764500
Pinack	765000
Pingley	765800
Pinkerton	765936
Pints	764000
Piper	779000
Pitton	736000
Pitts	740000
Pleasants	784640
Plenge	786500
Plinge	786500
Plumer	786900
Plumstead	786433
Plumsted	786433
Plumtsead	786430
Plunket	786530
Poak	705000
Pobjay	771000
Pobjay	774000
Pobjea	771000
Pobjea	774000
Pockle	745800
Pockle	758000
Poe	700000

Name	Code
Polander	786390
Pole	780000
Polke	785000
Pollex	785400
Pollock	784500
Pollock	785000
Pollox	785400
Polock	784500
Polock	785000
Pontius	763400
Porter	793900
Portter	793900
Potter	739000
Potts	740000
Poultney	708360
Powel	778000
Powell	778000
Power	779000
Powers	774000
Powers	779400
Prather	793900
Pratt	793000
Preater	793900
Preator	793900
Prentice	796340
Prentice	796350
Presser	794900
Preston	794360
Preveal	797800
Price	794000
Price	795000
Prickit	794530
Prickit	795300
Priestly	794380
Priser	794900
Probst	797430
Procter	794390
Procter	795390
Proctor	794390
Proctor	795390
Province	797640
Province	797650
Pryor	799000
Pugh	750000
Pulton	783600
Pumeroy	769000
Pumrey	769000
Pumroy	769000
Punroy	769000
Purcell	794800
Purcell	795800
Purdon	793600
Purviance	797640
Purviance	797650
Pusey	740000
Pussey	740000
Putty	730000
Quail	580000
Queen	560000
Quigley	558000
Raiguee	950000
Rainey	960000
Rairdon	993600
Raker	959000
Ralfe	987000
Ralins	986400
Ralph	987000
Ralse	984000
Ralston	984360
Ramsay	964000
Ramsey	964000
Randell	963800
Randles	963840
Rankan	965600
Rankin	965600
Rannels	968400
Raquet	953000
Ratan	936000
Rausch	940000
Rawle	978000
Ray	900000
Raybolt	978300
Rayl	980000
Reaborn	979600
Read	930000
Reader	939000
Reading	936500
Ready	930000
Reay	900000
Rebets	974000
Rebman	976600
Redick	934500
Redick	935000
Reed	930000
Reef	970000
Reemer	969000
Rees	940000
Reese	940000
Reger	959000
Rehrick	994500
Rehrick	995000
Reid	930000
Reiff	970000
Reig	950000
Reigar	959000
Reigart	959300
Reigert	959300
Reily	980000
Reitenaur	936900
Reith	930000
Rekas	954000
Remely	968000
Ren	960000
Renchler	964890
Renchler	965890
Renick	964500
Renick	965000
Renicks	964540
Renicks	965400
Rennalls	968400
Rennard	969300
Rennick	964500
Rennick	965000
Requate	953000
Rerich	994000
Rerich	995000
Resner	946900
Resnor	946900
Resoner	946900
Reyer	919000
Reynolds	968400
Rhea	950000
Rhoades	950340
Rhoads	950400
Rhodes	953400
Rice	940000
Rice	950000
Rich	940000
Rich	950000
Richards	949400
Richards	959400
Richardson	949460
Richardson	959460
Riche	940000
Riche	950000
Richey	940000
Richey	950000
Richie	940000
Richie	950000
Richmond	946630
Richmond	956630
Rickets	945400
Rickets	954000
Riddle	938000
Riddles	938400
Rider	939000
Riffer	979000
Riggs	954000
Right	953000
Rily	980000
Rinker	965900
Ripley	978000
Ripy	970000
Rishel	948000
Risk	945000
Ritchey	940000
Rittenhouse	936504
Ritter	939000

Name	Code
Rivington	976536
Roat	903000
Roatt	903000
Robb	970000
Roberdeau	979300
Robers	974000
Robers	979400
Roberts	979400
Robertson	979460
Robeson	974600
Robins	976400
Robinson	976460
Robison	974600
Rockman	945660
Rockman	956600
Roddy	930000
Rodger	935900
Rodgers	935400
Rodgers	935940
Rodgres	935940
Rodney	936000
Roes	904000
Roger	959000
Rogers	954000
Rogers	959400
Roher	959000
Rohrer	999000
Roletter	983900
Rolletes	983400
Rollettor	983900
Romters	963400
Romters	963940
Ronno	960000
Roodman	903660
Rooper	907900
Rora	990000
Rorer	999000
Rose	940000
Roseberry	947900
Ross	940000
Roston	943600
Rotery	939000
Rotten	936000
Rough	905000
Roush	904000
Rove	970000
Row	970000
Rowan	976000
Rowe	970000
Rowland	978630
Rowletter	978390
Rownd	976300
Royal	918000
Royer	919000
Royle	980000
Rubley	978000
Rudebaugh	937500
Rudolph	938700
Rudulph	938700
Rugh	950000
Rush	940000
Russel	948000
Russell	948000
Ruthanburger	936795
Rutherford	939793
Ryal	980000
Ryan	960000
Rybolt	978300
Ryerson	946000
Ryerson	994600
Rygar	959000
Rygart	959300
Ryles	984000
Ryne	960000
Ryor	990000
Saam	460000
Sager	459000
Salmon	486600
Salter	483900
Saltman	483660
Saltsman	484660
Sam	460000
Same	460000
Sample	467800
Sampson	467460
Samuel	468000
Samuels	468400
Sanders	463400
Sanders	463940
Sanderson	463460
Sanderson	463946
Sandwith	463730
Sassaman	446600
Sattaford	437930
Saum	460000
Savage	475000
Savoise	474000
Sayer	419000
Sayler	489000
Sayre	490000
Schaffner	476900
Schauffner	476900
Schimick	464500
Schimick	465000
Schinick	464500
Schinick	465000
Schneideer	463900
Schneider	463900
Scholfield	487830
Schooly	408000
Schornagle	496580
Schriver	497900
Schub	470000
Schwartz	479400
Sckinner	256900
Scot	230000
Scott	230000
Scudder	239000
Scull	280000
Scully	280000
Searle	498000
Seaton	436000
Seber	479000
Seckler	445890
Seckler	458900
Seebold	478300
Seely	480000
Seess	440000
Seever	479000
Segar	459000
Seger	459000
Sellers	484000
Sellers	489400
Semple	467800
Senff	467000
Server	497900
Settaford	437930
Sever	479000
Seybert	479300
Shaaf	470000
Shadde	430000
Shadden	436000
Shaddon	436000
Shaeffer	479000
Shaffer	479000
Shaffner	476900
Shafner	476900
Shakespear	454790
Shale	480000
Shallus	484000
Shandy	463000
Shank	465000
Shanks	465400
Shannon	466000
Shanon	466000
Sharon	496000
Sharp	497000
Sharpnack	497645
Sharpnack	497650
Sharron	496000
Shaub	470000
Shaw	470000
Sheafer	479000
Sheaffer	479000
Sheaphard	479300
Shearer	499000
Sheart	493000
Sheaver	479000

Name	Code
Stephens	276400
Stephenson	276460
Sterrat	293000
Stevens	276400
Stevenson	276460
Stevinson	276460
Steward	279300
Stewardson	279460
Stewart	279300
Stewert	279300
Sticker	245900
Sticker	259000
Stiene	260000
Stille	280000
Stimble	267800
Stine	260000
Stiret	293000
Stockberger	245795
Stockberger	257959
Stockbiger	245759
Stockbiger	257590
Stoie	210000
Stokely	258000
Stone	260000
Stoner	269000
Stones	264000
Stopher	279000
Story	290000
Stotler	238900
Stouffer	207900
Stout	203000
Stoute	203000
Stover	279000
Stratten	293600
Strauch	294000
Strauch	295000
Straugh	295000
Strawbridge	297935
Streeker	295900
Street	293000
Stricker	294590
Stricker	295900
Stringer	296590
Strode	293000
Stroud	290300
Stroude	290300
Stroup	290700
Strubel	297800
Struble	297800
Stuart	293000
Stuber	279000
Stucker	245900
Stucker	259000
Studebaker	237590
Stull	280000
Stump	267000
Sturdevant	293763
Sturgeon	295600
Sturges	295400
Styger	259000
Suber	479000
Sugar	459000
Sullivan	487600
Summers	464000
Summers	469400
Sunderland	463986
Supplee	478000
Sutherland	439863
Suttan	436000
Sutten	436000
Suttin	436000
Sutton	436000
Swaim	476000
Swales	478400
Swan	476000
Swany	476000
Swanzey	476400
Swanzy	476400
Swartz	479400
Swearingan	479656
Swearingen	479656
Swearingham	479656
Sweet	473000
Sweger	475900
Sweringham	479656
Swerington	479653
Swinford	476793
Swiper	477900
Swisher	474900
Swisser	474900
Swons	476400
Swort	479300
Sybert	479300
Sylverton	487936
Sympson	467460
Tagart	359300
Taggart	359300
Talbot	387300
Talbott	387300
Talbout	387030
Tamson	364600
Tanner	369000
Tate	330000
Taub	370000
Tayler	389000
Taylor	389000
Tayney	360000
Teagarden	359360
Tedmarsh	336400
Tedmarsh	336940
Teegarden	359360
Teeters	334000
Teeters	339400
Tegard	359300
Teines	364000
Templeton	367836
Tenist	364300
Tharp	397000
Thatcher	349000
Thatoher	335900
Thauley	380000
Thauly	380000
Theobald	378300
Thesh	340000
Tholey	380000
Thomas	364000
Thompson	367460
Thomson	364600
Thorn	396000
Thornhill	396580
Thoughtes	305340
Tice	340000
Tice	350000
Tilghman	385660
Tinbrock	367945
Tinbrock	367950
Toblor	378900
Toby	370000
Todd	330000
Tohog	355000
Tohogo	355000
Tohogod	355300
Tolbert	387930
Tollsman	384660
Tomkin	365600
Tompson	367460
Tomson	364600
Toochman	304660
Toochman	305660
Tooly	308000
Topham	376000
Torrance	396400
Torrance	396500
Torrence	396400
Torrence	396500
Torrey	390000
Toubson	307460
Touch	304000
Touch	305000
Toup	307000
Toupe	307000
Touseman	304660
Tramel	396800
Trapnall	397680
Trautner	393690
Travers	397400
Travers	397940
Travirs	397400

Name	Code
Travirs	397940
Travis	397400
Treat	393000
Tredwell	393780
Tremly	396800
Trester	394390
Trimble	396780
Trindle	396380
Trisler	394890
Trissler	394890
Troop	390700
Trotter	393900
Troupe	390700
Troutman	390366
Troy	390000
Truby	397000
Truman	396600
Trump	396700
Tuckness	345640
Tuckness	356400
Tumbald	367830
Tups	374000
Turbutt	397300
Turner	396900
Tush	340000
Tusler	348900
Tweed	373000
Tygarden	359360
Tyler	389000
Tyson	346000
Tzorn	496000
Uhre	090000
Uhri	090000
Ulmar	086900
Ulrich	089400
Ulrich	089500
Ulrick	089450
Ulrick	089500
Ulsh	084000
Umstead	064330
Umsted	064330
Updegraff	073597
Urguhart	095593
Urie	090000
Vale	780000
Van Cleave	764870
Van Cleave	765870
Van Devourt	763709
Van Meter	766390
Vanates	763400
Vanbuskirk	767459
Vance	764000
Vance	765000
Vancleave	764870
Vancleave	765870
Vancleve	764870
Vancleve	765870
Vandecrift	763497
Vandecrift	763597
Vanderbill	763978
Vanderbilt	763978
Vanderen	763960
Vanderhoof	763950
Vanderien	763960
Vanderpool	763970
Vanderver	763979
Vandike	763500
Vandunn	763600
Vaneken	765600
Vanhorn	765960
Vanhorne	765960
Vankirk	765950
Vanmeter	766390
Vanoorhis	760954
Varner	796900
Varvell	797800
Venble	767800
Venlore	768900
Vergin	795600
Vernon	796600
Virgin	795600
Vocht	743000
Vocht	753000
Volans	786400
Volen	786000
Vonmeter	766390
Vorner	796900
Wabel	778000
Waddell	738000
Waddle	738000
Wade	730000
Waggoner	756900
Wagle	758000
Wainwright	767953
Wakefield	757830
Wakeland	758630
Walis	784000
Walker	785900
Wall	780000
Wallace	784000
Wallace	785000
Waller	789000
Wallis	784000
Wallrad	789300
Walor	789000
Walradon	789360
Walsh	784000
Walter	783900
Walters	783400
Walters	783940
Walthower	783790
Waltman	783660
Walton	783600
Walts	784000
Ward	793000
Warden	793600
Warder	793900
Wargintin	795636
Warner	796900
Warnock	796450
Warnock	796500
Warren	796000
Washington	746536
Waterson	734600
Waterson	739460
Watherill	739800
Watkins	735640
Watson	746000
Watts	740000
Waugh	750000
Wayground	759063
Wayland	786300
Weakley	758000
Weaver	779000
Webb	770000
Webster	774390
Weddell	738000
Weed	730000
Weeks	754000
Weichel	748000
Weichel	758000
Weinn	760000
Weiser	749000
Weiss	740000
Weitzel	748000
Weitzell	748000
Welcker	784590
Welcker	785900
Welckle	784580
Welckle	785800
Welckley	784580
Welckley	785800
Wells	784000
Welsh	784000
Welty	783000
Werder	793900
Werly	798000
Werner	796900
West	743000
Westbay	743700
Wetherhill	739580
Wetherill	739800
Wetherington	739653
Wetherinton	739636
Weylan	786000
Weyland	786300
Weyner	769000
Whaley	758000

Name	Code
Wharry	759000
Wharton	759360
Whary	759000
Whealin	758600
Wheeler	758900
Whelin	758600
Wherry	759000
Whisler	754890
Whislor	754890
Whitacre	753490
Whitacre	753590
White	753000
Whitehead	753530
Whitehill	753580
Whitesell	753480
Whitley	753800
Whitly	753800
Whitman	753660
Whitmer	753690
Whitmore	753690
Whitner	753690
Whitson	754600
Wibbley	778000
Wickersham	745456
Wickersham	745945
Wickersham	754560
Wickersham	759456
Wickerson	745460
Wickerson	745946
Wickerson	754600
Wickerson	759460
Wickware	745790
Wickware	757900
Wiggant	756300
Wiggins	756400
Wikoff	757000
Wiley	780000
Wilkens	785640
Wilkin	785600
Wilkins	785640
Willcox	784540
Willcox	785540
Willets	784000
Willey	780000
Willhelm	785860
William	786000
Williams	786400
Williamson	786460
Willing	786500
Willisill	784800
Willits	784000
Wills	784000
Willson	784600
Wilson	784600
Wilts	784000
Winebidder	767390
Winebiddle	767380
Winemiller	766890
Winter	763900
Winters	763400
Winters	763940
Wirley	798000
Wirmly	796800
Wirt	793000
Wise	740000
Wiseman	746600
Wiser	749000
Wishad	743000
Wishard	749300
Wisman	746600
Wither	739000
Witherhill	739580
Witherington	739653
Withington	736536
Witmer	736900
Wittemoyer	736190
Witzel	748000
Wolf	787000
Wolfart	787930
Wolff	787000
Wonder	763900
Wood	703000
Woodhouse	703504
Woods	704000
Woodson	704600
Wooley	708000
Wooleys	708400
Woolman	708660
Work	795000
Worral	798000
Worthington	793653
Wotle	738000
Wray	790000
Wright	795300
Wunder	763900
Wyerbaugher	797590
Wynn	760000
Yarnell	196800
Yearl	198000
Yearly	198000
Yeates	134000
Yocum	146000
Yocum	156000
Yon	160000
Yoner	169000
Yost	143000
Young	106500
Yung	165000
Zane	460000
Zantzinger	464659
Zeiger	459000
Zeigler	458900
Zeinnet	463000
Zeinnot	463000
Zeller	489000
Zenes	464000
Zennit	463000
Zerbe	497000
Zigler	458900
Zimmerman	469660
Zinnet	463000
Zorn	496000

030000 Aday
035000 Edge
035460 Atkison
035600 Aitkin
035646 Atkinson
036000 Adam
036000 Eatten
036000 Eatton
036400 Adams
036540 Iddings
036643 Edminston
036643 Edmonstone
036646 Edmondson
036646 Edmunson
037940 Edwards
038000 Athel
039000 Edder
039000 Eder
039000 Odair
039400 Edires
043600 Ashton
043600 Austin
043796 Eastburne
044973 Ashcraft
045000 Askey
045593 Eckhard
045640 Askins
045700 Askew
045700 Ickawee
045840 Ackels
045966 Ackerman
045973 Ashcraft
046000 Ozean
046300 Auchmuty
046705 Achenbough
047000 Ashbee
047000 Espey
047000 Espy
047500 Ashbaugh
047890 Essweiler
047890 Esweiler
047890 Etswiler
047935 Ashbridge
047960 Osborn
047960 Osburn
048660 Eshelman
048660 Eshleman
049000 Acre
049300 Achert
049703 Isherwood
050000 Agey
050000 Ege
053600 Ogden
053600 Ogdon
054340 Augustus
055930 Eckhard
056000 Aiken
056000 Eaken
056300 Auchmuty
056590 Ehingeur
056700 Agnew
056705 Achenbough
057000 Ickawee
058000 Okeley
058000 Okely
058400 Ackels
058470 Ogelsvee
058700 Ogilvie
059000 Acre
059000 Eagar
059000 Eager
059000 Eaker
059000 O'Hara
059000 O'Harra
059300 Achert
059660 Ackerman
059660 Akerman
061900 Anjer
063400 Anders
063400 Antes
063400 Antis
063460 Anderson
063900 Andree
063940 Anders
063940 Andres
063946 Anderson
063974 Andrews
064000 Annis
064000 Ennis
064000 Enoch
064000 Innis
064330 Umstead
064330 Umsted
064570 Inskeep
064665 Ensminger
064900 Anjer
065000 Enoch
065840 Inglish
065863 England
066000 Enon
066000 Eyman
068000 O'Neil
069450 Emrick
069500 Emrick
070000 Evy
070000 Ewa
070000 Eby
073597 Updegraff
074000 Evers
074000 Eves
074900 Officer
075000 Ewig
075900 Officer
076000 Owen
076400 Evans
076400 Evens
076490 Ovenshire
076500 Ewing
076540 Ewings
076540 Owings
078000 Eppele
078300 Evalt
078300 Ewalt
078530 Aplegate
078530 Appelgate
078530 Applegate
078700 Appleby
079300 Everit
079400 Evers
079593 Everhart
079690 Overmire
079783 Overfield
079800 Eberly
079800 Everly
080000 All
080000 Allee
083000 Althoe
083000 Eliot
083000 Elliot
083000 Elliott
083000 Old
083040 Althouse
083660 Alteman
083660 Altman
083660 Oldman
083900 Elder
084000 Ales
084000 Ellis
084000 Ulsh
084300 Ellicott
084360 Alston
084600 Alison
084600 Allison
084600 Ellison
084793 Allsworth
084793 Elsworth
085300 Ellicott
085460 Alkison
085463 Alexander
086000 Alen
086000 Allen
086000 Eolen
086400 Allens
086600 Allman
086600 Allmen

086900 Ulmar
087030 Alwood
087630 Oliphant
087930 Alward
087943 Albrecht
087953 Albrecht
087953 Albright
089000 Oiller
089000 Olar
089400 Ulrich
089450 Ulrick
089454 Alricks
089500 Ulrich
089500 Ulrick
089540 Alricks
090000 Eyre
090000 Orr
090000 Uhre
090000 Uhri
090000 Urie
093000 Ord
093600 Arden
093800 Iredell
094600 Irisen
094600 Irison
094660 Erisman
094900 Archer
094930 Archert
095593 Urguhart
095900 Archer
095930 Archert
095930 Earhart
096300 Aurandt
096300 Aurnt
096350 Armitage
096439 Armstrong
096470 Ormsby
096540 Ourings
096830 Arnold
097000 Erb
097000 Orbey
097600 Erwin
097600 Irvin
097600 Irvine
097600 Irwin
098000 Eairl
098000 Earl
098000 Early
098630 Ireland
100000 Jay
100000 Joy
106400 Joans
106500 Young
134000 Yeates
139000 Ioder
139000 Joder

140000 Joice
143000 Yost
143400 Justice
143500 Justice
145000 Jack
145400 Jackes
145460 Jackson
145660 Jackman
146000 Yocum
147000 Jacob
147000 Jacoby
147400 Jacobs
150000 Jack
150000 Joice
154000 Jackes
154600 Jackson
156000 Yocum
156600 Jackman
157000 Jacob
157000 Jacoby
157400 Jacobs
160000 Jane
160000 John
160000 Yon
164000 James
164000 Johns
164000 Jones
164360 Johnston
164360 Johnstone
164600 Jameson
164600 Jamison
164600 Jemison
164600 Johnson
164600 Jonson
165000 Yung
165640 Jenkins
166400 Jennens
166540 Jennings
169000 Yoner
178000 Jewell
180000 Jolley
180000 Jolly
184540 Julicks
185400 Julicks
193600 Jardon
193600 Jordan
193600 Jurdan
196800 Yarnell
197400 Jarvis
197400 Jervis
198000 Yearl
198000 Yearly
203000 Stout
203000 Stoute
207900 Stouffer
210000 Stoie

230000 Scot
230000 Scott
234000 States
237590 Studebaker
238900 Stotler
239000 Scudder
245759 Stockbiger
245795 Stockberger
245900 Sticker
245900 Stucker
248900 St. Clair
250000 Stake
256900 Sckinner
257590 Stockbiger
257959 Stockberger
258000 Steigel
258000 Stokely
258900 St. Clair
259000 Sticker
259000 Stucker
259000 Styger
260000 Steen
260000 Stine
260000 Stone
260000 Stiene
264000 Stones
266400 Steinmetz
267000 Stamp
267000 Stump
267800 Stimble
267949 Steinbrecher
267959 Steinbrecher
269000 Stoner
276000 Stephan
276000 Stephen
276400 Stephens
276400 Stevens
276460 Stephenson
276460 Stevenson
276460 Stevinson
278900 Stapler
279000 Stauffer
279000 Stopher
279000 Stover
279000 Stuber
279300 Stafford
279300 Steward
279300 Stewart
279300 Stewert
279460 Stewardson
280000 Scull
280000 Scully
280000 Stahl
280000 Steel
280000 Steele
280000 Stille

280000 Stull
290000 Star
290000 Starr
290000 Story
290300 Stroud
290300 Stroude
290700 Stroup
293000 Starett
293000 Starret
293000 Starrett
293000 Starrit
293000 Sterrat
293000 Stiret
293000 Street
293000 Strode
293000 Stuart
293600 Stratten
293763 Sturdevant
294000 Strauch
294590 Stricker
294600 Steardson
295000 Strauch
295000 Straugh
295400 Sturges
295600 Sturgeon
295900 Streeker
295900 Stricker
296590 Stringer
297800 Strubel
297800 Struble
297935 Strawbridge
303300 Douthit
303800 Doudle
303800 Doutel
303800 Douthel
303800 Douthill
304000 Touch
304660 Toochman
304660 Touseman
305000 Touch
305340 Thoughtes
305360 Doughton
305600 Dougan
305660 Toochman
305800 Dougal
305840 Doughlas
305840 Douglas
305840 Douglass
305930 Dougherty
307000 Toup
307000 Toupe
307460 Toubson
308000 Tooly
330000 Death
330000 Doty
330000 Tate
330000 Todd
334000 Teeters
335900 Thatoher
336400 Tedmarsh
336940 Tedmarsh
339400 Teeters
340000 Diets
340000 Dorsey
340000 Dorsy
340000 Doz
340000 Thesh
340000 Tice
340000 Tush
340000 Daitch
344000 Dicas
344000 Dorsius
345000 Dickey
345000 Dick
345400 Dicks
345460 Dickson
345600 Dersham
345640 Tuckness
345900 Dacker
345900 Decker
345930 Deckert
346000 Dodson
346000 Tyson
346000 Dushane
348900 Tusler
349000 Thatcher
349400 Dorsiris
350000 Dickey
350000 Duke
350000 Tice
350000 Dick
354000 Dehaas
354000 DeHaas
354000 Dehaas
354000 Dehaus
354000 Dicas
354000 Dicks
354000 Diggs
354600 Dickson
354600 Dixon
355000 Tohog
355000 Tohogo
355300 Tohogod
356000 Dugan
356400 Tuckness
357630 Dehavent
357930 Dogworthey
359000 Dacker
359000 Decker
359300 Daugherty
359300 Deckert
359300 Tagart
359300 Taggart
359300 Tegard
359360 Teagarden
359360 Teegarden
359360 Tygarden
360000 Dane
360000 Dean
360000 Deaney
360000 Deney
360000 Denny
360000 Donne
360000 Dun
360000 Dunn
360000 Tayney
364000 Dennis
364000 Teines
364000 Thomas
364000 Dumars
364300 Tenist
364378 Dunstable
364600 Duncan
364600 Tamson
364600 Thomson
364600 Tomson
365600 Duncan
365600 Dungan
365600 Tomkin
366000 Donan
366500 Duning
367000 Donaway
367030 Dunwoody
367400 Dunwich
367450 Dunwick
367460 Thompson
367460 Tompson
367500 Dunwich
367500 Dunwick
367830 Dombalt
367830 Dunfield
367830 Tumbald
367836 Templeton
367945 Tinbrock
367950 Tinbrock
368000 Donnely
368400 Daniels
368460 Donaldson
368460 Donnaldson
368600 Donnellan
368600 Dunlaney
368600 Dunlany
368700 Dunlap
369000 Deimer
369000 Donar
369000 Tanner
369400 Dumars
369663 DeNormandie

369678 Dunrumple
370000 Davey
370000 Depuey
370000 Depuy
370000 Duff
370000 Taub
370000 Toby
373000 David
373000 Dewit
373000 Dewitt
373000 Dowde
373000 Tweed
373800 Dowdle
374000 Davis
374000 Dobbs
374000 Tups
374600 Davidson
374600 Davison
374600 Dobson
374650 Dabsong
376000 Downe
376000 Downey
376000 Topham
376397 Diffenderfer
376400 Dobbins
376400 Downs
376650 Downing
376930 Downard
378000 Deval
378000 Devale
378000 Devall
378000 Dowell
378300 Duffield
378300 Theobald
378900 Toblor
379000 Devoir
379000 Dwire
379300 Deyworthey
380000 Dailey
380000 Dale
380000 Deihl
380000 Diehl
380000 Dill
380000 Doil
380000 Doyl
380000 Doyle
380000 Thauley
380000 Thauly
380000 Tholey
383600 Dalton
384000 Dallas
384660 Tollsman
385660 Tilghman
386000 Dallam
387000 Delap
387030 Talbout
387300 Talbot
387300 Talbott
387600 Dillwyn
387930 Dillworth
387930 Dilworth
387930 Tolbert
389000 Tayler
389000 Taylor
389000 Tyler
389678 Dalrymple
390000 Dar
390000 Derr
390000 Dyar
390000 Torrey
390000 Troy
390366 Troutman
390500 Dorough
390700 Troop
390700 Troupe
393000 Treat
393400 Dordes
393690 Trautner
393780 Tredwell
393900 Trotter
394000 Dorsey
394000 Dorsy
394390 Trester
394400 Dorsius
394560 Dersham
394566 Druckenmiller
394745 Dreisback
394750 Dreisback
394890 Trisler
394890 Trissler
394940 Dorsiris
395000 Darrigh
395000 Darugh
395600 Durham
395668 Druckenmiller
396000 Doran
396000 Dorran
396000 Thorn
396380 Trindle
396400 Torrance
396400 Torrence
396500 Torrance
396500 Torrence
396580 Thornhill
396590 Drinker
396600 Drennin
396600 Truman
396630 Drummond
396630 Drumond
396650 Drenning
396700 Trump
396780 Trimble
396783 Drumfield
396800 Tramel
396800 Tremly
396900 Turner
397000 Tharp
397000 Truby
397300 Turbutt
397400 Travers
397400 Travirs
397400 Travis
397540 Drevox
397680 Trapnall
397900 Drewry
397940 Travers
397940 Travirs
398000 Drell
398600 Darlin
398653 Darlington
400000 Jay
400000 Joy
400000 Shee
403000 Shoot
403400 Souders
403900 Couder
403940 Souders
404000 Coats
404600 Courson
405000 Cook
405000 Cooke
405960 Coughran
406000 Coon
406400 Joans
406486 Counselman
406590 Shoemaker
406656 Counyngham
407900 Cooper
408000 Coale
408000 Schooly
408390 Coulter
409460 Courson
419000 Sayer
430000 Catt
430000 Codd
430000 Cuddy
430000 Shadde
430000 Sheed
430000 Shute
434000 Shutes
434930 Cathcart
434930 Cathcort
435930 Cathcart
435930 Cathcort
436000 Cotton
436000 Seaton
436000 Shadden
436000 Shaddon

436000 Sitton
436000 Suttan
436000 Sutten
436000 Suttin
436000 Sutton
436400 Catumus
436400 Cothamas
437400 Catfish
437450 Chadwick
437500 Chadwick
437839 Cadwalader
437839 Cadwalder
437839 Cadwallader
437930 Cuthbert
437930 Sattaford
437930 Settaford
438000 Shedle
438900 Shitler
439000 Cather
439000 Joder
439660 Catterman
439800 Cathrall
439800 Cottral
439863 Sutherland
440000 Cash
440000 Cassey
440000 Corsa
440000 Corso
440000 Joice
440000 Seess
440000 Sheets
443000 Cost
443400 Justice
443500 Justice
443866 Castleman
443900 Coster
443900 Costor
443930 Custard
445000 Jack
445000 Sisk
445400 Jackes
445460 Jackson
445638 Cockendal
445638 Cockendall
445660 Jackman
445840 Sickles
445864 Chickelamis
445890 Seckler
446000 Carson
446000 Cason
446000 Casson
446000 Chesney
446600 Sassaman
446900 Casner
446900 Cassner
447000 Jacob
447000 Jacoby
447030 Sherswood
447400 Jacobs
447900 Casper
448000 Corsale
448600 Chisholm
448660 Casselman
448660 Cosselman
449600 Cochran
449600 Cochrin
450000 Coke
450000 Jack
450000 Joice
454000 Cox
454000 Coxe
454000 Jackes
454400 Coxs
454600 Jackson
454790 Shakespear
455000 Skagoe
456380 Cockendal
456380 Cockendall
456600 Jackman
457000 Jacob
457000 Jacoby
457400 Jacobs
458000 Caghel
458000 Cahell
458000 Cahill
458000 Caughel
458400 Sickles
458640 Chickelamis
458900 Seckler
458900 Zeigler
458900 Zigler
459000 Sager
459000 Segar
459000 Seger
459000 Siger
459000 Sugar
459000 Zeiger
459600 Cochran
459600 Cochrin
460000 Cain
460000 Conn
460000 Jane
460000 John
460000 Saam
460000 Sam
460000 Same
460000 Saum
460000 Shinney
460000 Snee
460000 Zane
463000 Shandy
463000 Sinnet
463000 Sinnett
463000 Smith
463000 Zeinnet
463000 Zeinnot
463000 Zennit
463000 Zinnet
463000 Condy
463400 Sanders
463460 Sanderson
463594 Snodgrass
463730 Sandwith
463780 Cantwell
463900 Schneideer
463900 Schneider
463900 Sneider
463900 Snyder
463900 Snider
463940 Sanders
463946 Sanderson
463986 Sunderland
464000 Comes
464000 James
464000 Johns
464000 Jones
464000 Sims
464000 Summers
464000 Zenes
464360 Johnston
464360 Johnstone
464500 Connosque
464500 Schimick
464500 Schinick
464500 Smock
464589 Sinckler
464600 Jameson
464600 Jamison
464600 Jemison
464600 Johnson
464600 Jonson
464600 Simeson
464600 Simison
464600 Simson
464659 Zantzinger
464800 Concle
464890 Sinclair
465000 Schimick
465000 Schinick
465000 Shank
465000 Smock
465400 Shanks
465640 Jenkins
465800 Concle
465800 Shingle
465890 Sinckler
465890 Sinclair
465890 Sinkler

465900 Singer
466000 Cannon
466000 Canon
466000 Shannon
466000 Shanon
466000 Simon
466400 Cummins
466400 Jennens
466400 Simons
466500 Cumming
466540 Commings
466540 Cumings
466540 Cummings
466540 Jennings
466560 Cuningham
466560 Cunningham
467000 Champ
467000 Senff
467360 Cumpton
467360 Snowden
467360 Snowdon
467400 Chambers
467400 Compass
467460 Sampson
467460 Simpson
467460 Sympson
467600 Champin
467600 Champion
467800 Campbell
467800 Campble
467800 Sample
467800 Semple
467800 Snevely
467800 Snively
467800 Snivley
467800 Snivly
467940 Chambers
467960 Chamberain
467980 Chamberly
467986 Chamberlain
467986 Chamberlin
468000 Camel
468000 Comley
468000 Comly
468000 Conley
468000 Connally
468000 Connelly
468000 Connolly
468000 Samuel
468000 Small
468400 Samuels
468490 Smellser
468499 Smelserer
468660 Smallman
469000 Cammer
469000 Coner
469000 Conner
469000 Connor
469300 Conrad
469300 Cunrad
469400 Summers
469660 Zimmerman
470000 Chew
470000 Coffie
470000 Schub
470000 Shaaf
470000 Shaub
470000 Shaw
470000 Shub
470600 Spoon
473000 Cavet
473000 Cavett
473000 Cavit
473000 Cavitt
473000 Spadd
473000 Spayd
473000 Sweet
473000 Cavode
473000 Covde
473000 Covode
473600 Cowden
474000 Savoise
474000 Sipes
474000 Spears
474000 Speers
474900 Spicer
474900 Swisher
474900 Swisser
475000 Savage
475750 Cowhawk
475861 Speigelmoyer
475861 Speiglemeyer
475900 Spicer
475900 Sweger
476000 Chapham
476000 Covien
476000 Cowan
476000 Cowen
476000 Shippen
476000 Spohn
476000 Swaim
476000 Swan
476000 Swany
476400 Cavins
476400 Spence
476400 Swanzey
476400 Swanzy
476400 Swons
476490 Spencer
476500 Spence
476589 Spangler
476590 Spencer
476600 Chapman
476600 Chapmen
476600 Coffman
476600 Cofman
476600 Shipman
476793 Swinford
476900 Schaffner
476900 Schauffner
476900 Shaffner
476900 Shafner
477900 Swiper
478000 Cable
478000 Cawlley
478000 Jewell
478000 Shible
478000 Shively
478000 Supplee
478300 Seebold
478365 Spalding
478400 Swales
478900 Shufler
479000 Copper
479000 Seber
479000 Seever
479000 Sever
479000 Shaeffer
479000 Shaffer
479000 Sheafer
479000 Sheaffer
479000 Shever
479000 Shower
479000 Sober
479000 Spear
479000 Spiere
479000 Suber
479000 Sheaver
479000 Sower
479030 Sproat
479300 Seybert
479300 Sheaphard
479300 Shepard
479300 Shepherd
479300 Sheppard
479300 Shubard
479300 Swort
479300 Sybert
479373 Cowperthwait
479400 Schwartz
479400 Spears
479400 Speers
479400 Swartz
479530 Sievright
479530 Siewright
479530 Spright
479580 Sprogel
479580 Sprogell

479580 Sprogle
479653 Swerington
479656 Swearingan
479656 Swearingen
479656 Swearingham
479656 Sweringham
479659 Springer
480000 Call
480000 Celly
480000 Cole
480000 Jolley
480000 Jolly
480000 Seely
480000 Shale
480000 Sly
480300 Sloat
480500 Slough
480600 Sloan
483000 Clyde
483000 Colt
483400 Clydes
483600 Calyton
483600 Clayton
483660 Saltman
483780 Caldwell
483900 Colder
483900 Salter
484000 Cilts
484000 Shallus
484000 Shields
484000 Sills
484000 Soles
484000 Sellers
484500 Clock
484500 Slack
484540 Julicks
484660 Saltsman
484900 Slusher
485000 Clock
485000 Slack
485060 Calhoon
485060 Colhoon
485390 Slaughter
485400 Julicks
485436 Clogston
485436 Clogstone
485436 Clugston
485436 Clugstone
485476 Silkspinner
485600 Callahan
486000 Clin
486000 Cline
486000 Slone
486360 Clinton
486390 Calendar
486390 Callender
486400 Collins
486564 Clingansmith
486600 Coleman
486600 Salmon
486900 Colemore
486900 Clymer
487000 Clavoe
487000 Culp
487080 Claypoole
487400 Silvers
487600 Calvin
487600 Clapham
487600 Claphan
487600 Colvin
487600 Solovan
487600 Sullivan
487630 Chalfant
487640 Solovans
487800 Calwell
487800 Claypole
487830 Scholfield
487900 Silver
487930 Clifford
487936 Sylverton
487940 Silvers
487946 Culbertson
487946 Culbertsun
489000 Collier
489000 Sayler
489000 Shuler
489000 Soler
489000 Zeller
489400 Sellers
489500 Clark
489500 Clarke
489546 Clarkson
489660 Clarnen
490000 Care
490000 Carr
490000 Cherry
490000 Corey
490000 Correy
490000 Corry
490000 Cory
490000 Cree
490000 Currie
490000 Curry
490000 Sayre
490000 Shira
490540 Crookes
490540 Crooks
490560 Croughen
493000 Cord
493000 Crute
493000 Sheart
493400 Carothers
493400 Carrothars
493400 Carrothers
493400 Carruthers
493400 Carthers
493400 Caruthers
493400 Crutis
493600 Jardon
493600 Jordan
493600 Jurdan
493600 Sheradine
493600 Sheredin
493600 Sheredine
493900 Carether
493900 Carter
493900 Caruther
493900 Crider
493900 Shrater
493940 Carothers
493940 Carrothars
493940 Carrothers
493940 Carruthers
493940 Carthers
493940 Caruthers
494000 Church
494000 Corsa
494000 Corso
494000 Cross
494000 Crush
494165 Croseyong
494300 Christ
494300 Christie
494300 Christy
494300 Crist
494360 Crastin
494500 Sherack
494500 Sherrack
494500 Shryack
494500 Shryock
494530 Crocket
494600 Carson
494703 Sherswood
494780 Crosswell
494800 Corsale
494900 Crozer
495000 Church
495000 Crago
495000 Craig
495000 Craike
495000 Creag
495000 Creigh
495000 Crig
495000 Sherack
495000 Sherrack
495000 Shryack
495000 Shryock
495300 Crocket

495450 Shrihack
495500 Shrihack
495600 Crogham
495600 Croghan
495900 Croker
496000 Corn
496000 Corney
496000 Corren
496000 Cran
496000 Crane
496000 Creme
496000 Sharon
496000 Sharron
496000 Sherian
496000 Shram
496000 Tzorn
496000 Zorn
496000 Shrum
496000 Srum
496480 Carmichael
496560 Carnahan
496564 Curnahans
496580 Schornagle
496580 Carmichael
496600 Sherman
496736 Crampton
496736 Crompton
496760 Cramphon
496830 Carmalt
496900 Cramer
496900 Criner
497000 Croff
497000 Crow
497000 Sharp
497000 Zerbe
497030 Sherwood
497300 Corbett
497400 Crafts
497400 Crows
497400 Jarvis
497400 Jervis
497639 Carpenter
497645 Sharpnack
497650 Sharpnack
497900 Schriver
497900 Server
497900 Shriver
497930 Craford
497930 Crawford
498000 Carroll
498000 Searle
498000 Sorrel
498360 Charleton
498480 Carlisle
498600 Cearlin
499000 Shearer
499000 Sheerer
499000 Sherer
499300 Sherrerd
500000 Gay
500000 Guy
500000 Hay
500000 Hoy
503000 Good
503000 Goudey
503000 Goudie
503000 Goudy
503900 Couder
503900 Hooder
504000 Coats
504360 Houston
504590 Houseker
504590 Housseggor
504600 Courson
504900 Hoocher
504900 Koocher
505000 Cook
505000 Cooke
505000 Gough
505000 Hook
505900 Hoocher
505900 Koocher
505960 Coughran
506000 Coon
506486 Counselman
506656 Counyngham
507000 Hoape
507400 Hoops
507658 Hoofnagle
507900 Cooper
507900 Hoover
508000 Coale
508300 Hoult
508390 Coulter
508400 Hoults
508630 Hoalland
509300 Gourty
509460 Courson
510000 Hoye
519000 Guyer
519000 Hauer
530000 Catt
530000 Codd
530000 Cuddy
530000 Haddy
530000 Head
530000 Heath
530000 Heth
530000 Hite
530000 Keith
530000 Huthy
530000 Kade
534000 Gaddis
534000 Geddis
534930 Cathcart
534930 Cathcort
535000 Hodge
535460 Hodgson
535600 Gudgion
535930 Cathcart
535930 Cathcort
536000 Cotton
536000 Heaton
536000 Hutton
536300 Hudnot
536400 Catumus
536400 Cothamas
536900 Hittner
537400 Catfish
537450 Chadwick
537500 Chadwick
537830 Hatfield
537839 Cadwalader
537839 Cadwalder
537839 Cadwallader
537930 Cuthbert
539000 Cather
539000 Guthery
539000 Guthrey
539000 Guthrie
539000 Guthry
539000 Hadder
539300 Goddard
539660 Catterman
539800 Cathrall
539800 Cottral
539800 Katterly
540000 Cash
540000 Cassey
540000 Corsa
540000 Corso
540000 Goz
540000 Guice
540000 Hays
540000 Hess
540000 Hirsh
540000 Hise
540000 Hussey
540000 Hice
540000 Hyse
543000 Cost
543000 Gist
543000 Hurst
543600 Huston
543866 Castleman
543900 Coster
543900 Costor
543900 Hiester

543900 Keester
543900 Koster
543900 Kostor
543930 Custard
543966 Hosterman
544300 Gasst
544450 Hitchcock
544500 Hitchcock
544600 Hutcheson
544600 Hutchison
545000 Husk
545000 Kick
545300 Hacket
545400 Hicks
545450 Hitchcock
545450 Hickock
545500 Hitchcock
545500 Hickock
545600 Hackney
545638 Cockendal
545638 Cockendall
545660 Hickman
545673 Hickenbottom
545680 Hickenlooper
545800 Hockley
545864 Chickelamis
546000 Carson
546000 Cason
546000 Casson
546000 Chesney
546000 Gozin
546000 Heyshan
546000 Hudson
546000 Kitcham
546000 Kitchen
546400 Hutchins
546460 Hutchinson
546540 Hutchings
546590 Kissinger
546600 Gaseman
546900 Casner
546900 Cassner
546900 Kisner
547630 Husband
547900 Casper
547959 Hershberger
548000 Corsale
548000 Horsely
548360 Hazelton
548500 Godshalk
548543 Hazelhurst
548543 Hazlehurst
548594 Hazelhurst
548594 Hazlehurst
548600 Chisholm
548600 Kechlein
548600 Kechline
548660 Casselman
548660 Cosselman
548660 Gasselman
548660 Getzelman
548700 Heslip
548703 Hazelwood
548900 Kessler
548900 Kishler
549000 Gasser
549000 Heiser
549000 Hesser
549000 Hyser
549000 Keiser
549000 Keyser
549600 Cochran
549600 Cochrin
549600 Hartshorn
549600 Hartshorne
550000 Coke
550000 Guice
550000 Hoge
550000 Hogg
550000 Hoke
550000 Keagy
550000 Kick
550000 Hice
553000 Hacket
554000 Cox
554000 Coxe
554000 Hicks
554000 Hokes
554000 Hughes
554400 Coxs
554500 Hickock
555000 Hickock
556000 Hackney
556380 Cockendal
556380 Cockendall
556380 Kuykendale
556380 Kuykindall
556400 Higgens
556400 Higgins
556600 Hickman
556736 Hickenbottom
556736 Higinbotham
556807 Hickenlooper
556900 Hagener
557000 Highby
558000 Caghel
558000 Cahell
558000 Cahill
558000 Caughel
558000 Quigley
558000 Hockley
558600 Kechlein
558600 Kechline
558630 Hogeland
558640 Chickelamis
559000 Keiger
559000 Kugger
559300 Keigart
559600 Cochran
559600 Cochrin
560000 Cain
560000 Conn
560000 Gohn
560000 Guiney
560000 Hain
560000 Haine
560000 Hanah
560000 Haney
560000 Hanna
560000 Hannah
560000 Keen
560000 Keene
560000 Keim
560000 Keney
560000 Kinney
560000 Kinny
560000 Kuhn
560000 Queen
563000 Hand
563000 Hunt
563000 Kenneday
563000 Kennedy
563000 Condy
563460 Henderson
563600 Henton
563660 Hindman
563690 Kintner
563780 Cantwell
563800 Kendal
563800 Kendall
563800 Kindle
563900 Hunter
563945 Hendricks
563945 Hendrickson
563945 Kendrick
563946 Henderson
563950 Kendrick
563954 Hendricks
563954 Hendrickson
563954 Hendrix
563960 Henthorn
564000 Comes
564000 Goms
564000 Haines
564000 Hains
564000 Hans
564000 Hennessey
564000 Hynes

564000 Kuntz
564459 Huntzecker
564459 Huntzicker
564459 Hunsicker
564500 Connosque
564580 Hinckel
564580 Kunckle
564590 Huntzecker
564590 Huntzicker
564590 Hunsicker
564600 Kenson
564650 Kintzing
564800 Concle
564800 Hamersly
564800 Hammersly
564840 Gonsalus
564840 Gonzales
564840 Hammersleys
565000 Hank
565000 King
565300 Kinkead
565300 Knight
565400 Hinks
565400 Knox
565460 Hinkson
565479 Kingsberry
565800 Concle
565800 Hinckel
565800 Kunggel
565800 Kunkle
565800 Kunckle
566000 Cannon
566000 Canon
566000 Hammon
566300 Hammond
566400 Cummins
566500 Cumming
566500 Hening
566540 Commings
566540 Cumings
566540 Cummings
566560 Cuningham
566560 Cunningham
567000 Champ
567000 Knap
567360 Cumpton
567400 Chambers
567400 Compass
567600 Champin
567600 Champion
567800 Campbell
567800 Campble
567800 Gamwell
567800 Knable
567800 Kneible
567800 Knieble
567800 Knoble
567800 Gamble
567836 Hambelton
567836 Hambleton
567840 Knowles
567840 Knowls
567900 Humphrey
567940 Chambers
567940 Humphreys
567940 Humphries
567953 Hambright
567960 Chamberain
567980 Chamberly
567986 Chamberlain
567986 Chamberlin
567986 Gemberling
567986 Gimberling
568000 Camel
568000 Comley
568000 Comly
568000 Conley
568000 Connally
568000 Connelly
568000 Connolly
568000 Heinley
568000 Heinly
568000 Kenley
568000 Kenly
568000 Kimmel
568360 Hamilton
569000 Cammer
569000 Coner
569000 Conner
569000 Connor
569000 Henry
569300 Conrad
569300 Cunrad
569300 Kennard
569480 Hamersly
569480 Hammersly
569484 Hammersleys
569800 Hammerly
569800 Hemerly
570000 Chew
570000 Coffie
570000 Gibb
570000 Guffee
570000 Guffie
570000 Heap
570000 Hoff
570000 Hop
570000 Howe
570000 Howey
570000 Huff
570000 Kap
570000 Kapp
573000 Cavet
573000 Cavett
573000 Cavit
573000 Cavitt
573000 Govet
573000 Gowdey
573000 Hewett
573000 Hewitt
573000 Cavode
573000 Covde
573000 Covode
573600 Cowden
574000 Gibbs
574000 Hewes
574000 Hews
574000 Howsche
574345 Haberstick
574350 Haberstick
574400 Hewses
574600 Gibson
574900 Habichar
574973 Howcroft
575640 Hawkins
575640 Hopkins
575750 Cowhawk
575900 Habaker
575900 Habichar
575930 Gebhart
575973 Howcroft
576000 Chapham
576000 Covien
576000 Cowan
576000 Cowen
576000 Gawen
576000 Gibbon
576000 Giffen
576400 Cavins
576400 Gibbons
576400 Gibons
576500 Hewing
576580 Huffnagle
576600 Chapman
576600 Chapmen
576600 Coffman
576600 Cofman
576600 Hoffman
576600 Kaufman
578000 Cable
578000 Cawlley
578000 Gable
578000 Howell
578000 Hubley
578000 Hubly
578000 Kaple
578000 Keppel
578000 Keppele

Code	Name
578000	Keppell
578000	Kepple
578400	Havelitch
578765	Heffelfinger
578765	Hefflefinger
578900	Keppeler
579000	Copper
579000	Gover
579000	Hover
579000	Keffer
579300	Govert
579300	Hibberd
579300	Hibert
579300	Hubbert
579373	Cowperthwait
579434	Haberstick
579435	Haberstick
579600	Hepburn
579800	Gabriel
579860	Haverliny
580000	Call
580000	Celly
580000	Cole
580000	Gale
580000	Gall
580000	Galley
580000	Gill
580000	Hale
580000	Hall
580000	Haly
580000	Heil
580000	Hill
580000	Holly
580000	Hyle
580000	Kelley
580000	Kelly
580000	Kull
580000	Kyle
580000	Kyll
580000	Kylle
580000	Quail
583000	Clyde
583000	Colt
583000	Galt
583000	Gold
583000	Halladay
583000	Held
583000	Holladay
583000	Holliday
583000	Holodey
583000	Holt
583000	Hoyladay
583400	Clydes
583600	Calyton
583600	Clayton
583600	Hulton
583780	Caldwell
583790	Holdbrook
583900	Colder
584000	Cilts
584000	Glass
584000	Holes
584000	Holtz
584000	Kelso
584000	Kelsoe
584500	Clock
584569	Hiltzheimer
584570	Glasgow
584600	Gillson
584660	Hiltzeman
584690	Hiltzsimer
584700	Galespie
584700	Gelaspy
584700	Gelespey
584700	Gilespie
584700	Gillaspy
584700	Gillespie
584700	Gillespy
584700	Gillispie
584700	Golespy
584700	Gollespey
584790	Hillsborough
584863	Holtsland
584900	Gallacher
584940	Gilcrease
584940	Killcrese
584943	Gilcreast
584943	Kilcreest
584943	Kilcriest
584943	Kilcrist
584943	Killcrest
585000	Clock
585000	Klugh
585060	Calhoon
585060	Colhoon
585436	Clogston
585436	Clogstone
585436	Clugston
585436	Clugstone
585600	Callahan
585900	Galagher
585900	Galaher
585900	Gallacher
585900	Gallagher
585900	Gallahur
585900	Gallaugher
585940	Gilcrease
585940	Killcrese
585943	Gilcreast
585943	Kilcreest
585943	Kilcriest
585943	Kilcrist
585943	Killcrest
586000	Clin
586000	Cline
586000	Glen
586000	Glenn
586000	Helm
586000	Hulme
586000	Kellum
586000	Killum
586000	Klein
586000	Kline
586040	Gilmous
586300	Kulland
586360	Clinton
586390	Calendar
586390	Callender
586400	Collins
586400	Hillands
586400	Holmes
586465	Holmesing
586500	Huling
586500	Kling
586540	Hulings
586540	Hullings
586547	Hollingsworth
586564	Clingansmith
586579	Hollingworth
586600	Coleman
586600	Gillman
586600	Gilman
586600	Holman
586900	Colemore
586900	Gilmore
586900	Clymer
586900	Gilmer
587000	Clavoe
587000	Culp
587000	Galloway
587000	Galoway
587080	Claypoole
587400	Gleaves
587600	Calvin
587600	Clapham
587600	Claphan
587600	Colvin
587600	Gilpin
587630	Chalfant
587800	Calwell
587800	Claypole
587860	Gilfillen
587930	Clifford
587930	Galbraith
587930	Galbreath
587930	Gilbert
587930	Guliford
587946	Culbertson

Code	Name
587946	Culbertsun
587960	Hilborn
587960	Hilburn
587960	Hillborn
588630	Gilliland
589000	Collier
589000	Keller
589500	Clark
589500	Clarke
589546	Clarkson
589660	Clarnen
590000	Care
590000	Carr
590000	Cherry
590000	Corey
590000	Correy
590000	Corry
590000	Cory
590000	Cree
590000	Currie
590000	Curry
590000	Gray
590000	Hare
590000	Haur
590000	Heer
590000	Kehr
590000	Kerr
590000	Kohr
590000	Kore
590540	Crookes
590540	Crooks
590560	Croughen
591600	Grojean
593000	Cord
593000	Crute
593000	Girty
593000	Grady
593000	Greit
593000	Gurty
593000	Harety
593000	Harity
593000	Harriot
593000	Hart
593400	Carothers
593400	Carrothars
593400	Carrothers
593400	Carruthers
593400	Carthers
593400	Caruthers
593400	Crutis
593400	Kriteers
593600	Gordon
593600	Graydon
593600	Hardin
593650	Harding
593660	Hartman
593690	Gardener
593690	Gardner
593800	Gridley
593800	Hartley
593900	Carether
593900	Carter
593900	Caruther
593900	Crider
593900	Greiter
593900	Kreider
593900	Kreutter
593940	Carothers
593940	Carrothars
593940	Carrothers
593940	Carruthers
593940	Carthers
593940	Caruthers
593940	Kriteers
594000	Church
594000	Corsa
594000	Corso
594000	Cross
594000	Crush
594000	Gratz
594000	Gross
594000	Harris
594000	Hirsh
594000	Kurtz
594165	Croseyong
594300	Christ
594300	Christie
594300	Christy
594300	Crist
594300	Hurst
594360	Crastin
594500	Gearick
594530	Crocket
594590	Kricker
594600	Carson
594600	Harrison
594660	Gressman
594780	Crosswell
594795	Hershberger
594800	Corsale
594800	Horsely
594900	Crozer
594900	Karcher
594900	Kratzer
594960	Hartshorn
594960	Hartshorne
595000	Church
595000	Crago
595000	Craig
595000	Craike
595000	Creag
595000	Creigh
595000	Crig
595000	Gearick
595000	George
595000	Greag
595000	Greg
595000	Gregg
595000	Kirk
595300	Crocket
595600	Crogham
595600	Croghan
595600	Graham
595630	Harganot
595638	Kirkindall
595638	Kirkindoll
595640	Harkness
595739	Kirkpatrick
595793	Kirkbride
595830	Herhold
595900	Croker
595900	Gregory
595900	Gurhery
595900	Karcher
595900	Kricker
595930	Gearhart
596000	Corn
596000	Corney
596000	Corren
596000	Cran
596000	Crane
596000	Creme
596000	Grame
596000	Green
596000	Griem
596000	Gurney
596000	Heron
596000	Herron
596000	Kearney
596000	Kearny
596000	Kern
596000	Kerney
596000	Kirney
596000	Krum
596050	Greenough
596300	Grant
596300	Grundy
596360	Grandin
596375	Herndbaugh
596400	Graymes
596400	Grimes
596400	Kerns
596480	Carmichael
596536	Harington
596560	Carnahan
596560	Kernahan
596564	Curnahans
596580	Carmichael

596600 Garman
596600 Harmon
596646 Harminson
596650 Horning
596700 Grenow
596736 Crampton
596736 Crompton
596740 Grimbes
596760 Cramphon
596783 Greenfield
596790 Greenbury
596800 Gormly
596800 Gromly
596830 Carmalt
596900 Cramer
596900 Criner
596900 Krammer
596900 Kreamer
597000 Croff
597000 Crow
597000 Graff
597000 Griffey
597000 Groff
597000 Grove
597000 Harrow
597000 Harvey
597000 Hervey
597300 Corbett
597300 Griffith
597300 Harbet
597340 Griffiths
597350 Harbidge
597400 Crafts
597400 Crows
597400 Horbach
597439 Herbster
597450 Harwick
597458 Harwickel
597500 Harwick
597500 Horbach
597580 Harwickel
597600 Garven
597600 Griffin
597639 Carpenter
597800 Garbel
597800 Garbell
597800 Graybill
597800 Grebill
597800 Growell
597800 Horible
597800 Horoble
597900 Garber
597900 Gruber
597900 Harper
597930 Craford
597930 Crawford
597930 Harbert
597930 Herbert
598000 Carroll
598000 Gorell
598000 Gorrell
598000 Kerley
598300 Herold
598300 Herrold
598360 Charleton
598480 Carlisle
598600 Cearlin
598600 Kerlin
598600 Kirlin
598630 Garland
598650 Kirling
599000 Greer
599000 Greir
599000 Grier
600000 Ney
603000 Moodie
603000 Moote
603670 Noutimape
604000 Noetz
606000 Moon
609000 Moor
609000 Moore
609300 Noarth
609530 Moorehead
609530 Moorhead
609900 Mourer
614000 Mayes
614000 Meyers
619000 Mauer
619000 Meyer
619000 Moyer
619400 Meyers
633000 Mathiot
634870 Medcalf
635000 Nidok
635400 Maddox
635870 Medcalf
636400 Neetimis
636400 Nutimus
637000 Mathew
637400 Mathews
637400 Matthews
638360 Middleton
638450 Matlack
638479 Middlesworth
638500 Matlack
639000 Mather
640000 Mars
640000 Maus
640000 McCay
640000 McCoy
640000 Mears
640000 Mease
640000 Meirs
640000 Miers
640000 Motz
640000 Myers
640000 Nassey
640000 Nice
643000 McCady
643400 Masters
643460 Masterson
643600 Marsden
643600 Masden
643600 Maston
643680 McDonnal
643680 McDonnall
643680 McDonnel
643680 McDonnell
643683 McDonald
643780 McDowal
643780 McDowel
643780 McDowell
643900 Mitchetree
643940 Masters
643946 Masterson
643966 McDermont
644500 McCaskey
644500 McCasky
644500 McCoskeey
644500 McCoskey
644590 McCoskery
644590 McCoskry
644600 McCutchen
644630 Messersmith
644863 McCausland
645000 MacKay
645000 Mackay
645000 MacKey
645000 Mackey
645000 McGee
645000 McKay
645000 McKee
645000 Mckee
645000 McKee
645000 Mckee
645000 McKee
645000 Mckee
645000 McKee
645000 Mckee
645000 McKee
645000 McKoy
645300 Morshed
645400 McGachey
645450 McKoskey
645460 McKachney
645460 McKessen
645500 McGachey

645560 McKachney
645560 McGahan
645600 McKean
645600 McKeen
645600 McKenney
645600 McKim
645600 McKiney
645600 McKinney
645640 Mackenness
645640 McGines
645640 McGinnes
645640 McGinnis
645640 McKinzey
645640 McKinzy
645645 McKamisk
645653 McKnight
645660 McGannon
645678 Mickenfelder
645678 Mickenfilder
645680 McKinly
645750 McGuffog
645760 McGown
645760 McKibben
645760 McKibbin
645760 Mckibbin
645760 McKibbin
645760 McKown
645764 McKibbins
645800 Macklay
645800 Marshal
645800 Marshall
645839 McGlathery
645839 McGlathry
645858 McGlaughlin
645860 Mecklin
645890 Meckleroy
645890 Mockler
645900 McGery
645900 McGuire
645930 McGready
645945 McKroskey
645956 McGrogan
645959 McGreegar
645959 McGreeger
645959 McGregor
645959 McGruger
645970 McGraw
645970 McGrew
645976 McGriffin
646000 Machan
646000 Mason
646000 Matson
646000 McCoyne
646000 McCune
646000 Meason
646000 Muchnou
646000 Nearson
646050 McConoughy
646090 Machmoore
646300 McMath
646300 McNitt
646300 McNutt
646340 McIntosh
646390 McIntire
646390 McIntyre
646390 McMotry
646434 McMasters
646439 McMasters
646456 McMacken
646460 McMachan
646460 McMachen
646460 McMasen
646460 McNachon
646500 McCanahey
646500 McConaughy
646560 McMachan
646560 McMachen
646560 McMacken
646560 McMahan
646560 McMahon
646560 McNachon
646600 McMean
646600 McMeen
646640 McMeans
646658 McManegal
646660 McMannamy
646660 McMenimy
646700 McComb
646700 McNaw
646790 McNavare
646800 McConal
646800 McConnall
646800 McConnel
646800 McConnell
646800 McMull
646800 McNale
646800 McNaul
646800 McNeal
646860 McMillian
646860 McMullen
646860 McMullin
646860 McMullon
646900 McEmery
646900 McEmory
646900 McHenry
646900 McMurrey
646900 McNair
646900 Metzner
646900 Missinner
646900 Muchmore
646900 McMurray
646939 Macmurtry
646939 McMurtree
647000 McAfee
647000 McAvoy
647000 McVay
647300 McBath
647300 Neisbite
647300 Nesbit
647300 Nesbitt
647300 McBeth
647360 McFadden
647360 McFaddion
647360 McFaden
647360 McFadian
647360 McFadion
647460 McPherson
647500 McCuffog
647593 McFigart
647600 McEwen
647600 McSweeney
647800 McCawley
647800 McFall
647864 McWilliams
647930 McBride
647946 McPherson
647960 McFarren
647986 McFarlan
647986 McFarland
647986 McFarlane
647986 McFarlington
647990 McBrier
648000 Maclay
648000 McCall
648000 McClay
648000 McCulley
648000 McCully
648000 Michael
648000 Mitchel
648000 Mitchele
648000 Mitchell
648000 Nicely
648005 McCulloough
648050 McCullough
648390 Mitcheltree
648400 McLees
648400 Nicholas
648400 Nichols
648439 McAlister
648439 McCalester
648439 McCalister
648439 McCallester
648439 McCallister
648439 McColester
648439 McCollester
648439 McCollister
648439 McAllester
648450 McClasky

648450 McClosky
648450 McCollack
648450 McCollock
648450 McCullock
648450 McCulluck
648460 Nicholason
648460 Nicholson
648500 McCollack
648500 McCollock
648500 McCollogh
648500 McCullock
648500 McCullogh
648500 McCulluck
648569 McElhenry
648586 McLaughlin
648600 McAllen
648600 McCelen
648600 McClain
648600 McClean
648600 McCleane
648600 McCollem
648600 McCollum
648600 McLone
648630 McCalland
648634 McClintock
648635 McClintock
648646 McClanachan
648646 McClenachan
648646 McClinachan
648650 McClung
648656 McClanachan
648656 McClannegan
648656 McClenachan
648656 McClenegan
648656 McClinachan
648660 McColman
648663 McCalmont
648700 Metcalf
648760 McIlvaine
648760 McIlvane
648860 Maclellan
648860 McClalin
648860 McClelan
648860 McClellan
648860 McLellan
648863 MCClelland
648863 McClellandon
648900 Maclure
648900 McCleery
648900 McClure
648900 McElroy
648930 Nesselrode
648950 McClurg
648950 McClurgh
649000 McCrea
649000 McCrey
649000 McCroy
649000 Misser
649000 Musser
649000 Neisser
649300 McCarty
649300 McCord
649300 McCready
649300 McCurday
649300 McCurdy
649360 McCartney
649390 McCarter
649450 McCroskey
649450 McCrosky
649456 McCracken
649463 Messersmith
649560 McCracken
649580 McCorkle
649600 McCoron
649645 McCarmick
649645 McCormick
649650 McCarmick
649650 McCormick
649800 McCorely
649800 McCurly
649900 McCreery
649900 McCrerry
649900 McRory
649900 McCreary
650000 MacKay
650000 Mackay
650000 MacKey
650000 Mackey
650000 Magee
650000 Maggee
650000 McCay
650000 McCoy
650000 McKay
650000 McKee
650000 Mckee
650000 McKee
650000 Mckee
650000 McKee
650000 Mckee
650000 McKee
650000 Mckee
650000 McKee
650000 McKoy
650000 Meek
650000 Meeke
650000 Mike
650000 Nice
653000 McCady
653680 McDonnal
653680 McDonnall
653680 McDonnel
653680 McDonnell
653683 McDonald
653700 Mokotoff
653780 McDowal
653780 McDowel
653780 McDowell
653966 McDermont
654000 Meeks
654500 McCaskey
654500 McCasky
654500 McCoskeey
654500 McCoskey
654500 McKoskey
654590 McCoskery
654590 McCoskry
654600 McCutchen
654600 McKachney
654600 McKessen
654600 Nixon
654780 Maxwell
654863 McCausland
655000 McGee
655400 McGachey
655500 McGachey
655560 McGahan
655600 McKachney
655640 McGines
655640 McGinnes
655640 McGinnis
655660 McGannon
655750 McGuffog
655760 McGown
655839 McGlathery
655839 McGlathry
655858 McGlaughlin
655900 McGery
655900 McGuire
655930 McGready
655956 McGrogan
655959 McGreegar
655959 McGreeger
655959 McGregor
655959 McGruger
655970 McGraw
655970 McGrew
655976 McGriffin
656000 Machan
656000 Maghen
656000 Mahan
656000 Mahaun
656000 Makin
656000 Maughan
656000 Mauhan
656000 Mauhaun
656000 McCoyne
656000 McCune
656000 McKean

656000 McKeen
656000 McKenney
656000 McKim
656000 McKiney
656000 McKinney
656000 Muchnou
656050 McConoughy
656090 Machmoore
656300 McMath
656300 McNitt
656300 McNutt
656340 McIntosh
656390 McIntire
656390 McIntyre
656390 McMotry
656400 Mackenness
656400 McKinzey
656400 McKinzy
656400 Meginness
656434 McMasters
656439 McMasters
656450 McKamisk
656456 McMacken
656460 McMachan
656460 McMachen
656460 McMasen
656460 McNachon
656500 McCanahey
656500 McConaughy
656530 McKnight
656560 McMachan
656560 McMachen
656560 McMacken
656560 McMahan
656560 McMahon
656560 McNachon
656600 McMean
656600 McMeen
656640 McMeans
656658 McManegal
656660 McMannamy
656660 McMenimy
656700 McComb
656700 McNaw
656783 Mickenfelder
656783 Mickenfilder
656790 McNavare
656800 McConal
656800 McConnall
656800 McConnel
656800 McConnell
656800 McKinly
656800 McMull
656800 McNale
656800 McNaul
656800 McNeal
656860 McMillian
656860 McMullen
656860 McMullin
656860 McMullon
656900 McEmery
656900 McEmory
656900 McHenry
656900 McMurrey
656900 McNair
656900 Megamery
656900 Muchmore
656900 McMurray
656939 Macmurtry
656939 McMurtree
657000 Magaw
657000 McAfee
657000 McAvoy
657000 McVay
657300 McBath
657300 McBeth
657360 McFadden
657360 McFaddion
657360 McFaden
657360 McFadian
657360 McFadion
657460 McPherson
657500 McCuffog
657593 McFigart
657600 McEwen
657600 McKibben
657600 McKibbin
657600 Mckibbin
657600 McKibbin
657600 McKown
657640 McKibbins
657800 McCawley
657800 McFall
657864 McWilliams
657930 McBride
657946 McPherson
657960 McFarren
657986 McFarlan
657986 McFarland
657986 McFarlane
657986 McFarlington
657990 McBrier
658000 Macklay
658000 Maclay
658000 McCall
658000 McClay
658000 McCulley
658000 McCully
658000 Michael
658000 Nagle
658000 Negley
658000 Nicely
658005 McCulloough
658050 McCullough
658400 McLees
658400 Nicholas
658400 Nichols
658439 McAlister
658439 McCalester
658439 McCalister
658439 McCallester
658439 McCallister
658439 McColester
658439 McCollester
658439 McCollister
658439 McAllester
658450 McClasky
658450 McClosky
658450 McCollack
658450 McCollock
658450 McCullock
658450 McCulluck
658460 Nicholason
658460 Nicholson
658500 McCollack
658500 McCollock
658500 McCollogh
658500 McCullock
658500 McCullogh
658500 McCulluck
658569 McElhenry
658586 McLaughlin
658600 McAllen
658600 McCelen
658600 McClain
658600 McClean
658600 McCleane
658600 McCollem
658600 McCollum
658600 McLone
658600 Mecklin
658630 McCalland
658634 McClintock
658635 McClintock
658646 McClanachan
658646 McClenachan
658646 McClinachan
658650 McClung
658656 McClanachan
658656 McClannegan
658656 McClenachan
658656 McClenegan
658656 McClinachan
658660 McColman
658663 McCalmont
658760 McIlvaine
658760 McIlvane
658860 Maclellan

Code	Name
658860	McClalin
658860	McClelan
658860	McClellan
658860	McLellan
658863	MCClelland
658863	McClellandon
658900	Maclure
658900	McCleery
658900	McClure
658900	McElroy
658900	Meckleroy
658900	Mockler
658950	McClurg
658950	McClurgh
659000	McCrea
659000	McCrey
659000	McCroy
659000	Maguire
659300	Magrath
659300	McCarty
659300	McCord
659300	McCready
659300	McCurday
659300	McCurdy
659360	McCartney
659390	Magruder
659390	McCarter
659450	McCroskey
659450	McCrosky
659450	McKroskey
659456	McCracken
659560	McCracken
659580	McCorkle
659600	McCoron
659645	McCarmick
659645	McCormick
659650	McCarmick
659650	McCormick
659800	McCorely
659800	McCurly
659900	McCreery
659900	McCrerry
659900	McRory
659900	McCreary
660000	Man
660000	Mann
660000	Maun
660000	Nana
663000	Munday
663090	Montour
663400	Mendoch
663500	Mendoch
663569	Montgomery
663974	Manderbach
663975	Manderbach
663979	Manderbarch
664000	Means
664000	Menoch
664390	Minster
664536	Monckton
664783	Mansfield
664800	Maunsel
664800	Minshell
664800	Minssell
664900	Mentzer
665000	Menoch
665360	Monckton
665400	Menges
665400	Mengies
665400	Minges
665900	Meneher
665900	Munger
666500	Manning
666590	Memminger
666590	Meninger
667830	Manfield
669000	Miner
669000	Monroe
669000	Munro
669300	Meanard
670000	Nafe
670000	Neaf
670000	Neaff
670000	Neave
670000	Neff
673000	Moffit
673600	Newton
674590	Naftzger
674765	Newswanger
676000	Mabben
678000	Neifly
678000	Nevill
678000	Newale
678000	Newel
678000	Newell
678300	Mawfield
678560	Nawalegan
678600	Mifflin
678630	Nowland
679000	Neeper
680000	Neall
680000	Neely
680000	Neil
680000	Neill
684000	Miles
684600	Malcom
684600	Nellson
684600	Nelson
684600	Nilson
684600	Millison
684860	Malcolm
685600	Malcom
685600	Milligan
685600	Milliken
685600	Millikin
685600	Mulligan
685860	Malcolm
686000	Malone
686000	Maloney
686000	Melone
686000	Mullen
686300	Neeland
686795	Muhlenberg
686900	Milner
689000	Miller
689000	Nailor
689000	Myler
689600	Miliron
689600	Milliron
690000	More
690000	Muir
690000	Murray
690000	Murry
690000	Myer
690000	Myre
693000	North
693300	Meredith
693450	Murdock
693500	Murdock
693600	Martin
693600	Martinea
693600	Mertain
693600	Morton
694000	Marache
694000	March
694000	Mars
694000	Mears
694000	Meirs
694000	Merca
694000	Miers
694000	Mirca
694000	Moris
694000	Morris
694000	Myers
694000	Norris
694360	Marsden
694530	Morshed
694580	Marshal
694580	Marshall
694600	Morison
694600	Moroson
694600	Morrison
694600	Nearson
694630	Marchant
694630	Merchand
694630	Merchant
694900	Mercer
694940	Norcross

695000 Marache
695000 March
695000 Merca
695000 Mirca
695300 Morhead
695363 Margdant
695400 Marks
695600 Morgan
695630 Marchant
695630 Merchand
695630 Merchant
695683 Mauregnalt
695683 Maurignault
695793 Markwrite
695860 Merklin
695900 Mercer
695930 Margaret
695940 Norcross
696000 Marrion
696450 Marmock
696500 Marmock
697000 Morrow
697000 Murphy
697390 Merryweather
698000 Merrill
699000 Maurer
700000 Bay
700000 Bee
700000 Boay
700000 Poe
703000 Boude
703000 Fout
703000 Wood
703504 Woodhouse
703660 Footman
704000 Boos
704000 Fouts
704000 Foutz
704000 Woods
704600 Woodson
704660 Bousman
704900 Boucher
705000 Bouga
705000 Poak
705300 Bouquet
705300 Fought
705400 Bougs
705400 Fooks
705660 Boughanan
705900 Boucher
706000 Boon
706000 Boone
706190 Bounjure
706490 Bounjure
708000 Wooley
708360 Poultney
708400 Wooleys
708500 Foulk
708500 Foulke
708540 Foulks
708660 Woolman
708700 Foullew
709000 Boor
709660 Fourman
714000 Bayers
714000 Buyers
715400 Bayax
715400 Bayux
719000 Bauer
719000 Boyer
719300 Bayard
719400 Bayers
719400 Buyers
719800 Beyerly
730000 Batt
730000 Beatey
730000 Beattey
730000 Beatty
730000 Beaty
730000 Bidde
730000 Boyd
730000 Bud
730000 Budd
730000 Faith
730000 Path
730000 Patty
730000 Paty
730000 Piatt
730000 Piety
730000 Putty
730000 Wade
730000 Weed
733000 Pettit
734000 Beatis
734000 Peters
734000 Petters
734600 Paterson
734600 Patterson
734600 Pattison
734600 Petterson
734600 Waterson
734700 Batersby
735000 Badge
735600 Pidgen
735600 Pidgeon
735640 Watkins
735900 Badger
736000 Battom
736000 Boten
736000 Patton
736000 Pedan
736000 Pitton
736190 Wittemoyer
736400 Pedens
736536 Withington
736900 Witmer
738000 Bettel
738000 Biddle
738000 Bittel
738000 Bittle
738000 Fudle
738000 Waddell
738000 Waddle
738000 Weddell
738000 Wotle
738900 Battler
738900 Butler
738900 Buttler
739000 Pater
739000 Peter
739000 Potter
739000 Wither
739400 Peters
739400 Petters
739450 Patrick
739460 Paterson
739460 Patterson
739460 Petterson
739460 Waterson
739470 Batersby
739500 Butterage
739500 Patrick
739580 Wetherhill
739580 Witherhill
739636 Wetherinton
739653 Wetherington
739653 Witherington
739660 Peterman
739800 Watherill
739800 Wetherill
740000 Baush
740000 Bays
740000 Beass
740000 Botts
740000 Byers
740000 Peace
740000 Peairs
740000 Pearse
740000 Pitts
740000 Potts
740000 Pusey
740000 Pussey
740000 Watts
740000 Weiss
740000 Wise
743000 Forsith
743000 Forsyth
743000 Forsythe

743000 Vocht
743000 West
743000 Wishad
743700 Westbay
743800 Bechtel
743800 Bechtle
743900 Forster
743900 Foster
743900 Furster
744000 Fiscus
744500 Physick
745000 Beck
745000 Buck
745000 Fucke
745000 Physick
745400 Backus
745456 Wickersham
745460 Wickerson
745504 Backhouse
745560 Bickham
745640 Baskins
745660 Bickman
745783 Buckwalter
745790 Wickware
745800 Beckley
745800 Pickel
745800 Pockle
745890 Fockler
745900 Packer
745930 Pickert
745936 Beckerton
745945 Wickersham
745946 Wickerson
745983 Fitzgerald
746000 Beason
746000 Beeson
746000 Parson
746000 Pearson
746000 Person
746000 Watson
746000 Persian
746400 Parsons
746536 Washington
746600 Bauchman
746600 Bausman
746600 Baussman
746600 Bossman
746600 Buchanan
746600 Buchannon
746600 Buchanon
746600 Forsman
746600 Wiseman
746600 Wisman
746640 Fitzsimons
746900 Passmore
747000 Bishop
748000 Beessel
748000 Paschal
748000 Paschall
748000 Pashall
748000 Pearsall
748000 Persal
748000 Persall
748000 Weichel
748000 Weitzel
748000 Weitzell
748000 Witzel
748660 Fussleman
749000 Baucher
749000 Bishure
749000 Fisher
749000 Weiser
749000 Wiser
749000 Bucher
749300 Bossert
749300 Bussard
749300 Buzzard
749300 Wishard
750000 Beck
750000 Buck
750000 Fague
750000 Fucke
750000 Peace
750000 Pegg
750000 Pugh
750000 Waugh
753000 Boquet
753000 Vocht
753000 White
753480 Whitesell
753490 Whitacre
753530 Whitehead
753580 Whitehill
753590 Whitacre
753660 Whitman
753690 Whitmer
753690 Whitmore
753690 Whitner
753800 Bechtel
753800 Bechtle
753800 Whitley
753800 Whitly
754000 Backus
754000 Boggs
754000 Fox
754000 Weeks
754390 Baxter
754560 Wickersham
754600 Whitson
754600 Wickerson
754890 Whisler
754890 Whislor
755040 Backhouse
755600 Bickham
756300 Wiggant
756400 Wiggins
756600 Bauchman
756600 Bickman
756600 Buchanan
756600 Buchannon
756600 Buchanon
756900 Waggoner
757000 Wikoff
757830 Wakefield
757839 Buckwalter
757900 Wickware
758000 Beckley
758000 Feagley
758000 Pickel
758000 Pikly
758000 Pockle
758000 Wagle
758000 Weakley
758000 Weichel
758000 Whaley
758600 Whealin
758600 Whelin
758630 Wakeland
758660 Fogleman
758900 Fockler
758900 Wheeler
759000 Baker
759000 Baucher
759000 Packer
759000 Wharry
759000 Whary
759000 Wherry
759000 Bucher
759063 Wayground
759300 Bigert
759300 Boggert
759300 Pickert
759360 Beckerton
759360 Wharton
759456 Wickersham
759460 Wickerson
760000 Baum
760000 Been
760000 Bony
760000 Bunn
760000 Fame
760000 Fine
760000 Finney
760000 Penn
760000 Penny
760000 Pimm
760000 Weinn
760000 Wynn

760954 Vanoorhis
763000 Benat
763000 Bond
763000 Bennett
763400 Pontius
763400 Vanates
763400 Winters
763443 Penticost
763497 Vandecrift
763500 Vandike
763543 Penticost
763597 Vandecrift
763600 Baynton
763600 Vandunn
763709 Van Devourt
763800 Bentley
763800 Findlay
763800 Findley
763900 Bender
763900 Painter
763900 Winter
763900 Wonder
763900 Wunder
763940 Winters
763950 Vanderhoof
763959 Pendergrass
763960 Vanderen
763960 Vanderien
763970 Vanderpool
763978 Vanderbill
763978 Vanderbilt
763979 Vanderver
764000 Bantze
764000 Bayns
764000 Benetsh
764000 Fance
764000 Fence
764000 Pints
764000 Vance
764345 Bumstick
764350 Bumstick
764500 Pennock
764500 Pinack
764800 Bonsal
764800 Bonsall
764870 Van Cleave
764870 Vancleave
764870 Vancleve
764900 Bunsure
765000 Fance
765000 Fence
765000 Pennock
765000 Pinack
765000 Vance
765400 Banks
765600 Benham
765600 Bonham
765600 Vaneken
765660 Bingman
765700 Bunkhoff
765800 Fangle
765800 Pingley
765870 Van Cleave
765870 Vancleave
765870 Vancleve
765900 Banker
765936 Baumgartner
765936 Pinkerton
765950 Vankirk
765960 Vanhorn
765960 Vanhorne
766390 Van Meter
766390 Vanmeter
766390 Vonmeter
766590 Benninger
766890 Winemiller
767380 Winebiddle
767390 Winebidder
767459 Pennybecker
767459 Vanbuskirk
767590 Pennybecker
767800 Venble
767830 Banfield
767830 Bennefield
767953 Wainwright
768000 Bonnell
768000 Finley
768900 Venlore
769000 Boner
769000 Bonner
769000 Bunner
769000 Pamer
769000 Pumeroy
769000 Pumrey
769000 Pumroy
769000 Punroy
769000 Weyner
769400 Penrose
770000 Webb
771000 Pobjay
771000 Pobjea
773600 Bawden
773600 Bowden
773600 Bowdin
773600 Bowdon
774000 Beavers
774000 Phipps
774000 Pobjay
774000 Pobjea
774000 Powers
774390 Webster
774660 Bowsman
776000 Bowne
776500 Buyvank
776600 Bowman
776900 Pawmer
778000 Powel
778000 Powell
778000 Wabel
778000 Wibbley
778400 Peeples
778400 Peoples
778650 Pawling
778900 Fowler
779000 Beaver
779000 Beeber
779000 Beever
779000 Bower
779000 Pfeffer
779000 Piper
779000 Power
779000 Weaver
779300 Bevaird
779300 Bovard
779400 Beavers
779400 Powers
780000 Bailey
780000 Bale
780000 Ball
780000 Beale
780000 Beally
780000 Bell
780000 Boyle
780000 Bull
780000 Fall
780000 Paul
780000 Pauli
780000 Peal
780000 Pelley
780000 Phile
780000 Pole
780000 Vale
780000 Wall
780000 Wiley
780000 Willey
780530 Blooget
780600 Bloom
783000 Blyth
783000 Blythe
783000 Field
783000 Floyd
783000 Welty
783000 Fulthy
783400 Walters
783600 Baldin
783600 Bolden
783600 Fulten
783600 Fulton

783600 Pulton
783600 Walton
783660 Waltman
783690 Baltimore
783760 Baldwin
783760 Boldwin
783790 Walthower
783900 Bolter
783900 Walter
783940 Walters
784000 Bayles
784000 Bayless
784000 Bayloss
784000 Beels
784000 Blaze
784000 Bloss
784000 Boyles
784000 Boyls
784000 Fields
784000 Philes
784000 Walis
784000 Wallace
784000 Wallis
784000 Walsh
784000 Walts
784000 Wells
784000 Welsh
784000 Willets
784000 Willits
784000 Wills
784000 Wilts
784500 Black
784500 Pollock
784500 Polock
784540 Blacks
784540 Willcox
784543 Blackstone
784563 Blickendoffer
784564 Blickenstoffer
784566 Blackman
784579 Blackburn
784580 Welckle
784580 Welckley
784590 Blecker
784590 Welcker
784600 Willson
784600 Wilson
784640 Pleasants
784650 Blessing
784800 Willisill
784900 Flatcher
784900 Fletcher
784900 Flitcher
785000 Black
785000 Polke
785000 Pollock
785000 Polock
785000 Wallace
785400 Blacks
785400 Pollex
785400 Pollox
785436 Blackstone
785540 Willcox
785600 Wilkin
785637 Blickendoffer
785640 Wilkens
785640 Wilkins
785643 Blickenstoffer
785659 Flakingar
785660 Blackman
785760 Flagavan
785760 Flahavan
785760 Flahaven
785760 Flehaven
785796 Blackburn
785800 Bleakley
785800 Welckle
785800 Welckley
785860 Willhelm
785900 Blecker
785900 Walker
785900 Welcker
785930 Flaherty
786000 Blain
786000 Blaine
786000 Blane
786000 Blum
786000 Bolen
786000 Volen
786000 Weylan
786000 William
786300 Boland
786300 Wayland
786300 Weyland
786390 Polander
786400 Bolins
786400 Volans
786400 Williams
786430 Plumtsead
786433 Plumstead
786433 Plumsted
786456 Flenicken
786460 Williamson
786500 Blank
786500 Pauling
786500 Plenge
786500 Plinge
786500 Willing
786530 Plunket
786560 Flenegan
786560 Flenicken
786640 Fleamons
786650 Fleming
786650 Flemming
786900 Ballmore
786900 Fulmer
786900 Palmer
786900 Plumer
787000 Wolf
787000 Wolff
787300 Flewitt
787400 Philips
787400 Phillips
787460 Flipson
787930 Folbert
787930 Wolfart
787935 Balbridge
789000 Beeler
789000 Blair
789000 Blare
789000 Waller
789000 Walor
789300 Ballard
789300 Wallrad
789360 Fullerton
789360 Walradon
790000 Bar
790000 Bare
790000 Barr
790000 Baur
790000 Bear
790000 Bray
790000 Faree
790000 Farree
790000 Feree
790000 Ferree
790000 Ferry
790000 Frey
790000 Fry
790000 Frye
790000 Furry
790000 Par
790000 Parr
790000 Pear
790000 Perry
790000 Wray
790540 Brooks
790564 Brookens
793000 Baird
793000 Bard
793000 Barret
793000 Beard
793000 Biard
793000 Bird
793000 Brady
793000 Bratt
793000 Bready
793000 Bredy

793000 Burd
793000 Byrd
793000 Fruit
793000 Pratt
793000 Ward
793000 Wirt
793545 Brodhack
793550 Brodhack
793564 Bridgins
793600 Barton
793600 Braton
793600 Bratten
793600 Bratton
793600 Breadin
793600 Breden
793600 Purdon
793600 Warden
793600 Bratain
793600 Brattin
793600 Brittain
793653 Worthington
793705 Britebough
793730 Braithwaite
793740 Breidebach
793750 Breidebach
793793 Bradford
793800 Bradley
793867 Bartholomow
793900 Porter
793900 Portter
793900 Prather
793900 Preater
793900 Preator
793900 Warder
793900 Werder
793936 Brotherton
793945 Frederick
793945 Fredericks
793945 Fredrick
793950 Frederick
793950 Fredrick
793954 Fredericks
793960 Bartram
793960 Burtran
793963 Brotherntin
794000 Birch
794000 Brays
794000 Brice
794000 Bruce
794000 Byers
794000 Fearis
794000 Force
794000 Fries
794000 Paress
794000 Paris
794000 Parris
794000 Peairs
794000 Pearce
794000 Pearis
794000 Pearse
794000 Perroch
794000 Pierce
794000 Price
794300 Forsith
794300 Forsyth
794300 Forsythe
794360 Preston
794380 Priestly
794390 Bruster
794390 Forster
794390 Furster
794390 Procter
794390 Proctor
794500 Brock
794500 Frick
794500 Parrock
794530 Prickit
794560 Bracken
794566 Berckman
794569 Brackenridge
794569 Breckenridge
794578 Breckbill
794580 Barckley
794580 Brickley
794600 Brison
794600 Bryson
794600 Burcome
794600 Parson
794600 Pearson
794600 Person
794600 Persian
794640 Parsons
794660 Forsman
794660 Fritchman
794663 Parchment
794800 Barclay
794800 Parcel
794800 Pearsall
794800 Persal
794800 Persall
794800 Purcell
794900 Fraizer
794900 Fraser
794900 Frazer
794900 Frazier
794900 Presser
794900 Priser
795000 Bereke
795000 Birch
795000 Brice
795000 Brock
795000 Bruce
795000 Buergy
795000 Force
795000 Frick
795000 Park
795000 Parrock
795000 Pearce
795000 Perroch
795000 Pierce
795000 Price
795000 Work
795000 Burk
795300 Braght
795300 Bragth
795300 Bright
795300 Prickit
795300 Wright
795390 Procter
795390 Proctor
795400 Parks
795460 Burkcom
795460 Fergerson
795460 Ferguson
795460 Forgeson
795460 Forguson
795460 Furgeson
795460 Furguson
795560 Burkcom
795600 Borhen
795600 Burcome
795600 Burkem
795600 Burkham
795600 Vergin
795600 Virgin
795600 Bracken
795630 Bargamot
795636 Wargintin
795640 Perkins
795646 Parkinson
795660 Berckman
795660 Birgeman
795663 Parchment
795690 Burkheimer
795693 Brackenridge
795693 Breckenridge
795780 Breckbill
795800 Barckley
795800 Barclay
795800 Barkley
795800 Berkley
795800 Brickley
795800 Parcel
795800 Purcell
795839 Burkholder
795900 Parker
795930 Burgerd
795946 Fergerson

795950 Burkerk
796000 Boren
796000 Briney
796000 Bryan
796000 Burn
796000 Byram
796000 Byrne
796000 Fearon
796000 Frame
796000 Perian
796000 Warren
796300 Barnett
796300 Brand
796300 Brant
796300 Burnet
796300 Friend
796340 Prentice
796350 Prentice
796360 Brandon
796360 Brinton
796400 Barnes
796400 Barns
796400 Burens
796400 Burnes
796400 Burns
796400 Frantz
796436 Brunston
796440 Francis
796440 Frenches
796450 Warnock
796490 Brenizer
796500 Briniegh
796500 Brinigh
796500 Frank
796500 Warnock
796540 Francis
796540 Franks
796540 Frenches
796543 Bringhurst
796546 Frankson
796560 Bringham
796566 Bringman
796570 Brinkhoff
796580 Barnhill
796586 Franklin
796586 Franklinberry
796590 Berringer
796590 Brinker
796593 Barnhart
796594 Bringhurst
796600 Boreman
796600 Brannon
796600 Foreman
796600 Freeman
796600 Froman
796600 Furman
796600 Perryman
796600 Vernon
796660 Breniman
796660 Briniman
796730 Brumfit
796740 Barnabas
796783 Brumfield
796800 Wirmly
796900 Brenner
796900 Bruner
796900 Farmer
796900 Varner
796900 Vorner
796900 Warner
796900 Werner
797000 Farrow
797300 Browd
797360 Brewton
797400 Burrows
797400 Forbes
797430 Probst
797500 Burbige
797590 Wyerbaugher
797600 Brown
797640 Province
797640 Purviance
797650 Province
797650 Purviance
797658 Brownholtz
797678 Brownfield
797680 Brownlee
797800 Preveal
797800 Varvell
797900 Barber
797930 Forward
797935 Burbridge
798000 Bierly
798000 Byerley
798000 Byerly
798000 Pharley
798000 Werly
798000 Wirley
798000 Worral
798659 Brillinger
799000 Pierer
799000 Pryor
800000 Lea
800000 Lee
803000 Loud
803600 Louden
803968 Loutermilk
803974 Loutherback
803975 Loutherback
804000 Louch
805000 Louch
805900 Loughry
807000 Loaf
809000 Loury
830000 Lata
830000 Latta
830000 Leet
830000 Lloyd
830000 Lute
835000 Lodge
836000 Litton
836485 Lautenslager
836485 Lautensliger
836485 Lauttenschleiger
836900 Latemer
836900 Latimer
836900 Lattamor
836900 Lattimer
836900 Lattimore
838000 Leadley
838000 Leadly
838000 Ledlie
838000 Lidlie
838000 Little
838000 Lytle
838400 Ledlies
838530 Littlehead
839000 Leather
839300 Letart
839400 Letarts
839685 Lautermilk
840000 Latcha
840000 Leech
840000 Leetch
840000 Leich
840000 Luce
840000 Lush
840000 Lutz
840000 Lees
845900 Lockry
847000 Latchaw
847930 Letchworth
848000 Lesley
849000 Lasher
849000 Lazier
849000 Leashure
849000 Leasure
849000 Lesher
849000 Lochery
849000 Lochrey
849000 Lochry
850000 Lake
850000 Lauk
850000 Leech
850000 Leich
850000 Luce
853000 Leggat
853000 Liggit

853000 Light
853000 Ligat
853690 Lightner
853703 Lightfoot
854360 Logston
854700 Lightcap
854800 Loxley
856000 Logan
856000 Logane
856400 Lukens
856600 Laughman
858600 Laughlin
858600 Loghlan
858650 Laugling
859000 Laughier
859000 Lochery
859000 Lochrey
859000 Lochry
859000 Lockry
859000 Lugar
860000 Lian
860000 Linn
860000 Lynn
860000 Lyon
863400 Landes
863489 Landislyer
863690 Lintner
864000 Lands
864000 Lems
864000 Limes
864000 Lims
864000 Linch
864000 Lindsay
864000 Lindsey
864000 Lines
864000 Linnes
864000 Lyons
864600 Lymson
865000 Linch
865000 Long
865000 Longe
865300 Longhead
865400 Lenox
865600 Longane
865600 Lungan
865645 Longnacker
865659 Longnacker
865800 Lingly
865900 Longhery
865930 Leonhart
866000 Lauman
866000 Leamon
866000 Lemmon
866000 Lemon
866500 Laning
866500 Leming
866500 Loning
866590 Leyninger
867000 Lamb
867956 Lonabergen
868000 Lemly
869000 Lamar
870000 Leap
870000 Lebb
870000 Leef
870000 Levy
870000 Love
870000 Low
873600 Lowden
873600 Lowdon
874000 Levers
874000 Lewis
874000 Lowers
874600 Lawson
875000 Lebig
875970 Lovegrove
876400 Lowans
876400 Lownes
876430 Lippencott
876530 Lippencott
876543 Lippingcott
876553 Lippingcott
876590 Lavengair
876590 Lovengier
876600 Lowman
877900 Lafaver
877900 Lefever
878600 Lofflin
878900 Lefler
879000 Laveor
879000 Lawrie
879000 Lowery
879000 Lowrey
879000 Lowry
879400 Levers
879400 Lowers
879503 Livergood
879640 Lawrence
879650 Lawrence
880000 Lilley
887600 Lylbuin
890000 Laura
890000 Laurey
890000 Lehr
893000 Laird
893000 Lord
896400 Laurence
896500 Laurence
896600 Larimon
896900 Larimore
900000 Ray
900000 Reay
903000 Roat
903000 Roatt
903660 Roodman
904000 Roes
904000 Roush
905000 Rough
907900 Rooper
918000 Royal
919000 Reyer
919000 Royer
930000 Read
930000 Ready
930000 Reed
930000 Reid
930000 Reith
930000 Roddy
934500 Redick
935000 Redick
935400 Rodgers
935900 Rodger
935940 Rodgers
935940 Rodgres
936000 Ratan
936000 Rodney
936000 Rotten
936500 Reading
936504 Rittenhouse
936795 Ruthanburger
936900 Reitenaur
937500 Rudebaugh
938000 Riddle
938400 Riddles
938700 Rudolph
938700 Rudulph
939000 Reader
939000 Rider
939000 Ritter
939000 Rotery
939793 Rutherford
940000 Rausch
940000 Rees
940000 Reese
940000 Rice
940000 Rich
940000 Riche
940000 Richey
940000 Richie
940000 Ritchey
940000 Rose
940000 Ross
940000 Rush
943600 Roston
945000 Risk
945400 Rickets
945660 Rockman
946000 Ryerson

946630 Richmond
946900 Resner
946900 Resnor
946900 Resoner
947900 Roseberry
948000 Rishel
948000 Russel
948000 Russell
949400 Richards
949460 Richardson
950000 Raiguee
950000 Reig
950000 Rhea
950000 Rice
950000 Rich
950000 Riche
950000 Richey
950000 Richie
950000 Rugh
950340 Rhoades
950400 Rhoads
953000 Right
953000 Raquet
953000 Requate
953400 Rhodes
954000 Rekas
954000 Rickets
954000 Riggs
954000 Rogers
956600 Rockman
956630 Richmond
959000 Raker
959000 Reger
959000 Reigar
959000 Roger
959000 Roher
959000 Rygar
959300 Reigart
959300 Reigert
959300 Rygart
959400 Richards
959400 Rogers
959460 Richardson
960000 Rainey
960000 Ren
960000 Ronno
960000 Ryan
960000 Ryne
963400 Romters
963800 Randell
963840 Randles
963940 Romters
964000 Ramsay
964000 Ramsey
964500 Renick
964500 Rennick
964540 Renicks
964890 Renchler
965000 Renick
965000 Rennick
965400 Renicks
965600 Rankan
965600 Rankin
965890 Renchler
965900 Rinker
968000 Remely
968400 Rannels
968400 Rennalls
968400 Reynolds
969000 Reemer
969300 Rennard
970000 Reef
970000 Reiff
970000 Ripy
970000 Robb
970000 Rove
970000 Row
970000 Rowe
974000 Rebets
974000 Robers
974600 Robeson
974600 Robison
976000 Rowan
976300 Rownd
976400 Robins
976460 Robinson
976536 Rivington
976600 Rebman
978000 Rawle
978000 Ripley
978000 Rubley
978300 Raybolt
978300 Rybolt
978390 Rowletter
978630 Rowland
979000 Riffer
979300 Roberdeau
979400 Robers
979400 Roberts
979460 Robertson
979600 Reaborn
980000 Rayl
980000 Reily
980000 Royle
980000 Ryal
980000 Rily
983400 Rolletes
983900 Roletter
983900 Rollettor
984000 Ralse
984000 Ryles
984360 Ralston
986400 Ralins
987000 Ralph
987000 Ralfe
990000 Rora
990000 Ryor
993600 Rairdon
994000 Rerich
994500 Rehrick
994600 Ryerson
995000 Rehrick
995000 Rerich
999000 Rohrer
999000 Rorer

Alphabetical Index

Alphabetical Index

Alphabetical Index

Alphabetical Index

Alphabetical Index